Lecture Notes in Computer Science 12971

More information about this subseries at http://www.springer.com/series/7408

Zhe Hou · Vijay Ganesh (Eds.)

Automated Technology for Verification and Analysis

19th International Symposium, ATVA 2021
Gold Coast, QLD, Australia, October 18–22, 2021
Proceedings

 Springer

Editors
Zhe Hou ⓘ
Griffith University
Brisbane, QLD, Australia

Vijay Ganesh
University of Waterloo
Waterloo, ON, Canada

ISSN 0302-9743   ISSN 1611-3349   (electronic)
Lecture Notes in Computer Science
ISBN 978-3-030-88884-8   ISBN 978-3-030-88885-5   (eBook)
https://doi.org/10.1007/978-3-030-88885-5

LNCS Sublibrary: SL2 – Programming and Software Engineering

This Springer imprint is published by the registered company Springer Nature Switzerland AG
The registered company address is: Gewerbestrasse 11, 6330 Cham, Switzerland

Preface

This volume contains the papers presented at the 19th International Symposium on Automated Technology for Verification and Analysis (ATVA 2021). The ATVA series of symposia intends to promote research in theoretical and practical aspects of automated analysis, verification, and synthesis by providing a forum for interaction between the regional and international research communities and industry in related areas.

ATVA 2021 was planned to be hosted on the Gold Coast, Australia, in late October 2021. However, due to the COVID-19 pandemic and travel restrictions, the Steering Committee decided to host the conference virtually during October 18–22, 2021. ATVA 2021 received 75 submissions covering topics related to the theory of and applications in automated verification and analysis techniques. Each paper was reviewed by at least three reviewers, and the Program Committee (PC) accepted 19 regular papers and 4 tool papers, leading to a competitive and attractive scientific program.

This edition of ATVA was blessed by the presence of four prestigious keynote speakers. The first keynote was given by Sir Tony Hoare, a Turing Award and Kyoto Prize laureate. He discussed the link between algebra, geometry, and programming testing and verification using a unified theory. The second keynote speaker, Andrew Chi-Chih Yao from the Tsinghua University, is also a Turing Award and Kyoto Prize laureate. His expertise is in complexity theory and cryptography, and he presented novel ideas about computing and analysis from these angles. Moshe Vardi from the Rice University is another widely recognized top computer scientist and a Godel Prize winner. He talked about linear temporal logic and its applications in analysis and synthesis. Last, but not least, Jha from the University of Wisconsin presented insightful views on security, formal methods and adversarial machine learning. The four talks covered current hot research topics and revealed many new interesting research directions.

After the success of the workshops of the previous edition, we decided to co-host the conference with three workshops in related research areas: Security and Reliability of Machine Learning (SRML 2021), organized by Shiqi Wang, Huan Zhang, Kaidi Xu, and Suman Jana; the Workshop on Hyperproperties: Advances in Theory and Practice (HYPER 2021), organized by Daniel Fremont and Hazem Torfah; and the Workshop on Open Problems in Learning and Verification of Neural Networks 2021, organized by Anna Lukina, Guy Avni, Mirco Giacobbe, and Christian Schilling. All three workshops were hosted virtually on October 18, 2021. These workshops brought in additional participants to ATVA 2021 and helped make it an interesting and successful event. We thank all the workshop organizers for their hard work.

ATVA 2021 would not have been successful without the contributions and involvement of the Program Committee members as well as the external reviewers, who contributed to the review process (with more than 225 reviews) and the selection of the best contributions. This event would not exist if authors and contributors did not submit their proposals. We thank every person, reviewer, author, PC member and organizing committee member involved in the success of ATVA 2021.

The EasyChair system was set up for the management of ATVA 2021 and supported the submission, review, and volume preparation processes. It proved to be a powerful framework.

Although ATVA 2021 was hosted virtually, the local host and sponsor Griffith University provided tremendous help with the registration and online facilities. The other sponsors, Formal Methods Europe, Springer, and Destination Gold Coast, contributed in different forms to help the conference run smoothly. Many thanks to all the local organisers and sponsors.

We wish to express our special thanks to the General Chair and Steering Committee members, particularly Jing Sun, Farn Wang, Jie-Hong Roland Jiang, and Yu-Fang Chen, for their valuable support.

October 2021   Zhe Hou
                                                                      Vijay Ganesh

Organization

General Co-chairs

Jin Song Dong   National University of Singapore, Singapore
Jing Sun   University of Auckland, New Zealand

Program Co-chairs

Zhe Hou   Griffith University, Australia
Vijay Ganesh   University of Waterloo, Canada

Steering Committee

Teruo Higashino   Osaka University, Japan
Jie-Hong Roland Jiang   National Taiwan University, Taiwan
Doron A Peled   Bar Ilan University, Israel
Yu-Fang Chen   Institute of Information Science, Academia Sinica,
                                   Taiwan
Ichiro Hasuo   National Institute of Informatics, Japan
Yunja Choi   Kyungpook National University, South Korea

Advisory Committee

Insup Lee   University of Pennsylvania, USA
Allen Emerson   The University of Texas at Austin, USA
Hsu-Chun Yen   National Taiwan University, Taiwan
Farn Wang   National Taiwan University, Taiwan

Publicity Co-chairs

Giles Reger   The University of Manchester, UK
Meng Sun   Peking University, China

Workshop Co-chairs

Guy Katz   Hebrew University of Jerusalem, Israel
Rayna Dimitrova   CISPA Helmholtz Center for Information Security,
                                   Germany

Program Committee

Erika Abraham	RWTH Aachen University, Germany
Mohamed Faouzi Atig	Uppsala University, Sweden
Christel Baier	TU Dresden, Germany
Stanley Bak	Stony Brook University, USA
Ezio Bartocci	Vienna University of Technology, Austria
Saddek Bensalem	VERIMAG, France
Armin Biere	Johannes Kepler University Linz, Austria
Nikolaj Bjorner	Microsoft, USA
Udi Boker	Interdisciplinary Center (IDC) Herzliya, Israel
Borzoo Bonakdarpour	Michigan State University, USA
Luca Bortolussi	University of Trieste, Italy
Jalil Boudjadar	Aarhus University, Denmark
Martin Brain	University of Oxford, UK
Franck Cassez	ConsenSys and Macquarie University, Australia
Supratik Chakraborty	IIT Bombay, India
Krishnendu Chatterjee	Institute of Science and Technology (IST), UK
Yu-Fang Chen	Academia Sinica, Taiwan
Chih-Hong Cheng	Denso Automotive Deutschland GmbH, Germany
Alessandro Cimatti	Fondazione Bruno Kessler, Italy
Hung Dang Van	Vietnam National University, Vietnam
Tien V. Do	Budapest University of Technology and Economics, Hungary
Alexandre Duret-Lutz	LRDE, EPITA, France
Javier Esparza	Technical University of Munich, Germany
Bernd Finkbeiner	CISPA Helmholtz Center for Information Security, Germany
Pascal Fontaine	Université de Liège, Belgium
Martin Fränzle	Carl von Ossietzky Universität Oldenburg, Germany
Pierre Ganty	IMDEA Software Institute, Spain
Alberto Griggio	Fondazione Bruno Kessler, Italy
Dimitar Guelev	Bulgarian Academy of Sciences, Bulgaria
Keijo Heljanko	University of Helsinki, Finland
Guy Katz	The Hebrew University of Jerusalem, Israel
Siau-Cheng Khoo	National University of Singapore, Singapore
Xuandong Li	Nanjing University, China
Anthony Widjaja Lin	TU Kaiserslautern, Germany
Alexander Nadel	Intel, Israel
Pham Ngoc Hung	Vietnam National University, Vietnam
Aina Niemetz	Stanford University, USA
Tobias Nipkow	Technical University of Munich, Germany
Doron Peled	Bar Ilan University, Israel
Mathias Preiner	Stanford University, USA

Markus Rabe	Google, USA
Andrew Reynolds	University of Iowa, USA
Olli Saarikivi	Aalto University, Finland
Indranil Saha	Indian Institute of Technology Kanpur, India
Sven Schewe	University of Liverpool, UK
Anne-Kathrin Schmuck	Max-Planck-Institute for Software Systems, Germany
Daniel Selsam	Microsoft Research, USA
Gagandeep Singh	VMWare Research and University of Illinois at Urbana-Champaign, USA
Sadegh Soudjani	Newcastle University, UK
Jun Sun	Singapore Management University, Singapore
Sofiene Tahar	Concordia University, Canada
Michael Tautschnig	Queen Mary University of London, UK
Tachio Terauchi	Waseda University, Japan
Aditya Thakur	University of California, Davis, USA
Cesare Tinelli	University of Iowa, USA
Hoang Truong	Vietnam National University, Vietnam
Bow-Yaw Wang	Academia Sinica, Taiwan
Zhilin Wu	Chinese Academy of Sciences, China

Geometric Theory for Program Testing
(Abstract of a Keynote Talk)

Bernhard Möller[1], Tony Hoare[2] and Zhe Hou[3]

[1] Universität Augsburg
[2] University of Cambridge and Honorary Member of Griffith University
[3] Griffith University

Abstract. Formal methods for verification of programs are extended to testing of programs. Their combination is intended to lead to benefits in reliable program development, testing, and evolution. Our geometric theory of testing is intended to serve as the specification of a testing environment, included as the last stage of a toolchain that assists professional programmers, amateurs, and students of Computer Science. The testing environment includes an automated algorithm which locates errors in a test that has been run, and assists in correcting them. It does this by displaying, on a monitor screen, a stick diagram of causal chains in the execution of the program under test. The diagram can then be navigated backwards in the familiar style of a satnav following roads on a map. This will reveal selections of places at which the program should be modified to remove the error.

Summary

The relevant formal methods for testing are due to the pioneers who provided the ideas: Euclid and Descartes for geometry; Carl Adam Petri, whose nets model execution of programs; Noam Chomsky, whose structured method defines the syntax of many programming languages. Their pioneering theories are simplified and adapted to meet current needs of programmers.

A Euclidean diagram is formed by executing a set of constructors, whose feasibility is postulated by axioms and definitions. The geometric features of the diagram (axes, coordinates, points, lines, figures, ...) are labelled by identifiers chosen in drawing the diagram. These identifiers relate the diagram to the proof of a Euclidean proposition, or the text of a program under test.

As an example, we take a structured programming language, with program executions represented by Chomsky's Abstract Syntax Trees. A multiple simultaneous assignment labels the leaves of the tree with atomic commands, and constructors label the branching points. Operators are sequential composition, object class declaration, and concurrent composition of various kinds. Individual operations of the language are defined by specifying the properties of a correct interface between their operands. Errors in arithmetic expressions can be detected by labelling a tree by the value that it produces. Detection of zero divide is then just a matter of calculation. Other errors (eg. deadlock) can be defined by defining a pattern (eg. a cyclic chain of arrows).

This makes it easy to define a new language feature separately by a new constructor. A new language can be defined as the union of its features. A testing tool should be automatically extensible to deal with any combination of features.

Contents

Model Checking

Probabilistic Analysis

Software and Hardware Verification

System Synthesis and Approximation

Verification of Machine Learning

Invited Paper

Linear Temporal Logic – From Infinite to Finite Horizon

Lucas M. Tabajara and Moshe Y. Vardi[✉]

Rice University, Houston, USA
vardi@rice.edu

Abstract. Linear Temporal Logic (LTL), proposed by Pnueli in 1977 for reasoning about ongoing programs, was defined over infinite traces. The motivation for this was the desire to model arbitrarily long computations. While this approach has been highly successful in the context of model checking, it has been less successful in the context of reactive synthesis, due to the challenging algorithmics of infinite-horizon temporal synthesis. In this paper we show that focusing on finite-horizon temporal synthesis offers enough algorithmic advantages to compensate for the loss in expressiveness. In fact, finite-horizon reasonings is useful even in the context of infinite-horizon applications.

1 Reactive Systems and Reactive Synthesis

Reactive systems are widespread in modern society, from our personal computers to traffic control systems and factory robots, and we can expect them to become even more ubiquitous with the recent advent of new technologies such as autonomous vehicles and Internet of Things. A reactive system is any kind of computer system that operates in a continuous loop interacting with an external environment. This environment can be the physical world, another component of a larger system, or other systems connected in a network [25].

Because reactive systems interact with other systems and the real world, it is especially important to guarantee that such systems operate safely and correctly, since errors in their operation can have far reaching and often serious consequences. But designing such systems correctly can be especially challenging, since they can run for an unbounded amount of time, and their internal state at any given moment depends on the entire history of inputs received since they started operation. Therefore, the designer has to make sure that they respond correctly to a potentially infinite set of possible environment behaviors [25].

This challenge motivates the problem of *reactive synthesis* [40], which proposes an alternative to the manual design of reactive systems. Instead, reactive synthesis aims to automatically and algorithmically generate a reactive system from a specification of its desired behavior. This specification is usually given as

Work supported in part by NSF grants IIS-1527668, CCF-1704883,IIS-1830549, DoD MURI grant N00014-20-1-2787, and an award from the Maryland Procurement Office.

Z. Hou and V. Ganesh (Eds.): ATVA 2021, LNCS 12971, pp. 3–12, 2021.
https://doi.org/10.1007/978-3-030-88885-5_1

a formula in some type of temporal logic expressing the set of acceptable execution traces of the system. A reactive system is said to *realize* this specification if every execution trace produced by the system satisfies the formula, regardless of the inputs received from the environment. A reactive synthesis algorithm should be able to determine if the specification is realizable and, if so, synthesize a system realizing it.

Possibly the most common specification language for reactive synthesis is Linear Temporal Logic (LTL) [39], an extension of propositional logic with temporal operators such as "next", "until", "eventually" and "globally". The classic approach for reactive synthesis from an LTL specification is based on reducing the problem to a game played over a deterministic ω-automaton [42], a class of automata that accept languages over infinite words. This approach proceeds as follows:

1. Convert the LTL formula into some type of deterministic ω-automaton, such as a deterministic Rabin [42,43] or parity [20] automaton, that accepts exactly the language of traces that satisfy the formula.
2. Use the automaton as the arena for a two-player game between the system and the environment, where the system wins if it satisfies the acceptance condition of the automaton [40].
3. Solve the game to find out which player has a winning strategy (such games are always determined) [24]. If the system wins, the specification is realizable and the winning strategy can be used as a model for the reactive system.

Over the years, reactive synthesis has been extensively studied in the field of formal methods. Yet, not much of the progress in the area has translated into making reactive synthesis significantly more practical for real-world applications [31]. Techniques like bounded synthesis [19,21–23], symbolic algorithms [7,19] and on-the-fly game construction [35] have made implementation of synthesis algorithms more feasible, but tools for reactive synthesis still have limited scalability, which has largely prevented this problem from gaining traction for practical applications. Furthermore, many generalizations of reactive synthesis that would be of interest in real-world scenarios, such as quantitative synthesis [1,2] and synthesis with incomplete information [32], have not been able to be fully explored in practice so far, since they layer additional complexity on top of a problem that is already challenging to solve efficiently.

At first glance, it is easy to attribute this lack of practical impact to the worst-case complexity of reactive synthesis: the problem is 2EXPTIME-complete, meaning that deciding whether a specification is realizable may take doubly-exponential time in the size of the formula [41]. But this complexity analysis can be deceptive. First, it considers only the worst case, which rarely occurs in practice. In fact, many useful classes of specification can be synthesized in exponential or even polynomial time [4,6,12]. Second, the doubly-exponential upper bound speaks more of the succinctness of LTL as a specification language than anything else: some classes of LTL formulas specify properties that can only be realized by a system of doubly-exponential size [41].

Instead of the worst-case complexity, it might make more sense to attribute the poor practical performance of reactive-synthesis algorithms to the lack of efficient algorithms for ω-automata. Other applications of such automata in formal methods, like LTL model checking, tend to use nondeterministic Büchi automata (NBA) [48]. The classic approach to reactive synthesis, however, requires a *deterministic* automaton [40], which leads to a number of complications. Unlike NBAs, deterministic Büchi automata are not expressive enough to represent all LTL formulas [30], forcing determinization to produce an automaton with a more complex acceptance condition, such as a *parity automaton*. The classic algorithm for performing this procedure is Safra's algorithm [38, 42, 43], which is notoriously complex and difficult to understand, let alone implement efficiently [3, 47]. Furthermore, it is still an open problem whether games over parity automata can be solved in polynomial time [9], an issue that is compounded by the complexity of the state space generated by Safra's construction.

These observations suggest that in order for reactive synthesis to be efficiently implementable in practice, it is necessary to overcome the algorithmic barriers imposed by ω-automata. One of the most successful attempts to do this has been Generalized Reactivity(1) (GR(1)) synthesis [6], which has become maybe the only variant of reactive synthesis that has achieved widespread use in application domains, particularly robotics [29, 36]. Despite GR(1) being a more limited specification format, GR(1) synthesis has a number of advantages over synthesis from LTL specifications [6]:

- The state space of the game is directly encoded in the GR(1) specification, thus entirely avoiding having to use automaton construction and determinization.
- The winning condition of the game is a GR(1) condition, which is more general than a Büchi condition, but simpler than a parity condition. Unlike parity games, games with a GR(1) condition can be solved in polynomial (cubic) time.
- The game can be naturally represented symbolically, as states correspond to assignments to Boolean variables and the transition relation can be represented as a Boolean formula. This enables the use of efficient symbolic algorithms. In contrast, the games produced by Safra's construction have very complex state spaces which are not amenable to a symbolic encoding.

The success story of GR(1) demonstrates how, by trying to do less, we can accomplish more: by imposing limits on what types of problems can be specified and how, it becomes possible to attain a synthesis procedure that has hopes of being useful in practice. GR(1) achieves this by entirely avoiding the use of automata, but a more recently-proposed variant of reactive synthesis brings to light an alternative option: replacing ω-automata by the simpler and more tractable automata over finite words.

2   LTL Synthesis over Finite Traces

Classically, LTL is interpreted over infinite traces, which is consistent with the idea that a reactive system might operate continuously for an indeterminate amount of time [25]. Many applications, however, use LTL to specify finite-horizon behaviors, especially in areas such as robotics and planning in AI, where systems more often than not have a finite-horizon task to complete [11, 26, 37]. This has led to the formalization of LTL with finite-trace semantics, or LTL_f [16].

Reactive synthesis from LTL_f specifications has found promising applications in planning and robotics, where it is closely related to fully-observable nondeterministic (FOND) planning [10, 15]. In this context, LTL_f synthesis can be used to synthesize a policy for an autonomous agent to complete a task within an unpredictable environment. An example is when a robot needs to complete a task in the presence of humans, who can both aid and interfere in the completion of the task [26, 49]. Synthesis can be used to generate a policy that considers all possible behaviors of the humans and other components of the environment (within a set of assumptions) and chooses how to respond to each in order to fulfill the task. Using synthesis thus avoids the need for re-planning in the case of an uncooperative environment [33].

What makes LTL_f promising in the context of reactive synthesis is that it opens up the possibility of algorithms based on automata over *finite*, rather than infinite, words. LTL_f has the same expressive power as first-order logic (FOL) over finite sequences [16]. Both are strictly less expressive than monadic second-order logic (MSO) over finite sequences, which is equivalent to finite automata [8]. This means that every LTL_f formula can be converted into a deterministic finite automaton (DFA) that accepts exactly those finite traces that satisfy the formula.

As a consequence, when the specification can be expressed as an LTL_f formula, reactive synthesis can be solved using an algorithm based on DFAs instead than ω-automata: the LTL_f formula is converted into an equivalent DFA, and the system is synthesized by solving a reachability game over this DFA [17]. Although LTL_f synthesis has the same 2EXPTIME-complete complexity as LTL synthesis, this DFA-based algorithm has a number of advantages in relation to the classic algorithms for LTL synthesis [53]:

1. Determinization of automata over finite words can use the classic subset construction algorithm, which despite still being exponential is much simpler and more efficient than Safra's construction, as well as being very amenable to symbolic representation.
2. DFA minimization is much more viable than for ω-automata. While minimization of ω-automata is NP-complete [44], DFAs have a minimal canonical form, which can be computed efficiently in time $O(n \log n)$ [28].
3. Reachability games are much simpler than parity games, being solvable in linear time [34].

We have used this theoretical algorithm as the basis for SYFT, the first framework for performing LTL$_f$ synthesis in practice [53], which takes advantage of the benefits of DFAs outlined above. SYFT works in the following way:

1. The LTL$_f$ specification is converted into an equivalent formula in FOL over finite traces.
2. The FOL formula is given as input to the tool MONA [27], which constructs the minimal DFA for the language of the formula.
3. The DFA is converted to a compact symbolic representation, using Binary Decision Diagrams (BDDs) to represent the state sets and the transition function.
4. A reachability game is solved over this DFA using a symbolic fixpoint algorithm that constructs a BDD representing the set of winning states. If the game is winning for the system, a winning strategy is constructed using BDDs as well.

Our empirical results showed that, despite LTL$_f$ synthesis having the same 2EXPTIME complexity as LTL synthesis, SYFT performed far better in practice than converting the LTL$_f$ specification to an equivalent LTL formula and giving it as input to existing tools for LTL synthesis [53]. This difference in performance can be attributed to the benefits of DFAs previously mentioned:

- The reachability game played on the DFA can be solved in linear time, and the symbolic implementation further improves the performance.
- Thanks to the ease of DFA minimization, MONA is able to output a fully-minimized DFA, decreasing the state space of the reachability game and making it easier to solve.
- MONA furthermore constructs the DFA in stages, minimizing intermediate DFAs. This leads to better performance in terms of both time and memory for the DFA construction [51].

Despite the differences between the two approaches, LTL$_f$ synthesis is able to benefit from the same strategy as GR(1) synthesis: by limiting the scope of the problem (in this case, to finite-horizon tasks) it becomes possible to achieve success where classic reactive synthesis failed. The advantages are similar to those for GR(1): avoiding the expensive determinization of ω-automata, reducing the problem to a game that can be solved in polynomial time, and producing a simpler and more compact state space that is amenable to a symbolic representation. LTL$_f$ synthesis was able to achieve this by replacing the classic algorithms based on ω-automata with DFA-based methods, and the initial experiments using SYFT have demonstrated the potential of this approach.

It is only natural to now ask what other doors DFA algorithms have opened for reactive synthesis. For instance, can DFAs be used also for synthesis over infinite traces? Can we design better algorithms for constructing and manipulating DFAs in order to improve synthesis performance? And now that DFAs have allowed us to reach an algorithm with more practical potential, can we generalize it to extensions of reactive synthesis like synthesis with incomplete information, which were previously infeasible to explore in practice? These are some of the questions that our work seeks to answer.

3   Synthesis Using Finite-Word Automata

Over the last few years we have focused on several research directions on the topic of DFA-based approaches for reactive synthesis.

One such line of research is exploring how DFA algorithms can be extended beyond synthesis over finite traces into synthesis of infinite traces, by identifying classes of specifications involving infinite-trace semantics for which the synthesis problem can similarly be reduced to a game over a DFA. In this way, the algorithmic benefits of DFAs can be exploited also for these types of specifications. One such setting is synthesis of Safety LTL [52], a fragment of LTL that can only express safety properties, meaning properties where every violation occurs in a finite time. As a consequence, the synthesis problem for this fragment can be reduced to a safety game, the dual of a reachability game, which likewise can be solved in linear time. Furthermore, the arena for this game can be constructed as a DFA for the language of finite prefixes that violate the specification, allowing us to take advantage of MONA and the efficient algorithms for DFA construction. Another example is LTL$_f$ augmented with infinite-trace assumptions, including LTL and GR(1) assumptions [13,14,50]. In this line of work, the task the system has to complete is finite, but its satisfaction might depend on an assumption of infinite behavior on the part of the environment. This means that the system might need to wait an unbounded amount of time for the right conditions to complete its task. Similarly to Safety LTL, this class of specifications can lead to games that are simpler than parity games, for example, GR(1) games, and where the arena can also be constructed as a DFA. For both Safety LTL and infinitary-assumption LTL$_f$, the DFA-based algorithms outperform the use of tools for LTL synthesis.

Another direction focuses on attempting to improve DFA construction in a way that can lead to better performance of synthesis algorithms, based on the fact that early experiments indicated that DFA construction was the bottleneck of the SYFT pipeline [53]. In [46] we presented a solution that avoids the cost of constructing the full DFA explicitly by instead representing the reachability game by the implicit product of smaller DFAs. The experimental results showed, however, that although the construction of this partitioned game is more efficient, it does not compensate for the overhead incurred for solving the game over this representation. A deeper analysis identified the root cause of the issue to be the fact that, although the partitioned game is a more compact representation, it prevents taking full advantage of DFA minimization, leading to an enlarged implicit state space that makes the reachability game harder to solve. The insights obtained from the results and analysis in that work later allowed the design an improved algorithm that achieves a balance between partitioning and minimization [5].

Finally, in [45] we investigated how the properties of automata over finite words affect the performance in practice of LTL$_f$ synthesis under partial observability, a generalization of standard LTL$_f$ synthesis where the system must satisfy the specification even in the presence of unobservable inputs [18]. Our work presented the first practical implementation of synthesis under partial observability, making use of MONA and symbolic techniques to integrate two previously-proposed algorithms for partial observability [18] into the SYFT framework. In addition, a third algorithm was introduced that emerges naturally from the use of MONA for DFA construction. The empirical evaluation showed that the practical performance of the algorithms differs significantly from what the theoretical complexity analysis predicts, due to the absence in practice of the worst-case exponential gap between deterministic and nondeterministic finite automata. These results demonstrated that, especially when dealing with finite automata, worst-case complexity is not necessarily a good predictor of practical performance, highlighting the importance of complementing theoretical analysis with an experimental evaluation.

Each of these three research directions contributes to exploring the full potential of approaches based on automata over finite words for reactive synthesis. The results improve on the state of the art and demonstrate the benefits of DFA-based algorithms, such as the value of state-space minimization for synthesis performance. The insights obtained from these works will hopefully be useful as a guide for future research on DFA-based synthesis.

References

1. Almagor, S., Boker, U., Kupferman, O.: Formally reasoning about quality. J. ACM **63**(3), 24:1–24:56 (2016). https://doi.org/10.1145/2875421
2. Almagor, S., Kupferman, O.: High-quality synthesis against stochastic environments. In: Talbot, J., Regnier, L. (eds.) CSL. LIPIcs, vol. 62, pp. 28:1–28:17. Schloss Dagstuhl - Leibniz-Zentrum für Informatik (2016)
3. Althoff, C.S., Thomas, W., Wallmeier, N.: Observations on determinization of Büchi automata. In: Farré, J., Litovsky, I., Schmitz, S. (eds.) CIAA 2005. LNCS, vol. 3845, pp. 262–272. Springer, Heidelberg (2006). https://doi.org/10.1007/11605157_22
4. Alur, R., Torre, S.L.: Deterministic generators and games for LTL fragments. In: IEEE, pp. 291–300. IEEE Computer Society (2001). https://doi.org/10.1109/LICS.2001.932505
5. Bansal, S., Li, Y., Tabajara, L.M., Vardi, M.Y.: Hybrid compositional reasoning for reactive synthesis from finite-horizon specifications. In: AAAI, pp. 9766–9774 (2020)
6. Bloem, R., Jobstmann, B., Piterman, N., Pnueli, A., Sa'ar, Y.: Synthesis of reactive(1) designs. J. Comput. Syst. Sci. **78**(3), 911–938 (2012)
7. Bohy, A., Bruyère, V., Filiot, E., Jin, N., Raskin, J.-F.: Acacia+, a tool for LTL synthesis. In: Madhusudan, P., Seshia, S.A. (eds.) CAV 2012. LNCS, vol. 7358, pp. 652–657. Springer, Heidelberg (2012). https://doi.org/10.1007/978-3-642-31424-7_45
8. Büchi, J.R.: Weak second-order arithmetic and finite automata. In: Mac, L.S., Siefkes, D. (eds.) The Collected Works of J. Richard Büchi, pp. 398–424. Springer, New York (1990). https://doi.org/10.1007/978-1-4613-8928-6_22
9. Calude, C.S., Jain, S., Khoussainov, B., Li, W., Stephan, F.: Deciding parity games in quasipolynomial time. In: STOC, pp. 252–263 (2017)
10. Camacho, A., Baier, J.A., Muise, C.J., McIlraith, S.A.: Finite LTL synthesis as planning. In: ICAPS, pp. 29–38 (2018)

11. Camacho, A., Triantafillou, E., Muise, C., Baier, J.A., McIlraith, S.: Non-deterministic planning with temporally extended goals: LTL over finite and infinite traces. In: AAAI, pp. 3716–3724 (2017)
12. Cheng, C.-H., Hamza, Y., Ruess, H.: Structural synthesis for GXW specifications. In: Chaudhuri, S., Farzan, A. (eds.) CAV 2016. LNCS, vol. 9779, pp. 95–117. Springer, Cham (2016). https://doi.org/10.1007/978-3-319-41528-4_6
13. De Giacomo, G., Di Stasio, A., Tabajara, L.M., Vardi, M., Zhu, S.: Finite-trace and generalized-reactivity specifications in temporal synthesis. In: IJCAI (2021)
14. De Giacomo, G., Di Stasio, A., Vardi, M.Y., Zhu, S.: Two-stage technique for LTL$_f$ synthesis under LTL assumptions. In: KR (2020)
15. De Giacomo, G., Rubin, S.: Automata-theoretic foundations of FOND planning for LTL$_f$/LDL$_f$ Goals. In: IJCAI, pp. 4729–4735 (2018)
16. De Giacomo, G., Vardi, M.Y.: Linear temporal logic and linear dynamic logic on finite traces. In: IJCAI, pp. 854–860 (2013)
17. De Giacomo, G., Vardi, M.Y.: Synthesis for LTL and LDL on finite traces. In: IJCAI, pp. 1558–1564 (2015)
18. De Giacomo, G., Vardi, M.Y.: LTL$_f$ and LDL$_f$ synthesis under partial observability. In: IJCAI, pp. 1044–1050 (2016)
19. Ehlers, R.: Unbeast: symbolic bounded synthesis. In: Abdulla, P.A., Leino, K.R.M. (eds.) TACAS 2011. LNCS, vol. 6605, pp. 272–275. Springer, Heidelberg (2011). https://doi.org/10.1007/978-3-642-19835-9_25
20. Emerson, E., Jutla, C.: On simultaneously determinizing and complementing ω-automata. In: Proceedings of 4th IEEE Symposium on Logic in Computer Science, pp. 333–342 (1989)
21. Faymonville, P., Finkbeiner, B., Rabe, M.N., Tentrup, L.: Encodings of bounded synthesis. In: Legay, A., Margaria, T. (eds.) TACAS 2017. LNCS, vol. 10205, pp. 354–370. Springer, Heidelberg (2017). https://doi.org/10.1007/978-3-662-54577-5_20
22. Faymonville, P., Finkbeiner, B., Tentrup, L.: BoSy: an experimentation framework for bounded synthesis. In: Majumdar, R., Kunčak, V. (eds.) CAV 2017. LNCS, vol. 10427, pp. 325–332. Springer, Cham (2017). https://doi.org/10.1007/978-3-319-63390-9_17
23. Finkbeiner, B., Schewe, S.: Bounded synthesis. Int. J. Softw. Tools Technol. Transf. **15**(5–6), 519–539 (2013). https://doi.org/10.1007/s10009-012-0228-z
24. Grädel, E., Thomas, W., Wilke, T. (eds.): Automata, Logics, and Infinite Games: A Guide to Current Research [outcome of a Dagstuhl seminar, February 2001]. Lecture Notes in Computer Science, vol. 2500. Springer, Heidelberg (2002). https://doi.org/10.1007/3-540-36387-4
25. Harel, D., Pnueli, A.: On the development of reactive systems. In: Apt, K. (ed.) Logics and Models of Concurrent Systems, NATO Advanced Summer Institutes, vol. 13, pp. 477–498. Springer, Heidelberg (1985). https://doi.org/10.1007/978-3-642-82453-1_17
26. He, K., Wells, A.M., Kavraki, L.E., Vardi, M.Y.: Efficient symbolic reactive synthesis for finite-horizon tasks. In: ICRA, pp. 8993–8999. IEEE (2019)
27. Henriksen, J.G., et al.: MONA: monadic second-order logic in practice. In: TACAS, pp. 89–110 (1995)
28. Hopcroft, J.: An $n \log n$ algorithm for minimizing states in a finite automaton. In: Theory of machines and computations, pp. 189–196. Elsevier (1971)
29. Kress-Gazit, H., Fainekos, G.E., Pappas, G.J.: Temporal-logic-based reactive mission and motion planning. IEEE Trans. Rob. **25**(6), 1370–1381 (2009)

30. Krishnan, S.C., Puri, A., Brayton, R.K.: Deterministic ω automata vis-a-vis deterministic Buchi automata. In: Du, D.-Z., Zhang, X.-S. (eds.) ISAAC 1994. LNCS, vol. 834, pp. 378–386. Springer, Heidelberg (1994). https://doi.org/10.1007/3-540-58325-4_202

31. Kupferman, O.: Recent challenges and ideas in temporal synthesis. In: Bieliková, M., Friedrich, G., Gottlob, G., Katzenbeisser, S., Turán, G. (eds.) SOFSEM 2012. LNCS, vol. 7147, pp. 88–98. Springer, Heidelberg (2012). https://doi.org/10.1007/978-3-642-27660-6_8

32. Kupferman, O., Vardi, M.: Synthesis with incomplete informatio. In: ICTL, pp. 1044–1050 (1997)

33. Lahijanian, M., Maly, M.R., Fried, D., Kavraki, L.E., Kress-Gazit, H., Vardi, M.Y.: Iterative temporal planning in uncertain environments with partial satisfaction guarantees. IEEE Trans. Robot. **32**(3), 583–599 (2016)

34. Mazala, R.: Infinite games. In: Grädel, E., Thomas, W., Wilke, T. (eds.) Automata Logics, and Infinite Games. LNCS, vol. 2500, pp. 23–38. Springer, Heidelberg (2002). https://doi.org/10.1007/3-540-36387-4_2

35. Meyer, P.J., Sickert, S., Luttenberger, M.: Strix: explicit reactive synthesis strikes back! In: Chockler, H., Weissenbacher, G. (eds.) CAV 2018. LNCS, vol. 10981, pp. 578–586. Springer, Cham (2018). https://doi.org/10.1007/978-3-319-96145-3_31

36. Moarref, S., Kress-Gazit, H.: Automated synthesis of decentralized controllers for robot swarms from high-level temporal logic specifications. Auton. Robot. **44**(3–4), 585–600 (2020). https://doi.org/10.1007/s10514-019-09861-4

37. Pešić, M., Bošnački, D., van der Aalst, W.M.P.: Enacting declarative languages using LTL: avoiding errors and improving performance. In: van de Pol, J., Weber, M. (eds.) SPIN 2010. LNCS, vol. 6349, pp. 146–161. Springer, Heidelberg (2010). https://doi.org/10.1007/978-3-642-16164-3_11

38. Piterman, N.: From nondeterministic Büchi and streett automata to deterministic parity automata. Log. Methods Comput. Sci. **3**(3) (2007)

39. Pnueli, A.: The temporal logic of programs. In: 18th Annual Symposium on Foundations of Computer Science, pp. 46–57 (1977)

40. Pnueli, A., Rosner, R.: On the synthesis of a reactive module. In: POPL, pp. 179–190 (1989)

41. Rosner, R.: Modular synthesis of reactive systems. Ph.D. thesis, The Weizmann Institute of Science (1991)

42. Safra, S.: On the complexity of ω-automata. In: FOCS, pp. 319–327 (1988)

43. Safra, S.: Exponential determinization for ω-automata with a strong fairness acceptance condition. SIAM J. Comput. **36**(3), 803–814 (2006)

44. Schewe, S.: Beyond hyper-minimisation–minimising DBAs and DPAs is NP-complete. In: Proceedings of IARCS Annual Conference on Foundations of Software Technology and Theoretical Computer Science. LIPIcs, vol. 8, pp. 400–411. Schloss Dagstuhl - Leibniz-Zentrum für Informatik (2010)

45. Tabajara, L.M., Vardi, M.Y.: LTL_f synthesis under partial observability: from theory to practice. In: Raskin, J., Bresolin, D. (eds.) GandALF. EPTCS, vol. 326, pp. 1–17 (2020). https://doi.org/10.4204/EPTCS.326.1

46. Tabajara, L.M., Vardi, M.Y.: Partitioning techniques in LTL_f synthesis. In: IJCAI, pp. 5599–5606. AAAI Press (2019)

47. Taşiran, S., Hojati, R., Brayton, R.K.: Language containment of non-deterministic ω-automata. In: Camurati, P.E., Eveking, H. (eds.) CHARME 1995. LNCS, vol. 987, pp. 261–277. Springer, Heidelberg (1995). https://doi.org/10.1007/3-540-60385-9_16

48. Vardi, M.Y.: Automata-theoretic model checking revisited. In: Cook, B., Podelski, A. (eds.) VMCAI 2007. LNCS, vol. 4349, pp. 137–150. Springer, Heidelberg (2007). https://doi.org/10.1007/978-3-540-69738-1_10
49. Wells, A.M., Lahijanian, M., Kavraki, L.E., Vardi, M.Y.: LTL$_f$ synthesis on probabilistic systems. In: Raskin, J., Bresolin, D. (eds.) GandALF. EPTCS, vol. 326, pp. 166–181 (2020). https://doi.org/10.4204/EPTCS.326.11
50. Zhu, S., De Giacomo, G., Pu, G., Vardi, M.Y.: LTL$_f$ synthesis with fairness and stability assumptions. In: AAAI, pp. 3088–3095 (2020)
51. Zhu, S., Pu, G., Vardi, M.Y.: First-order vs. second-order encodings for LTL$_f$-to-automata translation. In: TAMC, pp. 684–705 (2019)
52. Zhu, S., Tabajara, L.M., Li, J., Pu, G., Vardi, M.Y.: A symbolic approach to safety LTL synthesis. In: HVC 2017. LNCS, vol. 10629, pp. 147–162. Springer, Cham (2017). https://doi.org/10.1007/978-3-319-70389-3_10
53. Zhu, S., Tabajara, L.M., Li, J., Pu, G., Vardi, M.Y.: Symbolic LTL$_f$ synthesis. In: IJCAI, pp. 1362–1369 (2017)

Automata Theory

Determinization and Limit-Determinization of Emerson-Lei Automata

Tobias John$^{(\boxtimes)}$, Simon Jantsch$^{(\boxtimes)}$, Christel Baier,
and Sascha Klüppelholz

Technische Universität Dresden, Dresden, Germany
tobiasj@posteo.de,
{simon.jantsch,christel.baier,sascha.klueppelholz}@tu-dresden.de

Abstract. We study the problem of determinizing ω-automata whose
acceptance condition is defined on the transitions using Boolean formulas, also known as *transition-based Emerson-Lei automata* (TELA). The
standard approach to determinize TELA first constructs an equivalent
generalized Büchi automaton (GBA), which is later determinized. We
introduce three new ways of translating TELA to GBA. Furthermore,
we give a new determinization construction which determinizes several
GBA separately and combines them using a product construction. An
experimental evaluation shows that the product approach is competitive when compared with state-of-the-art determinization procedures.
We also study limit-determinization of TELA and show that this can be
done with a single-exponential blow-up, in contrast to the known double-
exponential lower-bound for determinization. Finally, one version of the
limit-determinization procedure yields *good-for-MDP* automata which
can be used for quantitative probabilistic model checking.

1 Introduction

Automata on infinite words, also called ω-automata, play a fundamental role in
the fields of verification and synthesis of reactive systems [11,32,35,39]. They can
be used both to represent properties of systems and the systems themselves. For
logical specification languages such as linear temporal logic (LTL), many verification systems, such as SPIN [4] or PRISM [25], use logic-to-automata translations
internally to verify a given system against the specification.

A major research question in this area has been, and still is, the question
of whether and how ω-automata can be determinized efficiently [26,31,33,36,
37]. The first single-exponential and asymptotically optimal determinization for
Büchi automata was presented in [36]. Deterministic automata are important

This work was funded by DFG grant 389792660 as part of TRR 248, the Cluster of
Excellence EXC 2050/1 (CeTI, project ID 390696704, as part of Germany's Excellence
Strategy), DFG-projects BA-1679/11-1 and BA-1679/12-1, and the Research Training
Group QuantLA (GRK 1763).

Z. Hou and V. Ganesh (Eds.): ATVA 2021, LNCS 12971, pp. 15–31, 2021.
https://doi.org/10.1007/978-3-030-88885-5_2

from a practical point of view as classical automata-based solutions to reactive synthesis and probabilistic verification use deterministic automata [32,39].

The high complexity of determinization and most logic-to-automata translations have raised the question of more succinct representations of ω-automata. Using *generalized* acceptance conditions (e.g. generalized Büchi [12] or generalized Rabin [8,10]) and transition-based [18], rather than state-based, conditions are common techniques in this direction. An even more general approach has led to the HOA-format [1], which represents the acceptance condition as a positive Boolean formula over standard Büchi (Inf) and co-Büchi (Fin) conditions, also called Emerson-Lei conditions [16,35]. Together with a vast body of work on heuristics and dedicated procedures this standardized format has led to practically usable and mature tools and libraries such as SPOT [14] and OWL [24] which support a wide range of operations on ω-automata. Special classes of nondeterministic automata with some of the desired properties of deterministic automata have also been studied. The classes of good-for-MDP [20] and good-for-games [23] automata can be used for quantitative probabilistic model checking of Markov decision processes [19,38], while limit-deterministic Büchi automata can be used for qualitative model-checking [11]. Dedicated translations from LTL directly to deterministic and limit-deterministic automata have been considered in [17].

This paper considers determinization and limit-determinization of TELA. In contrast to limit-determinization, the theoretical complexity of determinization is well understood (a tight, double-exponential, bound was given in [35,36]). However, it has not been studied yet from a practical point of view.

Contribution. We propose three new translations from TELA to GBA (Sect. 3) and give an example in which they perform exponentially better than state-of-the-art implementations. We introduce a new determinization procedure for TELA based on a product construction (Sect. 4). Our experiments show that it often outperforms the approaches based on determinizing a single GBA (Sect. 6). A simple adaptation of the product construction produces *limit-deterministic* TELA of single-exponential size (in contrast to the double-exponential worst-case complexity of full determinization, Sect. 5.1). We show that deciding $\mathbf{Pr}_{\mathcal{M}}^{\max}(\mathcal{L}(\mathcal{A})) > 0$ is NP-complete for limit-deterministic TELA $\mathcal{A}$, and in P if the acceptance of $\mathcal{A}$ is fin-less (Proposition 5.9). Finally, we show how to limit-determinize TELA based on the breakpoint-construction. A version of this procedure yields *good-for-MDP* Büchi automata (Definition 5.6). Thereby $\mathbf{Pr}_{\mathcal{M}}^{\max}(\mathcal{L}(\mathcal{A}))$ is computable in single-exponential time for arbitrary MDP $\mathcal{M}$ and TELA $\mathcal{A}$ (Theorem 5.15).

Related Work. The upper-bound for TELA-determinization [35,36] relies on a translation to GBA which first transforms the acceptance formula into disjunctive normal form (DNF). We build on this idea. Another way of translating TELA to GBA was described in [13]. Translations from LTL to TELA have been proposed in [7,27,30], and all of them use product constructions to combine automata for subformulas. The emptiness-check for ω-automata under different types of acceptance conditions has been studied in [2,8,10,15], where [2] covers the general case of Emerson-Lei conditions and also considers qualitative probabilistic model checking using deterministic TELA. The generalized Rabin condition from [8,10] is equivalent to the special DNF that we use and a special case of the hyper-Rabin condition for which the emptiness problem is in P [9,16]. Probabilistic model checking for *deterministic* automata under this condition is considered in [10], while [8] is concerned with standard emptiness while allowing nondeterminism. A procedure to transform TELA into parity automata is presented in [34].[1]

2   Preliminaries

Automata. A *transition-based Emerson-Lei* automaton (TELA) $\mathcal{A}$ is a tuple $(Q, \Sigma, \delta, I, \alpha)$, where Q is a finite set of states, Σ is a finite alphabet, $\delta \subseteq Q \times \Sigma \times Q$ is the transition relation, $I \subseteq Q$ is the set of initial states and α is a symbolic acceptance condition over δ, which is defined by:

$$\alpha ::= t\!t \mid f\!f \mid \mathrm{Inf}(T) \mid \mathrm{Fin}(T) \mid (\alpha \vee \alpha) \mid (\alpha \wedge \alpha), \text{ with } T \subseteq \delta$$

If α is $t\!t$, $f\!f$, $\mathrm{Inf}(T)$ or $\mathrm{Fin}(T)$, then it is called *atomic*. We denote by $|\alpha|$ the number of atomic conditions contained in α, where multiple occurrences of the same atomic condition are counted multiple times. Symbolic acceptance conditions describe sets of transitions $T \subseteq \delta$. Their semantics is defined recursively as follows:

$$T \models t\!t \quad\quad T \models \mathrm{Inf}(T') \text{ iff } T \cap T' \neq \emptyset \quad\quad T \models \alpha_1 \vee \alpha_2 \text{ iff } T \models \alpha_1 \text{ or } T \models \alpha_2$$
$$T \not\models f\!f \quad\quad T \models \mathrm{Fin}(T') \text{ iff } T \cap T' = \emptyset \quad\quad T \models \alpha_1 \wedge \alpha_2 \text{ iff } T \models \alpha_1 \text{ and } T \models \alpha_2$$

Two acceptance conditions α and β are *δ-equivalent* ($\alpha \equiv_\delta \beta$) if for all $T \subseteq \delta$ we have $T \models \alpha \iff T \models \beta$. A *run* of $\mathcal{A}$ for an infinite word $u = u_0 u_1 \ldots \in \Sigma^\omega$ is an infinite sequence of transitions $\rho = (q_0, u_0, q_1)(q_1, u_1, q_2) \ldots \in \delta^\omega$ that starts with an initial state $q_0 \in I$. The set of transitions that appear infinitely often in ρ are denoted by $\inf(\rho)$. A run ρ is *accepting* ($\rho \models \alpha$) iff $\inf(\rho) \models \alpha$. The language of $\mathcal{A}$, denoted by $\mathcal{L}(\mathcal{A})$, is the set of all words for which there exists an accepting run of $\mathcal{A}$. The sets of infinite words which are the language of some TELA are called *ω-regular*. A TELA $\mathcal{A}$ is *deterministic* if the set of initial states contains exactly one state and the transition relation is a function $\delta : Q \times \Sigma \to Q$. It is *complete*, if for all $(q, a) \in Q \times \Sigma$: $\delta \cap \{(q, a, q') \mid q' \in Q\} \neq \emptyset$. A *Büchi condition* is an acceptance condition of the form $\mathrm{Inf}(T)$ and a *generalized Büchi condition* is a condition of the form $\bigwedge_{1 \leq i \leq k} \mathrm{Inf}(T_i)$. We call the sets T_i appearing in a generalized Büchi condition its *acceptance sets*. Rabin (resp. Street) conditions are of the form $\bigvee_{1 \leq i \leq k}(\mathrm{Fin}(F_i) \wedge \mathrm{Inf}(T_i))$ (resp. $\bigwedge_{1 \leq i \leq k}(\mathrm{Fin}(F_i) \vee \mathrm{Inf}(T_i))$).

Probabilistic Systems. A labeled *Markov decision process* (MDP) $\mathcal{M}$ is a tuple $(S, s_0, \mathrm{Act}, P, \Sigma, L)$ where S is a finite set of states, $s_0 \in S$ is the initial state, Act is a finite set of actions, $P : S \times \mathrm{Act} \times S \to [0, 1]$ defines the transition probabilities with $\sum_{s' \in S} P(s, \alpha, s') \in \{0, 1\}$ for all $(s, \alpha) \in S \times \mathrm{Act}$ and $L : S \to$

---

[1] All proofs are provided in the full version of the paper [21].

Σ is a labeling function of the states into a finite alphabet Σ. Action $\alpha \in \text{Act}$ is *enabled* in s if $\sum_{s' \in S} P(s, \alpha, s') = 1$, and $\text{Act}(s) = \{\alpha \mid \alpha \text{ is enabled in } s\}$. A *path* of $\mathcal{M}$ is an infinite sequence $s_0 \alpha_0 s_1 \alpha_1 \ldots \in (S \times \text{Act})^\omega$ such that $P(s_i, \alpha_i, s_{i+1}) > 0$ for all $i \geq 0$. The set of all paths of $\mathcal{M}$ is denoted by $\text{Paths}(\mathcal{M})$ and $\text{Paths}_{\text{fin}}(\mathcal{M})$ denotes the *finite paths*. Given a path $\pi = s_0 \alpha_0 s_1 \alpha_1 \ldots$, we let $L(\pi) = L(s_0) L(s_1) \ldots \in \Sigma^\omega$. A *Markov chain* is an MDP with $|\text{Act}(s)| \leq 1$ for all states s. A scheduler of $\mathcal{M}$ is a function $\mathfrak{S} : (S \times \text{Act})^* \times S \to \text{Act}$ such that $\mathfrak{S}(s_0 \alpha_0 \ldots s_n) \in \text{Act}(s_n)$. It induces a Markov chain $\mathcal{M}_\mathfrak{S}$ and thereby a probability measure over $\text{Paths}(\mathcal{M})$. The probability of a set of paths Π starting in s_0 under this measure is $\text{Pr}^\mathfrak{S}_\mathcal{M}(\Pi)$. For an ω-regular property $\Phi \subseteq \Sigma^\omega$ we define $\mathbf{Pr}^{\max}_\mathcal{M}(\Phi) = \sup_\mathfrak{S} \text{Pr}^\mathfrak{S}_\mathcal{M}(\{\pi \mid \pi \in \text{Paths}(\mathcal{M}) \text{ and } L(\pi) \in \Phi\})$. See [3, Chapter 10] for more details.

3   From TELA to Generalized Büchi Automata

3.1   Operations on Emerson-Lei Automata

The first operator takes a TELA and splits it along the top-level disjuncts of the acceptance condition. Let $\mathcal{A} = (Q, \Sigma, \delta, I, \alpha)$ be a TELA where $\alpha = \bigvee_{1 \leq i \leq m} \alpha_i$ and the α_i are arbitrary acceptance conditions. We define $\text{split}(\mathcal{A}) := (\mathcal{A}_1, \ldots, \mathcal{A}_m)$ with $\mathcal{A}_i = (Q, \Sigma, \delta, I, \alpha_i)$ for $1 \leq i \leq m$, and $\text{split}(\mathcal{A})[i] := \mathcal{A}_i$.

Lemma 3.1. *It holds that* $\mathcal{L}(\mathcal{A}) = \bigcup_{1 \leq i \leq m} \mathcal{L}(\text{split}(\mathcal{A})[i])$.

The analogous statement does not hold for conjunction and intersection (cf [21, Fig. 5]). We also need constructions to realize the union of a sequence of automata. This can either be done using the sum (i.e. disjoint union) or the disjunctive product of the state spaces. We define a general sum (simply called *sum*) operation and one that preserves GBA acceptance (called *GBA-specific sum*). The disjunctive product construction for TELA is mentioned in [13] and similar constructions are used in [27, 30]. While the sum operations yield smaller automata in general, only the product construction preserves determinism.

Definition 3.2. *Let $\mathcal{A}_i = (Q_i, \Sigma, \delta_i, I_i, \alpha_i)$, with $i \in \{0, 1\}$, be two complete TELA with disjoint state-spaces. The* sum *of $\mathcal{A}_0$ and $\mathcal{A}_1$ is defined as follows:*

$$\mathcal{A}_0 \oplus \mathcal{A}_1 = (Q_0 \cup Q_1, \Sigma, \delta_0 \cup \delta_1, I_0 \cup I_1, (\alpha_0 \wedge \text{Inf}(\delta_0)) \vee (\alpha_1 \wedge \text{Inf}(\delta_1)))$$

If $\alpha_i = \text{Inf}(T_1^i) \wedge \ldots \wedge \text{Inf}(T_k^i)$, with $i \in \{0, 1\}$, (i.e. both automata are GBA), then we can use the GBA-specific sum:

$$\mathcal{A}_0 \oplus_{GBA} \mathcal{A}_1 = (Q_0 \cup Q_1, \Sigma, \delta_0 \cup \delta_1, I_0 \cup I_1, (\text{Inf}(T_1^0 \cup T_1^1) \wedge \ldots \wedge \text{Inf}(T_k^0 \cup T_k^1)))$$

The disjunctive product *is defined as follows:*

$$\mathcal{A}_0 \otimes \mathcal{A}_1 = (Q_0 \times Q_1, \Sigma, \delta_\otimes, I_0 \times I_1, (\uparrow(\alpha_0) \vee \uparrow(\alpha_1)))$$

with $\delta_\otimes = \{((q_0, q_1), a, (q_0', q_1')) \mid (q_0, a, q_0') \in \delta_0 \text{ and } (q_1, a, q_1') \in \delta_1\}$ and $\uparrow(\alpha_i)$ is constructed by replacing every occurring set of transitions T in α_i by $\{((q_0, q_1), u, (q_0', q_1')) \in \delta_\otimes \mid (q_i, u, q_i') \in T\}$.

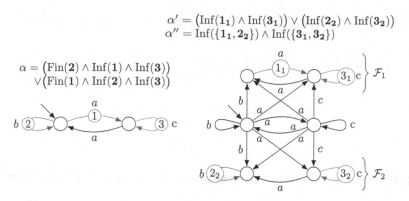

$$\alpha' = \big(\mathrm{Inf}(\mathbf{1_1}) \wedge \mathrm{Inf}(\mathbf{3_1})\big) \vee \big(\mathrm{Inf}(\mathbf{2_2}) \wedge \mathrm{Inf}(\mathbf{3_2})\big)$$
$$\alpha'' = \mathrm{Inf}(\{\mathbf{1_1}, \mathbf{2_2}\}) \wedge \mathrm{Inf}(\{\mathbf{3_1}, \mathbf{3_2}\})$$

$$\alpha = \big(\mathrm{Fin}(\mathbf{2}) \wedge \mathrm{Inf}(\mathbf{1}) \wedge \mathrm{Inf}(\mathbf{3})\big)$$
$$\vee\big(\mathrm{Fin}(\mathbf{1}) \wedge \mathrm{Inf}(\mathbf{2}) \wedge \mathrm{Inf}(\mathbf{3})\big)$$

Fig. 1. Example of applying removeFin and removeFin$_{\mathrm{GBA}}$ (Definition 3.4) to the automaton on the left. The result is the automaton on the right with acceptance α' (removeFin), respectively α'' (removeFin$_{\mathrm{GBA}}$).

The additional $\mathrm{Inf}(\delta_0)$ and $\mathrm{Inf}(\delta_1)$ atoms in the acceptance condition of $\mathcal{A}_0 \oplus \mathcal{A}_1$ are essential (see [21, Fig. 6]). We can apply the GBA-specific sum to any two GBA by adding $\mathrm{Inf}(\delta_i)$ atoms until the acceptance conditions are of equal length. Many of our constructions will require the acceptance condition of the TELA to be in DNF. We will use the following normal form throughout the paper (also called *generalized Rabin* in [8,10]).

Definition 3.3 (DNF for TELA). *Let $\mathcal{A} = (Q, \Sigma, \delta, I, \alpha)$ be a TELA. We say that $\mathcal{A}$ is in DNF if α is of the form $\alpha = \bigvee_{1 \leq i \leq m} \alpha_i$, with $\alpha_i = \mathrm{Fin}(T_0^i) \wedge \bigwedge_{1 \leq j \leq k_i} \mathrm{Inf}(T_j^i)$ and such that all $k_i \geq 1$.*

The reason that a single Fin atom in each disjunct is enough is that $\mathrm{Fin}(T_1) \wedge \mathrm{Fin}(T_2) \equiv_\delta \mathrm{Fin}(T_1 \cup T_2)$ for all T_1, T_2, δ. Taking $k_i \geq 1$ is also no restriction, as we can always add $\wedge \mathrm{Inf}(\delta)$ to any disjunct. Using standard Boolean operations one can transform a TELA with acceptance β into DNF by just translating the acceptance formula into a formula α of the above form, with $|\alpha| \leq 2^{|\beta|}$.

Fin-Less Acceptance. To transform a TELA in DNF (see Definition 3.3) into an equivalent one without Fin-atoms we use the idea of [8,13]: a main copy of $\mathcal{A}$ is connected to one additional copy for each disjunct α_i of the acceptance condition, in which transitions from T_0^i are removed. The acceptance condition ensures that every accepting run leaves the main copy eventually. Figure 1 shows an example.

Definition 3.4. *Let $\mathcal{F}_i = (Q_i, \Sigma, \delta_i, I_i, \phi_i)$, where $Q_i = \{q^{(i)} \mid q \in Q\}$, $\delta_i = \{(q^{(i)}, a, q'^{(i)}) \mid (q, a, q') \in \delta \setminus T_0^i\}$ and $\phi_i = \bigwedge_{1 \leq j \leq k_i} \mathrm{Inf}(U_j^i)$, where $U_j^i = \{(q^{(i)}, a, q'^{(i)}) \mid (q, a, q') \in T_j^i \setminus T_0^i\}$. Let removeFin$(\mathcal{A}) = (Q', \Sigma, \delta', I, \alpha')$ and removeFin$_{\mathrm{GBA}}(\mathcal{A}) = (Q', \Sigma, \delta', I, \alpha'')$, where $Q' = Q \cup \bigcup_{1 \leq i \leq m} Q_i$ and:*

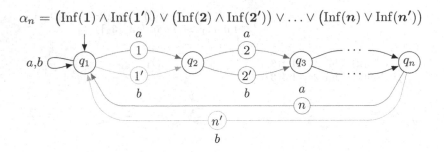

Fig. 2. A class of TELA where generating the CNF leads to 2^n many conjuncts.

- $\delta' = \delta \cup \bigcup_{1 \leq i \leq m} \left(\delta_i \cup \{(q, a, q'^{(i)}) \mid (q, a, q') \in \delta\} \right)$
- $\alpha' = \bigvee_{1 \leq i \leq m} \phi_i$
- $\alpha'' = \bigwedge_{1 \leq j \leq k} \mathrm{Inf}(U_j^1 \cup \ldots \cup U_j^m)$, with $k = \max_i k_i$ and $U_j^i = \delta_i$ if $k_i < j \leq k$.

Lemma 3.5. *It holds that* $\mathcal{L}(\mathcal{A}) = \mathcal{L}(\mathrm{removeFin}(\mathcal{A})) = \mathcal{L}(\mathrm{removeFin}_{\mathrm{GBA}}(\mathcal{A}))$.

While $\mathrm{removeFin}(\mathcal{A})$ is from [8,13], $\mathrm{removeFin}_{\mathrm{GBA}}(\mathcal{A})$ is a variant that differs only in the acceptance and always produces GBA. Both consist of $m + 1$ copies of $\mathcal{A}$ (with Fin-transitions removed).

3.2   Construction of Generalized Büchi Automata

Construction of Spot. The transformation from TELA to GBA from [13] is implemented in SPOT [14]. It transforms the automaton into DNF and then applies (an optimized version of) removeFin. The resulting fin-less acceptance condition is translated into conjunctive normal form (CNF). As $\mathrm{Inf}(T_1) \vee \mathrm{Inf}(T_2) \equiv_\delta \mathrm{Inf}(T_1 \cup T_2)$ holds for all δ, one can rewrite any fin-less condition in CNF into a conjunction of Inf-atoms, which is a generalized Büchi condition. When starting with a TELA $\mathcal{B}$ with acceptance β and N states, one gets a GBA with $N\, 2^{O(|\beta|)}$ states and $2^{O(|\beta|)}$ acceptance sets, as the fin-removal may introduce exponentially (in $|\beta|$) many copies, and the CNF may also be exponential in $|\beta|$.

Transforming a fin-less automaton into a GBA by computing the CNF has the advantage of only changing the acceptance condition, and in some cases it produces simple conditions directly. For example, SPOT's TELA to GBA construction transforms a Rabin into a Büchi automaton, and a Streett automaton with m acceptance pairs into a GBA with m accepting sets. However, computing the CNF may also incur an exponential blow-up (Fig. 2 shows such an example).

Copy-Based Approaches. We now describe three approaches (remFin→splitα, splitα→remFin and remFin→rewriteα), which construct GBA with at most $|\beta|$ acceptance sets. On the other hand, they generally produce automata with more states. They are based on [35] which first translates copies of $\mathcal{A}$ (corresponding to the disjuncts of the acceptance condition) to GBA, and then takes their sum. However, it is not specified in [35] how exactly Fin-atoms should be removed (they were concerned only with the theoretical complexity). We define:

$$\text{remFin}{\to}\text{split}\alpha(\mathcal{A}) := \bigoplus_{\substack{\text{GBA} \\ 1 \le i \le m}} \text{split}(\text{removeFin}(\mathcal{A}))[i]$$

$$\text{split}\alpha{\to}\text{remFin}(\mathcal{A}) := \bigoplus_{\substack{\text{GBA} \\ 1 \le i \le m}} \text{removeFin}(\text{split}(\mathcal{A})[i])$$

$$\text{remFin}{\to}\text{rewrite}\alpha(\mathcal{A}) := \text{removeFin}_{\text{GBA}}(\mathcal{A})$$

With removeFin as defined in Definition 3.4, the approaches remFin→splitα and splitα→remFin produce the same automata (after removing non-accepting SCC's in remFin→splitα), and all three approaches create $O(m)$ copies of $\mathcal{A}$. Our implementation uses an optimized variant of removeFin, as provided by SPOT, which leads to different results for all three approaches.

4 Determinization

Determinization via Single GBA. The standard way of determinizing TELA is to first construct a GBA, which is then determinized. Dedicated determinization procedures for GBA with N states and K acceptance sets produce deterministic Rabin automata with $2^{O(N(\log N + \log K))}$ states [37]. For a TELA $\mathcal{B}$ with n states and acceptance β, the above translations yield GBA with $N = n\, 2^{O(|\beta|)}$ and $K = 2^{O(|\beta|)}$ (SPOT's construction) or $N = n\, 2^{O(|\beta|)}$ and $K = O(|\beta|)$ (copy-based approaches). We evaluate the effect of the translations to GBA introduced in the previous chapter in the context of determinization in Sect. 6.

Determinization via a Product Construction. Another way to determinize a TELA $\mathcal{A}$ in DNF is to determinize the automata split($\mathcal{A}$)[i] one by one and then combining them with the disjunctive product construction of Definition 3.2:

$$\bigotimes_{1 \le i \le m} \det\big(\text{removeFin}(\text{split}(\mathcal{A})[i])\big)$$

where "det" is any GBA-determinization procedure. Let $\mathcal{B}$ be a TELA with acceptance β and n states, and let α be an equivalent condition in DNF with m disjuncts. Assuming an optimal GBA-determinization procedure, the product combines m automata with $2^{O(n(\log n + \log |\beta|))}$ states and hence has $\big(2^{O(n\,(\log n + \log |\beta|))}\big)^m = 2^{O(2^{|\beta|} \cdot n(\log n + \log |\beta|))}$ states.

5 Limit-Deterministic TELA

Limit-determinism has been studied mainly in the context of Büchi automata [11, 38, 39], and we define it here for general TELA.

Definition 5.1. *A TELA* $\mathcal{A} = (Q, \Sigma, \delta, I, \alpha)$ *is called* limit-deterministic *if there exists a partition* Q_N, Q_D *of* Q *such that*

1. $\delta \cap (Q_D \times \Sigma \times Q_N) = \varnothing$,
2. *for all* $(q, a) \in Q_D \times \Sigma$ *there exists at most one* q' *such that* $(q, a, q') \in \delta$,
3. *every accepting run* ρ *of* $\mathcal{A}$ *satisfies* $\inf(\rho) \cap (Q_N \times \Sigma \times Q_N) = \varnothing$.

This is a semantic definition and as checking emptiness of deterministic TELA is already coNP-hard, checking whether a TELA is limit-deterministic is also.

Proposition 5.2. *Checking limit-determinism for TELA is coNP-complete.*

An alternative syntactic definition for TELA in DNF, which implies limit-determinism, is provided in Definition 5.3.

Definition 5.3. *A TELA* $\mathcal{A} = (Q, \Sigma, \delta, \{q_0\}, \alpha)$ *in DNF, with* $\alpha = \bigvee_{1 \leq i \leq m} \alpha_i$, $\alpha_i = \mathrm{Fin}(T_0^i) \wedge \bigwedge_{1 \leq j \leq k_i} \mathrm{Inf}(T_j^i)$ *and* $k_i \geq 1$ *for all* i, *is syntactically limit-deterministic if there exists a partition* Q_N, Q_D *of* Q *satisfying 1. and 2. of Definition 5.1 and additionally* $T_j^i \subseteq Q_D \times \Sigma \times Q_D$ *for all* $i \leq m$ *and* $1 \leq j \leq k_i$.

5.1   Limit-Determinization

We first observe that replacing the product by a sum in the product-based determinization above yields limit-deterministic automata of single-exponential size (in contrast to the double-exponential lower-bound for determinization). Let $\mathcal{A}$ be a TELA in DNF with n states and acceptance $\alpha = \bigvee_{1 \leq i \leq m} \alpha_i$, where $\alpha_i = \mathrm{Fin}(T_0^i) \wedge \bigwedge_{1 \leq j \leq k_i} \mathrm{Inf}(T_j^i)$ (see Definition 3.3), and let $\mathcal{A}_i = \mathrm{split}(\mathcal{A})[i]$.

Proposition 5.4. $\bigoplus_{1 \leq i \leq m} \det(\mathrm{removeFin}(\mathcal{A}_i))$ *is limit-deterministic and of size* $\sum_{1 \leq i \leq m} |\det(\mathcal{A}_i)| = m \cdot 2^{O(n (\log n + \log k))}$, *where* $k = \max\{k_i \mid 1 \leq i \leq m\}$.

If "det" is instantiated by a GBA-determinization that produces Rabin automata, then the result is in DNF and syntactically limit-deterministic. Indeed, in this case the only nondeterminism is the choice of the initial state. But "det" can, in principle, also be replaced by any limit-determinization procedure for GBA.

We now extend the limit-determinization constructions of [11] (for Büchi automata) and [5,6,19] (for GBA) to Emerson-Lei conditions in DNF. These constructions use an *initial* component and an *accepting breakpoint component* [28] for $\mathcal{A}$, which is deterministic. The following construction differs in two ways: there is one accepting component per disjunct of the acceptance condition, and the accepting components are constructed from $\mathcal{A}$ without considering the Fin-transitions of that disjunct. To define the accepting components we use the subset transition function θ associated with δ: $\theta(P, a) = \bigcup_{q \in P} \{q' \mid (q, a, q') \in \delta\}$ for $(P, a) \in 2^Q \times \Sigma$, and additionally we define $\theta|_T(P, a) = \bigcup_{q \in P} \{q' \mid (q, a, q') \in \delta \cap T\}$. These functions are extended to finite words in the standard way.

Definition 5.5. *Let* $\theta_i = \theta|_{\delta \setminus T_0^i}$ *and define* $\mathcal{BP}_i = (Q_i, \Sigma, \delta_i, \{p_0\}, \mathrm{Inf}(\delta_i^{\mathrm{break}}))$
with: $Q_i = \{(R, B, l) \in 2^Q \times 2^Q \times \{0, \ldots, k_i\} \mid B \subseteq R\}$, $p_0 = (I, \varnothing, 0)$ *and*

$$\delta_i^{\mathrm{main}} = \left\{ ((R_1, B_1, l), a, (R_2, B_2, l)) \,\middle|\, \begin{array}{l} R_2 = \theta_i(R_1, a), \\ B_2 = \theta_i(B_1, a) \cup \theta_i|_{T_l^i}(R_1, a) \end{array} \right\}$$

$$\delta_i^{\mathrm{break}} = \left\{ ((R_1, B_1, l), a, (R_2, \varnothing, l')) \,\middle|\, \begin{array}{l} ((R_1, B_1, l), a, (R_2, B_2, l)) \in \delta_i^{\mathrm{main}}, \\ R_2 = B_2, \\ l' = (l+1) \bmod (k_i + 1) \end{array} \right\}$$

$$\delta_i = \{((R_1, B_1, l), a, (R_2, B_2, l)) \in \delta_i^{\mathrm{main}} \mid R_2 \neq B_2\} \cup \delta_i^{\mathrm{break}}$$

In state (R, B, l), intuitively R is the set of states reachable for the prefix word in $\mathcal{A}$ without using transitions from T_0^i, while B are the states in R which have seen a transition in T_l^i since the last "breakpoint". The breakpoint-transitions are $\delta_i^{\mathrm{break}}$, which occur when all states in R have seen an accepting transition since the last breakpoint (namely if $R = B$). The breakpoint construction under-approximates the language of a given GBA, in general.

We define two limit-deterministic Büchi automata (LDBA) $\mathcal{G}_{\mathcal{A}}^{\mathrm{LD}}$ and $\mathcal{G}_{\mathcal{A}}^{\mathrm{GFM}}$ where $\mathcal{G}_{\mathcal{A}}^{\mathrm{GFM}}$ is additionally *good-for-MDP* (GFM) [20]. This means that $\mathcal{G}_{\mathcal{A}}^{\mathrm{GFM}}$ can be used to solve certain quantitative probabilistic model checking problems (see Sect. 5.2). Both use the above breakpoint automata as accepting components. While $\mathcal{G}_{\mathcal{A}}^{\mathrm{LD}}$ simply uses a copy of $\mathcal{A}$ as initial component, $\mathcal{G}_{\mathcal{A}}^{\mathrm{GFM}}$ uses the determin-istic subset-automaton of $\mathcal{A}$ (it resembles the *cut-deterministic* automata of [5]). Furthermore, to ensure the GFM property, there are more transitions between initial and accepting copies in $\mathcal{G}_{\mathcal{A}}^{\mathrm{GFM}}$. The construction of $\mathcal{G}_{\mathcal{A}}^{\mathrm{GFM}}$ extends the approach for GBA in [19] (also used for probabilistic model checking) to TELA. We will distinguish elements from sets Q_i for different i from Definition 5.5 by using subscripts (e.g. $(R, P, l)_i$) and assume that these sets are pairwise disjoint.

Definition 5.6. $(\mathcal{G}_{\mathcal{A}}^{\mathrm{LD}}$ *and* $\mathcal{G}_{\mathcal{A}}^{\mathrm{GFM}})$. *Let* $Q_{\mathrm{acc}} = \bigcup_{1 \le i \le m} Q_i$, $\delta_{\mathrm{acc}} = \bigcup_{1 \le i \le m} \delta_i$ *and* $\alpha_{\mathrm{acc}} = \mathrm{Inf}(\bigcup_{1 \le i \le m} \delta_i^{\mathrm{break}})$. *Define*

$$\mathcal{G}_{\mathcal{A}}^{\mathrm{LD}} = (Q \cup Q_{\mathrm{acc}}, \Sigma, \delta^{\mathrm{LD}}, I, \alpha') \quad \text{and} \quad \mathcal{G}_{\mathcal{A}}^{\mathrm{GFM}} = (2^Q \cup Q_{\mathrm{acc}}, \Sigma, \delta^{\mathrm{GFM}}, \{I\}, \alpha')$$

with

$$\delta^{\mathrm{LD}} = \delta \cup \delta_{\mathrm{bridge}}^{\mathrm{LD}} \cup \delta_{\mathrm{acc}} \quad \text{and} \quad \delta^{\mathrm{GFM}} = \theta \cup \delta_{\mathrm{bridge}}^{\mathrm{GFM}} \cup \delta_{\mathrm{acc}}$$

$$\delta_{\mathrm{bridge}}^{\mathrm{LD}} = \{(q, a, (\{q'\}, \varnothing, 0)_i) \mid (q, a, q') \in \delta \text{ and } 1 \le i \le m\}$$

$$\delta_{\mathrm{bridge}}^{\mathrm{GFM}} = \{(P, a, (P', \varnothing, 0)_i) \mid P' \subseteq \theta(P, a) \text{ and } 1 \le i \le m\}$$

As $\delta_i^{\mathrm{break}} \subseteq \delta_{\mathrm{acc}}$ for all i, both $\mathcal{G}_{\mathcal{A}}^{\mathrm{LD}}$ and $\mathcal{G}_{\mathcal{A}}^{\mathrm{GFM}}$ are syntactically limit-deterministic. The proofs of correctness are similar to ones of the corresponding constructions for GBA [5, Thm. 7.6]. We show later in Proposition 5.14 that $\mathcal{G}_{\mathcal{A}}^{\mathrm{GFM}}$ is GFM.

Theorem 5.7. $\mathcal{G}_{\mathcal{A}}^{\text{LD}}$ and $\mathcal{G}_{\mathcal{A}}^{\text{GFM}}$ are syntactically limit-deterministic and satisfy $\mathcal{L}(\mathcal{G}_{\mathcal{A}}^{\text{LD}}) = \mathcal{L}(\mathcal{G}_{\mathcal{A}}^{\text{GFM}}) = \mathcal{L}(\mathcal{A})$. Their number of states is in $O(n + 3^n\, m\, k)$ for $\mathcal{G}_{\mathcal{A}}^{\text{LD}}$ and $O(2^n + 3^n\, m\, k) = O(|\alpha|^2 \cdot 3^n)$ for $\mathcal{G}_{\mathcal{A}}^{\text{GFM}}$, where $k = \max\{k_i \mid 1 \le i \le m\}$.

Corollary 5.8. Given TELA $\mathcal{B}$ (not necessarily in DNF) with acceptance condition β and N states, there exists an equivalent LDBA with $2^{O(|\beta|+N)}$ states.

5.2 Probabilistic Model Checking

We now discuss how these constructions can be used for probabilistic model checking. First, consider the *qualitative* model checking problem to decide $\mathbf{Pr}^{\max}(\mathcal{L}(\mathcal{A})) > 0$, under the assumption that $\mathcal{A}$ is a limit-deterministic TELA. While NP-hardness follows from the fact that the problem is already hard for deterministic TELA [29, Thm. 5.13], we now show that it is also in NP. Furthermore, it is in P for automata with a fin-less acceptance condition. This was already known for LDBA [11], and our proof uses similar arguments.

Proposition 5.9. Deciding $\mathbf{Pr}_{\mathcal{M}}^{\max}(\mathcal{L}(\mathcal{A})) > 0$, given an MDP $\mathcal{M}$ and a limit-deterministic TELA $\mathcal{A}$, is NP-complete. If $\mathcal{A}$ has a fin-less acceptance condition, then the problem is in P.

Now we show that $\mathcal{G}_{\mathcal{A}}^{\text{GFM}}$ is good-for-MDP [20]. In order to define this property, we introduce the product of an MDP with a nondeterministic automaton in which, intuitively, the scheduler is forced to resolve the nondeterminism by choosing the next state of the automaton (see [20,23]). We assume that the automaton used to build the product has a single initial state, which holds for $\mathcal{G}_{\mathcal{A}}^{\text{GFM}}$.

Definition 5.10. Given an MDP $\mathcal{M} = (S, s_0, \text{Act}, P, \Sigma, L)$ and TELA $\mathcal{G} = (Q, \Sigma, \delta, \{q_0\}, \alpha)$ we define the MDP $\mathcal{M} \times \mathcal{G} = (S \times Q, (s_0, q_0), \text{Act} \times Q, P^\times, \Sigma, L^\times)$ with $L^\times((s, q)) = L(s)$ and

$$P^\times\big((s, q), (\alpha, p), (s', q')\big) = \begin{cases} P(s, \alpha, s') & \text{if } p = q' \text{ and } (q, L(s), q') \in \delta \\ 0 & \text{otherwise} \end{cases}$$

We define the *accepting paths* Π_{acc} of $\mathcal{M} \times \mathcal{G}$ to be:

$$\Pi_{acc} = \{(s_0, q_0)\alpha_0(s_1, q_1)\alpha_1 \ldots \in \text{Paths}(\mathcal{M} \times \mathcal{G}) \mid q_0, L(s_0), q_1, L(s_1) \ldots \models \alpha\}$$

A Büchi automaton $\mathcal{G}$ is good-for-MDP (GFM) if $\mathbf{Pr}_{\mathcal{M}}^{\max}(\mathcal{L}(\mathcal{G})) = \mathbf{Pr}_{\mathcal{M} \times \mathcal{G}}^{\max}(\Pi_{acc})$ holds for all MDP $\mathcal{M}$ [20]. The inequality "$\ge$" holds for all automata [23, Thm. 1], but the other direction requires, intuitively, that a scheduler on $\mathcal{M} \times \mathcal{G}$ is able to safely resolve the nondeterminism of the automaton based on the prefix of the run. This is trivially satisfied by deterministic automata, but *good-for-games* automata also have this property [23]. Limit-deterministic Büchi automata are not GFM in general, for example, $\mathcal{G}_{\mathcal{A}}^{\text{LD}}$ may not be (see Example 5.12).

We fix an arbitrary MDP $\mathcal{M}$ and show that $\mathbf{Pr}_{\mathcal{M}}^{\max}(\mathcal{L}(\mathcal{A})) \le \mathbf{Pr}_{\mathcal{M} \times \mathcal{G}_{\mathcal{A}}^{\text{GFM}}}^{\max}(\Pi_{acc})$. To this end we show that for any finite-memory scheduler

$\mathfrak{S}$ on $\mathcal{M}$ we find a scheduler $\mathfrak{S}'$ on $\mathcal{M} \times \mathcal{G}_{\mathcal{A}}^{\text{GFM}}$ such that $\text{Pr}_{\mathcal{M}}^{\mathfrak{S}}(\mathcal{L}(\mathcal{A})) \leq$
$\text{Pr}_{\mathcal{M} \times \mathcal{G}_{\mathcal{A}}^{\text{GFM}}}^{\mathfrak{S}'}(\Pi_{acc})$. The restriction to finite-memory schedulers is allowed because
the maximal probability to satisfy an ω-regular property is always attained
by such a scheduler [3, Secs. 10.6.3 and 10.6.4]. Let $\mathcal{M}_{\mathfrak{S}} \times \mathcal{D}$ be the product of the induced finite Markov chain $\mathcal{M}_{\mathfrak{S}}$ with $\mathcal{D} = \bigotimes_{1 \leq i \leq m} \mathcal{D}_i$, where
$\mathcal{D}_i = \det\left(\text{removeFin}(\text{split}(\mathcal{A})[i]) \right)$ and "det" is the GBA-determinization procedure from [37], which makes $\mathcal{D}$ a deterministic Rabin automaton. The scheduler
$\mathfrak{S}'$ is constructed as follows. It stays inside the initial component of $\mathcal{M} \times \mathcal{G}_{\mathcal{A}}^{\text{GFM}}$
and mimics the action chosen by $\mathfrak{S}$ until the corresponding path in $\mathcal{M}_{\mathfrak{S}} \times \mathcal{D}$
reaches an accepting bottom strongly connected component (BSCC) B. This
means that the transitions of $\mathcal{D}$ induced by B satisfy one of the Rabin pairs.
The following lemma shows that in this case there exists a state in one of the
breakpoint components to which $\mathfrak{S}'$ can safely move.

Lemma 5.11. *Let $\mathfrak{s}$ be a state in an accepting BSCC B of $\mathcal{M}_{\mathfrak{S}} \times \mathcal{D}$ and π_1 be
a finite path that reaches $\mathfrak{s}$ from the initial state of $\mathcal{M}_{\mathfrak{S}} \times \mathcal{D}$. Then, there exists
$1 \leq i \leq m$ and $Q' \subseteq \theta\big(I, L(\pi_1)\big)$ such that:*

$$\text{Pr}_{\mathfrak{s}}(\{\pi \mid L(\pi) \text{ is accepted from } (Q', \varnothing, 0) \text{ in } \mathcal{BP}_i\}) = 1$$

The lemma does not hold if we restrict ourselves to singleton $\{q\} \subseteq \theta\big(I, L(\pi_1)\big)$
(see Example 5.12). Hence, restricting $\delta_{\text{bridge}}^{\text{GFM}}$ to such transitions (as for $\delta_{\text{bridge}}^{\text{LD}}$,
see Definition 5.6) would not guarantee the GFM property.

Example 5.12. Consider the automaton $\mathcal{A}$ with states $\{a_i b_j \mid i, j \in \{1, 2\}\} \cup$
$\{b_i a_j \mid i, j \in \{1, 2\}\}$, where $a_i b_j$ has transitions labeled by a_i to $b_j a_1$ and
$b_j a_2$. Transitions of states $b_i a_j$ are defined analogously, and all states in $\{a_i b_j \mid$
$i, j \in \{1, 2\}\}$ are initial (Fig. 3a shows the transitions of $a_1 b_1$). All transitions are
accepting for a single Büchi condition, and hence $\mathcal{L}(\mathcal{A}) = (\{a_i b_j \mid i, j \in \{1, 2\}\})^{\omega}$.

Consider the Markov chain $\mathcal{M}$ in Fig. 3b (transition probabilities are all $1/2$
and omitted in the figure). Clearly, $\text{Pr}_{\mathcal{M}}(\mathcal{L}(\mathcal{A})) = 1$. Figure 3c shows a part of
the product of $\mathcal{M}$ with the breakpoint automaton $\mathcal{BP}$ for $\mathcal{A}$ (Definition 5.5)
starting from $\big(a_1, (\{a_1 b_1\}, \varnothing, 0)\big)$. The state $\big(b_2, (\{b_1 a_1, b_1 a_2\}, \varnothing, 0)\big)$ is a trap
state as $b_1 a_1$ and $b_1 a_2$ have no b_2-transition. Hence, $\big(a_1, (\{a_1 b_1\}, \varnothing, 0)\big)$ generates an accepting path with probability at most $1/2$. This is true for all states
$\big(s, (P', \varnothing, 0)\big)$ of $\mathcal{M} \times \mathcal{BP}$ where P' is a singleton. But using $\delta_{\text{bridge}}^{\text{LD}}$ to connect initial and accepting components implies that any accepting path sees such a state.
Hence, using $\delta_{\text{bridge}}^{\text{LD}}$ to define $\mathcal{G}_{\mathcal{A}}^{\text{GFM}}$ would not guarantee the GFM property.

Using Lemma 5.11 we can define $\mathfrak{S}'$ such that the probability accepting paths
under $\mathfrak{S}'$ in $\mathcal{M} \times \mathcal{G}_{\mathcal{A}}^{\text{GFM}}$ is at least as high as that of paths with label in $\mathcal{L}(\mathcal{A})$
in $\mathcal{M}_{\mathfrak{S}}$. This is the non-trivial direction of the GFM property.

Lemma 5.13. *For every finite-memory scheduler $\mathfrak{S}$ on $\mathcal{M}$, there exists a scheduler $\mathfrak{S}'$ on $\mathcal{M} \times \mathcal{G}_{\mathcal{A}}^{\text{GFM}}$ such that:*

$$\text{Pr}_{\mathcal{M} \times \mathcal{G}_{\mathcal{A}}^{\text{GFM}}}^{\mathfrak{S}'}(\Pi_{acc}) \geq \text{Pr}_{\mathcal{M}}^{\mathfrak{S}}(\mathcal{L}(\mathcal{A}))$$

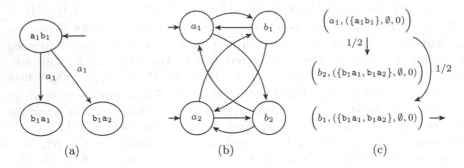

Fig. 3. Restricting $\delta_{\text{bridge}}^{\text{GFM}}$ to transitions with endpoints of the form $(s, (\{q\}, \varnothing, 0))$ (similar to $\delta_{\text{bridge}}^{\text{LD}}$) would not guarantee the GFM property (see Example 5.12).

Proposition 5.14. *The automaton $\mathcal{G}_{\mathcal{A}}^{\text{GFM}}$ is good-for-MDP.*

To compute $\mathbf{Pr}_{\mathcal{M}}^{\max}(\mathcal{L}(\mathcal{B}))$ one can translate $\mathcal{B}$ into an equivalent TELA $\mathcal{A}$ in DNF, then construct $\mathcal{G}_{\mathcal{A}}^{\text{GFM}}$ and finally compute $\mathbf{Pr}_{\mathcal{M} \times \mathcal{G}_{\mathcal{A}}^{\text{GFM}}}^{\max}(\Pi_{\text{acc}})$. The automaton $\mathcal{G}_{\mathcal{A}}^{\text{GFM}}$ is single-exponential in the size of $\mathcal{B}$ by Theorem 5.7, and $\mathbf{Pr}_{\mathcal{M} \times \mathcal{G}_{\mathcal{A}}^{\text{GFM}}}^{\max}(\Pi_{\text{acc}})$ can be computed in polynomial time in the size of $\mathcal{M} \times \mathcal{G}_{\mathcal{A}}^{\text{GFM}}$ [3, Thm. 10.127].

Theorem 5.15. *Given a TELA $\mathcal{B}$ (not necessarily in DNF) and an MDP $\mathcal{M}$, the value $\mathbf{Pr}_{\mathcal{M}}^{\max}(\mathcal{L}(\mathcal{B}))$ can be computed in single-exponential time.*

6   Experimental Evaluation

The product approach combines a sequence of deterministic automata using the disjunctive product. We introduce the *langcover heuristic*: the automata are "added" to the product one by one, but only if their language is not already subsumed by the automaton constructed so far. This leads to substantially smaller automata in many cases, but is only efficient if checking inclusion for the considered automata types is efficient. In our case this holds (the automata are deterministic with a disjunction of parity conditions as acceptance), but it is not the case for arbitrary deterministic TELA, or nondeterministic automata.

Implementation. We compare the following implementations of the constructions discussed above.[2] SPOT uses the TELA to GBA translator of SPOT, simplifies (using SPOT's `postprocessor` with preference `Small`) and degeneralizes the result and then determinizes using a version of Safra's algorithm [14,33]. The removeFin function that is used is an optimized version of Definition 3.4. In `remFin→splitα`, `splitα→remFin` and `remFin→rewriteα`, the first step is replaced by the corresponding TELA to GBA construction (using SPOT's

---

[2] The source code and data of all experiments are available at [22].

Table 1. Evaluation of benchmarks *random* and *DNF*. Columns "States", "Time" and "Acceptance" refer to the respective median values, where mem-/timeouts are counted as larger than the rest. Values in brackets refer to the subset of input automata for which at least one determinization needed more than 0.5 s (447 (182) automata for benchmark *random* (*DNF*)).

	Algorithm	Timeouts	Memouts	States	Time	Acceptance	Intermediate GBA States	Acceptance
random	Spot	0.5%	9.9%	3,414 (59,525)	<1 (1.5)	10 (17)	71	2
	remFin→splitα	0.5%	15.2%	8,639 (291,263)	<1 (9.7)	14 (24)	109	2
	splitα→remFin	0.7%	17.8%	14,037 (522,758)	<1 (21.0)	14 (24)	119	2
	remFin→rewriteα	1.6%	18.7%	15,859 (1,024,258)	<1 (40.2)	14 (26)	116	2
	product	1.3%	7.9%	3,069 (43,965)	<1 (1.2)	18 (29)		
	product (no langcover)	0.7%	9.0%	3,857 (109,908)	<1 (1.1)	24 (38)		
	limit-det.	0.0%	0.0%	778 (3,346)	<1 (<1)	1 (1)		
	limit-det. via GBA	1.6%	0.3%	463 (1,556)	<1 (1.6)	1 (1)		
	good-for-MDP	9.3%	13.4%	5,069 (192.558)	2.0 (139.6)	1 (1)		
	good-for-MDP via GBA	5.5%	44.0%	71,200 (–)	836.9 (–)	1 (–)		
DNF	Spot	0.4%	6.2%	5,980 (692,059)	<1 (18.3)	11 (25)	30	3
	product	0.0%	3.8%	2,596 (114,243)	<1 (4.6)	13 (24)		

removeFin). The product approach (also implemented using the Spot-library) is called product and product (no langcover) (without the langcover heuristic). The intermediate GBA are also simplified. The construction $\mathcal{G}_{\mathcal{A}}^{LD}$ is implemented in limit-det., using the Spot-library and parts of Seminator. We compare it to limit-det. via GBA, which concatenates the TELA to GBA construction of Spot with the limit-determinization of Seminator. Similarly, good-for-MDP and good-for-MDP via GBA are the construction $\mathcal{G}_{\mathcal{A}}^{GFM}$ applied to $\mathcal{A}$ directly, or to the GBA as constructed by Spot. Both constructions via GBA are in the worst case double-exponential. No post-processing is applied to any output automaton.

Experiments. Computations were performed on a computer with two Intel E5-2680 CPUs with 8 cores each at 2.70 GHz running Linux. Each individual experiment was limited to a single core, 15 GB of memory and 1200 s. We use versions 2.9.4 of Spot (configured to allow 256 acceptance sets) and 2.0 of Seminator.

Our first benchmark set (called *random*) consists of 1000 TELA with 4 to 50 states and 8 sets of transitions $T_1, \ldots, T_8$ used to define the acceptance conditions. They are generated using Spot's procedure random_graph() by specifying probabilities such that: a triple $(q, a, q') \in Q \times \Sigma \times Q$ is included in the transition relation $(3/|Q|)$ and such that a transition t is included in a set T_j (0.2). We use only transition systems that are nondeterministic. The acceptance condition is generated randomly using Spot's procedure acc_code::random(). We transform the acceptance condition to DNF and keep those acceptance conditions whose lengths range between 2 and 21 and consist of at least two disjuncts. To quantify the amount of nondeterminism, we divide the number of pairs of transitions of the form $(q, a, q_1), (q, a, q_2)$, with $q_1 \neq q_2$, of the automaton by its number of states.

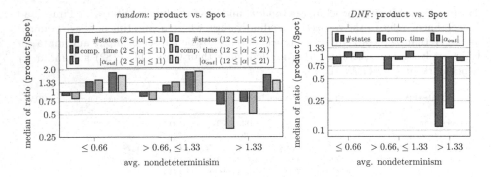

Fig. 4. Comparison of Spot and product, with input automata grouped by the size of the DNF of their acceptance condition and the amount of nondeterminism.

Table 1 shows that the product produces smallest deterministic automata overall. Spot produces best results among the algorithms that go via a single GBA. One reason for this is that after GBA-simplifications of Spot, the number of acceptance marks of the intermediate GBA are comparable. Figure 4 (left) compares Spot and product and partitions the input automata according to acceptance complexity (measured in the size of their DNF) and amount of nondeterminism. Each subset of input automata is of roughly the same size (159–180) (see [21, Tab. 2]). The graph depicts the median of the ratio (product/Spot) for the measured values. For time- or memouts of Spot (product) we define the ratio as 0 (∞). If both failed, the input is discarded. The number of time- and memouts grows with the amount of nondeterminism and reaches up to 42%. The approach product performs better for automata with more nondeterminism and complex acceptance conditions as the results have fewer states and the computation times are smaller compared to Spot.

The limit-deterministic automata are generally much smaller than the deterministic ones, and limit-det via GBA. performs best in this category. However, the construction $\mathcal{G}_{\mathcal{A}}^{\text{LD}}$ (limit-det.) resulted in fewer time- and memouts.

For GFM automata we see that computing $\mathcal{G}_{\mathcal{A}}^{\text{GFM}}$ directly, rather than first computing a GBA, yields much better results (good-for-MDP vs. good-for-MDP via GBA). However, the GFM automata suffer from significantly more time- and memouts than the other approaches. The automata sizes are comparable on average with Spot's determinization (see [21, Fig. 7]). Given their similarity to the pure limit-determinization constructions, and the fact that their acceptance condition is much simpler than for the deterministic automata, we believe that future work on optimizing this construction could make it a competitive alternative for probabilistic model checking using TELA.

The second benchmark (called *DNF*) consists of 500 TELA constructed randomly as above, apart from the acceptance conditions. They are in DNF with 2–3 disjuncts, with 2–3 Inf-atoms and 0–1 Fin-atoms each (all different). Such formulas tend to lead to larger CNF conditions, which benefits the new approaches. Figure 4 (right) shows the median ratio of automata sizes, computation times and acceptance sizes, grouped by the amount of nondeterminism. We do not consider different lengths of acceptance conditions because the subsets of input automata are already relatively small (140–193). Again, product performs better for automata with more nondeterminism.

7   Conclusion

We have introduced several new approaches to determinize and limit-determinize automata under the Emerson-Lei acceptance condition. The experimental evaluation shows that in particular the product approach performs very well. Furthermore, we have shown that the complexity of limit-determinizing TELA is single-exponential (in contrast to the double-exponential blow-up for determinization). One of our constructions produces limit-deterministic good-for-MDP automata, which can be used for quantitative probabilistic verification.

This work leads to several interesting questions. The presented constructions would benefit from determinization procedures for GBA which trade a general acceptance condition (rather than Rabin or parity) for a more compact state-space of the output. Similarly, translations from LTL to compact, nondeterministic TELA would allow them to be embedded into (probabilistic) model-checking tools for LTL (a first step in this direction is made in [27]). It would be interesting to study, in general, what properties can be naturally encoded directly into nondeterministic TELA. Another open point is to evaluate the good-for-MDP automata in the context of probabilistic model checking in practice.

Acknowledgments. We thank David Müller for suggesting to us the problem of determinizing Emerson Lei automata and many discussions on the topic.

References

1. Babiak, T., et al.: The Hanoi omega-automata format. In: Kroening, D., Păsăreanu, C.S. (eds.) CAV 2015. LNCS, vol. 9206, pp. 479–486. Springer, Cham (2015). https://doi.org/10.1007/978-3-319-21690-4_31
2. Baier, C., Blahoudek, F., Duret-Lutz, A., Klein, J., Müller, D., Strejček, J.: Generic emptiness check for fun and profit. In: Chen, Y.-F., Cheng, C.-H., Esparza, J. (eds.) ATVA 2019. LNCS, vol. 11781, pp. 445–461. Springer, Cham (2019). https://doi.org/10.1007/978-3-030-31784-3_26
3. Baier, C., Katoen, J.P.: Principles of Model Checking. Representation and Mind Series, The MIT Press, Cambridge (2008)
4. Ben-Ari, M.: Principles of the Spin Model Checker. Springer, London (2008). https://doi.org/10.1007/978-1-84628-770-1
5. Blahoudek, F.: Automata for formal methods: little steps towards perfection. Ph.D. thesis, Masaryk University, Faculty of Informatics (2018)
6. Blahoudek, F., Duret-Lutz, A., Klokocka, M., Kretínský, M., Strejcek, J.: Semi-nator: a tool for semi-determinization of omega-automata. In: International Conference on Logic for Programming, Artificial Intelligence and Reasoning (LPAR). EPiC Series in Computing (2017)

7. Blahoudek, F., Major, J., Strejček, J.: LTL to smaller self-loop alternating automata and back. In: Hierons, R.M., Mosbah, M. (eds.) ICTAC 2019. LNCS, vol. 11884, pp. 152–171. Springer, Cham (2019). https://doi.org/10.1007/978-3-030-32505-3_10

8. Bloemen, V., Duret-Lutz, A., van de Pol, J.: Model checking with generalized Rabin and Fin-less automata. Int. J. Softw. Tools Technol. Transfer **21**(3), 307–324 (2019)

9. Boker, U.: Why these automata types? In: Logic for Programming, Artificial Intelligence and Reasoning (LPAR). EPiC Series in Computing (2018)

10. Chatterjee, K., Gaiser, A., Křetínský, J.: Automata with generalized Rabin pairs for probabilistic model checking and LTL synthesis. In: Sharygina, N., Veith, H. (eds.) CAV 2013. LNCS, vol. 8044, pp. 559–575. Springer, Heidelberg (2013). https://doi.org/10.1007/978-3-642-39799-8_37

11. Courcoubetis, C., Yannakakis, M.: The complexity of probabilistic verification. J. ACM **42**(4), 857–907 (1995)

12. Couvreur, J.-M.: On-the-fly verification of linear temporal logic. In: Wing, J.M., Woodcock, J., Davies, J. (eds.) FM 1999. LNCS, vol. 1708, pp. 253–271. Springer, Heidelberg (1999). https://doi.org/10.1007/3-540-48119-2_16

13. Duret-Lutz, A.: Contributions to LTL and ω-automata for model checking. Habilitation thesis, Université Pierre et Marie Curie (2017)

14. Duret-Lutz, A., Lewkowicz, A., Fauchille, A., Michaud, T., Renault, É., Xu, L.: Spot 2.0—a framework for LTL and ω-automata manipulation. In: Artho, C., Legay, A., Peled, D. (eds.) ATVA 2016. LNCS, vol. 9938, pp. 122–129. Springer, Cham (2016). https://doi.org/10.1007/978-3-319-46520-3_8

15. Duret-Lutz, A., Poitrenaud, D., Couvreur, J.-M.: On-the-fly emptiness check of transition-based Streett automata. In: Liu, Z., Ravn, A.P. (eds.) ATVA 2009. LNCS, vol. 5799, pp. 213–227. Springer, Heidelberg (2009). https://doi.org/10.1007/978-3-642-04761-9_17

16. Emerson, E.A., Lei, C.L.: Modalities for model checking: branching time logic strikes back. Sci. Comput. Program. **8**(3), 275–306 (1987)

17. Esparza, J., Křetínský, J., Sickert, S.: One theorem to rule them all: a unified translation of LTL into ω-automata. In: Logic in Computer Science (LICS). ACM (2018)

18. Giannakopoulou, D., Lerda, F.: From states to transitions: improving translation of LTL formulae to Büchi automata. In: Peled, D.A., Vardi, M.Y. (eds.) FORTE 2002. LNCS, vol. 2529, pp. 308–326. Springer, Heidelberg (2002). https://doi.org/10.1007/3-540-36135-9_20

19. Hahn, E.M., Li, G., Schewe, S., Turrini, A., Zhang, L.: Lazy probabilistic model checking without determinisation. In: Concurrency Theory (CONCUR) (2015)

20. Hahn, E.M., Perez, M., Schewe, S., Somenzi, F., Trivedi, A., Wojtczak, D.: Good-for-MDPs automata for probabilistic analysis and reinforcement learning. In: Biere, A., Parker, D. (eds.) TACAS 2020. LNCS, vol. 12078, pp. 306–323. Springer, Cham (2020). https://doi.org/10.1007/978-3-030-45190-5_17

21. John, T., Jantsch, S., Baier, C., Klüppelholz, S.: Determinization and limit-determinization of Emerson-Lei automata. arXiv:2106.15892 [cs], June 2021

22. John, T., Jantsch, S., Baier, C., Klüppelholz, S.: Determinization and limit-determinization of Emerson-Lei automata. Supplementary material (ATVA 2021) (2021). https://doi.org/10.6084/m9.figshare.14838654.v2

23. Klein, J., Müller, D., Baier, C., Klüppelholz, S.: Are good-for-games automata good for probabilistic model checking? In: Dediu, A.-H., Martín-Vide, C., Sierra-Rodríguez, J.-L., Truthe, B. (eds.) LATA 2014. LNCS, vol. 8370, pp. 453–465. Springer, Cham (2014). https://doi.org/10.1007/978-3-319-04921-2_37

24. Křetínský, J., Meggendorfer, T., Sickert, S.: Owl: a library for ω-words, automata, and LTL. In: Lahiri, S.K., Wang, C. (eds.) ATVA 2018. LNCS, vol. 11138, pp. 543–550. Springer, Cham (2018). https://doi.org/10.1007/978-3-030-01090-4_34

25. Kwiatkowska, M., Norman, G., Parker, D.: PRISM 4.0: verification of probabilistic real-time systems. In: Gopalakrishnan, G., Qadeer, S. (eds.) CAV 2011. LNCS, vol. 6806, pp. 585–591. Springer, Heidelberg (2011). https://doi.org/10.1007/978-3-642-22110-1_47

26. Löding, C., Pirogov, A.: Determinization of Büchi automata: unifying the approaches of Safra and Muller-Schupp. In: International Colloquium on Automata, Languages, and Programming (ICALP). LIPIcs (2019)

27. Major, J., Blahoudek, F., Strejček, J., Sasaráková, M., Zbončáková, T.: ltl3tela: LTL to small deterministic or nondeterministic Emerson-Lei automata. In: Chen, Y.-F., Cheng, C.-H., Esparza, J. (eds.) ATVA 2019. LNCS, vol. 11781, pp. 357–365. Springer, Cham (2019). https://doi.org/10.1007/978-3-030-31784-3_21

28. Miyano, S., Hayashi, T.: Alternating finite automata on ω-words. Theoret. Comput. Sci. **32**(3), 321–330 (1984)

29. Müller, D.: Alternative automata-based approaches to probabilistic model checking. Ph.D. thesis, Technische Universität Dresden, November 2019

30. Müller, D., Sickert, S.: LTL to deterministic Emerson-Lei automata. In: Games, Automata, Logics and Formal Verification (GandALF). EPTCS (2017)

31. Muller, D.E., Schupp, P.E.: Simulating alternating tree automata by nondeterministic automata: new results and new proofs of the theorems of Rabin, McNaughton and Safra. Theoret. Comput. Sci. **141**(1), 69–107 (1995)

32. Pnueli, A., Rosner, R.: On the synthesis of a reactive module. In: Symposium on Principles of Programming Languages (POPL). Association for Computing Machinery (ACM), New York, NY, USA (1989)

33. Redziejowski, R.R.: An improved construction of deterministic omega-automaton using derivatives. Fund. Inform. **119**(3–4), 393–406 (2012)

34. Renkin, F., Duret-Lutz, A., Pommellet, A.: Practical "paritizing" of Emerson-Lei automata. In: Hung, D.V., Sokolsky, O. (eds.) ATVA 2020. LNCS, vol. 12302, pp. 127–143. Springer, Cham (2020). https://doi.org/10.1007/978-3-030-59152-6_7

35. Safra, S., Vardi, M.Y.: On omega-automata and temporal logic. In: Symposium on Theory of Computing (STOC). Association for Computing Machinery (ACM), New York, NY, USA (1989)

36. Safra, S.: Complexity of automata on infinite objects. Ph.D. thesis, Weizmann Institute of Science, Rehovot, Israel (1989)

37. Schewe, S., Varghese, T.: Tight bounds for the determinisation and complementation of generalised Büchi automata. In: Chakraborty, S., Mukund, M. (eds.) ATVA 2012. LNCS, pp. 42–56. Springer, Heidelberg (2012). https://doi.org/10.1007/978-3-642-33386-6_5

38. Sickert, S., Esparza, J., Jaax, S., Křetínský, J.: Limit-deterministic Büchi automata for linear temporal logic. In: Chaudhuri, S., Farzan, A. (eds.) CAV 2016. LNCS, vol. 9780, pp. 312–332. Springer, Cham (2016). https://doi.org/10.1007/978-3-319-41540-6_17

39. Vardi, M.Y.: Automatic verification of probabilistic concurrent finite state programs. In: Symposium on Foundations of Computer Science (SFCS) (1985)

Automatic Discovery of Fair Paths in Infinite-State Transition Systems

Alessandro Cimatti[1], Alberto Griggio[1], and Enrico Magnago[1,2]($\boxtimes$)

[1] Fondazione Bruno Kessler, Trento, Italy
{cimatti,griggio,magnago}@fbk.eu
[2] University of Trento, Trento, Italy

Abstract. Proving existential properties of infinite-state systems (e.g. software non-termination, model checking of hybrid automata) comes with a key challenge: differently from the finite-state case, witnesses may not be in form of lasso-shaped fair paths. In this paper we propose an approach to automatically prove existential properties for infinite state transition systems, presenting witnesses in an indirect way. The approach is based on the notion of *well-founded funnel*, where a ranking function guarantees that the states in the source set are guaranteed to inevitably reach the destination set. We show that, under suitable conditions, a sequence of funnels ensures the existence of a fair path. We propose an algorithm that, working in an abstract space induced by a set of predicates, identifies candidate funnels, proves their well-foundedness, and searches for a sequencing order.

An experimental evaluation shows that the approach is effective in proving existential properties on a wide range of examples taken from both software and LTL model checking, and outperforms various competitor tools.

Keywords: LTL model checking · LTL falsification · Infinite-state systems · SMT

1 Introduction

Temporal logic model checking for infinite-state transition systems is a very important direction in verification. Most of the works have been devoted to proving universal properties, i.e. properties holding on all the traces. The dual problem of proving existential properties, used for example for software non-termination and model checking of hybrid automata, comes with a fundamental difficulty: differently from the finite-state case, witnesses may not be in form of lasso-shaped fair paths.

In this paper we propose an approach to automatically prove existential properties for infinite state transition systems, presenting witnesses in an indirect way. Our approach is based on the notion of *well-founded funnel*. A (well-founded) funnel fnl comprises two sets of (source and target) states S and D,

© Springer Nature Switzerland AG 2021
Z. Hou and V. Ganesh (Eds.): ATVA 2021, LNCS 12971, pp. 32–47, 2021.
https://doi.org/10.1007/978-3-030-88885-5_3

an underapproximation of the transition relation, and a ranking function proving that all paths of fnl from S will eventually reach D. A sequence of funnels $fnl_0, \ldots, fnl_{n-1}$ ensures the existence of a fair path if certain conditions are met. These include that D_{n-1} must be contained in the fairness condition, the destination D_i of fnl_i must be contained in the source S_{i+1} of the next funnel for all $i > 1$, and D_{n-1} must be contained in S_0.

We propose an algorithm that identifies candidate funnels, proves their well-foundedness, and searches for the right sequencing order so that the existence of a corresponding fair path is ensured. The algorithm works in an abstraction of the infinite-state transition system induced by a set of suitable predicates. Specifically, it uses a liveness-to-safety construction to generate lasso-shaped paths in the abstract space. At its core, the proof of well-foundedness of each funnel is carried out by synthesizing a suitable ranking function.

A key difference with respect to predicate abstraction is that here abstract traces are not required to have the same number of transitions of their concretizations – in fact, each abstract state is implicitly associated with an arbitrarily high (but finite) number of self-transitions in its concretization.

We implemented the approach in a prototype called F3, built on top of the SMT solvers MathSAT and Z3. We carried out an extensive experimental evaluation, on a wide range of examples taken from both software and LTL model checking, comparing F3 with several competitor systems. The results shows that the proposed approach has two key advantages: first, it is very general, in that none of the competitor tools is able to cover all the benchmarks; second, it is very effective in proving a large number of existential properties.

The paper is structured as follows. In Sect. 2 we present some preliminaries. Then, in Sect. 3 we define funnels and prove their properties. In Sect. 4 we present the algorithm, and in Sect. 5 we discuss the related work. In Sect. 6 we briefly describe some implementation details and then discuss our experimental results. In Sect. 7 we draw some conclusions and outline the directions for future work. The proofs of all the theorems are reported in the extended version of this document[1].

2   Background

We work in the setting of SMT, with the theory of quantified real arithmetic. We assume the standard notions of interpretation, model, satisfiability, validity and logical consequence. A symbolic fair transition system M is a tuple $\langle V, I, T, F \rangle$, where V is the set of state variables; I and F are formulae over V, representing respectively the initial and fair states; T is a formula over V and V' representing the transitions, where $V' \doteq \{v' | v \in V\}$ and the primed version of a variable refers to the next state. We write $I(V)$, $F(V)$ and $T(V, V')$ to explicitly state that they are formulae over the symbols in V (I and F) and $V \cup V'$ (T) respectively.

---

[1] The extended version is available at https://enricomagnago.com/automatic_discovery_of_fair_paths_in_infinite-state_transition_systems_extended.pdf.

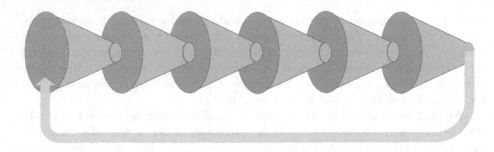

Fig. 1. Funnels combined into chain forming a funnel-loop.

We denote with v a total assignment over V, i.e. a state. A fair path of M is an infinite sequence of states, $v_0, v_1, \ldots$, such that $v_0 \models I$, $v_i v'_{i+1} \models T$ for all i, and for each i there exists $j > i$ such that $v_j \models F$. Given a formula $\phi(V)$ we also write $\phi(v)$ for the evaluation of ϕ obtained by replacing every symbol in V with its corresponding assignment in v. We also assume the standard notions of trace, reachability, and temporal logic model checking, using the usual definitions of $\mathbf{U}, \mathbf{G}, \mathbf{F}$ for the "until", "always" and "eventually" temporal operators (LTL [35]) (Fig. 1).

We overload the $\models$ symbol: when ϕ and ψ are SMT formulae, then $\phi \models \psi$ stands for entailment in SMT; when M is a fair transition system and ψ is a linear temporal property, then $M \models \psi$ is to be interpreted with the LTL semantics. If ψ is a quantifier-free SMT formula and ϕ is a conjunction of (a subset of) the atoms of ψ, then ϕ is an implicant of ψ iff $\phi \models \psi$.

Given a fair transition system M, we are interested in the problem of determining whether M admits at least one fair path. Notice that the existential LTL model checking problem, i.e. the problem of determining whether a system $M \doteq \langle V, I, T, \top \rangle$ admits at least a path that satisfies a given LTL formula φ, can be reduced to checking for the existence of a fair path in the fair transition system $M \times M_\varphi \doteq \langle V \cup V_\varphi, I \wedge I_\varphi, T \wedge T_\varphi, F_\varphi \rangle$, where $M_\varphi \doteq \langle V_\varphi, I_\varphi, T_\varphi, F_\varphi \rangle$ is a symbolic encoding of an automaton accepting the language of φ [36], which can be obtained e.g. with the procedure of [10].

A binary relation $\rho \subseteq Q \times Q$ is well-founded if every non-empty subset $U \subseteq Q$ has a minimal element wrt. ρ, i.e. there is $m \in U$ such that no $u \in U$ satisfies $\rho(u, m)$. Given a (transition) relation T over symbols $V \cup V'$, a ranking function $\mathrm{RF}(V)$ is a function from the assignments to the symbols V to some set Q, such that the relation $\{\langle \mathrm{RF}(v_0), \mathrm{RF}(v_1)\rangle \mid v_0, v'_1 \models T\}$ is well-founded.

3   Funnels and Funnel Loops

We identify fair paths by means of a composition of elements called *funnels* that, like actual funnels, take items from a source and constrain them to follow a path leading to a destination. Each funnel characterizes a set of finite paths, each starting from the source region, remaining in it for a bounded number of steps, and eventually ending in the destination region. Funnels are concatenated in chains such that the destination region of a funnel is contained in the source region of the following one. Funnel-loops are chains of funnels in which the destination region of the last funnel is included in the source region of first one.

We show that under certain conditions the existence of one such funnel-loop implies the existence of a fair path for a fair transition system M.

Given a set of symbols V, a funnel is a 4-tuple $\langle S(V), T(V, V'), D(V), \mathrm{RF}(V) \rangle$. S and D are formulae representing respectively the source and destination regions, T is the transition relation and RF is a ranking function for S with respect to the transition relation T. Intuitively, this structure represents a terminating loop over S where D are the end states of the loop. Depending on the shape of the ranking function, the loop might correspond to a simple loop or to more complex termination arguments such as nested loops. Each path through the funnel starts from a state in S, it remains in S by following transition T while the ranking function RF remains greater than the minimal element $\mathbf{0}$ and finally reaches D when the ranking function becomes $\mathbf{0}$. If we consider a trivial ranking function that is always equal to the minimal element $\mathbf{0}$ the 4-tuple simply asserts that every state in S is mapped into D by a single transition T.

Definition 1 (Funnel). *Given a set of symbols V, a funnel is defined as the 4-tuple*

$$Funnel \doteq \langle S(V), T(V, V'), D(V), \mathrm{RF}(V) \rangle$$

where: S and D are SMT formulae that represent abstract states; T is a boolean formula with symbols in $V \cup V'$ over some combination of SMT-theories representing a transition relation; RF is a function from the assignments to the symbols in V to some well-founded set with minimal element $\mathbf{0}$. Every funnel fnl satisfies the following hypotheses.

F.1. *The transition relation is total relative to the source region.*

$$\forall V \exists V' : S(V) \rightarrow T(V, V')$$

F.2. *Every funnel keeps iterating on the source region as long as its ranking function is greater than the minimal element.*

$$\forall V, V' : (S(V) \wedge \mathrm{RF}(V) > \mathbf{0} \wedge T(V, V')) \rightarrow S(V')$$

F.3. *Every step from the source region decreases the ranking function.*

$$\forall V, V' : (S(V) \wedge \mathrm{RF}(V) > \mathbf{0} \wedge T(V, V')) \rightarrow \mathrm{RF}(V) > \mathrm{RF}(V')$$

F.4. *Once the ranking function is equal to $\mathbf{0}$ the funnel reaches its destination region.*

$$\forall V, V' : (S(V) \wedge \mathrm{RF}(V) = \mathbf{0} \wedge T(V, V')) \rightarrow D(V')$$

Given a funnel fnl_i we write S_i, T_i, D_i and RF_i to refer to its components. We define the transition system corresponding to a funnel $fnl \doteq \langle S, T, D, \text{RF} \rangle$ over symbols V as $M_{fnl} \doteq \langle V, S, T, \top \rangle$. We refer to the paths through a funnel fnl with $\mathcal{L}(fnl)$ meaning the paths in the language of the corresponding transition system that end in D and write $fnl \models \phi$ meaning that ϕ holds in every path in $\mathcal{L}(fnl)$. From the definition it easily follows that every funnel fnl satisfies the following:

$$fnl \models S \textbf{ U } D$$

We define a funnel-loop as a chain of funnels $[fnl_i]_{i=0}^{n-1}$ such that the destination region of each funnel is included in the source region of the following one and the destination region of the last funnel is included in the source region of the first one.

Definition 2 (Funnel-loop). *A sequence of $n \geq 1$ of funnels $[fnl_i]_{i=0}^{n-1}$ over symbols V is a funnel-loop iff the following hold.*

FL.1. *The destination region of a funnel is included in the source region of the following funnel.*

$$\forall 0 \leq i < n - 1, V : D_i(V) \to S_{i+1}(V)$$

FL.2. *The destination region of the last funnel D_{n-1} is contained in the source region of the first funnel S_0.*

$$\forall V : D_{n-1}(V) \to S_0(V)$$

We define the paths through a funnel-loop $floop$, $\mathcal{L}(floop)$, as the infinite paths obtained by infinite concatenation of the paths of the funnels in the corresponding chain and write $floop \models \phi$ meaning that ϕ holds in all such paths. For every funnel different from the last one, Hyp. FL.1 ensures that we can extend every path of such funnel, ending in its destination region, by following the transition relation of the next funnel. Therefore, every path starting in any source region will eventually reach the destination region of the last funnel:

$$floop \models (\bigvee_{i=0}^{n-1} S_i) \textbf{ U } D_{n-1}$$

By Hyp. FL.2 every time we reach the destination region of the last funnel associated with $floop$ we are also in the source region of the first funnel. Therefore, we can extend the execution by appending another finite number of steps: a finite path starting from S_0 and ending in the last destination region D_{n-1}. We can do this infinitely many times obtaining infinite paths.

$$floop \models \textbf{G}((\bigvee_{i=0}^{n-1} S_i) \textbf{ U } D_{n-1})$$

We propose to identify a non-empty set of fair paths for a transition system M as a funnel-loop $floop$; every path through $floop$ must correspond to an

infinite fair execution of M. The totality of the transition relation of each funnel
(F.1) and their chaining (FL.1, FL.2) ensure that all the paths in $\mathcal{L}(floop)$ are
infinite. We need such paths to be fair paths, hence they must visit the fairness
condition infinitely often. By construction of $floop$ we know that every path goes
through each S_i and each D_i infinitely many times. Since by FL.1 and FL.2 for
every source region S_i, there exists a destination region D_j that is contained in
it, it is sufficient to require one of the destination regions to contain only fair
states. Without loss of generality we assume such a region to be the last one.
These conditions ensure that $floop$ represents a set of fair paths of M. However,
such set might be empty or non-reachable in M. Therefore, we finally require
the union of the source regions to contain at least one state reachable in M.
The existence of such state is sufficient to conclude non-emptiness of $\mathcal{L}(floop)$
because the transition relation of each funnel always allows for a successor state
(F.1) and, by induction, this ensures that every region and the language of
$floop$ are not empty. Theorem 1 shows that these requirements are sufficient for
a funnel-loop to prove the existence of a fair path in M.

Theorem 1. *Let $M \doteq \langle V, I_M, T_M, F_M \rangle$ be a fair transition system. Let $floop$ be
a funnel-loop of length n over the symbols V and funnels $[fnl_i]_{i=0}^{n-1}$ such that:*

FF.1. *There is at least one state reachable in M in the union of the source
regions of $floop$:*

$$M \not\models \mathbf{G}\neg \bigvee_{i=0}^{n-1} S_i$$

FF.2. *The destination region of the last funnel must contain only fair states of
M.*

$$\forall V \ : \ D_{n-1}(V) \rightarrow F_M(V)$$

FF.3. *Every transition of every funnel underapproximates the transition relation
of M. For every funnel fnl_i in $[fnl_i]_{i=0}^{n-1}$:*

$$\forall V, V' \ : \ S_i(V) \wedge T_i(V, V') \rightarrow T_M(V, V')$$

Then M admits at least one fair path.

4   Automated Synthesis of Funnel Loops

This section describes our approach to automate the synthesis of a funnel loop.
Algorithm 1 describes the main steps of the procedure. We reduce the synthesis
problem to a sequence of SMT queries. In order to reduce the search space, we
only look for deterministic funnel loops by requiring that each transition relation
of each funnel is deterministic. More in detail, Algorithm 1 enumerates candidate
conjunctive fair loops of the fair transition system and, for each loop, it generates
a sequence of parameterised candidate funnel loops. The procedure then tries to
find an assignment to the parameters such that the candidate funnel loop meets
all the hypotheses of Definitions 1 and 2 and of Theorem 1.

Algorithm 1. SEARCH-FUNNEL(M)

1: **for** $\langle v_0, abst\_s, abst\_t \rangle \in$ GENERATE-ABSTRACT-LOOPS(M) **do**
2:    **for** $fnl\_template \in$ GENERATE-TEMPLATES($v_0, abst\_s, abst\_t$) **do**
3:       $ef\_constrs \leftarrow fnl\_template.ef\_constraints()$
4:       $\langle found, model \rangle \leftarrow$ SEACH-PARAMETER-ASSIGNMENT($ef\_constrs$)
5:       **if** $found == \top$ **then**
6:          **return** $\langle model, fnl\_template \rangle$
7:       **end if**
8:    **end for**
9: **end for**
10: **return** $unknown$

In the following we consider parametric expressions that are linear combinations of the variables of the system, i.e. $\sum_{v_i \in V} \lambda_i \cdot v_i$, where λ_i are the parameters. We use a method called NEW-PARAMETRIC-EXPR to generate such linear combinations of symbols and parameters, and we refer to the set of all parameters as P.

The procedure relies on ranking functions to perform 2 different tasks. Algorithm 2 tries to synthesise ranking functions to avoid considering candidate abstract loops for which we know a ranking function exists. The existence of the ranking function proves that the loop must eventually terminate, hence it cannot correspond to an infinite path. Then, ranking function templates are also used as components for the funnels of the funnel-loop template generated by Algorithm 3. In both cases as template for the ranking functions we consider the PR-ranking template described in [31].

We first describe how we represent and enumerate candidate abstract loops for the transition system M. Then, we describe how a funnel-loop template is generated from a candidate abstract loop and the search problem associated with a funnel-loop template. Finally, we describe the approach we adopt to perform the search.

Given a fair transition system $M \doteq \langle V, I_M, T_M, F_M \rangle$ we describe a candidate conjunctive fair abstract loop of length n for M as a sequence of abstract states $abst\_s \doteq [abst\_s_i(V)]_{i=0}^{n-1}$, transitions $abst\_t \doteq [abst\_t_i(V, V')]_{i=0}^{n-2}$ and an initial state v_0 such that: (i) $v_0 \models abst\_s_0(V)$, (ii) v_0 is reachable in M, (iii) one of the abstract states underapproximates the fair states, and (iv) the abstract path is an implicant for a path of the same length in M:

$$\forall V_0, \ldots, V_{n-1} : (\bigwedge_{i=0}^{n-1} abst\_s_i(V_i) \wedge \bigwedge_{i=0}^{n-2} abst\_t_i(V_i, V_{i+1})) \rightarrow \bigwedge_{i=0}^{n-2} T_M(V_i, V_{i+1})$$

$$\exists i \, \forall V : abst\_s_i(V) \rightarrow F_M(V).$$

Both the abstract states and the abstract transitions are built as formulae over a finite set of predicates. Without loss of generality, and to simplify the presentation, we assume the fair abstract state to be the first one. The enumeration of abstract loops is performed by Algorithm 2. The procedure is based on Bounded

---

Algorithm 2. GENERATE-ABSTRACT-LOOPS(M)

1: $\langle V, I, T, bad \rangle \leftarrow$ ENCODE-BMC-FAIR-ABSTRACT-LOOP(M)
2: **for** $k \in [0, 1, 2, \ldots]$ **do**
3:     $query \leftarrow I(V_0) \wedge \bigwedge_{i=0}^{k-1} T(V_i, V_{i+1}) \wedge bad(V_k)$
4:     $\langle sat, model \rangle \leftarrow$ SMT-SOLVE($query$)
5:     $refs \leftarrow []$
6:     **while** sat **do**
7:         $\langle abst\_s, abst\_t \rangle \leftarrow$ GET-IMPLICANT($model, query$)
8:         $\langle is\_ranked, rf \rangle \leftarrow$ RANK-LOOP($abst\_s, abst\_t$)
9:         **if** is_ranked **then**
10:           $\langle V, I, T, bad \rangle \leftarrow$ REMOVE-RANKED-LOOPS(V, I, T, bad, rf)
11:         **else**
12:           $v_0 \leftarrow$ GET-LOOPBACK-STATE($model$)
13:           **yield** $\langle v_0, abst\_s, abst\_t \rangle$
14:           $refs.append(\neg(\bigwedge_{s \in abst\_s} s \wedge \bigwedge_{t \in abst\_t} t))$
15:         **end if**
16:         $query \leftarrow I(V_0) \wedge \bigwedge_{i=0}^{k-1} T(V_i, V_{i+1}) \wedge bad(V_k) \wedge \bigwedge_{ref \in refs} ref$
17:         $\langle sat, model \rangle \leftarrow$ SMT-SOLVE($query$)
18:     **end while**
19: **end for**

Model Checking (BMC) [3], for the enumeration of candidate paths, and on the computation of an implicant for each path.

Line 1 performs the usual BMC encoding for the search of a fair loop, where the loop-back state is identified in the abstract space defined by the predicates in the transition relation and fairness condition of M. The last state and the loop-back state must agree on the truth assignment of all the predicates in the transition relation and fairness condition, hence they may not be the very same assignment. We then rely on a SMT-solver to identify fair lasso paths of increasing length k, as done for the abstract liveness-to-safety algorithm of [14]. Then, at line 8 we first try to synthesise a ranking function for such abstract loop. The method RANK-LOOP implements the procedure described in [31] for PR-ranking templates. If we succeed in identifying a ranking function, we refine our transition system such that we avoid enumerating other loops ranked by the same function, as described in [14] (REMOVE-RANKED-LOOPS, line 10). Otherwise, from the path we extract the assignment to the loop-back state and return it together with the current abstract path. If no abstract loop of length k exists, we clear the list of refinements and enumerate the candidate loops of length $k + 1$.

Algorithm 3 shows the procedure we use to generate a funnel-loop template from a candidate abstract loop. We generate a funnel-loop of the same length as the abstract loop. Line 1 selects a list of natural numbers to be used to generate the funnel-loop templates. Each number corresponds to the amount of parametric inequalities added to each abstract state to define the corresponding source region of a funnel template (line 6). The higher the number the more freedom will the template have in shrinking the regions, but in the search problem we will have more parameters and a larger space to explore. Notice that, since

---

Algorithm 3. GENERATE-TEMPLATES($v_0, abst\_s, abst\_t$)

1: $ineqs \leftarrow$ HEURISTIC-PICK-NUM-INEQS($abst\_s, abst\_t$)
2: **for** $ineq \in ineqs$ **do**
3:    $n \leftarrow len(abst\_s)$
4:    $funnels \leftarrow []$
5:    **for** $i \in [0..n-2]$ **do**
6:       $src \leftarrow abst\_s[i] \wedge \bigwedge_{j=0}^{ineq-1}$ NEW-PARAMETRIC-EXPR(V) ≥ 0
7:       $rf \leftarrow$ NEW-PARAMETRIC-EXPR(V)
8:       $t \leftarrow \top$
9:       **for** $v_{i+1} \in V_{i+1}$ **do**
10:          **if** $v_{i+1} = f(V_i) \in abst\_t[i]$ for some function f **then**
11:             $t \leftarrow t \wedge v_{i+1} = f(V_i)$
12:          **else**
13:             $t \leftarrow t \wedge v_{i+1} =$ NEW-PARAMETRIC-EXPR(V_i)
14:          **end if**
15:       **end for**
16:       $dst(V) \leftarrow \forall V_0 : src(V_0) \wedge rf(V_0) = \mathbf{0} \wedge t(V_0, S)$
17:       $funnels.append(Funnel(src, t, rf, dst))$
18:    **end for**
19:    **yield** FUNNEL-LOOP($funnels, v_0$)
20: **end for**

---

by construction of the abstract loop one of the $abst\_s$ is fair, then also the corresponding destination region in the funnel-loop template will be fair. We create the funnel template corresponding to the ith abstract state $abst\_s[i]$ and transition $abst\_t[i]$ in lines 5–18. We define the transition relation t of the funnel as a deterministic functional assignment as follows. For each symbol $v_{i+1} \in V_{i+1}$, if $abst\_t_i$ already contains a functional assignment for v_{i+1}, then we use that (line 11). Otherwise, we generate a functional assignment for v_{i+1} as a parametric expression over the symbols in V (line 13). We define the destination region of a funnel implicitly as the set of states reachable in one step from $S(V) \wedge \text{RF}(V) = \mathbf{0}$ (line 16). Finally, the procedure returns the funnel-loop template associated with the list of parametric funnels and initial state v_0.

We now describe the $\exists \forall$ quantified formula that corresponds to the synthesis problem of a funnel-loop template and the procedure we use to solve it. Every instance of the funnel-loop template must satisfy all hypotheses of Definitions 1, and 2 and of Theorem 1. In the hypotheses, for every funnel $fnl_i \doteq \langle S_i, T_i, D_i, \text{RF}_i \rangle$, we replace each destination region D_i with the quantified formula:

$$\forall V_0 : S_i(V_0) \wedge \text{RF}_i(V_0) = \mathbf{0} \wedge T_i(V_0, V). \tag{1}$$

Every instance of the funnel-loop template must contain a fair region since $abst\_s_0$ is a subset of the fair states and S_0, by construction, underapproximates $abst\_s_0$. We ensure that Hyp. FF.1 holds by requiring that v_0 is in the source region of the first funnel fnl_0 with the constraint:

$$\exists P : S_0(v_0, P). \tag{2}$$

Hyp. F.1 holds by construction since each transition relation T_i of every funnel template fnl_i is a functional assignment without any circular dependency. Hyp. F.4 holds since we implicitly defined the destination region of each funnel fnl_i as the set of states reachable in one step from $S_i \wedge \text{RF}_i = \mathbf{0}$. Then, we ensure that every instantiation of every funnel template fnl_i in the funnel-loop template satisfies hypotheses F.2 and F.3 by requiring that the following hold:

$$\exists P \; \forall V, V' : (S_i(V, P) \wedge \text{RF}_i(V, P) > \mathbf{0} \wedge T_i(V, V', P)) \rightarrow S_i(V', P) \tag{3}$$

$$\exists P \; \forall V, V' : (S_i(V, P) \wedge \text{RF}_i(V, P) > \mathbf{0} \wedge T_i(V, V', P)) \rightarrow \text{RF}_i(V, P) > \text{RF}_i(V', P) \tag{4}$$

The funnels must be correctly chained for Hyp. FL.1 to hold. For this reason we require every two consecutive funnel templates fnl_i and fnl_{i+1} in the funnel-loop template to satisfy the following:

$$\exists P \; \forall V, V' : (S_i(V, P) \wedge \text{RF}_i(V, P) = \mathbf{0} \wedge T_i(V, V', P)) \rightarrow S_{i+1}(V', P) \tag{5}$$

Similarly, considering the first and last funnels fnl_0 and fnl_{n-1}, for Hyp. FL.2 we require:

$$\exists P \; \forall V, V' : (S_{n-1}(V, P) \wedge \text{RF}_{n-1}(V, P) = \mathbf{0} \wedge T_{n-1}(V, V', P)) \rightarrow S_0(V', P) \tag{6}$$

This ensures that D_{n-1} is a subset of S_0. We have observed above that S_0 contains only fair states, hence FF.2 holds. Finally, we require each funnel-loop instance to underapproximate M (Hyp. FF.3) by requiring the following to hold for every funnel fnl:

$$\exists P \; \forall V, V' : S(V, P) \wedge T(V, V', P) \rightarrow T_M(V, V'). \tag{7}$$

The final synthesis problem is then given by the conjunction of all the constraints (1)–(7). In order to solve it, we apply a combination of the EF-SMT procedure of [16] and the application of Motzkin's transposition theorem [33] to reduce the problem into a purely existentially-quantified one which can then be solved via standard quantifier-free SMT reasoning: we first try to apply EF-SMT, and resort to the elimination of universal quantifiers only if this fails to provide a definite answer.

5 Related Work

Most of the literature in verification of temporal properties of infinite-state transition systems, hybrid automata and termination analysis focuses on the universal case, while the existential one has received relatively little attention. The most closely related work is [6]. The key difference is that the procedure we presented in [6] is partly interactive, while the approach presented here is fully automatic. Furthermore, there is a difference at the technical level in the way the approaches partition the problem. In [6], the idea is to synthesise a partitioned structure called $\mathcal{R}$-abstraction out of a set of components, called $\mathcal{AG}$-skeletons. Each component is obtained by considering only a subset of the symbols of the system, and is used to describe a set of infinite paths for such symbols. Here, instead, we act on the monolithic system, but partition the fair path into funnels.

Also related are the works concerned with proving *program non-termination*. [21] and [11] are based on the notion of closed recurrence set, that corresponds to proving the non-termination of a relation. [5] and [30] search for non-terminating executions via a sequence of safety queries. Other approaches look for specific classes of programs ([18] and [24] prove the decidability of termination for linear loops over the integers), or specific non-termination arguments (in [32] non-termination is seen as the sum of geometric series). However, none of these works deals with fairness and they rely on the existence of a control flow graph, whereas we work at the level of transition system.

[13] reduces the verification of the universal fragment of CTL on a infinite-state transition system to the problem of deciding whether a program always returns true. The approach can be applied also on LTL properties by relying on a reduction based on prophecy variables and it relies on some off-the-shelf tool for the analysis of the program. Therefore, its capability of proving or identifying a counterexample for some property depends on the ones of the considered underlying tool.

[12] explicitly deals with fairness for infinite-state programs supporting full CTL*: it is able to deal with existential properties and to provide fair paths as witnesses. The approach focuses on programs manipulating integer variables, with an explicit control-flow graph, rather than more general symbolic transition systems expressed over different theories (including real arithmetic). Another approach supporting full CTL* is proposed in [25]. The work presents a model checking algorithm for the verification of CTL* on finite-state systems and a deductive proof system for CTL* on infinite-state systems. In the first case they reduce the verification of CTL* properties to the verification of properties without temporal operators and a single fair path quantifier in front of the formula. To the best of our knowledge there is no generalisation of this algorithm, first reported in [26] and then also in [27], to the infinite-state setting. The rules presented in the second case have been exploited in [2] to implement a procedure for the verification of CTL properties, while our objective is the falsification of LTL properties. Moreover, in these settings [12,25] there is no notion of non-zenoness.

The works on *timed automata* are less relevant: although the concrete system may exhibit no lasso-shaped witnesses, due to the divergence of clocks, the problem is decidable, and lasso-shaped counterexamples exist in finite bi-simulating abstractions. This view is adopted, for example, in UPPAAL [1]. Other tools directly search for non lasso-shaped counterexamples, but the proposed techniques are specific for the setting of timed automata [7,28] and lack the generality of the method proposed in this paper. Finally, our approach can be applied also to *hybrid systems*. However, the implementation relies on an approximation of the nonlinearities which, from our experiments, appears too coarse for this context.

6   Experimental Evaluation

Implementation. We have implemented these procedures in a prototype, called F3[2] (for FINDFAIRFUNNEL), written in Python. F3 uses MATHSAT5 [9] and Z3 [34] as underlying SMT engines, interacting with them through PYSMT [19]. F3 takes as input a transition system M and a fairness condition F, and tries to identify a funnel that proves that M admits at least 1 path that visits F infinitely-often. We then employ the usual tableau construction to support LTL specifications via reduction to the previous case. In order to support timed systems, we use the product construction described in [8] to remove all zeno-paths of the model. F3 enumerates funnel templates in increasing order of complexity. By default, F3, considers a minimum of 0 and a maximum of 2 inequalities in the implementation of HEURISTIC-PICK-NUM-INEQS of Algorithm 3. An important optimization is that F3 generates ranking function templates (line 6 of Algorithm 3) only when it finds a pair of abstract states that prescribe the same assignment to the boolean variables of M; if the abstract states differ in their boolean variables, rf is simply set to the constant $\mathbf{0}$. This avoids the introduction of unnecessary parameters for funnels which do not need an explicit ranking function. Finally, when applying the Motzkin's transposition theorem to solve the parameter synthesis problems, F3 replaces non-linear terms with fresh symbols, in order to obtain a linear system. This simple way of handling non-linearities has the benefit of being very easy to implement; on the other hand, however, it can produce very coarse approximations, which can prevent F3 from finding counterexamples in cases where non-linearities play a significant role.

Benchmarks. In order to evaluate the effectiveness of our method, we have evaluated F3 on a wide range of benchmarks coming from different domains, from software (non)termination to timed automata and infinite-state symbolic transition systems. More specifically, we considered a total of 455 benchmarks, divided into 6 categories:

LS consists of 52 nonterminating linear software benchmarks taken from the C programs of the software termination competition;

NS contains 30 nonlinear software programs, of which 29 have been taken from [11] and one from [6];

ITS are 70 LTL falsification problems on infinite-state systems; 2 of such problems are proof obligations generated in the verification of a contract-based design, 29 come from the scaling to up to 30 processes of a model of the bakery mutual exclusion protocol in which we introduced a bug, other 29 come from the scaling to up to 30 processes of a semaphore-based synchronisation protocol, and the last 10 are instances we created;

---

[2] The tool and the benchmarks can be downloaded from https://github.com/EnricoMagnago/F3.

TA contains 174 LTL falsification problems on timed automata; we consider 6 different protocols taken from [17] (*critical, csma, fddi, fischer, lynch* and *train*) and scale each of them from 1 to 30 processes;

TTS consists of 120 LTL falsification problems on timed transition systems, of which 116 come from the scaling from 1 to 30 processes of 4 protocols (inspired by the *csma, fischer, lynch* and *token ring* protocols), and 4 are handcrafted instances;

HS are 9 LTL falsification problems on hybrid systems (encoded as nonlinear infinite-state transition systems) taken from [6].

F3 only handles symbolic transition systems, and not software programs; therefore, we have encoded the software benchmarks as infinite-state transition systems by introducing an explicit program counter as state variable. Moreover, since F3 only supports systems with boolean, integer and real variables, we have not considered programs that involve recursion or dynamic memory allocation.

Competitor Tools. We compare F3 with the following state-of-the-art tools: ANANT [11], APROVE [20], DIVINE3 [22], MITLBMC [29], NUXMV [7], T2 [4], ULTIMATE [23] and UPPAAL [15]. Most of the other tools are however not able to handle all the benchmarks we have considered. Therefore, we limit their application as follows:

- we ran ANANT, APROVE and T2 only on the software nontermination problems (LS and NS groups);
- we ran DIVINE3, MITLBMC and UPPAAL only on the time automata (TA) benchmarks; moreover, since UPPAAL supports only a fragment of LTL which is not sufficient to express the properties of the *fischer* and *lynch* benchmarks, we could run it only on 116 of the 174 TA instances;
- as ULTIMATE doesn't support non-linear arithmetic, we didn't run it on the NA family. Moreover, since it supports LTL specifications but works on programs rather than transition systems, we translated the benchmarks to LTL verification problems on software programs, using the same approach described in [14].
- NUXMV is the only other tool (besides F3) that supports all the benchmarks. Since our focus is falsification of universal properties (or dually verification of existential ones), we ran NUXMV using only its BMC engine.

Results. We performed our experiments on a machine running Ubuntu 20.04 equipped with an Intel(R) Xeon(R) Gold 6226R 2.90 GHz CPU, using a 1 h timeout and a memory limit of 30 GB for each benchmark. A summary of the evaluation results is reported in Table 1. The table shows, for each tool, the number of solved instances in each benchmark family. When a tool is not applicable to a specific family, this is marked with "-". From the table, we can see that F3 not only solved the highest number (by far) of instances overall, but it is also the tool that solved the highest number of instances in all categories

Table 1. Summary of experimental results (number of solved instances per benchmark family).

Benchmark family	F3	ANANT	APROVE	DIVINE3	MITLBMC	NUXMV	T2	ULTIMATE	UPPAAL
LS (52)	**52**	38	43	–	–	28	38	49	–
NS (30)	**29**	25	5	–	–	14	2	–	–
ITS (70)	**57**	–	–	–	–	4	–	8	–
TA (174)	137	–	–	43	**151**	90	–	0	103
TTS (120)	**55**	–	–	–	–	8	–	1	–
HS (9)	0	–	–	–	–	0	–	–	–
Total (455)	**330**	63	48	43	151	144	40	58	103

Entries marked with "–" denote that the tool cannot handle the given benchmarks.

with the exception of timed automata. In this category F3 is outperformed only by MITLBMC, which implements a technique explicitly developed for timed automata. This demonstrates the generality of our approach, although (unsurprisingly) it is possible to define more efficient procedures to target specific classes of problems. On the software benchmarks (linear and non-linear) F3 fails to provide an answer in only 1 case (the nonlinear one taken from[6]). Therefore, while being coarse-grained, the approximation of the nonlinear terms used by F3 appears to be sufficient in these cases. However, the hybrid benchmarks highlight the limitations of such approximation. In fact, F3 was unable to provide an answer in all 9 cases. These instances can be solved successfully with the approach of [6], which however requires user guidance and is therefore not fully automatic. In fact, we are not aware of any automatic tool that is able to solve them. Finally, we should remark that unlike F3 several of the competitor tools (with the exception of MITLBMC and NUXMV in BMC mode) are also able to prove that a universal property holds, whereas F3 can only find counterexamples. On the other hand, however, our techniques can be easily integrated with approaches focusing on proving properties, such as [8,14].

7 Conclusions and Future Work

In this paper we presented an automated approach to the verification of existential properties for infinite-state systems. We adopt an approach to build an implicit presentation of fair paths, that may not have a lasso-shape structure, using an abstract representation of the trace in form of a sequence of funnels. The approach alternates between finding candidate counterexample skeleta in the abstract space, and proving whether they admit a concretization.

The experimental evaluation, carried out on a wide set of benchmarks, demonstrates that the approach is very effective, being able to solve realistic benchmarks from many different domains, and also general, being competitive with other specialized tools.

In the future, we plan to integrate the partitioning techniques presented in [6] in an automated setting, and to explore the possibility of hierarchically decomposed proofs.

References

1. Behrmann, G., David, A., Larsen, K.G.: A tutorial on UPPAAL. In: Bernardo, M., Corradini, F. (eds.) SFM-RT 2004. LNCS, vol. 3185, pp. 200–236. Springer, Heidelberg (2004). https://doi.org/10.1007/978-3-540-30080-9_7
2. Beyene, T.A., Popeea, C., Rybalchenko, A.: Solving existentially quantified horn clauses. In: Sharygina, N., Veith, H. (eds.) CAV 2013. LNCS, vol. 8044, pp. 869–882. Springer, Heidelberg (2013). https://doi.org/10.1007/978-3-642-39799-8_61
3. Biere, A., Cimatti, A., Clarke, E.M., Strichman, O., Zhu, Y.: Bounded model checking. Adv. Comput. **58**, 1–27 (2003)
4. Brockschmidt, M., Cook, B., Ishtiaq, S., Khlaaf, H., Piterman, N.: T2: temporal property verification. In: Chechik, M., Raskin, J.-F. (eds.) TACAS 2016. LNCS, vol. 9636, pp. 387–393. Springer, Heidelberg (2016). https://doi.org/10.1007/978-3-662-49674-9_22
5. Chen, H.-Y., Cook, B., Fuhs, C., Nimkar, K., O'Hearn, P.: Proving nontermination via safety. In: Ábrahám, E., Havelund, K. (eds.) TACAS 2014. LNCS, vol. 8413, pp. 156–171. Springer, Heidelberg (2014). https://doi.org/10.1007/978-3-642-54862-8_11
6. Cimatti, A., Griggio, A., Magnago, E.: Proving the existence of fair paths in infinite-state systems. In: Henglein, F., Shoham, S., Vizel, Y. (eds.) VMCAI 2021. LNCS, vol. 12597, pp. 104–126. Springer, Cham (2021). https://doi.org/10.1007/978-3-030-67067-2_6
7. Cimatti, A., Griggio, A., Magnago, E., Roveri, M., Tonetta, S.: Extending nuXmv with timed transition systems and timed temporal properties. In: Dillig, I., Tasiran, S. (eds.) CAV 2019. LNCS, vol. 11561, pp. 376–386. Springer, Cham (2019). https://doi.org/10.1007/978-3-030-25540-4_21
8. Cimatti, A., Griggio, A., Mover, S., Tonetta, S.: Verifying LTL properties of hybrid systems with K-LIVENESS. In: Biere, A., Bloem, R. (eds.) CAV 2014. LNCS, vol. 8559, pp. 424–440. Springer, Cham (2014). https://doi.org/10.1007/978-3-319-08867-9_28
9. Cimatti, A., Griggio, A., Schaafsma, B.J., Sebastiani, R.: The MathSAT5 SMT solver. In: Piterman, N., Smolka, S.A. (eds.) TACAS 2013. LNCS, vol. 7795, pp. 93–107. Springer, Heidelberg (2013). https://doi.org/10.1007/978-3-642-36742-7_7
10. Clarke, E.M., Grumberg, O., Hamaguchi, K.: Another look at LTL model checking. Formal Methods Syst. Des. **10**(1), 47–71 (1997)
11. Cook, B., Fuhs, C., Nimkar, K., O'Hearn, P.W.: Disproving termination with over-approximation. In: FMCAD. IEEE (2014)
12. Cook, B., Khlaaf, H., Piterman, N.: Verifying increasingly expressive temporal logics for infinite-state systems. J. ACM **64**(2), 1–39 (2017)
13. Cook, B., Koskinen, E., Vardi, M.Y.: Temporal property verification as a program analysis task - extended version. Formal Methods Syst. Des. **41**(1), 66–82 (2012)
14. Daniel, J., Cimatti, A., Griggio, A., Tonetta, S., Mover, S.: Infinite-state liveness-to-safety via implicit abstraction and well-founded relations. In: Chaudhuri, S., Farzan, A. (eds.) CAV 2016. LNCS, vol. 9779, pp. 271–291. Springer, Cham (2016). https://doi.org/10.1007/978-3-319-41528-4_15
15. David, A., Larsen, K.G., Legay, A., Mikučionis, M., Poulsen, D.B.: Uppaal SMC tutorial. Int. J. Softw. Tools Technol. Transfer **17**(4), 397–415 (2015)
16. Dutertre, B.: Solving exists/forall problems with yices. In: SMT Workshop (2015)
17. Farkas, R., Bergmann, G.: Towards reliable benchmarks of timed automata. In: Proceedings of the 25th PhD Mini-Symposium (2018)

18. Frohn, F., Giesl, J.: Termination of triangular integer loops is decidable. In: Dillig, I., Tasiran, S. (eds.) CAV 2019. LNCS, vol. 11562, pp. 426–444. Springer, Cham (2019). https://doi.org/10.1007/978-3-030-25543-5_24

19. Gario, M., Micheli, A.: PySMT: a solver-agnostic library for fast prototyping of SMT-based algorithms. In: SMT Workshop (2015)

20. Giesl, J., et al.: Proving termination of programs automatically with AProVE. In: Demri, S., Kapur, D., Weidenbach, C. (eds.) IJCAR 2014. LNCS (LNAI), vol. 8562, pp. 184–191. Springer, Cham (2014). https://doi.org/10.1007/978-3-319-08587-6_13

21. Gupta, A., Henzinger, T.A., Majumdar, R., Rybalchenko, A., Xu, R.: Proving non-termination. In: POPL. ACM (2008)

22. Havlíček, J.: Untimed LTL model checking of timed automata. Ph.D. thesis, Masaryk University (2013)

23. Heizmann, M., et al.: Ultimate automizer with SMTInterpol. In: Piterman, N., Smolka, S.A. (eds.) TACAS 2013. LNCS, vol. 7795, pp. 641–643. Springer, Heidelberg (2013). https://doi.org/10.1007/978-3-642-36742-7_53

24. Hosseini, M., Ouaknine, J., Worrell, J.: Termination of linear loops over the integers. In: ICALP. LIPIcs, vol. 132 (2019)

25. Kesten, Y., Pnueli, A.: A compositional approach to CTL* verification. Theor. Comput. Sci. **331**(2-3), 397–428 (2005)

26. Kesten, Y., Pnueli, A., Raviv, L.: Algorithmic verification of linear temporal logic specifications. In: Larsen, K.G., Skyum, S., Winskel, G. (eds.) ICALP 1998. LNCS, vol. 1443, pp. 1–16. Springer, Heidelberg (1998). https://doi.org/10.1007/BFb0055036

27. Kesten, Y., Pnueli, A., Raviv, L., Shahar, E.: Model checking with strong fairness. Formal Methods Syst. Des. **28**(1), 57–84 (2006)

28. Kindermann, R., Junttila, T., Niemelä, I.: Beyond lassos: complete SMT-based bounded model checking for timed automata. In: Giese, H., Rosu, G. (eds.) FMOODS/FORTE -2012. LNCS, vol. 7273, pp. 84–100. Springer, Heidelberg (2012). https://doi.org/10.1007/978-3-642-30793-5_6

29. Kindermann, R., Junttila, T.A., Niemelä, I.: Bounded model checking of an MITL fragment for timed automata. In: ACSD. IEEE Computer Society (2013)

30. Larraz, D., Nimkar, K., Oliveras, A., Rodríguez-Carbonell, E., Rubio, A.: Proving non-termination using max-SMT. In: Biere, A., Bloem, R. (eds.) CAV 2014. LNCS, vol. 8559, pp. 779–796. Springer, Cham (2014). https://doi.org/10.1007/978-3-319-08867-9_52

31. Leike, J., Heizmann, M.: Ranking templates for linear loops. Log. Methods Comput. Sci. **11**(1) (2015)

32. Leike, J., Heizmann, M.: Geometric nontermination arguments. In: Beyer, D., Huisman, M. (eds.) TACAS 2018. LNCS, vol. 10806, pp. 266–283. Springer, Cham (2018). https://doi.org/10.1007/978-3-319-89963-3_16

33. Motzkin, T.S.: Two consequences of the transposition theorem on linear inequalities. Econometrica (pre-1986) **19**(2), 184 (1951)

34. de Moura, L., Bjørner, N.: Z3: an efficient SMT solver. In: Ramakrishnan, C.R., Rehof, J. (eds.) TACAS 2008. LNCS, vol. 4963, pp. 337–340. Springer, Heidelberg (2008). https://doi.org/10.1007/978-3-540-78800-3_24

35. Pnueli, A.: The temporal logic of programs. In: 18th Annual Symposium on Foundations of Computer Science. IEEE Computer Society (1977)

36. Vardi, M.Y.: An automata-theoretic approach to linear temporal logic. In: Moller, F., Birtwistle, G. (eds.) Logics for Concurrency. LNCS, vol. 1043, pp. 238–266. Springer, Heidelberg (1996). https://doi.org/10.1007/3-540-60915-6_6

Certifying DFA Bounds for Recognition and Separation

Orna Kupferman, Nir Lavee, and Salomon Sickert[✉]

School of Computer Science and Engineering, The Hebrew University,
Jerusalem, Israel
orna@cs.huji.ac.il, {nir.lavee,salomon.sickert}@mail.huji.ac.il

Abstract. The automation of decision procedures makes certification essential. We suggest to use determinacy of turn-based two-player games with regular winning conditions in order to generate certificates for the number of states that a deterministic finite automaton (DFA) needs in order to recognize a given language. Given a language L and a bound k, recognizability of L by a DFA with k states is reduced to a game between Prover and Refuter. The interaction along the game then serves as a certificate. Certificates generated by Prover are minimal DFAs. Certificates generated by Refuter are faulty attempts to define the required DFA. We compare the length of offline certificates, which are generated with no interaction between Prover and Refuter, and online certificates, which are based on such an interaction, and are thus shorter. We show that our approach is useful also for certification of separability of regular languages by a DFA of a given size. Unlike DFA minimization, which can be solved in polynomial time, separation is NP-complete, and thus the certification approach is essential. In addition, we prove NP-completeness of a strict version of separation.

1 Introduction

Deterministic finite automata (DFAs) are among the most studied computation models in theoretical computer science. In addition to serving as an abstract mathematical concept, they are often the basis for specification and implementation of finite-state hardware and software designs [22]. In particular, the theory of DFAs applies also to deterministic automata of infinite words that recognize *safety* languages, which are characterized by finite forbidden behaviors [2,14].

A fundamental problem about DFAs is their *minimization*: For $k \geq 1$, we say that a language $L \subseteq \Sigma^*$ is *k-DFA-recognizable* if there is a k-DFA, namely a DFA with at most k states, that recognizes L. In the minimization problem, we are given a DFA $\mathcal{A}$ and a bound $k \geq 1$, and decide whether $L(\mathcal{A})$, namely the language of $\mathcal{A}$, is k-DFA-recognizable. DFAs enjoy a clean (and beautiful) theory of canonicity and minimization, based on a *right-congruence* relation: A

The full version of this article is available from [13]. Orna Kupferman is supported in part by the Israel Science Foundation, grant No. 2357/19. Salomon Sickert is supported by the Deutsche Forschungsgemeinschaft (DFG) under project number 436811179.

© Springer Nature Switzerland AG 2021
Z. Hou and V. Ganesh (Eds.): ATVA 2021, LNCS 12971, pp. 48–64, 2021.
https://doi.org/10.1007/978-3-030-88885-5_4

language $L \subseteq \Sigma^*$ induces a relation $\sim_L \subseteq \Sigma^* \times \Sigma^*$, where for every two words $h_1, h_2 \in \Sigma^*$, we have that $h_1 \sim_L h_2$ iff for all words $t \in \Sigma^*$, we have that $h_1 \cdot t \in L$ iff $h_2 \cdot t \in L$. By the Myhill-Nerode Theorem [17,19], the language L is k-DFA-recognizable iff the number of equivalence classes of $\sim_L$ is at most k. Moreover, a given DFA $\mathcal{A}$ can be minimized in polynomial time, by a fixed-point algorithm that merges states associated with the same equivalence class of $\sim_{L(\mathcal{A})}$.

Another fundamental problem about DFAs is *separation*: Given DFAs $\mathcal{A}_1$ and $\mathcal{A}_2$, and a bound $k \geq 1$, decide whether there is a k-DFA $\mathcal{A}$ that *separates* $\mathcal{A}_1$ and $\mathcal{A}_2$. That is, $L(\mathcal{A}_1) \subseteq L(\mathcal{A})$ and $L(\mathcal{A}) \cap L(\mathcal{A}_2) = \emptyset$. Finding a separator for $\mathcal{A}_1$ and $\mathcal{A}_2$ is closely related to the *DFA identification* problem. There, given sets $S_1, S_2 \subseteq \Sigma^*$ of positive and negative words, and a bound $k \geq 1$, we seek a k-DFA that accepts all words from S_1 and no word from S_2. DFA identification is NP-complete [10], with numerous heuristics and applications [11,25]. NP-hardness of DFA separation can be obtained by a reduction from DFA identification, but for DFA separation with additional constraints, in particular strict separation, NP-hardness is open [9]. Studies of separation include a search for regular separators of general languages [6], as well as separation of regular languages by weaker classes of languages, e.g., FO-definable languages [21] or piecewise testable languages [7].

Let us return to the problem of DFA minimization, and assume we want to *certify* the minimality of a given DFA. That is, we are given a DFA $\mathcal{A}$ and a bound $k \geq 1$, and we seek a proof that $L(\mathcal{A})$ is not k-DFA-recognizable. The need to accompany results of decision procedures by a certificate is not new, and includes certification of a "correct" decision of a model checker [15, 23], reachability certificates in complex multi-agent systems [1], and explainable reactive synthesis [4]. Certifying that $L(\mathcal{A})$ is not k-DFA-recognizable, we can point to $k + 1$ words $h_1, \ldots, h_{k+1} \in \Sigma^*$ that belong to different equivalence classes of the relation $\sim_{L(\mathcal{A})}$, along with an explanation why they indeed belong to different classes, namely words $t_{i,j} \in \Sigma^*$, for all $1 \leq i \neq j \leq k + 1$, such that $h_i \cdot t_{i,j}$ and $h_j \cdot t_{i,j}$ do not agree on their membership in $L(\mathcal{A})$.

The above certification process is *offline*: Refuter (that is, the entity proving that $L(\mathcal{A})$ is not k-DFA-recognizable) generates and outputs the certificate without an interaction with Prover (that is, the entity claiming that $L(\mathcal{A})$ is k-DFA-recognizable). In this work we describe an *interactive certification protocol*:[1] Given $\mathcal{A}$ and $k \geq 1$, Refuter and Prover interact, aiming to convince each other about the (non-)existence of a k-DFA for $L(\mathcal{A})$. Our approach offers two advantages over offline certification. First, the length of the certificate is shorter. Second, the interactive protocol can also be used for efficiently certifying bounds on the size of DFA separators. In addition, we solve the open problem of the complexity of deciding strict separation by a k-DFA. We show that it is NP-

---

[1] Note that while our certification protocol is interactive, the setting is different from that of an interactive proof system in computational complexity theory. In particular, our Prover and Refuter are both finite-state, they have complementary objectives, and no probability is involved.

complete, and so are variants requiring only one side of the separation to be strict.

The underlying idea behind the interactive certification protocol is simple: Consider a language $L \subseteq \Sigma^*$ and a bound $k \geq 1$. We consider a *turn-based two-player game* between Refuter and Prover. In each round in the game, Prover provides a letter from a set $[k] = \{1, 2, \ldots, k\}$ that describes the state space of a DFA for L that Prover claims to exist, and Refuter responds with a letter in $\Sigma \cup \{\#\}$, for a special reset letter $\# \notin \Sigma$. Thus, during the interaction, Prover generates a word $y \in [k]^\omega$ and Refuter generates a word $x \in (\Sigma \cup \{\#\})^\omega$. The word x describes an infinite sequence of words in Σ^*, separated by $\#$'s, and the word y aims to describe runs of a k-DFA on the words in the sequence. Prover wins if the described runs are legal: They all start with the same initial state and follow some transition function, and are consistent with L: There is a way to classify the states in $[k]$ to accepting and rejecting such that Prover responds with an accepting state whenever the word generated by Refuter since the last $\#$ is in L. Clearly, if there is a k-DFA for L, then Prover can win by following its runs. Likewise, a winning strategy for Prover induces a k-DFA for L. The key idea behind our contribution is that since the above described game is determined [5], Refuter has a winning strategy iff no k-DFA for L exists. Moreover, since the game is regular, this winning strategy induces a finite-state transducer, which we term an (L, k)-*refuter*, and which generates interactive certificates for $L(\mathcal{A})$ not being k-DFA-recognizable.

Consider a language L with index N. Recall that the interaction between Refuter and Prover generates words $x \in (\Sigma \cup \{\#\})^\omega$ and $y \in [k]^\omega$. If $k < N$, Refuter can generate x for which the responses of Prover in y must contain a violation of legality or agreement with L. Once a violation is detected, the interaction terminates and it constitutes a certificate: an *informative bad prefix* [14] of the safety language of interactions in which Prover's responses are legal and agree with L. We show that the length of certificates generated by offline refuters is at most $O(k^2 \cdot N)$, whereas interaction reduces the length to $O(k^2 + N)$. We show that both bounds are tight. For separation, we describe a refuter that generates certificates of length at most $O(k^2 \cdot |\Sigma| + k \cdot (N_1 + N_2))$, where N_1 and N_2 are the indices of the separated languages.

Our interactive certification protocol has similarities with the interaction that takes place in *learning* of regular languages [3], (see recent survey in [8]). There, a Learner is tasked to construct a DFA $\mathcal{A}$ for an unknown regular set L by asking a Teacher queries of two types: Membership ("$w \in L?$") and equivalence ("$L(\mathcal{A}) = L?$"). In our setting, Refuter also wants to "learn" the k-DFA for L that Prover claims to possess, but she needs to learn only a fraction of it from Prover – a fraction that reveals that it does not actually recognize L. This is done with a single type of query ("what is the next state?"), which may give Refuter more information than the information gained in the learning setting.

Due to the lack of space, some proofs are omitted and can be found in the full version [13].

2   Preliminaries

Automata. A *deterministic automaton on finite words* (DFA, for short) is $\mathcal{A} = \langle \Sigma, Q, q_0, \delta, F \rangle$, where Q is a finite set of states, $q_0 \in Q$ is an initial state, $\delta : Q \times \Sigma \to Q$ is a partial transition function, and $F \subseteq Q$ is a set of final states. We sometimes refer to δ as a relation $\Delta \subseteq Q \times \Sigma \times Q$, with $\langle q, \sigma, q' \rangle \in \Delta$ iff $\delta(q, \sigma) = q'$. A *run* of $\mathcal{A}$ on a word $w = w_1 \cdot w_2 \cdots w_m \in \Sigma^*$ is the sequence of states $q_0, q_1, \ldots, q_m$ such that $q_{i+1} = \delta(q_i, w_{i+1})$ for all $0 \leq i < m$. The run is accepting if $q_m \in F$. A word $w \in \Sigma^*$ is accepted by $\mathcal{A}$ if the run of $\mathcal{A}$ on w is accepting. The *language* of $\mathcal{A}$, denoted $L(\mathcal{A})$, is the set of words that $\mathcal{A}$ accepts. We define the *size* of $\mathcal{A}$, denoted $|\mathcal{A}|$, as the number of states that $\mathcal{A}$ has. For a language $L \subseteq \Sigma^*$, we use $comp(L)$ to denote the language complementing L, thus $comp(L) = \Sigma^* \setminus L$.

Consider a language $L \subseteq \Sigma^*$. For two finite words h_1 and h_2, we say that h_1 and h_2 are *right L-indistinguishable*, denoted $h_1 \sim_L h_2$, if for every $t \in \Sigma^*$, we have that $h_1 \cdot t \in L$ iff $h_2 \cdot t \in L$. Thus, $\sim_L$ is the Myhill-Nerode right congruence used for minimizing DFAs. For $h \in \Sigma^*$, let $[h]$ denote the equivalence class of h in $\sim_L$ and let $\langle L \rangle$ denote the set of all equivalence classes. When L is regular, the set $\langle L \rangle$ is finite and we use index(L) to denote $|\langle L \rangle|$. The set $\langle L \rangle$ induces the *residual automaton* of L, defined by $\mathcal{R}_L = \langle \Sigma, \langle L \rangle, \Delta_L, [\epsilon], F \rangle$, with $\langle [h], a, [h \cdot a] \rangle \in \Delta_L$ for all $[h] \in \langle L \rangle$ and $a \in \Sigma$. Also, F contains all classes $[h]$ with $h \in L$. The DFA $\mathcal{R}_L$ is well defined and is the unique minimal DFA for L.

Lemma 1. *Consider a regular language L of index N. For every $1 \leq k \leq N$, there is a set $H_k = \{h_1, \ldots, h_k\}$ of words $h_i \in \Sigma^*$ such that $h_i \not\sim_L h_j$ for all $1 \leq i \neq j \leq k$ and $|h_i| \leq k - 1$ for all $1 \leq i \leq k$.*

Safety Languages. Consider a language $L \subseteq \Sigma^\omega$ of infinite words. Here, the language complementing L is $comp(L) = \Sigma^\omega \setminus L$. A finite word $x \in \Sigma^*$ is a *bad prefix* for L if for every $y \in \Sigma^\omega$, we have that $x \cdot y \notin L$. That is, x is a bad prefix if all its extensions are words not in L. A language $L \subseteq \Sigma^\omega$ is a *safety* language if every word not in L has a bad prefix. A language L is a *co-safety* language if $comp(L)$ is safety. Equivalently, every word $w \in L$ has a *good prefix*, namely a prefix $x \in \Sigma^*$ such that for every $y \in \Sigma^\omega$, we have that $x \cdot y \in L$.

Transducers and Realizability. Consider two finite alphabets Σ_I and Σ_O. For two words $x = x_1 \cdot x_2 \cdots \in \Sigma_I^\omega$ and $y = y_1 \cdot y_2 \cdots \in \Sigma_O^\omega$, we define $x \oplus y$ as the word in $(\Sigma_I \times \Sigma_O)^\omega$ obtained by merging x and y. Thus, $x \oplus y = (x_1, y_1) \cdot (x_2, y_2) \cdots$.

A (Σ_I / Σ_O)-*transducer* models a finite-state system that generates letters in Σ_O while interacting with an environment that generates letters in Σ_I. Formally, a (Σ_I / Σ_O)-transducer is $\mathcal{T} = \langle \Sigma_I, \Sigma_O, \iota, S, s_0, \rho, \tau \rangle$, where $\iota \in \{sys, env\}$ indicates who initiates the interaction – the system or the environment, S is a set of states, $s_0 \in S$ is an initial state, $\rho : S \times \Sigma_I \to S$ is a transition function, and $\tau : S \to \Sigma_O$ is a labeling function on the states. Consider an input word $x = x_1 \cdot x_2 \cdots \in \Sigma_I^\omega$. The *run* of $\mathcal{T}$ on x is the sequence $s_0, s_1, s_2 \ldots$ such that for all $j \geq 0$, we have that $s_{j+1} = \rho(s_j, x_{j+1})$. The *annotation of x by $\mathcal{T}$*, denoted $\mathcal{T}(x)$, depends on ι. If $\iota = sys$, then $\mathcal{T}(x) = \tau(s_0) \cdot \tau(s_1) \cdot \tau(s_2) \cdots \in \Sigma_O^\omega$. Note that the first letter in $\mathcal{T}(x)$ is the output of $\mathcal{T}$ in s_0. This reflects the fact that the system initiates the interaction. If $\iota = env$, then $\mathcal{T}(x) = \tau(s_1)\cdot\tau(s_2)\cdot\tau(s_3)\cdots \in \Sigma_O^\omega$. Note that now, the output in s_0 is ignored, reflecting the fact that the environment initiates the interaction. Then, the *computation* of $\mathcal{T}$ on x is the word $x \oplus \mathcal{T}(x) \in (\Sigma_I \times \Sigma_O)^\omega$.

We say that a (Σ_I/Σ_O)-transducer is *offline* if its behavior is independent of inputs from the environment. Formally, its transition function ρ satisfies $\rho(s, x) = \rho(s, x')$ for all states $s \in S$ and input letters $x, x' \in \Sigma_I$. Note that an offline transducer has exactly one run, and it annotates all words by the same lasso-shaped word $u \cdot v^\omega$, with $u \in \Sigma_O^*$ and $v \in \Sigma_O^+$. We sometimes refer to general transducers as *online* transducers, to emphasize they are not offline.

Consider a ω-regular language $L \subseteq (\Sigma_I \times \Sigma_O)^\omega$. We say that L is (Σ_I/Σ_O)-*realizable by the system* if there exists a (Σ_I/Σ_O)-transducer $\mathcal{T}$ with $\iota = sys$ all whose computations are in L. Thus, for every $x \in \Sigma_I^\omega$, we have that $x \oplus \mathcal{T}(x) \in L$. We then say that $\mathcal{T}$ (Σ_I/Σ_O)-*realizes* L. Then, L is (Σ_O/Σ_I)-*realizable by the environment* if there exists a (Σ_O/Σ_I)-transducer $\mathcal{T}$ with $\iota = env$ all whose computations are in L. When Σ_I and Σ_O are clear from the context, we omit them.

When the language L is ω-regular, realizability reduces to deciding a game with a regular winning condition. Then, by determinacy of games and due to the existence of finite-memory winning strategies [5], we have the following.

Proposition 1. *For every ω-regular language $L \subseteq (\Sigma_I \times \Sigma_O)^\omega$, exactly one of the following holds.*

1. *L is (Σ_I/Σ_O)-realizable by the system.*
2. *$comp(L)$ is (Σ_O/Σ_I)-realizable by the environment.*

3   Proving and Refuting Bounds on DFAs

Consider a regular language $L \subseteq \Sigma^*$ and a bound $k \geq 1$. We view the problem of deciding whether L can be recognized by a k-DFA as the problem of deciding a turn-based two-player game between Refuter and Prover. In each round in the game, Prover provides a letter from a set $[k] = \{1, 2, \ldots, k\}$ that describes the state space of a DFA for L that Prover claims to exist, and Refuter responds with a letter in $\Sigma \cup \{\#\}$, for a special reset letter $\# \notin \Sigma$. Thus, during the interaction, Prover generates a word $y \in [k]^\omega$ and Refuter generates a word $x \in (\Sigma \cup \{\#\})^\omega$. The word x describes an infinite sequence of words in Σ^*, separated by $\#$'s, and the word y aims to describe runs of the claimed DFA on them.

Below we formalize this intuition. Let $\Sigma' = \Sigma \cup \{\#\}$, for a letter $\# \notin \Sigma$. Consider a (finite or infinite) word $w = x \oplus y \in (\Sigma' \times [k])^* \cup (\Sigma' \times [k])^\omega$. Let $x = x_1 \cdot x_2 \cdots$ and $y = y_1 \cdot y_2 \cdots$. We say that w is *legal* if the following two conditions hold:

1. For all $1 \leq j < |w|$ with $x_j = \#$, we have $y_{j+1} = y_1$.
2. There exists a function $\delta : [k] \times \Sigma \to [k]$ such that $y_{j+1} = \delta(y_j, x_j)$ for all $1 \leq j < |w|$ with $x_j \in \Sigma$.

The first condition ensures that Prover starts all runs in the same state $y_1 \in [k]$, which serves as the initial state in her claimed DFA. The second condition ensures that there exists a deterministic transition relation that Prover follows in all her transitions.

A word w being legal guarantees that Prover follows some k-DFA. We now add conditions on w in order to guarantee that this DFA recognizes L. Consider a position $1 \leq j < |w|$. Let $\#(j) = \max\{j' : (j' < j \text{ and } x_{j'} = \#) \text{ or } j' = 0\}$ be the last position before j in which Refuter generates the reset letter $\#$ (or 0, if no such position exists). When the interaction is in position j, we examine the word w^j that starts at position $\#(j) + 1$ and ends at position $j - 1$. Thus, $w^j = x_{\#(j)+1} \cdot x_{\#(j)+2} \cdots x_{j-1} \in \Sigma^*$. The run that Prover suggests to w^j is then $y_{\#(j)+1}, y_{\#(j)+2}, \ldots, y_j$, and we say that y *maps* w^j to y_j. When y is clear from the context, we also say that Prover maps w^j to y_j. Note that if j_1 and j_2 are such that $w^{j_1} = w^{j_2}$, then w being legal ensures that w^{j_1} and w^{j_2} are mapped to the same state. Now, we say that $w = x \oplus y \in (\Sigma' \times [k])^* \cup (\Sigma' \times [k])^\omega$ *agrees with L* if there exists a set $F \subseteq [k]$ such that for all $1 \leq j < |w|$, Prover maps w^j to an element in F iff $w^j \in L$.

Remark 1. Note that a word w agrees with L iff w agrees with $comp(L)$. Indeed, our definition of agreement with L only guarantees we can define an acceptance condition on top of the claimed k-DFA for either L and $comp(L)$. Since these DFAs dualize each other, they have the same index, and so it makes sense not to distinguish between them in our study.   □

Example 1. Let $\Sigma = \{a, b\}$ and $k = 2$. An interaction between Prover and Refuter may generate the prefix of a computation in $(\{a, b, \#\} \times \{1, 2\})^\omega$ described in Table 1. Note that while w fixes $\delta(1, a)$, $\delta(2, a)$, and $\delta(2, b)$, it does not fix $\delta(1, b)$.   □

Table 1. $x \oplus y$ and its analysis.

$w = x \oplus y =$	$(a, 1)$	$(b, 2)$	$(\#, 2)$	$(a, 1)$	$(a, 2)$	$(a, 1)$	$(b, 2)$	$(\#, 2)$	$(\#, 1)$	$(a, 1)$	$(a, 2)$
$j =$	1	2	3	4	5	6	7	8	9	10	11
$\#(j) =$	0	0	0	3	3	3	3	3	8	9	9
$w^j =$	ϵ	a	ab	ϵ	a	aa	aaa	$aaab$	ϵ	ϵ	a

The language $\mathrm{DFA}(L, k) \subseteq (\Sigma' \times [k])^\omega$ of words with correct annotations is then $\mathrm{DFA}(L, k) = \{x \oplus y \in (\Sigma' \times [k])^\omega : x \oplus y \text{ is legal and agrees with } L\}$. Then, $\mathrm{NoDFA}(L, k)$ is the language of words with incorrect annotations, thus $\mathrm{NoDFA}(L, k) = comp(\mathrm{DFA}(L, k))$.

By Proposition 1, we have the following:

Proposition 2. *Consider a language $L \subseteq \Sigma^*$. Exactly one of the following holds:*

- *L can be recognized by a k-DFA, in which case $\mathrm{DFA}(L, k)$ is $(\Sigma'/[k])$-realizable by the system.*

- L cannot be recognized by a k-DFA, in which case $\text{NoDFA}(L, k)$ is $([k]/\Sigma')$-realizable by the environment.

By Proposition 2, the language $\text{DFA}(L, k)$ is $(\Sigma'/[k])$-realizable by the system whenever $k \geq \text{index}(L)$. Moreover, a $(\Sigma'/[k])$-transducer T that realizes $\text{DFA}(L, k)$ induces a k-DFA for L. To see this, consider the word $x \in (\Sigma')^* = w_1 \cdot \# \cdot w_2 \cdots \# \cdot w_{|\Sigma|^k} \cdot \#$ obtained by concatenating all words $w_i \cdot \# \in \Sigma^k \cdot \#$ in some order. Since every transition in a k-DFA is reachable by traversing a word of length at most $k - 1$, the computation of T on x must commit on all the transitions in a transition function $\delta : [k] \times \Sigma \to [k]$, and must also induce a single classification of the states in $[k]$ to accepting and rejecting. Note also that if $k > \text{index}(L)$, the transducer may induce several different DFAs for L.

By Proposition 2, we also have that the language $\text{NoDFA}(L, k)$ is $([k]/\Sigma')$-realizable by the environment whenever $k < \text{index}(L)$. A $([k]/\Sigma')$-transducer that realizes $\text{NoDFA}(L, k)$ is termed an (L, k)-*refuter*.

4   Certifying Bounds on Recognizability

Recall that $\text{DFA}(L, k)$ contains exactly all words that are legal and agree with L. Accordingly, if a word $x \oplus y \in (\Sigma' \times [k])^\omega$ is not in $\text{DFA}(L, k)$, it contains a violation of legality or agreement with L, and thus has a bad prefix for $\text{DFA}(L, k)$. Formally, we define the language $\text{Violate}(L, k) \subseteq (\Sigma' \times [k])^*$ of words that include a violation of legality or agreement with L as follows.

$$\text{Violate}(L, k) = \{x \oplus y : \text{there is } j \geq 1 \text{ such that } x_j = \# \text{ and } y_{j+1} \neq y_1, \text{ or}$$
$$\text{there are } j_1, j_2 \geq 1 \text{ such that}$$
$$y_{j_1} = y_{j_2}, x_{j_1} = x_{j_2}, \text{ and } y_{j_1+1} \neq y_{j_2+1},$$
$$\text{or } w^{j_1} \in L, w^{j_2} \notin L \text{ and } y_{j_1} = y_{j_2}\}.$$

Note that while all the words in $\text{Violate}(L, k)$ are bad prefixes for $\text{DFA}(L, k)$, there are bad prefixes for $\text{DFA}(L, k)$ that are not in $\text{Violate}(L, k)$. For example, if $L = \{a^{2n} : n \geq 0\}$, then the word $(a, 1)$ is a bad prefix for $\text{DFA}(L, 1)$, as both $(a, 1)(a, 1)$ and $(a, 1)(\#, 1)$, which are the only possible extensions of $(a, 1)$ by a single letter, are in $\text{Violate}(L, 1)$, yet $(a, 1)$ itself is not in $\text{Violate}(L, 1)$. Formally, using the terminology of [14], the language $\text{Violate}(L, k)$ contains all the *informative bad prefixes* of $\text{DFA}(L, k)$, namely these that contain an explanation to the prefix being bad. Since every infinite word not in $\text{DFA}(L, k)$ has a bad prefix in $\text{Violate}(L, k)$, then restricting attention to bad prefixes in $\text{Violate}(L, k)$ is appropriate in the context of certificates. Also, as we show in the full version [13], a bad prefix of $\text{DFA}(L, k)$ that is not informative can be made informative by concatenating to it any letter in $\Sigma' \times [k]$.

Refuting recognizability of L by a k-DFA, we consider two approaches. In the first, we consider the interaction of Prover with an offline (L, k)-refuter. Such a refuter has to generate a word $x \in (\Sigma')^*$ such that for all $y \in [k]^{|x|}$, we have that $x \oplus y \in \text{Violate}(L, k)$. We call x a *universal informative bad prefix* (see [16] for a study of bad prefixes for safety languages in an interactive setting). In the second approach, we consider the interaction of Prover with an online (L, k)-refuter. There, the goal is to associate every sequence $y \in [k]^\omega$ that is generated by Prover with a sequence $x \in (\Sigma')^\omega$ such that $x \oplus y$ has a prefix in $\text{Violate}(L, k)$. In Sects. 4.1 and 4.2 we compare the two approaches in terms of the length of the certificate (namely the word in $\text{Violate}(L, k)$) that they generate.

4.1 Certification with Offline Refuters

Recall that a word $x \in (\Sigma')^*$ is a *universal informative bad prefix* for $\text{DFA}(L, k)$ if for all $y \in [k]^{|x|}$, we have that $x \oplus y \in \text{Violate}(L, k)$.

Theorem 1. *Consider a regular language $L \subseteq \Sigma^*$ and let $N = \text{index}(L)$. For every $k < N$, the length of a shortest universal informative bad prefix for $\text{DFA}(L, k)$ is at most $O(k^2 \cdot N)$. This bound is tight: There is a family of regular languages $L_1, L_2, \ldots$ such that for every $n \geq 1$, the length of a shortest universal informative bad prefix for $\text{DFA}(L_n, N_n - 1)$ is $\Omega(N_n^3)$, where $N_n = \text{index}(L_n)$.*

Proof. We start with the upper bound and construct, for every $k < N$, a universal informative bad prefix for $\text{DFA}(L, k)$ of length $O(k^2 \cdot N)$.

Let $H = \{h_1, \ldots, h_{k+1}\}$ be representatives of $k + 1$ distinct Myhill-Nerode classes. Since $k < N$, such a set H exists. Moreover, by Lemma 1, we can assume that $|h_i| \leq k$, for all $1 \leq i \leq k+1$. For each pair $\langle h_i, h_j \rangle$, there is a distinguishing tail $t_{i,j}$ of length at most N. Let x be the concatenation of all words of the form $h_i \cdot t_{i,j} \cdot \#$ and $h_j \cdot t_{i,j} \cdot \#$, for all pairs. There are $k \cdot (k+1)$ such words, each of length at most $k + N + 1$, so $|x| \leq (k + N + 1) \cdot k \cdot (k+1)$, which is $O(k^2 \cdot N)$. In the full version [13] we prove that x is a universal informative bad prefix.

For a matching lower bound, we describe a family of regular languages $L_1, L_2, \ldots$ such that for every $n \geq 1$, the length of a shortest universal informative bad prefix for $\text{DFA}(L_n, N_n-1)$ is $\Omega(N_n^3)$, where $N_n = \text{index}(L_n)$. For $n \geq 1$, let $\Sigma_n = \{a, b_1, \ldots, b_n\}$ and consider the language $L_n = \{a^n b_i^2 : 1 \leq i \leq n\}$. Let A_n be a minimal DFA for L_n. For example, $L_3 = \{aaab_1b_1, aaab_2b_2, aaab_3b_3\}$, and the DFA A_3 for L_3 appears in Fig. 1.

It is easy to see that $\text{index}(L_n) = N_n = 2n + 3$, corresponding to (see Fig. 1) $n + 1$ states $q_0, \ldots, q_n$, n states $r_1, \ldots, r_n$, an accepting state, and a rejecting sink, which we omit from the figure.

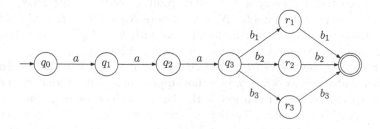

Fig. 1. A DFA for L_3.

Let $k = N_n - 1$, and consider some prefix $x \in (\Sigma')^*$. For $1 \le i \ne j \le n$, the words $a^n b_i$ and $a^n b_j$ belong to different Myhill-Nerode classes, corresponding to the states r_i and r_j, respectively. The distinguishing tails are b_i and b_j. In the full version [13] we prove that if x is a universal informative bad prefix for DFA(L, k), then for every $1 \le i \ne j \le n$, it contains the subwords $a^n b_i b_j$ or $a^n b_j b_i$, which are of length $n + 2$. There are $n \cdot (n-1)/2$ such subwords and they are disjoint. Therefore, $|x| \ge (n+2) \cdot n \cdot (n-1)/2$, which is $\Omega(N_n^3)$.   □

4.2   Certification with Online Refuters

We now consider refuters that take Prover's choices into account when outputting letters. We show that this capability allows an interactive refuter to win in fewer rounds than an offline refuter.

Theorem 2. *Consider a regular language $L \subseteq \Sigma^*$ and let $N = \text{index}(L)$. For every $k < N$, there exists an (L, k)-refuter that generates a word in Violate(L, k) within $O(k^2 + N)$ rounds. This bound is tight: There is a family of regular languages $L_1, L_2, \ldots$ such that for every $n \ge 1$, every (L, k)-refuter needs at least $\Omega(N_n^2)$ rounds to construct a word in Violate$(L_n, N_n - 1)$, where $N_n = \text{index}(L_n)$.*

Proof. We start with the upper bound, by describing a winning strategy. As in the offline case, let $H = \{h_1, \ldots, h_{k+1}\}$ be representatives of distinct Myhill-Nerode classes, each of length at most k. Unlike the offline case, where Refuter outputs all pairs of heads and distinguishing tails, here a single pair suffices to achieve the same effect. Refuter starts the interaction by outputting $h_1 \cdot \# \cdots \# \cdot h_{k+1} \cdot \#$. By the pigeonhole principle, there are distinct words h_i and h_j that are mapped by Prover to the same state. Refuter then outputs $h_i \cdot t_{i,j} \cdot \# \cdot h_j \cdot t_{i,j} \cdot \#$. If Prover does not violate the conditions of legality, it maps $h_i \cdot t_{i,j}$ and $h_j \cdot t_{i,j}$ to the same state. Exactly one of them is in L, so there is no $F \subseteq [k]$ that can satisfy agreement with L, and so the generated word is in Violate(L, k). We now analyze its length. Recall that Refuter first outputs $k+1$ words of length at most k each, separated by $\#$'s, and then two words of length at most $k + N$ each, again separated by $\#$. Thus, the length of the prefix is $k(k+1)+2(k+N)+k+3$, which is $O(k^2 + N)$.

For a matching lower bound, we describe a family of regular languages $L_1, L_2 \ldots$ such that for every $n \ge 1$, every refuter needs at least $\Omega(N_n^2)$ rounds to generate a word in Violate$(L_n, N_n - 1)$, where $N_n = \text{index}(L_n)$. Consider the DFA $\mathcal{A}_n$ from the offline lower bound, again with $k = N_n - 1$. We claim that $\Omega(N_n^2)$ rounds are required to generate a word in Violate$(L_n, N_n - 1)$.

Let $x \in (\Sigma')^*$ be the word generated by Refuter. Assume there exists $1 \le i \le n$ such that the subword $a^n b_i$ does not appear in x. The state corresponding to $a^n b_i$ is r_i. Hence, Prover can follow the DFA obtained by removing the state r_i from $\mathcal{A}_n$ without violating legality or agreement with L. Therefore, in order to guarantee a generation of a word in Violate$(L_n, N_n - 1)$, Refuter must output all the words $a^n b_1, \ldots, a^n b_n$ in some order. Each of these n words has length

$n + 1$, and they are disjoint. Their total length is therefore at least $n \cdot (n + 1)$, which is $\Omega(N_n^2)$.   □

Remark 2. **Fixed alphabet.** In the proofs of Theorems 1 and 2, we use languages L_n over an alphabet Σ_n that depends on n. By replacing the letters $b_1, \ldots, b_n$ by words in $\{a, b\}^{\lfloor \log n \rfloor}$, one gets languages over the fixed alphabet $\Sigma = \{a, b\}$ that exhibit the claimed lower bounds for both online and offline refuters.   □

Remark 3. **Optimal Survival Strategies for Provers.** Assume that L is not k-DFA recognizable. Then, there is an (L, k)-refuter, and Refuter is going to win a game against Prover and generate a word in Violate(L, k). Suppose that Prover aims at prolonging the interaction. It is tempting to think that the following greedy strategy is optimal for such an objective: Prover follows the transitions of $\mathcal{R}_L$. If $k < \text{index}(L)$, then Prover may be forced to deviate from $\mathcal{R}_L$ and make a "mistake", namely choose to output one of the k states that have already been exposed. Using this strategy, Prover can prolong the game at least until $k + 1$ different states are exposed. In the full version [13] we describe an example showing that this strategy is not optimal at prolonging the game as long as possible (no matter how clever the choice when a "mistake" is forced is).   □

5   Bounds on DFA Separation

Consider three languages $L_1, L_2, L \subseteq \Sigma^*$. We say that L is a *separator* for $\langle L_1, L_2 \rangle$ if $L_1 \subseteq L$ and $L \cap L_2 = \emptyset$. Equivalently, $L_1 \subseteq L \subseteq comp(L_2)$. For $k \geq 1$, we say that a pair of languages $\langle L_1, L_2 \rangle$ is k-*DFA-separable* iff there is a k-DFA $\mathcal{A}$ such that $L(\mathcal{A})$ separates $\langle L_1, L_2 \rangle$. We extend the definition to DFAs and say that two DFAs $\mathcal{A}_1$ and $\mathcal{A}_2$ are separated by a DFA $\mathcal{A}$, if their languages are separated by $L(\mathcal{A})$.

In this section we study refuting and certifying bounds on DFA separation. We first give proofs that deciding (strict and non-strict) k-DFA-separability, is NP-complete. The problem being NP-hard suggests that there is no clean theory of equivalence classes that is the base for offline certification. We continue and describe interactive certification protocol for k-DFA-separability.

5.1   Hardness of Separation

The following Theorem 3 is considered by the literature (e.g., [18]) to be a consequence of [20]. Since we also investigate the strict-separation case and there is a progression of techniques, we describe below an alternative and explicit proof.

Theorem 3. *Given DFAs $\mathcal{A}_1$ and $\mathcal{A}_2$, and a bound $k \geq 1$, deciding whether $\langle \mathcal{A}_1, \mathcal{A}_2 \rangle$ is k-DFA-separable is NP-complete.*

Proof. Membership in NP is easy, as given a candidate separator $\mathcal{A}$ of size k, we can verify that $L(\mathcal{A}_1) \subseteq L(\mathcal{A})$ and $L(\mathcal{A}) \cap L(\mathcal{A}_2) = \emptyset$ in polynomial time. Note that if $k \geq \text{index}(L(\mathcal{A}_1))$, then $\langle \mathcal{A}_1, \mathcal{A}_2 \rangle$ is k-DFA-separable by $\mathcal{A}_1$. Thus, we can assume that $k < \mathrm{index}(L(\mathcal{A}_1))$, and so membership in NP applies also for the case k is given in binary.

For NP-hardness, we reduce from the *DFA identification* problem. Recall that there, given sets $S_1, S_2 \subseteq \Sigma^*$ of positive and negative words, and a bound $k \geq 1$, we seek a k-DFA that accepts all words in S_1 and no word in S_2. By [10], DFA identification is NP-complete. Given S_1, S_2, and k, our reduction constructs DFAs $\mathcal{A}_1$ and $\mathcal{A}_2$ such that $L(\mathcal{A}_1) = S_1$ and $L(\mathcal{A}_2) = S_2$. Clearly, a k-DFA solves the DFA identification problem for S_1, S_2, and k, iff it solves the k-DFA-separation of $\mathcal{A}_1$ and $\mathcal{A}_2$.

Constructing a DFA $\mathcal{A}_S$ such that $L(\mathcal{A}_S) = S$, for some finite set $S \subseteq \Sigma^*$ can be done in polynomial time, by traversing prefixes of words in S. Formally, we define $\mathcal{A}_S = \langle \Sigma, Q, q_0, \delta, F \rangle$, where $Q = \{w : w \text{ is a prefix of a word in } S\}$, $q_0 = \epsilon$, and for all $w \in Q$ and $\sigma \in \Sigma$, we have that $\delta(w, \sigma) = w \cdot \sigma$ if $w \cdot \sigma \in S$, and $\delta(w, \sigma)$ is undefined otherwise. Finally, $F = S$. It is easy to see that $L(\mathcal{A}_S) = S$ and that $|\mathcal{A}_S| \leq \sum_{w \in S} |w|$.   □

Consider three languages $L_1, L_2, L \subseteq \Sigma^*$. We say that L is a *strict separator* for $\langle L_1, L_2 \rangle$ if $L_1 \subset L$, $L \cap L_2 = \emptyset$, and $L \cup L_2 \subset \Sigma^*$. Equivalently, $L_1 \subset L \subset comp(L_2)$. For $k \geq 1$, we say that a pair of languages $\langle L_1, L_2 \rangle$ is *k-DFA-strictly-separable* iff there is a k-DFA $\mathcal{A}$ such that $L(\mathcal{A})$ strictly separates $\langle L_1, L_2 \rangle$. Again, we extend the definition to DFAs.

Theorem 4. *Given DFAs $\mathcal{A}_1$ and $\mathcal{A}_2$, and a bound $k \geq 1$, deciding whether $\langle \mathcal{A}_1, \mathcal{A}_2 \rangle$ is k-DFA-strictly-separable is NP-complete.*

Proof. We start with membership in NP. As in the proof of Theorem 3, a witness k-DFA $\mathcal{A}$ can be checked in polynomial time. However, if k is given in binary and greater than $\mathrm{index}(L(\mathcal{A}_1))$ and $\mathrm{index}(L(\mathcal{A}_2))$, we cannot base a separator on $\mathcal{A}_1$ or $\mathcal{A}_2$. We fill this gap by showing that if a DFA strictly separates $\langle \mathcal{A}_1, \mathcal{A}_2 \rangle$, then there also exists one that is polynomial in $|\mathcal{A}_1|$ and $|\mathcal{A}_2|$.

Assume that $\langle \mathcal{A}_1, \mathcal{A}_2 \rangle$ are strictly separable. Let $T = comp(L(\mathcal{A}_1) \cup L(\mathcal{A}_2))$. Note that $\langle \mathcal{A}_1, \mathcal{A}_2 \rangle$ being strictly separable implies that $|T| > 1$. Let $\mathcal{A}_T$ be a minimal DFA for T. Note that $|\mathcal{A}_T| \leq |\mathcal{A}_1| \cdot |\mathcal{A}_2|$. Consider a word $w \in T$ that is accepted along a simple path in $\mathcal{A}_T$. Thus, $|w|$ is polynomial in $|\mathcal{A}_T|$. Consider a DFA $\mathcal{A}_1^w$ with $L(\mathcal{A}_1^w) = L(\mathcal{A}_1) \cup \{w\}$. Note that $|\mathcal{A}_1^w|$ is polynomial in $|\mathcal{A}_1|$ and $|w|$. It is not hard to see that $\mathcal{A}_1^w$ is a strict separator for $\langle \mathcal{A}_1, \mathcal{A}_2 \rangle$. Indeed, $L(\mathcal{A}_1^w)$ strictly contains $L(\mathcal{A}_1)$, it is contained in $comp(L(\mathcal{A}_2))$, and as $|T| > 1$, the latter containment is strict. Hence, $\langle \mathcal{A}_1, \mathcal{A}_2 \rangle$ are strictly separable by a DFA that is polynomial in $|\mathcal{A}_1|$ and $|\mathcal{A}_2|$.

For NP-hardness, we describe a reduction from k-DFA-separability, proved to be NP-hard in Theorem 3. Consider two DFAs $\mathcal{A}_1$ and $\mathcal{A}_2$ over Σ, and assume that $0 \notin \Sigma$. Assume also that $L(\mathcal{A}_1), L(\mathcal{A}_2) \neq \emptyset$, and that $L(\mathcal{A}_1), L(\mathcal{A}_2)$ are finite, and thus have rejecting sinks. Clearly, k-DFA-separability is NP-hard also in this case. Let $\mathcal{A}_1'$ and $\mathcal{A}_2'$ be DFAs obtained from $\mathcal{A}_1$ and $\mathcal{A}_2$ by extending the alphabet to $\Sigma \cup \{0\}$ and adding a transition labeled 0 from every state to the rejecting sink. Note that $L(\mathcal{A}_1') = L(\mathcal{A}_1)$ and $comp(L(\mathcal{A}_2')) = (\Sigma \cup \{0\})^* \setminus L(\mathcal{A}_2)$.

In the full version [13], we prove that for every $k \geq 1$, we have that $\langle \mathcal{A}_1, \mathcal{A}_2 \rangle$ is k-DFA-separable iff $\langle \mathcal{A}'_1, \mathcal{A}'_2 \rangle$ is k-DFA-strictly-separable. □

The reduction described in the proof of Theorem 4 can be used to prove NP-completeness also for *one-sided strict separation* problems. Formally, we have the following, which generalizes Conjecture 1 from [9] (see proof in the full version [13]).

Theorem 5. *Given DFAs $\mathcal{A}_1$ and $\mathcal{A}_2$, and a bound $k \geq 1$, the problems of deciding whether there exists a k-DFA $\mathcal{A}$ such that $L(\mathcal{A}_1) \subset L(\mathcal{A}) \subseteq comp(L(\mathcal{A}_2))$ and whether there exists a k-DFA $\mathcal{A}'$ such that $L(\mathcal{A}_1) \subseteq L(\mathcal{A}') \subset comp(L(\mathcal{A}_2))$ are NP-complete.*

5.2 Certifying Bounds on Separation

Consider two regular languages $L_1, L_2 \subseteq \Sigma^*$ and a bound $k \geq 1$. Certifying bounds on separation, we again consider a turn-based two-player game between Prover and Refuter. This time we are interested in whether L_1 and L_2 can be separated by a k-DFA. Consider a word $x \oplus y \in (\Sigma' \times [k])^\omega$. We say that $x \oplus y$ *agrees with* $\langle L_1, L_2 \rangle$ if there exists $F \subseteq [k]$ such that for every $j \geq 1$, if $w^j \in L_1$, then Prover maps w^j to F and if $w^j \in L_2$, then Proven does not map w^j to F.

Accordingly, we define the language $\text{SepDFA}(L_1, L_2, k) \subseteq (\Sigma' \times [k])^\omega$ of words with correct annotations as follows:

$$\text{SepDFA}(L_1, L_2, k) = \{x \oplus y : x \oplus y \text{ is legal and agrees with } \langle L_1, L_2 \rangle\}.$$

Then, $\text{NoSepDFA}(L_1, L_2, k) = comp(\text{SepDFA}(L_1, L_2, k))$ is the language of all words with incorrect annotations.

Proposition 3. *Consider two regular languages $L_1, L_2 \subseteq \Sigma^*$ and $k \geq 1$. Exactly one of the following holds:*

- *$\langle L_1, L_2 \rangle$ is k-DFA-separable, in which case $\text{SepDFA}(L_1, L_2, k)$ is $(\Sigma'/[k])$-realizable by the system.*
- *$\langle L_1, L_2 \rangle$ is not k-DFA-separable, in which case $\text{NoSepDFA}(L_1, L_2, k)$ is $([k]/\Sigma')$-realizable by the environment.*

A transducer that $([k]/\Sigma')$-realizes $\text{NoSepDFA}(L, k)$ is termed an (L_1, L_2, k)-refuter, and we seek refuters that generate short certificates. As has been the case in Sect. 4, such a certificate is an informative bad prefix for $\text{SepDFA}(L_1, L_2, k)$. Formally, we define the language $\text{Violate}(L_1, L_2, k) \subseteq (\Sigma' \times [k])^*$ of words that include a violation of legality or agreement with L_1 and L_2 as follows.

$$\text{Violate}(L_1, L_2, k) = \{x \oplus y : \text{there is } j \geq 1 \text{ such that } x_j = \# \text{ and } y_{j+1} \neq y_1, \text{ or}$$
$$\text{there are } j_1, j_2 \geq 1 \text{ such that}$$
$$y_{j_1} = y_{j_2}, x_{j_1} = x_{j_2}, \text{ and } y_{j_1+1} \neq y_{j_2+1},$$
$$\text{or } w^{j_1} \in L_1, w^{j_2} \in L_2, \text{ and } y_{j_1} = y_{j_2}\}.$$

Before constructing an (L_1, L_2, k)-refuter that generates short certificates, we first need some notations and observations. Let $\mathcal{A} = \langle \Sigma, Q, q_0, \delta, F \rangle$ and

$\mathcal{A}' = \langle \Sigma, Q', q_0', \delta', F' \rangle$ be DFAs. We define the set $F_{\mathcal{A},\mathcal{A}'}$ of states of $\mathcal{A}$ that are reachable by traversing a word in $L(\mathcal{A}')$. Formally, $q \in F_{\mathcal{A},\mathcal{A}'}$ iff there is $w \in L(\mathcal{A}')$ such that $\delta^*(q_0, w) = q$, where δ^* is the extension of δ to words. Note that $F_{\mathcal{A},\mathcal{A}'}$ does not depend on the acceptance condition of $\mathcal{A}$.

Lemma 2. *For every DFAs $\mathcal{A}$ and $\mathcal{A}'$, we have that $L(\mathcal{A}') \subseteq L(\mathcal{A})$ iff $F_{\mathcal{A},\mathcal{A}'} \subseteq F$, and $L(\mathcal{A}) \cap L(\mathcal{A}') = \emptyset$ iff $F_{\mathcal{A},\mathcal{A}'} \subseteq Q \setminus F$.*

Proof. We start with the first claim. If $F_{\mathcal{A},\mathcal{A}'} \subseteq F$, then for every word $w \in L(\mathcal{A}')$, we have that $\delta^*(q_0, w) \in F$, and so $w \in L(\mathcal{A})$ and $L(\mathcal{A}') \subseteq L(\mathcal{A})$. If $F_{\mathcal{A},\mathcal{A}'} \not\subseteq F$, then there exists a word $w \in L(\mathcal{A}')$ such that $\delta^*(q_0, w) \in Q \setminus F$. Then, $w \in L(\mathcal{A}') \setminus L(\mathcal{A})$, and so $L(\mathcal{A}') \not\subseteq L(\mathcal{A})$.

For the second claim, note that $L(\mathcal{A}) \cap L(\mathcal{A}') = \emptyset$ iff $L(\mathcal{A}') \subseteq comp(L(\mathcal{A}))$. Let $\tilde{\mathcal{A}}$ be $\mathcal{A}$ with $Q \setminus F$ being the set of accepting states. By the first claim, we have that $L(\mathcal{A}') \subseteq L(\tilde{\mathcal{A}})$ iff $F_{\tilde{\mathcal{A}},\mathcal{A}'} \subseteq Q \setminus F$. Since $\mathcal{A}$ and $\tilde{\mathcal{A}}$ differ only in the acceptance condition, $F_{\tilde{\mathcal{A}},\mathcal{A}'} = F_{\mathcal{A},\mathcal{A}'}$, and so we are done. $\square$

Lemma 2 implies the following characterization of separability by a DFA with a given structure:

Theorem 6. *Consider DFAs $\mathcal{A}_1$, $\mathcal{A}_2$, and $\mathcal{A}$. Let $\mathcal{A} = \langle \Sigma, Q, q_0, \delta, \emptyset \rangle$. For a set $F \subseteq Q$, define $\mathcal{A}_F = \langle \Sigma, Q, q_0, \delta, F \rangle$. Then, $F_{\mathcal{A},\mathcal{A}_1} \cap F_{\mathcal{A},\mathcal{A}_2} = \emptyset$ iff there exists a set $F \subseteq Q$ such that $\mathcal{A}_F$ separates $\langle \mathcal{A}_1, \mathcal{A}_2 \rangle$.*

Proof. By Lemma 2, the DFA $\mathcal{A}_F$ is a separator for $\langle \mathcal{A}_1, \mathcal{A}_2 \rangle$ iff $F_{\mathcal{A},\mathcal{A}_1} \subseteq F$ and $F_{\mathcal{A},\mathcal{A}_2} \subseteq Q \setminus F$. If $F_{\mathcal{A},\mathcal{A}_1} \cap F_{\mathcal{A},\mathcal{A}_2} = \emptyset$, then $F = F_{\mathcal{A},\mathcal{A}_1}$ satisfies both containments. In the other direction, if there exists a set F that satisfies both containments, then $F_{\mathcal{A},\mathcal{A}_1} \cap F_{\mathcal{A},\mathcal{A}_2} = \emptyset$. $\square$

Consider a DFA $\mathcal{A} = \langle \Sigma, Q, q_0, \delta, \emptyset \rangle$. If there is no set F such that $\mathcal{A}_F$ is a separator for $\langle \mathcal{A}_1, \mathcal{A}_2 \rangle$, there exists a state $q \in F_{\mathcal{A},\mathcal{A}_1} \cap F_{\mathcal{A},\mathcal{A}_2}$. That is, there are words $w_1 \in L(\mathcal{A}_1)$ and $w_2 \in L(\mathcal{A}_2)$ such that $\delta^*(q_0, w_1) = \delta^*(q_0, w_2) = q$. Note that if Prover follows $\mathcal{A}$, then Refuter can cause the interaction to be a word in $Violate(L(\mathcal{A}_1), L(\mathcal{A}_2), k)$ by generating $w_1 \cdot \# \cdot w_2 \cdot \#$. Indeed, then the resulting prefix cannot agree with $L(\mathcal{A}_1)$ and $L(\mathcal{A}_2)$. Accordingly, Refuter's strategy is to first force Prover to commit on the transitions of a k-DFA, and then to generate $w_1 \cdot \# \cdot w_2 \cdot \#$, for the appropriate words w_1 and w_2. Next, we show how Refuter can force Prover to commit on the transitions of a k-DFA.

A legal word $w = x \oplus y$ induces a partial function $\delta_w : [k] \times \Sigma \to [k]$, where for all $j \geq 1$, we have that $y_{j+1} = \delta_w(y_j, x_j)$. Forcing Prover to commit on the transitions of a k-DFA amounts to generating a word w for which δ_w is complete.

Lemma 3. *For every $k \geq 1$, there is a strategy for Refuter that forces Prover to commit on the transitions of a k-DFA in $O(k^2 \cdot |\Sigma|)$ rounds.*

Proof. Refuter maintains a set $S \subseteq [k]$ of discovered states, and a set $\Delta \subseteq [k] \times \Sigma \times [k]$ of discovered transitions. Note that for every discovered state $q \in S$,

Refuter can construct a word $w \in \Sigma^*$ that Prover maps to q using transitions in Δ. Initially, the sets S and Δ are empty. Prover starts the interaction outputting an initial state q_0, and Refuter sets $S = \{q_0\}$.

Assume that there is an undiscovered transition from one of the discovered states. That is, there exist $q \in S$ and $\sigma \in \Sigma$ such that $\langle q, \sigma, r \rangle \notin \Delta$ for all $r \in [k]$. Refuter outputs $w \cdot \sigma \cdot \#$, where w is a word Prover maps to q. Then, Prover answers with a state q', and Refuter adds q' to S, and $\langle q, \sigma, q' \rangle$ to Δ.

Refuter repeats the above process until Δ is complete. Each of the k states has $|\Sigma|$ outgoing transitions. Refuter exposes one new transition in at most $k+1$ rounds: A shortest word w that Prover maps to q has length at most $k-1$, then she outputs the letter σ, and then $\#$. Overall, the number of rounds is at most $k \cdot (k+1) \cdot |\Sigma|$, which is $O(k^2 \cdot |\Sigma|)$. $\qquad\square$

Theorem 7. *Let $L_1, L_2 \subseteq \Sigma^*$ be regular languages, and let $N_1 = \text{index}(L_1)$ and $N_2 = \text{index}(L_2)$. For every $k \geq 1$, if $\langle L_1, L_2 \rangle$ is not k-DFA-separable, then Refuter can generate a word in $\text{Violate}(L_1, L_2, k)$ in $O(k^2 \cdot |\Sigma| + k \cdot N_1 + k \cdot N_2)$ rounds.*

Proof. As described in Lemma 3, Refuter can force Prover to commit on a k-DFA $\mathcal{A}$ in $O(k^2 \cdot |\Sigma|)$ rounds. Since $\langle L_1, L_2 \rangle$ is not k-DFA-separable, there are words $w_1 \in L_1, w_2 \in L_2$ such that the runs of $\mathcal{A}$ on w_1 and on w_2 both end in the same state. In the full version [13] we show that there exist such words satisfying $|w_1| \leq k \cdot N_1$ and $|w_2| \leq k \cdot N_2$. Refuter maintains a pair of such words for every k-DFA. After the DFA $\mathcal{A}$ is exposed, Refuter outputs the corresponding string $w_1 \cdot \# \cdot w_2 \cdot \#$, which has length at most $k \cdot N_1 + k \cdot N_2 + 2$. Overall, the interaction requires $O(k^2 \cdot |\Sigma| + k \cdot N_1 + k \cdot N_2)$ rounds. $\qquad\square$

Recall that when $L_2 = comp(L_1)$, separation coincides with recognizability, with $N_1 = N_2 = N$. Hence, the $O(N^2)$ lower bound on the length of certificates in Theorem 2, applies also for $(N-1)$-DFA-separation. Our upper bound for $(N-1)$-DFA-separation in Theorem 7 includes an extra $|\Sigma|$ factor, as Refuter first forces Prover to commit on all transitions of the claimed DFA. We conjecture that Refuter can do better and force Prover to only to commit on a relevant part of the claimed DFA; namely one in which we can still point to a state $q \in F_{\mathcal{A},\mathcal{A}_1} \cap F_{\mathcal{A},\mathcal{A}_2}$ that is reachable via two words $w_1 \in L(\mathcal{A}_1)$ and $w_2 \in L(\mathcal{A}_2)$. Thus, rather than forcing Prover to commit on all $|\Sigma|$ successors of each state, Refuter forces Prover to commit only on transitions that reveal new states or reveal the required state q. Then, the prefix of the certificate that is generated in Lemma 3 is only of length $O(N^2)$, making the bound tight. Note that such a lazy exposure of the claimed DFA could be of help also in implementations of algorithms for the DFA identification problem [11].

6   Discussion and Directions for Future Research

On the Size of Provers and Refuters. Our study of certification focused on the *length* of certificates. We did not study the *size* of the transducers used by Prover and Refuter in order to generate these certificates. A naive upper bound on the size of such transducers follows from the fact that they are winning strategies in a game played on a deterministic looping automaton for Violate(L, k). Such an automaton has to store in its state space the set of transitions committed by Prover, and is thus exponential in k. The (L, k)-refuter we used for generating short certificates is also exponential in k, as it stores in its state space a mapping from the $k + 1$ words in H to $[k]$ (see Theorem 2). On the other hand, it is easy to see that Prover can do with a transducer that is polynomial in k, as she can follow the transitions of $\mathcal{R}_L$.

Interestingly, with a slight change in the setting, we can shift the burden of maintaining the set of transitions committed by Prover from Refuter to Prover. We do this by requiring Prover to reveal new states in her claimed k-DFA in an *ordered* manner: Prover can respond with a state $i \in [k]$ only after she has responded with states $\{1, \ldots, i - 1\}$. Formally, we say that $w = x \oplus y \in (\Sigma' \times [k])^* \cup (\Sigma' \times [k])^\omega$, with $x = x_1 \cdot x_2 \cdots$ and $y = y_1 \cdot y_2 \cdots$ is *ordered* iff for all $1 \leq j \leq |w|$ we have $y_j \leq \max\{y_l : 1 \leq l < j\} + 1$. Note that if Prover has a winning strategy in a game on DFA(L, k), she also has a winning strategy in a game in which DFA(L, k) is restricted to ordered words. In such a game, however, Refuter can make use of $\mathcal{R}_L$ and circumvent the maintenance of subsets of transitions, whereas Prover has to maintain a mapping from the states in $\mathcal{R}_L$ to their renaming imposed by the order condition. We leave the analysis of this setting as well as the study of trade-offs between the size of transducers and the length of the certificates to future research.

Infinite Words. Our setting considers automata on finite words, and it focuses on the number of states required for recognizing a regular language. In [12], we used a similar methodology for refuting the recognizability of ω-regular languages by automata with limited expressive power. For example, deterministic *Büchi* automata (DBAs) are less expressive than their non-deterministic counterpart, and a DBA-refuter generates certificates that a given language cannot be recognized by a DBA. Thus, the setting in [12] is of automata on infinite words, and it focuses on expressive power.

Unlike DFAs, which allow polynomial minimization, minimization of DBAs is NP-complete [24]. Combining our setting here with the one in [12] would enable the certification and refutation of k-*DBA-recognizability*, namely recognizability by a DBA with k states. The NP-hardness of DBA minimization makes this combination very interesting. In particular, there are interesting connections between polynomial certificates and possible membership of DBA minimization in co-NP, as well as connections between size of certificates and succinctness of the different classes of automata.

References

1. Almagor, S., Lahijanian, M.: Explainable multi agent path finding. In: Proceedings of 19th AAMAS, pp. 34–42 (2020)
2. Alpern, B., Schneider, F.B.: Recognizing safety and liveness. Distrib. Comput. **2**, 117–126 (1987)

3. Angluin, D.: Learning regular sets from queries and counterexamples. Inf. Comput. **75**(2), 87–106 (1987)
4. Baumeister, T., Finkbeiner, B., Torfah, H.: Explainable reactive synthesis. In: Hung, D.V., Sokolsky, O. (eds.) ATVA 2020. LNCS, vol. 12302, pp. 413–428. Springer, Cham (2020). https://doi.org/10.1007/978-3-030-59152-6_23
5. Büchi, J.R., Landweber, L.H.: Solving sequential conditions by finite-state strategies. Trans. AMS **138**, 295–311 (1969)
6. Czerwiński, W., Lasota, S., Meyer, R., Muskalla, S., Kumar, K.N., Saivasan, P.: Regular separability of well-structured transition systems. In: Proceedings of 29th CONCUR. LIPIcs, vol. 118, pp. 35:1–35:18 (2018)
7. Czerwiński, W., Martens, W., Masopust, T.: Efficient separability of regular languages by subsequences and suffixes. In: Fomin, F.V., Freivalds, R., Kwiatkowska, M., Peleg, D. (eds.) ICALP 2013. LNCS, vol. 7966, pp. 150–161. Springer, Heidelberg (2013). https://doi.org/10.1007/978-3-642-39212-2_16
8. Fisman, D.: Inferring regular languages and ω-languages. J. Log. Algebraic Methods Program. **98**, 27–49 (2018)
9. Gange, G., Ganty, P., Stuckey, P.J.: Fixing the state budget: approximation of regular languages with small DFAs. In: D'Souza, D., Narayan Kumar, K. (eds.) ATVA 2017. LNCS, vol. 10482, pp. 67–83. Springer, Cham (2017). https://doi.org/10.1007/978-3-319-68167-2_5
10. Gold, E.M.: Complexity of automaton identification from given data. Inf. Control **37**(3), 302–320 (1978)
11. Heule, M.J.H., Verwer, S.: Exact DFA identification using SAT solvers. In: Sempere, J.M., García, P. (eds.) ICGI 2010. LNCS (LNAI), vol. 6339, pp. 66–79. Springer, Heidelberg (2010). https://doi.org/10.1007/978-3-642-15488-1_7
12. Kupferman, O., Sickert, S.: Certifying inexpressibility. In: FOSSACS 2021. LNCS, vol. 12650, pp. 385–405. Springer, Cham (2021). https://doi.org/10.1007/978-3-030-71995-1_20
13. Kupferman, O., Lavee, N., Sickert, S.: Certifying DFA bounds for recognition and separation (2021). Full version archived at arXiv:2107.01566
14. Kupferman, O., Vardi, M.Y.: Model checking of safety properties. Formal Methods Syst. Des. **19**(3), 291–314 (2001)
15. Kupferman, O., Vardi, M.Y.: From complementation to certification. Theoret. Comput. Sci. **305**, 591–606 (2005)
16. Kupferman, O., Weiner, S.: Environment-friendly safety. In: Biere, A., Nahir, A., Vos, T. (eds.) HVC 2012. LNCS, vol. 7857, pp. 227–242. Springer, Heidelberg (2013). https://doi.org/10.1007/978-3-642-39611-3_22
17. Myhill, J.: Finite automata and the representation of events. Technical report WADD TR-57-624, pp. 112–137. Wright Patterson AFB, Ohio (1957)
18. Neider, D.: Computing minimal separating DFAs and regular invariants using SAT and SMT solvers. In: Chakraborty, S., Mukund, M. (eds.) ATVA 2012. LNCS, pp. 354–369. Springer, Heidelberg (2012). https://doi.org/10.1007/978-3-642-33386-6_28
19. Nerode, A.: Linear automaton transformations. Proc. Am. Math. Soc. **9**(4), 541–544 (1958)
20. Pfleeger, C.P.: State reduction in incompletely specified finite-state machines. IEEE Trans. Comput. **22**(12), 1099–1102 (1973)
21. T. Place and M. Zeitoun. Separating regular languages with first-order logic. Log. Methods Comput. Sci. **12**(1) (2016)
22. ESF Network Programme: Automata: from mathematics to applications (AutoMathA) (2010). http://www.esf.org/index.php?id=1789

23. Almagor, S., Chistikov, D., Ouaknine, J., Worrell, J.: O-minimal invariants for linear loops. In: Proceedings of 45th ICALP. LIPIcs, vol. 107, pp. 114:1–114:14 (2018)
24. Schewe, S.: Beyond hyper-minimisation–minimising DBAs and DPAs is NP-complete. In: Proceedings of 30th FST & TCS. LIPIcs, vol. 8, pp. 400–411 (2010)
25. Trakhtenbrot, B.A., Barzdin, Y.M.: Finite Automata. North Holland, Amsterdam (1973)

Machine Learning for Formal Methods

AALpy: An Active Automata Learning Library

Edi Muškardin[1,2]([✉]) [iD], Bernhard K. Aichernig[2] [iD], Ingo Pill[1] [iD],
Andrea Pferscher[2], and Martin Tappler[1,2] [iD]

[1] Silicon Austria Labs, TU Graz - SAL DES Lab, Graz, Austria
edi.muskardin@silicon-austria.com
[2] Institute of Software Technology, Graz University of Technology, Graz, Austria

Abstract. AALPY is an extensible open-source Python library providing efficient implementations of active automata learning algorithms for deterministic, non-deterministic, and stochastic systems. We put a special focus on the conformance testing aspect in active automata learning, as well as on an intuitive and seamlessly integrated interface for learning automata characterizing real-world reactive systems. In this manuscript, we present AALPY's core functionalities, illustrate its usage via examples, and evaluate its learning performance.

Keywords: Active automata learning · Model inference · Python

1 Introduction

Whenever facing an unknown system, we strive to learn more about its behavior, which in computer science terms often translates to learning its *language*. Regular language inference, a.k.a automata learning or model mining, is thus a well-studied topic and has been an active field ever since Anguin's seminal paper [4]. The topic has gained special interest in the context of model checking [12] and software testing [3] of black-box systems.

Despite the growing interest, there are few libraries or frameworks for automata learning available. The most notable one is LearnLib [9], an open-source Java library that is the de-facto standard when it comes to tools. Compared to LearnLib, our AALPY[1] extends the scope to learning of deterministic Moore machines, observable non-deterministic finite-state machines (ONFSMs), and Markov decision processes (MDPs).

Due to Python's popularity in software engineering and AI, we chose to implement AALPY in Python such as to target a wide audience, supported also by an open-source MIT license. Especially important for learning models of black-box systems is the fact that Python increasingly serves as interface language for a wide range of software and systems on chip.

---

[1] Code, documentation, interactive examples, and a comprehensive Wiki can be found at https://github.com/DES-Lab/AALpy.

Z. Hou and V. Ganesh (Eds.): ATVA 2021, LNCS 12971, pp. 67–73, 2021.
https://doi.org/10.1007/978-3-030-88885-5_5

2   AALpy – Intuitive Automata Learning in Python

Key features of our library are its modular design, a seamlessly integrated deployment process, efficient implementations of state-of-the-art learning algorithms for deterministic, non-deterministic, and stochastic automata, and efficient conformance testing. AALPY accessibility and usability is enhanced via extensive documentation and multiple demonstrating examples for each of the library's functionalities—complemented by visualization and logging capabilities. The latter may be of special interest for educational purposes.

The query-based automata learning algorithms implemented in AALPY are based on the minimally adequate teacher framework by Angluin [4]. We particularly focus on learning models of reactive systems (s.t. their input-output behavior can be captured by regular languages) via a test-based concept. To this end, AALPY interfaces the system under learning (SUL) and a selected learning algorithm via a step-based interface. In an individual step, the input stimulus is provided to the SUL and then the resulting output is observed. For real-world SULs, interfacing the SUL and the algorithm may involve some abstraction and concretization, e.g., implemented via a mapper [1]. When employing AALPY, a user thus in principle only has to define the functionality for a step, as well as a proper reset for the SUL (in order to be able to start a query from the initial state). AALPY implements queries as sequences of steps and resets. If required, a user can implement queries directly.

When employing AALPY, a user follows a three stage process: (a) define the SUL interface for the learning engine, (b) select an equivalence oracle, and (c) select, customize and execute the learning algorithm. In (a), three methods are to be defined: `pre`, `post`, and `step` (see also Example 1). With `pre`, we initialize and setup the SUL, while `post` shall support a graceful shutdown/memory cleanup. As informally suggested above, `step` encapsulates a single step in the query execution, such that formally some $\sigma \in \Sigma$ for the input alphabet Σ is mapped to a concrete input/or action for the SUL, and the SUL's output is observed and reported back as a letter γ in some output alphabet Γ. Note that we do not limit alphabets to integers, characters, or strings. In particular, Σ and Γ can be lists of hashable objects, or even class methods with appropriate arguments.

Example 1 (Learning a regular expression). Listing 1.1 implements active learning of a deterministic finite automaton (DFA) conforming to a regular expression.

In Lines 1–14, we show a simple SUL that parses regular expressions. In Lines 16 and 17, we define a regular expression over a binary alphabet. In Line 19, we select the equivalence oracle used for answering equivalence queries via conformance testing, and in Line 20 we select the learning algorithm and execute it. When finished, AALPY prints the learning statistics and visualizes the automaton as shown in Fig. 1.

Let us now describe the supported learning algorithms, starting with the support of **deterministic learning of DFA, Mealy and Moore machines**. We extended the original L^* algorithm [4] with two counterexample processing

Listing 1.1. Learning regural expressions with AALPY

```
1   class RegexSUL(SUL):
2     # System under learning for regular expressions
3     def __init__(self, regex: str):
4       super().__init__()
5       self.regex = regex if regex[-1] == '$' else regex + '$'
6       self.string = ""
7     def pre(self):
8       self.string = ""
9     def post(self):
10      pass
11    def step(self, letter):
12      if letter is not None:
13        self.string += str(letter)
14      return True if re.match(self.regex, self.string) else False\\
15  # complement of Tomita 3 grammar
16  regex = '((0|1)*0)*1(11)*(0(0|1)*1)*0(00)*(1(0|1)*)*'
17  alphabet = [0, 1]
18  regex_sul = RegexSUL(regex)
19  eq_oracle = RandomWMethodEqOracle(alphabet, regex_sul)
20  learned_automaton = run_Lstar(alphabet, regex_sul, eq_oracle,
21                                  automaton_type='dfa')
22  visualize_automaton(learned_automaton)
```

techniques [14, 15] as well as query caching. The cache reduces the number of SUL interactions performed for membership queries. It encodes membership query results as a tree that is updated during learning as well as equivalence checking.

We also support **learning of ONFSMs** [5] and the more recent **abstracted non-deterministic finite-state machines** [13]. These algorithms overcome the limitation of classical algorithms where deterministic behavior of the SUL is required. In addition, the latter reduces the state-space of the learned system via abstraction, resulting in smaller models and faster learning.

AALPY's support of **active learning of stochastic systems** draws on L^*_{MDP} [16] and formalizes their behavior as MDPs or as stochastic Mealy machines. While the previously discussed learning approaches rely on membership and equivalence queries, L^*_{MDP} implements a "stochastic" teacher that is able to answer *complete queries, frequency queries, refine queries* and *equivalence queries* (see [16] for more information on query types). Additionally, we implemented a slight adaptation of the L^*_{MDP} algorithm that requires fewer parameters and is more robust to sparse observations. In practice, users only have to implement the SUL interface as discussed in Sect. 2.

We address equivalence queries via conformance testing. Equivalence checking in automata learning should try "finding counterexample fast" instead of "proving equivalence" between SUL and hypothesis [8]. Therefore, we focus on efficient random-testing heuristics rather than expensive deterministic conformance testing, such as the W-method. AALPY provides ten equivalence oracles and new ones can be easily added. To this end, AALPY supports the user by providing a (non-necessarily minimal) characterization set of the hypothesis, shortest path to each state, and a set of previously observed traces (cache). Currently, AALPY implements the following equivalence oracles:

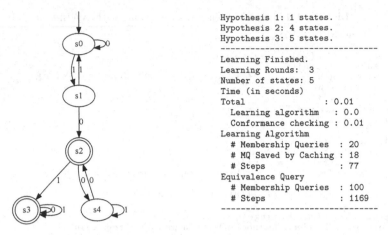

```
Hypothesis 1: 1 states.
Hypothesis 2: 4 states.
Hypothesis 3: 5 states.
-------------------------------
Learning Finished.
Learning Rounds:  3
Number of states: 5
Time (in seconds)
Total               : 0.01
  Learning algorithm   : 0.0
  Conformance checking : 0.01
Learning Algorithm
  # Membership Queries  : 20
  # MQ Saved by Caching : 18
  # Steps               : 77
Equivalence Query
  # Membership Queries  : 100
  # Steps               : 1169
-------------------------------
```

Fig. 1. Output of Listing 1.1

- W-Method
- Random Walk
- Cache-Tree Based Exploration
- Fixed Prefix Random Walk
- k-Way Transition Coverage

- Random W-Method
- Random Word
- Transition/Same state Focus
- Breath-First Exploration.
- User Input Oracle

We refer the interested reader to AALPY's documentation and Wiki for descriptions, suggested use cases, and parameter explanations for each of these oracles.

For an enhanced user experience, AALPY can save learned automata to files (following community's syntax [11]), visualize them, and display information about the learning progress and the observation table. For evaluation, a user may generate random automata, define them as an SUL and then learn them. For verification, AALPY provides a translation of MDPs into PRISM [10] format.

3   Experimental Evaluation

In order to showcase AALPY's performance, we conducted several experiments on a Dell Lattitude 5410 with an Intel Core i7-10610U processor, 8 GB of RAM running Windows 10 and using PyPy 3.9. In particular, we experienced a performance benefit of using PyPy over CPython.

Deterministic Automata Learning efficiency was evaluated with extensive experiments on random automata. We conducted two types of experiments, one in which we increased the number of states of the target automata while keeping the size of the input alphabet constant, and one where we increased the size of the input alphabet whilst keeping the size of the target automata constant. Each experiment was repeated 20 times to obtain average values. Figure 2 shows the results. We observed that the automaton size affects DFA learning more than Mealy and Moore machine learning. On the other hand, DFA learning is least

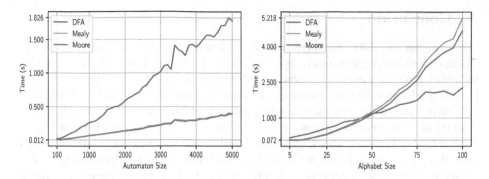

Fig. 2. Runtime of the deterministic L^* with respect to automata size (for an alphabet of size 10) and alphabet size (for an automaton with 1000 states).

affected by the increase in the input alphabet. Furthermore, we see that the runtime increases linearly with the number of states and almost linearly with the size of the alphabet. Results are consistent with LearnLib's findings [9].

Stochastic Automata Learning was evaluated with the same experiments as the original Java version of L^*_{MDP} [16]. Figure 3 shows the average runtime and the average model-checking errors measured in the experiments. The latter is the average absolute difference between probabilistic model-checking on a learned model and the true model. We can see that AALPY and the Java implementation are generally similarly fast and produce similarly accurate models. Evaluation differences can be attributed to minor implementation details.

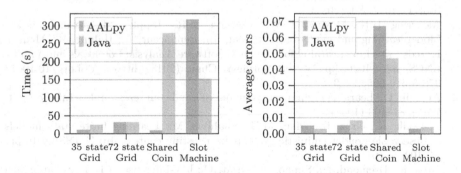

Fig. 3. Runtime measurements and probabilistic model-checking errors on learned models for the AALPY implementation and the Java implementation of L^*_{MDP}.

4   Conclusion

We presented AALPY, an active automata learning library. AALPY efficiently learns deterministic, non-deterministic, and stochastic systems. AALPY provides its users a set of equivalence oracles, different configurations of learning algorithms, and the ability to visualize the learning process and results. AALPY is currently successfully used to learn the protocols of MQTT and Bluetooth. These learned models serve as a basis for learning-based testing [3] and fuzzing [2].

AALPY is for researchers, educators, and industry alike. Its modular design provides a solid basis for experimentation with new learning algorithms, equivalence oracles, and counterexample processing. In future, we intend to extend these functionalities, with SAT-based learning [7] and learning without reset [6]. We hope that the community will recognize AALPY as an attractive foundation for further research, and welcome suggestions and extensions.

Acknowledgments. This work has been supported by the "University SAL Labs" initiative of Silicon Austria Labs (SAL) and its Austrian partner universities for applied fundamental research for electronic based systems and by the TU Graz LEAD project "Dependable Internet of Things in Adverse Environments".

References

1. Aarts, F., Jonsson, B., Uijen, J.: Generating models of infinite-state communication protocols using regular inference with abstraction. In: Petrenko, A., Simão, A., Maldonado, J.C. (eds.) ICTSS 2010. LNCS, vol. 6435, pp. 188–204. Springer, Heidelberg (2010). https://doi.org/10.1007/978-3-642-16573-3_14
2. Aichernig, B., Muškardin, E., Pferscher, A.: Learning-based fuzzing of IoT message brokers. In: ICST (2021)
3. Aichernig, B.K., Mostowski, W., Mousavi, M.R., Tappler, M., Taromirad, M.: Model learning and model-based testing. In: Bennaceur, A., Hähnle, R., Meinke, K. (eds.) Machine Learning for Dynamic Software Analysis: Potentials and Limits. LNCS, vol. 11026, pp. 74–100. Springer, Cham (2018). https://doi.org/10.1007/978-3-319-96562-8_3
4. Angluin, D.: Learning regular sets from queries and counterexamples. Inf. Comput. **75**(2), 87–106 (1987)
5. El-Fakih, K., Groz, R., Irfan, M.N., Shahbaz, M.: Learning finite state models of observable nondeterministic systems in a testing context. In: ICTSS 2010, pp. 97–102 (2010)
6. Groz, R., Bremond, N., Simao, A., Oriat, C.: hW-inference: a heuristic approach to retrieve models through black box testing. JSS **159**, 110426 (2020)
7. Heule, M.J.H., Verwer, S.: Exact DFA identification using SAT solvers. In: Sempere, J.M., García, P. (eds.) ICGI 2010. LNCS (LNAI), vol. 6339, pp. 66–79. Springer, Heidelberg (2010). https://doi.org/10.1007/978-3-642-15488-1_7
8. Howar, F., Steffen, B., Merten, M.: From ZULU to RERS. In: Margaria, T., Steffen, B. (eds.) ISoLA 2010. LNCS, vol. 6415, pp. 687–704. Springer, Heidelberg (2010). https://doi.org/10.1007/978-3-642-16558-0_55
9. Isberner, M., Howar, F., Steffen, B.: The open-source LearnLib. In: Kroening, D., Păsăreanu, C.S. (eds.) CAV 2015. LNCS, vol. 9206, pp. 487–495. Springer, Cham (2015). https://doi.org/10.1007/978-3-319-21690-4_32

10. Kwiatkowska, M., Norman, G., Parker, D.: PRISM 4.0: verification of probabilistic real-time systems. In: Gopalakrishnan, G., Qadeer, S. (eds.) CAV 2011. LNCS, vol. 6806, pp. 585–591. Springer, Heidelberg (2011). https://doi.org/10.1007/978-3-642-22110-1_47

11. Neider, D., Smetsers, R., Vaandrager, F., Kuppens, H.: Benchmarks for automata learning and conformance testing. In: Margaria, T., Graf, S., Larsen, K.G. (eds.) Models, Mindsets, Meta: The What, the How, and the Why Not? LNCS, vol. 11200, pp. 390–416. Springer, Cham (2019). https://doi.org/10.1007/978-3-030-22348-9_23

12. Peled, D.A., Vardi, M.Y., Yannakakis, M.: Black box checking. J. Autom. Lang. Comb. **7**(2), 225–246 (2002)

13. Pferscher, A., Aichernig, B.K.: Learning abstracted non-deterministic finite state machines. In: Casola, V., De Benedictis, A., Rak, M. (eds.) ICTSS 2020. LNCS, vol. 12543, pp. 52–69. Springer, Cham (2020). https://doi.org/10.1007/978-3-030-64881-7_4

14. Rivest, R.L., Schapire, R.E.: Inference of finite automata using homing sequences. Inf. Comput. **103**(2), 299–347 (1993)

15. Shahbaz, M., Groz, R.: Inferring mealy machines. In: Cavalcanti, A., Dams, D.R. (eds.) FM 2009. LNCS, vol. 5850, pp. 207–222. Springer, Heidelberg (2009). https://doi.org/10.1007/978-3-642-05089-3_14

16. Tappler, M., Aichernig, B.K., Bacci, G., Eichlseder, M., Larsen, K.G.: L^*-based learning of Markov decision processes. In: ter Beek, M.H., McIver, A., Oliveira, J.N. (eds.) FM 2019. LNCS, vol. 11800, pp. 651–669. Springer, Cham (2019). https://doi.org/10.1007/978-3-030-30942-8_38

Learning Linear Temporal Properties from Noisy Data: A MaxSAT-Based Approach

Jean-Raphaël Gaglione[1], Daniel Neider[2], Rajarshi Roy[2(✉)], Ufuk Topcu[3], and Zhe Xu[4]

[1] Ecole Polytechnique, Palaiseau, France
[2] Max Planck Institute for Software Systems, Kaiserslautern, Germany
rajarshi@mpi-sws.org
[3] University of Texas at Austin, Austin, TX, USA
[4] Arizona State University, Tempe, AZ, USA

Abstract. We address the problem of inferring descriptions of system behavior using Linear Temporal Logic (LTL) from a finite set of positive and negative examples. Most of the existing approaches for solving such a task rely on predefined templates for guiding the structure of the inferred formula. The approaches that can infer arbitrary LTL formulas, on the other hand, are not robust to noise in the data. To alleviate such limitations, we devise two algorithms for inferring concise LTL formulas even in the presence of noise. Our first algorithm infers minimal LTL formulas by reducing the inference problem to a problem in maximum satisfiability and then using off-the-shelf MaxSAT solvers to find a solution. To the best of our knowledge, we are the first to incorporate the usage of MaxSAT solvers for inferring formulas in LTL. Our second learning algorithm relies on the first algorithm to derive a decision tree over LTL formulas based on a decision tree learning algorithm. We have implemented both our algorithms and verified that our algorithms are efficient in extracting concise LTL descriptions even in the presence of noise.

Keywords: Linear temporal logic · Specification mining · Explainable AI

1 Introduction

Explaining the behavior of complex systems in a form that is interpretable to humans has become a central problem in Artificial Intelligence. Applications where having concise system descriptions are essential include debugging, reverse engineering, motion planning, specification mining for formal verification, to name just a few examples.

For inferring descriptions of a system, we rely on a set of positive examples and a set of negative examples generated from the underlying system. Given

© Springer Nature Switzerland AG 2021
Z. Hou and V. Ganesh (Eds.): ATVA 2021, LNCS 12971, pp. 74–90, 2021.
https://doi.org/10.1007/978-3-030-88885-5_6

such data, the objective is to infer a concise model in a suitable formalism that is consistent with the data; that is, the model must satisfy the positive examples and not satisfy the negative ones.

Most of the data representing AI systems consist of sequences since, more often than not, the properties of these systems evolve over time. For representing data consisting of sequences, temporal logic has emerged to be a successful and popular formalism. Among temporal logics, Linear Temporal Logic (LTL), developed by Pnueli [16], enjoys being both mathematically rigorous and human interpretable for describing system properties. Moreover, LTL displays a resemblance to natural language and simultaneously eliminates the ambiguities existing in natural language. To this end, LTL uses modal operators such as **F** ("eventually"), **G** ("globally"), **U** ("until"), and several others to describe naturally occurring sequences based on their temporal aspect. One can use these operators to easily describe properties such as "the robot should reach the goal and not touch a wall or step into the water in the process" using (¬water ∧ ¬wall)**U**goal or "every request should be followed by a grant eventually" using **G**(request → (**F**grant)).

The task of inferring temporal logic formulas consistent with a given data has been studied extensively [4,13,20,24]. Most of the existing inference methods, however, typically impose syntactic restrictions on the inferred formula. In particular, these methods only derive formulas whose structures are based on certain handcrafted templates, and this leads to several drawbacks. First, handcrafting templates by users may not be a straightforward task, since it requires adequate knowledge about the underlying system. Second, by restricting the structure of inferred formulas, we potentially increase the size of the inferred formula.

Nevertheless, there are approaches [6,15] that avoid the use of templates. These works present algorithms that rely on reducing the learning problem to a Boolean satisfiability problem (SAT) to infer LTL formulas that perfectly classify the input data. However, such exact algorithms suffer from the limitation that they are susceptible to failure in the presence of noise which is ubiquitous in real-world data. Furthermore, trying to infer formulas that perfectly classify a noisy sample often results in complex formulas, hampering interpretability.

To alleviate the limitation of the earlier approaches, in this paper we present two novel algorithms for inferring LTL formulas from data provided as a sample consisting of system traces labeled as positive and negative. The goal of algorithms is to infer concise LTL formulas that achieve a low *loss* on the sample, where loss $l(S, \varphi)$ refers to the fraction of examples in the sample S that the inferred formula φ misclassified. Precisely, the problem we solve is the following: given a sample S and a threshold κ, find a minimal LTL formula φ that has $l(S, \varphi) \leq \kappa$. Our algorithms are built upon the SAT-based learning algorithms introduced by Neider and Gavran [15]. Our first algorithm tackles this problem by reducing the search of an LTL formula to a problem in Maximum Satisfiability (MaxSAT). Roughly speaking, we construct formulas in propositional logic with appropriate weights assigned to various clauses. We then search for assignments to the propositional formula that maximize the total weight of the satisfied clauses. Finally, using an assignment that maximizes the weights of the satisfied clauses, we construct an LTL formula minimizing loss in a straightforward manner.

Our first algorithm constructs series of monolithic propositional formulas to tackle the inference problem and is, thus, often inefficient for inferring larger formulas. Our second algorithm solves the inference problem by dividing the problem into smaller subproblems based on a decision tree learning algorithm. Instead of finding LTL formulas that achieve a loss less than κ in one step, for each decision node in the tree we exploit our first algorithm to infer small LTL formulas. Neider and Gavran also propose a similar decision tree based learning algorithm for LTL. However, our algorithm outperforms theirs in two aspects. First, our algorithm is robust to noise in the data. Second, we incorporate a systematic search of LTL formulas for each decision node, while theirs rely on simple heuristics for searching without termination guarantees.

We have implemented a prototype of both of our algorithms, and compared them to the algorithms by Neider and Gavran. To effectuate the evaluation, we used benchmarks that model typical LTL patterns used in practice. From our observations, we conclude that our algorithms outperform that of Neider and Gavran in terms of running time and formula size, especially in the benchmarks containing noise.

Related Work. Our approach builds upon that of Neider and Gavran [15] who exploit a SAT-based inference method. Similar to this is the work of Camacho et al. [6] which uses a SAT-based approach to construct Alternating Finite Automaton consistent with data and extract an LTL formula from it. Most of the other works require templates for inferring LTL formulas. Among those, one prominent work is that of Kim et al. [12] as they infer satisfactory LTL formulas from noisy data, exploiting the Bayesian inference problem.

For the inference of temporal logic formulas, a number of works also utilize decision tree learning algorithms. One notable example is the work of Bombara et al. [4] which infers Signal Temporal Logic (STL) classifiers based on decision trees. While their work can infer STL formulas with arbitrary misclassification error on the data, the STL primitives used for the decision nodes in their trees are derived only from a predefined set. Closely related is the work of Brunello et al. [5] which infers decision trees over Interval Temporal Logic. The decision nodes in their trees, as well, are simple formulas; usually consisting of a single temporal relation with a proposition.

The inference problem of temporal logic, in general, has gained popularity in the recent years. Apart from LTL, this problem has been looked at for a variety of logics, including Past Time Linear Temporal Logic (PLTL) [1], Signal Temporal Logic (STL) [2,10,11,13,20,21], Property Specification Language (PSL) [18] and several others [22,23,25].

2 Preliminaries

In this section, we introduce the necessary background required for the paper.

Propositional Logic. Let *Var* be a set of propositional variables, which take Boolean values $\{0, 1\}$ (0 represents *true*, 1 represents *false*). Formulas in propositional logic—denoted by capital Greek letters—are defined inductively as follows:

$$\Phi := x \in Var \mid \neg\Phi \mid \Phi \vee \Phi$$

Moreover, we add syntactic sugar and allow the formulas *true*, *false*, $\Phi \wedge \Psi$, $\Phi \rightarrow \Psi$ and $\Phi \leftrightarrow \Psi$ which are defined in the standard manner.

A propositional valuation is a mapping $v\colon Var \mapsto \{0, 1\}$, which maps propositional variables to Boolean values. We define the semantics of propositional logic using a valuation function $V(v, \Phi)$ that is inductively defined as follows: $V(v, x) = v(x)$, $V(v, \neg\Psi) = 1 - V(v, \Psi)$, and $V(v, \Psi \vee \Phi) = max\{V(v, \Psi), V(v, \Phi)\}$. We say that v satisfies Φ if $V(v, \Phi) = 1$, and call v as a model of Φ. A propositional formula Φ is satisfiable if there exists a model v of Φ.

The satisfiability problem of propositional formula—abbreviated as SAT—is the problem of determining whether a propositional formula is satisfiable or not. For the SAT problem, usually propositional formulas are assumed to be provided in Conjunctive Normal Form (CNF). Formulas in CNF are represented as conjunction of clauses C_i, where each clause is a disjunction of literals; a literal being a propositional variable x or its complement $\neg x$.

Finite Traces. Formally, a *trace* over a set $\mathcal{P}$ of propositional variables (which represent interesting system properties) is a finite sequence of symbols $u = a_0 a_1 \ldots a_n$, where $a_i \in 2^{\mathcal{P}}$ for $i \in \{0, \cdots, n\}$. For instance, $\{p, q\}\{p\}\{q\}$ is a trace over the propositional variables $\mathcal{P} = \{p, q\}$. The empty trace, denoted by ϵ, is an empty sequence. The length of a trace is given by $|u|$ (note $|\epsilon| = 0$). Moreover, given a trace u and $i \in \mathbb{N}$, we use $u[i]$ to denote the symbol at position i (counting starts from 0). Finally, we denote the set of all traces by $(2^{\mathcal{P}})^*$.

Linear Temporal Logic. Linear Temporal Logic (LTL) is a logic that enables reasoning about sequences of events by extending propositional Boolean logic with temporal modalities. Given a finite set $\mathcal{P}$ of propositional variables, formulas in LTL—denoted by small greek letters—are defined inductively by:

$$\varphi := p \in \mathcal{P} \mid \neg\varphi \mid \varphi \vee \varphi \mid \mathbf{X}\varphi \mid \varphi \mathbf{U}\varphi$$

As syntactic sugar, we allow the use of additional constants and operators used in propositional logic. Additionally, we include temporal operators $\mathbf{F}$ ("future") and $\mathbf{G}$ ("globally") by $\mathbf{F}\varphi := true\mathbf{U}\varphi$ and $\mathbf{G}\varphi := \neg\mathbf{F}\neg\varphi$. The set of all operators is defined as $\Lambda = \{\neg, \vee, \wedge, \rightarrow, \mathbf{X}, \mathbf{U}, \mathbf{F}, \mathbf{G}\} \cup \mathcal{P}$ (propositional variables are considered to be nullary operators). We define the size $|\varphi|$ of an LTL formula φ to be the number of its unique subformulas. For instance, size of formula $\varphi = (p\mathbf{U}\mathbf{X}q) \vee \mathbf{X}q$ is 5, since, the distinct subformulas of φ are $p, q, \mathbf{X}q, p\mathbf{U}\mathbf{X}q$ and $(p\mathbf{U}\mathbf{X}q) \vee \mathbf{X}q$.

We interpret LTL over finite traces[1] as is done in several applications related to AI [3]. We define the semantics of LTL on finite traces based on the definition by Giacomo and Vardi [9]. For the semantics, we use a valuation function V, that maps a formula, a finite trace and a position in the trace to a Boolean value. Formally we define V as follows: $V(p, u, i) = 1$ if and only if $p \in u[i]$, $V(\neg\varphi, u, i) = 1 - V(\varphi, u, i)$, $V(\varphi \lor \psi, u, i) = max\{V(\varphi, u, i), V(\psi, u, i)\}$, $V(\mathbf{X}\varphi, u, i) = min\{i < |u|, V(\varphi, u, i+1)\}$, $V(\varphi\mathbf{U}\psi, u, i) = max_{i \leq j \leq |u|}\{V(\psi, u, j), min_{i \leq k < j}V(\varphi, u, k)\}$. We say that a trace $u \in (2^{\mathcal{P}})^*$ satisfies a formula φ if $V(u, \varphi, 0) = 1$. For the sake of brevity, we use $V(u, \varphi)$ to denote $V(u, \varphi, 0)$.

3   Problem Formulation

The input data is provided as a sample $S \subset (2^{\mathcal{P}})^* \times \{0, 1\}$ consisting of labeled traces. Precisely, sample S is a set of pairs (u, b), where $u \in (2^{\mathcal{P}})^*$ is a trace and $b \in \{0, 1\}$ is its classification label. The traces labeled 1 are called positive traces, while the ones labeled 0 are called negative traces. We assume that in a sample $(u, b_1) = (u, b_2)$ implies $b_1 = b_2$, indicating that no trace can be both positive and negative. Further, we denote the size of S, that is, the number of traces in a sample, by $|S|$.

We define a *loss* function which assigns a real value to a given sample S and an LTL formula φ. Intuitively, a loss function evaluates how "well" the LTL formula φ classifies a sample. While there are numerous ways of defining loss functions (e.g., quadratic loss function, regret, etc.), we use the definition:

$$l(S, \varphi) = \sum_{(u,b) \in S} \frac{|V(\varphi, u) - b|}{|S|},$$

which calculates the fraction of traces in S which the LTL formula φ misclassified.

Having defined the setting, we now formally describe the problem we solve:

Problem 1. Given a sample $S \subset (2^{\mathcal{P}})^* \times \{0, 1\}$ and threshold $\kappa \in [0, 1]$, find an LTL formula φ such that $l(S, \varphi) \leq \kappa$.

Generally speaking, the above problem is trivial if no constraint is imposed on the size of the output formula since, one can always find a large LTL formula with zero loss on a given sample, as indicated by the following remark.

Remark 1. Given sample S, there exists an LTL formula φ such that $l(S, \varphi) = 0$.

To construct such a formula, one needs to perform the following steps: construct formulas $\varphi_{u,v}$ for all $(u, 1) \in S$ and $(v, 0) \in S$, such that $V(\varphi_{u,v}, u) = 1$ and $V(\varphi_{u,v}, u) = 0$, using a sequence of **X**-operators and an appropriate propositional formula to describe the first symbol where u and v differ; now $\varphi = \bigvee_{(u,1) \in S} \bigwedge_{(v,0) \in S} \varphi_{u,v}$ is the desired formula. The formula φ, however, is

---

[1] LTL, when interpreted over finite traces, is sometimes referred to as LTL$_f$.

large in size (of the order of $|S|^2 \times max_{(u,b) \in S} |u|$) and it does not help towards the goal of inferring a concise description of the data.

Our first algorithm for solving Problem 1, in fact, infers an LTL formula that is minimal among the ones that achieve $l(S, \varphi) \leq \kappa$. We describe the algorithm in Sect. 4. Our second algorithm, described in Sect. 5, infers a decision tree over LTL formulas which, however, is not guaranteed to be of minimal size. Nevertheless, decision trees are considered to be structures that provide interpretable explanations of the underlying system. Further, in the algorithm, we introduce a tunable parameter which makes it possible to adjust the size of the decision tree based on user requirements.

4   Learning Minimal LTL Formulas

Our solution to Problem 1 relies on MaxSAT solvers which we introduce next.

4.1   MaxSAT

MaxSAT—a variant of the SAT (Boolean satisfiability) problem—is the problem of finding an assignment that maximizes the number of satisfied clauses in a given propositional formula provided in CNF. For solving our problem, we use a more general variant of MaxSAT, known as Partial Weighted MaxSAT. In this variant, a weight function $w: \mathcal{C} \mapsto \mathbb{R} \cup \{\infty\}$ assigns a weight to every clause in the set of clauses $\mathcal{C}$ of a propositional formula. The problem is to then find a valuation v that maximises $\Sigma_{C_i \in \mathcal{C}} w(C_i) \cdot V(v, C_i)$.

While the MaxSAT problem and its variants can be solved using dedicated solvers, standard SMT solvers like Z3 [14] are also able to handle such problems. According to terminology derived from the theory behind such solvers, clauses C_i for which $w(C_i) = \infty$ are termed as *hard* constraints, while clauses C_i for which $w(C_i) < \infty$ are termed as *soft* constraints. Given a propositional formula with weights assigned to clauses, MaxSAT solvers try to find a valuation that satisfies all the hard constraints and maximizes the total weight of the soft constraints that can be satisfied.

4.2   The Learning Algorithm

Given that we are using MaxSAT solvers that possess the capability of handling Partial Weighted MaxSAT problems, we can solve a stronger version of Problem 1. In this stronger version, the loss based on which we search for LTL formulas takes the following form:

$$wl(S, \varphi, \Omega) = \sum_{(u,b) \in S} \Omega(u) |V(\varphi, u) - b|,$$

where Ω is a function that assigns a positive real-valued weight to each u in the sample in such a way that $\sum_{(u,b) \in S} \Omega(u) = 1$. Observe that by considering

---

Algorithm 1: MaxSAT-based LTL learning algorithm

Input: A sample S, Ω function, Threshold κ
1 $n \leftarrow 0$
2 **repeat**
3 | $n \leftarrow n + 1$
4 | Construct formula $\Phi_n^S = \Phi_n^{str} \wedge \Phi_n^{stf}$
5 | Assign weights to soft constraints in Φ_n^S:
6 | $w(y_{n,0}^u) = \Omega(u)$ for$(u, 1) \in S$, and $w(\neg y_{n,0}^u) = \Omega(u)$ for $(u, 0) \in S$
7 | Find assignment v using MaxSAT solver
8 **until** *Sum of weights of soft constraints* $\geq 1 - \kappa$
9 **return** φ_v

$\Omega(u) = 1/|S|$ for all traces in the sample, we have exactly $wl(S, \varphi, \Omega) = l(S, \varphi)$ which is used in Problem 1. In this section, we will solve the stronger version since, not only does it enable us to solve Problem 1 but also provides us with a versatile algorithm that we can exploit for learning decision trees over LTL formulas in Sect. 5.

For solving this problem, we devise an algorithm based on ideas from the learning algorithm of Neider and Gavran for inferring LTL formulas that perfectly classify a sample. Following their algorithm, we translate the problem of inferring LTL formulas into problems in Partial Weighted MaxSAT and then use an optimized MaxSAT solver to find a solution. More precisely, we construct a propositional formula Φ_n^S and assign weights to its clauses in such a way that an assignment v of Φ_n^S that satisfies all the hard constraints, satisfies two properties:

1. Φ_n^S contains sufficient information to extract an LTL formula φ_v of size n, and
2. the sum of weights of the soft constraints satisfied by it is equal to $1 - wl(S, \varphi_v, \Omega)$.

To obtain a complete algorithm, we increase the value of n (starting from 1) until we find an assignment v of Φ_n^S that satisfies the hard constraints and ensures that sum of weights of the soft constraints is greater than $1 - \kappa$. The termination of this algorithm is guaranteed by the existence of an LTL formula with zero loss on the sample (see Remark 1).

On a technical level, the formula Φ_n^S in Algorithm 1 is the conjunction $\Phi_n^S = \Phi_n^{str} \wedge \Phi_n^{stf}$, where Φ_n^{str} encodes the *structure* of the prospective LTL formula (of size n) and Φ_n^{stf} tracks the satisfaction of the prospective LTL formula with traces in S. We now explain each of the conjuncts in greater detail.

Structural Constraints. For designing the formula Φ_n^{str}, we rely on a canonical syntactic representation of LTL formulas, which we refer to as *syntax DAGs*.

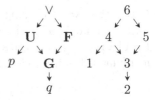

Fig. 1. Syntax DAG and identifiers of the formula $(p\mathbf{U}\mathbf{G}q) \vee \mathbf{F}\mathbf{G}q$

A syntax DAG is essentially a syntax tree (i.e., the unique tree that arises from the inductive definition of an LTL formula) in which common subformulas are shared. As a result, the number of the unique subformulas of an LTL formula coincides with the number of nodes, which we term as the size of its syntax DAG.

In a syntax DAG, to uniquely identify the nodes, we assign identifiers $1, \ldots, n$ in such a way that the root node is always indicated by n and every node has an identifier larger than that of its children, if it has any. An example of a syntax DAG is shown in Fig. 1.

To encode the structure of a syntax DAG using propositional logic, we introduce the following propositional variables: $x_{i,\lambda}$ for $i \in \{1, \cdots, n\}$ and $\lambda \in \Lambda$, which encode that Node i is labeled by operator λ (includes propositional variables); and $< ij$ and $r_{i,j'}$, for $i \in \{2, \cdots, n\}$ and $j, j' \in \{1, \cdots, i-1\}$, which encode that the left and right child of Node i is Node j and Node j', respectively. For instance, we must have variables $x_{6,\wedge}$, < 64, and $r_{6,5}$ to be true in order to obtain a syntax DAG where Node 6 is labeled with $\wedge$, has the left child to be Node 4, and the right child to be Node 5 (similar to the syntax DAG in Fig. 1).

We now introduce constraints on the variables to ensure that they encode a valid syntax DAG. First, we ensure that each node of the syntax DAG has a unique label using the following constraint:

$$\left[\bigwedge_{1 \le i \le n} \bigvee_{\lambda \in \Lambda} x_{i,\lambda} \right] \wedge \left[\bigwedge_{1 \le i \le n} \bigwedge_{\lambda \ne \lambda' \in \Lambda} \neg x_{i,\lambda} \vee \neg x_{i,\lambda'} \right] \tag{1}$$

Next, we need constraints to ensure that each node of a syntax DAG has a unique left and right child, which can be done similar to Formula 1. Moreover, we must ensure that Node 1 is labeled by a propositional variable; we refer the readers to an extended version of the paper [8] for the remaining structural constraints. The overall formula Φ_n^{str} is obtained by taking conjunction of all the structural constraints discussed above.

Observe that from a valuation v satisfying Φ_n^{str} one can extract an unique syntax DAG describing an LTL formula φ_v as follows: label Node p of the syntax DAG with the unique λ for which $v(x_{p,\lambda}) = 1$; assign Node n to be the root node; and assign edges from a node to its children based on the values of $l_{p,q}$ and $r_{p,q}$.

Semantic Constraints. Towards the definition of the formula Φ_n^{stf}, we define propositional formulas Φ_u^n for each trace u that tracks the valuation of the LTL formula encoded by Φ_n^{str} on u. These formulas are built using variables $y_{i,\tau}^u$, where $i \in \{1, \ldots, n\}$ and $\tau \in \{1, \ldots, |u|-1\}$, that corresponds to the value of $V(\varphi_i, u, \tau)$ (φ_i is the LTL formula rooted at Node i). Now, to make sure that these variables have the desired meaning, we impose constraints based on the semantics of the LTL operators. For instance, for the **X**-operator, we impose the following constraint:

$$\bigwedge_{1 < i \le n, \, 1 \le j < i} [x_{i,\mathbf{X}} \wedge < ij] \rightarrow \left[\bigwedge_{0 \le \tau \le |u|-1} \left[y_{i,\tau}^u \leftrightarrow y_{i,\tau+1}^u \right] \right], \tag{2}$$

This constraint states that if Node i is labeled with $\mathbf{X}$ and its left child is Node j, then the satisfaction of the formula rooted at Node i at time τ (i.e., $y_{i,\tau}^u$) equals the satisfaction of the subformula rooted at Node j at time $\tau + 1$ (i.e., $y_{j,\tau+1}^u$). The constraints for the remaining operators can again be found in the extended version [8]. Formula Φ_u^n is the conjunction of all such semantic constraints.

We now define Φ_n^{stf} to be:

$$\Phi_n^{stf} = \bigwedge_{(u,b)\in S} \Phi_u^n \wedge \bigwedge_{(u,1)\in S} y_{n,0}^u \wedge \bigwedge_{(u,0)\in S} \neg y_{n,0}^u \tag{3}$$

Weight Assignment. For assigning weights to the clauses of Φ_n^S, we first convert the formulas Φ_n^{str} and Φ_n^{stf} into CNF. Towards this, we simply exploit the Tseitin transformation [19] which converts a formula into an equivalent formula in CNF whose size is linear in the size of the original formula.

We now assign weights to constraints starting with the hard constraints as follows: $w(\Phi_n^{str}) = \infty, w(\Phi_u^n) = \infty$ for all $(u,b) \in S$. Here, $w(\Phi) = w$ is a shorthand to denote $w(C_i) = w$ for all clauses C_i in Φ. The constraint Φ_n^{str} is a hard one since, it ensures that we obtain a valid syntax DAG of an LTL formula. Φ_u^n ensures that the prospective LTL formula is evaluated on the trace u according to the semantics of LTL and thus, also needs to be a hard constraint.

The soft constraints are the ones that enforce correct classification and we assign them weights as follows: $w(y_{n,0}^u) = \Omega(u)$ for all $(u,1) \in S$, and $w(\neg y_{n,0}^u) = \Omega(u)$ for all $(u,0) \in S$. Recall that Ω refers to the function assigning weights to the traces.

To prove the correctness of our learning algorithm, we first ensure that the formula Φ_n^S along with the weight assigned to its clauses serves our purpose.

Lemma 1. *Let S be a sample, Ω the weight function, $n \in \mathbb{N} \setminus \{0\}$ and Φ_n^S the formula with the associated weights as defined above. Then,*

1. *the hard constraints of Φ_n^S are satisfiable; and*
2. *if v is an assignment that satisfies the hard constraints of Φ_n^S and maximizes the sum of weight of the satisfied soft constraints of Φ_n^S, then φ_v is an LTL formula of size n that achieves the minimum wl value among all LTL formulas of size n.*

The termination and the correctness of Algorithm 1, which is established using the following theorem, is a consequence of Lemma 1.

Theorem 1. *Given a sample S and threshold $\kappa \in [0,1]$, Algorithm 1 computes an LTL formula φ that has $wl(\varphi, S, \Omega) \leq \kappa$ and is the minimal one among all LTL formulas that have $wl(\varphi, S, \Omega) \leq \kappa$.*

5   Learning Decision Trees over LTL Formulas

In this section, we first introduce decision trees over LTL formulas and then discuss how to infer them from given data.

5.1   Decision Trees over LTL Formulas

A decision tree over LTL formulas is a tree-like structure where all nodes of the tree are labeled by LTL formulas. While the leaf nodes of a decision tree are labeled by either *true* or *false*, the inner nodes are labeled by (non-trivial) LTL formulas which represent decisions to predict the class of a trace. Each inner node leads to two subtrees connected by edges, where the left edge is represented with a solid edge and the right edge with a dashed one. Figure 2 depicts a decision tree over LTL formulas.

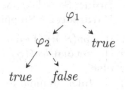

Fig. 2. A decision tree over LTL formulas

A decision tree t over LTL formula corresponds to an LTL formula $\varphi_t :=$ $\bigvee_{\rho \in \Pi} \bigwedge_{\varphi \in \rho} \varphi'$, where Π is the set of paths that originate in the root node and end in a leaf node labeled by *true* and $\varphi' = \varphi$ if it appears before a solid edge in $\rho \in \Pi$, otherwise $\varphi' = \neg\varphi$. For the decision tree in Fig. 2, the equivalent LTL formula is $(\varphi_1 \wedge \varphi_2) \vee \neg\varphi_1$.

For evaluating a decision tree t on a trace u, we use the valuation $V(\varphi_t, u)$ of the equivalent LTL formula φ on u. We can, in fact, extend the valuation function and loss function for LTL formulas to decision trees as $V(t, u) = V(\varphi_t, u)$ and $l(t, \varphi) = l(S, \varphi)$.

5.2   The Learning Algorithm

Our decision tree learning algorithm shares similarity with the class of decision tree learning algorithms known as Top-Down Induction of Decision Trees (TDIDT) [17]. Popular decision tree learning algorithms such as ID3, C4.5, CART are all part of the TDIDT algorithm family. In such algorithms, decision trees are constructed in a top-down fashion by finding suitable features (i.e., predicates over the attributes) of the data to partition it and then applying the same method inductively to the individual partitions.

Algorithm 2 outlines our approach to infer a decision tree over LTL formulas. In our algorithm, we first check the stopping criterion (Line 1) that is responsible for the termination of the algorithm. If the stopping criterion is met, we return a leaf node. We discuss the exact stopping criterion used in our algorithm in Sect. 5.4.

If the stopping criterion fails, we search for an appropriate LTL formula φ using Algorithm 1 for the current node of the decision tree. Our search for φ is based on a score function and we infer the minimal one that achieves a score greater than a user-defined minimum score μ on the sample. The choice of the score function and parameter μ is a crucial aspect of the algorithm, and we discuss more about this in Sect. 5.3.

Having inferred formula φ, next we split the sample into two sub-samples S_1 and S_2 with respect to φ as follows: $S_1 = \{(u, b) \mid V(\varphi, u) = 1\}$, and $S_2 = \{(u, b) \mid V(\varphi, u) = 0\}$. The final step is to recursively apply the decision tree learning on each of the resulting sub-samples (Line 6) to obtain trees t_1 and t_2. The decision tree returned is a tree with root node φ and subtrees t_1 and t_2.

Algorithm 2: Decision tree learning algorithm

Input: Sample S, Minimum score value μ, Threshold κ
Parameter : Stopping criterion *stop*, Score function s

1 **if** $stop(S, \kappa)$ **then**
2 | **return** $leaf(S)$
3 **else**
4 | Infer minimal formula φ with $s(S, \varphi) \geq \mu$ using Algorithm 1
5 | Split S into S_1, S_2 using φ
6 | Infer trees t_1, t_2 by recursively applying algorithm to S_1 and S_2
7 | **return** *decision tree with root node φ and subtrees t_1, t_2*

5.3 LTL Formulas for Decision Nodes

Ideally, we aim to infer LTL formulas at each decision node, that in addition to being small, also ensure that the resulting sub-samples after a split is as "homogenous" as possible. In simpler words, we want the sub-samples obtained after a split to predominantly consist of traces of one particular class. More homogenous splits result in early termination of the algorithm resulting in small decision trees. To achieve this, one can simply infer a minimal LTL formula that perfectly classifies the sample. While in principle, this solves our problem, in practice inferring an LTL formula that perfectly classifies a sample is a computationally expensive process [15]. Moreover, it results in a trivial decision tree consisting of a single decision node. Thus, to avoid that, we wish to infer concise LTL formulas that classify most traces correctly on the given sample.

To mechanize the search for concise LTL formulas for the splits, we measure the quality of an LTL formula using a *score* function. In our algorithm, we use this function to infer a minimal LTL formula having score greater than a user-defined threshold μ. The parameter μ regulates the tradeoff between the height of the tree and the size of the LTL formulas in the decision nodes of a tree. While all TDIDT algorithms involve certain metrics (e.g., gini impurity, entropy) to measure the efficacy of a feature to perform a split, these metrics are based on non-linear operations on the fraction of examples of each class in a sample. Searching LTL formulas, however, based on such metrics cannot be handled using a MaxSAT framework.

One possible choice of score $s_l(S, \varphi) = 1 - l(S, \varphi)$, which relies on the loss function. A formula φ with $s_l(S, \varphi) \geq \mu$ is a formula with $l(S, \varphi) \leq 1 - \mu$. Thus, for inferring LTL formulas with score greater than μ, we invoke Algorithm 1 to produce a minimal LTL formula φ with $l(S, \varphi) \leq 1 - \mu$. Note that, for this score, one must choose the μ to be smaller than $1 - \kappa$, else one will end up with a trivial decision tree with a single decision node.

While s_l as the metric seems to be an obvious choice, it often results in a problem which we refer to as *empty splits*. Precisely, the problem of empty splits occurs when one of the sub-samples, i.e., either S_1 or S_2 becomes empty. Empty splits lead to an unbounded recursion branch of the learning algorithm since, using the best LTL formula (w.r.t. s_l) does not produce any meaningful splits. This problem is more prominent in examples where the sample is skewed towards one class of examples. For instance, consider a sample $S = \{(u,1)\} \cup \{(v_1,0),(v_2,0),\cdots(v_{99},0)\}$; for this sample if one searches for an LTL formula with $\mu = 0.9$, *false* is a minimal formula; this formula, however, results in empty splits, since $S_1 = \emptyset$.

To address this problem, we use a score that relies on wl with a weight function Ω_r defined as follows:

$$\Omega_r(u) = \frac{0.5}{|\{(u,b)|b = 1\}|} \text{ for } (u,1) \in S, \Omega_r(u) = \frac{0.5}{|\{(u,b)|b = 0\}|} \text{ for } (u,0) \in S$$

Intuitively, the above Ω_r function normalizes the weight provided to traces, based on the number of examples in its class.

Our final choice of score, based on the above Ω_r function, is $s_r(S,\varphi) = max\{wl(S,\varphi,\Omega_r), 1 - wl(S,\varphi,\Omega_r)\}$. Using such a score, we also avoid having *asymmetric splits*. We say a split is asymmetric when the fraction of positive examples in S_1 is greater than or equal 0.5. Choosing the score to be $1 - wl(S,\varphi,\Omega_r)$ always leads to asymmetric splits, since φ in order to minimize $wl(S,\varphi,\Omega_r)$ several positive traces need to end up in S_1. Now, for finding an LTL formula based on s_r, we need to invoke Algorithm 1 twice with $\kappa = 1 - \mu$; once with the original sample and once with the same sample but with class labels inverted and then, choosing the one that provides a formula with a better split.

While any score function that avoids the problem of empty and asymmetric splits is sufficient for our learning algorithm, we have used s_r as a score function in our experiments. We show that if we infer an LTL formula φ such that $s_r(S,\varphi) > 0.5$, we never encounter empty splits using the following lemma.

Lemma 2. *Given a sample S and an LTL formula φ, if $s_r(S,\varphi) > 0.5$, there exists traces u_1, u_2 in S such that $V(u_1,\varphi) = 1$ and $V(u_2,\varphi) = 0$.*

5.4 Stopping Criterion

The stopping criterion is essential for the termination of the algorithm. Towards the definition of the stopping criterion, we define the following two quantities: $p_1(S) = |\{(u,b) \mid b = 1\}|/|S|$ and $p_2(S) = |\{(u,b) \mid b = 0\}|/|S|$. We now define the stopping criterion as follows: $stop(S) = true$ if $p_1(S) \leq \kappa$ or $p_2(S) \leq \kappa$, and *false* otherwise. Intuitively, the stopping criterion ensures that the algorithm terminates when the fraction of positive examples or fraction of negative examples in a resulting sample is less or equal to κ. When the stopping criterion holds, the algorithm halts and returns a leaf node labeled by *leaf(S)* where *leaf* is defined as $leaf(S) = false$ if $p_1(S) \leq \kappa$ and *true* if $p_2(S) \leq \kappa$.

The following theorem ensures the correctness and termination of Algorithm 2.

Theorem 2. *Given sample S and threshold $\kappa \in [0,1]$, Algorithm 2 terminates and returns a decision tree over LTL formula t such that $l(S,t) \leq \kappa$.*

Table 1. Summary of all the tested algorithms – comparison of numbers of timeouts, running times in seconds, inferred formula sizes

Algorithm	Benchmark without noise			Benchmark with 5% noise		
	Timeouts	Avg. time	Avg. size	Timeouts	Avg. time	Avg. size
SAT-flie	36/148	293.31	3.76	124/148	780.51	5.96
MaxSAT-flie($\kappa = 0.001$)	47/148	357.26	3.47	130/148	801.03	4.89
MaxSAT-flie($\kappa = 0.05$)	27/148	218.46	2.86	87/148	548.65	2.95
MaxSAT-flie($\kappa = 0.1$)	26/148	211.81	2.59	40/148	275.97	2.54
SAT-DT($\kappa = 0.05$)	51/148	342.35	5.92	127/148	786.16	9.62
MaxSAT-DT($\kappa = 0.05, \mu = 0.8$)	23/148	174.58	6.77	85/148	543.50	7.05
MaxSAT-DT($\kappa = 0.05, \mu = 0.6$)	7/148	74.97	30.91	38/148	281.60	56.55

6   Experimental Evaluation

In this section, we aim to evaluate the performance of our proposed algorithms and compare them to the SAT-based learning algorithms by Neider and Gavran [15]. We compare the following four algorithms: *SAT-flie*: the SAT-based learning algorithms introduced by Neider and Gavran (Algorithm 1 from [15]), *MaxSAT-flie*: our MaxSAT-based algorithm (Algorithm 1), *SAT-DT*: the decision tree based learning algorithm introduced by Neider and Gavran (Algorithm 2 from [15])[2] and *MaxSAT-DT*: our decision tree learning algorithm (Algorithm 2).

We implement all learning algorithms in a Python tool[3] using Microsoft Z3 [14]. All experiments were conducted on a Debian machine with Intel Xeon E7-8857 CPU at 3 GHz using upto 6 GB of RAM.

We generate samples based on common LTL patterns [7] such as: absence patterns like $\mathbf{G}(\neg p_0)$ and $\mathbf{F}(p_1) \rightarrow (\neg p_0 \mathbf{U} p_1)$, existence patterns like $\mathbf{F}(p_0)$ and $\mathbf{G}(\neg p_0) \vee \mathbf{F}(p_0 \wedge \mathbf{F}(p_1))$, universality patterns like $\mathbf{G}(p_0)$ and $\mathbf{G}(p_1 \rightarrow \mathbf{G}(p_0))$, and several others. In a first benchmark (without noise), we generate 148 samples with the generation method proposed by Neider and Gavran [15]. The size of the generated samples ranges between 12 and 1000, consisting of traces of length up to 15. Furthermore, we derive a second benchmark from the first one, by introducing 5% noise: for each sample of the benchmark, we invert the labels of up to 5% of the traces, randomly.

We evaluate the performance of all the algorithms on the two benchmarks previously defined. We set a timeout of 900s on each run. Table 1 presents the parameters of the algorithms, as well as their respective performances.

We first compare *MaxSAT-flie* (proposed in this paper) and *SAT-flie* (proposed in [15]). Figure 3 presents a comparison of the running time of these two algorithms, on each sample of the benchmark. With $\kappa = 0.001$, *MaxSAT-flie* performs worse than *SAT-flie*. This is largely due to the fact that SAT solvers

---

[2] We adapted *SAT-DT* to learn decision trees with a similar stopping criteria as ours.
[3] https://github.com/cryhot/samples2LTL.

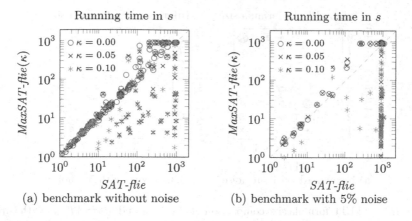

Fig. 3. Running time comparison of *SAT-flie* and *MaxSAT-flie*

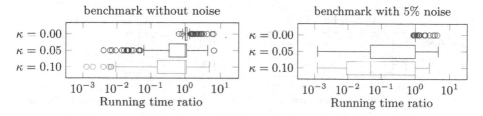

Fig. 4. Comparison of the ratio of the running time of *MaxSAT-flie*(κ) over the running time of *SAT-flie* for all samples in the benchmarks.

are specifically designed to handle this type of problem. For greater values of κ, *MaxSAT-flie* performs better than *SAT-flie*, especially on the benchmark with noise (Fig. 3b). To affirm this claim, we calculate the ratio of the running times of *MaxSAT-flie* and *SAT-flie* for each sample of the benchmarks (Fig. 4). For example, given a sample S, this ratio would be the running time of *MaxSAT-flie* on S divided by the running time of *SAT-flie* on S.

We evaluate the size of the inferred LTL formula by *MaxSAT-flie* and *SAT-flie* on each sample of the benchmark in Fig. 5. The size of the formula inferred by *MaxSAT-flie* will by design be less than or equal to the size of the formula inferred by *SAT-flie*. As the running time of both algorithms grows exponentially with the number of iterations, it is lower for *MaxSAT-flie* when the inferred formula size is strictly smaller than the size of the formula inferred by *SAT-flie*. However, when both inferred formulas have the same size, there is no running time gain, hence the median running time often being equal to 1 in Fig. 4.

We now compare the two algorithms proposed in this paper: did *MaxSAT-DT* perform any better than *MaxSAT-flie*? To be able to compare learned decision trees to learned LTL formulas, we measure the size of a tree t in terms of the size of the formula φ_t this tree encodes. Figure 6 presents a comparison of the running time ratio as well as the inferred formula size ratio of these two algorithms,

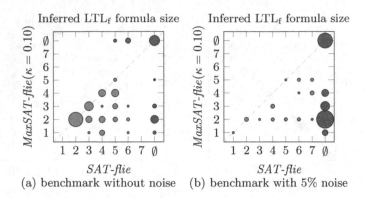

Fig. 5. Inferred LTL formula size comparison of *SAT-flie* and *MaxSAT-flie* with threshold $\kappa = 0.10$ on all samples. The surface of a bubble is proportional to the number of samples it represents. The timed out instances are represented by $\emptyset$.

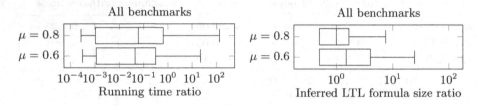

Fig. 6. On each sample of the benchmarks, comparison of the ratio of the performances of *MaxSAT-DT*(μ) over the performances of *MaxSAT-flie*, with $\kappa = 0.05$ for both algorithms, and where both algorithms did not time out.

on each sample of the benchmark that did not time out with both algorithms. We observe that the running time is generally lower for *MaxSAT-DT* than for *MaxSAT-flie*. However, *MaxSAT-DT* tends to infer larger formulas than formulas inferred by *MaxSAT-flie*. This trade-off between running time and inferred formula size is more pronounced for lower values of μ.

Regarding *SAT-DT* (proposed in [15]), we observe a large number of timeouts, especially when evaluated on the benchmark with 5% noise.

7   Conclusion

We developed two novel algorithms for inferring LTL_f formulas from a set of labeled traces allowing misclassifications. Moreover, we demonstrated that our algorithms are efficient in inferring formulas, especially from noisy data. As a part of future work, we like to apply our MaxSAT-based approach for inferring models in other formalisms that incorporate SAT-based learning (e.g. [18]).

Acknowledgements. This work has been supported by the Defense Advanced Research Projects Agency (DARPA) under Contract no. HR001120C0032, ARL W911NF2020132, ARL ACC-APG-RTP W911NF, NSF 1646522 and DFG Grant no. 434592664.

References

1. Arif, M.F., Larraz, D., Echeverria, M., Reynolds, A., Chowdhury, O., Tinelli, C.: SYSLITE: syntax-guided synthesis of PLTL formulas from finite traces. In: FMCAD, pp. 93–103. IEEE (2020)
2. Asarin, E., Donzé, A., Maler, O., Nickovic, D.: Parametric identification of temporal properties. In: Khurshid, S., Sen, K. (eds.) RV 2011. LNCS, vol. 7186, pp. 147–160. Springer, Heidelberg (2012). https://doi.org/10.1007/978-3-642-29860-8_12
3. Bacchus, F., Kabanza, F.: Using temporal logics to express search control knowledge for planning. Artif. Intell. **116**(1–2), 123–191 (2000)
4. Bombara, G., Vasile, C.I., Penedo, F., Yasuoka, H., Belta, C.: A decision tree approach to data classification using signal temporal logic. In: Proceedings of International Conference on Hybrid Systems: Computation and Control, pp. 1–10. ACM (2016)
5. Brunello, A., Sciavicco, G., Stan, I.E.: Interval temporal logic decision tree learning. In: Calimeri, F., Leone, N., Manna, M. (eds.) JELIA 2019. LNCS (LNAI), vol. 11468, pp. 778–793. Springer, Cham (2019). https://doi.org/10.1007/978-3-030-19570-0_50
6. Camacho, A., McIlraith, S.A.: Learning interpretable models expressed in linear temporal logic. In: ICAPS, pp. 621–630. AAAI Press (2019)
7. Dwyer, M.B., Avrunin, G.S., Corbett, J.C.: Property specification patterns for finite-state verification. In: Proceedings of the Second Workshop on Formal Methods in Software Practice, pp. 7–15. FMSP 1998. Association for Computing Machinery (1998)
8. Gaglione, J., Neider, D., Roy, R., Topcu, U., Xu, Z.: Learning linear temporal properties from noisy data: a maxsat approach. CoRR abs/2104.15083 (2021)
9. Giacomo, G.D., Vardi, M.Y.: Linear temporal logic and linear dynamic logic on finite traces. In: IJCAI, pp. 854–860. IJCAI/AAAI (2013)
10. Hoxha, B., Dokhanchi, A., Fainekos, G.: Mining parametric temporal logic properties in model-based design for cyber-physical systems. Int. J. Softw. Tools Technol. Transf. **20**(1), 79–93 (2017). https://doi.org/10.1007/s10009-017-0447-4
11. Jin, X., Donzé, A., Deshmukh, J.V., Seshia, S.A.: Mining requirements from closed-loop control models. IEEE Trans. Comput. Aided Des. Integr. Circuits Syst. **34**(11), 1704–1717 (2015)
12. Kim, J., Muise, C., Shah, A., Agarwal, S., Shah, J.: Bayesian inference of linear temporal logic specifications for contrastive explanations. In: IJCAI, pp. 5591–5598. ijcai.org (2019)
13. Kong, Z., Jones, A., Belta, C.: Temporal logics for learning and detection of anomalous behavior. IEEE Trans. Autom. Control **62**(3), 1210–1222 (2017)
14. de Moura, L., Bjørner, N.: Z3: an efficient SMT solver. In: Ramakrishnan, C.R., Rehof, J. (eds.) TACAS 2008. LNCS, vol. 4963, pp. 337–340. Springer, Heidelberg (2008). https://doi.org/10.1007/978-3-540-78800-3_24

15. Neider, D., Gavran, I.: Learning linear temporal properties. In: Bjørner, N., Gurfinkel, A. (eds.) 2018 Formal Methods in Computer Aided Design, FMCAD 2018, pp. 1–10. IEEE (2018)
16. Pnueli, A.: The temporal logic of programs. In: Proceedings of 18th Annual Symposium on Foundations of Computer Science, pp. 46–57 (1977)
17. Quinlan, J.R.: Induction of decision trees. Mach. Learn. **1**(1), 81–106 (1986). https://doi.org/10.1007/BF00116251
18. Roy, R., Fisman, D., Neider, D.: Learning interpretable models in the property specification language. In: IJCAI, pp. 2213–2219. ijcai.org (2020)
19. Tseitin, G.S.: On the complexity of derivation in propositional calculus. In: Siekmann, J.H., Wrightson, G. (eds.) Automation of Reasoning. Symbolic Computation (Artificial Intelligence), pp. 466–483. Springer, Heidelberg (1983). https://doi.org/10.1007/978-3-642-81955-1_28
20. Xu, Z., Birtwistle, M., Belta, C., Julius, A.: A temporal logic inference approach for model discrimination. IEEE Life Sci. Lett. **2**(3), 19–22 (2016)
21. Xu, Z., Julius, A.A.: Census signal temporal logic inference for multiagent group behavior analysis. IEEE Trans. Autom. Sci. Eng. **15**(1), 264–277 (2018)
22. Xu, Z., Nettekoven, A.J., Agung Julius, A., Topcu, U.: Graph temporal logic inference for classification and identification. In: 2019 IEEE 58th Conference on Decision and Control (CDC), pp. 4761–4768 (2019)
23. Xu, Z., Ornik, M., Julius, A.A., Topcu, U.: Information-guided temporal logic inference with prior knowledge. In: 2019 American Control Conference (ACC), pp. 1891–1897 (2019)
24. Xu, Z., Belta, C., Julius, A.: Temporal logic inference with prior information: an application to robot arm movements. In: IFAC Conference on Analysis and Design of Hybrid Systems (ADHS), pp. 141–146 (2015)
25. Xu, Z., Julius, A.A.: Robust temporal logic inference for provably correct fault detection and privacy preservation of switched systems. IEEE Syst. J. **13**(3), 3010–3021 (2019)

Mining Interpretable Spatio-Temporal Logic Properties for Spatially Distributed Systems

Sara Mohammadinejad[1]([⊠]) [iD], Jyotirmoy V. Deshmukh[1] [iD],
and Laura Nenzi[2,3] [iD]

[1] University of Southern California, Los Angeles, USA
{saramoha,jdeshmuk}@usc.edu
[2] University of Trieste, Trieste, Italy
lnenzi@units.it
[3] TU Wien, Vienna, Austria

Abstract. The Internet-of-Things, complex sensor networks, multi-agent cyber-physical systems are all examples of spatially distributed systems that continuously evolve in time. Such systems generate huge amounts of spatio-temporal data, and system designers are often interested in analyzing and discovering structure within the data. There has been considerable interest in learning causal and logical properties of temporal data using logics such as Signal Temporal Logic (STL); however, there is limited work on discovering such relations on *spatio-temporal* data. We propose the first set of algorithms for *unsupervised learning* for spatio-temporal data. Our method does automatic feature extraction from the spatio-temporal data by projecting it onto the parameter space of a *parametric spatio-temporal reach and escape logic* (PSTREL). We propose an agglomerative hierarchical clustering technique that guarantees that each cluster satisfies a distinct STREL formula. We show that our method generates STREL formulas of bounded description complexity using a novel decision-tree approach which generalizes previous unsupervised learning techniques for Signal Temporal Logic. We demonstrate the effectiveness of our approach on case studies from diverse domains such as urban transportation, epidemiology, green infrastructure, and air quality monitoring.

Keywords: Distributed systems · Unsupervised learning ·
Spatio-temporal data · Interpretability · Spatio-temporal reach and escape logic

1 Introduction

Due to rapid improvements in sensing and communication technologies, embedded systems are now often spatially distributed. Such spatially distributed

J. V. Deshmukh and L. Nenzi—Equal contribution.

© Springer Nature Switzerland AG 2021
Z. Hou and V. Ganesh (Eds.): ATVA 2021, LNCS 12971, pp. 91–107, 2021.
https://doi.org/10.1007/978-3-030-88885-5_7

systems (SDS) consist of heterogeneous components embedded in a specific topological space, whose time-varying behaviors evolve according to complex mutual
inter-dependence relations [16]. In the formal methods community, tremendous
advances have been achieved for verification and analysis of distributed systems.
However, most formal techniques abstract away the specific spatial aspects of
distributed systems, which can be of crucial importance in certain applications.
For example, consider the problem of developing a bike-sharing system (BSS)
in a "sharing economy." Here, the system consists of a number of bike stations
that would use sensors to detect the number of bikes present at a station, and
use incentives to let users return bikes to stations that are running low. The
bike stations themselves could be arbitrary locations in a city, and the design
of an effective BSS would require reasoning about the distance to nearby locations, and the time-varying demand or supply at each location. For instance, the
property "there is always a bike and a slot available at distance d from a bike
station" depends on the distance of the bike station to its nearby stations. Evaluating whether the BSS functions correctly is a verification problem where the
specification is a *spatio-temporal* logic formula. Similarly, consider the problem
of coordinating the movements of multiple mobile robots, or a HVAC controller
that activates heating or cooling in parts of a building based on occupancy.
Given spatio-temporal execution traces of nodes in such systems, we may be
interested in analyzing the data to solve several classical formal methods problems such as fault localization, debugging, invariant generation or specification
mining. It is increasingly urgent to formulate methods that enable reasoning
about spatially-distributed systems in a way that explicitly incorporates their
spatial topology.

In this paper, we focus on one specific aspect of spatio-temporal reasoning:
mining interpretable logical properties from data in an SDS. We model a SDS
as a directed or undirected graph where individual compute nodes are vertices,
and edges model either the connection topology or spatial proximity. In the past,
analytic models based on partial differential equations (e.g. diffusion equations)
[6] have been used to express the spatio-temporal evolution of these systems.
While such formalisms are incredibly powerful, they are also quite difficult to
interpret. Traditional machine learning (ML) approaches have also been used
to uncover the structure of such spatio-temporal systems, but these techniques
also suffer from the lack of interpretability. Our proposed method draws on
a recently proposed logic known as *Spatio-Temporal Reach and Escape Logic*
(STREL) [2]. Recent research on STREL has focused on efficient algorithms
for runtime verification and monitoring of STREL specifications [2,3]. However,
there is no existing work on mining STREL specifications.

Mined STREL specifications can be useful in many different contexts in the
design of spatially distributed systems; an incomplete list of usage scenarios
includes the following applications: (1) Mined STREL formulas can serve as
spatio-temporal invariants that are satisfied by the computing nodes, (2) STREL
formulas could be used by developers to characterize the properties of a deployed
spatially distributed system, which can then be used to monitor any subsequent

updates to the system, (3) Clustering nodes that satisfy similar STREL formulas can help debug possible bottlenecks and violations in communication protocols in such distributed systems.

There is considerable amount of recent work on learning temporal logic formulas from data [8,11,14,15]. In particular, the work in this paper is closest to the work on unsupervised clustering of time-series data using Signal Temporal Logic [11]. In this work, the authors assume that the user provides a Parametric Signal Temporal Logic (PSTL) formula, and the procedure projects given temporal data onto the parameter domain of the PSTL formula. The authors use off-the-shelf clustering techniques to group parameter values and identify STL formulas corresponding to each cluster. There are a few hurdles in applying such an approach to spatio-temporal data. First, in [11], the authors assume a monotonic fragment of PSTL: there is no such fragment identified in the literature for STREL. Second, in [11], the authors assume that clusters in the parameter space can be separated by axis-aligned hyper-boxes. Third, given spatio-temporal data, we can have different choices to impose the edge relation on nodes, which can affect the formula we learn.

To address the shortcomings of previous techniques, we introduce PSTREL, by treating threshold constants in signal predicates, time bounds in temporal operators, and distance bounds in spatial operators as parameters. We then identify a monotonic fragment of PSTREL, and propose a multi-dimensional binary-search based procedure to infer *tight* parameter valuations for the given PSTREL formula. We also explore the space of implied edge relations between spatial nodes, proposing an algorithm to define the most suitable graph. After defining a projection operator that maps a given spatio-temporal signal to parameter values of the given PSTREL formula, we use an agglomerative hierarchical clustering technique to cluster spatial locations into hyperboxes. We improve the method of [11] by introducing a decision-tree based approach to systematically split overlapping hyperbox clusters. The result of our method produces axis-aligned hyperbox clusters that can be compactly described by an STREL formula that has length proportional to the number of parameters in the given PSTREL formula (and independent of the number of clusters). Finally, we give human-interpretable meanings for each cluster. We show the usefulness of our approach considering four benchmarks: COVID-19 data from LA County, Outdoor air quality data, BSS data and movements of the customer in a Food Court.

Running Example: A Bike Sharing System (BSS). To ease the exposition of key ideas in the paper, we use an example of a BSS deployed in the city of Edinburgh, UK. The BSS consists of a number of bike stations, distributed over a geographic area. Each station has a fixed number of bike slots. Users can pick up a bike, use it for a while, and then return it to another station in the area. The data that we analyze are the number of bikes (B) and empty slots (S) at each time step in each bike station. With the advent of electric bikes, BSS have become an important aspect in urban mobility, and such systems make use of embedded devices for diverse purposes such as tracking bike usage, billing, and displaying information about availability to users over apps. Figure 1b shows the

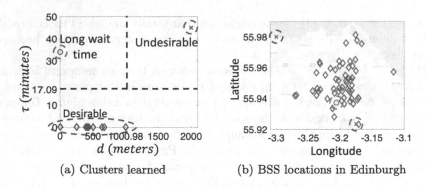

(a) Clusters learned   (b) BSS locations in Edinburgh

Fig. 1. Interpretable clusters automatically identified by our technique.

map of the Edinburgh city with the bike stations. Different colors of the nodes represent different learned clusters as can be seen in Fig. 1a. For example, using our approach, we learn that stations in *orange* cluster have a long wait time, and stations in *red* cluster are the most undesirable stations as they have long wait time and do not have nearby stations with bike availability. If we look at the actual location of *red* points in Fig. 1b, they are indeed far away stations.

2   Background

In this section, we introduce the notation and terminology for spatial models and spatio-temporal traces and we describe Spatio-Temporal Reach and Escape Logic (STREL).

Definition 1 (Spatial Model). *A spatial model S is defined as a pair $\langle L, W \rangle$, where L is a set of nodes or locations and $W \subseteq L \times \mathbb{R} \times L$ is a nonempty relation associating each distinct pair $\ell_1, \ell_2 \in L$ with a label $w \in \mathbb{R}$ (also denoted $\ell_1 \xrightarrow{w} \ell_2$).*

There are many different choices possible for the proximity relation W; for example, W could be defined in a way that the edge-weights indicate spatial proximity, communication network connectivity etc. Given a set of locations, unless there is a user-specified W, we note that there are several graphs (and associated edge-weights) that we can use to express spatial models. We explore these possibilities in Sect. 3. For the rest of this section, we assume that W is defined using the notion of (δ, d)-connectivity graph as defined in Definition 2.

Definition 2 ((δ, d)-connectivity spatial model). *Given a compact metric space M with the distance metric $d : M \times M \to \mathbb{R}^{\geq 0}$, a set of locations L that is a finite subset of M, and a fixed $\delta \in \mathbb{R}, \delta > 0$, a (δ, d)-connectivity spatial model is defined as $\langle L, W \rangle$, where $(\ell_1, w, \ell_2) \in W$ iff $d(\ell_1, \ell_2) = w$, and $w < \delta$.*

Example 1. In the BSS, each bike station is a node/location in the spatial model, where locations are assumed to lie on the metric space defined by the 3D spherical manifold of the earth's surface; each location is defined by its latitude and longitude, and the distance metric is the *Haversine distance*[1]. Figure 2b shows the δ-connectivity graph of the Edinburgh BSS, with $\delta = 1$ km.

Definition 3 (Route). *For a spatial model $S = \langle L, W \rangle$, a route τ is an infinite sequence $\ell_0 \ell_1 \cdots \ell_k \cdots$ such that for any $i \geq 0$, $\ell_i \xrightarrow{w_i} \ell_{i+1}$.*

For a route τ, $\tau[i]$ denotes the ith node ℓ_i in τ, $\tau[i..]$ indicates the suffix route $\ell_i \ell_{i+1}...$, and $\tau(\ell)$ denotes $\min i \mid \tau[i] = \ell$, i.e. the first occurrence of ℓ in τ. Note that $\tau(\ell) = \infty$ if $\forall i \tau[i] \neq \ell$. We use $\mathcal{T}(S)$ to denote the set of routes in S, and $\mathcal{T}(S, \ell)$ to denote the set of routes in S starting from $\ell \in L$. We can use routes to define the route distance between two locations in the spatial model as follows.

Definition 4 (Route Distance and Spatial Model Induced Distance). *Given a route τ, the route distance along τ up to a location ℓ denoted $d_S^\tau(\ell)$ is defined as $\sum_{i=0}^{\tau(\ell)} w_i$. The spatial model induced distance between locations ℓ_1 and ℓ_2 (denoted $d_S(\ell_1, \ell_2)$) is defined as: $d_S(\ell_1, \ell_2) = \min_{\tau \in \mathcal{T}(S, \ell_1)} d_S^\tau(\ell_2)$.*

Note that by the above definition, $d_S^\tau(\ell) = 0$ if $\tau[0] = \ell$ and ∞ if ℓ is not a part of the route (i.e. $\tau(\ell) = \infty$), and $d_S(\ell_1, \ell_2) = \infty$ if there is no route from ℓ_1 to ℓ_2.

Spatio-temporal Time-Series. A spatio-temporal trace associates each location in a spatial model with a time-series trace. Formally, a time-series trace x is a mapping from a time domain $\mathbb{T}$ to some bounded and non-empty set known as the value domain $\mathcal{V}$. Given a spatial model $S = \langle L, W \rangle$, a spatio-temporal trace σ is a function from $L \times \mathbb{T}$ to $\mathcal{V}$. We denote the time-series trace at location ℓ by $\sigma(\ell)$.

Example 2. Consider a spatio-temporal trace σ of the BSS defined such that for each location ℓ and at any given time t, $\sigma(\ell, t)$ is $(B(t), S(t))$, where $B(t)$ and $S(t)$ are respectively the number of bikes and empty slots at time t.

2.1 Spatio-temporal Reach and Escape Logic (STREL)

Syntax. STREL is a logic that was introduced in [2] as a formalism for monitoring spatially distributed cyber-physical systems. STREL extends Signal Temporal Logic [12] with two spatial operators, *reach* and *escape*, from which is possible to derive other three spatial modalities: *everywhere, somewhere* and *surround*. The syntax of STREL is given by:

$$\varphi ::= true \mid \mu \mid \neg\varphi \mid \varphi_1 \wedge \varphi_2 \mid \varphi_1 \, U_I \, \varphi_2 \mid \varphi_1 \, \mathcal{R}_D \, \varphi_2 \mid \mathcal{E}_D \, \varphi.$$

---

[1] Haversine Formula gives minimum distance between any two points on sphere by using their latitudes and longitudes.

Here, μ is an atomic predicate (AP) over the value domain $\mathcal{V}$. Negation $\neg$ and conjunction $\wedge$ are the standard Boolean connectives, while U_I is the temporal operator *until* with I being a non-singular interval over the time-domain $\mathbb{T}$. The operators $\mathcal{R}_D$ and $\mathcal{E}_D$ are spatial operators where D denotes an interval over the distances induced by the underlying spatial model, i.e., an interval over $\mathbb{R}^{\geq 0}$.

Semantics. A STREL formula is evaluated piecewise over each location and each time appearing in a given spatio-temporal trace. We use the notation $(\sigma, \ell) \vDash \varphi$ if the formula φ holds true at location ℓ for the given spatio-temporal trace σ. The interpretation of atomic predicates, Boolean operations and temporal operators follows standard semantics for Signal Temporal Logic: E.g., for a given location ℓ and a given time t, the formula $\varphi_1 U_I \varphi_2$ holds at ℓ iff there is some time t' in $t \oplus I$ where φ_2 holds, and for all times t'' in $[t, t')$, φ_1 holds. Here the $\oplus$ operator defines the interval obtained by adding t to both interval end-points. We use standard abbreviations $\mathbf{F}_I \varphi = true U_I \varphi$ and $\mathbf{G}_I \varphi = \neg \mathbf{F}_I \varphi$, for the *eventually* and *globally* operators. The reachability ($\mathcal{R}_D$) and escape ($\mathcal{E}_D$)operators are spatial operators. The formula $\varphi_1 \mathcal{R}_D \varphi_2$ holds at a location ℓ if there is a route τ starting at ℓ that reaches a location ℓ' that satisfies φ_2, with a route distance $d_S^\tau(\ell')$ that lies in the interval D, and for all preceding locations, including ℓ, φ_1 holds true. The escape formula $\mathcal{E}_D \varphi$ holds at a location ℓ if there exists a location ℓ' at a route distance $d_S(\ell_1, \ell_2)$ that lies in the interval D and a route starting at ℓ and reaching ℓ' consisting of locations that satisfy φ. We define two other operators for notational convenience: The *somewhere* operator, denoted $\diamondsuit_{[0,d]} \varphi$, is defined as $true \mathcal{R}_{[0,d]} \varphi$, and the *everywhere* operator, denoted $\boxdot_{[0,d]} \varphi$ is defined as $\neg \diamondsuit_{[0,d]} \neg \varphi$, where d is a real positive value; their meaning is described in the next example.

Example 3. In the BSS, we use atomic predicates $S > 0$ and $B > 10$, and the formula $\mathbf{G}_{[0,3hours]} \diamondsuit_{[0,1km]} (B > 10)$ is true if always within the next 3 h, at a location ℓ, there is some location ℓ' at most 1 km from ℓ where, the number of bikes available exceed 10. Similarly, the formula $\boxdot_{[0,1km]} \mathbf{G}_{[0,30min]}(S > 0)$ is true at a location ℓ if for all locations within 1 km, for the next 30 mins, there is no empty slot.

3   Constructing a Spatial Model

In this section, we present four approaches to construct a spatial model, and discuss the pros and cons of each approach.

1. (∞, d)-**connectivity spatial model**: This spatial model corresponds to the (δ, d)-connectivity spatial model as presented in Definition 2, where we set $\delta = \infty$. We note that this gives us a fully connected graph, i.e. where $|W|$ is $O(|L|^2)$. We remark that our learning algorithm uses monitoring STREL formulas as a sub-routine, and from Lemma 2 in Appendix[2], we can see that

---

[2] **Algorithms and Appendix of the paper are provided in the** arXiv **version due to lack of space.**

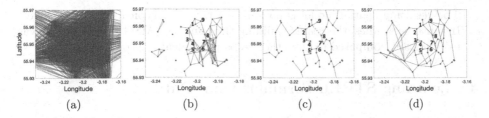

Fig. 2. Different approaches for constructing the spatial model for the BSS. (a) shows an $(\infty, d_{\mathrm{hvrsn}})$-connectivity spatial model where d_{hvrsn} is the Haversine distance between locations. (b) shows a $(\delta, d_{\mathrm{hvrsn}})$-connectivity spatial model where $\delta = 1\,\mathrm{km}$. Observe that the spatial model is disconnected. (c) shows an MST-spatial model. (d) shows an $(\alpha, d_{\mathrm{hvrsn}})$ enhanced MSG spatial model with $\alpha = 2$. Observe that this spatial model is sparse compared even to the $(\delta, d_{\mathrm{hvrsn}})$-connectivity spatial model.

as the complexity of monitoring a STREL formula is linear in $|W|$, a fully connected graph is undesirable.

2. (δ, d)-**connectivity spatial model**: This is the model presented in Definition 2, where δ is heuristically chosen in an application-dependent fashion. Typically, the δ we choose is much smaller compared to the distance between the furthest nodes in the given topological space. This gives us W that is sparse, and thus with a lower monitoring cost; however, a small δ can lead to a disconnected spatial model which can affect the accuracy of the learned STREL formulas. Furthermore, this approach may overestimate the spatial model induced distance between two nodes (as in Definition 4) that are not connected by a direct edge. For instance, in Fig. 2b, nodes 1 and 8 are connected through the route $1 \to 9 \to 8$, and sum of the edge-weights along this route is larger than the actual (metric) distance of 1 and 8.

3. **MST-spatial model**: To minimize the number of edges in the graph while keeping the connectivity of the graph, we can use Minimum Spanning Tree (MST) as illustrated in Fig. 2c. This gives us $|W|$ that is $O(|L|)$, which makes monitoring much faster, while resolving the issue of disconnected nodes in the (δ, d)-spatial model. However, an MST can also lead to an overestimate of the spatial model induced distance between some nodes in the graph. For example, in Fig. 2c, the direct distance between nodes 1 and 8 is much smaller than their route distance (through the route $1 \to 2 \to 3 \to 4 \to 5 \to 6 \to 7 \to 8$).

4. (α, d)-**Enhanced MSG Spatial Model**: To address the shortcomings of previous approaches, we propose constructing a spatial model that we call the (α, d)-*Enhanced Minimum Spanning Graph* Spatial model. First, we construct an MST over the given set of locations and use it to define W and pick α as some number greater than 1. Then, for each distinct pair of locations ℓ_1, ℓ_2, we compute the shortest route distance $d_{\mathcal{S}}(\ell_1, \ell_2)$ between them in the constructed MST, and compare it to their distance $d(\ell_1, \ell_2)$ in the metric space. If $d_{\mathcal{S}}(\ell_1, \ell_2) > \alpha \cdot d(\ell_1, \ell_2)$, then we add an edge $(\ell_1, d(\ell_1, \ell_2), \ell_2)$ to W.

The resulting spatial model is no longer a tree, but typically is still sparse[3]. In our case studies, the cost of building the enhanced MSG spatial model was insignificant compared to the other steps in the learning procedure[4].

4   Learning STREL Formulas from Data

In this section, we first introduce Parametric Spatio-Temporal Reach and Escape Logic (PSTREL) and the notion of monotonicity for PSTREL formulas. Then, we introduce a projection function π that maps a spatio-temporal trace to a valuation in the parameter space of a given PSTREL formula. We then cluster the trace-projections using Agglomerative Hierarchical Clustering, and finally learn a compact STREL formula for each cluster using Decision Tree techniques.

Parametric STREL (PSTREL). Parametric STREL (PSTREL) is a logic obtained by replacing one or more numeric constants appearing in STREL formulas by parameters; parameters appearing in atomic predicates are called *magnitude* parameters $\mathcal{P}_\mathcal{V}$, and those appearing in temporal and spatial operators are called *timing* $\mathcal{P}_\mathbb{T}$ and *spatial* parameters $\mathcal{P}_{d_S}$ respectively. Each parameter in $\mathcal{P}_\mathcal{V}$ take values from $\mathcal{V}$, those in $\mathcal{P}_\mathbb{T}$ take values from $\mathbb{T}$, and those in $\mathcal{P}_{d_S}$ take values from $\mathbb{R}^{\geq 0}$ (i.e. the set of values that the d_S metric can take for a given spatial model). We define a valuation function ν that maps all parameters in a PSTREL formula to their respective values.

Example 4. Consider the PSTREL versions of the STREL formulas introduced in Example 3 $\varphi(\mathbf{p}_\tau, \mathbf{p}_d, \mathbf{p}_c) = \mathbf{G}_{[0,\mathbf{p}_\tau]} \circledast_{[0,\mathbf{p}_d]} (B > \mathbf{p}_c)$. The valuation ν: $\mathbf{p}_\tau \mapsto 3\,\mathrm{h}$, $\mathbf{p}_d \mapsto 1\mathrm{km}$, and $\mathbf{p}_c \mapsto 10$ returns the STREL formula introduced in Example 3.

Definition 5 (Parameter Polarity, Monotonic PSTREL). *A polarity function γ maps a parameter to an element of $\{+, -\}$, and is defined as follows:*

$$\gamma(\mathbf{p}) = + \overset{\text{def}}{=} \nu'(\mathbf{p}) > \nu(\mathbf{p}) \wedge (\sigma, \ell) \vDash \varphi(\nu(\mathbf{p})) \Rightarrow (\sigma, \ell) \vDash \varphi(\nu'(\mathbf{p}))$$

$$\gamma(\mathbf{p}) = - \overset{\text{def}}{=} \nu'(\mathbf{p}) < \nu(\mathbf{p}) \wedge (\sigma, \ell) \vDash \varphi(\nu(\mathbf{p})) \Rightarrow (\sigma, \ell) \vDash \varphi(\nu'(\mathbf{p}))$$

The monotonic fragment of PSTREL consists of PSTREL formulas where all parameters have either positive or negative polarity.

---

[3] The complete algorithm, Algorithm 1 is provided in the arXiv version. Algorithm 1 is a simple way of constructing an (α, d)-enhanced MSG spatial model, and incurs a one-time cost of $O(|L|^2 \cdot (|L| + |W| \cdot \log(|L|)))$. We believe that the time complexity can be further improved using a suitable dynamic programming based approach.

[4] The runtimes of our learning approach for different kinds of spatial models on various case studies is illustrated in Table 1 in the arXiv version.

In simple terms, the polarity of a parameter $\mathbf{p}$ is positive if it is easier to satisfy φ as we increase the value of $\mathbf{p}$ and is negative if it is easier to satisfy φ as we decrease the value of $\mathbf{p}$. The notion of polarity for PSTL formulas was introduced in [1], and we extend this to PSTREL and spatial operators. The polarity for PSTREL formulas $\varphi(d_1, d_2)$ of the form $\diamondsuit_{[d_1,d_2]}\psi$, $\psi_1 \mathcal{R}_{[d_1,d_2]}\psi_2$, and $\mathcal{E}_{[d_1,d_2]}\psi$ are $\gamma(d_1) = -$ and $\gamma(d_2) = +$, i.e. if a spatio-temporal trace satisfies $\varphi(\nu(d_1), \nu(d_2))$, then it also satisfies any STREL formula over a strictly larger spatial model induced distance interval, i.e. by decreasing $\nu(d_1)$ and increasing $\nu(d_2)$. For a formula $\boxdot_{[d_1,d_2]}\psi$, $\gamma(d_1) = +$ and $\gamma(d_2) = -$, i.e. the formula obtained by strictly shrinking the distance interval. The proofs are simple, and provided in Appendix for completeness.

Definition 6 (Validity Domain, Boundary). *Let* $P = \mathcal{V}^{|\mathcal{P}_V|} \times \mathbb{T}^{|\mathcal{P}_T|} \times (\mathbb{R}^{\geq 0})^{|\mathcal{P}_{d_S}|}$ *denote the space of parameter valuations, then the validity domain* V *of a PSTREL formula at a location* ℓ *with respect to a set of spatio-temporal traces* Σ *is defined as follows:* $V(\varphi(\mathbf{p}), \ell, \Sigma) = \{\nu(\mathbf{p}) \mid \mathbf{p} \in P, \sigma \in \Sigma, (\sigma, \ell) \vDash \varphi(\nu(\mathbf{p}))\}$ *The validity domain boundary* $\partial V(\varphi(\varphi), \ell, \Sigma)$ *is defined as the intersection of* $V(\varphi, \ell, \Sigma)$ *with the closure of its complement.*

Spatio-temporal Trace Projection. We now explain how a monotonic PSTREL formula $\varphi(\mathbf{p})$ can be used to automatically extract features from a spatio-temporal trace. The main idea is to define a total order $>_{\mathcal{P}}$ on the parameters $\mathbf{p}$ (i.e. parameter priorities) that allows us to define a lexicographic projection of the spatio-temporal trace σ at each location ℓ to a parameter valuation $\nu(\mathbf{p})$ (this is similar to assumptions made in [8,11]). We briefly remark how we can relax this assumption later. Let ν_j denote the valuation of the jth parameter.

Definition 7 (Parameter Space Ordering, Projection). *A total order on parameter indices* $j_1 > \ldots > j_n$ *imposes a total order* $\prec_{\text{lex}}$ *on the parameter space defined as:*

$$\nu(\mathbf{p}) \prec_{\text{lex}} \nu'(\mathbf{p}) \Leftrightarrow \exists j_k \ s.t. \begin{cases} \gamma(\mathbf{p}_{j_k}) = + \Rightarrow \nu_{j_k} < \nu'_{j_k} \\ \gamma(\mathbf{p}_{j_k}) = - \Rightarrow \nu_{j_k} > \nu'_{j_k} \end{cases} \ and \ \forall m <_{\mathcal{P}} k, \nu_m = \nu'_m.$$

Given above total order, $\pi_{\text{lex}}(\sigma, \ell) = \inf_{\prec_{\text{lex}}} \{\nu(\mathbf{p}) \in \partial V(\varphi(\mathbf{p}), \{\sigma\}\}.$

In simple terms, given a total order on the parameters, the lexicographic projection maps a spatio-temporal trace to valuations that are least permissive w.r.t. the parameter with the greatest priority, then among those valuations, to those that are least permissive w.r.t. the parameter with the next greater priority, and so on. Finding a lexicographic projection can be done by sequentially performing binary search on each parameter dimension [11][5]. It is easy to show that π_{lex} returns a valuation on the validity domain boundary.

---

[5] Algorithm 2 is provided in the arXiv version.

Remark 1. The order of parameters is assumed to be provided by the user and is important as it affects the unsupervised learning algorithms for clustering that we apply next. Intuitively, the order corresponds to what the user deems as more important. For example, consider the formula $\mathbf{G}_{[0,3\text{hours}]} \diamondsuit_{[0,d]} (B > c)$. Note that $\gamma(d) = +$, and $\gamma(c) = -$. Now if the user is more interested in the radius around each station where the number of bikes exceeds some threshold (possibly 0) within 3 h, then the order is $d >_P c$. If she is more interested in knowing what is the largest number of bikes available in any radius (possibly ∞) always within 3 h, then $c >_P d$.

Remark 2. Similar to [18], we can compute an approximation of the validity domain boundary for a given trace, and then apply a clustering algorithm on the validity domain boundaries. This does not require the user to specify parameter priorities. In all our case studies, the parameter priorities were clear from the domain knowledge, and hence we will investigate this extension in the future.

Clustering. The projection operator $\pi_{\text{lex}}(\sigma, \ell)$ maps each location to a valuation in the parameter space. These valuation points serve as features for off-the-shelf clustering algorithms. In our experiments, we use the *Agglomerative Hierarchical Clustering* (AHC) technique [5] to automatically cluster similar valuations. AHC is a bottom-up approach that starts by assigning each point to a single cluster, and then merging clusters in a hierarchical manner based on a similarity criteria[6]. An important hyperparameter for any clustering algorithm is the number of clusters to choose. In some case studies, we use domain knowledge to decide the number of clusters. Where such knowledge is not available, we use the *Silhouette metric* to compute the optimal number of clusters. Silhouette is a ML method to interpret and validate consistency within clusters by measuring how well each point has been clustered. The silhouette metric ranges from -1 to $+1$, where a high silhouette value indicates that the object is well matched to its own cluster and poorly matched to neighboring clusters [17].

Example 5. Figure 1a shows the results of projecting the spatio-temporal traces from BSS through the PSTREL formula $\varphi(\tau, d)$ shown in Eq. (1).

$$\varphi(\tau, d) = \mathbf{G}_{[0,3]}(\varphi_{\text{wait}}(\tau) \vee \varphi_{\text{walk}}(d)) \tag{1}$$

In the above formula, $\varphi_{\text{wait}}(\tau)$ is defined as $\mathbf{F}_{[0,\tau]}(B \geq 1) \wedge (\mathbf{F}_{[0,\tau]}S \geq 1)$, and $\varphi_{\text{walk}}(d)$ is $\diamondsuit_{[0,d]}(B \geq 1) \wedge \diamondsuit(S \geq 1)$. $\varphi(\tau, d)$ means that for the next 3 h, either $\varphi_{\text{wait}}(\tau)$ or $\varphi_{\text{walk}}(d)$ is true. Locations with large values of τ have long wait times or with large d values are typically far from a location with bike/slot availability (and are thus undesirable). Locations with small τ, d are desirable. Each point in Fig. 1a shows $\pi_{\text{lex}}(\sigma, \ell)$ applied to each location and the result of applying AHC with 3 clusters.

---

[6] We used complete-linkage criteria which assumes the distance between clusters equals the distance between those two elements (one in each cluster) that are farthest away from each other.

Let $numC$ be the number of clusters obtained after applying AHC to the parameter valuations. Let C denote the labeling function mapping $\pi_{\text{lex}}(\sigma, \ell)$ to $\{1, \ldots, numC\}$. The next step after clustering is to represent each cluster in terms of an easily interpretable STREL formula. Next, we propose a decision tree-based approach to learn an interpretable STREL formula from each cluster.

Learning STREL Formulas from Clusters. The main goal of this subsection is to obtain a compact STREL formula to describe each cluster identified by AHC. We argue that bounded length formulas tend to be human-interpretable, and show how we can automatically obtain such formulas using a decision-tree approach. Decision-trees (DTs) are a non-parametric supervised learning method used for classification and regression[13]. Given a finite set of points $X \subseteq \mathbb{R}^m$ and a labeling function $\mathcal{L}$ that maps each point $x \in X$ to some label $\mathcal{L}(x)$, the DT learning algorithm creates a tree whose non-leaf nodes n_j are annotated with constraints ϕ_j, and each leaf node is associated with some label in the range of $\mathcal{L}$. Each path $n_1, \ldots, n_i, n_{i+1}$ from the root node to a leaf node corresponds to a conjunction $\bigwedge_{j=1}^{i} h_j$, where $h_j = \neg\phi_j$ if h_{j+1} is the left child of h_j and ϕ_j otherwise. Each label thus corresponds to the disjunction over the conjunctions corresponding to each path from the root node to the leaf node with that label.

Recall that after applying the AHC procedure, we get one valuation $\pi_{\text{lex}}(\sigma, \ell)$ for each location, and its associated cluster label. We apply a DT learning algorithm to each point $\pi_{\text{lex}}(\sigma, \ell)$, and each DT node is associated with a ϕ_j of the form $p_j \geq v_j$ for some $p_j \in \mathbf{p}$.

Lemma 1. *Any path in the DT corresponds to a STREL formula of length that is* $O((|\mathcal{P}| + 1) \cdot |\varphi|)$.

Proof. Any path in the DT is a conjunction over a number of formulas of the kind $p_j \geq v_j$ or its negation. Because $\varphi(\mathbf{p})$ is monotonic in each of its parameters, if we are given a conjunction of two conjuncts of the type $p_j \geq v_j$ and $p_j \geq v_j'$, then depending on $\gamma(p_j)$, one inequality implies the other, and we can discard the weaker inequality. Repeating this procedure, for each parameter, we will be left with at most 2 inequalities (one specifying a lower limit and the other an upper limit on p_j). Thus, each path in the DT corresponds to an axis-aligned hyperbox in the parameter space. Due to monotonicity, an axis-aligned hyperbox in the parameter space can be represented by a formula that is a conjunction of $|\mathcal{P}| + 1$ STREL formulas (negations of formulas corresponding to the $|\mathcal{P}|$ vertices connected to the vertex with the most permissive STREL formula, and the most permissive formula itself) [11] (see Fig. 3a for an example in a 2D parameter space). Thus, each path in the DT can be described by a formula of length $O((|\mathcal{P}| + 1) \cdot |\varphi|)$, where $|\varphi|$ is the length of φ.

Example 6. The result of applying the DT algorithm to the clusters identified by AHC (shown in dotted lines in Fig. 1a) is shown as the axis-aligned hyperboxes. Using the meaning of $\varphi(\tau, d)$ as defined in Eq. (1), we learn the formula $\neg\varphi(17.09, 2100) \wedge \neg\varphi(50, 1000.98) \wedge \varphi(50, 2100)$ for the red cluster. The last of these conjuncts is essentially the formula *true*, as this formula corresponds to

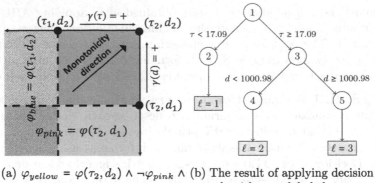

(a) $\varphi_{yellow} = \varphi(\tau_2, d_2) \wedge \neg\varphi_{pink} \wedge$ (b) The result of applying decision
$\neg\varphi_{blue}$.   tree algorithm on labeled parame-
ter valuations shown in Fig. 1a

Fig. 3. Illustration of clustering on the BSS locations

the most permissive formula over the given parameter space. Thus, the formula
we learn is:

$$\varphi_{red} = \neg\mathbf{G}_{[0,3]}(\varphi_{\text{wait}}(17.09) \vee \varphi_{\text{walk}}(2100)) \wedge \neg\mathbf{G}_{[0,3]}(\varphi_{\text{wait}}(50) \vee \varphi_{\text{walk}}(1000.98))$$

The first of these conjuncts is associated with a short wait time and the second is
associated with short walking distance. As both are not satisfied, these locations
are the least desirable.

Pruning the Decision Tree. If the decision tree algorithm produces several
disjuncts for a given label (e.g., see Fig. 4a), then it can significantly increase the
length and complexity of the formula that we learn for a label. This typically
happens when the clusters produced by AHC are not clearly separable using
axis-aligned hyperplanes. We can mitigate this by pruning the decision tree to a
maximum depth, and in the process losing the bijective mapping between cluster
labels and small STREL formulas. We can still recover an STREL formula that
is satisfied by most points in a cluster using a k-fold cross validation approach
(The formal procedure is presented in Algorithm 3 in the arXiv version.) The
idea is to loop over the maximum depth permitted from 1 to N, where N is user
provided, and for each depth performing k-fold cross validation to characterize
the accuracy of classification at that depth. If the accuracy is greater than a
threshold (90% in our experiments), we stop and return the depth as a limit
for the decision tree. Figure 4b illustrates the hyper-boxes obtained using this
approach. For this example, we could decrease the number of hyper-boxes from
11 to 3 by miss-classifying only a few data points (less than 10% of the data).

5   Case Studies

We now present the results of applying the clustering techniques developed on
three benchmarks: (1) COVID-19 data from Los Angeles County, USA, [9] (2)

Outdoor Air Quality data from California, and (3) BSS data from the city of Edinburgh [10] (running example)[7]. A summary of the computational aspects of the results is provided in Table 1. The numbers indicate that our methods scale to spatial models containing hundreds of locations, and still learn interpretable STREL formulas for clusters.

Table 1. Summary of results.

Case	$|L|$	$|W|$	Run-time (secs)	$numC$	$|\varphi_{cluster}|$
COVID-19	235	427	813.65	3	$3 \cdot |\varphi| + 4$
BSS	61	91	681.78	3	$2 \cdot |\varphi| + 4$
Air Quality	107	60	136.02	8	$5 \cdot |\varphi| + 7$
Food Court*	20	35	78.24	8	$3 \cdot |\varphi| + 4$

COVID-19 Data from LA County. Understanding the spread pattern of COVID-19 in different areas is vital to stop the spread of the disease. While this example is not related to a software system, it is nevertheless a useful example to show the versatility of our approach to spatio-temporal data. The PSTREL formula $\varphi(c, d) = \diamondsuit_{[0,d]}\{\mathbf{F}_{[0,\tau]}(x > c)$ allows us to number of cases exceeding a threshold c within $\tau = 10$ days in a neighborhood of size d for a given location[8]. Locations with small value of d and large value of c are unsafe as there is a large number of new positive cases within a small radius around them.

We illustrate the clustering results in Fig. 4. Each location in Fig. 4a is associated with a geographic region in LA county (shown in Fig. 4c), and the *red* cluster corresponds to hot spots (small d and large c). Applying the DT classifier on the learned clusters (shown in Fig. 4a) produces 11 hyperboxes, some of which contain only a few points. Hence we apply our DT pruning procedure to obtain the largest cluster that gives us at least 90% accuracy. Figure 4b shows the results after pruning the Decision Tree. We learn the following formula:

$$\varphi_{red} = \diamondsuit_{[0,4691.29]}(\mathbf{F}_{[0,10]}(x > 3180)) \vee \diamondsuit_{[0,15000]}(\mathbf{F}_{[0,10]}(x > 5611.5)),$$

---

[7] We provide results on a fourth benchmark consisting of a synthetic dataset for tracking movements of people in a food court building and detailed descriptions for each benchmark in the Appenidx. All experiments were performed on an Intel Core-i7 Macbook Pro with 2.7 GHz processor and 16 GB RAM. We use an existing monitoring tool MoonLight [3] in Matlab for computing the robustness of STREL formulas. For Agglomerative Hierarchical Clustering and Decision Tree techniques we use scikit-learn library in Python and the Statistics and Machine Learning Toolbox in Matlab.

[8] We fix τ to 10 days and focus on learning the values of c and d for each location.

This formula means that within 4691.29 m from any *red* location, within 10 days, the number of new positive cases exceeds 3180. The COVID-19 data that we used is for September 2020[9].

Outdoor Air Quality Data from California. We next consider Air Quality data from California gathered by the US Environmental Protection Agency (EPA). Among reported pollutants we focus on $PM2.5$ contaminant, and try to learn the patterns in the amount of $PM2.5$ in the air using STREL formulas. Consider a mobile sensing network consisting of UAVs to monitor pollution, such a STREL formula could be used to characterize locations that need increased monitoring.

We use the PSTREL formula $\varphi(c,d) = \mathbf{G}_{[0,10]}(\mathcal{E}_{[d,16000]}(PM2.5 < c))$ and project each location in California to the parameter space of c, d. A location ℓ satisfies this property if it is always true within the next 10 days, that there exists a location ℓ' at a distance more than d, and a route τ starting from ℓ and reaching ℓ' such that all the locations in the route satisfy the property $PM2.5 < c$. Hence, it might be possible to escape to a location at a distance greater than d always satisfying property $PM2.5 < c$. The results are shown in Fig. 5a. Cluster 8 is the best cluster as it has a small value of c and large value of d which means that there exists a long route from the locations in cluster 8 with low density of $PM2.5$. Cluster 3 is the worst as it has a large value of c and a small value of d. The formula for cluster 3 is $\varphi_3 = \varphi(500,0) \wedge \neg\varphi(500,2500) \wedge \neg\varphi(216,0)$. φ_3 holds in locations where, in the next 10 days, $PM2.5$ is always less than 500, but at least in 1 day $PM2.5$ reaches 216 and there is no safe route (i.e. locations along the route have $PM2.5 < 500$) of length at least 2500.

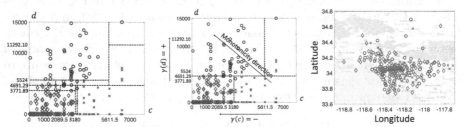

(a) The learned hyper-boxes before pruning DT.   (b) The learned hyper-boxes after pruning the DT.   (c) Red-color points: hot spots.

Fig. 4. Procedure to learn STREL formulas from COVID-19 data

---

[9] In Fig. 6 in the appendix of the arXiv version, we show the results of STREL clustering for 3 different months in 2020, which confirms the rapid spread of the COVID-19 virus in LA county from April 2020 to September 2020. Furthermore, we can clearly see spread of the virus around the hot spots during the time, a further validation of our approach.

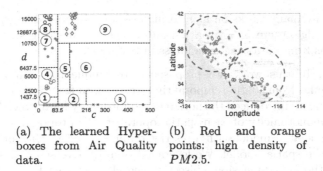

(a) The learned Hyper-
boxes from Air Quality
data.

(b) Red and orange
points: high density of
$PM2.5$.

Fig. 5. Clustering experiments on the California Air Quality Data

6   Related Work and Conclusion

Traditional ML Approaches for Time-Series Clustering. Time-series
clustering is a popular area in the domain of machine learning and data mining. Some techniques for time-series clustering combine clustering methods such
as KMeans [7], Hierarchical Clustering, agglomerative clustering [4] and etc.,
with similarity metrics between time-series data such as the Euclidean distance,
dynamic time-warping (DTW) distance, and statistical measures (such as mean,
median, correlation, etc.). Some recent works such as the works on shapelets
automatically identify distinguishing shapes in the time-series data [19]. Such
shapelets serve as features for ML tasks. All these approaches are based on
shape-similarity which might be useful in some applications; however, for applications that the user is interested in mining temporal information from data,
dissimilar traces might be clustered in the same group [11]. Furthermore, such
approaches may lack interpretability as we showed in BSS case study.

STL-Based Clustering of Time-Series Data. There is considerable amount
of recent work on learning temporal logic formulas from time-series data using
logics such as Signal Temporal Logic (STL) [8,11,14,15]; however, there is no
work on discovering such relations on spatio-temporal data. In particular, the
work in [11] which addresses unsupervised clustering of time-series data using
Signal Temporal Logic is closest to our work. There are a few hurdles in applying
such an approach to spatio-temporal data as explained in Sect. 1. We address
all the hurdles in the current work.

Monitoring Spatio-temporal Properties. There is considerable amount of
recent work such as [2,3] on monitoring spatio-temporal properties. Particularly,
MoonLight [3] is a recent tool for monitoring of STREL properties, and in our
current work, we use MoonLight for computing the robustness of spatio-temporal
data with respect to STREL formulas. MoonLight uses (δ, d)-connectivity approach for creating a spatial model, which has several issues, including dis-
connectivity and distance overestimation. We resolve these issues by proposing
our new method for creating the spatial graph, which we call Enhanced MSG.

While there are many works on monitoring of spatio-temporal logic, to the best of our knowledge, there is no work on automatically inferring spatio-temporal logic formulas from data that we address in this work.

Conclusion. In this work, we proposed a technique to learn interpretable STREL formulas from spatio-temporal time-series data for Spatially Distributed Systems. First, we introduced the notion of monotonicity for a PSTREL formula, proving the monotonicity of each spatial operator. We proposed a new method for creating a spatial model with a restrict number of edges that preserves connectivity of the spatial model. We leveraged quantitative semantics of STREL combined with multi-dimensional bisection search to extract features for spatio-temporal time-series clustering. We applied Agglomerative Hierarchical clustering on the extracted features followed by a Decision Tree based approach to learn an interpretable STREL formula for each cluster. We then illustrated with a number of benchmarks how this technique could be used and the kinds of insights it can develop. The results show that while our method performs slower than traditional ML approaches, it is more interpretable and provides a better insight into the data. For future work, we will study extensions of this approach to supervised and active learning.

Acknowledgments. We thank the anonymous reviewers for their comments. The authors also gratefully acknowledge the support by the National Science Foundation under the Career Award SHF-2048094, the NSF FMitF award CCF-1837131, the Austrian FWF projects ZK-35, and a grant from Toyota R&D North America.

References

1. Asarin, E., Donzé, A., Maler, O., Nickovic, D.: Parametric identification of temporal properties. In: Khurshid, S., Sen, K. (eds.) RV 2011. LNCS, vol. 7186, pp. 147–160. Springer, Heidelberg (2012). https://doi.org/10.1007/978-3-642-29860-8_12
2. Bartocci, E., Bortolussi, L., Loreti, M., Nenzi, L.: Monitoring mobile and spatially distributed cyber-physical systems. In: Proceedings of MEMOCODE (2017)
3. Bartocci, E., Bortolussi, L., Loreti, M., Nenzi, L., Silvetti, S.: MoonLight: a lightweight tool for monitoring spatio-temporal properties. In: Deshmukh, J., Ničković, D. (eds.) RV 2020. LNCS, vol. 12399, pp. 417–428. Springer, Cham (2020). https://doi.org/10.1007/978-3-030-60508-7_23
4. Cobo, G., García-Solórzano, D., Santamaría, E., Morán, J.A., Melenchón, J., Monzo, C.: Modeling students' activity in online discussion forums: a strategy based on time series and agglomerative hierarchical clustering. In: Educational Data Mining (2010)
5. Day, W.H., Edelsbrunner, H.: Efficient algorithms for agglomerative hierarchical clustering methods. J. Classif. **1**(1), 7–24 (1984)
6. Fiedler, B., Scheel, A.: Spatio-temporal dynamics of reaction-diffusion patterns. In: Kirkilionis, M., Krömker, S., Rannacher, R., Tomi, F. (eds.) Trends in Nonlinear Analysis, pp. 23–152. Springer, Heidelberg (2003). https://doi.org/10.1007/978-3-662-05281-5_2

7. Huang, X., Ye, Y., Xiong, L., Lau, R.Y., Jiang, N., Wang, S.: Time series k-means: a new k-means type smooth subspace clustering for time series data. Inf. Sci. **367**, 1–13 (2016)
8. Jin, X., Donzé, A., Deshmukh, J.V., Seshia, S.A.: Mining requirements from closed-loop control models. IEEE Trans. CAD **34**(11), 1704–1717 (2015)
9. Kiamari, M., Ramachandran, G., Nguyen, Q., Pereira, E., Holm, J., Krishna-machari, B.: Covid-19 risk estimation using a time-varying sir-model. In: Proceedings of the 1st ACM SIGSPATIAL International Workshop on Modeling and Understanding the Spread of COVID-19, pp. 36–42 (2020)
10. Kreikemeyer, J.N., Hillston, J., Uhrmacher, A.: Probing the performance of the Edinburgh bike sharing system using SSTL. In: Proceedings of the 2020 ACM SIGSIM Conference on Principles of Advanced Discrete Simulation, pp. 141–152 (2020)
11. Vazquez-Chanlatte, M., Deshmukh, J.V., Jin, X., Seshia, S.A.: Logical clustering and learning for time-series data. In: Majumdar, R., Kunčak, V. (eds.) CAV 2017. LNCS, vol. 10426, pp. 305–325. Springer, Cham (2017). https://doi.org/10.1007/978-3-319-63387-9_15
12. Maler, O., Nickovic, D.: Monitoring temporal properties of continuous signals. In: Lakhnech, Y., Yovine, S. (eds.) FORMATS/FTRTFT -2004. LNCS, vol. 3253, pp. 152–166. Springer, Heidelberg (2004). https://doi.org/10.1007/978-3-540-30206-3_12
13. Mitchell, T.M.: Machine Learning, 1st edn. McGraw-Hill Inc., New York (1997)
14. Mohammadinejad, S., Deshmukh, J.V., Puranic, A.G.: Mining environment assumptions for cyber-physical system models. In: Proceedings of ICCPS (2020)
15. Mohammadinejad, S., Deshmukh, J.V., Puranic, A.G., Vazquez-Chanlatte, M., Donzé, A.: Interpretable classification of time-series data using efficient enumerative techniques. In: Proceedings of HSCC (2020)
16. Nenzi, L., Bortolussi, L., Ciancia, V., Loreti, M., Massink, M.: Qualitative and quantitative monitoring of spatio-temporal properties with SSTL. LMCS **14**(4) (2018)
17. Rousseeuw, P.J.: Silhouettes: a graphical aid to the interpretation and validation of cluster analysis. J. Comput. Appl. Math. **20**, 53–65 (1987)
18. Vazquez-Chanlatte, M., Ghosh, S., Deshmukh, J.V., Sangiovanni-Vincentelli, A., Seshia, S.A.: Time-series learning using monotonic logical properties. In: Colombo, C., Leucker, M. (eds.) RV 2018. LNCS, vol. 11237, pp. 389–405. Springer, Cham (2018). https://doi.org/10.1007/978-3-030-03769-7_22
19. Zakaria, J., Mueen, A., Keogh, E.: Clustering time series using unsupervised-shapelets. In: 2012 IEEE 12th International Conference on Data Mining, pp. 785–794. IEEE (2012)

Theorem Proving and Tools

A Formal Semantics of the GraalVM Intermediate Representation

Brae J. Webb$^{(\boxtimes)}$ ⓘ, Mark Utting ⓘ, and Ian J. Hayes ⓘ

The University of Queensland, Brisbane, Australia
{B.Webb,M.Utting,Ian.Hayes}@uq.edu.au

Abstract. The optimization phase of a compiler is responsible for transforming an intermediate representation (IR) of a program into a more
efficient form. Modern optimizers, such as that used in the GraalVM compiler, use an IR consisting of a sophisticated graph data structure that
combines data flow and control flow into the one structure. As part of a
wider project on the verification of optimization passes of GraalVM, this
paper describes a semantics for its IR within Isabelle/HOL. The semantics consists of a big-step operational semantics for data nodes (which
are represented in a graph-based static single assignment (SSA) form)
and a small-step operational semantics for handling control flow including heap-based reads and writes, exceptions, and method calls. We have
proved a suite of canonicalization optimizations and conditional elimination optimizations with respect to the semantics.

1 Introduction

Compilers are an essential ingredient of the computing base. Software developers
need to be able to trust their compilers because an error in a compiler can manifest
as erroneous generated code for any of the myriad of programs it compiles.

This paper forms the first steps of a wider project that focuses on the verification of compiler optimization passes, a common source of compiler errors. The
project does not cover initial parsing, type checking and intermediate representation (IR) construction passes, nor the final machine-dependent code generation
pass.

The multi-pass structure of a compiler affords verification on a pass-by-pass
basis. An optimization pass transforms a program represented in the IR. The
verification of a pass involves proving that, for every IR input program, the
transformation implemented by the pass preserves the semantics of the program.
This task can be partitioned into:

- defining a formal semantics for the IR,
- defining the optimizations as transformations of the IR, and
- verifying that the transformations are semantics preserving.

In this paper, we embark on the process of verifying the optimization passes
of an existing production compiler, GraalVM [14], using Isabelle/HOL [13].

© Springer Nature Switzerland AG 2021
Z. Hou and V. Ganesh (Eds.): ATVA 2021, LNCS 12971, pp. 111–126, 2021.
https://doi.org/10.1007/978-3-030-88885-5_8

We present a formalization of the IR used by the GraalVM compiler (Sects. 3, 4, 5 and 6). We briefly describe the validation of this semantics against the existing compiler implementation (Sect. 7), then show the effectiveness of the semantics by proving two kinds of local optimizations (Sect. 8).

The main contribution of this paper is to devise a formal semantics of the GraalVM IR in Isabelle/HOL [13]. The IR combines control flow and data flow into a single 'sea-of-nodes' graph structure [3], rather than a more conventional control-flow graph with basic blocks representing sequential flow. Section 2 gives further details of the GraalVM Compiler. As far as we are aware, this is the first formal semantics of a sea-of-nodes IR that covers method calls, with exceptions, as well as object reads and writes. The semantics of the IR consists of the following components:

- the graph representation corresponding to the GraalVM IR (Sect. 3),
- data-flow semantics that handles expression evaluation using a big-step operational semantics (Sect. 4),
- local control-flow semantics that handles control flow within a single method using a small-step operational semantics (Sect. 5),
- global control-flow semantics that handles method invocation and return, exceptions handling, and promotes the local control-flow semantics to a small-step operational semantics (Sect. 6).

Each stage builds on the previous. Note that expression evaluation within the GraalVM IR is side-effect-free and terminating, so it is appropriate to use a big-step semantics that just returns the result, whereas for the control-flow semantics we use a small-step operational semantics to account for non-terminating programs and to accurately model the order of all side-effects, including object reads and writes, method calls, etc.

2   GraalVM IR

The GraalVM Intermediate Representation (IR) is a sophisticated graph structure that is designed to support implementation of efficient code optimizing transformations (see Fig. 6b for an example graph). A side-effect-free expression is represented by a data-flow subgraph that is acyclic (i.e. it is a DAG), so that common subexpressions are represented by shared subgraphs (instead of by value numbering in traditional SSA form). This has the advantage that data-flow dependencies are explicitly represented in the graph [6]. Expressions with potentially observable side-effects, such as method invocations or field accesses, are incorporated into the control-flow graph.

The IR combines both data-flow and control-flow aspects of a program within a single graph structure. This graphical representation allows efficient implementation of optimizations equivalent to global value numbering and global code motion optimization strategies [2].

The GraalVM IR graph consists of many different kinds of nodes (over 200) with two main kinds of edges:

Listing 1.1. A simplified AddNode class definition in GraalVM

```
class AddNode extends Node {
    @Input ValueNode x;
    @Input ValueNode y;
}
```

- *input* edges that specify the data inputs of a node;
- *successor* edges that specify the control-flow successors of a node.

Nodes of the GraalVM IR are implemented in Java as a collection of Java classes which inherit from a base Node class. Each subclass of Node can specify their possible edge connections, either input or successor edges, by annotating fields that store references to other Node subclasses. Listing 1.1 shows a simplified example of one such Node subclass for an addition expression. AddNode has two input edges x and y but it has no successors because it is a pure data-flow node.

3   Graph Model in Isabelle/HOL

Our Isabelle/HOL model of the GraalVM IR graph has a close correspondence with the Java Node subclasses but still supports efficient reasoning and pattern matching in Isabelle. We use natural numbers[1] to identify nodes of the graph, and define an Isabelle datatype *IRNode* (see Fig. 1) to model the concrete subclasses of the Java Node class. We developed a tool that uses Java reflection to traverse the GraalVM Node subclasses and generate the *IRNode* datatype, including within each branch of the datatype the input edges, successor edges, and selected data attributes of each node, using the same names as in the Java source code but prefixed with "*ir_*" to avoid name clashes (field names are global functions in Isabelle). We currently translate 45 of the concrete subclasses of the Java Node class into Isabelle, which corresponds to over 85% of the nodes used to compile the Dacapo Java benchmark[2] and is enough to handle simple example programs. For the 60+ interface classes and abstract Java subclasses of Node, such as BinaryArithmeticNode, we also generate a corresponding Isabelle boolean function[3] over the *IRNode* type, such as:

$$\textit{is-BinaryArithmeticNode} :: \textit{IRNode} \Rightarrow \textit{bool}$$

Figure 1 gives the Isabelle representation of the graph nodes.[4] *ConstantNode* corresponds to a Java constant, so has a value constant as its only field, with

---

[1] A more abstract representation would be better but using natural numbers allows us to utilise Isabelle code generation facilities.

[2] https://github.com/dacapobench/dacapobench.

[3] In Isabelle/HOL "$S \Rightarrow T$" is the type of a function from S to T.

[4] All theories are available at https://github.com/uqcyber/veriopt-releases/tree/atva2021.

type_synonym *ID* = *nat*
type_synonym *INPUT* = *ID*
type_synonym *SUCC* = *ID*

datatype *IRNode* =
NoNode
(* Subclasses of FloatingNode *)
| *ConstantNode*(*ir_const* : *Value*)
| *ParameterNode*(*ir_index* : *nat*)
| *ValuePhiNode*(*ir_nid* : *ID*)(*ir_values* : *INPUT list*)(*ir_merge* : *INPUT*)
| *NegateNode*(*ir_value* : *INPUT*)
| *AddNode*(*ir_x* : *INPUT*)(*ir_y* : *INPUT*)
| *MulNode*(*ir_x* : *INPUT*)(*ir_y* : *INPUT*)
| *IntegerLessThanNode*(*ir_x* : *INPUT*)(*ir_y* : *INPUT*)
| ...
(* Control flow (fixed) nodes *)
| *StartNode* ... (*ir_next* : *SUCC*)
| *IfNode*(*ir_condition* : *INPUT*)
        (*ir_trueSuccessor* : *SUCC*)(*ir_falseSuccessor* : *SUCC*)
| *BeginNode*(*ir_next* : *SUCC*)
| *EndNode*
| *LoopBeginNode*(*ir_ends* : *INPUT list*) ... ... (*ir_next* : *SUCC*)
| *LoopEndNode*(*ir_loopBegin* : *INPUT*)
| *LoopExitNode*(*ir_loopBegin* : *INPUT*) ... (*ir_next* : *SUCC*)
| *MergeNode*(*ir_ends* : *INPUT list*) ... (*ir_next* : *SUCC*)
| *NewInstanceNode*(*ir_nid* : *ID*)(*ir_instanceClass* : *string*) ... (*ir_next* : *SUCC*)
| *LoadFieldNode*(*ir_nid* : *ID*)(*ir_field* : *string*)(*ir_object_opt* : *INPUT option*)
        (*ir_next* : *SUCC*)
| *StoreFieldNode*(*ir_nid* : *ID*)(*ir_field* : *string*)(*ir_value* : *INPUT*) ...
        (*ir_object_opt* : *INPUT option*)(*ir_next* : *SUCC*)
| *RefNode*(*ir_next* : *SUCC*)
(* Interprocedural nodes *)
| *ReturnNode*(*ir_result_opt* : *INPUT option*) ...
| *InvokeNode*(*ir_nid* : *ID*)(*ir_callTarget* : *INPUT*) ... ... (*ir_next* : *SUCC*)
| *InvokeWithExceptionNode*(*ir_nid* : *ID*)(*ir_callTarget* : *INPUT*) ... ...
        (*ir_next* : *SUCC*)(*ir_exceptionEdge* : *SUCC*)
| *MethodCallTargetNode*(*ir_targetMethod* : *string*)(*ir_arguments* : *INPUT list*)
| *UnwindNode*(*ir_exception* : *INPUT*)

Fig. 1. An extract of the Isabelle datatype definition of the IR graph nodes (some node types and fields are omitted or abbreviated to save space).

no input or successor edges. Similarly, *ParameterNode* has a single natural number field that is an index into the list of parameter values of the current method. Binary expression nodes (like *AddNode*) have two input expression edges, named *ir_x* and *ir_y*. The data-flow aspects of merging multiple control-flow paths are handled by a ϕ-node (abbreviating *ValuePhiNode*) for each value that is dependent on the path used to reach an associated merge node (e.g. *MergeNode*). The semantics of ϕ-nodes is explained more fully in Sect. 5, but note that a ϕ-node has a pseudo-input edge called ir_merge that references the merge node associated with the ϕ-node, and a list of input edges ir_values that is in one-to-one correspondence with the control-flow edges into that merge node. To illustrate how the structure of a node influences its semantics, consider an $IfNode$. An $IfNode$ has one input edge for its boolean condition, and two successor edges, one to take when the condition evaluates to true and the other successor edge to take when it evaluates to false.

In addition to explicit (named) input and successor fields, the Java Node classes use annotations and meta-data in each subclass to provide *generic* access functions for accessing the list of all inputs of an arbitrary subclass, and similarly for all successors. Such generic access is helpful for implementing visitor patterns that walk the graph, etc. In Isabelle, we provide the equivalent functionality by defining two functions over $IRNode$, *inputs-of* and *successors-of*, in the following style, in which "·" represents list cons.

$inputs\text{-}of$ :: $IRNode \Rightarrow nat\ list$
$inputs\text{-}of\ (ConstantNode\ const) = []$
$inputs\text{-}of\ (ParameterNode\ index) = []$
$inputs\text{-}of\ (ValuePhiNode\ nid\ values\ merge) = merge \cdot values$
$inputs\text{-}of\ (AddNode\ x\ y) = [x,\ y]$
$inputs\text{-}of\ (IfNode\ condition\ trueSuccessor\ falseSuccessor) = [condition]$

We model an IR graph for a single method as a partial map ($\rightharpoonup$) from node IDs to $IRNodes$ with a finite domain.

typedef $IRGraph = \{g :: ID \rightharpoonup IRNode\ .\ finite\ (dom\ g)\}$

A finite domain is a requisite property for code generation used by validation efforts (see Sect. 7), however, we have found reasoning to be more straightforward with total functions and hence we introduce the kind function, denoted $g\langle\langle nid\rangle\rangle$, that is a total function that performs lookup on the underlying partial function, g, resulting in $NoNode$ for identifiers with no mapping. In addition, we lift the domain function to the function ids and introduce functions $inputs$, $succ$, $usages$, and $predecessors$ that, given a graph and a node identifier, produce the sets of input, successor, usage, and predecessor node ids, respectively.

There are several conditions that a graph g should satisfy to be well-formed, such as being closed, i.e. all inputs and successors identify nodes within the graph (that is, within $ids\ g$). The key invariants that we have needed so far are shown in Fig. 2, and include the edge-closure properties, as well as the requirement that node zero should be the $StartNode$ for the method represented by the graph, and that all the nodes in the graph are proper nodes, rather than $NoNode$. Additionally, end nodes need to have at least one usage which is treated as the pseudo-successor edge for an end node. The input edges of a merge node are used by ϕ nodes to determine the value for a ϕ node, the number of input edges of any ϕ node must match the number of input edges of its associated merge node to ensure correct execution. We expect to add further invariants in the future as we prove deeper properties of the graph. Indeed, one of the expected benefits of this project is to discover important IR invariants that are currently implicit in the way that the GraalVM compiler constructs and uses the graph, and to:

- prove that those invariants are preserved by the graph transformations that represent optimizations;
- document those invariants explicitly and implement them in the Java code base so that they can be checked at runtime during test runs of the compiler.

$wf\text{-}start\ g =$
$(0\ \in\ ids\ g\ \land\ is\text{-}StartNode\ g\langle\!\langle 0\rangle\!\rangle)$

$wf\text{-}phis\ g =$
$(\forall\, n{\in}ids\ g.$
$\quad is\text{-}PhiNode\ g\langle\!\langle n\rangle\!\rangle\ \longrightarrow$
$\quad |ir\text{-}values\ g\langle\!\langle n\rangle\!\rangle| =$
$\quad |ir\text{-}ends\ g\langle\!\langle ir\text{-}merge\ g\langle\!\langle n\rangle\!\rangle\rangle\!\rangle|)$

$wf\text{-}ends\ g =$
$(\forall\, n{\in}ids\ g.$
$\quad is\text{-}AbstractEndNode\ g\langle\!\langle n\rangle\!\rangle\ \longrightarrow$
$\quad 0 < |usages\ g\ n|)$

$wf\text{-}closed\ g =$
$(\forall\, n{\in}ids\ g.$
$\quad inputs\ g\ n\ \subseteq\ ids\ g\ \land$
$\quad succ\ g\ n\ \subseteq\ ids\ g\ \land\ g\langle\!\langle n\rangle\!\rangle\ \neq\ NoNode)$

$wf\text{-}graph\ ::\ IRGraph\ \Rightarrow\ bool$
$wf\text{-}graph\ g = (wf\text{-}start\ g\ \land\ wf\text{-}closed\ g\ \land\ wf\text{-}phis\ g\ \land\ wf\text{-}ends\ g)$

Fig. 2. Isabelle well-formedness graph invariants.

An *IRGraph* represents a single method. In the GraalVM compiler, to uniquely identify a method, one needs not only its name but the class in which it is defined and the types of its parameters to handle method overloading (as in Java [11]). Together these form the method's signature, which is represented by the type *Signature*. Programs are represented as a partial function from method signatures to their *IRGraph*.

$$\textbf{\textit{type-synonym}}\ Program = Signature \rightharpoonup IRGraph$$

4   Data-Flow Semantics

In a programming language like Java, expression evaluation may involve side effects, such as calling a method. The GraalVM, and hence our semantics, treats nodes that may have a side effect differently. These nodes are included in the control-flow graph so that they are evaluated as part of the control-flow semantics (see Sect. 5) and hence the order of their evaluation is preserved. When one of these nodes (with node identifier *nid*, say) is evaluated as part of the control flow semantics, the calculated value is saved under the node identifier *nid* in a mapping m from node identifiers to values, which we refer to as the *method state*.

The data-flow semantics handles the evaluation of side-effect-free expressions, which are represented by a directed acyclic (sub-)graph (DAG), in which internal nodes are operators (with input arguments that are graph node ids) and leaf nodes are either constant nodes, parameter nodes, or control-flow nodes representing expressions that may have had side effects, e.g. a method invocation node. These control-flow nodes have their current value stored in the method state m under their node identifier, with m nid giving the current value associated with (leaf) node nid. The values of the parameters are given by a list of values p, with $p_{[i]}$ giving the value of the ith parameter.

$$[g,\ m,\ p] \vdash ConstantNode\ c \mapsto c \tag{3.1}$$

$$\frac{[g,\ m,\ p] \vdash g\langle x\rangle \mapsto v1 \qquad [g,\ m,\ p] \vdash g\langle y\rangle \mapsto v2}{[g,\ m,\ p] \vdash AddNode\ x\ y \mapsto v1 + v2} \tag{3.2}$$

$$[g,\ m,\ p] \vdash ParameterNode\ i \mapsto p_{[i]} \tag{3.3}$$

$$[g,\ m,\ p] \vdash ValuePhiNode\ nid\ uu\ uv \mapsto m\ nid \tag{3.4}$$

$$[g,\ m,\ p] \vdash InvokeNode\ nid\ vh\ vi\ vj\ vk\ vl \mapsto m\ nid \tag{3.5}$$

$$[g,\ m,\ p] \vdash NewInstanceNode\ nid\ vs\ vt\ vu \mapsto m\ nid \tag{3.6}$$

$$[g,\ m,\ p] \vdash LoadFieldNode\ nid\ vv\ vw\ vx \mapsto m\ nid \tag{3.7}$$

Fig. 3. Data-flow semantics for a subset of nodes

For a graph g, method state m, and list of parameter values p, in our big-step operational semantics for expressions, an evaluation of a node n to a value v is represented as

$$[g,\ m,\ p] \vdash n \mapsto v.$$

A sample of the 27 evaluation rules for data nodes is given in Fig. 3. Note that for the $AddNode$, the $+$ is overloaded to use the Isabelle/HOL WORD library to add two fixed-size integers, so that integer arithmetic follows Java's twos-complement semantics with wrapping upon overflow.

Each parameter node contains the index i of its parameter in the formal parameter list, with $p_{[i]}$ giving the parameter's value. Control-flow nodes for expressions with side effects (such as $ValuePhiNode$, $InvokeNode$, $NewInstanceNode$, $LoadFieldNode$) extract the current value of the node from the method state m. Each of these node types also has a rule in the control-flow semantics that triggers their evaluation and updates m with the result (see Sect. 5). The control-flow semantics requires the ability to evaluate a list of expressions, $nids$, to a list of values, vs, written,

$$[g,\ m,\ p] \vdash nids \longmapsto vs,$$

(note the longer arrow), which is the obvious lifting of evaluation of a single expression to evaluate each expression in the list (not detailed for space reasons).

5 Local Control-Flow Semantics

To support object orientation, the semantics requires a heap to store objects. We define a heap in the form of a function h that for an object reference r and a field name f gives the value of that field for that object, $h\ r\ f$ [1]. Note that while the heap is always finite, its size is unbounded. Figure 4 defines our heap representation. *Heap* is a type that maps object references and field names to values. *DynamicHeap* expands *Heap* to track the next free object reference[5] in the heap, *Free*, each time a new object is instantiated the next free object reference is incremented and the current free object reference is used. The supporting definitions, *h-load-field*, *h-store-field*, and *h-new-inst*, are used by the semantics of the load (5.5) and store (5.6) field nodes in Fig. 5.

> **type-synonym** *Heap = objref ⇒ string ⇒ Value*
> **type-synonym** *Free = nat*
> **type-synonym** *DynamicHeap = Heap × Free*
>
> *h-load-field* :: *objref ⇒ string ⇒ DynamicHeap ⇒ Value*
> *h-load-field r f (h, n) = h r f*
>
> *h-store-field* :: *objref ⇒ string ⇒ Value ⇒ DynamicHeap ⇒ DynamicHeap*
> *h-store-field r f v (h, n) = (h(r := (h r)(f := v)), n)*
>
> *h-new-inst* :: *DynamicHeap ⇒ (DynamicHeap × Value)*
> *h-new-inst (h, n) = ((h, n + 1), ObjRef (Some n))*

Fig. 4. Isabelle model of a heap and supporting definitions

The control-flow semantics local to a method is given by a small-step operational semantics. A configuration consists of a triple of the current node id, nid, the method state, m, as used in expression evaluation, and the heap, h. The transition

$$[g,\ p] \vdash (nid,\ m,\ h) \to (nid',\ m',\ h'),$$

can be read as, within the context of graph, g, and list of parameter values, p, an execution step can transition from configuration (nid, m, h) to configuration (nid', m', h'). The node id acts as a program counter for the graph representation of the method. For a configuration, (nid, m, h), to be valid, nid must be a control flow node within g, p must give values for all parameters to the current method, and m gives the values for all control-flow nodes that represent expressions with side effects that have been reached in the current invocation of the method.

---

[5] The operation for allocating a new object could nondeterministically choose any unused object reference, but we have made it a deterministic function that allocates the next location to facilitate the use of Isabelle code generation facilities.

$$\frac{is\text{-}sequential\text{-}node \; g\langle nid\rangle \qquad nid' = (successors\text{-}of \; g\langle nid\rangle)_{[0]}}{[g,\, p] \vdash (nid,\, m,\, h) \rightarrow (nid',\, m,\, h)} \qquad (5.1)$$

$$\frac{g\langle nid\rangle = IfNode \; cond \; tb \; fb}{[g,\, m,\, p] \vdash g\langle cond\rangle \mapsto val \qquad nid' = (if \; val\text{-}to\text{-}bool \; val \; then \; tb \; else \; fb)}{[g,\, p] \vdash (nid,\, m,\, h) \rightarrow (nid',\, m,\, h)} \qquad (5.2)$$

$$\frac{\begin{array}{c} is\text{-}AbstractEndNode \; g\langle nid\rangle \\ merge = any\text{-}usage \; g \; nid \qquad is\text{-}AbstractMergeNode \; g\langle merge\rangle \\ i = find\text{-}index \; nid \; (inputs\text{-}of \; g\langle merge\rangle) \qquad phis = phi\text{-}list \; g \; merge \\ inps = phi\text{-}inputs \; g \; i \; phis \qquad [g,\, m,\, p] \vdash inps \longmapsto vs \qquad m' = set\text{-}phis \; phis \; vs \; m \end{array}}{[g,\, p] \vdash (nid,\, m,\, h) \rightarrow (merge,\, m',\, h)} \qquad (5.3)$$

$$\frac{\begin{array}{c} g\langle nid\rangle = NewInstanceNode \; nid \; class \; frame \; nid' \\ (h',\, ref) = h\text{-}new\text{-}inst \; h \qquad m' = m(nid := ref) \end{array}}{[g,\, p] \vdash (nid,\, m,\, h) \rightarrow (nid',\, m',\, h')} \qquad (5.4)$$

$$\frac{g\langle nid\rangle = LoadFieldNode \; nid \; f \; (Some \; obj) \; nid'}{[g,\, m,\, p] \vdash g\langle obj\rangle \mapsto ObjRef \; ref \qquad h\text{-}load\text{-}field \; ref \; f \; h = v \qquad m' = m(nid := v)}{[g,\, p] \vdash (nid,\, m,\, h) \rightarrow (nid',\, m',\, h)} \qquad (5.5)$$

$$\frac{\begin{array}{c} g\langle nid\rangle = StoreFieldNode \; nid \; f \; newval \; uu \; (Some \; obj) \; nid' \\ [g,\, m,\, p] \vdash g\langle newval\rangle \mapsto val \qquad [g,\, m,\, p] \vdash g\langle obj\rangle \mapsto ObjRef \; ref \\ h' = h\text{-}store\text{-}field \; ref \; f \; val \; h \qquad m' = m(nid := val) \end{array}}{[g,\, p] \vdash (nid,\, m,\, h) \rightarrow (nid',\, m',\, h')} \qquad (5.6)$$

Fig. 5. Control node semantics

Figure 5 shows most of the rules for the local control-flow semantics —to save space we omit the load and store rules for static fields, where the object pointer is *None* rather than (*Some obj*). A number of nodes have a control-flow behaviour of a no-op; we group them together as sequential nodes. Their semantics (5.1) is a transition from the current node to the node attached to the only successor edge. An *IfNode* (5.2) chooses to transition to the first (*tb*) or second (*fb*) successor edge based on the evaluation of the condition expression.

Our approach to handling ϕ nodes is similar to that used by Demange *et al.* for their formalization of reasoning about the sea of nodes in Coq [4]. End nodes (5.3) represent the end of a basic block in SSA terminology. Each end node forms an input to a merge node and each merge node has an associated set of ϕ nodes, each of which represents a value that is dependent on which path was taken to reach the end node, and hence the merge node. When an end node is reached, the method state m of each associated ϕ node is updated with the value of its associated expression DAG in the current state, m. This process is best explained via the example in Fig. 6b, in which nodes 3, 10 and 19 are constant nodes, node 20 is an AddNode, node 18 is a MulNode, node 11 is a IntegerLessThanNode, ϕ-node 8 represents the value of the local variable result, and node 1 corresponds to the parameter n, which provides the initial value of ϕ-node 7, which represents the variable n within the loop. The ProxyNode 15

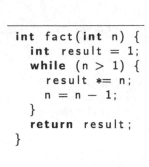

```
int fact(int n) {
    int result = 1;
    while (n > 1) {
        result *= n;
        n = n - 1;
    }
    return result;
}
```

(a) Java factorial program

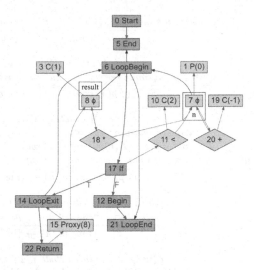

(b) Factorial program IR graph

Fig. 6. Example factorial program transformed into a GraalVM IR graph

is the value of the ϕ-node 8 (i.e. result) but has an additional dependency on the LoopExitNode 14 to ensure the value is that after loop exit. Note that the value of AddNode 20 is calculated using the inputs constant -1 and the ϕ-node 7, representing the previous value of n, to give the new value of the ϕ-node 7 (hence the double-headed arrow between nodes 7 and 20). Given

- $merge$, the id of the merge node LoopBegin $\boxed{6}$,
- usage ϕ nodes of $merge$, $phis = [\phi_1 \boxed{7}, \phi_2 \boxed{8}]$
- input end nodes of $merge$, $ends = [\text{End } \boxed{5}, \text{LoopEnd } \boxed{21}]$
- inputs of $\phi_1 \boxed{7}$ excluding $merge$, [ParameterNode P(0) $\boxed{1}$, AddNode + $\boxed{20}$]
- inputs of $\phi_2 \boxed{8}$ excl. $merge$, [ConstantNode C(1) $\boxed{3}$, MultiplyNode * $\boxed{18}$]

when

- $End \boxed{5}$ is reached
  1. evaluate the first input edge to all $phis$ in the original method state, m, i.e. for $\boxed{1}$, $[g, m, p] \vdash P(0) \mapsto r_1$ and for $\boxed{3}$ $[g, m, p] \vdash C(1) \mapsto 1$.
  2. update m to map the values of the evaluated expressions to each ϕ node, i.e. $m'(\phi_1) = r_1$ and $m'(\phi_2) = 1$.
- $LoopEnd \boxed{21}$ is reached
  1. evaluate the second input edge to all $phis$ in the original method state, m, i.e. for $\boxed{20}$ $[g, m, p] \vdash AddNode(\boxed{7}, \boxed{19}) \mapsto r_1$ and for $\boxed{18}$ $[g, m, p] \vdash MulNode(\boxed{8}, \boxed{7}) \mapsto r_2$. Note that when the evaluation reaches a ϕ node, it refers to the (previous) value of the ϕ node in m, i.e. $m(\phi)$.
  2. update m to map the values of the evaluated expressions to each ϕ node, i.e. $m'(\phi_1) = r_1$ and $m'(\phi_2) = r_2$.

More generally, a merge node may have a list of input end nodes, ns, and any number of associated ϕ nodes, each of which has a list of input expressions, each of which is of the same length as ns. When the merge node is reached via its ith input end node, the value of each associated ϕ node is updated within m to the value of the $(i + 1)^{th}$ input expression of the ϕ node using method state m (the $i + 1$ offset is because input edge zero of a ϕ node is used to connect to its merge node).

When a $NewInstanceNode$ is reached in the control flow (5.4), space is allocated in the heap for a new object ref using the function $h\text{-}new\text{-}inst$ function (Fig. 4). The value associated with the $NewInstanceNode$ is updated in m' to the new object reference ref so that subsequent data-flow evaluations of the $NewInstanceNode$ evaluate to ref.

A $LoadFieldNode$ (5.5) contains a field name f and an optional input edge to a node that must evaluate to an object reference, obj. The $h\text{-}load\text{-}field$ function (Fig. 4) reads the value from the heap based on the object reference and field name. The resulting value, v, is then stored in m' under the node id of $LoadFieldNode$ so that subsequent data-flow evaluations of the $LoadFieldNode$ result in v.

Similar to the $LoadFieldNode$, the $StoreFieldNode$ (5.6) contains a field identifier, f, and an optional input edge to a node which must evaluate to an object reference, obj. A $StoreFieldNode$ also has an input edge to a node, $newval$, that is evaluated to a value, val and stored in the heap. The $h\text{-}store\text{-}field$ function (Fig. 4) stores val in the updated heap, h', corresponding to the field f and object reference, obj. Note that null pointer dereferences are checked by a separate (dominating) $GuardNode$ (not covered in this paper) and hence null pointer dereferences are not an issue for load and store field. To save space, we omit load and store for static fields—these do not evaluate an object reference.

6   Global Control-Flow Semantics

The semantics in Sect. 5 only handles control flow within a single method. To handle method calls and returns, we lift the semantics to a richer global configuration that consists of a pair, (stk, h), containing a stack, stk, of local configurations for each called but not yet returned method and a global heap, h. The stack contains tuples of the form (g, nid, m, p), in which g represents the method's graph, nid is a node id (the program counter) within g, m is the method state, and p is the list of of parameter values, as for the data-flow semantics. The $IRGraph$ of the method with signature s in program P (of type $Program$) is given by $P\ s$.

Figure 7 gives a small-step semantics for global control flow. Given a program P, a transition of the form $P \vdash (stk, h) \longrightarrow (stk', h')$ represents a step from a configuration stack stk and heap h to a new stack stk' and heap h'. Stacks are represented as lists, so $(g, nid, m, p) \cdot stk$ represents a stack with top as the local configuration (g, nid, m, p) and remainder of the stack, stk.

$$\frac{[g,\, p] \vdash (nid,\, m,\, h) \to (nid',\, m',\, h')}{P \vdash ((g,\, nid,\, m,\, p) \cdot stk,\, h) \longrightarrow ((g,\, nid',\, m',\, p) \cdot stk,\, h')} \tag{7.1}$$

$$\frac{\begin{array}{c} is\text{-}Invoke\ g\langle nid\rangle \qquad callTarget = ir\text{-}callTarget\ g\langle nid\rangle \\ g\langle callTarget\rangle = MethodCallTargetNode\ targetMethod\ arguments \\ Some\ targetGraph = P\ targetMethod \\ m' = new\text{-}map\text{-}state \qquad [g,\, m,\, p] \vdash arguments \longmapsto p' \end{array}}{P \vdash ((g,\, nid,\, m,\, p) \cdot stk,\, h) \longrightarrow ((targetGraph,\, 0,\, m',\, p') \cdot (g,\, nid,\, m,\, p) \cdot stk,\, h)} \tag{7.2}$$

$$\frac{\begin{array}{c} g\langle nid\rangle = ReturnNode\ (Some\ expr)\ uu \qquad [g,\, m,\, p] \vdash g\langle expr\rangle \mapsto v \\ cm' = cm(cnid := v) \qquad cnid' = (successors\text{-}of\ cg\langle cnid\rangle)_{[0]} \end{array}}{P \vdash ((g,\, nid,\, m,\, p) \cdot (cg,\, cnid,\, cm,\, cp) \cdot stk,\, h) \longrightarrow ((cg,\, cnid',\, cm',\, cp) \cdot stk,\, h)} \tag{7.3}$$

$$\frac{\begin{array}{c} g\langle nid\rangle = UnwindNode\ exception \qquad [g,\, m,\, p] \vdash g\langle exception\rangle \mapsto e \\ cg\langle cnid\rangle = InvokeWithExceptionNode\ uw\ ux\ uy\ uz\ va\ vb\ exEdge \\ cm' = cm(cnid := e) \end{array}}{P \vdash ((g,\, nid,\, m,\, p) \cdot (cg,\, cnid,\, cm,\, cp) \cdot stk,\, h) \longrightarrow ((cg,\, exEdge,\, cm',\, cp) \cdot stk,\, h)} \tag{7.4}$$

Fig. 7. Interprocedural semantics

Local control-flow transitions are promoted to global control-flow transitions in which the top of stack is updated according to the local transition step (7.1).

For an *InvokeNode* (7.2), its list of actual parameter expressions, *arguments*, is evaluated to give the list of parameter values, p'. The method state m' for the invoked method is initially empty (*new_map_state*). The method being invoked is determined by the *MethodCallTargetNode*, which is attached via an input edge to an *InvokeNode*. The *MethodCallTargetNode* contains the signature, *targetMethod*, of the invoked method. A new local configuration consisting of the graph of the invoked method, *targetGraph*, a method start node id of zero, the method state m', and the list of parameter values p' is pushed onto the stack.

For a *ReturnNode* (7.3), the return expression is optional. Here we only consider the case in which there is some return expression. The return value, v, is calculated using the top-of-stack graph g, method state m and parameters p (i.e. the called method). The second stack element is a local configuration containing the graph of the calling method, *cg*, id of the invocation node, *cnid*, the method state at the point of call, *cm*, and the parameters of the calling method, *cp*. The top two elements of the stack are replaced by a single local configuration consisting of the calling method's graph *cg*, the successor *cnid'* of invocation node *cnid*, a new method state *cm'* that updates *cm* to map the invocation node *cnid* to the returned value, v, and the parameters to the calling method, *cp*.

Certain methods can result in exceptions rather than regular returned values. Calls to these methods are made using the *InvokeWithExceptionNode*. The invocation of these methods is handled with the same semantics as *InvokeNode*. An *UnwindNode* (7.4) indicates that an exception has been thrown. The control-flow path when an *UnwindNode* is reached is determined by the *exEdge* successor of the calling *InvokeWithExceptionNode*. The *InvokeWithExceptionNode* is the node on the second top of the stack when an *UnwindNode* is reached. The top two elements of the stack are replaced by a single local configuration consisting of the graph of the calling method, cg, the *exEdge* successor of the *InvokeWithExceptionNode*, and the method state cm updated so that the *InvokeWithExceptionNode* maps to the object reference e of the exception that was thrown.

7   Validation of Execution Semantics

The GraalVM compiler contains thousands of unit test cases, and many of these define a standalone method. Each test checks that its unoptimized and optimized execution give the same result. We have added code to intercept such tests and translate the unoptimized IR graph, the input parameter values, and the expected result into our Isabelle IR graph notation. We can then use Isabelle's code generation mechanism to execute the Isabelle IR graph of the method with the given input parameters, and check if the result matches.

We have translated and executed over 1400 of these unit tests so far, and after fixing a minor boolean-to-integer conversion issue and adding support for initializing static fields before the method is called, they all return the expected result. This gives us some initial confidence that our execution semantics corresponds to the GraalVM IR semantics. Any remaining differences will become apparent during the correctness proofs of optimizations.

8   Proving Optimizations

The GraalVM compiler contains a comprehensive canonicalization phase. Subsequent optimization phases rely on the canonicalization phase to minimize the forms which an IR can take. The majority of the canonicalization optimizations do not rely on additional static analysis processes, so are good case studies for the process of proving local optimizations. A canonicalization of a data-flow node within a graph g_1, replaces a data-flow node in g_1 at nid with a new node and may introduce additional new nodes with fresh node ids to form a new graph g_2. The replacement must maintain the property that the subgraph is acyclic. While the new node at nid may no longer reference some node ids that the original node at that position did, the unreferenced nodes are left in the graph because there may be other references to those nodes elsewhere in graph. To show the correctness of these forms of canonicalization optimizations, noting that expression evaluation has been shown to be deterministic, it is sufficient to show that for all method states m, evaluating the new node at nid gives the same value as evaluating the old node at nid, i.e.

$$\forall m, p \ . \ ([g_1, \ m, \ p] \ \vdash g_1 \langle\!\langle nid \rangle\!\rangle \mapsto v) \longrightarrow ([g_2, \ m, \ p] \ \vdash g_2 \langle\!\langle nid \rangle\!\rangle \mapsto v).$$

For example, we have completed proofs of correctness of optimizations of conditional expressions (Java's (c ? v1 : v2)).

As an example of a canonicalization of the control-flow graph, we define a set of optimizations for the $IfNode$ in Fig. 8. We show the optimization where an $IfNode$ with a constant condition is replaced by a $RefNode$ to either the true or false branch, where a $RefNode$ is a sequential node that just transitions to its successor. In addition, we give the optimization where both successor edges of the $IfNode$ are equal, replacing with a $RefNode$ to one of the (equal) branches. Note that these optimizations bypass the condition evaluation but as that is side effect free, it is of no consequence.

$$\frac{g\langle\!\langle cond \rangle\!\rangle \; = \; ConstantNode \; condv \qquad val\text{-}to\text{-}bool \; condv}{CanonicalizeIf \; g \; (IfNode \; cond \; tb \; fb) \; (RefNode \; tb)}$$

$$\frac{g\langle\!\langle cond \rangle\!\rangle \; = \; ConstantNode \; condv \qquad \neg \; val\text{-}to\text{-}bool \; condv}{CanonicalizeIf \; g \; (IfNode \; cond \; tb \; fb) \; (RefNode \; fb)}$$

$$\frac{\neg \; is\text{-}ConstantNode \; g\langle\!\langle cond \rangle\!\rangle \qquad tb = fb}{CanonicalizeIf \; g \; (IfNode \; cond \; tb \; fb) \; (RefNode \; tb)}$$

Fig. 8. Canonicalization rules for an $IfNode$

We prove that the canonicalization rules are correct by showing that, given:

- a node, $before$, where $g\langle\langle nid \rangle\rangle = before$;
- that $before$ can be canonicalized to the node $after$;
- a graph, g', where the node at nid has been replaced by $after$;

then we can prove that g' has the same behaviour as g starting from node nid in both graphs.

Thus far, we have encoded and proved exploratory components of the canonicalization phase and the entirety of the conditional elimination phase allowed by our subset of nodes. The techniques used for the requisite static analysis during the conditional elimination phase are to be the subject of future papers.

9   Related Work

The closest research to that presented here is the work of Demange *et al.* [4] who provide the semantics of an abstract sea-of-nodes representation in Coq, which focuses on the semantics of ϕ nodes and regions. The semantics is used to prove a semantic property and a simple optimization transformation. Their formalization allows properties of the abstract sea-of-nodes representation to be proven in isolation. We offer a variant of this semantics that matches the concrete implementation of a production compiler, and we extend the approach to handle interprocedural calls and a heap-based object model.

Two notable verified compiler projects are CompCert [9], for a subset of C verified in Coq, and CakeML [7], for a subset of ML verified in HOL4. These are both substantial projects verifying end-to-end correctness of their respective compilers from source code to generated machine code. Unlike these projects, this project targets only the optimization phase of the compiler, a common source of issues, rather than full end-to-end verification.

JinjaThreads [12] is a substantial formalization effort of the Java language semantics in Isabelle/HOL. Unlike our project, JinjaThreads focuses on directly formalizing the language semantics, rather than a language-agnostic IR. As the GraalVM IR is implemented in Java, one plausible approach to our project would be to use the JinjaThreads formalization to prove optimizations correct. However, such proofs would have been undoubtedly laborious, so we have instead chosen to introduce a semantics to capture the IR semantics directly and allow optimizations to be more easily expressed and proved.

VeLLVM [15] formalizes the LLVM [8] IR semantics using the Coq proof assistant. While the approach is similar, the target IR is substantially different. LLVM shares some common properties such as being in SSA form, but the GraalVM IR is a sea-of-nodes graph structure that unifies a program's control-flow and data-flow, while the LLVM IR is in traditional basic block SSA form.

K-LLVM [10] is another formalization effort for the LLVM IR that does not directly expand on VeLLVM but expands the formalized feature set by offering a separate formalization implemented in $\mathbb{K}$. $\mathbb{K}$ is a framework designed for formalizing language semantics, which can produce language interpreters as well as export to Isabelle/HOL to allow proofs based on the specification.

10   Conclusions

We have described an Isabelle model and execution semantics for the sophisticated sea-of-nodes graph structure [3] that is used as the internal representation in the GraalVM optimizing compiler [5]. Additionally, we have proved several suites of local optimizations correct according to the semantics.

In future work, we plan to tackle more global optimizations that transform the input graph in more complex ways. In the longer term, we also want to explore expressing optimizations in a high-level notation that can more easily be transformed into Isabelle (for correctness proof purposes) as well as into Java code that implements the graph transformation, in order to have a tight connection between the Java and Isabelle graph transformations.

Acknowledgements. Mark Utting's position and Brae Webb's scholarship are both funded in part by a gift from Oracle Labs. Thanks especially to Cristina Cifuentes, Paddy Krishnan and Andrew Craik from Oracle Labs Brisbane for their helpful feedback, and to the Oracle GraalVM compiler team for answering questions. Thanks to Chris Seaton for helping us extend the SeaFoam IR visualization tool to output the graph in Isabelle syntax. Thanks also to Kristian Thomassen for his work on the semantics of ϕ-nodes and Sadra Bayat Tork who investigated IR graph invariants in the GraalVM compiler.

References

1. Böhme, S., Moskal, M.: Heaps and data structures: a challenge for automated provers. In: Bjørner, N., Sofronie-Stokkermans, V. (eds.) CADE 2011. LNCS (LNAI), vol. 6803, pp. 177–191. Springer, Heidelberg (2011). https://doi.org/10.1007/978-3-642-22438-6_15
2. Click, C.: Global code motion/global value numbering. In: PLDI 1995, pp. 246–257. ACM Press (1995). https://doi.org/10.1145/207110.207154
3. Click, C., Cooper, K.D.: Combining analyses, combining optimizations. TOPLAS **17**(2), 181–196 (1995). https://doi.org/10.1145/201059.201061
4. Demange, D., Fernández de Retana, Y., Pichardie, D.: Semantic reasoning about the sea of nodes. In: CC 2018, pp. 163–173. ACM, New York (2018). https://doi.org/10.1145/3178372.3179503
5. Duboscq, G., et al.: An intermediate representation for speculative optimizations in a dynamic compiler. In: VMIL 2013, pp. 1–10 (2013)
6. Ferrante, J., Ottenstein, K.J., Warren, J.D.: The program dependence graph and its use in optimization. ACM TOPLAS **9**(3), 319–349 (1987). https://doi.org/10.1145/24039.24041
7. Kumar, R., Myreen, M.O., Norrish, M., Owens, S.: CakeML: a verified implementation of ML. In: POPL 2014, pp. 179–191. ACM Press, January 2014. https://doi.org/10.1145/2535838.2535841
8. Lattner, C., Adve, V.: LLVM: a compilation framework for lifelong program analysis & transformation. In: CGO 2004, pp. 75–86. IEEE Computer Society (2004)
9. Leroy, X., Blazy, S., Kästner, D., Schommer, B., Pister, M., Ferdinand, C.: CompCert - a formally verified optimizing compiler. In: ERTS 2016. SEE, Toulouse, January 2016. https://hal.inria.fr/hal-01238879
10. Li, L., Gunter, E.L.: K-LLVM: a relatively complete semantics of LLVM IR. In: Hirschfeld, R., Pape, T. (eds.) ECOOP 2020, vol. 166, pp. 7:1–7:29. Dagstuhl, Germany (2020). https://doi.org/10.4230/LIPIcs.ECOOP.2020.7
11. Lindholm, T., Yellin, F., Bracha, G., Buckley, A.: The Java virtual machine specification, February 2013. https://docs.oracle.com/javase/specs/jvms/se7/html/jvms-4.html. Chapter 4. The class File Format
12. Lochbihler, A.: Mechanising a type-safe model of multithreaded Java with a verified compiler. J. Autom. Reason. **63**(1), 243–332 (2018)
13. Nipkow, T., Paulson, L.C., Wenzel, M.: Isabelle/HOL: A Proof Assistant for Higher-Order Logic. LNCS, vol. 2283. Springer, Heidelberg (2002). https://doi.org/10.1007/3-540-45949-9
14. Oracle: GraalVM: Run programs faster anywhere (2020). https://github.com/oracle/graal
15. Zhao, J., Nagarakatte, S., Martin, M.M., Zdancewic, S.: Formalizing the LLVM intermediate representation for verified program transformations. In: POPL 2012, pp. 427–440. ACM, New York (2012). https://doi.org/10.1145/2103656.2103709

A Verified Decision Procedure for Orders in Isabelle/HOL

Lukas Stevens$^{(\boxtimes)}$ ⓘ and Tobias Nipkow ⓘ

Fakultät für Informatik, Technische Universität München, Munich, Germany
`lukas.stevens@in.tum.de`

Abstract. We present the first verified implementation of a decision procedure for the quantifier-free theory of partial and linear orders. We formalise the procedure in Isabelle/HOL and provide a specification that is made executable using Isabelle's code generator. The procedure is already part of the development version of Isabelle as a sub-procedure of the simplifier.

1 Introduction

Powerful proof automation facilities, e.g. `auto` in Isabelle, are crucial to make an interactive theorem prover practical. These tools fill in the logical steps that are trivial to humans and thus enable the users of interactive theorem provers to write formal proofs that resemble the less formal pen-and-paper proofs. Their efficacy in an interactive environment is judged by their completeness ("How many problems do they solve?") and their performance ("How fast do they solve the problems?"). Many of theses problems are undecidable in general; hence, incomplete heuristics, which are fast in practice, are used to tackle them. In decidable theories we can do better since they admit decision procedures, i.e. methods that always prove or disprove the goal at hand. Nevertheless, theorem provers sometimes still employ heuristics even for decidable theories. Isabelle in particular uses an unverified and incomplete ML procedure[1], which interprets a given set of (in)equalities as a graph, to decide partial and linear orders. As an example, the procedure fails to prove the goal

lemma assumes ¬ x < y and x = y and ¬ x ≤ y shows **False**

where ≤ is a partial order. Note that ¬ x < y is equivalent to x ≠ y ∨ x ≤ y for partial orders ≤. With that in mind, we investigate partial and linear order relations and develop decision procedures for them, which we prove to be sound and complete.

1.1 Related Work

The decidability of the first-order theory of linear orders was posed as a problem in a article by Janiczak [5] that was posthumously published. In a review of

---

[1] File path of the procedure in the Isabelle2021 distribution: `src/Provers/order.ML`.

© Springer Nature Switzerland AG 2021
Z. Hou and V. Ganesh (Eds.): ATVA 2021, LNCS 12971, pp. 127–143, 2021.
https://doi.org/10.1007/978-3-030-88885-5_9

the article from 1954, Kreisel [6] answers the question by reducing the theory of linear order to first-order monadic predicate calculus assuming no limit points in the order. Janiczak had died in 1951, though, and Kreisel's proof apparently went unnoticed in the literature. Subsequently, Ehrenfeucht [3] submitted an abstract that proposed a proof using model-theoretic methods; however, the result was never published. The problem was settled by Läuchli and Leonard [7], who proved decidability by showing both the set of valid and refutable sentences to be recursively enumerable.

More recently, Negri et al. [8] performed a proof-theoretical analysis of order relations in terms of a contraction-free sequent calculus. Their analysis showed that the quantifier-free theory of partial orders has the subterm property. Due to the nature of the calculus, it follows that the proof search is terminating thus yielding a decision procedure. The result also extends to linear orders.

1.2   Contributions

In this paper, we develop decision procedures for the quantifier-free theory of partial and linear orders and provide an executable specification in Isabelle/HOL [10], i.e. we can generate code from the specification using the code generator of Isabelle. More specifically, our procedure determines whether the conjunction $\bigwedge_{i=1}^{n} L_i$ is contradictory where each literal L_i is an (potentially negated) atom of the form $x = y$, $x \le y$ or $x < y$. Note that it is possible to generalise this to arbitrary propositional formulas ϕ by taking their disjunctive normal form (DNF) and applying the procedure to each clause: the formula ϕ is a contradiction if and only if all clauses of the DNF lead to a contradiction. The restriction to a single clause is reasonable because we integrated the procedure as a sub-procedure of the simplifier and by extension of the classical reasoning tactics of Isabelle. As they eliminate disjunctions by performing case distinctions, an explicit conversion to DNF is not necessary.

Unlike Negri et al. [8], whose proof-theoretic procedure is too far removed from an actual implementation to give an accurate bound on the running time, we provide an implementation of the decision procedure and state its complexity. We also define a proof system that provides us with a framework to certify any contradiction that the procedure finds. Soundness and completeness of the executable specification is fully verified in Isabelle/HOL.

The paper is structured as follows: we start by giving a formal semantics for order (in)equalities in Sect. 2. To determine whether a set of (in)equalities is contradictory, we present abstract decision procedures for partial and linear orders in Sect. 3 and 4, respectively. The executable specification presented in Sect. 6 uses the proof terms introduced in Sect. 5 to certify contradictions. The final Sect. 7 gives an overview of how the exported code obtained from the executable specification is used to implement a tactic that can be applied to proof goals in Isabelle.

· A copy of the formalisation is available online [12].

1.3   Notation

Isabelle/HOL conforms to everyday mathematical notation for the most part. For the benefit of the reader that is unfamiliar with Isabelle/HOL, we establish notation and in particular some essential datatypes together with their primitive operations that are specific to Isabelle/HOL. We write t :: 'a to specify that the term t has the type 'a and 'a ⇒ 'b for the type of a total function from 'a to 'b. The types for booleans, natural numbers, and in integers are bool, nat, and int, respectively. Sets with elements of type 'a have the type 'a set. Analogously, we use 'a list to describe lists, which are constructed as the empty list [] or with the infix constructor #, and are appended with the infix operator @. The function set converts a list into a set. For optional values, Isabelle/HOL offers the type option where a term opt :: 'a option is either None or Some a with a :: 'a. Finally, we remark that **iff** is equivalent to = on type bool and ≡ is definitional equality of the meta-logic of Isabelle/HOL, which is called Isabelle/Pure.

2   A Semantics for Orders

Since we only deal with a single conjunction $\bigwedge_{i=1}^{n} L_i$ of order literals, it is convenient to represent it in clause form, i.e. just as a set of literals. A literal consists of a boolean polarity and an order atom. If the boolean is True, they are called positive; conversely, when the boolean is False, we call them negative. Altogether we define the type of order atoms and literals as follows:

    type_synonym var = int

    datatype order_atom = var ≤ var | var < var | var = var

    type_synonym order_literal = bool × order_atom

The **boldface** symbols ≤, <, and = are ordinary constructors of the datatype chosen to resemble the (in)equalities they represent. Depending on context, we will abuse the notation for literals, e.g. we use x ≤ y to mean (True, x ≤ y) and x ≮ y to mean (False, x < y). We arbitrarily chose to represent variables with int for straightforward code generation but any linearly ordered type would do.

Semantically, a given order literal corresponds to a proposition that the (in)equality holds. To this end, we assign each variable x a value v x :: 'a and interpret the literals relative to a relation r :: 'a rel where 'a rel is a synonym for ('a × 'a) set. This allows us to apply the semantics in the context of any order relation by suitably constraining r. For example, we would demand that r is reflexive, transitive, and antisymmetric in the context of partial orders. We call a pair (r, v) a *model* of a literal a if (r, v) ⊨$_o$ a, as defined below, holds. If r is constrained to a specific kind of order relation, say a partial order, we will speak of a *partial order model* (r, v). The same notation is used for sets of literals A where (r, v) ⊨$_o$ A is equivalent to ∀a ∈ A. (r, v) ⊨$_o$ a.

```
fun ⊨ₒ :: 'a rel × (var ⇒ 'a) ⇒ order_literal ⇒ bool where
  (r, v) ⊨ₒ (p, x ≤ y) = (p ⟷ (v x, v y) ∈ r)
| (r, v) ⊨ₒ (p, x < y) = (p ⟷ (v x, v y) ∈ r ∧ v x ≠ v y)
| (r, v) ⊨ₒ (p, x = y) = (p ⟷ v x = v y)
```

3 Deciding Partial Orders

In this section, we will derive an abstract specification for a procedure that decides the theory of partial orders. For the time being, we assume that the set of (in)equalities A does not contain any strict inequalities and instead deal with them later in Sect. 5.2. In order to satisfy the (in)equalities, we need to come up with a partial order r and a variable assignment v that are a model of A, i.e. $(r, v) \models_o A$. We build a syntactic model where the variable assignment maps every variable to itself, i.e. we set v = (λx. x). To find the accompanying relation, we first define a relation leq1 A that contains all pairs that are directly given by the set of (in)equalities; for example, we add (x, y) if x ≤ y ∈ A. A partial order has to be reflexive and transitive so we define leq A as the smallest reflexive and transitive relation that contains leq1 A.

definition leq1 A ≡ {(x, y). x ≤ y ∈ A ∨ x = y ∈ A ∨ y = x ∈ A}
definition leq A ≡ (leq1 A)*

Since we chose v to be the identity, we can directly read off all inequalities that must hold from leq A. Furthermore, we can use the same inequalities to derive all equalities that must hold by antisymmetry: the equality x = y must hold if both (x, y) ∈ leq A and (y, x) ∈ leq A. Bossert and Suzumura [2] call this subset of a relation the symmetric factor.

definition sym_factor r ≡ r ∩ r⁻¹

The symmetric factor is clearly a symmetric relation. Considering that reflexivity and transitivity is invariant under inversion and intersection, we conclude that sym_factor r is an equivalence relation for any relation r that is reflexive and transitive. The symmetric factor of leq A, called eq A, is thus an equivalence relation.

abbreviation eq A ≡ sym_factor (leq A)

Equipped with the relations leq A and eq A, we are ready to define the abstract decision procedure. It uses these relations, which are derived from the positive literals in A, and checks for consistency with the negative literals in A.

definition contr :: order_literal set ⇒ bool where
contr A ⟷ (∃ x y. x ≰ y ∈ A ∧ (x, y) ∈ leq A) ∨
                   (∃ x y. x ≠ y ∈ A ∧ (x, y) ∈ eq A)

We claim that contr is a decision procedure for the theory of partial orders. To verify this claim, we have to prove soundness and completeness of contr with respect to our semantics $\models_o$. More precisely, we have to show that contr A evaluates to `True` if and only if `A` is contradictory, i.e. there exists no partial order model `(r, v)` of `A`. We prove both directions in contrapositive form, starting with soundness.

```
theorem contr_sound:
  assumes refl r and trans r and antisym r and (r, v) ⊨ₒ A
  shows ¬ contr A
```

The soundness proof, which is sketched below, uses the following lemma.

```
lemma assumes (x, y) ∈ leq A and (r, v) ⊨ₒ A shows (v x, v y) ∈ r*
```

Proof (Soundness). We assume `contr` `A` and therefore must show `False`. It holds by definition of `contr` `A` that a negative literal in `A` contradicts with either `leq` `A` or `eq` `A`.

We first consider the case where $x \not\leq y \in$ `A` and `(x, y)` $\in$ `leq A` for some `x` and `y`. Using the assumption `(r, v)` $\models_o$ `A`, we can apply the above lemma to conclude that `(v x, v y)` $\in$ `r*`. Moreover, we have that `r*` = `r` because we assumed that `r` is reflexive and transitive. But this is a contradiction to the assumption `(r, v)` $\models_o$ `A` which requires `(r, v)` $\models_o$ $(x \not\leq y) \longleftrightarrow$ `(v x, v y)` $\notin$ `r` to hold.

In the remaining case we have $x \neq y \in$ `A` and `(x, y)` $\in$ `eq A`. Remember that we defined `eq A` as the symmetric factor of `leq A` which implies that `(x, y)` $\in$ `leq A` and `(y, x)` $\in$ `leq A`. With the same argument as above it follows that `(v x, v y)` $\in$ `r` and `(v y, v x)` $\in$ `r`, and, by antisymmetry, `v x = v y`; however, this contradicts the assumption `(r, v)` $\models_o$ `A` which entails `(r, v)` $\models_o$ $(x \neq y) \longleftrightarrow$ `v x` $\neq$ `v y`. ⊓

For completeness, on the other hand, we have to show that there exists a partial order model `(r, v)` for `A` if ¬ `contr A`. A tempting candidate for `r` would be `leq A` but then again `leq A` is only a preorder: it is not antisymmetric because it captures the relation between distinct variables, not their values. This means that `v` must map distinct variables `x` and `y` to the same value `v x = v y` if `(x, y)` $\in$ `leq A` and `(y, x)` $\in$ `leq A`. In other words, we have to take the quotient set of `leq A` with respect to the equivalence relation `eq A`.

Viewing `leq A` more abstractly as a preorder `r` on some set `C`, we have to map each variable `x` to its equivalence class in the equivalence relation `sym_factor r`. Lifting `r` to the quotient set `C // sym_factor r`, where `//` is Isabelle notation for the quotient, yields an antisymmetric relation and therefore a partial order.

```
definition sym_class r x ≡ {y | (x, y) ∈ sym_factor r}
definition sym_class_rel r ≡ {(sym_class r x, sym_class r y) |
                             (x, y) ∈ r}
```

We confirm that the lifting works as intended with the following lemma.

```
lemma assumes preorder_on C r
       shows (x, y) ∈ r ⟷
                   (sym_class r x, sym_class r y) ∈ sym_class_rel r
```

Now, we apply these ideas to the relation `leq A` to obtain the partial order `Leq A`. Additionally, we take the reflexive closure of `Leq A` to obtain a partial order on the whole universe `UNIV` of the type `var set`.

> **abbreviation** Eq :: (bool × atom) set ⇒ var ⇒ var set
>   where Eq A x ≡ sym_class (leq A) x

> **abbreviation** Leq :: (bool × atom) set ⇒ var rel
>   where Leq A ≡ sym_class_rel (leq A)

> **abbreviation** Leq_refl ≡ (Leq A)⁼

We show that, if ¬ `contr A`, then the interpretation (`Leq_refl A`, `Eq A`) is a model of A thus proving completeness of `contr`.

> **theorem** contr_complete:
>   assumes ¬ contr A shows (Leq_refl A, Eq A) ⊨$_o$ A

Proof. We show that for any a ∈ A it holds that (`Leq_refl A`, `Eq A`) ⊨$_o$ a. By case distinction on a, we prove that the statement holds for any kind of literal a. The proofs of the different cases are similar so we only present the case a = x ≰ y for some x and y. Considering the definition of `contr` it follows from the assumption ¬ `contr A` that (x, y) ∉ `leq A`. This means that x ≠ y because `leq A` is reflexive. Moreover, we apply the above lemma to obtain (Eq A x, Eq A y) ∉ `Leq A`. Again, `Leq A` is reflexive on `UNIV // eq A` so we have Eq A x ≠ Eq A y. Since `Leq_refl A` only adds reflexive pairs to `Leq A`, we can conclude that (Eq A x, Eq A y) ∉ `Leq_refl A`. This gives us our goal (`Leq_refl A`, `Eq A`) ⊨$_o$ x ≤ y ⟷ (Eq A x, Eq A y) ∉ `Leq_refl A`. □

4   Deciding Linear Orders

We now show that the procedure `contr` can be modified to decide linear orders. Recall that the soundness of `contr` assumes that the underlying relation r is a partial order. This means that the soundness of `contr` for linear orders is trivial as every linear order is a partial order. Again, completeness is more involved since we have to construct a linear order model for A if ¬ `contr A` holds. Thus, we cannot reuse `Leq_refl A` because it is only a partial order. All is not lost, though: we can appeal to a classical result from order theory, namely Szpilrajn's extension theorem [13]. The original theorem states that every relation that is transitive and asymmetric, i.e. is a strict partial order, can be extended to a relation that is also total. A more general version of the theorem, which in particular applies to non-strict partial orders, was formalised in Isabelle/HOL by Zeller and Stevens in an AFP entry [14]. Using this result, we can prove that every partial order can be extended to a linear order.

> **theorem** partial_order_extension:
>   assumes **partial_order** r shows ∃ R. linear_order R ∧ r ⊆ R

We use Hilbert's ε-operator in the form of SOME to obtain an arbitrary extension Leq_ext A of the partial order Leq_refl A.

definition Leq_ext A ≡ (SOME r. linear_order r ∧ Leq_refl A ⊆ r)

Theorem partial_order_extension guarantees that such an extension exists so Leq_ext A is well-defined.

theorem linear_order (Leq_ext A) and Leq_refl A ⊆ Leq_ext A

Both Leq_refl A and Leq_ext A are reflexive and antisymmetric, which means that for any x, y with Eq A x = Eq A y we have

(Eq A x, Eq A y) ∈ Leq_refl A ⟷ (Eq A x, Eq A y) ∈ Leq_ext A.

Therefore, Leq_ext A is consistent with negative literals of the form x ≠ y ∈ A. The other case, that is to say literals of the form x ≰ y ∈ A, is not so easy: how can we ensure that the extension from Leq_refl A to Leq_ext A does not introduce (Eq A x, Eq A y) ∈ Leq_ext? Fortunately, we can sidestep the problem by exploiting the properties of linear orders: for any linear order r it holds that

$$(r, v) \vDash_o (x \not\leq y) \longleftrightarrow (v\ x, v\ y) \notin r$$
$$\longleftrightarrow v\ x \neq v\ y \wedge (v\ y, v\ x) \in r$$
$$\longleftrightarrow (r, v) \vDash_o x \neq y, y \leq x.$$

In other words, we can replace all literals of the form x ≰ y by the two literals x ≠ y and y ≤ x while maintaining the completeness of contr. Employing this preprocessing step, we obtain a sound and complete decision procedure for linear orders.

5   Certification with Proof Terms

We aim to generate an executable specification of the decision procedure in order to automatically generate code from it; however, we do not want to trust the code generation facilities of Isabelle. Instead, the executable specification has to certify any contradiction it finds with a proof term, which is then replayed through Isabelle's inference kernel to obtain a theorem.

5.1   Basic Proof System for Partial Orders

The proof system we define is very limited as the only kind of provable propositions are order literals. Since we chose to define order literals without an explicit constructor representing the boolean value False but ultimately want to deduce a contradiction, we define False in terms of the order literal 0 ≠ 0, that is Fls ≡ 0 ≠ 0. With this, we define the proof system $\vdash_P$ for partial orders (see Fig. 1), where A $\vdash_P$ p : l means that the proof term p proves the proposition l under the set of assumptions A. For now, we will pretend that proof terms are defined as a datatype with one constructor for each rule as shown below. We will discuss the actual definition of proof terms in Sect. 5.

$$\frac{\mathtt{x} \leq \mathtt{y} \in \mathtt{A}}{\mathtt{A} \vdash_P \mathtt{AssmP} \ (\mathtt{x} \leq \mathtt{y}) \ : \ \mathtt{x} \leq \mathtt{y}} \ \text{Assm} \qquad \frac{}{\mathtt{A} \vdash_P \mathtt{ReflP} \ \mathtt{x} \ : \ \mathtt{x} \leq \mathtt{x}} \ \text{Refl}$$

$$\frac{\mathtt{A} \vdash_P \mathtt{p1} \ : \ \mathtt{x} \leq \mathtt{y} \qquad \mathtt{A} \vdash_P \mathtt{p2} \ : \ \mathtt{y} \leq \mathtt{z}}{\mathtt{A} \vdash_P \mathtt{TransP} \ \mathtt{p1} \ \mathtt{p2} \ : \ \mathtt{x} \leq \mathtt{z}} \ \text{Trans}$$

$$\frac{\mathtt{A} \vdash_P \mathtt{p1} \ : \ \mathtt{x} \leq \mathtt{y} \qquad \mathtt{A} \vdash_P \mathtt{p2} \ : \ \mathtt{y} \leq \mathtt{x}}{\mathtt{A} \vdash_P \mathtt{AntisymP} \ \mathtt{p1} \ \mathtt{p2} \ : \ \mathtt{x} = \mathtt{y}} \ \text{Antisym}$$

$$\frac{\mathtt{x} = \mathtt{y} \in \mathtt{A}}{\mathtt{A} \vdash_P \mathtt{EQE1P} \ (\mathtt{x} = \mathtt{y}) \ : \ \mathtt{x} \leq \mathtt{y}} \ \text{EqE1} \qquad \frac{\mathtt{x} = \mathtt{y} \in \mathtt{A}}{\mathtt{A} \vdash_P \mathtt{EQE2P} \ (\mathtt{x} = \mathtt{y}) \ : \ \mathtt{y} \leq \mathtt{x}} \ \text{EqE2}$$

$$\frac{(\mathtt{False, \ a}) \in \mathtt{A} \qquad \mathtt{A} \vdash_P \mathtt{p} \ : \ (\mathtt{True, \ a})}{\mathtt{A} \vdash_P \mathtt{ContrP} \ (\mathtt{False, \ a}) \ \mathtt{p} \ : \ \mathtt{Fls}} \ \text{Contr}$$

Fig. 1. The proof system $\vdash_P$ for partial orders

```
datatype prf_trm = AssmP order_literal | ReflP order_literal |
  TransP prf_trm prf_trm | AntisymP prf_trm prf_trm |
  EQE1P order_literal | EQE2P order_literal |
  Contr order_literal prf_trm | ...
```

Every proof rule corresponds to a step the procedure `contr` takes:

- The relation `leq1 A` contains those pairs $(\mathtt{x}, \mathtt{y})$ for which we can prove $\mathtt{A} \vdash_P \mathtt{p} : \mathtt{x} \leq \mathtt{y}$ directly by assumption using one of Assm, EqE1, or EqE2.
- We obtain `leq A` from `leq1 A` by taking the reflexive transitive closure. Put another way, $(\mathtt{x}, \mathtt{y}) \in$ `leq A` holds if and only if $\mathtt{A} \vdash_P \mathtt{p} : \mathtt{x} \leq \mathtt{y}$ can be proved by repeatedly applying the rules Refl and Trans.
- Since `eq A` is the symmetric factor of `leq A`, it contains exactly those pairs $(\mathtt{x}, \mathtt{y})$ for which $\mathtt{A} \vdash_P \mathtt{p} : \mathtt{x} = \mathtt{y}$ is provable by the rule Antisym.
- Finally, we check if the negative literals are consistent with the relations `leq A` and `eq A`. Any inconsistency can be certified by the rule Contr.

Due to this close correspondence it is not surprising that we can prove the following lemmas.

```
lemma (x, y) ∈ leq A ⟷ ∃p. A ⊢_P p : x ≤ y
lemma (x, y) ∈ eq A ⟷ ∃p. A ⊢_P p : x = y
```

Using these lemmas, the soundness and completeness of the proof system relative to `contr`—and by extension to $\models_o$—follow easily.

theorem $\vdash_P$_sound: assumes $\mathtt{A} \vdash_P \mathtt{p} : \mathtt{Fls}$ shows `contr A`
theorem $\vdash_P$_complete: assumes `contr A` shows $\exists \mathtt{p}. \ \mathtt{A} \vdash_P \mathtt{p} : \mathtt{Fls}$

5.2 Dealing with Strict Literals Through Rewriting

Until now, we assumed that the set of literals A does not contain any strict literals, i.e. literals of the form x $<$ y or x $\not<$ y. For the case of linear orders r, dealing with those literals is just a matter of replacing them by equivalent, non-strict literals:

- $(r, v) \vDash_o (x < y) \longleftrightarrow (v\ x, v\ y) \in r \land v\ x \neq v\ y$
$$\longleftrightarrow (r, v) \vDash_o x \leq y, x \neq y$$

- $(r, v) \vDash_o (x \not< y) \longleftrightarrow (v\ x, v\ y) \notin r \lor v\ x = v\ y$
$$\longleftrightarrow (v\ y, v\ x) \in r \lor v\ x = v\ y$$
$$\longleftrightarrow (r, v) \vDash_o (y \leq x)$$

Now, if r is a partial order, the same holds for the former case but in the latter case we are stuck after the first step: $(v\ x, v\ y) \notin r \leftrightarrow (v\ y, v\ x) \in r$ does not hold. A possible solution is that we (recursively) check whether both contr ($\{x \not\leq y\} \cup A - \{x \not< y\}$) and contr ($\{x = y\} \cup A - \{x \not< y\}$) hold. This was the first approach we tried but we ultimately found that the matching proof rule made reasoning about the proof terms tedious. Following Nipkow [9], we took a more general approach and introduced a type of propositional formulae with order literals as propositional atoms. Both replacement of literals and conversion to DNF are represented as rewrite rules on formulae. The semantics of order literals naturally generalises to formulae but, for brevity, we forgo discussing how we proved the soundness of the rewrite rules with respect to the semantics. A formula is either an atom or one of the logical connectives conjunction, disjunction, or negation:

```
datatype 'a fm = Atom 'a |
    And ('a fm) ('a fm) | Or ('a fm) ('a fm) | Neg ('a fm)
```

Motivated by the need to replace the order literals in the formula by other literals respectively formulae, we define amap$_{fm}$ which allows us to apply a replacement function to all atoms of a formula.

```
fun amap_fm :: ('a ⇒ 'b fm) ⇒ 'a fm ⇒ 'b fm where
    amap_fm f (Atom a) = f a
|  amap_fm f (And φ₁ φ₂) = And (amap_fm f φ₁) (amap_fm f φ₂)
|  amap_fm f (Or φ₁ φ₂) = Or (amap_fm f φ₁) (amap_fm f φ₂)
|  amap_fm f (Neg φ) = Neg (amap_fm f φ)
```

We now define a function deless for partial orders that transforms a strict literal into a formula without strict literals.

```
fun deless :: order_literal ⇒ order_literal fm where
    deless (x < y) = And (Atom (x ≤ y)) (Atom (x ≠ y))
|  deless (x ≮ y) = Or (Atom (x ≰ y)) (Atom (x = y))
|  deless a = Atom a
```

We use the rules of the proof systems in Fig. 2 to certify the rewrite steps that amap$_{\text{fm}}$ deless performs. The proof system for formulae $\equiv_{\text{fm}}$ is parametrised by a proof system for atoms $\equiv_{\text{a}}$. Again, you may imagine that the datatype of proof terms has a constructor for each rule of the proof systems.

$$\frac{}{\text{LessLe : } x < y \equiv_{\text{a}} \text{And (Atom } (x \leq y)) \text{ (Atom } (x \neq y))} \quad \text{LessLe}$$

$$\frac{}{\text{NlessLe : } x \not< y \equiv_{\text{a}} \text{Or (Atom } (x \not\leq y)) \text{ (Atom } (x = y))} \quad \text{NlessLe}$$

$$\frac{p \; : \; a \equiv_{\text{a}} \phi}{\text{AtomConv } p \; : \; \text{Atom } a \equiv_{\text{fm}} \phi} \quad \text{AtomConv} \qquad \frac{}{\text{AllConv} \; : \; \phi \equiv_{\text{fm}} \phi} \quad \text{AllConv}$$

$$\frac{p \; : \; \phi \equiv_{\text{fm}} \psi}{\text{NegConv } p \; : \; \text{Neg } \phi \equiv_{\text{fm}} \text{Neg } \psi} \quad \text{NegConv}$$

$$\frac{\text{bop} \in \{\text{And, Or}\} \qquad \text{p1} \; : \; \phi_1 \equiv_{\text{fm}} \psi_1 \qquad \text{p2} \; : \; \phi_2 \equiv_{\text{fm}} \psi_2}{\text{BinopConv p1 p2} \; : \; \text{bop } \phi_1 \; \phi_2 \equiv_{\text{fm}} \text{bop } \psi_1 \; \psi_2} \quad \text{BinopConv}$$

Fig. 2. Proof system $\equiv_{\text{fm}}$ for conversions of formulae

We use the above rules to define functions that produce a proof term for amap$_{\text{fm}}$ deless.

```
fun amapfm_prf :: ('a ⇒ prf_trm) ⇒ 'a fm ⇒ prf_trm where
   amapfm_prf ap (Atom a) = AtomConv (ap a)
|  amapfm_prf ap (And φ1 φ2) =
      BinopConv (amapfm_prf ap φ1) (amapfm_prf ap φ2)
|  amapfm_prf ap (Or φ1 φ2) =
      BinopConv (amapfm_prf ap φ1) (amapfm_prf ap φ2)
|  amapfm_prf ap (Neg φ) = ArgConv (amapfm_prf ap φ)

fun deless_prf :: order_literal ⇒ prf_trm where
   deless (x < y) = LessLe
|  deless (x ≮ y) = NlessLe
|  deless_prf _ = AllConv
```

We can show that $\phi \equiv_{\text{fm}} \text{amap}_{\text{fm}} \text{ deless } \phi \; : \; \text{amap}_{\text{fm}}\text{\_prf deless\_prf } \phi$ by a simple inductive proof. After this conversion, the resulting formula may contain disjunctions but our decision procedure can only deal with conjunctions; thus, we first have to compute the DNF of ψ and apply the procedure to each clause. Certifying the conversion to DNF follows a similar approach to amap$_{\text{fm}}$ so we refer to the formalisation for the details. This conversion also eliminates negations in the formula by pushing them into the atoms. Now assume that we are given a formula ϕ in DNF without negations, we still need to apply the decision procedure to each clause of the formula. As conversions alone are not sufficient, we build a proof system for propositional logic on top of conversions.

Similarly to the system $\equiv_{\mathtt{fm}}$, the proof system $\vdash$ in Fig. 3 is parametrised by a proof system for atoms $\vdash_a$ (with the same type as $\vdash_P$).

$$\frac{A \vdash_a p : \phi}{A \vdash p : \phi} \text{ LIFT} \qquad \frac{\text{And } c\ d \in A \qquad A,c,d \vdash p : \phi}{A \vdash \text{ConjE } c\ d\ p : \phi} \text{ CONJE}$$

$$\frac{\text{Or } c\ d \in A \qquad A,c \vdash p1 : \phi \qquad A,d \vdash p2 : \phi}{A \vdash \text{DisjE } c\ d\ p1\ p2 : \phi} \text{ DISJE}$$

$$\frac{c \in A \qquad c \equiv_{\mathtt{fm}} d : cp \qquad A,d \vdash p : \phi}{A \vdash \text{Conv } cp\ p : \phi} \text{ CONV}$$

Fig. 3. Propositional proof system for formulae.

A clause C of a formula in DNF consists of nested applications of the constructor **And** with **Atom** constructors as leaves. We first define a function `conj_list` that computes the atoms of C. Along with it, we define a function `from_conj_prf` that uses the rule CONJE to convert the proof p that assumes every atom in `from_conj` C into a proof that just assumes C.

```
fun conj_list :: 'a fm ⇒ 'a list where
   conj_list (And φ₁ φ₂) = conj_list φ₁ @ conj_list φ₂
 | conj_list (Atom a) = [a]
```

```
fun from_conj_prf :: prf_trm ⇒ 'a fm ⇒ prf_trm where
   from_conj_prf p (And a b) =
     ConjE a b (from_conj_prf (from_conj_prf p b) a)
 | from_conj_prf p (Atom a) = p
```

Let `contr_prf`$_a$ `:: 'a list ⇒ prf_trm option` be a function that tries to derive a contradiction from a list of atoms. We will define an instance `contr_list` of `contr_prf`$_a$ that refines the abstract procedure `contr` in the upcoming section. In order to prove that ϕ is contradictory, we first recurse down to its clauses and apply `contr_prf`$_a$ to each clause. Then, if each clause is contradictory, we combine those inductively with the rule DISJE to obtain a proof for the whole formula.

```
fun contr_fm_prf :: 'a fm ⇒ prf_trm option where
   contr_fm_prf (Or c d) = case (contr_fm_prf c, contr_fm_prf d) of
     (Some p1, Some p2) ⇒ Some (DisjE c d p1 p2) | _ ⇒ None
 | contr_fm_prf (And a b) = case contr_prfₐ (conj_list (And a b)) of
     Some p ⇒ Some (from_conj_prf p (And a b)) | None ⇒ None
 | contr_fm_prf (Atom a) = contr_prfₐ [a]
```

To summarise, we now have the tools to preprocess a conjunction of partial order literals such that we can apply the decision procedure `contr` to the clauses of the resulting formula. By introducing appropriate proof terms, the same tools can be applied to linear orders where it is not necessary to convert to DNF.

The functions as defined above are amenable to code generation; thus, the only missing part is an executable specification for `contr`, which is the topic of the next section.

6 Refinement to Executable Specification

The executable specification utilises the abstract datatype (`'a`, `'b`) `mapping`, which is a partial map `'a` ⇒ `'b` `option` from keys to values. Isabelle's library conveniently provides a refinement of `mapping` to red-black trees, thereby making `mapping` executable [4]. We will need the following operations on this datatype:

– `Mapping.keys` m give us all keys of the map m that have an associated value.
– `Mapping.entries` m gives us the entries of the map m, i.e. all key-value pairs.
– `Mapping.of_alist` as converts the association list as into a map.

The prefix `Mapping` will be dropped in what follows.

Remember that, at its core, the decision procedure computes the relation `leq A` where for each (x, y) ∈ `leq A`, there exists a proof p such that A ⊢$_P$ p : x ≤ y. Computing `leq A` boils down to computing the transitive closure of the finite relation `leq1 A` while keeping track of the corresponding proof terms. Note that we only assume finiteness for the sake of executability; the abstract decision procedure does not make this assumption. This in turn allows us to only consider a finite number of terms of (`leq1 A`)$^+$ = $\bigcup_{i=0}^{\infty}$ (`leq1 A`)$^{i+1}$. More specifically, if `leq1 A` contains n pairs, then it is sufficient to only consider the first n terms. We implement this naively by iterating over n while accumulating the n-fold relational composition. We claim (without formal proof) that this yields a running time of $\mathcal{O}(n^4 \log(n))$ where the logarithmic component is due to the implementation being based on red-black trees. Using the Floyd-Warshall-Algorithm and arrays instead of red-black trees, the running time could be improved to $\mathcal{O}(v^3) \subseteq \mathcal{O}(n^3)$ where v is the number of distinct variables in the set of (in)equalities A. This optimisation, however, is unlikely to pay off since the goals tend to be small: throughout the whole basic library of Isabelle/HOL the number of order literals never exceeds 13. Although computing the transitive closure dominates the running time of the procedure, it must be noted that case analyses on literals of the form x ≮ y incur an exponential number of calls to the procedure. Altogether we obtain a function `trancl_mapping` that computes the transitive closure.

```
lemma assumes finite (keys m)
        shows keys (trancl_mapping m) = trancl (keys m)
```

and keeps track of the proof terms:

```
lemma assumes finite (keys m)
            and ∀((x, y), p) ∈ entries m. A ⊢P p : x ≤ y
        shows ∀((x, y), p) ∈ entries (trancl_mapping m). A ⊢P p : x ≤ y
```

As explained above we assume the set of order literals to be finite so we represent it as list. This makes defining an executable refinement for leq1 straightforward. Here, computing the intermediate leq1_list is done strictly to simplify the proofs as one could use a fold over the mapping to obtain leq1_mapping directly.

```
fun leq1_member_list :: order_literal
                     ⇒ ((var × var) × prf_trm) list where
  leq1_member_list (x ≤ y) = [ ((x, y), AssmP (x ≤ y)) ]
| leq1_member_list (x = y) =
    [ ((x, y), EQE1P (x = y)), ((y, x), EQE2P (x = y)) ]
| leq1_member_list _ = []

definition leq1_list A ≡ concat (map leq1_member_list A)
definition leq1_mapping A ≡ of_alist (leq1_list A)
```

Equipped with the above functions, we can compute the transitive closure trancl_mapping (leq1_mapping A); thus, we are only missing the reflexive closure to have a refinement of leq. The reflexive closure for an infinite carrier type, however, would yield an infinite set. Therefore, we only represent the set implicitly with the predicate is_in_leq that, for a given pair (x, y), returns some proof $A \vdash_P p : x \leq y$ if and only if $(x, y) \in$ leq A. Similarly, we define is_in_eq by combining the proofs we get from is_in_leq with the rule ANTISYM. We pass around trancl_mapping (leq1_mapping A) as the argument leqm to avoid recomputing it.

```
definition is_in_leq leqm (x, y) ≡
  if x = y then Some (ReflP x) else lookup leqm l

definition is_in_eq leqm (x, y) ≡
  case (is_in_leq leqm (x, y), is_in_leq leqm (y, x)) of
    (Some p1, Some p2) ⇒ Some (AntisymP p1 p2) | _ ⇒ None
```

Putting things together, we try to find the first negative literal in A that stands in contradiction to either is_in_leq or is_in_eq. In case we find one, we produce a proof of contradiction by mapping Contr over the value with map_option :: ('a ⇒ 'b) ⇒ 'a option ⇒ 'b option.

```
fun contr1_list :: ((var × var), prf_trm) mapping ⇒ order_literal
                ⇒ prf_trm option where
  contr1_list leqm (x ≤ y) =
    map_option (ContrP (x ≤ y)) (is_in_leq leqm (x, y))
| contr1_list leqm (x ≠ y) =
    map_option (ContrP (x ≠ y)) (is_in_eq leqm (x, y))
| contr1_list _ _ = None

fun contr_list_aux where
  contr_list_aux leqm [] = None
| contr_list_aux leqm (l#ls) = case contr1_list leqm l of
    Some p ⇒ Some p | None ⇒ contr_list_aux leqm ls
```

```
definition contr_list A ≡
  contr_list_aux (trancl_mapping (leq1_mapping A)) A
```

The executable specification `contr_list` refines `contr`.

```
theorem contr (set A) ⟷ (∃p. contr_list A = Some p)
```

7   From Exported Code to Integrated Proof Tactic

In the previous sections, we demonstrated how to refine the abstract decision procedure down to an executable specification. We can now generate Standard ML code from it that, assuming the code generator to be correct, implements the specification. Nevertheless, the procedure only works on a simple term language of propositional formulas with order literals as their atoms. To integrate the procedure back into Isabelle as a full-blown tactic, we have to convert a goal given in the higher-order term language of Isabelle into our simple term language on the one hand and replay the proof terms produced by the procedure through Isabelle's inference kernel on the other hand. The first aspect is taken care of by some hand-written ML code that

- brings the goal into a form where we have to prove `False`,
- extracts those assumptions that are order literals,
- converts the literals into our simple representation, e.g. for the term $s \leq t$ it replaces $\leq$ by the constructor $\leq$ and s and t by integer variables,
- and builds conjunction from the converted literals using `And`.

Passing the conjunction of literals to the exported code produces a proof term in the format that we sketched in Sect. 5. There, we pretended that each rule of the proof system has a designated proof term constructor, which would require replay code for every constructor. In reality we use a more general format for the proof terms, namely a simplified version of Isabelle's proof terms as introduced by Berghofer and Nipkow [1]. Both terms and proof terms are less expressive in our representation. First, terms only consist of constants, function application, and variables, where each variable stands for an Isabelle term as explained above. In particular, there is no function abstraction.

```
datatype trm = Const String.literal | App trm trm | Var var
```

As for the proof terms, they are less expressive as well: we have proof constants, proof variables bound by an enclosing proof abstraction, proof application, proof abstraction, term application, and conversions but no term abstractions and no instantiation of proof constants. In contrast to Isabelle's proof terms, we refer to bound proofs by their proposition, i.e. with a term, instead of using variables. This is to avoid dealing with bound variable indices, which simplifies reasoning about proof terms. Conversion proofs are strictly for convenience as the other constructors would be sufficient to represent equational proofs.

```
datatype prf_trm = PThm String.literal | Bound trm
  | AppP prf_trm prf_trm | AbsP trm prf_trm
  | Appt prf_trm trm | Conv trm prf_trm prf_trm
```

In Fig. 4, we define a proof system where we write $\Gamma \vdash \mathtt{p} : \phi$ to mean that, in the context Γ, the proof term $\mathtt{p}$ proves the proposition ϕ. The context Γ contains propositions and conversions but no terms because we omitted term abstractions. Quoting bound proof variables in Γ by their term requires us to convert the simple terms to Isabelle terms. For this, we use the function $\mathtt{dr}$ that maps constants to Isabelle constants and variables back to their corresponding Isabelle terms. Proof constants $\mathtt{PThm}$ $\mathtt{c}$ are interpreted by the environment $\Sigma(\mathtt{c})$, which maps them to the corresponding propositions. Finally, we use the function $\mathtt{rpc(cp)}$ to convert a conversion proof into an Isabelle conversion.

$$\frac{\Sigma(\mathtt{c}) = \phi}{\Gamma \vdash \mathtt{PThm}\ \mathtt{c} : \phi}\ \text{PThm} \qquad \frac{}{\Gamma, \mathtt{dr}(\phi) \vdash \mathtt{Bound}\ \phi : \mathtt{dr}(\phi)}\ \text{Bound}$$

$$\frac{\Gamma, \phi \vdash \mathtt{p} : \psi}{\Gamma \vdash \mathtt{AbsP}\ \phi\ \mathtt{p} : \phi \Longrightarrow \psi}\ \text{AbsP} \qquad \frac{\Gamma \vdash \mathtt{p} : \phi \Longrightarrow \psi \qquad \Gamma \vdash \mathtt{q} : \phi}{\Gamma \vdash \mathtt{AppP}\ \mathtt{p}\ \mathtt{q} : \psi}\ \text{AppP}$$

$$\frac{\Gamma \vdash \mathtt{p} : \bigwedge \mathtt{x}.\ \phi}{\Gamma \vdash \mathtt{Appt}\ \mathtt{p}\ \mathtt{t} : \phi[\mathtt{dr}(\mathtt{t})/\mathtt{x}]}\ \text{Appt}$$

$$\frac{\mathtt{rpc(cp)} = \mathtt{cv} \qquad \mathtt{cv}(\mathtt{dr}(\pi)) = (\mathtt{dr}(\pi) \equiv \sigma) \qquad \Gamma, \mathtt{dr}(\pi), \sigma \vdash \mathtt{p} : \phi}{\Gamma, \mathtt{dr}(\pi) \vdash \mathtt{Conv}\ \pi\ \mathtt{cp}\ \mathtt{p} : \phi}\ \text{Conv}$$

Fig. 4. Proof system for proof terms

The rules for proof abstraction AbsP and for proof application AppP correspond to introduction respectively elimination of Isabelle's meta-implication $\Longrightarrow$. Similarly, applying a term to a proof with Appt is equivalent to elimination of the universal meta-quantification $\bigwedge$. Those rules are modelled after primitives of the Isabelle's inference kernel so they are straightforward to replay. The remaining rules, on the other hand, require retrieving information from the context Γ, which is implemented as follows: mapping from theorem and conversion constants $\mathtt{PThm}$ $\mathtt{c}$ to the respective theorems and conversions is realised with association lists. Likewise, we save the bound proof terms in a map from terms to theorems, recursively extending the map with assumptions introduced by AbsP while replaying the proof term. The function $\mathtt{rpc}$ that constructs a conversion from proof applications and conversion constants is straightforward to implement. Applying the resulting conversion to the specified bound proof term and adding the new theorem to the context completes the implementation of Conv.

The procedure is already part of the development version of Isabelle[2] where it is registered to the simplifier as a so-called solver. As such, the procedure is

---

[2] Introduced in commit https://isabelle-dev.sketis.net/rISABELLEa3cc9fa129.

called whenever the simplifier is out of applicable rewrite rules. This is helpful when, for example, the simplifier wants to apply a conditional rewrite rule whose premises talk about set inclusion (which is a partial order). Since our procedure is more powerful than the old one, more rewrite rules apply which resulted in some broken proofs that had to be fixed. There were no significant changes in performance in comparison to the old procedure.

8   Conclusion

We provided the first verified implementation of a decision procedure for the quantifier-free theory of partial and linear orders. Although we closely followed the Isabelle/HOL formalisation in our presentation, the findings are not specific to Isabelle: any reasonably powerful theorem prover could use the code exported from the specification and replay the proof terms that it produces. In future work, we plan to apply the methodology presented here to the quantifier-free theory of (reflexive) transitive closure. Another direction is to replace our terms and proof terms by those from the formalisation of Isabelle's meta-logic [11], allowing us to reason about higher-order terms directly instead of translating between them and our simple terms.

Acknowledgements. We thank Kevin Kappelmann and the anonymous reviewers for their comments.

References

1. Berghofer, S., Nipkow, T.: Proof terms for simply typed higher order logic. In: Aagaard, M., Harrison, J. (eds.) TPHOLs 2000. LNCS, vol. 1869, pp. 38–52. Springer, Heidelberg (2000). https://doi.org/10.1007/3-540-44659-1_3
2. Bossert, W., Suzumura, K.: Consistency, Choice, and Rationality. Harvard University Press, Cambridge (2010)
3. Ehrenfeucht, A.: Decidability of the theory of linear order. Not. Am. Math. Soc. **6**, 268–269 (1959)
4. Haftmann, F., Krauss, A., Kunčar, O., Nipkow, T.: Data refinement in Isabelle/HOL. In: Blazy, S., Paulin-Mohring, C., Pichardie, D. (eds.) ITP 2013. LNCS, vol. 7998, pp. 100–115. Springer, Heidelberg (2013). https://doi.org/10.1007/978-3-642-39634-2_10
5. Janiczak, A.: Undecidability of some simple formalized theories. Fundam. Math. **40**, 131–139 (1953)
6. Kreisel, G.: Review of "Undecidability of some simple formalized theories". Math. Rev. **15**, 669–670 (1954)
7. Läuchli, H., Leonard, J.: On the elementary theory of linear order. Fundam. Math. **59**, 109–116 (1966)
8. Negri, S., Von Plato, J., Coquand, T.: Proof-theoretical analysis of order relations. Arch. Math. Logic **43**(3), 297–309 (2004)
9. Nipkow, T.: Linear quantifier elimination. In: Armando, A., Baumgartner, P., Dowek, G. (eds.) IJCAR 2008. LNCS (LNAI), vol. 5195, pp. 18–33. Springer, Heidelberg (2008). https://doi.org/10.1007/978-3-540-71070-7_3

10. Nipkow, T., Wenzel, M., Paulson, L.C.: Isabelle/HOL–A Proof Assistant for Higher-Order Logic. LNCS, vol. 2283. Springer, Heidelberg (2002). https://doi.org/10.1007/3-540-45949-9

11. Nipkow, T., Roßkopf, S.: Isabelle's metalogic: Formalization and proof checker (2021). https://arxiv.org/abs/2104.12224

12. Stevens, L., Nipkow, T.: A verified decision procedure for orders. https://www21.in.tum.de/team/stevensl/assets/atva-2021-artifact.zip. Formal proof development

13. Szpilrajn, E.: Sur l'extension de l'ordre partiel. Fundam. Math. 1(16), 386–389 (1930)

14. Zeller, P., Stevens, L.: Order extension and Szpilrajn's theorem. Archive of Formal Proofs (2021). https://devel.isa-afp.org/entries/Szpilrajn.html. Formal proof development

PJBDD:
A BDD Library for Java and Multi-Threading

Dirk Beyer, Karlheinz Friedberger, and Stephan Holzner

LMU Munich, Munich, Germany

Abstract. PJBDD is a flexible and modular Java library for binary decision diagrams (BDD), which are a well-known data structure for performing efficient operations on compressed sets and relations. BDDs have practical applications in composing and analyzing boolean functions, e.g., for computer-aided verification. Despite its importance, there are only a few BDD libraries available. PJBDD is based on a slim object-oriented design, supports multi-threaded execution of the BDD operations (internal) as well as thread-safe access to the operations from applications (external). It provides automatic reference counting and garbage collection. The modular design of the library allows us to provide a uniform API for binary decision diagrams, zero-suppressed decision diagrams, and also chained decision diagrams. This paper includes a compact evaluation of PJBDD, to demonstrate that concurrent operations on large BDDs scale well and parallelize nicely on multi-core CPUs.

Keywords: BDD · Java Library · Concurrency · Multi-threaded Application

1 Introduction

Binary Decision Diagrams (BDDs) [1,8] enabled a major break-through in applying model checking to large hardware models [9]. In our own previous work, we applied BDDs to model checking of timed automata [2] and C programs [5]. Most of the existing, state-of-the-art BDD libraries are not designed in thread-safe manner (CuDD [15], BuDDy [10], and JDD [16]), do not support multi-threaded execution of the BDD operations (BeeDeeDee [14]), or require effort to manually update reference counters for BDD nodes (Sylvan [11]). Therefore, application developers of, e. g., verification tools based on BDDs, have to implement code for cleaning up unused nodes or cannot directly use multi-threaded verification algorithms with BDDs in a thread-safe manner.

PJBDD contributes to closing this gap and offers a full-fledged BDD library with support for convenient usage from Java applications. Table 1 lists the programming and BDD features that we identified as important in our development work on the verification framework CPACHECKER, which uses BDDs as a central data structure. For our work it is more important to have a convenient and thread-safe development environment with an *easy-to-read code basis*, than to

© Springer Nature Switzerland AG 2021
Z. Hou and V. Ganesh (Eds.): ATVA 2021, LNCS 12971, pp. 144–149, 2021.
https://doi.org/10.1007/978-3-030-88885-5_10

Table 1. Different BDD libraries and their features

	last main-tained	thread-safe access	parallel operations	automatic reference counting	dynamic variable reordering	further supported diagrams
BuDDy [10]	2014	-	-	✓	✓	-
CuDD [15]	(2016)	-	-	-	✓	ADD, ZBDD, CBDD
PJBDD	2021	✓	✓	✓	-	ZBDD, CBDD
JDD [16]	2019	-	-	-	-	ZBDD
Sylvan [11]	2020	(✓)	✓	-	-	ADD, LDD, TBDD
BeeDeeDee [14]	2018	✓	-	-	-	-

leverage the maximal possible performance. This makes the library easier to maintain and extend for us and our students. PJBDD is also an interesting choice for teaching. PJBDD is the only available BDD library (Table 1) that

- is actively maintained by the developers,
- ensures thread-safe concurrent calls from user applications in Java,
- supports multi-threaded execution of BDD operations,
- provides automatic reference counting, and
- supports zero-suppressed BDDs (ZBDD) and chained BDDs (CBDD).

Related Work. BDDs are practically relevant since the seminal paper by Bryant in 1986 [7]. Several highly tuned BDD libraries became available since that time, written in different programming languages. Well-known examples are the C/C++ libraries BuDDy [10], CuDD [15], and Sylvan [11], as well as the Java libraries BeeDeeDee [14], and JDD [16].

The performance of a BDD library depends on several low-level design choices, which makes it difficult for researchers to develop new design approaches in existing highly optimized code. Furthermore, existing libraries often lack support for multi-threaded algorithms, concurrent access, or automatic reference counting. The Java-based implementation BeeDeeDee allows to perform thread-safe parallel operations. The library Sylvan [11] achieved great speed-up in large-scale scenarios with multi-threaded execution of BDD operations. However, due to a bug in the Java wrapper, thread-safe access from Java is not possible (An issue was reported at https://github.com/utwente-fmt/jsylvan/issues/3). While several tools support automated garbage collection, BuDDy and PJBDD are the only tools that support automated reference counting. The last date of official maintenance of CuDD is unknown, because the official FTP server is offline (The mirror at https://github.com/ivmai/cudd does not show activity since 2016.)

The implementation of ZBDDs is only available in the oldest (and thus most advanced) implementations; and unfortunately missing in newer libraries like BeeDeeDee and Sylvan. PJBDD closes this gap by providing all of the features described above in a well-known platform-independent programming language.

2   Design and Implementation Details

This section gives a compact overview of PJBDD's design and implementation.

Shared Graph Representation. In an application, there is not only one single BDD, but there are multiple of them. For overall efficiency, it is required that all common sub-graphs are shared in one central data structure, i.e., in a large hash table. In our BDD library, this shared data structure, called UniqueTable, is usable from multiple threads in concurrent manner, and we took care of minimal synchronization overhead. Therefore, read and write accesses are implemented as atomic compare-and-swap operations (CAS). Our hash tables use a prime-hashing function, which is a common choice for BDD libraries.

Operations Cache. For efficient BDD manipulation, a cache for computed operation results is necessary. Since the cache heavily reduces workload and achieves huge speed up, we implemented one central caching instance which all worker threads share. To enable thread-safe accesses we use atomic CAS accesses.

Concurrent BDD Operations. For concurrent operations, we use a fork-join parallelism. The Shannon expansion in the BDD applies its operations such that the two recursive calls run in parallel. We keep the implementation as simple as possible and use the Java-native fork-join framework to avoid overthreading and respect the execution order (the two recursive calls have to finish before returning).

Memory Management. Automatic memory management relieves the developer from the error-prone and tedious job of manually allocating and deallocating memory, which is one of the advantages of high-level programming languages like Java. An automatic garbage collection clears all memory objects that are no longer reachable from the user application. However, one problem remains that is crucial for long-running applications: The application can leak memory if the user forgets to remove object references in a central data structure. PJBDD offers automated cleaning of unused nodes. We chose to use *WeakReferences* and *ReferenceQueues* as provided by the JDK for fine-grained, but automatic and efficient memory control.

3   Architecture of the Library

Our library is written in Java. In comparison to other BDD libraries, PJBDD does not work with integer indices as internal BDD representations, but with Java objects. This allows us to use the object-oriented approach, but at the price of slightly heavier memory consumption. More implementation details and results of preliminary experiments are available in the Master's thesis by Holzner [13].

Design Criteria. Instead of developing another Java clone of an existing C library, we started from scratch and thoroughly considered the design criteria. Our development of a new BDD library is motivated by several requirements that are not addressed by existing BDD libraries.

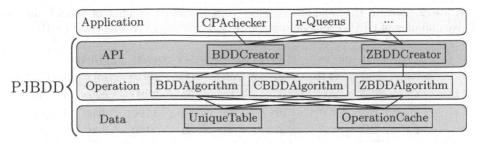

Fig. 1. Overview of the components of PJBDD

First, we desire a *simple to use API* and an *easy-to-read code basis*, such that future developers (including students) can experiment with and extend the existing code without requiring expert knowledge about optimizations, such as low-level bit-operations and reference counting. Of course, memory management is important for a highly optimized library. However, memory management by the user of a library is error prone and modern programming languages tend to already include automatic garbage collection. We decided for the standard Java garbage collector and do not provide an explicit way for the user to remove BDD nodes from the cache. Second, to minimize development time and maintenance costs, we used components from the Java standard API, such as the default fork-join framework for efficient multi-threaded computations.

Overview. Our library offers two distinct APIs: one for working with BDDs and one for ZBDDs. Due to their theoretical different nature, it is not possible to directly combine those types of decision diagrams. The API for BDDs provides typical boolean operations, such as conjunction, implication, or negation. Our library supports to configure chaining [6] with the same interface. The API for ZBDD has typical operations on ZBDDs, such as union and intersection.

Both APIs access the same kind of data structures: An operation layer, a node implementation, and a central cache. Figure 1 gives an overview of the layers and used components. The operation layer contains the basic algorithms on BDDs, and their implementation is optimized for multi-threaded computation. A BDD node itself represents an independent subtree and its implementation is as slim as possible to minimize memory consumption. A BDD node references its variable, the end of its chain in case of CBDD, and its two child nodes along the high and low edge. The central components of a BDD library are the node caches, which are divided into the global UniqueTable for node references given to the user, and the operation cache that is utilized in all internal algorithms. The operation cache is a crucial ingredient for BDD operations and responsible for the overall performance of the library.

With our modular approach, we can exchange several components to analyze the effect of different implementations without changing the user's application that is built on top of our library. For example, we can select from different cache and UniqueTable implementations or enable BDD chaining. For the experiment, we have set the currently best choices as default to evaluate the impact of concurrent computation on a scaling application.

Table 2. Solving the n-queens problem with a limited number of threads and a given number of CPU cores (wall time in seconds, memory consumption in MB)

cores	10-queens (s)	(MB)	11-queens (s)	(MB)	12-queens (s)	(MB)	13-queens (s)	(MB)
1	3.5	200	15	480	93	2 200	620	12 000
2	3.3	400	10	1 200	54	4 700	490	13 000
4	2.3	430	6.3	1 800	32	5 100	220	13 000
8	1.7	400	4.5	1 600	19	5 800	140	12 000

4   Experimental Evaluation

Our evaluation was executed with PJBDD, version v1.0.9 on an Intel Xeon E3-1230 CPU with 8 processing units. To guarantee reproducibility we isolated the benchmark runs with BENCHEXEC [4], restricted the memory to 15 GB and set the maximal Java heap size to 12 GB. The *n-queens problem* is a typical satisfiability problem, which can be represented as BDD. To correctly solve the problem, one needs to place n chess queens on a chess board of size $n \times n$, such that no queen can be beaten by others (according to chess rules). BDDs can represent all the problem's different possible solutions in one BDD. To evaluate whether PJBDD scales well on multiple CPU cores, we analyzed the n-queens problem and measured the consumed memory and response time, when PJBDD uses a given number of CPU cores. The results in Table 2 show a significant impact of the parallelization. PJBDD's memory usage increased with multi-threaded computations (up to four times for $N = 11$). In terms of response time, our library can achieve a speed-up of up to five times for this application.

5   Conclusion

The abundance of multi-core environments makes it meaningful to invest in multi-threaded verification algorithms. This, however, requires the availability of thread-safe and multi-threaded data-structure libraries. The advent of SYLVAN showed that this is possible and can lead to a considerable speed-up. Our motivation is to provide a Java implementation of a BDD library that guarantees thread-safe operation and supports multi-threaded execution of the BDD operations. PJBDD is such a BDD package. We use the n-queens problem as a load test and showed that the parallelization works well, as the work nicely distributes over the cores.

There are lots of additional features that can be implemented in the future. Due to the modular implementation, slim and flexible ZBDD and CBDD implementations are included already. This design could be used to support more different types of decision diagrams, such as CZBDDs [6] or tagged BDDs [12]. Improvements in performance or memory consumption without introducing additional code complexity is also a major goal of the developers.

Data Availability Statement. PJBDD is licensed under Apache 2.0 and available on GitLab: https://gitlab.com/sosy-lab/software/paralleljbdd. The repository contains examples and instructions how to install and use the tool. A reproduction package for the n-queens experiment and some software-verification experiments is available on Zenodo [3].

Funding. This project was supported by the Deutsche Forschungsgemeinschaft (DFG) – 378803395 (ConVeY).

References

1. Akers, S.B.: Binary decision diagrams. IEEE Trans. Computers **27**(6), 509–516 (1978). https://doi.org/10.1109/TC.1978.1675141
2. Beyer, D.: Improvements in BDD-based reachability analysis of timed automata. In: Proc. FME. pp. 318–343. LNCS 2021, Springer (2001). https://doi.org/10.1007/3-540-45251-6_18
3. Beyer, D., Friedberger, K., Holzner, S.: Reproduction package for article 'PJBDD: A BDD library for Java and multi-threading' in Proc. ATVA 2021. Zenodo (2021). https://doi.org/10.5281/zenodo.5070156
4. Beyer, D., Löwe, S., Wendler, P.: Reliable benchmarking: Requirements and solutions. Int. J. Softw. Tools Technol. Transfer **21**(1), 1–29 (2019). https://doi.org/10.1007/s10009-017-0469-y
5. Beyer, D., Stahlbauer, A.: BDD-based software model checking with CPACHECKER. In: Proc. MEMICS. pp. 1–11. LNCS 7721, Springer (2013). https://doi.org/10.1007/978-3-642-36046-6_1
6. Bryant, R.E.: Chain reduction for binary and zero-suppressed decision diagrams. J. Autom. Reasoning **64**(7), 1361–1391 (2020). https://doi.org/10.1007/s10817-020-09569-6
7. Bryant, R.E.: Graph-based algorithms for boolean function manipulation. IEEE Trans. Computers **35**(8), 677–691 (1986). https://doi.org/10.1109/TC.1986.1676819
8. Bryant, R.E.: Binary decision diagrams. In: Handbook of Model Checking, pp. 191–217. Springer (2018). https://doi.org/10.1007/978-3-319-10575-8_7
9. Burch, J.R., Clarke, E.M., McMillan, K.L., Dill, D.L., Hwang, L.J.: Symbolic model checking: 10^{20} states and beyond. In: Proc. LICS. pp. 428–439. IEEE (1990). https://doi.org/10.1109/LICS.1990.113767
10. Cohen, H., Whaley, J., Wildt, J., Gorogiannis, N.: BuDDy: A BDD package. http://sourceforge.net/p/buddy/
11. van Dijk, T.: Sylvan: Multi-core decision diagrams. Ph.D. thesis, University of Twente, Enschede, Netherlands (2016)
12. van Dijk, T., Wille, R., Meolic, R.: Tagged BDDs: Combining reduction rules from different decision diagram types. In: Proc. FMCAD. pp. 108–115. IEEE (2017). https://doi.org/10.23919/FMCAD.2017.8102248
13. Holzner, S.: Design und Implementierung einer parallelen BDD-Bibliothek. Master's Thesis, LMU Munich, Software Systems Lab (2019)
14. Lovato, A., Macedonio, D., Spoto, F.: A thread-safe library for binary decision diagrams. In: Proc. SEFM. pp. 35–49. LNCS 8702, Springer (2014). https://doi.org/10.1007/978-3-319-10431-7_4
15. Somenzi, F.: Colorado University decision diagram package (1998)
16. Vahidi, A.: JDD: A pure Java BDD and Z-BDD library. https://bitbucket.org/vahidi/jdd (2003)

Model Checking

Live Synthesis

Bernd Finkbeiner, Felix Klein, and Niklas Metzger[✉]

CISPA Helmholtz Center for Information Security, Saarbrücken, Germany
{finkbeiner,felix.klein,niklas.metzger}@cispa.de

Abstract. Synthesis automatically constructs an implementation that satisfies a given logical specification. In this paper, we study the *live synthesis* problem, where the synthesized implementation replaces an already running system. In addition to satisfying its own specification, the synthesized implementation must guarantee a sound transition from the previous implementation. This version of the synthesis problem is highly relevant in "always-on" applications, where updates happen while the system is running. To specify the correct handover between the old and new implementation, we introduce an extension of linear-time temporal logic (LTL) called *LiveLTL*. A LiveLTL specification defines separate requirements on the two implementations and ensures that the new implementation satisfies, in addition to its own requirements, any obligations left unfinished by the old implementation. For specifications in LiveLTL, we show that the live synthesis problem can be solved within the same complexity bound as standard reactive synthesis, i.e., in 2EXPTIME. Our experiments show the necessity of live synthesis for LiveLTL specifications created from benchmarks of SYNTCOMP and robot control.

1 Introduction

The past decade has brought remarkable progress in the automatic synthesis of reactive systems from temporal specifications [5,13,17]. Traditionally, synthesis is seen as a one-off method: the generated implementation is guaranteed, by construction, to satisfy the specification. If the specification changes, the process is repeated from the start. For systems that are *always-on*, like banking systems, or controllers in power plants, this may, however, not be an option: when the requirements change, the system must be updated while it is still running, and the control must transition to the new version without disrupting the safety or functionality of the running system. While such *live updates* are a well-studied concern in operating systems research (cf. [9]), they are, somewhat surprisingly, still a novelty in formal methods.

An extended version of this paper is available at [6].

This work was partially supported by the German Research Foundation (DFG) as part of the Collaborative Research Center "Foundations of Perspicuous Software Systems" (TRR 248, 389792660), by the European Research Council (ERC) Grant OSARES (No. 683300), and by the German Israeli Foundation (GIF) Grant "Knowledge-based Synthesis" (No. I-1513-407./2019).

Z. Hou and V. Ganesh (Eds.): ATVA 2021, LNCS 12971, pp. 153–169, 2021.
https://doi.org/10.1007/978-3-030-88885-5_11

In this paper, we define a *live system* as sequence of implementations, each with a corresponding specification. The last element in the sequence is the currently executed system. Performing a live update terminates the currently active system and extends the sequence with a new implementation. The key challenge of live updates is that any obligations imposed by the specification of the terminated system that are not yet satisfied at the time of the update must be taken care of by the newly active system. This transfer of obligations is important to make the update transparent from the user's perspective. Consider, for example, an arbiter specified as the LTL formula $\square(request \rightarrow \lozenge\, grant)$, which requires that every *request* is eventually followed by a *grant*. If the update occurs after some *request*, but before the corresponding *grant*, then the new implementation must still guarantee the occurrence of the *grant*.

The problem of *model checking* live updates is to check whether a given new implementation will result in a correct live update; the *synthesis* problem is to automatically find such an implementation. To specify the correct handover between the old and new implementation, we introduce an extension of linear-time temporal logic (LTL) called *LiveLTL*. A LiveLTL specification defines requirements on the two implementations and ensures that the new implementation satisfies, in addition to its own requirements, any obligations left unfinished by the old implementation. We consider two variants of the model checking and synthesis problems. In *finite-trace live updates*, we only require the update to be correct in a specific situation, i.e., after a specific execution of the previous implementation. In *universal updates*, we require that the update can occur at any time. We show that model checking live updates is PSPACE-complete in the initial and update specification. Synthesis is 2EXPTIME-complete in the combination of the specifications for both update variants.

We report on experience with a prototype implementation of our approach on a range of benchmarks, including examples taken from the synthesis competition and a robotic case study. In our experiments, live synthesis is used to construct live updates built on reasonable pairs of specifications. The results show the necessity of verifying live updates with the adapted semantics of LiveLTL and that every considered specification states obligations for the update.

2   Running Example – Relay Station

Consider the following setup: a satellite has been positioned in the orbit of Mars in combination with multiple base stations on the planet. The base stations take samples from the extraterrestrial environment, analyze them and submit their findings to the satellite. After the data has been sent by a station, it waits for instructions from the satellite: whether the sample must be further analysed, or whether it can be discarded and a new sample must be taken. The satellite, on the other hand, provides the stations with the corresponding instructions and collects the data of all stations for relaying it back to earth. To this end, the satellite takes care that always some data of all base stations has been collected to be present in the report for earth.

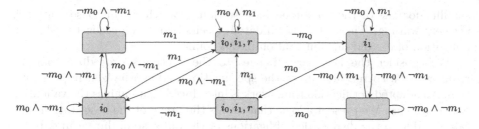

Fig. 1. Synthesized LTS for the satellite specification.

We formalize this behavior of the satellite in LTL. On the input side, the satellite receives n *measurements* m_j of every base station, where $0 \leq j < n$ ranges over the n deployed base stations on the planet. On the output side, the satellite outputs *instructions* i_j and can create a *report* r to be sent back to earth. The behavior is formalized using the following guarantees: First of all, every measurement m_i must be responded to eventually and instructions are only sent in response to received measurements.

$$\varphi_1 := \bigwedge_{j=0}^{n} m_j \rightarrow \bigcirc\Diamond i_j \qquad \varphi_2 := \bigwedge_{j=0}^{n} \Box\neg m_j \rightarrow \Diamond\Box\neg i_j$$

Furthermore, a report is generated as long as every base station submits a measurement regularly, while no report needs to be generated as long as some measurements are still missing.

$$\varphi_3 := (\bigwedge_{j=0}^{n} \Diamond m_j) \rightarrow \Diamond r \qquad \varphi_4 := (\bigvee_{j=0}^{n} \Box\neg m_j) \rightarrow \Diamond\Box\neg r$$

All guarantees φ_j must be satisfied at every point in time. We obtain the overall specification $\varphi := \bigwedge_{j=1}^{4} \Box\varphi_j$. The specification is realizable, as witnessed by the synthesized labeled transition system (LTS) for two base stations in Fig. 1. We follow the transition system for $\Box\varphi_1$. Starting in the initial state, if m_0 and m_1 is received, we stay in the same state and $\bigcirc\Diamond m_0$ as well as $\bigcirc\Diamond m_1$ is satisfied. The transition system follows the $\neg m_0$ edge to the state labeled with i_1 to satisfy the subformula $\bigcirc\Diamond i_1$. Note that $m_1 \rightarrow \Diamond i_1$ would be directly satisfied in the initial state since the Moore semantics evaluates the formula based on the current state and next edge label. The states at the top right and bottom left ensure that φ_2 is satisfied, i.e., it waits for inputs before the corresponding output is set. Corresponding to φ_4, the top left and bottom right states control the output r which is only allowed to be true as long as all measurements are received. Consider a situation, where one of the base stations fails. The satellite controller must be updated, since the satellite would wait indefinitely for the data of the broken base station otherwise. The report generation would also be broken. However, we cannot just eliminate the broken base station from the original specification, synthesize again and restart the satellite with the new result. The reason is that there still may be an outstanding instruction of the satellite for one of the remaining base stations, for which this base station is actively waiting. Therefore, the updated specification still needs to take this obligation of the old implementation into account.

We consider the necessary changes to the synthesis procedure that are required for a correct update of the specification and synthesized implementation. An adapted verification framework is introduced that enables the validation of live systems. We present a logic that avoids the break of the base stations and satellite due to the disregarded obligations of the old system during update.

3 Preliminaries

Linear Temporal Logic. Linear temporal logic (LTL) [19] is a logic for specifying correctness of linear-time systems. The syntax is a combination of state and path operators over a set of atomic propositions (AP) that define behavior over infinite time. Formulas in LTL are built according to the grammar $\varphi ::= \top \mid \perp \mid a \mid \neg\varphi \mid \varphi_1 \wedge \varphi_2 \mid \bigcirc\varphi \mid \varphi_1 \mathcal{U} \varphi_2$ where $a \in AP$. Temporal operators are *next* $\bigcirc$ and *until* $\mathcal{U}$, all other operators are boolean connectives. We assume every LTL formula to be in release positive normal form (PNF) where negations are only allowed in front of atomic propositions. For readability, implication $\rightarrow$ and equivalence $\leftrightarrow$ as well as the common abbreviations *eventually* $\Diamond a$ for $\top \mathcal{U} a$ and *globally* $\square a$ for $\neg\Diamond\neg a$ are used throughout this paper. Defining the LTL semantics, the operator $\vDash$ evaluates infinite traces σ and explicit index i against LTL formulas φ where traces are words over letters $\sigma \in (2^{AP})^\omega$. For example, σ satisfies $\bigcirc a$ if in the next step a holds in σ and $a \mathcal{U} b$ if a holds until b holds. A trace $\sigma = A_0 A_1 A_2 \ldots$ with $A_i \in 2^{AP}$ is an infinite sequence of sets of atomic propositions. We use the infix notation $\sigma[n, m]$ to crop the trace to the sub-trace from position n to m, $\sigma[n, m] = A_n A_{n+1} \ldots A_{m-1}$, where $A_i \in 2^{AP}$, and concatenate the finite trace σ_1 with the possibly infinite trace σ_2 with $\sigma_1 \cdot \sigma_2$. The semantic operator $\vDash$ builds a language of a specification φ with $\text{Words}(\varphi) = \{\sigma \in (2^{AP})^\omega \mid \sigma, 0 \vDash \varphi\}$. A trace σ that is terminated at an arbitrary position m, i.e., $\sigma[0, m]$, is a finite trace and denoted by η. The function $expand : LTL \rightarrow LTL$ uses the standard LTL expansion rules to unroll the given formula, $expand_n$ repeats $expand$ n times. For example, $expand_1(aUb) = b \vee (a \wedge \bigcirc(a \mathcal{U} b))$. The function $after : LTL \times 2^{AP} \rightarrow LTL$ evaluates the formula on a given atomic proposition assignment and returns the remaining formula, e.g. $after(a \mathcal{U} b, \{a\}) = a \mathcal{U} b$ and $after(a \mathcal{U} b, \{b\}) = \top$. $after(\varphi, \sigma[0, n])$ is defined as $after(after(\varphi, \sigma_0), \sigma[1, n])$ with $after(\varphi, \epsilon) = \varphi$. Explicit definitions of $expand$ and $after$ can be found in [6].

Transition Systems. The reactive model for LTL are transition systems where state labels correspond to the output of systems and transition labels correspond to the input of the environment. Given a finite set of directions Υ and a finite set of labels Σ, a Σ-labeled Υ-transition system is a tuple $TS = (T, t_0, \tau, o)$, consisting of a finite set of states T, an initial state $t_0 \in T$, a transition function $\tau : T \times \Upsilon \rightarrow T$, and a labeling function $o : T \rightarrow \Sigma$. Given AP and partition $AP = O \cup I$ for output and input atomic propositions, implementations for LTL specifications are 2^O-labeled 2^I-transition systems (TS). The paths of a transition system start in t_0 and follow the transition function τ collecting input and output labels with the output function o. The traces of a transition system $Traces(TS)$ omit the state information of paths. We assume transition systems without terminal states and a deterministic transition function.

Model Checking and Synthesis. Model checking a transition system TS against a specification φ checks the relation $Traces(TS) \subseteq Words(\varphi)$. The problem of automatically constructing a transition system that satisfies the model checking property is referred to as *synthesis*. In the course of this paper, we refer to the algorithms of LTL model checking and synthesis as black box algorithms. Similar to $Traces(TS)$, we denote the set of finite traces of TS by $FinTraces(TS)$.

4   Live Updates

Common formalisms for verification agree on the following assumption: different system versions are analyzed in isolation, i.e., everything that happened before the initial state of the new implementation is irrelevant for its correctness. For updates at runtime, this assumption is infeasible. The update system has to satisfy *obligations* that were stated during the execution of the previous system to be correct. In this section, we set the foundations for a specification language that is able to express correctness of a live update by defining the structure of two live update problems. We identify the factors affecting the update process and formalize the interplay of the components. The definitions are independent of specific temporal logics and can be adapted to various logics and system models.

Proving the correctness of systems either by model checking or synthesis assumes the existence of a starting point that is handled as the initial state. For live updates, the starting point of verification is not the initial state of the update system, but the initial state of the system running beforehand. Running systems create obligations that cannot be discarded when updated live, otherwise, for example, an observer would starve waiting for its response. The recent development of live systems enforces the sensibility of correctness algorithms to validate systems w.r.t. the *context* they are started in. For linear-time systems given as transition systems, we define the context as the finite execution of the previous system combined with its specification. The finite execution implicitly changes the state of the formula which we refer to as *active* formula. We capture this change to the formula with a function Ψ, which, given a finite trace and a specification, returns a specification that captures the obligations needed for the satisfaction of the update system. With defining Ψ, one is able to vary the impact of the initial system to the update system. Verifying an update system with standard LTL, one implicitly defines Ψ to be $\top$ for every input, enforcing no obligations on the update system.

Definition 1 (Finite Trace Live Update). *Let TS_I be an initial system, TS_U be an update system, φ be an initial specification, ψ be an update specification, and η be a finite trace of TS_I. TS_U is considered correct if it is correct w.r.t. ψ and the result of $\Psi(\eta, \varphi)$ for the function $\Psi : (2^{AP})^* \times LTL \to LTL$ defining the obligation.*

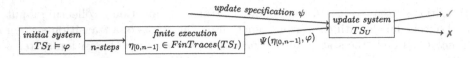

Fig. 2. The finite trace live update with φ as the initial specification, ψ as the update specification, and Ψ as the function computing the obligation for TS_U.

The finite trace live update handles the context of the update as white-box: the finite execution of the previous system is fully known. For this explicit execution, the obligation is computed and, together with the specification of the update system, verified against the update. Figure 2 shows the dependencies built by the finite trace live update where n is the number of discrete time-steps of the finite execution. However, the explicit finite execution of the initial system is not always available. Therefore, Definition 2 introduces update correctness for all possible finite paths of the initial system.

Definition 2 (Universal Live Update). *Let TS_I be an initial system, TS_U be an update system, φ be an initial specification, and ψ be an update specification. TS_U is considered correct if it is correct w.r.t. ψ and $\Psi(\eta, \varphi)$ for all possible finite traces η of TS_I.*

The context of the update is handled as black-box in the universal case. The explicit execution and the system's state of the update is unknown. Nevertheless, if all possible obligations are satisfied by the update system, the update is guaranteed to be correct. Definition 2 increases the number of possibilities to be verified, since arguing over an infinite set of finite traces cannot be performed directly. In comparison to the explicit live update, the length n is kept arbitrary since every finite trace may enforce its particular obligation.

Since we consider reactive systems, it is natural to aim for an update system that reacts to the update context, i.e., for each result of $\Psi(\eta, \varphi)$ the update system starts differently. This problem is covered by the finite trace live update if the number of different contexts is finite. One can solve the update problem for each context and combine the resulting update systems accordingly. In general, multiple other meaningful models of update correctness can be designed, e.g., enforcing the existence of an update point in the initial system's future. Nevertheless, finite trace and universal live updates suffice for the course of this paper and build a justifiable framework for live updates.

5   A Temporal Language for Live Updates

With the two live update problems defined, we introduce LiveLTL to state and verify the correctness of live updates. LiveLTL is an extension to LTL and specifies live update properties that automatically enforce the obligations of the previous execution on the update system. The syntax and semantics of LiveLTL as well as the language equivalence to LTL are shown. Moreover, we identify the class of obligations that can be stated by LiveLTL specifications.

5.1   LiveLTL

LiveLTL is designed according to three aspects: (1) the initial system is not able to enforce new obligations after termination, (2) all obligations stated before termination are satisfied by the update system, and (3) obligations are satisfiable in finite time. This guideline is a trade-off between independence of the previous system and incurring obligations from the initial specification to the update system. The definition of LiveLTL follows the finite trace update structure and builds the language for inputs as a combination of a finite and an infinite trace evaluation. The syntax is taken from LTL and we assume the set of atomic proposition for the initial system to be a subset of the atomic propositions of the update system. As extension to the semantic operator $\vDash$ of LTL, the operators $\vDash_{|\eta|,\mathcal{I}}$ and $\vDash_{|\eta|,\mathcal{U}}$ form the language for the initial system and the update system respectively. $\vDash_{|\eta|,\mathcal{U}}$ performs an index shift from time-step 0 to the update position and evaluates the changed formula with the LTL operator and is defined as $\sigma, i \vDash_{|\eta|,\mathcal{U}} \varphi$ iff $\sigma, i + |\eta| \vDash \varphi$. Since the update specification is only relevant for the update system, the shift of size $|\eta|$ enables the correct evaluation of the update system's part of the trace. $\vDash_{|\eta|,\mathcal{I}}$ inserts $|\eta|$ as upper bound for recurrent formulas, i.e., formulas with the *release* operator:

$\sigma, i \vDash_{|\eta|,\mathcal{I}} \top$ $\qquad\qquad$ $\sigma, i \nvDash_{|\eta|,\mathcal{I}} \bot$

$\sigma, i \vDash_{|\eta|,\mathcal{I}} a$ $\qquad\qquad$ iff $A_i \vDash a$, i.e. $a \in A_i$

$\sigma, i \vDash_{|\eta|,\mathcal{I}} \neg a$ $\qquad\qquad$ iff $A_i \nvDash a$, i.e. $a \notin A_i$

$\sigma, i \vDash_{|\eta|,\mathcal{I}} \varphi_1 \wedge \varphi_2$ $\quad$ iff $\sigma, i \vDash_{|\eta|,\mathcal{I}} \varphi_1$ and $\sigma, i \vDash_{|\eta|,\mathcal{I}} \varphi_2$

$\sigma, i \vDash_{|\eta|,\mathcal{I}} \varphi_1 \vee \varphi_2$ $\quad$ iff $\sigma, i \vDash_{|\eta|,\mathcal{I}} \varphi_1$ or $\sigma, i \vDash_{|\eta|,\mathcal{I}} \varphi_2$

$\sigma, i \vDash_{|\eta|,\mathcal{I}} \bigcirc \varphi$ $\qquad\quad$ iff $\sigma, i + 1 \vDash_{|\eta|,\mathcal{I}} \varphi$

$\sigma, i \vDash_{|\eta|,\mathcal{I}} \varphi_1 \mathcal{U} \varphi_2$ $\quad$ iff $\exists j, j \geq i.\ \sigma, j \vDash_{|\eta|,\mathcal{I}} \varphi_2$ and $\forall k, i \leq k < j.\ \sigma, k \vDash_{|\eta|,\mathcal{I}} \varphi_1$

$\sigma, i \vDash_{|\eta|,\mathcal{I}} \varphi_1 \mathcal{R} \varphi_2$ $\quad$ iff $\forall j, |\eta| > j \geq i.\ \sigma, j \vDash_{|\eta|,\mathcal{I}} \varphi_2$ or

$\qquad\qquad\qquad\qquad\qquad \exists k, |\eta| > k \geq i.\ (\sigma, k \vDash_{|\eta|,\mathcal{I}} \varphi_1 \wedge \forall l, i \leq l \leq k.\ \sigma, l \vDash_{|\eta|,\mathcal{I}} \varphi_2)$

Informally, $\varphi_1 \mathcal{R} \varphi_2$ opens the *obligation* φ_2 in every execution step which contradicts (1) if evaluated after the update. As standard LTL semantics enables the specification to infinitely open new obligations, $\vDash_{|\eta|,\mathcal{I}}$ is built to limit this behavior to the actual finite execution of the initial system. The definition of $\vDash_{|\eta|,\mathcal{I}}$ mostly follows the definition of $\vDash$, except for the evaluation of *release* formulas. For all indices greater or equal to the length of the trace, $\varphi_1 \mathcal{R} \varphi_2$ is immediately satisfied, thus imposing the end of newly created obligations from the initial implementation. Therefore, the initial operator permits the transfer of finitely satisfiable obligations to the update system (2), but forbids the impact of the initial system after its termination (1). Note that for LTL formulas in PNF, all operators except *release* only specify finite behavior and all open obligations are satisfiable in finite time (3). The two operators define the language of LiveLTL.

Definition 3 (Language of LiveLTL). *Let φ, ψ be LTL formulas and let $\eta \in (2^{AP})^*$. The linear time property induced by φ, ψ, and η is*

$$Words(\varphi, \psi, \eta) = \{\eta \cdot \sigma \in (2^{AP})^\omega \mid \eta \cdot \sigma, 0 \vDash_{|\eta|,\mathcal{I}} \varphi \ \wedge \eta \cdot \sigma, 0 \vDash_{|\eta|,\mathcal{U}} \psi\}.$$

The language is dependent on the initial specification, the update specification, and the finite trace. Evaluating the inclusion of an infinite trace with the first $|\eta|$ elements being fixed consists of a combination of the operators $\vDash_{|\eta|,\mathcal{I}}$ and $\vDash_{|\eta|,\mathcal{U}}$. The initial LiveLTL operator is defined on the syntactic structure of the initial formula and is insensitive with respect to syntactic tautologies. Providing formulas without syntactic ambiguity that cannot be dissolved in $|\eta|$ time steps is left to the specifier. The following theorem relates LiveLTL and LTL.

Theorem 1. *LiveLTL and LTL are equally expressive.*

The proof is a reduction via encoding the initial trace into the LTL formula and is presented in the full version [6]. While being equally expressive, LiveLTL enables the direct evaluation of the newly introduced live update problems on a given context. Correctness for finite trace live updates follows from standard language inclusion.

Definition 4 (Finite Trace LiveLTL Update). *Let TS_U be an update system, φ be an initial specificaiton, ψ be an update specification, and η be a finite trace. TS_U is correct w.r.t. finite trace LiveLTL if $\eta \cdot Traces(TS_U) \subseteq Words(\varphi, \psi, \eta)$.*

Example 1. Interpreting the running example as finite trace LiveLTL update, we can obtain the finite trace $\eta = \{m_1, i_0, i_1, r\}, \{i_1\}, \{m_0, m_1\}$ as execution of the relay station. Evaluating η with $\vDash_{|\eta|,\mathcal{I}}$ shows that $\Diamond i_0$, $\Diamond i_1$, and $\Diamond r$ need to be satisfied by the update system, since both measurements are unanswered and no report was given after both base stations sent their measurements. Note that changing the last trace element to $\{m_0\}$ eliminates the obligations for the base station i_1 and the report r.

The finite trace update directly translates to the definition of LiveLTL, whereas the universal live update adds a level of quantification.

Definition 5 (Universal Live LTL Update). *Let TS_I be an initial system, TS_U be an update system, φ be an initial specification, and ψ be an update specification. TS_U is correct w.r.t. universal LiveLTL if*

$$\forall \eta \in FinTraces(TS_I) : \eta \cdot Traces(TS_U) \subseteq \bigcup_{\eta \in FinTraces(TS_I)} Words(\varphi, \psi, \eta).$$

To satisfy the universal update condition, the update system needs to be robust against every possible obligation of the initial system. We explore the model checking and synthesis problems of LiveLTL in Sect. 6.

5.2 Obligations

The impact of the initial system on the update system is declared by the operator $\vDash_{|\eta|,\mathcal{I}}$ and forms a class of temporal properties. We investigate this class and build a monitor that traces the open obligations during the execution of a system. In

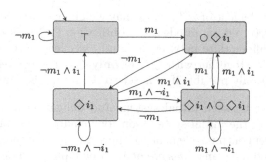

Fig. 3. The obligation monitor for φ_1 with one base station.

practice, the explicit update to be performed is unknown during the design of the initial system. Therefore, one approach to face live updates is keeping track of *open* obligations while the system is executed. To obtain the expressivity of the obligations possibly enforced by LiveLTL, we introduce the *obligation property*.

Definition 6 (Obligation Property). *A linear time property P_{obl} over AP is called an obligation property if for all words $\sigma \in P_{obl}$ there exists a good prefix, i.e., for every $\sigma \in P_{obl}$ there exists a word $\sigma[0, m]$ s.t. $\forall x.x \in (2^{AP})^\omega : \sigma[0, m] \cdot x \in P_{obl}$. Obligation properties coincide with the class of co-safety properties.*

Obligations and co-safety properties describing the same language is a natural outcome of the LiveLTL semantics. To obtain the open obligations with constant cost during runtime, the construction of a monitor tracking the obligations provides a space bounded solution. The monitor is meant to be constructed simultaneously to the initial system.

Definition 7 (Obligation Monitor). *Let $strip : LTL \rightarrow LTL$ be a function syntactically substituting every $\mathcal{R}$ by $\top$. A deterministic obligation monitor for an LTL formula φ is the tuple $\mathcal{OM}_\varphi = (T, t_0, \Upsilon, after, o)$, where $T = \{\varphi' \mid \omega \in (2^{AP})^* : \varphi' = after(\varphi, \omega)\}$ is the set of states, $t_0 = strip(\varphi)$ is the initial state, $\Upsilon = 2^{AP}$ is the set of directions, after is the transition function defined over T and Υ, and $o(t) = strip(t)$ is the labeling function.*

Since the state space of $\mathcal{OM}_\varphi$ corresponds to the state exploration of φ, converting the formulas to obligations is achieved by *strip* and stored in the labeling function. This can be interpreted as the obligations that have to be satisfied by the update system if an update is initiated in this state. The obligation monitor only tracks states and does not guarantee that every reachable state corresponds to a reachable state of a correct implementation of φ. We justify this property by assuming TS_I is correct.

Example 2. Figure 3 displays the obligation monitor for $\varphi_1 = \Box(m_1 \rightarrow \bigcirc\Diamond i_1)$ of our running example with one base station. The monitor starts in an obligation free state corresponding to the state before the system is started and contains one direction for every element of 2^{AP}. Note that we denote directions symbolically. Whenever m_1 is received on an edge, the obligation $\bigcirc\Diamond i_1$ is raised. From the $\bigcirc\Diamond i_1$ state, we differentiate between m_1 and $\neg m_1$ leading to another raise of the $\bigcirc\Diamond i_1$ obligation together with $\Diamond i_1$ or only $\Diamond i_1$ respectively. Returning to the obligation $\top$ is only possible if i_1 is set to $\top$ and m_1 is $\bot$ in the same step.

Note that an offset between initial system and obligation monitor is created. While transitions of the initial system consider environment inputs and states correspond to system outputs, elements of the state space of the obligation monitor are formulas and the transitions are defined by inputs and outputs combined. Residing in a state in the obligation monitor can be interpreted as taking a transition in the system and not yet reaching the next state. Figure 3 shows a monitor for a specification, where the implementation is unknown during construction and the obligation monitor over-approximates the reachable states of the implementation. One can limit the reachable states of the monitor to the paths in the transition system. Indeed, in regard of completeness, unreachable obligations need to be eliminated from the obligation monitor during verification.

6   Model Checking and Synthesis

In this section we solve the problems of model checking live updates and synthesis of live updates, i.e., live synthesis. We explore finite trace and universal updates for the problems and show the complexity of each result and multiple parameters.

6.1   Model Checking Live Updates

Model checking a transition system TS against an LTL formula φ corresponds to answering the question if TS satisfies φ, i.e., $TS \vDash \varphi$. For live systems, the evaluation of the update transition system starts with the initial finite execution and switches to the update system afterwards. Model checking the update system is therefore a language inclusion check of the traces of the transition system combined with η against the LiveLTL semantics.

Definition 8 (Model Checking Finite Trace Live Updates). *Let TS_U be an update system, φ be an initial specification, ψ be an update specification, and η be a finite trace. The problem of model checking finite trace live updates is defined as $\eta \cdot Traces(TS_U) \subseteq Words(\varphi, \psi, \eta)$.*

The model checking problem can be split into two separate parts, directly identifying the newly introduced conditions for live systems with the operators $\vDash_{|\eta|,\mathcal{I}}$ and $\vDash_{|\eta|,\mathcal{U}}$. In addition to that, TS_U combined with η needs to satisfy the update semantics of LiveLTL. Since both tasks can possibly be performed in isolation of each other, the overhead given by the live update semantics under the assumption of an update system already verified with LTL is an interesting topic but left open for future work. The complexity of the problem is stated w.r.t. the length of the trace and the combination of initial and update formula:

Theorem 2 (Complexity in φ, ψ, and η). *The model checking problem for finite trace live updates is PSPACE-complete in $|\varphi| + |\psi|$ and in NL in $\eta \cdot TS_U$.*

The proof is based on model checking the combination of η and TS_U and can be found in [6]. The universal live update is verified independently of specific initial traces. The condition is stronger than for finite trace updates, and the number of compatible initial and update systems is smaller. Given that the context is unknown, the executions starting in the initial state of TS_U need to satisfy every possible open obligation. Universal updates are relevant if neither the trace nor the obligation monitor are stored and computed respectively. Given the initial system, model checking universal update compatibility obtains the same complexity as finite trace updates.

Definition 9 (Model Checking Universal Live Updates). *Let TS_I be an initial system, TS_U be an update system, φ be an initial specification, and ψ be an update specification. The problem of model checking universal live updates is defined as $\forall \eta \in FinTraces(TS_I) : \eta \cdot Traces(TS) \subseteq Words(\varphi, \psi, \eta)$.*

The implicit update points in TS_I allow for the connection of both transition systems and model checking with a linearly increased formula.

Theorem 3 (Complexity in $\varphi + \psi$, and $TS_I \cdot TS_U$). *The model checking problem for universal live updates is PSPACE-complete in $|\varphi| + |\psi|$ and NL in $TS_I \cdot TS_U$.*

The complexity results from encoding the live update in the combined transition system $TS_I \cdot TS_U$ and an adapted formula. Based on the model checking results we introduce live synthesis, the major contribution of this paper.

6.2   Live Synthesis

In this section, we introduce the problem of live synthesis and show the complexity of synthezising live systems. Synthesis of live updates during the runtime of the initial system promises correct-by-definition updates that can substitute the executed system instantaneously. In contrast to model checking, the synthesis procedure returns an implementation or *unrealizable*, proving that the finite trace or initial system and initial specification are incompatible with the update specification. We begin with live updates for an explicit finite trace of the initial system – the update system needs to react to the explicit context and open obligation. The definition follows the model checking problem, but searches for a transition system satisfying the live update.

Definition 10 (Finite Trace Live Synthesis). *Let φ be an initial specification, ψ be an update specification, and η be a finite trace. The finite trace live synthesis problem is the computation of a transition system TS s.t. $\eta \cdot Traces(TS) \subseteq Words(\varphi, \psi, \eta)$.*

We additionally call a live update *realizable* if there exists a transition system that satisfies the finite trace live update. The complexity of the update synthesis is expressed w.r.t. φ and ψ and aligns to existing LTL synthesis bounds.

Theorem 4 (Complexity in φ and ψ). *The finite trace live synthesis problem is 2EXPTIME-complete in $|\varphi|$ and $|\psi|$.*

The proof is subsumed by the proof of Theorem 5. The universal update is again of interest if the context of the live update is unknown. Synthesizing a transition system that satisfies the universal live update enables the user to plug-in the new system at any time-step without further analysis.

Definition 11 (Universal Live Synthesis). *Let φ be an initial specification, TS_I be an initial system, and ψ be an update specification. The universal live synthesis problem is the computation of a transition system TS s.t. $\forall \eta \in FinTraces(TS_I) : \eta \cdot Traces(TS) \subseteq Words(\varphi, \psi, \eta)$.*

Again, we call the problem of the existence of a solution realizability. In general, the universal update obtains a conjunction of double exponentially many conjuncted obligations. To avoid the expansion of the update system, we combine the parity games of the initial and update system. Again, the initial formula conducts the impact on the update system and provides the complexity results.

Theorem 5 (Complexity in φ and ψ). *The universal update synthesis problem is 2EXPTIME-complete in $|\varphi|$ and $|\psi|$.*

Hardness follows from Theorem 1, the completeness proof is a reduction from LiveLTL to LTL. Therefore, a parity game is built for the combination of the formulas, where the environment controls all edges before the update, thereby choosing the update context. The full proof is given in [6].

7   Case Study

We explore the live update problems on benchmarks from the reactive synthesis competition [13] and robot control communities [16]. Our goal is a qualitative analysis of pairs of specifications that can be updated live according to the finite trace live update and the universal live update. In more detail, we aim to answer the following questions: For specifications that can potentially be updated to each other, does the LiveLTL semantics state universally updatable obligations? And if not, in how many obligation states is a finite trace update possible?

A prototype for the live synthesis procedure is implemented on top of BoSy [5], a tool that synthesizes implementations for LTL formulas[1]. We use Spot [3] for LTL formula manipulation and implemented the obligation monitor construction for arbitrary LTL formulas. For our experiments, the following structure is used: BoSy synthesizes a system for the initial specification which is used to build the obligation monitor. Therefore, the result of the synthesis query, i.e., a transition system satisfying the formula, is parsed and cut with the obligation monitor to eliminate unreachable states. Since the result of BoSy may

---

[1] The prototype and experiments are available online at https://github.com/reactive-systems/LiveSynthesisArtifact.

differ per execution, we may obtain different sizes of the obligation monitor for different benchmark runs. Based on the obligation monitor, we perform explicit trace live synthesis for every monitor state label and universal live synthesis for all monitor states combined. Therefore, we build the conjunction of obligation formula and update formula and execute BoSy to check realizability.

For the benchmarks in Sect. 7.1, Table 1 shows multiple results: The number of obligation monitor states built by the initial system and specification, the number of finite trace updates that are realizable, and the result of the universal update. Despite the finite trace live update stating updates from every possible finite execution of the initial system, we use the state representation of the obligation monitor to symbolically represent every execution. The runtime in seconds for the update specification without update constraints and the universal update conclude the table. All experiments were executed on an Intel i7 processor with 2,8 GHz and 16 GB RAM.

7.1   Benchmark Families

The upper part of Table 1 shows the results for live updates from specification patterns introduced by Menghi et al. [16], where **Reactivity** implements additional interaction with the environment. The specifications define the behavior of a robot that is able to travel between n different locations and needs to satisfy different specifications on the way. Our second set of benchmarks is taken from the annual synthesis competition SYNTCOMP [13]. The results for live updates in the reactive synthesis setting are shown in the lower part of Table 1.

- **Visit, Seq. Visit**, and **Patrolling** enforce the robot to visit every location once, in a sequence, and infinitely often respectively.
- **Reactivity.** The reactivity specification forces the robot to react to an event after two steps at latest by driving to a delineated location, e.g., for refueling. The Reactivity specification can be added to arbitrary specifications.
- **Relay Station.** The running example of this paper. The relay station communicates with n satellites and forwards the message if clients acknowledged.
- **Arbiter.** An arbiter controls the access of multiple clients to a shared resource. It ensures that every request to the resource is eventually granted. We consider three variants of arbiter, a simple arbiter (**s**) only iterating over grants, a full arbiter (**f**) only granting access if requested beforehand, and a prioritized arbiter (**p**) that prioritizes the requests of client 0.
- **ABP.** The alternating bit protocol consists of a receiver **ABPReceiver** and a transmitter **ABPTransmitter** specifying the data link layer in the OSI communication network.
- **Load Balancer.** The load balancer distributes workload over n worker.

In addition to the specifications, we denote updates with an increased parameter with $n \rightarrow n + 1$. This property is of interest if the parameter may change during the execution, e.g., increasing the number of clients of an arbiter.

Table 1. Results of live updates for robot and SYNTCOMP specifications.

Robot specification patterns						
Ben.	Update	#OM-states	#Fin. trace	Universal	Time ψ	Time univ.
Visit	Seq. visit	4	4	real.	0.75	0.75
	Patrolling	6	6	real.	0.68	0.68
	Seq. patrolling	6	6	real.	0.64	0.72
	Reactivity	7	7	real.	0.49	0.49
Seq. visit	Patrolling	14	14	real.	0.56	0.59
	Seq. patrolling	16	16	real.	0.57	0.59
	Reactivity	5	5	real.	0.44	0.44
Patrolling	Ord. visit	6	6	real.	0.61	0.67
	Reactivity	7	7	real.	0.49	0.52
SYNTCOMP						
Relay station	1 → 2	4	4	real.	16.26	17.23
	2 → 1	19	19	real.	0.61	0.61
Arbiter	2f → 3f	11	6	unreal.	5.30	–
	2s → 2f	4	2	unreal.	0.56	–
	2s → 4s	4	4	real.	0.69	0.79
	2s → 2p	13	13	real.	0.46	0.48
	2f → 2p	10	10	real.	0.45	0.52
	2p → 3p	6	6	real.	0.65	0.74
ABPReceiver	1 → 2	5	4	unreal.	0.55	–
	2 → 3	9	3	unreal.	0.43	–
ABPTransmitter	1 → 2	5	5	real.	2.70	2.82
Load balancer	2 → 4	7	7	real.	0.72	0.75

7.2   Observations

Throughout all experiments, the minor runtime overhead of the universal update synthesis shows that the additional cost for live update correctness is feasible. The robot specifications provide insight of obligations raised during execution. Since most of the benchmarks obtain the same structural behavior, i.e., the robot visits the locations under some restrictions, the universal live updates are realizable. Even when adding requests, e.g., the robot has to refuel in two steps after requested, the live update is realizable by satisfying the open obligations after the update. Changes to the visiting sequence or infinitely often reaching a location with patrolling increases the size of the obligation monitor (#OM-States) but does not lead to unrealizability. Nevertheless, the sizes of the obligation monitors indicate that tracking the behavior of the system is necessary to obtain the correct obligation. Altogether, our results show that although robot specifications raise obligations, synthesizing correct live updates is often feasible due to the absence of conflicts between the specifications. Most interestingly for the reactive systems benchmarks are arbiter live updates. Changing a specification to a simple arbiter is realizable since the arbiter does not additionally restrict the behavior. However, live updates to full arbiter are only possible from some obligation monitor states, shown by the difference of #OM-States and #finite *trace updates.* Unrealizability follows from obligation states forcing a grant - an unrequested grant of the update system would be spurious. Since the prioritized arbiter does not include non-spuriousness, a live update from and to this arbiter is realizable. The relay station can be universally updated to the one more and one less base stations. Once computed, the obligations can be satisfied in finite time-steps and synthesizing a solution that reacts to all obligations is possible.

The experiments answer the questions stated at the beginning of this section: Specifications that are meaningful live updates state obligations for the update system, shown by the large number of states of the obligation monitors. Realizability of the update system depends on the restrictiveness of the specification, even if the universal update is unrealizable, our results show that in all benchmarks some finite trace live updates are realizable.

8 Related Work

The necessity of live updates in always-on systems is long known and was introduced as [4,7]. Dynamic updates for programming languages, e.g., in C++ [12] and Java [10], enable developers to update *dynamic classes* during runtime and are called *dynamic software updates* (DSU). The proposed frameworks implement functionality and are unable to ensure temporal correctness of the updates. Live kernel patches received huge attention in the operating system community [1,9], where bug-fixes and features of the kernel can be deployed without reboot. Recent work in live updates for operating systems achieved real-life implementations, e.g. for Linux [14] and Android [2] kernels. Implementations of dynamic updates raised the need for verification: Following the idea of observability by the user, Hayden et al. [11] introduce *client-oriented specifications* (CO-specs) to define and verify against client-visible behavior. Closest to our work are dynamic updates in controller verification and synthesis. Ghezzi et al. [8] introduce a controller synthesis approach based on Modal Sequence Diagrams (MSD). The update is a synthesized MSD that takes over the execution when a safe state is reached. While reaching a safe state is also necessary in [15], the authors omit the obligations of the previous system. Where [8] also relies on the existence of a safe state for the live update, [18] also proves the reachability of the update state. Therefore, the condition of the handover between the systems is defined as LTL specification. The main difference is stating the correctness as LTL formula and not observing the update condition semantically from the initial formula.

9 Conclusion

We introduced live synthesis, a synthesis framework for dynamic updates in reactive systems. We identified *obligations* of a running system as the currently open *co-safety* formulas and defined LiveLTL to specify the correct handover between two systems. The presented obligation monitor enables tracking of obligations during system execution and continuously shows the open obligations. We explored synthesis and model-checking for two update problems, *finite trace live updates* and *universal update*, which consider full information and zero information of the currently open obligations respectively. Our case study on robot specifications and reactive synthesis benchmarks show that it is necessary to verify live updates in *always-on* systems and *live synthesis* is able to automatically generate correct update systems if realizable. We believe that live updates play a crucial role in *high-availability* system verification and can benefit from existing techniques for reactive systems.

References

1. Baumann, A., et al.: Providing dynamic update in an operating system. In: USENIX (2005)
2. Chen, Y., Zhang, Y., Wang, Z., Xia, L., Bao, C., Wei, T.: Adaptive android kernel live patching. In: Kirda, E., Ristenpart, T. (eds.) USENIX Security 2017 (2017)
3. Duret-Lutz, A., Lewkowicz, A., Fauchille, A., Michaud, T., Renault, É., Xu, L.: Spot 2.0—a framework for LTL and ω-automata manipulation. In: Artho, C., Legay, A., Peled, D. (eds.) ATVA 2016. LNCS, vol. 9938, pp. 122–129. Springer, Cham (2016). https://doi.org/10.1007/978-3-319-46520-3_8
4. Fabry, R.S.: How to design a system in which modules can be changed on the fly. In: ICSE 1976. IEEE Computer Society (1976)
5. Faymonville, P., Finkbeiner, B., Tentrup, L.: BoSy: an experimentation framework for bounded synthesis. In: Majumdar, R., Kunčak, V. (eds.) CAV 2017. LNCS, vol. 10427, pp. 325–332. Springer, Cham (2017). https://doi.org/10.1007/978-3-319-63390-9_17
6. Finkbeiner, B., Klein, F., Metzger, N.: Live synthesis (full version) (2021). http://arxiv.org/abs/2107.01136
7. Frieder, O., Segal, M.E.: On dynamically updating a computer program: from concept to prototype. JSS **14**, 111–128 (1991). https://doi.org/10.1016/0164-1212(91)90096-O
8. Ghezzi, C., Greenyer, J., Manna, V.P.L.: Synthesizing dynamically updating controllers from changes in scenario-based specifications. In: SEAMS 2012. IEEE Computer Society (2012). https://doi.org/10.1109/SEAMS.2012.6224401
9. Giuffrida, C., Kuijsten, A., Tanenbaum, A.S.: Safe and automatic live update for operating systems. SIGPLAN Not. **48**, 279–292 (2013). https://doi.org/10.1145/2499368.2451147
10. Gregersen, A.R., Jørgensen, B.N.: Dynamic update of java applications - balancing change flexibility vs programming transparency. JSWM **21**, 81–112 (2009). https://doi.org/10.1002/smr.406
11. Hayden, C.M., Magill, S., Hicks, M., Foster, N., Foster, J.S.: Specifying and verifying the correctness of dynamic software updates. In: Joshi, R., Müller, P., Podelski, A. (eds.) VSTTE 2012. LNCS, vol. 7152, pp. 278–293. Springer, Heidelberg (2012). https://doi.org/10.1007/978-3-642-27705-4_22
12. Hjalmtysson, G., Gray, R.: Dynamic C++ classes - a lightweight mechanism to update code in a running program. In: USENIX 1998. USENIX Association (1998)
13. Jacobs, S., et al.: SYNTCOMP 2017. In: SYNT@CAV 2017 (2017). https://doi.org/10.4204/EPTCS.260.10
14. Makris, K., Ryu, K.D.: Dynamic and adaptive updates of non-quiescent subsystems in commodity operating system kernels. In: EuroSys 2007. ACM (2007). https://doi.org/10.1145/1272996.1273031

15. Manna, V.P.L., Greenyer, J., Ghezzi, C., Brenner, C.: Formalizing correctness criteria of dynamic updates derived from specification changes. In: SEAMS 2013. IEEE Computer Society (2013). https://doi.org/10.1109/SEAMS.2013.6595493
16. Menghi, C., Tsigkanos, C., Berger, T., Pelliccione, P., Ghezzi, C.: Property specification patterns for robotic missions. In: ICSE 2018. ACM (2018)
17. Meyer, P.J., Sickert, S., Luttenberger, M.: Strix: explicit reactive synthesis strikes back! In: Chockler, H., Weissenbacher, G. (eds.) CAV 2018. LNCS, vol. 10981, pp. 578–586. Springer, Cham (2018). https://doi.org/10.1007/978-3-319-96145-3_31
18. Nahabedian, L., et al.: Assured and correct dynamic update of controllers. In: SEAMS@ICSE 2016. ACM (2016). https://doi.org/10.1145/2897053.2897056
19. Pnueli, A.: The temporal logic of programs. In: SFCS 1977, October 1977. https://doi.org/10.1109/SFCS.1977.32

Faster Pushdown Reachability Analysis with Applications in Network Verification

Peter Gjøl Jensen[1], Stefan Schmid[2], Morten Konggaard Schou[1], Jiří Srba[1(✉)], Juan Vanerio[2], and Ingo van Duijn[1]

[1] Department of Computer Science, Aalborg University, Aalborg, Denmark
srba@cs.aau.dk
[2] Faculty of Computer Science, University of Vienna, Vienna, Austria

Abstract. Reachability analysis of pushdown systems is a fundamental problem in model checking that comes with a wide range of applications. We study performance improvements of pushdown reachability analysis and as a case study, we consider the verification of the policy-compliance of MPLS (Multiprotocol Label Switching) networks, an application domain that has recently received much attention. Our main contribution are three techniques that allow us to speed up the state-of-the-art pushdown reachability tools by an order of magnitude. These techniques include the combination of classic pre^* and $post^*$ saturation algorithms into a dual-search algorithm, an on-the-fly technique for detecting the possibility of early termination, as well as a counter-example guided abstraction refinement technique that improves the performance in particular for the negative instances where the early termination technique is not applicable. As a second contribution, we describe an improved translation of MPLS networks to pushdown systems and demonstrate on an extensive set of benchmarks of real internet wide-area networks the efficiency of our approach.

1 Introduction

Pushdown systems are a widely-used formalism with applications in, e.g., inter-procedural control-flow analysis of recursive programs [7,10] and model checking [3,11,19,20]. Pushdown systems have recently also received attention in the context of communication networks. Modern communication networks rely on increasingly complex router configurations which are difficult to manage by human administrators. Indeed, over the last years, several major network outages were due to human errors [1,2,8,15], and researchers are hence developing more automated and formal approaches to ensure policy compliance in networks. In particular, pushdown systems have been shown to enable fast automated what-if analysis of the policy compliance of an important and widely-deployed type of network, namely Multiprotocol Label Switching (MPLS) networks [17].

Research supported by the Vienna Science and Technology Fund (WWTF), ICT19-045 (WHATIF), and the DFF project QASNET.

Z. Hou and V. Ganesh (Eds.): ATVA 2021, LNCS 12971, pp. 170–186, 2021.
https://doi.org/10.1007/978-3-030-88885-5_12

We are motivated by the objective to improve the performance of reachability analysis in pushdown systems, which typically relies on automata-theoretic approach for computing the pre^* and $post^*$ of a regular set of pushdown configurations [18]. Time is the most critical performance aspect of reachability analysis in general, and in particular, in the context of the increasingly large communication networks that need to be frequently reconfigured.

Our Contributions. We show that there is a significant potential to improve the state-of-the-art in reachability analysis of pushdown systems. In particular, we propose a fast on-the-fly early termination technique as well as an algorithm that provides a novel combination of the classic pre^* and $post^*$ algorithms in order to harvest the benefits of both methods. We also suggest a specialization of the counter-example guided abstraction refinement (CEGAR) [5] technique that leverages equivalence classes on stack symbols as well as control states in order to improve the reachability analysis of MPLS networks that contain significant redundancy in the IP prefixes and produce a large number of MPLS labels (modeled as stack symbols). All techniques are general and apply to arbitrary pushdown systems, and are hence of interest in a wide range of applications. Finally, we also suggest a novel encoding approach of an MPLS communication network into a pushdown system that not only renders the pushdown analysis faster but also simpler compared to the recent approaches [13,14,17]. We report on our C++ prototype implementation and our empirical evaluation showing that the techniques can reduce the runtime by almost an order of magnitude compared to the state-of-the-art tools AalWiNes [14] and Moped [19].

Background and Related Work. We are motivated by the application of pushdown systems in order to perform automated what-if analysis of communication networks. In a nutshell, we consider a communication network interconnecting a set of routers which forward packets. The forwarding behavior of each router is defined by its pre-installed routing table which consists of a set of forwarding rules. To provide a dependable service, the network needs to fulfill a number of properties, such as reachability or loop-freedom, even under link failures.

Schmid and Srba recently showed in [17] that policy compliance of the widely-deployed MPLS networks can be verified in polynomial time, when overapproximating the possible link failures. Their approach leverages the fact that routing in MPLS networks is based on *label stacks*: packets contain stacks of labels which can be pushed and popped, and routers forward packets based on the top-of-stack label. Accordingly, these networks can be modelled as pushdown systems. In [13], the tool P-Rex was presented which implements the approach from [17]. P-Rex is implemented in Python, relies on the Moped model checker, and allows to verify complex network queries on network topologies with 20–30 routers in a matter of hours. The AalWiNes tool [14] is a follow-up work that improves the performance by an order of magnitude compared to P-Rex and replaces Moped with a tailored reachability engine written in C++.

In this paper, we show how to improve the performance by another order of magnitude compared to AalWiNes, by using three novel reachability techniques, including an early termination algorithm, a combined dual computation of pre^* and $post^*$, and a CEGAR approach. The CEGAR [5] technique was investigated in the context of symbolic pushdown systems before by Esparza et al. [9] who consider sequential (recursive) programs whose statements are given as binary decision diagrams (BDDs). However, the CEGAR application is not used to speed up the reachability analysis but to refine the abstractions of the programs. Moped [18] is a model checker for linear-time logic on pushdown systems and has been adapted to many use cases. For instance, jMoped [20] models java byte-code as symbolic pushdown systems allowing automated analysis and verification of invariant properties with Moped.

2   Preliminaries

A *Labelled Transition System (LTS)* is a triple $(S, \Sigma, \rightarrow)$ where S is the set of *states*, Σ is the set of *labels* and $\rightarrow \subseteq S \times \Sigma \times S$ is a *transition relation*. If $(s, a, s') \in \rightarrow$ then we write $s \xrightarrow{a} s'$. We also write $s \rightarrow s'$ if there is an $a \in \Sigma$ such that $s \xrightarrow{a} s'$ and let $\rightarrow^*$ be the reflexive and transitive closure of $\rightarrow$. The relation $\rightarrow^*$ can be annotated by the sequence of labels $w \in \Sigma^*$ as follows: $s \xrightarrow{\varepsilon}^* s$ for any $s \in S$ where ε is the empty word, and $s \xrightarrow{aw}^* s'$ for $a \in \Sigma$ and $w \in \Sigma^*$ if $s \xrightarrow{a} s''$ and $s'' \xrightarrow{w}^* s'$ for some $s'' \in S$.

Definition 1. *A Nondeterministic Finite Automaton (NFA) is a tuple* $\mathcal{N} = (Q, \Sigma, \rightarrow, I, F)$ *where* Q *is a finite set of* states, Σ *is a finite input alphabet,* $\rightarrow \subseteq Q \times (\Sigma \cup \{\varepsilon\}) \times Q$ *is the* transition relation, $I \subseteq Q$ *is the set of* initial states, *and* $F \subseteq Q$ *is the set of* accepting states.

An NFA $\mathcal{N}$ *accepts* a word $w \in \Sigma^*$ if the LTS $(Q, \Sigma, \rightarrow)$ satisfies $q_0 \xrightarrow{w}^* q_f$ for an initial state $q_0 \in I$ and an accepting state $q_f \in F$. The language $Lang(\mathcal{N})$ is the set of all words that $\mathcal{N}$ accepts.

Definition 2. *A Pushdown System (PDS) is a tuple* $\mathcal{P} = (P, \Gamma, \Delta)$*, where* P *is a finite set of* control locations (states), Γ *is a* stack alphabet, *and the set of rules* Δ *is a finite subset of* $(P \times \Gamma) \times (P \times \Gamma^*)$*. If* $((p, \gamma), (p', w)) \in \Delta$ *then we write* $\langle p, \gamma \rangle \hookrightarrow_{\mathcal{P}} \langle p', w \rangle$*.*

A *configuration* of a pushdown system is a pair $\langle p, w \rangle$ where $p \in P$ and $w \in \Gamma^*$. The set of all configurations is denoted $Conf(\mathcal{P})$. The semantics of a pushdown system $\mathcal{P}$ is given by the LTS $\mathcal{T}_{\mathcal{P}} = (Conf(\mathcal{P}), \Delta, \Rightarrow_{\mathcal{P}})$ where $\langle p, \gamma w' \rangle \xrightarrow{r}_{\mathcal{P}} \langle p', ww' \rangle$ for all $w' \in \Gamma^*$ whenever there is $r = ((p, \gamma), (p', w)) \in \Delta$. If $\mathcal{P}$ is clear from the context, we may omit it from $\hookrightarrow_{\mathcal{P}}$ and $\Rightarrow_{\mathcal{P}}$. We only consider normalized PDS in which all rules $\langle p, \gamma \rangle \hookrightarrow \langle p', w \rangle$ satisfy $|w| \leq 2$. Note that any PDS can be normalized by adding at most $\mathcal{O}(|P|)$ auxiliary states [18].

Definition 3. *Let* $\mathcal{P} = (P, \Gamma, \Delta)$ *be a PDS. A* $\mathcal{P}$*-automaton is an NFA* $\mathcal{A} = (Q, \Gamma, \rightarrow, P, F)$ *with the stack symbols of* $\mathcal{P}$ *as its input alphabet and with the initial states being the control locations of* $\mathcal{P}$*.*

A $\mathcal{P}$-automaton accepts a pushdown configuration $\langle p, w \rangle$ of $\mathcal{P}$ if $p \xrightarrow{w}{}^* q$ for some $q \in F$. The set of all configurations accepted by $\mathcal{A}$ is denoted by $Lang(\mathcal{A})$. A set of configurations is called *regular* if it is accepted by some $\mathcal{P}$-automaton.

Problem 1 (Pushdown Reachability Problem). For a PDS $\mathcal{P}$ and two regular sets of configurations C and C', is there $c \in C$ and $c' \in C'$ such that $c \xRightarrow{\sigma}{}^*_{\mathcal{P}} c'$ for some sequence of rules σ? In the affirmative case return a witness trace (c, σ).

Given a PDS $\mathcal{P}$ and a set of configurations $C \subseteq Conf(\mathcal{P})$ the *predecessors* are defined as $pre^*(C) = \{c \mid \exists c' \in C, c \Rightarrow^* c'\}$ and the *successors* as $post^*(C) = \{c \mid \exists c' \in C, c' \Rightarrow^* c\}$. If C is a regular set of configurations, then both $pre^*(C)$ and $post^*(C)$ are also regular sets of configurations [4].

Construction of pre^*. Given a $\mathcal{P}$-automaton $\mathcal{A} = (Q, \Gamma, \rightarrow_0, P, F)$, we construct a $\mathcal{P}$-automaton $\mathcal{A}_{pre^*} = (Q, \Gamma, \rightarrow, P, F)$ where $\rightarrow$ is obtained by repeatedly adding transitions to $\rightarrow_0$ according to the following saturation rule: if $\langle p, \gamma \rangle \hookrightarrow \langle p', w \rangle$ and $p' \xrightarrow{w} q$ in the current automaton, add a transition $p \xrightarrow{\gamma} q$.

Theorem 1 ([3,12,18]). *An automaton $\mathcal{A}_{pre^*}$ that satisfies $Lang(\mathcal{A}_{pre^*}) = pre^*(Lang(\mathcal{A}))$ can be built in $\mathcal{O}(|Q|^2 \cdot |\Delta|)$ time and $\mathcal{O}(|Q| \cdot |\Delta| + |\rightarrow_0|)$ space.*

There is a slightly more complicated saturation procedure for $\mathcal{A}_{post^*}$.

Theorem 2 ([3,12,18]). *An automaton $\mathcal{A}_{post^*}$ that satisfies $Lang(\mathcal{A}_{post^*}) = post^*(Lang(\mathcal{A}))$ can be built in $\mathcal{O}(|P| \cdot |\Delta| \cdot (n_1 + n_2) + |P| \cdot |\rightarrow_0|)$ time and space, where $n_1 = |Q \setminus P|$ and n_2 is the number of different pairs (p, γ) such that there is a rule of the form $\langle p', \gamma' \rangle \hookrightarrow \langle p, \gamma\gamma'' \rangle$ in Δ.*

Problem 1 can now be solved in polynomial time using either the pre^* or $post^*$ algorithm by computing e.g. $pre^*(C')$ and checking if $C \cap pre^*(C') \neq \emptyset$, similarly for $post^*$, relying on the fact that regular languages are closed under intersection. A witness trace σ can be computed by storing metadata during the saturation procedures (see e.g. [18] for details).

3   Formal Model of MPLS Networks

An MPLS network consists of a topology and forwarding rules.

Definition 4. *A network topology is a directed multigraph (V, E, s, t) where V is a set of routers, E is a set of links between routers, $s : E \rightarrow V$ assigns the source router to each link, and $t : E \rightarrow V$ assigns the target router.*

We assume that links in the network can fail. This is modelled by a set $F \subseteq E$ of *failed* links. A link is *active* if it belongs to $E \setminus F$.

For a nonempty set of MPLS labels L, we define the set of *MPLS operations* on packet headers as $Op(L) = \{\mathtt{swap}(\ell) \mid \ell \in L\} \cup \{\mathtt{push}(\ell) \mid \ell \in L\} \cup \{\mathtt{pop}\}$. We define the semantics of MPLS operations $[\cdot] : Op(L) \rightarrow (L \rightarrow L^*)$ by $[\mathtt{pop}](\ell) = \varepsilon$, $[\mathtt{swap}(\ell')](\ell) = \ell'$ and $[\mathtt{push}(\ell')](\ell) = \ell'\ell$ for all $\ell, \ell' \in L$.

The forwarding of a packet in an MPLS network depends on the interface (link) that the packet arrives on, which determines the forwarding table used, and the top MPLS label in the packet header, which is used for lookup in the forwarding table. When a packet enters the MPLS domain, it does not yet have any MPLS label, and the forwarding depends only on the link that it arrives on as well as the type of the protocol that is used for the packet forwarding (this is abstracted away by the use of nondeterminism).

Definition 5. *An* MPLS *network is a tuple* $N = (V, E, s, t, L, \tau)$ *where* (V, E, s, t) *is a network topology, L is a finite set of MPLS labels, and τ :* $E \cup (E \times L) \rightarrow \left(2^{E \times Op(L)^+}\right)^*$ *is the routing table.*

For every link $e \in E$ and for every link-label pair $(e, \ell) \in E \times L$, the routing table returns a sequence of *traffic engineering groups* $O_1 O_2 \dots O_n$ where each group is a set of the form $\{(e_1, \omega_1), \dots, (e_m, \omega_m)\}$ where e_j is the outgoing link such that $t(e) = s(e_j)$ and $\omega_j \in Op(L)^+$ is a nonempty sequence of MPLS operations to be performed on the packet header. Figure 1a gives an example of an MPLS network with its routing table in Fig. 1b. Here the priority column refers to the index of the corresponding traffic engineering group.

The semantics of a traffic engineering group is that any pair of active link and operation sequence in the group can be nondeterministically chosen, hence abstracting away from various specific routing policies that allow e.g. splitting a flow along multiple paths. The group O_i has a higher priority than O_{i+1}, and during forwarding the router always selects the traffic engineering group with the highest priority and at least one active link.

For a traffic engineering group $O = \{(e_1, \omega_1), (e_2, \omega_2), \dots, (e_m, \omega_m)\}$ let $E(O) = \{e_1, e_2, \dots, e_m\}$ denote the set of outgoing links in the group.

Definition 6. *For a set of failed links $F \subseteq E$ we define the* active routing table $\tau_F : E \cup (E \times L) \rightarrow 2^{E \times Op(L)^+}$ *as* $\tau_F(u) = \{(e', \omega) \in \mathcal{A}_F(\tau(u)) \mid e' \in E \setminus F\}$, *where $u = e$ or $u = (e, \ell)$ and $\mathcal{A}_F$ is the* active traffic engineering group *defined as* $\mathcal{A}_F(O_1 O_2 \dots O_n) = O_j$ *if j is the lowest index such that $E(O_j) \setminus F \neq \emptyset$, or* $\mathcal{A}(O_1 O_2 \dots O_n) = \emptyset$ *if no such j exists.*

Definition 7. *The semantics of MPLS operations is a* partial *header rewrite function* $\mathcal{H} : L^* \times Op(L)^* \rightharpoonup L^*$, *where $\omega, \omega' \in Op(L)^*$, $h \in L^*$ and ε is the empty sequence of operations:*

$$\mathcal{H}(h, \omega) = \begin{cases} h & \text{if } \omega = \varepsilon \\ \mathcal{H}([op](\ell) \circ h', \omega') & \text{if } \omega = op \circ \omega' \text{ and } h = \ell \circ h' \text{ with } \ell \in L, h' \in L^* \\ \text{undefined} & \text{otherwise} . \end{cases}$$

Using the example from Fig. 1, the operation sequence $\mathsf{swap}(12) \circ \mathsf{push}(20)$ applied to the header $10 \circ 30$ yields $\mathcal{H}(10 \circ 30, \mathsf{swap}(12) \circ \mathsf{push}(20)) = 20 \circ 12 \circ 30$.

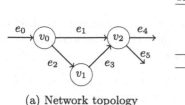

Router	e_{in}	Label	Priority	e_{out}	Operation
v_0	e_0	–	1	e_1	push(11)
	e_0	–	2	e_2	push(11) ∘ push(20)
	e_0	10	1	e_1	swap(12)
	e_0	10	2	e_2	swap(12) ∘ push(20)
v_1	e_2	20	1	e_3	pop
v_2	e_1	11	1	e_4	pop
	e_1	12	1	e_5	pop
	e_3	11	1	e_4	pop
	e_3	12	1	e_5	pop

(a) Network topology

(b) Routing table

$$\sigma_1 = (e_0, \varepsilon)(e_1, 11)(e_4, \varepsilon) \qquad\qquad\qquad \text{for } F = \emptyset$$
$$\sigma_2 = (e_0, 10 \circ 30)(e_2, 20 \circ 12 \circ 30)(e_3, 12 \circ 30)(e_5, 30) \qquad \text{for } F = \{e_1\}$$
$$\varphi = \langle 10 \cdot^* \rangle\ e_0 \ \cdot^* \ e_5 \ \langle 30 \rangle\ 1 \qquad\qquad\qquad \text{is satisfied by } \sigma_2$$

(c) Example traces σ_1 and σ_2 under a set of failed links F, and an example query φ

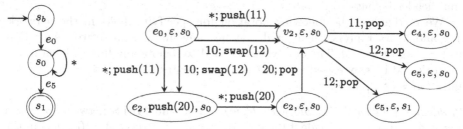

(d) Corresponding pushdown system for the query φ. Left: the NFA $\mathcal{N}_b$ for φ. Right: the generated PDS $\mathcal{P}$. The labelled arrow $(p) \xrightarrow{\ell;op} (p')$ denotes the rule $\langle p, \ell \rangle \hookrightarrow \langle p', [op](\ell) \rangle$. The state (v_2, ε, s_0) is merged from (e_1, ε, s_0) and (e_3, ε, s_0).

$$P_i = \{(e_0, \varepsilon, s_0)\} \qquad\qquad \langle (e_0, \varepsilon, s_0), 10 \circ 30 \circ \bot \rangle \Rightarrow_{\mathcal{P}}$$
$$P_f = \{(e_5, \varepsilon, s_1)\} \qquad\qquad \langle (e_2, \mathbf{push}(20), s_0), 12 \circ 30 \circ \bot \rangle \Rightarrow_{\mathcal{P}}$$
$$Lang(\mathcal{N}_i) = \{10 \circ w \circ \bot \mid w \in L^*\} \qquad \langle (e_2, \varepsilon, s_0), 20 \circ 12 \circ 30 \circ \bot \rangle \Rightarrow_{\mathcal{P}}$$
$$Lang(\mathcal{N}_f) = \{30 \circ \bot\} \qquad\qquad \langle (v_2, \varepsilon, s_0), 12 \circ 30 \circ \bot \rangle \Rightarrow_{\mathcal{P}} \langle (e_5, \varepsilon, s_1), 30 \circ \bot \rangle$$

(e) Initial/final configurations for φ (f) Computation in PDS $\mathcal{P}$ corresponding to σ_2

Fig. 1. Example of a small network and its encoding into a pushdown system

Definition 8. *A* trace *in a network* $N = (V, E, s, t, L, \tau)$, *given a set of failed links* $F \subseteq E$, *is any finite sequence* $(e_1, h_1)(e_2, h_2) \ldots (e_n, h_n) \in ((E \backslash F) \times L^*)^*$ *of link-header pairs where for all* i, $1 \leq i < n$, $h_{i+1} = \mathcal{H}(h_i, \omega)$ *for some* $(e_{i+1}, \omega) \in \tau_F(u)$, *where either* $u = e_i$ *or* $u = (e_i, head(h_i))$, *where* $head(h_i)$ *is the top (leftmost) label of* h_i. *If* $h_i = \varepsilon$ *then* $head(h_i)$ *is undefined.*

In Fig. 1c we can see a trace σ_1 in the network without any failed links, while for the failure set $F = \{e_1\}$ we notice that σ_1 is not a trace, while σ_2 is.

3.1   MPLS Network Verification

Similar to prior work [13,14], we present a powerful query language that allows us to specify regular trace properties, both regarding the initial and final label-stacks as well as the sequence of links in the trace.

Definition 9. *A reachability query for an MPLS network $N = (V, E, s, t, L, \tau)$ is of the form $\langle a \rangle \, b \, \langle c \rangle \, k$ where a and c are regular expressions over the set of labels L, b is a regular expression over the set of links E, and $k \geq 0$ specifies the maximum number of failures to be considered.*

We assume here a standard syntax for regular expressions and by $Lang(a)$, $Lang(b)$ and $Lang(c)$ we understand the regular language defined by the expressions a, b and c, respectively. Intuitively, the query $\langle a \rangle \, b \, \langle c \rangle \, k$ asks if there is a network trace such that the initial header (stack of labels) belongs to $Lang(a)$, the sequence of visited links belongs to $Lang(b)$ and at the end of the trace the final header belongs to $Lang(c)$.

We further use the following notation for specifying links in the network. If v and u are routers, then $[v\#u]$ matches any link e from v to u such that $s(e) = v$ and $t(e) = u$. The dot-syntax is used to denote any link or label in the network and it is extended to match also any router so that $[v\#\cdot] = \bigcup_{u \in V} [v\#u]$ and $[\cdot\#u] = \bigcup_{v \in V} [v\#u]$.

Problem 2 (Query Satisfiability Problem).   Given an MPLS network N and a query $\varphi = \langle a \rangle \, b \, \langle c \rangle \, k$, decide if there exists a trace $\sigma = (e_1, h_1) \ldots (e_n, h_n)$ in the network N for some set of failed links F such that $|F| \leq k$ where $h_1 \in Lang(a)$, $e_1 \ldots e_n \in Lang(b)$, and $h_n \in Lang(c)$. If this is the case, the query φ is *satisfied* and we call σ a *witness trace*.

In Fig. 1c the query φ asks if a packet with the top most label 10 can be forwarded from the link e_0 to e_5, while just leaving the label 30 on the label-stack. This query is satisfied and the trace σ_2 serves as a witness trace. On the other hand, the query $\langle \, \cdot^* \rangle \, [\cdot\#v_1] \, \cdot^* e_3 \, \langle \, \cdot^* \rangle \, 0$ is not satisfied as it asks if a packet (with any header) arriving on some link to the router v_1 (note that e_0 is the only such link) can reach the link e_3 if no links fail. Such a trace exists only if we allow for at least one failed link.

3.2   From Query Satisfiability to Pushdown Reachability

We now solve the query satisfiability problem by translation to the pushdown reachability problem. This is an over-approximation, so in a few cases a positive result cannot be transfered back to the query satisfiability problem. Notice that our construction is different from the one in [13]. In particular, we model the initial and final headers directly as NFA rather than simulating them with PDSs, which makes the reduction simpler and more efficient at the same time.

The behavior of the network for a fixed set of failed links F is given by the active routing table τ_F, however to represent the possible behavior for any set of failed links F with $|F| \leq k$, we use the following definition.

Definition 10. *For a network $N = (V, E, s, t, L, \tau)$ and number k, we define the overapproximating routing table $\tau^k(u) = \bigcup_{j=1}^{i} O_j$, where $\tau(u) = O_1 O_2 \ldots O_n$ and i is the smallest index such that $|\bigcup_{j=1}^{i} E(O_j)| > k$.*

The routing table τ^k overapproximates all possible routing table entries if up to k links fail at any router.

Given a network $N = (V, E, s, t, L, \tau)$ and a query $\varphi = \langle a \rangle \, b \, \langle c \rangle \, k$, let $\mathcal{N}_a = (S_a, L, \rightarrow_a, \{s_a\}, F_a)$, $\mathcal{N}_b = (S_b, E, \rightarrow_b, \{s_b\}, F_b)$ and $\mathcal{N}_c = (S_c, L, \rightarrow_c, \{s_c\}, F_c)$ be the NFAs corresponding to the regular expressions a, b and c. Let $L_\perp = L \cup \{\perp\}$ where $\perp$ is used to represent the bottom of the stack. We construct a PDS $\mathcal{P} = (P, L_\perp, \Delta)$ where $P = E \times \overline{Ops} \times S_b$ and $\overline{Ops}$ is the set of all operation sequences and suffixes hereof occurring in τ^k. The set of rules Δ is defined by:

a) $\langle (e, \varepsilon, s), \ell \rangle \hookrightarrow \langle (e', \omega, s'), [op](\ell) \rangle$ if $s \xrightarrow{e'}_b^* s'$ and $(e', op \circ \omega) \in \tau^k(u)$ where either (i) $u = (e, \ell)$, or (ii) $u = e$, $\ell \in L$, or (iii) $u = e$, $\ell = \perp$, $op = \text{push}(\ell')$.

b) $\langle (e, op \circ \omega, s), \ell \rangle \hookrightarrow \langle (e, \omega, s), [op](\ell) \rangle$ for $\ell \in L$ and for $\ell = \perp$ if $op = \text{push}(\ell')$.

Finally, we define the initial states $P_i = \{(e, \varepsilon, s) \mid e \in E, s \in S_b, s_b \xrightarrow{e}_b^* s\}$, and the final states $P_f = \{(e, \varepsilon, s_f) \mid e \in E, s_f \in F_b\}$. Let $\mathcal{N}_\perp$ be an NFA such that $Lang(\mathcal{N}_\perp) = \{\perp\}$. Let $\mathcal{N}_i = \mathcal{N}_a \circ \mathcal{N}_\perp$ and $\mathcal{N}_f = \mathcal{N}_c \circ \mathcal{N}_\perp$ where $\circ$ is the standard NFA concatenation operator. For the running example this is shown in Fig. 1e. Now the query satisfiability problem is reduced to the problem of finding configurations $c \in P_i \times Lang(\mathcal{N}_i)$ and $c' \in P_f \times Lang(\mathcal{N}_f)$ such that $c \xrightarrow{\sigma}_\mathcal{P}^* c'$, and in the positive case outputting the trace (c, σ).

Optimizations. To reduce the size of the PDS we use the following optimizations. We merge control locations (e, ω, s) and (e', ω, s) for which $t(e) = t(e')$, $\tau(e) = \tau(e')$ and $\tau(e, \ell) = \tau(e', \ell)$ for all $\ell \in L$, i.e. the lookup is independent of which interface on the router the packet arrives on, which is often the case in many existing networks. We only construct control states that are reachable from P_i. If a rule $\langle p, \ell \rangle \hookrightarrow \langle p', [op](\ell) \rangle$ is added for all $\ell \in L_\perp$, we represent it succinctly as $\langle p, * \rangle \hookrightarrow \langle p', [op](*) \rangle$ where $*$ is a wildcard representing any label. The wildcard can be handled efficiently by our $post^*$ algorithm, while for pre^* it needs to be unfolded. In Fig. 1d we can see the generated pushdown system for our running example and in Fig. 1f we show an execution of the pushdown system corresponding to the network trace σ_2.

We can now show that if there is a network trace satisfying a given query then the constructed pushdown system provides a positive answer in the reachability analysis.

Theorem 3. *Given a network N and a query φ, if there exists a witness trace in the network satisfying φ, then there exist $c \in P_i \times Lang(\mathcal{N}_i)$, $c' \in P_f \times Lang(\mathcal{N}_f)$ and $\sigma \in \Delta^*$ such that $c \xrightarrow{\sigma}_\mathcal{P}^* c'$.*

Proof (Sketch). By induction on the length of the witness trace we construct the corresponding pushdown execution following the construction of the pushdown rules Δ. One step in the network trace can be simulated by a sequence of push-down transitions as the rules of type b) apply the MPLS operations sequentially one by one.   □

For the other direction, we have to first make sure that the trace obtained from the execution in the pushdown system is indeed a valid network trace (since the pushdown system overapproximates the set of all valid traces as it assumes that at any router, up to k links can fail).

Reconstruction of Network Traces. The reachability analysis for the pushdown system $\mathcal{P}$ returns (in the affirmative case) a trace $\langle p_0, w_0 \rangle \overset{r_1}{\Rightarrow}_{\mathcal{P}} \dots \overset{r_m}{\Rightarrow}_{\mathcal{P}} \langle p_m, w_m \rangle$. We extract (e, h) for every i such that $p_i = (e, \omega, s)$ and $w_i = h \circ \bot$ where $\omega = \varepsilon$, producing a network trace $(e_0, h_0) \dots (e_n, h_n)$. For each rule r of type a) that was added due to $(e', \omega) \in \tau^k(u)$, we define $F^\tau(r) = \bigcup_{j=1}^{i-1} E(O_j)$ where $\tau(u) = O_1 O_2 \dots$ and i is the smallest index such that $(e', \omega) \in O_i$. Let $F = \bigcup_{i=1}^{n} F^\tau(r_i)$ be the set of failed links in order to enable the execution of the trace. Now we have to check that $\{e_0, \dots, e_n\} \cap F = \emptyset$ and $|F| \leq k$ in order to guarantee that the corresponding network trace is executable; otherwise the overapproximation returns an inconclusive answer.

Theorem 4. *Given a network N and a query φ, if in the constructed pushdown system there exist $c \in P_i \times Lang(\mathcal{N}_i)$, $c' \in P_f \times Lang(\mathcal{N}_f)$ and $\sigma \in \Delta^*$ s.t. $c \overset{\sigma}{\Rightarrow}_{\mathcal{P}}^* c'$ from which a valid network trace σ' can be reconstructed, then σ' satisfies φ.*

Proof (Sketch). From the construction of the pushdown system and the encoding of MPLS operations by a series of pushdown transitions, we can see that if the reconstructed trace only uses active links, i.e. $\{e_0, \dots, e_n\} \cap F = \emptyset$, then it corresponds to a correct network trace for the routing table τ^k. However, as τ^k allows for up to k link failures at any router along the trace, the total number of failed links along the reconstructed trace may exceed the bound k. This is detected in the trace reconstruction procedure.   □

4   Improving Pushdown System Reachability Analysis

We now describe our improvements to the pushdown reachability analysis.

4.1   Early Termination of Reachability Algorithms

In Sect. 2 we showed that for a given PDS $\mathcal{P} = (P, \Gamma, \Delta)$ and $\mathcal{P}$-automaton $\mathcal{A}$ that represents a set of configurations in $\mathcal{P}$, we can construct the $\mathcal{A}_{post*}$ and $\mathcal{A}_{pre*}$ automata by iteratively adding additional transitions to the existing automaton $\mathcal{A}$. During this saturation procedure, the language of the current $\mathcal{P}$-automaton $\mathcal{A}$ can only increase (w.r.t. subset inclusion). Hence if at any point the current $\mathcal{P}$-automaton has a nonempty intersection with some set of target configurations, it will have the nonempty intersection also after the saturation procedure

---

Algorithm 1. On-the-fly computation of product automaton

Input: $\mathcal{P}$-automata $\mathcal{A}_1 = (Q_1, \Gamma, \rightarrow_1, P, F_1)$ and $\mathcal{A}_2 = (Q_2, \Gamma, \rightarrow_2, P, F_2)$

1: Initialize $R \subseteq Q_1 \times Q_2$ to $\emptyset$
2: Let $\mathcal{A}_\cap \leftarrow (Q_1 \times Q_2, \Gamma, \rightarrow, \{(p, p) \mid p \in P\}, F_1 \times F_2)$ where $\rightarrow$ initially does not contain any transitions

3: **function** ADDSTATE(q_1, q_2)
4:     **if** $(q_1, q_2) \notin R$ **then**
5:         $R \leftarrow R \cup (q_1, q_2)$
6:         **if** $q_1 \in F_1$ and $q_2 \in F_2$ **then exit and return true**
7:         **for all** $q_1' \in Q_1, q_2' \in Q_2, \gamma \in \Gamma$ s.t. $q_1 \xrightarrow{\gamma}_1 q_1'$ and $q_2 \xrightarrow{\gamma}_2 q_2'$ **do**
8:             add $(q_1, q_2) \xrightarrow{\gamma} (q_1', q_2')$ to $\mathcal{A}_\cap$
9:             ADDSTATE(q_1', q_2')

10: **function** ADDTRANSITION($q_i \xrightarrow{\gamma}_i q_i'$)   ▷ with $i \in \{1, 2\}$
11:     add $q_i \xrightarrow{\gamma}_i q_i'$ to $\mathcal{A}_i$
12:     **for all** $q_{3-i}, q_{3-i}' \in Q_{3-i}$ s.t. $(q_1, q_2) \in R$ and $q_{3-i} \xrightarrow{\gamma}_{3-i} q_{3-i}'$ **do**
13:         add $(q_1, q_2) \xrightarrow{\gamma} (q_1', q_2')$ to $\mathcal{A}_\cap$
14:         ADDSTATE(q_1', q_2')

---

terminates. We can hence allow for an early termination as we can return a witness trace before completing the saturation procedure.

We further generalize this idea by considering $\mathcal{P}$-automata $\mathcal{A}_1 = (Q_1, \Gamma, \rightarrow_1, P, F_1)$ and $\mathcal{A}_2 = (Q_2, \Gamma, \rightarrow_2, P, F_2)$ that can be step-by-step saturated by calling (in arbitrary order) the functions ADDTRANSITION($q_1 \xrightarrow{\gamma}_1 q_1'$) and ADDTRANSITION($q_2 \xrightarrow{\gamma}_2 q_2'$), respectively. Each such call will add the corresponding transition in its argument to the automaton $\mathcal{A}_1$ resp. $\mathcal{A}_2$ and at the same time compute the reachable part (stored in the nondecreasing set R of pairs of states in $\mathcal{A}_1$ and $\mathcal{A}_2$) of the product automaton $\mathcal{A}_\cap$ representing the current intersection of $\mathcal{A}_1$ and $\mathcal{A}_2$. The function call ADDTRANSITION($q_i \xrightarrow{\gamma}_i q_i'$) where $i \in \{1, 2\}$ relies on the function ADDSTATE(q_1, q_2) given in Algorithm 1 and before any calls to ADDTRANSITION are made, it is assumed that the product automaton is initialized by calling ADDSTATE(p, p) for all states $p \in P$. The algorithm exits (early terminates) and returns true as soon as the product automaton accepts at least one string.

Proposition 1. *Let $\mathcal{A}_1$ and $\mathcal{A}_2$ be two initial $\mathcal{P}$-automata and let $\mathcal{A}_1'$ and $\mathcal{A}_2'$ be the resulting $\mathcal{P}$-automata after an arbitrary number of calls to the function* ADDTRANSITION *given in Algorithm 1. Then $Lang(\mathcal{A}_\cap) = Lang(\mathcal{A}_1') \cap Lang(\mathcal{A}_2')$ and as soon as $Lang(\mathcal{A}_\cap) \neq \emptyset$, the algorithm returns true.*

This on-the-fly detection of nonemptiness of the intersection between two $\mathcal{P}$-automata can be used to allow for early termination when deciding the reachability in pushdown systems using the *pre** and *post** approach described in Sect. 2. Here only one of the two $\mathcal{P}$-automata is saturated while the other

---

Algorithm 2. Dual search

    Input: $\mathcal{P}$-automata $\mathcal{A}$ and $\mathcal{A}'$

1: **for** p in P **do** ADDSTATE(p, p)
2: Initialize pre^* algorithm for $\mathcal{A}'$ and $post^*$ for $\mathcal{A}$ (incl. $worksets$ of transitions)
3: **while** $workset_{pre^*} \neq \emptyset$ and $workset_{post^*} \neq \emptyset$ **do**
4:     pop t from $workset_{pre^*}$
5:     execute one step of pre^* using t
6:     **for** t' newly added to $workset_{pre^*}$ **do** ADDTRANSITION(t')   (can return **true**)
7:     pop t from $workset_{post^*}$
8:     execute one step of $post^*$ using t
9:     **for** t' newly added to $workset_{post^*}$ **do** ADDTRANSITION(t')   (can return **true**)
10: **return false**

---

automaton remains unchanged. We now show that this on-the-fly detection of nonemptiness can be applied, with significant performance improvements, also when both approaches are combined.

4.2 Combining Forward and Backward Search

Our experiments show that none of the two approaches, pre^* and $post^*$, is superior to the other one. Our aim is to further improve the reachability analysis of pushdown systems by combining these two methods into $dual*$ algorithm. We first observe the following facts.

Proposition 2. *Given a PDS $\mathcal{P} = (P, \Gamma, \Delta)$ and regular sets C and C' of its configurations, the following statements are equivalent: a) $c \Rightarrow^* c'$ for some $c \in C$ and $c' \in C'$, b) $C \cap pre^*(C') \neq \emptyset$, c) $post^*(C) \cap C' \neq \emptyset$, and d) $post^*(C) \cap pre^*(C') \neq \emptyset$.*

Let the $\mathcal{P}$-automata $\mathcal{A}$ and $\mathcal{A}'$ represent the sets of configurations C and C', respectively. The classical approach to the reachability problem, formulated in Proposition 2a, either uses the equivalent formulation in b) and iteratively constructs $\mathcal{A}'_{pre^*}$ while checking whether its language has a nonempty intersection with the set C, or it uses part c) and constructs $\mathcal{A}_{post^*}$ while checking for nonempty intersection with C'.

We suggest a novel combination of these two methods while relying on Proposition 2d. In Algorithm 2, we (sequentially) interleave the executions of the $post^*$ saturation procedure on $\mathcal{A}$ and the pre^* procedure on $\mathcal{A}'$. The intersection of the two automata is computed on-the-fly using Algorithm 1 where each of the saturation procedures calls its respective ADDTRANSITION function and Algorithm 2 terminates with **true** as soon as the intersection becomes nonempty. Once one of the saturation algorithms completes its execution, the algorithm returns **false**. Notice that this approach is different from running pre^* and $post^*$ independently in parallel since our algorithm allows the two search directions to 'meet in the middle'. In Sect. 5 we document a gain of almost an order of magnitude compared to saturating exclusively $\mathcal{A}$ or $\mathcal{A}'$.

4.3 Abstraction Refinement for Pushdown System Reachability

We now explore an abstraction technique [6] in order to reduce the size of the verified PDS. We suggest (in a heuristic way) an initial abstraction by collapsing selected stack symbols and control states and use counter-example guided abstraction refinement [5] in case we obtain spurious traces.

Abstraction of Pushdown Model of MPLS Network. As described in Sect. 3.2, we consider a network $N = (V, E, s, t, L, \tau)$, NFAs that originate from the given query $\mathcal{N}_a = (S_a, L, \to_a, s_a, F_a)$, $\mathcal{N}_b = (S_b, E, \to_b, s_b, F_b)$ and $\mathcal{N}_c = (S_c, L, \to_c, s_c, F_c)$, and the overapproximating routing table τ^k.

Let $\mathbb{L}$ and $\mathbb{E}$ be the sets of abstract labels resp. edges that are possibly smaller than the sets L and E. A *network abstraction* is a surjective function $\alpha : L \cup E \to \mathbb{L} \cup \mathbb{E}$ such that $\alpha(\ell) \in \mathbb{L}$ for all $\ell \in L$ and $\alpha(e) \in \mathbb{E}$ for all $e \in E$.

Example 1. Let $\mathbb{L} = \{\bullet\}$ and $\mathbb{E} = \{\star\}$ such that $\alpha(\ell) = \bullet$ for $\ell \in L$ and $\alpha(e) = \star$ for $e \in E$. This is the coarsest abstraction that does not distinguish between any labels nor edges. On the other hand, if $\mathbb{L} = L$ and $\mathbb{E} = E$ then the abstraction $\alpha(x) = x$ for $x \in L \cup E$ is the most fine-grained one.

We extend α in a straightforward way to apply to headers and sequences of MPLS operations. We now construct an α-abstracted PDS $\mathcal{P} = (P, \mathbb{L}_\perp, \Delta)$ similar to Sect. 3.2 such that $P = \mathbb{E} \times \overline{Ops} \times S_b$ where $\overline{Ops} = \{\alpha(\omega) \mid \omega \in \overline{Ops}\}$ and Δ is defined as above except that rule of type a) now uses the abstraction:

a) $\langle (\alpha(e), \varepsilon, s), \alpha(\ell) \rangle \hookrightarrow \langle (\alpha(e'), \alpha(\omega), s'), [\alpha(op)](\alpha(\ell)) \rangle$ if $(e', op \circ \omega) \in \tau^k(u)$
   and $s \xrightarrow{e'}{}^*_b s'$ where either (i) $u = (e, \ell)$, or (ii) $u = e$ and $\ell \in L$, or (iii) $op = \mathrm{push}(\ell')$, $u = e$ and $\ell = \perp$.

We also define α-abstracted initial states $P_i = \{(\alpha(e), \varepsilon, s) \mid e \in E, s \in S_b, s_b \xrightarrow{e}{}^*_b s\}$ and final states $P_f = \{(\alpha(e), \varepsilon, s_f) \mid e \in E, s_f \in F_b\}$. Finally, we define an abstraction of an NFA $\mathcal{N} = (S, L, \to, \{s_0\}, F)$ as $\alpha(\mathcal{N}) = (S, \mathbb{L}, \to_\alpha, \{s_0\}, F)$ where $s \xrightarrow{\alpha(\ell)}_\alpha s'$ in $\alpha(\mathcal{N})$ iff $s \xrightarrow{\ell} s'$ in $\mathcal{N}$. Using this, let $\mathcal{N}_i = \alpha(\mathcal{N}_a) \circ \mathcal{N}_\perp$ and $\mathcal{N}_f = \alpha(\mathcal{N}_c) \circ \mathcal{N}_\perp$. Theorem 3 can now be shown to hold also for this α-abstracted PDS.

We now show how to reconstruct a concrete network trace from the α-abstracted pushdown trace. The reconstruction may finish with a success (a concrete network trace is found) or it suggests a refinement of the abstraction function α and the whole verification process is repeated (CEGAR).

Reconstruction of Network Traces. Given a trace $\langle p_0, w_0 \rangle \xRightarrow{r_1}_\mathcal{P} \dots \xRightarrow{r_m}_\mathcal{P} \langle p_m, w_m \rangle$ in the α-abstracted PDS, we take the subsequence of rules in the trace of type a), and for each such rule r_i define T_i as the set of forwarding rules (u, e', ω) such that r_i was added due to $(e', \omega) \in \tau^k(u)$.

For each set T_i, define $[T_i]$ as a mapping between sets of link-header pairs:
$[T_i](C) = \bigcup_{(e,h) \in C} \{(e', h') \mid (u, e', \omega) \in T_i, \mathcal{H}(h, \omega) = h', \text{and } u = e \text{ or } u =$

$(e, head(h))\}$. If $C' = [T_i](C)$ then we write $C \underset{T_i}{\Longrightarrow} C'$. The initial set of link-header pairs is $C_0 = \{(e, h) \in E \times L^* \mid p_0 = (\alpha(e), \varepsilon, s), s_b \xrightarrow{e}_b^* s, w_0 = \alpha(h) \circ \bot, h \in Lang(\mathcal{N}_a)\}$. The set of reachable link-header pairs is now found by $C_0 \underset{T_1}{\Longrightarrow} C_1 \underset{T_2}{\Longrightarrow} \dots \underset{T_n}{\Longrightarrow} C_n$. If $C_n \neq \emptyset$ and there exists $(e, h) \in C_n$ such that $h \in Lang(\mathcal{N}_c)$, then we have a concrete network trace, where we finally compute and check the set of failed links against the trace as in Sect. 3.2. Otherwise the PDS trace is a spurious counter-example that will guide the refinement of the abstraction α.

Refinement From Pushdown System Rules. If $C_n = \emptyset$ then we compute the refinement based on the rules of the pushdown system: let i be such that $C_i \neq \emptyset$ and $C_{i+1} = \emptyset$, and we must have some $(e, h) \in C_i$ and $(u, e'', \omega) \in T_{i+1}$ such that $u = (e', \ell')$ and $head(h) = \ell$ where $(\alpha(e), \alpha(\ell)) = (\alpha(e'), \alpha(\ell'))$ but $(e, \ell) \neq (e', \ell')$, or that $u = e'$ where $\alpha(e) = \alpha(e')$ but $e \neq e'$. In the refined abstraction α' we ensure that for all such $(e, \ell) \neq (e', \ell')$ we have $(\alpha'(e), \alpha'(\ell)) \neq (\alpha'(e'), \alpha'(\ell'))$, and similarly for such $e \neq e'$ we have $\alpha'(e) \neq \alpha'(e')$. The refined abstraction α' should preferably be as coarse as possible. In the appendix, we present a greedy algorithm (used in our experiments) for computing one such suitable refinement.

Refinement From Final Headers. If $C_n \neq \emptyset$ but for all $(e, h) \in C_n$ we have $h \notin Lang(\mathcal{N}_c)$ then we compute the refinement based on the transitions in the NFA encoding the final headers: for all pairs $(e, h) \in C_n$ we must have $\alpha(h) \in Lang(\alpha(\mathcal{N}_c))$ but $h \notin Lang(\mathcal{N}_c)$. That is we have in $\alpha(\mathcal{N}_c)$: $s_c \xrightarrow{\alpha(\ell_1)}_\alpha s_1 \xrightarrow{\alpha(\ell_2)}_\alpha \dots \xrightarrow{\alpha(\ell_n)}_\alpha s_n$ with $h = \ell_1 \ell_2 \dots \ell_n$, but in $\mathcal{N}_c$: $s_c \xrightarrow{\ell_1} s_1 \xrightarrow{\ell_2} \dots \xrightarrow{\ell_i} s_i \xrightarrow{\ell_{i+1}}\mkern-20mu\big/\ \ $, for some i with $i < n$. Now there must be another label ℓ' such that $\alpha(\ell_{i+1}) = \alpha(\ell')$ and $s_i \xrightarrow{\ell'} s_{i+1}$, but $\ell_{i+1} \neq \ell'$. In the refined abstraction α' we ensure that for all such ℓ' we have $\alpha'(\ell_{i+1}) \neq \alpha'(\ell')$ and we do this for all relevant h.

Heuristics for Initial Abstraction. We use a heuristic to construct the initial abstraction. We group labels based on their next-hop links, i.e. $\mathbb{L} \subseteq 2^E$ and $\alpha(\ell) = \{e' \mid (e', \omega) \in \tau^k(e, \ell) \text{ for some } e\}$. We group links based on their explicit mention in the path expression of the query, i.e. $\mathbb{E} \subseteq 2^{S_b \times S_b}$ and $\alpha(e) = \{(s, s') \mid s \xrightarrow{e}_b s'\}$.

5   Implementation and Experiments

We implemented the translation of MPLS networks to pushdown automata as well as the three improvements to the reachability analysis in our prototype tool written in C++. In our experimental evaluation, we use real-world network topologies from the Internet Topology Zoo [16]. We implemented a Python tool that for a given network topology distributes the MPLS labels and configures the forwarding tables by following the commonly used Label Distribution Protocol (LDP), the Resource Reservation Protocol with Traffic Engineering extensions

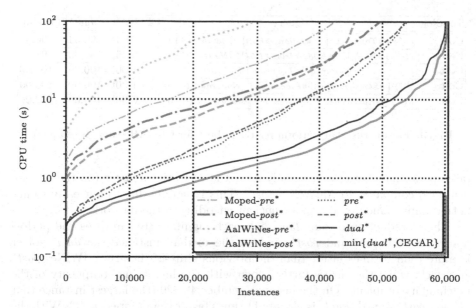

Fig. 2. Comparison of solvers; all 60,800 instances (x-axis) are for each solver independently sorted by the verification time (y-axis, note the logarithmic scale).

(RSVP-TE), as well as the industry-standard MPLS VPN services. We generate the forwarding tables using four different parameter settings for the ten largest topologies from [16] (ranging from 100 nodes up to 700 nodes). This results in 40 MPLS data planes, each with 1,520 queries that are randomly instantiated from a set of query templates describing reachability, waypointing, loop-freedom, service-chaining and transparency [13], with the maximum number of failures $k \in \{0, 1, 2, 3\}$. We balance the benchmark in order to obtain an even distribution between positive and negative queries. The whole benchmark consists of 60,800 queries that are verified by each of the solvers, in particular our algorithms referred to as $post^*$, pre^* and $dual^*$ (all without CEGAR), compared to the state-of-the-art pushdown reachability algorithms implemented in Moped [19] (Moped-pre^* and Moped-$post^*$) and in AalWiNes [14] (AalWiNes-pre^* and AalWiNes-$post^*$). The experiments were run on a cluster with AMD EPYC 7551 processors at 2.55 GHz (boost disabled) with 32 GB memory limit and 100 s timeout. Time spent on parsing files is excluded. The source code, experimental benchmark and all data are available at https://doi.org/10.5281/zenodo.5005893.

The results are presented in Fig. 2 in terms of performance plots where all instances for the competing approaches are independently sorted by their running times and plotted on the x-axis while the y-axis contains (on logarithmic scale) the respective running times in seconds.

The performance curve for AalWiNes-pre^* and Moped-pre^* are significantly slower than the other methods, including Moped-$post^*$ and AalWines-$post^*$, which are comparable. Our new improved pre^* and $post^*$ methods are compa-

Topology	Query	CEGAR	$dual^*$	Speedup
Colt	$\langle\cdot^*\rangle$ $[\cdot\#\,Toulouse]$ $[\,\hat{}\,\cdot\#Milan, \cdot\#Poit]^*$ $[Bari\#\cdot]$ $\langle\cdot^*\rangle$ 0	0.94	90.54	96.42
Pern	$\langle\cdot^*\rangle$ $[\cdot\#N56]$ $[\,\hat{}\,\cdot\#N38, \cdot\#Isla, \cdot\#N54]^*$ $[N99\#\cdot]$ $\langle\cdot^*\rangle$ 0	0.35	34.30	97.10
Colt	$\langle\cdot\rangle$ $[\cdot\#Paris]$ $\cdot^*$ $[Livorno\#\cdot]$ $\langle\cdot^+\cdot\rangle$ 0	1.00	>100.00	>100.00
Colt	$\langle\cdot?\rangle$ $[\cdot\#Strasbourg]$ $\cdot^*$ $[\cdot\#Piacenza]$ $\cdot^*$ $[Novara\#\cdot]$ $\langle\cdot?\rangle$ 0	1.00	>100.00	>100.00
Colt	$\langle\cdot?\rangle$ $[\cdot\#Karlsruhe]$ $\cdot^*$ $[\cdot\#Ostend]$ $\cdot^*$ $[Brindisi\#\cdot]$ $\langle\cdot?\rangle$ 0	0.98	>100.00	>102.04

Fig. 3. The queries that perform relatively best for CEGAR (time in seconds)

rable performance-wise and already more than two times faster (on the median instance) compared to AalWiNes-$post^*$. This is mainly due to our early termination improvement and a more efficient encoding of the network.

The introduction of our $dual^*$ approach significantly improves the performance of both pre^* and $post^*$, and on the median instance the $dual^*$ solver is more than 6 times faster than the previous state-of-the-art AalWiNes-$post^*$ approach, while the curves further open with the increasing complexity of the reachability problems. On the instance number 49,629 (the largest instance that Moped-$post^*$ solved) $dual^*$ is already 11 times faster than Moped-$post^*$. With the harder instances $dual^*$ performs increasingly better than both pre^* and $post^*$.

The performance of the CEGAR approach is incomparable with $dual^*$ as on 27% of all instances CEGAR is faster (sometimes even by two orders of magnitude) but on the remaining instances it can be significantly slower. We noticed that the CEGAR approach is considerably better performing on negative queries (without any trace) where it is faster on 47% cases. The best cases for CEGAR with two orders of magnitude speedup are listed in Fig. 3 and we remark that CEGAR solved 249 queries where $dual^*$ timed out. The number of CEGAR iterations where the method is faster than $dual^*$ ranges between 1 to 61 but typically less than 10 iterations are required to get a conclusive answer. As $dual^*$ and CEGAR are incomparable, we use the pragmatic approach where we can run both of them in parallel and terminate as soon as one of the methods provides an answer. This is depicted by the curve min{$dual^*$, CEGAR} that further improves the performance by additional 20–30%. In particular this combined method is 7.5 times faster than AalWiNes-$post^*$ on the median case and 17 times faster than Moped-$post^*$ on the instance number 49,629.

Finally, as both the network encoding in AalWiNes [14] as well as in our paper overapproximate the set of network traces, they can provide inconclusive answers. On our benchmark, AalWiNes-$post^*$ returned 2,024 inconclusive answers, whereas our encoding approach reported only 7 inconclusive answers for $dual^*$ and 6 inconclusive answers for $dual^*$ combined with CEGAR.

6   Conclusion

While more automated approaches to verify and operate communication networks can significantly improve their dependability, this requires efficient algorithms which can deal with the large scale and complexity of today's networks.

We presented an efficient translation from MPLS routing tables into pushdown systems. We also revisited the problem of fast reachability analysis of pushdown systems and presented three techniques improving the performance over the state-of-the-art solution by an order of magnitude. In the future work we plan to study fast algorithms for verifying quantitative reachability properties (related to latency or network congestion) via weighted pushdown automata.

Acknowledgements. We thank to Bernhard Schrenk for updating the AalWiNes online demo at https://demo.aalwines.cs.aau.dk with the improved verification engine described in this paper.

References

1. Anderson, C.J., et al.: NetKAT: semantic foundations for networks. In: POPL 2014, pp. 113–126. ACM (2014)
2. Beckett, R., Mahajan, R., Millstein, T., Padhye, J., Walker, D.: Don't mind the gap: bridging network-wide objectives and device-level configurations. In: ACM SIGCOMM 2016, pp. 328–341. ACM (2016)
3. Bouajjani, A., Esparza, J., Maler, O.: Reachability analysis of pushdown automata: application to model-checking. In: Mazurkiewicz, A., Winkowski, J. (eds.) CONCUR 1997. LNCS, vol. 1243, pp. 135–150. Springer, Heidelberg (1997). https://doi.org/10.1007/3-540-63141-0_10
4. Büchi, J.R.: Regular canonical systems. Archiv für mathematische Logik und Grundlagenforschung **6**(3–4), 91–111 (1964)
5. Clarke, E., Grumberg, O., Jha, S., Lu, Y., Veith, H.: Counterexample-guided abstraction refinement. In: Emerson, E.A., Sistla, A.P. (eds.) CAV 2000. LNCS, vol. 1855, pp. 154–169. Springer, Heidelberg (2000). https://doi.org/10.1007/10722167_15
6. Clarke, E.M., Grumberg, O., Long, D.E.: Model checking and abstraction. ACM Trans. Prog. Lang. Syst. **16**(5), 1512–1542 (1994)
7. Conway, C.L., Namjoshi, K.S., Dams, D., Edwards, S.A.: Incremental algorithms for inter-procedural analysis of safety properties. In: Etessami, K., Rajamani, S.K. (eds.) CAV 2005. LNCS, vol. 3576, pp. 449–461. Springer, Heidelberg (2005). https://doi.org/10.1007/11513988_45
8. El-Hassany, A., Tsankov, P., Vanbever, L., Vechev, M.: Network-wide configuration synthesis. In: Majumdar, R., Kunčak, V. (eds.) CAV 2017. LNCS, vol. 10427, pp. 261–281. Springer, Cham (2017). https://doi.org/10.1007/978-3-319-63390-9_14
9. Esparza, J., Kiefer, S., Schwoon, S.: Abstraction refinement with Craig interpolation and symbolic pushdown systems. J. Satisf. Boolean Model. Comput. **5**(1–4), 27–56 (2009)
10. Esparza, J., Knoop, J.: An automata-theoretic approach to interprocedural dataflow analysis. In: Thomas, W. (ed.) FoSSaCS 1999. LNCS, vol. 1578, pp. 14–30. Springer, Heidelberg (1999). https://doi.org/10.1007/3-540-49019-1_2
11. Esparza, J., Schwoon, S.: A BDD-based model checker for recursive programs. In: Berry, G., Comon, H., Finkel, A. (eds.) CAV 2001. LNCS, vol. 2102, pp. 324–336. Springer, Heidelberg (2001). https://doi.org/10.1007/3-540-44585-4_30
12. Finkel, A., Willems, B., Wolper, P.: A direct symbolic approach to model checking pushdown systems. In: INFINITY 1997. ENTCS, vol. 9, pp. 27–37. Elsevier (1997)

13. Jensen, J.S., Krøgh, T.B., Madsen, J.S., Schmid, S., Srba, J., Thorgersen, M.T.: P-Rex: fast verification of MPLS networks with multiple link failures. In: CoNEXT, pp. 217–227. ACM (2018)

14. Jensen, P.G., Kristiansen, D., Schmid, S., Schou, M.K., Schrenk, B.C., Srba, J.: AalWiNes: a fast and quantitative what-if analysis tool for MPLS networks. In: CoNEXT 2020, pp. 474–481. ACM (2020)

15. Kazemian, P., Varghese, G., McKeown, N.: Header space analysis: static checking for networks. In: Proceedings of the NSDI, pp. 113–126 (2012)

16. Knight, S., Nguyen, H., Falkner, N., Bowden, R., Roughan, M.: The internet topology Zoo. IEEE J. Sel. Areas Commun. **29**(9), 1765–1775 (2011)

17. Schmid, S., Srba, J.: Polynomial-time what-if analysis for prefix-manipulating MPLS networks. In: IEEE INFOCOM 2018, pp. 1799–1807. IEEE (2018)

18. Schwoon, S.: Model-checking pushdown systems. Ph.D. thesis, Technische Universität München (2002)

19. Schwoon, S.: Moped (2002). http://www2.informatik.uni-stuttgart.de/fmi/szs/tools/moped/

20. Suwimonteerabuth, D., Schwoon, S., Esparza, J.: jMoped: a java bytecode checker based on moped. In: Halbwachs, N., Zuck, L.D. (eds.) TACAS 2005. LNCS, vol. 3440, pp. 541–545. Springer, Heidelberg (2005). https://doi.org/10.1007/978-3-540-31980-1_35

Verifying Verified Code

Siddharth Priya[1]([✉]), Xiang Zhou[1], Yusen Su[1], Yakir Vizel[2], Yuyan Bao[1],
and Arie Gurfinkel[1]

[1] University of Waterloo, Waterloo, Canada
s2priya@uwaterloo.ca
[2] The Technion, Haifa, Israel

Abstract. A recent case study from AWS by Chong et al. proposes an effective methodology for Bounded Model Checking in industry. In this paper, we report on a followup case study that explores the methodology from the perspective of three research questions: (a) can proof artifacts be used across verification tools; (b) are there bugs in verified code; and (c) can specifications be improved. To study these questions, we port the verification tasks for aws-c-common library to SEAHORN and KLEE. We show the benefits of using compiler semantics and cross-checking specifications with different verification techniques, and call for standardizing proof library extensions to increase specification reuse. The verification tasks discussed are publicly available online.

1 Introduction

Bounded Model Checking (BMC) is an effective static analysis technique that reduces program analysis to propositional satisfiability (SAT) or Satisfiability Modulo Theories (SMT). It works directly on the source code. It is very precise, e.g., accounting for semantics of the programming language, memory models, and machine arithmetic. There is a vibrant ecosystem of tools from academia (e.g., SMACK [24], CPAChecker [4], ESBMC [12]), industrial research labs (e.g., Corral [19], F-SOFT [15]), and industry (e.g., CBMC [9], Crux [13], QPR [5]). There is an annual software verification competition, SV-COMP [3], with many participants. However, with a few exceptions, BMC is not actively used in software industry. Especially, when compared to dynamic analysis techniques such as fuzzing [25], or light-weight formal methods such as static analysis [2].

Transitioning research tools into practice requires case-studies, methodology, and best-practices to show how the tools are best applied. Until recently, there was no publicly available industrial case study on successful application of BMC for continuous verification[1] of C code. This has changed with [7] – a case study from the Automated Reasoning Group (ARG) at Amazon Web Services

---

[1] By *continuous verification*, we mean verification that is integrated with continuous integration (CI) and is checked during every commit.

This research was supported by grants from WHJIL and NSERC CRDPJ 543583-19.

Z. Hou and V. Ganesh (Eds.): ATVA 2021, LNCS 12971, pp. 187–202, 2021.
https://doi.org/10.1007/978-3-030-88885-5_13

(AWS) on the use of CBMC for proving memory safety (and other properties) of several AWS C libraries. This case study proposes a verification methodology with two core principles: (a) verification tasks structured around units of functionality (i.e., around a single function, as in a unit test), and (b) the use of code to express specifications (i.e., pre-, post-conditions, and other contextual assumptions). We refer to these as *unit proofs*, and *Code as Specification (CaS)*, respectively. The methodology is efficient because small verification tasks help alleviate scalability issues inherent in BMC. More significantly, developers adopt, own, extend and even use specifications (as code) in other contexts, e.g., unit tests. Admirably, AWS has released all of the verification artifacts (code, specifications and verification libraries)[2]. Moreover, these are maintained and integrated into Continuous Integration (CI). This gave us a unique opportunity to study, validate, and refine the methodology of [7]. In this paper, we report on our experience on adapting the verification tasks of [7] to two new verification tools: a Bounded Model Checking engine of SEAHORN, and the symbolic execution tool KLEE. We present our experience as a case study that is organized around three Research Questions (RQ):

RQ1: Does CaS Empower Multiple Tools for a Common Verification Task? Code is the *lingua franca* among developers, compilers, and verification tools. Thus, CaS makes specifications understandable by multiple verification tools. To validate effectiveness of this hypothesis, we adapted the unit proofs from AWS to different tools, and report on the experience in Sect. 3.1. While giving a positive answer to RQ1, we highlight the importance of the semantics used to interpret CaS, and that effectiveness of each tool depends on specification styles.

RQ2: Are there Bugs in Verified Code? Specifications written by humans may have errors. Do such errors hide bugs in verified implementations? What sanity checks are helpful to find bugs in implementations *and* specifications? The public availability of [7] is a unique opportunity to study this question. In contrast to [7], we found no new bugs in the library being verified (`aws-c-common`). However, we have found multiple errors in specifications! Reporting them to AWS triggered a massive review of existing unit proofs with many similar issues found and fixed. We report the bugs, and techniques that helped us discover them, in Sect. 3.2.

RQ3: Can Specifications be Improved While Maintaining CaS Philosophy? Some mistakes in specifications can be prevented by improvements to the specification language. We propose a series of improvements that significantly reduce specification burden. They are mostly in the form of built-in functions, thus, familiar to developers. In particular, we show how to make the verification of the `linked_list` data structure in `aws-c-common` significantly more efficient, while making the proofs unbounded (i.e., correct for linked list of any size).

   In our case study, we used the BMC engine of SEAHORN [14] and symbolic execution tool KLEE [6]. We have chosen SEAHORN because it is conceptually

---

[2] https://github.com/awslabs/aws-c-common/tree/main/verification/cbmc.

similar to CBMC that was used in [7]. Thus, it was reasonable to assume that all verification tasks can be ported to it. We are also intimately familiar with SEAHORN. Thus, we did not only port verification tasks, but proposed improvements to SEAHORN to facilitate the process. We have chosen KLEE because it is a well-known representative of symbolic execution – an approach that is the closest alternative to Bounded Model Checking.

Overall, we have ported all of the 169 unit proofs of `aws-c-common` to SEAHORN, and 153 to KLEE. The case study represents a year of effort. The time was divided between porting verification tasks, improving SEAHORN to allow for a better comparison, and, many manual and semi-automated sanity checks to increase confidence in specifications. Additionally, we have experimented with using unit proofs as fuzz targets using LLVM fuzzing library `libFuzzer` [25] and adapted 146 of the unit proofs to `libFuzzer`.

We make all results of our work publicly available and reproducible at https://github.com/seahorn/verify-c-common. In addition to what is reported in this paper, we have developed an extensive CMAKE build system that simplifies integration of additional tools. The case study is *live* in the sense that it is integrated in CI and is automatically re-run nightly. Thus, it is synchronized both with the tools we use and the AWS library we verify.

We hope that our study inspires researchers to adapt their tools to industrial code, and inspires industry to release verification efforts to study.

Caveats and Non-goals. We focus on the issues of methodology and sharing verification tasks between different tools. The tools that we use have different strengths and weaknesses. While they all validate user-supplied assertions, they check for different built-in properties (e.g., numeric overflow, undefined behaviours, memory safety). The goal is not to compare the tools head-to-head, or to find the best tool for a given task. We have not attempted to account for the differences between the tools. Nor have we tried to completely cover all verification tasks by all tools. Our goal was to preserve the unit proofs of [7] as much as possible to allow for a better comparison. For that reason, while we do report on performance results for the different tools, we do not describe them in detail. An interested reader is encouraged to look at the detailed data we make available on GitHub. Furthermore, while we have applied fuzzing to the unit proofs, we do not focus on effectiveness and applicability of static vs dynamic verification but only on the issues of methodology.

To summarize, we make the following contributions: (a) we validate that CaS can be used to share specifications between multiple tools, especially tools that share the same techniques (i.e., BMC), or tools with related techniques (i.e., BMC and Symbolic Execution); (b) we describe in details bugs that are found in verified code (more specifically, in specifications), some are quite surprising; (c) we suggest a direction to improve CaS with additional built-in functions that simplify common specification; and (d) we make our system publicly available allowing other researches to integrate their tools, use it as a benchmark, and to validate new verification approaches on industrial code.

The rest of the paper is structured as follows. Section 2 recalls the methodology of unit proof and CaS. And Sect. 3 presents the architecture of the case study

```
1   void aws_array_list_get_at_ptr_harness() {
2     struct aws_array_list list;
3     /* memhavoc(&list, sizeof(struct aws_array_list))); */
4     __CPROVER_assume(aws_array_list_is_bounded(&list));
5     ensure_array_list_has_allocated_data_member(&list);
6     void **val = can_fail_malloc(sizeof(void *));
7     size_t index /* = nd_size_t() */;
8     __CPROVER_assume(aws_array_list_is_valid(&list) && val != NULL);
9     if (aws_array_list_get_at_ptr(&list, val, index) == AWS_OP_SUCCESS)
10      assert(list.data != NULL && index < list.length);
11    assert(aws_array_list_is_valid(&list)); }
```

Fig. 1. The unit proof of `aws_array_list_get_at_ptr` from [7].

and answers the three research questions. We discuss related work in Sect. 4 and offer concluding remarks in Sect. 5.

2 Unit Proofs with Code-as-Specification

In [7], a methodology for program verification is proposed that allows developers to write specifications and proofs using the C programming language. The core of the methodology are *unit proof*[3] and *Code as Specification (CaS)*. A *unit proof* is similar to a *unit test* in that it is a piece of a code (usually a method) that invokes another piece of code (under test) and checks its correctness [23]. Figure 1 shows an example of a unit proof for the method `aws_array_list_get_at_ptr`, from `aws-c-common` library. It has three parts: (1) the specification of `aws_array_list_get_at_ptr`, i.e., pre- (line 8) and post-conditions (lines 10–11); (2) a call to the function under verification (line 9); and (3) the specification of the program context that the method is called from (lines 2–7). Note that all specifications are written directly in C. We call this specification style – CaS. Assumptions (or pre-conditions) correspond to `__CPROVER_assume`, and assertions (or post-conditions) correspond to **assert**. Specifications are factored into functions. For example, `aws_array_list_is_valid` specifies a representation invariant of the array list. In this unit proof, the context is restricted to a list of bounded size but with unconstrained elements and an **index** with (intentionally) unspecified value of type **size_t**. Even without expanding the code further, its meaning is clear to any C developer familiar with the library.

The unit proof is verified with CBMC [9]. CBMC uses a custom SMT solver to check that there are no executions that satisfy the pre-conditions and violate at least one of the assertions (i.e., a counterexample). Together with the explicit assertions, CBMC checks built-in properties: memory safety and integer overflow.

According to [7], CaS and unit proofs are a practical and productive verification methodology. It has been used successfully to verify memory safety (and other properties) of multiple AWS projects, including the `aws-c-common` library that we use in our case study. The library provides cross platform configuration,

---

[3] In [7], these are called *proof harnesses*.

category	num	LOC avg	LOC min	LOC max	CBMC (s) avg	CBMC (s) std	SeaHorn (s) avg	SeaHorn (s) std	KLEE (s) count	KLEE (s) avg	KLEE (s) std
arithmetic	6	33	11	40	3.8	0.8	0.6	0.1	6	0.9	0.3
array	4	97	78	112	5.6	0.0	1.7	0.7	4	32.3	6.0
array_list	23	126	77	181	35.8	60.8	2.5	3.3	23	55.4	49.3
byte_buf	29	97	50	188	17.6	47.3	1.0	0.8	27	75.3	124.1
byte_cursor	24	98	47	179	6.9	3.8	1.0	0.5	17	12.8	14.4
hash_callback	3	115	49	198	9.7	5.5	4.9	3.6	3	64.0	45.5
hash_iter	4	177	169	185	12.8	9.2	9.2	15.0	3	20.8	9.7
hash_table	19	172	36	328	23.5	33.3	5.3	7.5	15	104.6	333.4
linked_list	18	115	17	219	58.9	209.4	2.0	2.1	18	0.7	0.1
others	2	15	10	21	3.5	0.0	0.5	0.0	1	0.7	–
priority_queue	15	187	136	258	208.1	303.4	10.6	16.9	15	46.4	11.6
ring_buffer	6	155	56	227	20.0	19.5	29.5	34.2	6	48.1	26.4
string	15	87	11	209	6.3	1.3	2.9	1.8	15	139.7	159.7
Total	168	Loc	20,190		Time	6,475	Time	691	Time	8,577	

Fig. 2. Verification results for CBMC, SeaHorn and KLEE.

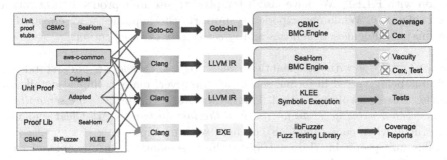

Fig. 3. Architecture of the case study.

data structures, and error handling support to a range of other AWS C libraries and SDKs. It is the foundation of many security related libraries, such as the AWS Encryption SDK for C [7]. It contains 13 data structures, 169 unit proofs that verify over 20K lines of code (LOC). Figure 2 shows the LOC and running time for each data structure.

3 Case Study

The architecture of our case study is shown in Fig. 3. To compare with CBMC, we use two tools based on the LLVM framework [20]: SeaHorn and KLEE. SeaHorn [14] is a verification framework. We used the bit- and memory-precise BMC developed during the case study. Its techniques are closest to CBMC. KLEE [6] is a well-known symbolic execution tool. It is an alternative to BMC for bounded exhaustive verification. In addition, we have experimented with libFuzzer – a coverage-guided random testing framework. It does no symbolic reasoning, and, together with address sanitizer, is known to be effective at discovering memory errors. Fuzzing results are available online.[4]

The rest of the section describes the research questions and our findings.

3.1   RQ1: Does CaS Empower Multiple Tools?

Hypothetically, CaS methodology enables sharing the same formal specification among multiple, potentially distinct, tools and techniques. For example, semantic analyses of IDEs and compilers can catch simple semantics bugs and inconsistencies in specifications. Fuzzers can validate specifications through testing. Symbolic execution can supplement BMC by capitalizing on a different balance in performance versus precision. Static analysis tools can be used to compute inductive invariants. However, is the hypothesis true in practice?

To validate the hypothesis, we adapted the unit proofs from `aws-c-common` to two distinct verification techniques: BMC with SEAHORN and symbolic execution with KLEE. We have also attempted to use unit proofs as fuzz targets for `libFuzzer`. While our experience supports the hypothesis, we encountered two major challenges: *semantics* and *effectiveness of specifications*.

Semantics. Code without semantics is meaningless. Developers understand code without being versed in formal semantics, however, many technical details and "corner cases" are often debated. This is especially true for C – *"the semantics of C has been a vexed question for much of the last 40 years"* [21]. Clear semantics are crucial when code (and CaS) are used with multiple tools.

The unit proofs in [7] do not follow the C semantics. For example, consider the proof in Fig. 1. According to C, it has no meaning as both `list` (line 2) and `index` (line 7) are used uninitialized. CBMC treats uninitialized variables as non-deterministic. So it is well-defined for CBMC, but not for other tools.

What is a good choice of semantics for CaS? In [21], two semantics are described – the ISO C Standard and the *de facto* semantics of compilers. Developers understand (and use) the de facto semantics. For example, comparison of arbitrary pointers is undefined according to ISO C, but defined consistently in mainstream compilers (and used in `aws-c-common`!). Therefore, we argue that CaS must use the de facto semantics. Furthermore, unit proofs must be compilable and, therefore, executable, so developers can execute them not *just* in their heads (like with [7]). Note that de facto semantics is not complete with regards to C semantics, but is a commonly agreed upon subset. What de facto semantics does not cover is compiler dependent semantics.

In our experience, using CaS with the de facto semantics is not hard. For example, to adapt Fig. 1, we introduced `memhavoc` and `nd_size_t`, shown as comments, that fills a memory region at a given address with non-deterministic bytes, and returns a non-deterministic value of type `size_t`, respectively.

---

[4] https://seahorn.github.io/verify-c-common/fuzzing_coverage/index.html.

```
1   size_t len = nd_size_t();      size_t cap = nd_size_t();
2   size_t cap = nd_size_t();      assume(cap <= MAX_BUFFER);        size_t len = nd_size_t();
3   assume(len <= cap);            buf->buffer = can_fail_malloc(    size_t cap = nd_size_t();
4   assume(cap <= MAX_BUFFER);       cap * sizeof(*(buf->buffer)));   cap len = (cap == 0) ? 0 : len
5                                  if (buf->buffer) {
6   buf->len = len;                  size_t len = nd_size_t();       buf->len = len;
7   buf->capacity = cap;             assume(len <= cap);             buf->capacity = cap;
8   buf->buffer = can_fail_malloc(   buf->len = len;                 buf->buffer = can_fail_malloc(
9     cap * sizeof(*(buf->buffer)));  buf->capacity = cap;            cap * sizeof(*(buf->buffer)));
10  buf->allocator = sea_allocator();  }                             buf->allocator = sea_allocator();
11                                 else {
12                                   buf->len = 0;
13                                   buf->capacity = 0;
14                                 }
15                                 buf->allocator = sea_allocator();
```

(a) for SEAHORN   (b) for KLEE   (c) for libFuzzer

Fig. 4. Tool-specific implementations for `initialize_byte_buf`.

Effectiveness of Specifications. We used three different tools on the same unit proof. Each tool requires slightly different styles of specifications to be effective. We believe that these stylistic differences between specifications can be captured by traditional code refactoring techniques (i.e., functions, macros, etc.). However, this is not easy whenever the specifications have not been written with multiple tools (and with their strengths and weaknesses) in mind. A significant part of our work has been in refactoring unit proofs from [7] to be more modular.

We illustrate this with the pre-condition for the `byte_buf` data-structure. In [7], data structures are assumed to be initially non-deterministic, and various assumptions throughout the unit proof are used to restrict it (e.g., lines 2–5 in Fig. 1). This impedes specification re-use since different tools work well with different styles of pre-conditions. For example, symbolic execution and fuzzing require memory to be explicitly allocated, and all tools that use de-facto semantics require all memory be initialized before use.

For `byte_buf`, we factored out its pre-conditions into a function `init_byte_buf`.[5] Its implementations for SEAHORN, KLEE, and `libFuzzer` are shown in Fig. 4. It takes `buf` structure as input, and initializes its fields to be consistent with the representation invariant of `byte_buf`.

SeaHorn initialization is closest to the original of [7]. Fields are initialized via calls to external functions (`nd_<type>`) that are assumed to return arbitrary values. Representation invariants (i.e., length is less or equal to capacity), as well as any upper bounds on buffer size are specified with *assumptions*. Note that `can_fail_malloc` internally initializes allocated memory via a call to `memhavoc`, ensuring that reading `buf->buffer` is well-defined.

KLEE initialization is similar to SEAHORN, but special care must be taken about the placement of assumptions, and implementation of `can_fail_malloc`. In particular, KLEE prefers that memory allocation functions are given explicit size, otherwise, it picks a concrete size non-deterministically. Special cases, like `buf->buffer` being `NULL`, are split in the initialization to aid KLEE during symbolic execution. Similar changes can be done for SEAHORN, but are not as effective. For that reason, we chose to keep SEAHORN initialization as close to [7] as possible, but adjusted the one for KLEE to be most effective.

---

[5] Similarly, we introduced `init_array_list` to replace lines 2–5 in Fig. 1.

libFuzzer initialization is the most different since non-determinisim must be replaced by randomness. In this case, nd_<type> functions are implemented using the random inputs generated by **libFuzzer**. *Assumptions* are implemented by aborting the current fuzzing run if the condition evaluates to **false**. Of course, this limits fuzzing effectiveness since the fuzzer must randomly guess inputs to pass all of the assumptions. For that reason, as many assumptions as possible are modeled by an explicit initialization. For example, in line 3 of Fig. 4c, **cap** is re-assigned to the modulo of **MAX_BUFFER** if **libFuzzer** generated a value exceeding **MAX_BUFFER**. This way, code after line 3 always executes regardless of the return value of **nd_size_t()** in line 2.

Overall, our results indicate that CaS empowers multiple verification tools to share specifications among them. Common refactoring techniques make specifications sharing effective. Specifications are easiest to share among tools that use similar techniques.

Discussion. We conclude this section with a discussion of our experience in using de facto semantics. First, the code of **aws-c-common** is written with de facto semantics in mind. We found that in [7] it had to be extended with many conditional compilation flags to provide alternative implementations that are compatible with CBMC or that instruct CBMC to ignore some seemingly undefined behavior. However, we have not changed any lines of **aws-c-common**. We analyze the code exactly how it is given to the compiler – improving coverage. Second, a compiler may generate different target code for different architectures. By using the compiler as front-end, we check that the code is correct as compiled on different platforms. This is another advantage of CaS. Third, compilers may provide additional safety checks. For example, **aws-c-common** uses GCC/Clang built-in functions for overflow-aware arithmetic. By using de facto semantics, all the tools used in the case study were able to deal with this in both CaS and code seamlessly. Fourth, **aws-c-common** uses inline assembly to deal with speculative execution-based vulnerabilities [17]. While inline assembly is not part of the ISO C standard, it is supported by compilers. Thus, it is not a problem for **libFuzzer**. We developed techniques to handle inline asm in SEAHORN. For KLEE, we had to ignore such unit proofs.

3.2   Are There Bugs in Verified Code?

Specifications may have errors as they are just programs: "Writing specifications can be as error-prone as writing programs". [22] Although [7] suggests to use code coverage and code review to increase the confidence in specifications, we still found non-trivial bugs. We summarize three most interesting ones below.

Bug 1. Figure 5a shows the definition of **byte buffer** that is a length delimited byte string. Its data representation should be either the buffer (**buf**) is **NULL** or its capacity (**cap**) is 0 (not the **len** as defined in **BB_is_ok**). We found this bug by a combination of sanity checks in SEAHORN and our model of the memory allocator (i.e., **malloc**). The bug did not manifest in [7] because other pre-conditions

```
1   typedef
2   struct byte_buf {
3       char* buf;
4       int len, cap;
5   } BB;
6   bool BB_is_ok(BB *b)
7   { return (b->len == 0
8            || b->buf);  }
```

(a) bug 1

```
1   assume(0 <= b && b <= 10);
2   if (a < (b - 5) &&
3        a >= (b + 5))
4   {
5       assert(c > 0);
6   }
7
8
9
```

(b) bug 2

```
1   void ht_del_over(HASH_TB *t) {
2       /* remove entry */
3       /* t->entry_count--; */
4   }
5
6
7
8
```

(c) bug 3

Fig. 5. Simplified code for specification bugs.

ensured that **buf** is always allocated. Our report of this bug to AWS triggered a massive code auditing effort in **aws-c-common** and related libraries where many related issues were found.[6]

Bug 2. Figure 5b shows a verification pattern where a property (line 5) is checked on the program path (from lines 1 to 5). As the condition at lines 2 and 3 can never be true, the property cannot be checked either. Our vacuity detection (discussed later) found the bugs occurring in this pattern. Note that the bug was missed by the code coverage detection used by CBMC, thus, may have been present for several years.

Bug 3. To make verification scalable, the verification of method A that calls another method B may use a *specification stub* that approximates the functionality of B. AWS adopts this methodology when verifying the iterator of a hash table. The iterator calls a function **ht_del** to remove an element in a hash table. During verification **ht_del** is approximated by a specification stub shown in Fig. 5c. However, the approximation does not decrement **entry_count**, i.e., line 3 should be added to the spec for correct behavior. In [7], the use of the buggy stub hides an error in the specification.

Discussion. Code coverage of a unit proof is, at best, a sanity check for CaS. It reports which source lines of the specification and code under verification are covered under execution. However, because source lines can remain uncovered for legitimate reasons e.g., dead code, interpreting a coverage report is not straightforward. There is no obvious *pass/fail* criterion. Thus, we found that code coverage may be insufficient to detect bugs in CaS reliably. In fact, bugs exist for multiple years even after code coverage failures. To help find bugs in CaS with SEAHORN, we adapted *vacuity detection* [18] to detect unreachable post-conditions. Vacuity detection checks that every assert statement is reachable. We encountered engineering challenges when developing vacuity detection. For example, we received spurious warnings due to code duplication. We silenced such warnings by only reporting a warning if all duplicate asserts reported a vacuity failure. In addition, due to CaS, an unreachable assertions may be removed by compiler's dead code elimination. This is not desirable for vacuity detection.

---

[6] An example is https://github.com/awslabs/aws-c-common/pull/686/commits.

```
1   linked_list l;
2   Node *p = malloc(sizeof(Node));
3   l.head.next = p;
4   for (int idx=0; idx < MAX; idx++) {
5     Node *n = malloc(sizeof(Node));
6     p->next = n;
7     p = n; }
8   p->next = &l.tail;
9   l.tail.prev = p;
10  list_front(l);
11  Node *nnode = l.head.next;
12  for (int idx=0; idx < MAX; idx++) {
13    nnode = nnode->next;  }
14  assert(nnode == l.tail);
```

(a) Spec in the style of [7]

```
1   linked_list l;
2   Node *n = malloc(sizeof(Node));
3   n->next = nd_voidp();
4   l.head.next = n;
5   l.tail.prev = nd_voidp();
6   list_front(l);
7   assert(l.head.next == n);
```

(b) New specification

Fig. 6. Simplified code for differing CaS specifications.

```
1   char buf[SZ];
2   init_buf(buf, SZ);
3   int idx = nd_int();
4   assume(0 <= idx && idx < SZ);
5   char saved = buf[idx];
6   read_only_op(buf);
7   assert(saved == buf[idx]);
```

(a) Spec in style of [7]

```
1   char buf[SZ];
2   init_buf(buf, SZ);
3   tracking_on();
4   read_only_op(buf);
5   assert(!is_mod(buf));
```

(b) Spec using a built-in is_mod

Fig. 7. Two styles of specifications for a read only buffer operation.

To mitigate this issue, we report when dead code is eliminated. However, since many eliminations are unrelated to specs, there is noise in the report which makes it un-actionable. Interaction between dead code removal by the compiler and vacuity detection remains an open challenge for us.

We have found bugs in specifications, but we do not know what bugs remain. As shown in this section, the bugs were found with a combination of manual auditing and tools. However, these techniques are far from complete.

3.3 Can Specifications Be Improved While Maintaining the CaS Philosophy?

There are many alternative ways to express a specification in CaS. In this section, we illustrate how to make proofs more efficient and make specs more readable. For example, a unit proof can fully instantiate a data structure (as in a unit test), or minimally constrain it (as in [7]). In this section, we illustrate this by describing our experience in making `linked_list` unit proofs unbounded (and more efficient). Furthermore, we believe that extending the specification language with additional verifier-supported built-in functions simplifies specs while making them easier to verify. We illustrate this with the built-ins developed for SEAHORN to specify absence of side-effects.

Linked List. A common pattern in *unit proofs* is to assume the representation invariant of a data structure, and to assert it after invocation of the function under verification along with other properties that must be maintained by the function. For example, a simplified version of its unit proof from [7] is shown in Fig. 6a. The pre-conditions are specified by (explicitly) creating a list in lines 4–7 using a loop. The post-condition is checked by completely traversing the list in lines 12–14. This specification is simple since it closely follows the style of unit tests. However, it is inefficient for BMC: (a) unrolling the loops in the pre- and post-conditions blows up the symbolic search space; (b) it makes verification of the loop-free function list_front bounded, i.e., verification appears to depend on the size of the list in the pre-conditions.

Our alternative formulation is to construct a partially defined linked list stub as shown in Fig. 8a. This stub can be used to verify list_front since it is expected that only the first node after head is accessed. The resulting CaS is shown in Fig. 6b. The next field of n points to a potentially invalid address (returned by nd_voidp). Either list_front never touches n->next or has a memory fault. Finally, the assert on line 7 in Fig. 6b checks that list_front did not modify the head of the list either. If there is no memory fault, then list_front did not modify the linked list after the node n. Our specification is not inductive. It uses the insight that the given linked list API only ever accesses a single element. It, therefore, avoids loops in both the pre- and post-conditions and verifies list_front for linked lists of any size.

Unfortunately, our new spec in Fig. 7b is difficult to understand by non-experts because it relies on the interplay between nd_voidp and memory safety checking. To make the spec accessible, we hide the details behind a helper API. Figure 9 shows the unit proof for aws_linked_list_front with this API. The function sea_nd_init_aws_linked_list_from_head constructs partial aws_linked_list instances with non-deterministic length (as shown in Fig. 8a). The function aws_linked_list_save_to_tail saves concrete linked list nodes from the partial aws_linked_list. Finally, the function is_aws_list_unchanged_to_tail is used in post-conditions to check that linked list nodes are not modified. The unit proof for aws_linked_list_front is not only more efficient than the original CBMC proof, but it is also a *stronger* specification. For example, if aws_linked_list_front removes or modifies a linked list node, our unit proof catches this as a violation, while the original proof only checks whether the returned value is valid and whether the linked list is well formed. The API we devised is generalized to work with all linked list operations in aws-c-common. For operations which access the node before the tail we construct a partially defined stub as shown in Fig. 8b while Fig. 8c is constructed for operations which access the list from both ends. We provide corresponding versions of the above API to save and check immutability of linked list nodes for each kind of stub.

Increasing CaS Expressiveness. Verification tools should provide built-ins to aid in concise specifications. Moreover, such built-ins enable specifications that are not otherwise expressible in CaS. For example, Fig. 7b uses a SEAHORN built-in, is_mod, to specify that read_only_op does not change the buffer. This built-in returns true if memory pointed by its argument is modified since the last call to tracking_on. In contrast, the original specification for CBMC in Fig. 7a is tricky. It saves a byte from some position in the buffer (lines 3–5), and checks that it is

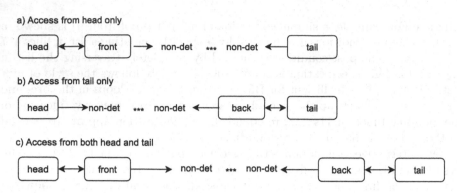

Fig. 8. Linked list stubs for proofs.

```
1      void aws_linked_list_front_harness() {
2        /* data structure */
3        struct aws_linked_list list;
4        struct saved_aws_linked_list to_save = {0};
5        size_t size;
6
7        sea_nd_init_aws_linked_list_from_head(&list, &size);
8        struct aws_linked_list_node *start = &list.head;
9        aws_linked_list_save_to_tail(&list, size, start, &to_save);
10
11       // precondition in function does not accept empty linked list
12       assume(!aws_linked_list_empty(&list));
13
14       /* perform operation under verification */
15       struct aws_linked_list_node *front = aws_linked_list_front(&list);
16
17       /* assertions */
18       sassert(list.head.next == front);
19       sassert(aws_linked_list_node_prev_is_valid(front));
20       sassert(aws_linked_list_node_next_is_valid(front));
21       sassert(is_aws_list_unchanged_to_tail(&list, &to_save));
22
23       return 0;
24     }
```

Fig. 9. SEAHORN unit proof for `aws_linked_list_front`.

not changed (line 7). This example illustrates that built-ins make specifications simpler and more direct. They ease specification writing for users and might be exploited efficiently by verification tools. As another example, SEAHORN provides a built-in **is_deref** to check that a memory access is within bounds, which is not (easily) expressible in C.

Discussion. CaS enables concise specifications and efficient proofs. As advanced verification techniques may not generalize, a standard extension is needed, such as verification-specific built-in functions. The semantics of these can be provided by a run-time library, validated by fuzzing and supported by multiple verification tools. Additional case studies are needed to identify a good set of built-ins. A standard extension can increase specification reuse and make verification more productive and effective.

4 Related Work

To our knowledge, [7] is the first significant, publicly available, example of an application of BMC on industrial code that is actively maintained with the code. Thus, our work is the first exploration of potential issues with software verified in this way. The closest verification case studies are `coreutils` with KLEE [6] and `busybox ls` with CBMC [16]. However, those focus on the scalability of a specific verification technology, while we focus on methodology, reuse, and what bugs might be hidden in the verification effort.

As we mentioned in the introduction, the Software Verification Competition (SV-COMP) [3] provides a large collection of benchmarks, and, an annual evaluation of many verification tools. However, it is focused on performance and soundness of the tools. The benchmarks are pre-processed to fit the competition format. At that stage, it is impossible to identify and evaluate the specifications, or to modify the benchmarks to increase efficiency of any particular tool. We hope that our case study can serve as an alternative benchmark to evaluate suitability of verification tools for industrial transition.

In addition to [7], there has been number of other recent applications of BMC at AWS, including [8,10,11]. However, they are either not publicly available, too specialized, or not as extensive as the case study in [7].

Using code as specification has a long history in verification tools, one prominent example is Code Contracts introduced in Spec$^\sharp$ [1]. One important difference is that in our case CaS is used to share specifications between completely different tools that only share the semantics of the underlying programming language, and the language itself is used to adapt specifications to the tools.

5 Conclusion

This case study would not have been possible without artifacts released by AWS in [7]. To our knowledge, it is the first publicly available application of BMC (to software) in industry. Related case studies on verification are those on `coreutils` with KLEE [6] and on `busybox ls` with CBMC [16]. SV-COMP is a large repository of benchmarks, but its goals are different from an actively maintained industrial project. The availability of both methodology and artifacts has given us a unique opportunity to study how verification is applied in industry and to improve verification methodology. We encourage industry to release more benchmarks to enable further studies by the research community.

In addition to answering the research questions, we are contributing a complete working system that might be of interest to other researchers. We have implemented a custom build system using CMAKE that simplifies integrating new tools. We provide Docker containers to reproduce all of the results. We created continuous integration (CI) on GitHub that nightly re-runs all the tools on the current version of `aws-c-common`. Since we use standard tools, the project integrates seamlessly into IDEs and refactoring tools. The CI runs are done in parallel by CTEST. Running SEAHORN takes under 8 min!

While comparing different tools on performance is not our primary concern, in Fig. 2, we show the running time for all of the verification tools, collected on the same machine. For libFuzzer, we make the detailed coverage report available online. We stress that while the tools check the same explicit assertions, they check different built-in properties. Thus, running time comparison must be taken with a grain of salt.

Our main conclusion is in agreement with [7], and we strengthen the evidence for it. CaS is a practical and scalable approach for specifications that is easy to understand and empowers many tools. We argue that using de facto compiler semantics in CaS is key for enabling many verification tools, each with its own characteristic, to be used on the same verification problem. We find that specifications can be written in different ways and specification writer must account for both verification efficiency and developer readability. We suggest that a set of common built-ins be shared by different verification tools. Such built-ins improve the expressive power of CaS while retaining portability across verification tools. With built-ins defined in a specification library, software developers will be able to write unit proofs in a way no difference than programming with libraries provided by some framework.

Today, formal verification is not the primary means of building confidence in software quality. Our hope is that case studies like this one are useful to both software engineering researchers and practitioners who want to make formal methods an integral part of software development. To further this agenda, we plan to continue applying the CaS methodology to larger and more complex code bases (and languages) in the future.

References

1. Barnett, M., Fähndrich, M., Leino, K.R.M., Müller, P., Schulte, W., Venter, H.: Specification and verification: the Spec# experience. Commun. ACM **54**(6), 81–91 (2011)
2. Bessey, A., et al.: A few billion lines of code later: using static analysis to find bugs in the real world. Commun. ACM **53**(2), 66–75 (2010). https://doi.org/10.1145/1646353.1646374
3. Beyer, D.: Advances in automatic software verification: SV-COMP 2020. In: TACAS 2020. LNCS, vol. 12079, pp. 347–367. Springer, Cham (2020). https://doi.org/10.1007/978-3-030-45237-7_21
4. Beyer, D., Keremoglu, M.E.: CPAchecker: a tool for configurable software verification. In: Gopalakrishnan, G., Qadeer, S. (eds.) CAV 2011. LNCS, vol. 6806, pp. 184–190. Springer, Heidelberg (2011). https://doi.org/10.1007/978-3-642-22110-1_16
5. Kleine Büning, M., Sinz, C., Faragó, D.: QPR verify: a static analysis tool for embedded software based on bounded model checking. In: Christakis, M., Polikarpova, N., Duggirala, P.S., Schrammel, P. (eds.) NSV/VSTTE -2020. LNCS, vol. 12549, pp. 21–32. Springer, Cham (2020). https://doi.org/10.1007/978-3-030-63618-0_2

6. Cadar, C., Dunbar, D., Engler, D.R.: KLEE: unassisted and automatic generation of high-coverage tests for complex systems programs. In: 8th USENIX Symposium on Operating Systems Design and Implementation, OSDI 2008, 8–10 December 2008, San Diego, California, USA, Proceedings, pp. 209–224. USENIX Association (2008)

7. Chong, N., et al.: Code-level model checking in the software development workflow. In: ICSE-SEIP 2020: 42nd International Conference on Software Engineering, Software Engineering in Practice, Seoul, South Korea, 27 June–19 July 2020, pp. 11–20. ACM (2020)

8. Chudnov, A., et al.: Continuous formal verification of Amazon s2n. In: Chockler, H., Weissenbacher, G. (eds.) CAV 2018. LNCS, vol. 10982, pp. 430–446. Springer, Cham (2018). https://doi.org/10.1007/978-3-319-96142-2_26

9. Clarke, E., Kroening, D., Lerda, F.: A tool for checking ANSI-C programs. In: Jensen, K., Podelski, A. (eds.) TACAS 2004. LNCS, vol. 2988, pp. 168–176. Springer, Heidelberg (2004). https://doi.org/10.1007/978-3-540-24730-2_15

10. Cook, B., et al.: Using model checking tools to triage the severity of security bugs in the Xen hypervisor. In: 2020 Formal Methods in Computer Aided Design, FMCAD 2020, Haifa, Israel, 21–24 September 2020, pp. 185–193. IEEE (2020). https://doi.org/10.34727/2020/isbn.978-3-85448-042-6_26

11. Cook, B., Khazem, K., Kroening, D., Tasiran, S., Tautschnig, M., Tuttle, M.R.: Model checking boot code from AWS data centers. In: Chockler, H., Weissenbacher, G. (eds.) CAV 2018. LNCS, vol. 10982, pp. 467–486. Springer, Cham (2018). https://doi.org/10.1007/978-3-319-96142-2_28

12. Gadelha, M.Y.R., Monteiro, F.R., Morse, J., Cordeiro, L.C., Fischer, B., Nicole, D.A.: ESBMC 5.0: an industrial-strength C model checker. In: Proceedings of the 33rd ACM/IEEE International Conference on Automated Software Engineering, ASE 2018, Montpellier, France, 3–7 September 2018, pp. 888–891. ACM (2018)

13. Galois: Crux: A Tool for Improving the Assurance of Software Using Symbolic Testing. https://crux.galois.com/

14. Gurfinkel, A., Kahsai, T., Komuravelli, A., Navas, J.A.: The seahorn verification framework. In: Kroening, D., Păsăreanu, C.S. (eds.) CAV 2015. LNCS, vol. 9206, pp. 343–361. Springer, Cham (2015). https://doi.org/10.1007/978-3-319-21690-4_20

15. Ivančić, F., Yang, Z., Ganai, M.K., Gupta, A., Shlyakhter, I., Ashar, P.: F-Soft: software verification platform. In: Etessami, K., Rajamani, S.K. (eds.) CAV 2005. LNCS, vol. 3576, pp. 301–306. Springer, Heidelberg (2005). https://doi.org/10.1007/11513988_31

16. Kim, Y., Kim, M.: SAT-based bounded software model checking for embedded software: a case study. In: 21st Asia-Pacific Software Engineering Conference, APSEC 2014, Jeju, South Korea, 1–4 December 2014. Volume 1: Research Papers, pp. 55–62. IEEE Computer Society (2014)

17. Kocher, P., et al.: Spectre attacks: exploiting speculative execution (2018). http://meltdownattack.com/

18. Kupferman, O.: Sanity checks in formal verification. In: Baier, C., Hermanns, H. (eds.) CONCUR 2006. LNCS, vol. 4137, pp. 37–51. Springer, Heidelberg (2006). https://doi.org/10.1007/11817949_3

19. Lal, A., Qadeer, S.: Powering the static driver verifier using Corral. In: Proceedings of the 22nd ACM SIGSOFT International Symposium on Foundations of Software Engineering, (FSE-22), Hong Kong, China, 16–22 November 2014, pp. 202–212. ACM (2014)

20. Lattner, C., Adve, V.S.: LLVM: a compilation framework for lifelong program analysis & transformation. In: 2nd IEEE/ACM International Symposium on Code Generation and Optimization (CGO 2004), 20–24 March 2004, San Jose, CA, USA, pp. 75–88. IEEE Computer Society (2004)
21. Memarian, K., et al.: Into the depths of C: elaborating the de facto standards. In: Proceedings of the 37th ACM SIGPLAN Conference on Programming Language Design and Implementation, PLDI 2016, Santa Barbara, CA, USA, 13–17 June 2016, pp. 1–15. ACM (2016)
22. Moy, Y., Wallenburg, A.: Tokeneer: beyond formal program verification. Embed. Real Time Softw. Syst. **24** (2010)
23. Osherove, R.: The Art of Unit Testing: With Examples in .Net. Manning Publications Co., Shelter Island (2009)
24. Rakamarić, Z., Emmi, M.: SMACK: decoupling source language details from verifier implementations. In: Biere, A., Bloem, R. (eds.) CAV 2014. LNCS, vol. 8559, pp. 106–113. Springer, Cham (2014). https://doi.org/10.1007/978-3-319-08867-9_7
25. Serebryany, K.: libFuzzer: a library for coverage-guided fuzz testing. https://llvm.org/docs/LibFuzzer.html

Probabilistic Analysis

Probabilistic Causes in Markov Chains

Christel Baier[ID], Florian Funke[ID], Simon Jantsch[ID], Jakob Piribauer[ID], and Robin Ziemek[(✉)][ID]

Technische Universität Dresden, Dresden, Germany
{christel.baier,florian.funke,simon.jantsch,jakob.piribauer, robin.ziemek}@tu-dresden.de

Abstract. The paper studies a probabilistic notion of causes in Markov chains that relies on the *counterfactuality* principle and the *probability-raising* property. This notion is motivated by the use of causes for monitoring purposes where the aim is to detect faulty or undesired behaviours *before* they actually occur. A cause is a set of finite executions of the system *after which* the probability of the effect exceeds a given threshold. We introduce multiple types of costs that capture the consump-tion of resources from different perspectives, and study the complexity of computing cost-minimal causes.

1 Introduction

The study of cause-effect relationships in formal systems has received considerable attention over the past 25 years. Notions of causality have been proposed within various models, including structural equation models [26,27,37], temporal logics in Kripke structures [4,11] and Markov chains [34,35], and application areas have been identified in abundance, ranging from finance [32] to medicine [33] to aeronautics [30]. These approaches form an increasingly powerful toolkit aimed at explaining *why* an observable phenomenon (the effect) has happened, and which previous events (the causes) are logically linked to its occurrence. As such, causality plays a fundamental building block in determining moral responsibility [6,10] or legal accountability [20], and ultimately fosters user acceptance through an increased level of transparency [36].

Despite the variety of models, application areas, and involved disciplines, all approaches essentially rely on (one of) two central paradigms that dictate how causes are linked to their effects: the *counterfactuality* principle and the *probability-raising* property. Counterfactual reasoning prescribes that an effect would not have happened if the cause had not occurred. Probability-raising states that the probability of the effect is higher whenever the cause has been observed.

This work was funded by DFG grant 389792660 as part of TRR 248, the Cluster of Excellence EXC 2050/1 (CeTI, project ID 390696704, as part of Germany's Excellence Strategy), DFG-projects BA-1679/11-1 and BA-1679/12-1, and the Research Training Group QuantLA (GRK 1763).

Z. Hou and V. Ganesh (Eds.): ATVA 2021, LNCS 12971, pp. 205–221, 2021.
https://doi.org/10.1007/978-3-030-88885-5_14

	expcost	pexpcost	maxcost
non-negative weights accumulated	in P (4.2)	pseudo-polyn. (4.5) PP-hard (4.6)	in P (4.8)
arbitrary weights accumulated	in P (4.2)	PP-hard (4.6)	pseudo-polyn. in NP ∩ coNP (4.8)
arbitrary weights instantaneous	in P (4.9)	in P (4.9)	in P (4.9)

Fig. 1. Summary of complexity results for different kinds of cost.

The contribution of this paper is twofold: First, we define a novel notion of *cause* for ω-regular properties in stochastic operational models. Second, we study the complexity of computing optimal causes for cost mechanisms motivated by monitoring applications.

The causes presented in this paper combine the two prevailing causality paradigms mentioned above into a single concept. More specifically, a p-cause for an ω-regular property $\mathcal{L}$ in a discrete-time Markov chain is a set of finite executions π of the system such that the probability that $\mathcal{L}$ occurs after executing π is at least p, where p is typically larger than the overall probability of $\mathcal{L}$. The counterfactuality principle is invoked through the additional requirement that almost every execution exhibiting the event $\mathcal{L}$ contains a finite prefix which is a member of the p-cause. This condition makes our approach amenable to the needs of monitoring a system at runtime.

Imagine a critical event that the system should avoid (e.g., a fully automated drone crashing onto the ground), and assume that a p-cause for this event is known (e.g., physical specifications foreshadowing a crash). Typically, the probability threshold p – which can be thought of as the sensitivity of the monitor – should be lower if the criticality of the event is higher. As the system is running, as soon as the execution seen so far is part of the p-cause, the monitor can trigger an alarm and suitable countermeasures can be taken (e.g., manual control instead of automated behavior). As such, our approach can be *preventive* in nature.

The monitoring application outlined above suggests computing a p-cause from the model before the system is put to use. However, multiple p-causes may exist for the same property, which raises the question which one to choose. Cyber-physical systems consume time, energy and other resources, which are often subject to budget restrictions. Furthermore, the intended countermeasures may incur different costs depending on the system state. Such costs can be modelled using state weights in the Markov chain, which induce weight functions on the finite executions either in an accumulative (total resource consumption) or instantaneous (current consumption intensity) fashion. On top of this model, we present three cost mechanisms for causes: (1) The *expected cost* measures the expected resource consumption until the monitor triggers an alarm or reaches a safe state, (2) the *partial expected cost* measures the expected consumption where executions reaching a safe state do not incur any cost, and (3) the *maximal cost* measures the maximal consumption that can occur until an alarm is triggered.

Figure 1 summarizes our results regarding the complexity of computing cost-minimal p-causes for the different combinations of weight type and cost mechanism. To obtain these results we utilize a web of connections to the rich landscape of computational problems for discrete-time Markovian models. More precisely, the results for the expected cost rely on connections to the *stochastic shortest path problem* (SSP) studied in [5]. The pseudo-polynomial algorithm for partial expected costs on non-negative, accumulated weights uses *partial expectations* in Markov decision processes [38]. The PP-hardness result is proved by reduction from the *cost problem* for acyclic Markov chains stated in [24]. The pseudo-polynomial algorithm for the maximal cost on arbitrary, accumulated weights applies insights from *total-payoff games* [7,9].

Full proofs missing in the main document can be found in the appendix.

Related Work. The structural model approach to actual causality [27] has sparked notions of causality in formal verification [4,11]. The complexity of computing actual causes has been studied in [16,17]. A probabilistic extension of this framework has been proposed in [21]. Recent work on checking and inferring actual causes is given in [29], and an application-oriented framework for it is presented in [30]. The work [34] builds a framework for actual causality in Markov chains and applies it to infer causal relationships in data sets. It was later extended to continuous time data [32] and to token causality [35] and has been refined using new measures for the significance of actual and token causes [28,44].

A logic for probabilistic causal reasoning is given in [1] in combination with logical programming. The work [43] compares this approach to Pearl's theory of causality involving Bayesian networks [37]. The CP-logic of [1] is close to the representation of causal mechanisms of [14]. The probability-raising principle goes back to Reichenbach [39]. It has been identified as a key ingredient to causality in various philosophical accounts, see e.g. [15].

Monitoring ω-regular properties in stochastic systems modeled as Hidden Markov Chains (HMCs) was studied in [23,40] and has recently been revived [18]. The trade-off between accuracy and overhead in runtime verification has been studied in [3,31,41]. In particular [3] uses HMCs to estimate how likely each monitor instance is to violate a temporal property. Monitoring the evolution of finite executions has also been investigated in the context of statistical model checking of LTL properties [13]. How randomization can improve monitors for non-probabilistic systems has been examined in [8]. The safety level of [19] measures which portion of a language admits bad prefixes, in the sense classically used for safety languages.

2 Preliminaries

Markov Chains. A *discrete-time Markov chain* (DTMC) M is a tuple $(S, s_0, \mathbf{P})$, where S is a finite set of *states*, $s_0 \in S$ is the *initial state*, and $\mathbf{P} \colon S \times S \to [0, 1]$ is the *transition probability function* where we require $\sum_{s' \in S} \mathbf{P}(s, s') = 1$ for all $s \in S$. For algorithmic problems all transition probabilities are assumed to be rational. A *finite path* $\hat{\pi}$ in M is a sequence $s_0 s_1 \ldots s_n$ of states such that $\mathbf{P}(s_i, s_{i+1}) > 0$ for all $0 \leq i \leq n - 1$. Let $\text{last}(s_0 \ldots s_n) = s_n$. Similarly one defines the notion of an *infinite path* π. Let $\text{Paths}_{\text{fin}}(M)$ and $\text{Paths}(M)$ be the set of finite and infinite paths. The set of prefixes of a path π is denoted by $\text{Pref}(\pi)$. The *cylinder set* of a finite path $\hat{\pi}$ is $\text{Cyl}(\hat{\pi}) = \{\pi \in \text{Paths}(M) \mid \hat{\pi} \in \text{Pref}(\pi)\}$. We consider $\text{Paths}(M)$ as a probability space whose σ-algebra is generated by such cylinder sets and whose probability measure is induced by $\text{Pr}(\text{Cyl}(s_0 \ldots s_n)) = \mathbf{P}(s_0, s_1) \cdot \ldots \cdot \mathbf{P}(s_{n-1}, s_n)$ (see [2, Chapter 10] for more details).

For an ω-regular language $\mathcal{L} \subseteq S^\omega$ let $\text{Paths}_M(\mathcal{L}) = \text{Paths}(M) \cap \mathcal{L}$. The probability of $\mathcal{L}$ in M is defined as $\text{Pr}_M(\mathcal{L}) = \text{Pr}(\text{Paths}_M(\mathcal{L}))$. Given a state $s \in S$, let $\text{Pr}_{M,s}(\mathcal{L}) = \text{Pr}_{M_s}(\mathcal{L})$, where M_s is the DTMC obtained from M by replacing the initial state s_0 with s. If M is clear from the context, we omit the subscript. For a finite path $\hat{\pi} \in \text{Paths}_{\text{fin}}(M)$, define the conditional probability

$$\text{Pr}_M(\mathcal{L} \mid \hat{\pi}) = \frac{\text{Pr}_M(\text{Paths}_M(\mathcal{L}) \cap \text{Cyl}(\hat{\pi}))}{\text{Pr}_M(\text{Cyl}(\hat{\pi}))}.$$

Given $E \subseteq S$, let $\Diamond E = \{s_0 s_1 \ldots \in \text{Paths}(M) \mid \exists i \geq 0.\ s_i \in E\}$. For such reachability properties we have $\text{Pr}_M(\Diamond E \mid s_0 \ldots s_n) = \text{Pr}_{M, s_n}(\Diamond E)$ for any $s_0 \ldots s_n \in \text{Paths}_{\text{fin}}(M)$. We assume $\text{Pr}_{s_0}(\Diamond s) > 0$ all states $s \in S$. Furthermore, define a *weight function* on M as a map $c \colon S \to \mathbb{Q}$. We typically use it to induce a weight function $c \colon \text{Paths}_{\text{fin}}(M) \to \mathbb{Q}$ (denoted by the same letter) by accumulation, i.e., $c(s_0 \cdots s_n) = \sum_{i=0}^n c(s_i)$. Finally, a set $\Pi \subseteq \text{Paths}_{\text{fin}}(M)$ is called *prefix-free* if for every $\hat{\pi} \in \Pi$ we have $\Pi \cap \text{Pref}(\hat{\pi}) = \{\hat{\pi}\}$.

Markov Decision Processes. A *Markov decision process* (MDP) $\mathcal{M}$ is a tuple $(S, \text{Act}, s_0, \mathbf{P})$, where S is a finite set of *states*, Act is a finite set of *actions*, s_0 is the *initial state*, and $\mathbf{P} \colon S \times \text{Act} \times S \to [0, 1]$ is the *transition probability function* such that for all states $s \in S$ and actions $\alpha \in \text{Act}$ we have $\sum_{s' \in S} \mathbf{P}(s, \alpha, s') \in \{0, 1\}$. An action α is *enabled* in state $s \in S$ if $\sum_{s' \in S} \mathbf{P}(s, \alpha, s') = 1$ and we define $\text{Act}(s) = \{\alpha \mid \alpha \text{ is enabled in } s\}$. We require $\text{Act}(s) \neq \emptyset$ for all states $s \in S$.

An infinite *path* in $\mathcal{M}$ is an infinite sequence $\pi = s_0 \alpha_1 s_1 \alpha_2 s_2 \cdots \in (S \times \text{Act})^\omega$ such that for all $i \geq 0$ we have $\mathbf{P}(s_i, \alpha_{i+1}, s_{i+1}) > 0$. Any finite prefix of π that ends in a state is a finite path. A *scheduler* $\mathfrak{S}$ is a function that maps a finite path $s_0 \alpha_1 s_1 \ldots s_n$ to an enabled action $\alpha \in \text{Act}(s_n)$. Therefore it resolves the nondeterminism of the MDP and induces a (potentially infinite) Markov chain $\mathcal{M}_\mathfrak{S}$. If the chosen action only depends on the last state of the path, i.e., $\mathfrak{S}(s_0 \alpha_1 s_1 \ldots s_n) = \mathfrak{S}(s_n)$, then the scheduler is called *memoryless* and naturally induces a finite DTMC. For more details on DTMCs and MDPs we refer to [2].

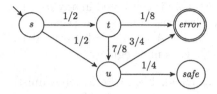
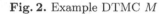

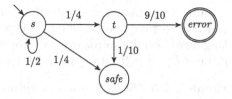

Fig. 2. Example DTMC M

Fig. 3. Infinite and non-regular $1/2$-causes

3   Causes

This section introduces a notion of *cause* for ω-regular properties in Markov chains. For the rest of this section we fix a DTMC M with state space S, an ω-regular language $\mathcal{L}$ over the alphabet S and a threshold $p \in (0,1]$.

Definition 3.1 (p-critical prefix). *A finite path $\hat{\pi}$ is a p-critical prefix for $\mathcal{L}$ if* $\Pr(\mathcal{L} \mid \hat{\pi}) \geq p$.

Definition 3.2 (p-cause). *A p-cause for $\mathcal{L}$ in M is a prefix-free set of finite paths $\Pi \subseteq \mathrm{Paths}_{\mathrm{fin}}(M)$ such that*

(1) almost every $\pi \in \mathrm{Paths}_M(\mathcal{L})$ has a prefix $\hat{\pi} \in \Pi$, and
(2) every $\hat{\pi} \in \Pi$ is a p-critical prefix for $\mathcal{L}$.

Note that condition (1) and (2) are in the spirit of completeness and soundness as used in [12]. The first condition is our invocation of the counterfactuality principle: Almost every occurrence of the effect (for example, reaching a target set) is preceded by an element in the cause. If the threshold is chosen such that $p > \mathrm{Pr}_{s_0}(\mathcal{L})$, then the second condition reflects the probability-raising principle in that seeing an element of Π implies that the probability of the effect $\mathcal{L}$ has increased over the course of the execution. For monitoring purposes as described in the introduction it would be misleading to choose p below $\mathrm{Pr}_{s_0}(\mathcal{L})$ as this could instantly trigger an alarm before the system is put to use. Also p should not be too close to 1 as this may result in an alarm being triggered too late.

If $\mathcal{L}$ coincides with a reachability property one could equivalently remove the *almost* from (1) of Definition 3.2. In general, however, ignoring paths with probability zero is necessary to guarantee the existence of p-causes for all p.

Example 3.3. Consider the DTMC M depicted in Fig. 2. For $p = 3/4$, a possible p-cause for $\mathcal{L} = \Diamond \mathit{error}$ in M is given by the set $\Pi_1 = \{st, su\}$ since both t and u reach *error* with probability greater or equal than p. The sets $\Theta_1 = \{st, su, stu\}$ and $\Theta_2 = \{sterror, su\}$ are not p-causes: Θ_1 is not prefix-free and for Θ_2 the path *stuerror* has no prefix in Θ_2. Another p-cause is $\Pi_2 = \{sterror, su, stu\}$.

Example 3.4. It can happen that there does not exist any finite p-cause. Consider Fig. 3 and $p = 1/2$. Since $\mathrm{Pr}_s(\Diamond \mathit{error}) < p$, the singleton $\{s\}$ is not a

p-cause. Thus, for every $n \geq 0$ either $s^n t$ or $s^n terror$ is contained in any p-cause, which must therefore be infinite. There may also exist non-regular p-causes (as languages of finite words over S). For example, for $A = \{n \in \mathbb{N} \mid n \text{ prime}\}$ the p-cause $\Pi_A = \{s_0^n t \mid n \in A\} \cup \{s_0^m terror \mid m \notin A\}$ is non-regular.

Remark 3.5 *(Reduction to reachability properties)*. Let $\mathcal{A}$ be a deterministic Rabin automaton for $\mathcal{L}$ and consider the product Markov chain $M \otimes \mathcal{A}$ as in [2, Section 10.3]. For any finite path $\hat{\pi} = s_0 \dots s_n \in \text{Paths}_{\text{fin}}(M)$ there is a unique path $a(\hat{\pi}) = (s_0, q_1)(s_1, q_2) \dots (s_n, q_{n+1}) \in \text{Paths}_{\text{fin}}(M \otimes \mathcal{A})$ whose projection onto the first factor is $\hat{\pi}$. Under this correspondence, a bottom strongly connected component (BSCC) of $M \otimes \mathcal{A}$ is either *accepting* or *rejecting*, meaning that for every finite path reaching this BSCC the corresponding path $\hat{\pi}$ in M satisfies $\text{Pr}_M(\mathcal{L} \mid \hat{\pi}) = 1$, or respectively, $\text{Pr}_M(\mathcal{L} \mid \hat{\pi}) = 0$ [2, Section 10.3]. This readily implies that almost every $\pi \in \text{Paths}_M(\mathcal{L})$ has a 1-critical prefix and that, therefore, p-causes exist for any p.

Moreover, if U is the union of all accepting BSCCs in $M \otimes \mathcal{A}$, then

$$\text{Pr}_M(\mathcal{L} \mid \hat{\pi}) = \text{Pr}_{M \otimes \mathcal{A}}(\Diamond U \mid a(\hat{\pi})) \tag{1}$$

holds for all finite paths $\hat{\pi}$ of M [2, Theorem 10.56]. Hence every p-cause Π_1 for $\mathcal{L}$ in M induces a p-cause Π_2 for $\Diamond U$ in $M \otimes \mathcal{A}$ by taking $\Pi_2 = \{a(\hat{\pi}) \mid \hat{\pi} \in \Pi_1\}$. Vice versa, given a p-cause Π_2 for $\Diamond U$ in $M \otimes \mathcal{A}$, then the set of projections of paths in Π_2 onto their first component is a p-cause for $\mathcal{L}$ in M. In summary, the reduction of ω-regular properties on M to reachability properties on the product $M \otimes \mathcal{A}$ also induces a reduction on the level of causes.

Remark 3.5 motivates us to focus on reachability properties henceforth. To apply the algorithms presented in Sect. 4 to specifications given in richer formalisms such as LTL, one would first have to apply the reduction to reachability given above, which increases the worst-case complexity exponentially.

In order to align the exposition with the monitoring application we are targeting, we will consider the target set as representing an erroneous behavior that is to be avoided. After collapsing the target set, we may assume that there is a unique state $error \in S$, so $\mathcal{L} = \Diamond error$ is the language we are interested in. Further, we collapse all states from which $error$ is not reachable to a unique state $safe \in S$ with the property $\text{Pr}_{safe}(\Diamond error) = 0$. After this pre-processing, we have $\text{Pr}_{s_0}(\Diamond\{error, safe\}) = 1$. Define the set

$$S_p := \{s \in S \mid \text{Pr}_s(\Diamond error) \geq p\}$$

of all acceptable final states for p-critical prefixes. This set is never empty as $error \in S_p$ for all $p \in (0, 1]$.

There is a partial order on the set of p-causes defined as follows: $\Pi \preceq \Phi$ if and only if for all $\phi \in \Phi$ there exists $\pi \in \Pi$ such that $\pi \in \text{Pref}(\phi)$. The reflexivity and transitivity are straightforward, and the antisymmetry follows from the fact that p-causes are prefix-free. However, this order itself has no influence on the probability. In fact for two p-causes Π, Φ with $\Pi \preceq \Phi$ it can happen that for

$\pi \in \Pi, \phi \in \Phi$ we have $\Pr(\Diamond error \mid \pi) \geq \Pr(\Diamond error \mid \phi)$. This partial order admits a minimal element which is a regular language over S and which plays a crucial role for finding optimal causes in Sect. 4.

Proposition 3.6 (Canonical p-cause). *Let*

$$\Theta = \big\{ s_0 \cdots s_n \in \mathrm{Paths}_{\mathrm{fin}}(M) \mid s_n \in S_p \text{ and for all } i < n\colon\ s_i \notin S_p \big\}.$$

Then Θ is a regular p-cause (henceforth called the canonical p-cause*) and for all p-causes Π we have $\Theta \preceq \Pi$.*

We now introduce an MDP associated with M whose schedulers correspond to the p-causes of M. This is useful both to represent p-causes and for algorithmic questions we consider later.

Definition 3.7 (p-causal MDP). *For the DTMC $M = (S, s_0, \mathbf{P})$ define the p-causal MDP $\mathcal{C}_p(M) = (S, \{continue, pick\}, s_0, \mathbf{P}')$ associated with M, where $\mathbf{P}'$ is defined as follows:*

$$\mathbf{P}'(s, continue, s') = \mathbf{P}(s, s') \text{ for all } s, s' \in S$$

$$\mathbf{P}'(s, pick, error) = \begin{cases} 1 & \text{if } s \in S_p \\ 0 & \text{otherwise} \end{cases}$$

Given a weight function c on M, we consider c also as weight function on $\mathcal{C}_p(M)$.

Example 3.8. Figure 4 demonstrates the p-causal MDP construction of $\mathcal{C}_p(M)$. The black edges are transitions of M, probabilities are omitted. Let us assume $S_p \backslash \{error\} = \{s_1, s_3, s_4\}$. To construct $\mathcal{C}_p(M)$ one adds transitions for the action *pick*, as shown by red edges.

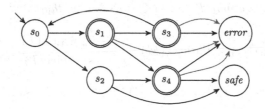

Fig. 4. Illustration of the p-causal MDP construction (Color figure online)

Technically, schedulers are defined on all finite paths of an MDP $\mathcal{M}$. However, under any scheduler, there are usually paths that cannot be obtained under the scheduler. Thus we define an equivalence relation $\equiv$ on the set of schedulers of $\mathcal{M}$ by setting $\mathfrak{S} \equiv \mathfrak{S}'$ if $\mathrm{Paths}(\mathcal{M}_\mathfrak{S}) = \mathrm{Paths}(\mathcal{M}_{\mathfrak{S}'})$. Note that two schedulers equivalent under $\equiv$ behave identically.

Lemma 3.9. *There is a one-to-one correspondence between equivalence classes of schedulers in* $\mathcal{C}_p(M)$ *w.r.t.* $\equiv$ *and p-causes in* M *for* $\Diamond error$.

Proof. Given a p-cause Π for $\Diamond error$ in M, we construct the equivalence class of scheduler $[\mathfrak{S}_\Pi]$ by defining $\mathfrak{S}_\Pi(\hat{\pi}) = pick$ if $\hat{\pi} \in \Pi$, and otherwise $\mathfrak{S}_\Pi(\hat{\pi}) = continue$. Vice versa, given an equivalence class $[\mathfrak{S}]$ of schedulers, we define the p-cause

$$\Pi_\mathfrak{S} = \left\{ \hat{\pi} \in \text{Paths}_{\text{fin}}(M) \;\middle|\; \begin{array}{l} \mathfrak{S}(\hat{\pi}) = pick \text{ or } \hat{\pi} \text{ ends in } error \text{ and} \\ \mathfrak{S} \text{ does not choose } pick \text{ on any prefix of } \hat{\pi} \end{array} \right\}$$

Since $pick$ can only be chosen once on every path in $\text{Paths}(\mathcal{M}_\mathfrak{S})$, it is easy to see that $\mathfrak{S} \equiv \mathfrak{S}'$ implies $\Pi_\mathfrak{S} = \Pi_{\mathfrak{S}'}$. Note that every $\hat{\pi} \in \Pi_\mathfrak{S}$ is a p-critical prefix since it ends in S_p and every path in $\Diamond error$ is covered since either $pick$ is chosen or $\hat{\pi}$ ends in $error$. Furthermore, the second condition makes Π prefix-free. □

3.1   Types of *p*-causes and Induced Monitors

We now introduce two classes of p-causes which have a comparatively simple representation, and we explain what classes of schedulers they correspond to in the p-causal MDP and how monitors can be derived for them.

Definition 3.10 (State-based *p*-cause). *A p-cause* Π *is* state-based *if there exists a set of states* $Q \subseteq S_p$ *such that* $\Pi = \{s_0 \ldots s_n \in \text{Paths}_{\text{fin}}(M) \mid s_n \in Q \text{ and } \forall i < n : s_i \notin Q\}$.

State-based p-causes correspond to memoryless schedulers of $\mathcal{C}_p(M)$ which choose $pick$ exactly for paths ending in Q. For DTMCs equipped with a weight function we introduce *threshold-based p-causes*:

Definition 3.11 (Threshold-based *p*-cause). *A p-cause* Π *is* threshold-based *if there exists a map* $T : S_p \to \mathbb{Q} \cup \{\infty\}$ *such that*

$$\Pi = \left\{ s_0 \cdots s_n \in \text{Paths}_{\text{fin}}(M) \;\middle|\; \begin{array}{l} s_0 \cdots s_n \in \text{pick}(T) \text{ and} \\ s_0 \cdots s_i \notin \text{pick}(T) \text{ for } i < n \end{array} \right\}$$

where $\text{pick}(T) = \{s_0 \ldots s_n \in \text{Paths}_{\text{fin}}(M) \mid s_n \in S_p \text{ and } c(s_0 \ldots s_n) < T(s_n)\}$.

Threshold-based p-causes correspond to a simple class of *weight-based* schedulers of the p-causal MDP, which base their decision in a state only on whether the current weight exceeds the threshold or not. Intuitively, threshold-based p-causes are useful if triggering an alarm causes costs while reaching a safe state does not (see Sect. 4.2): The idea is that cheap paths (satisfying $c(s_0 \ldots s_n) < T(s_n)$) are picked for the p-cause, while expensive paths are continued in order to realize the chance (with probability $\leq 1-p$) that a safe state is reached and therefore the high cost that has already been accumulated is avoided.

The concept of p-causes can be used as a basis for monitors that raise an alarm as soon as a state sequence in the p-cause has been observed. State-based p-causes have the advantage that they are realizable by "memoryless" monitors that only need the information on the current state of the Markov chain. Threshold-based monitors additionally need to track the weight that has been accumulated so far until the threshold value of the current state is exceeded. So, the memory requirements of monitors realizing a threshold-based p-cause are given by the logarithmic length of the largest threshold value for S_p-states. All algorithms proposed in Sect. 4 for computing cost-minimal p-causes will return p-causes that are either state-based or threshold-based with polynomially bounded memory requirements.

3.2   Comparison to Prima Facie Causes

The work [34] presents the notion of *prima facie causes* in DTMCs where both causes and events are formalized as PCTL state formulae. In our setting we can equivalently consider a state *error* $\in S$ as the effect and a state subset $C \subseteq S$ constituting the cause. We then reformulate [34, Definition 4.1] to our setting.

Definition 3.12 (cf. [34]). *A set $C \subseteq S$ is a p-prima facie cause of $\lozenge error$ if the following three conditions hold:*

(1) The set C is reachable from the initial state and error $\notin C$.
(2) $\forall s \in C : \mathrm{Pr}_s(\lozenge error) \geq p$
(3) $\mathrm{Pr}_{s_0}(\lozenge error) < p$

The condition $p > \mathrm{Pr}_{s_0}(\lozenge error)$ we discussed for p-causes is hard-coded here as (3). In [34] the value p is implicitly existentially quantified and thus conditions (2) and (3) can be combined to $\mathrm{Pr}_s(\lozenge error) > \mathrm{Pr}_{s_0}(\lozenge error)$ for all $s \in C$. This encapsulates the probability-raising property. However, *error* may be reached while avoiding the cause C, so p-prima facie causes do not entail the *counterfactuality* principle. Definition 3.2 can be seen as an extension of p-prima facie causes by virtue of the following lemma:

Lemma 3.13. *For $p > \mathrm{Pr}_{s_0}(\lozenge error)$ every p-prima facie cause induces a state-based p-cause.*

Proof. Let $C \subseteq S$ be a p-prima facie cause. By condition (1) and (2) of Definition 3.12 we have $C \subseteq S_p \backslash \{error\}$. Since every path reaching *error* trivially visits a state in $Q := C \cup \{error\} \subseteq S_p$, the set $\Pi = \{s_0 \ldots s_n \in \mathrm{Paths}_{\mathrm{fin}}(M) \mid s_n \in Q$ and $\forall i < n : s_i \notin Q\}$ is a state-based p-cause. $\qquad \square$

4   Costs of p-causes

In this section we fix a DTMC M with state space S, unique initial state s_0, unique target and safe state *error*, *safe* $\in S$ and a threshold $p \in (0, 1]$. As motivated in the introduction, we equip the DTMC of our model with a *weight function* $c : S \to \mathbb{Q}$ on states and consider the induced accumulated weight function $c : \mathrm{Paths}_{\mathrm{fin}}(M) \to \mathbb{Q}$. These weights typically represent resources spent, e.g., energy, time, material, etc.

4.1   Expected Cost of a p-cause

Definition 4.1 (Expected cost). *Given a p-cause Π for $\Diamond$ error in M consider the random variable $\mathcal{X}$: Paths$(M) \rightarrow \mathbb{Q}$ with*

$$\mathcal{X}(\pi) = c(\hat{\pi}) \ for \ \begin{cases} \hat{\pi} \in \Pi \cap \mathrm{Pref}(\pi) & if \ such \ \hat{\pi} \ exists \\ \hat{\pi} \in \mathrm{Pref}(\pi) \ minimal \ with \ \mathrm{last}(\hat{\pi}) = safe & otherwise. \end{cases}$$

Since $\mathrm{Pr}_{s_0}(\Diamond\{error, safe\}) = 1$, *paths not falling under the two cases above have measure 0. Then the* expected cost expcost(Π) *of Π is the expected value of $\mathcal{X}$.*

The expected cost is a means by which the efficiency of causes for monitoring purposes can be estimated. Assume a p-cause Π is used to monitor critical scenarios of a probabilistic system. This means that at some point either a critical scenario is predicted by the monitor (i.e., the execution seen so far lies in Π), or the monitor reports that no critical scenario will arise (i.e., *safe* has been reached) and can therefore be turned off. If the weight function on the state space is chosen such that it models the cost of monitoring the respective states, then expcost(Π) estimates the average total resource consumption of the monitor.

We say that a p-cause Π is expcost-*minimal* if for all p-causes Φ we have expcost$(\Pi) \leq$ expcost(Φ). By expcost^{min}, we denote the value expcost(Π) of any expcost-minimal p-cause Π.

Theorem 4.2. *(1) Given a non-negative weight function $c : S \rightarrow \mathbb{Q}_{\geq 0}$, the canonical p-cause Θ from Proposition 3.6 is expcost-minimal.*
(2) For an arbitrary weight function $c : S \rightarrow \mathbb{Q}$, an expcost-minimal and state-based p-cause Π and expcost^{min} *can be computed in polynomial time.*

Proof sketch. The statement (1) follows from the fact that if $\Pi \preceq \Phi$ holds for two p-causes, then we have expcost$(\Pi) \leq$ expcost(Φ), which is shown in the appendix. The value expcost$^{\mathrm{min}} =$ expcost(Θ) can then be computed in polynomial time using methods for expected rewards in Markov chains [2, Section 10.5].

To show (2), we reduce our problem to the *stochastic shortest path problem* (SSP) [5] from s_0 to $\{error, safe\}$. By Lemma 3.9 equivalence classes of schedulers in $\mathcal{C}_p(M)$ are in one-to-one correspondence with p-causes in M. Let $\Pi_{\mathfrak{S}}$ be a p-cause associated with a representative scheduler $\mathfrak{S}$. One can show that expcost$(\Pi_{\mathfrak{S}})$ is equal to the expected accumulated weight of paths under scheduler $\mathfrak{S}$ in $\mathcal{C}_p(M)$ upon reaching $\{error, safe\}$. A scheduler $\mathfrak{S}^*$ minimizing this value can be computed in polynomial time by solving the SSP in $\mathcal{C}_p(M)$ [5], and the algorithm returns a memoryless such $\mathfrak{S}^*$. It follows that $\Pi_{\mathfrak{S}^*}$ is an expcost-minimal and state-based p-cause.   □

4.2   Partial Expected Cost of a p-cause

In this section we study a variant of the expected cost where paths with no prefix in the p-cause are attributed zero costs. A use case for this cost mechanism arises if the costs are not incurred by monitoring the system, but by the countermeasures taken upon triggering the alarm. For example, an alarm might be followed by a downtime of the system, and the cost of this may depend on the current state and history of the execution. In such cases there are no costs incurred if no alarm is triggered.

Definition 4.3 (Partial expected cost). *For a p-cause Π for $\Diamond error$ in M consider the random variable $\mathcal{X} : \text{Paths}(M) \to \mathbb{Q}$ with*

$$\mathcal{X}(\pi) = \begin{cases} c(\hat{\pi}) & \text{for } \hat{\pi} \in \Pi \cap \text{Pref}(\pi) \text{ if such } \hat{\pi} \text{ exists} \\ 0 & \text{otherwise.} \end{cases}$$

The partial expected cost pexpcost(Π) *of Π is the expected value of $\mathcal{X}$.*

The analogous statement to Theorem 4.2 (1) does not hold for partial expected costs, as the following example shows.

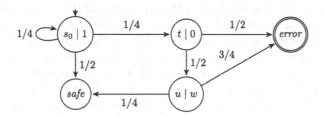

Fig. 5. An example showing that the partial expected cost is not monotonous on *p*-causes when c is non-negative.

Example 4.4. Consider the Markov chain depicted in Fig. 5. For $p = 1/2$ and $\Diamond error$ we have $S_p = \{t, u, error\}$. The canonical p-cause is $\Theta = \{s_0^k t \mid k \geq 1\}$ with pexpcost$(\Theta) = \sum_{k \geq 1} (1/4)^k \cdot k = 4/9$. Now let Π be any p-cause for $\Diamond error$. If the path $s_0^\ell t$ belongs to Π, then it contributes $(1/4)^\ell \cdot \ell$ to pexpcost(Π). If instead the paths $s_0^\ell terror$ and $s_0^\ell tuerror$ belong to Π, they contribute $(1/4)^\ell \cdot 1/2 \cdot \ell + (1/4)^\ell \cdot 1/2 \cdot 3/4 \cdot (\ell + w)$. So, the latter case provides a smaller pexpcost if $l > 3w$, and the pexpcost-minimal p-cause is therefore

$$\Pi = \{s_0^k t \mid 1 \leq k \leq 3w\} \cup \{s_0^k terror, s_0^k tu \mid 3w < k\}.$$

For $w = 1$, the expected cost of this p-cause is $511/1152 = 4/9 - 1/1152$. So, it is indeed smaller than pexpcost(Θ).

Theorem 4.5. *Given a non-negative weight function $c\colon S \to \mathbb{Q}_{\geq 0}$, a pexpcost-minimal and threshold-based p-cause Π, and the value pexpcost$^{\min}$, can be computed in pseudo-polynomial time. Π has a polynomially bounded representation.*

Proof sketch. For the pseudo-polynomial time bound we apply the techniques from [38] to optimize the partial expected cost in MDPs to the p-causal MDP $\mathcal{C}_p(M)$. It is shown in [38] that there is an optimal scheduler whose decision depends only on the current state and accumulated weight and that such a scheduler and its partial expectation can be computed in pseudo-polynomial time. It is further shown that a rational number K can be computed in polynomial time such that for accumulated weights above K, an optimal scheduler has to minimize the probability to reach *error*. In our case, this means choosing the action *continue*. Due to the special structure of $\mathcal{C}_p(M)$, we can further show that there is indeed a threshold $T(s)$ for each state s such that action *pick* is optimal after a path $\hat{\pi}$ ending in s if and only if $c(\hat{\pi}) < T(s)$. So, a threshold-based pexpcost-minimal p-cause can be computed in pseudo-polynomial time. Furthermore, we have $T(s) < K$ for each state s and as K has a polynomially bounded representation the same applies to the values $T(s)$ for all states s.   □

Since the causal MDP $\mathcal{C}_p(M)$ has a comparatively simple form, one could expect that one can do better than the pseudo-polynomial algorithm obtained by reduction to [38]. Nevertheless, in the remainder of this section we argue that computing a pexpcost-minimal p-cause is computationally hard, in contrast to expcost (cf. Theorem 4.2). For this we recall that the complexity class PP [22] is characterized as the class of languages $\mathcal{L}$ that have a probabilistic polynomial-time bounded Turing machine $M_{\mathcal{L}}$ such that for all words τ one has $\tau \in \mathcal{L}$ if and only if $M_{\mathcal{L}}$ accepts τ with probability at least $1/2$ (cf. [25]). We will use polynomial Turing reductions, which, in contrast to many-one reductions, allow querying an oracle that solves the problem we reduce to a polynomial number of times. A polynomial time algorithm for a problem that is PP-hard under polynomial Turing reductions would imply that the polynomial hierarchy collapses [42]. We reduce the PP-complete cost-problem stated in [24, Theorem 3] to the problem of computing pexpcost$^{\min}$.

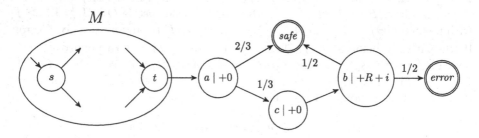

Fig. 6. The DTMCs N_i for $i = 0, 1$

Theorem 4.6. *Given an acyclic DTMC M, a weight function $c\colon S \to \mathbb{N}$ and a rational $\vartheta \in \mathbb{Q}$, deciding whether pexpcost$^{\min} \leq \vartheta$ is PP-hard under Turing reductions.*

Proof sketch. We sketch a Turing reduction from the following problem which is shown to be PP-hard in [24]: Given an acyclic DTMC M over state space S with initial state s, absorbing state t such that $\text{Pr}_s(\lozenge t) = 1$, weight function $c : S \to \mathbb{N}$ and natural number $R \in \mathbb{N}$, decide whether

$$\text{Pr}_M(\{\pi \in \text{Paths}(M) \mid c(\pi) \le R\}) \ge 1/2.$$

In an acyclic Markov chain M the values of pexpcost have a polynomially bounded binary representation as shown in the appendix. This allows for a binary search to compute pexpcost^{min} with polynomially many calls to the corresponding threshold problem. We use this procedure in a polynomial-time Turing reduction.

Let now M be a Markov chain as in [24, Theorem 3] and let R be a natural number. We construct two Markov chains N_0 and N_1 depicted in Fig. 6. The pexpcost-minimal p-cause in both Markov chains consists of all paths reaching c with weight $\le R$ and all paths reaching *error* that do not have a prefix reaching c with weight $\le R$. The difference between the values pexpcost^{min} in the two Markov chains depends only on the probability of paths in the minimal p-cause collecting the additional weight $+1$ in N_1. This probability is $\frac{1}{6}\text{Pr}_M(\{\pi \in \text{Paths}(M) \mid c(\pi) \le R\})$. By repeatedly using the threshold problem to compute pexpcost^{min} in N_0 and N_1 as described above, we can hence decide the problem from [24, Theorem 3]. More details can be found in the appendix. $\qquad\square$

4.3   Maximal Cost of a p-cause

In practice, the weight function on the Markov chain potentially models resources for which the available consumption has a *tight* upper bound. For example, the amount of energy a drone can consume from its battery is naturally limited. Instead of just knowing that *on average* the consumption will lie below a given bound, it is therefore often desirable to find monitors whose costs are guaranteed to lie below this limit for (almost) any evolution of the system.

Definition 4.7 (Maximal cost). *Let Π be a p-cause for $\lozenge error$ in M. We define the* maximal cost *of Π to be*

$$\text{maxcost}(\Pi) = \sup\{c(\hat{\pi}) \mid \hat{\pi} \in \Pi\}.$$

The maximal cost of a p-cause is a measure for the worst-case resource consumption among executions of the system. Therefore, by knowing the minimal value maxcost^{min} for p-causes one can ensure that there will be no critical scenario arising from resource management.

Theorem 4.8. *(1) Given a non-negative weight function $c : S \to \mathbb{Q}_{\ge 0}$, the canonical p-cause Θ is maxcost-minimal and maxcost^{min} can be computed in time polynomial in the size of M.*

(2) For an arbitrary weight function $c : S \to \mathbb{Q}$ a maxcost-minimal and state-based p-cause Π and maxcost^{min} can be computed in pseudo-polynomial time.

(3) Given a rational $\vartheta \in \mathbb{Q}$, deciding whether maxcost$^{\text{min}} \le \vartheta$ is in NP $\cap$ coNP.

Proof sketch. To show (1) it suffices to note that for non-negative weight functions maxcost is monotonous with respect to the partial order $\preceq$ on p-causes. Therefore Θ is maxcost-minimal. For (2) we reduce the problem to a max-cost reachability game as defined in [7]. The algorithm from [7] computes the lowest maximal cost and has a pseudo-polynomial time bound. By virtue of the fact that the minimizing player has a memoryless strategy we can compute a set of states $Q \subseteq S_p$ on which a maxcost-minimal p-cause Π is based upon. In order to show (3) we reduce the max-cost reachability game from (2) further to mean-payoff games, as seen in [9]. Mean-payoff games are known to lie in NP $\cap$ coNP [9]. □

4.4   Instantaneous Cost

The given weight function c on states can also induce an instantaneous weight function $c_{\text{inst}} : \text{Paths}_{\text{fin}}(M) \to \mathbb{Q}$ which just takes the weight of the state visited last, i.e., $c_{\text{inst}}(s_0 \cdots s_n) = c(s_n)$. This yields an alternative cost mechanism intended to model the situation where the cost of repairing or rebooting only depends on the current state, e.g., the altitude an automated drone has reached.

We add the subscript 'inst' to the three cost variants, where the accumulative weight function c has been replaced with the instantaneous weight function c_{inst}, the error state is replaced by an error set E and the safe state is replaced by a set of terminal safe states F. Thus we optimize p-causes for $\lozenge E$ in M.

Theorem 4.9. *For* $\text{expcost}_{\text{inst}}$, $\text{pexpcost}_{\text{inst}}$, *and* $\text{maxcost}_{\text{inst}}$ *a cost-minimal p-cause Π and the value of the minimal cost can be computed in time polynomial in M. In all cases Π can be chosen to be a state-based p-cause.*

Proof sketch. We first note that $\text{pexpcost}_{\text{inst}}$ can be reduced to $\text{expcost}_{\text{inst}}$ by setting the weight of all states in F to 0. We then construct an MDP (different from $\mathcal{C}_p(M)$) which emulates the instantaneous weight function using an accumulating weight function. Thus, finding an $\text{expcost}_{\text{inst}}$-minimal p-cause Π reduces to the SSP from [5], which can be solved in polynomial time. The solution admits a memoryless scheduler and thus Π is state-based in this case.

For $\text{maxcost}_{\text{inst}}$ we order the states in S_p by their cost and then start iteratively removing the states with lowest cost until E is not reachable anymore. The set Q of states which where removed induce a state-based $\text{maxcost}_{\text{inst}}$-minimal p-cause Π. This gives us a polynomial time procedure to compute $\text{maxcost}_{\text{inst}}^{\min}$ and Π. □

5   Conclusion

We combined the counterfactuality principle and the probability-raising property into the notion of p-causes in DTMCs. In order to find suitable p-causes we defined different cost models and gave algorithms to compute corresponding cost-minimal causes.

Cyber-physical systems are often not fully probabilistic, but involve a certain amount of control in form of decisions depending on the system state. Such systems can be modeled by MDPs, to which we intend to generalize the causality framework presented here. Our approach also assumes that the probabilistic system described by the Markov chain is fully observable. By observing execution traces instead of paths of the system, generalizing the notion of p-causes to hidden Markov models is straightforward. However, the corresponding computational problems exhibit additional difficulties which we address in future work.

References

1. CP-logic: A language of causal probabilistic events and its relation to logic programming 9
2. Baier, C., Katoen, J.P.: Principles of Model Checking (Representation and Mind Series). The MIT Press, Cambridge (2008)
3. Bartocci, E., et al.: Adaptive runtime verification. In: Qadeer, S., Tasiran, S. (eds.) RV 2012. LNCS, vol. 7687, pp. 168–182. Springer, Heidelberg (2013). https://doi.org/10.1007/978-3-642-35632-2_18
4. Beer, I., Ben-David, S., Chockler, H., Orni, A., Trefler, R.: Explaining counterexamples using causality. In: Bouajjani, A., Maler, O. (eds.) CAV 2009. LNCS, vol. 5643, pp. 94–108. Springer, Heidelberg (2009). https://doi.org/10.1007/978-3-642-02658-4_11
5. Bertsekas, D.P., Tsitsiklis, J.N.: An analysis of stochastic shortest path problems, 16(3), 580–595 (1991)
6. Braham, M., van Hees, M.: An anatomy of moral responsibility. Mind 121(483), 601–634 (2012)
7. Brihaye, T., Geeraerts, G., Haddad, A., Monmege, B.: To reach or not to reach? efficient algorithms for total-payoff games. In: Proceedings of the 26th International Conference on Concurrency Theory (CONCUR'15). LIPIcs, vol. 42, pp. 297–310 (2015)
8. Chadha, R., Sistla, A.P., Viswanathan, M.: On the expressiveness and complexity of randomization in finite state monitors, 56(5) (2009)
9. Chatterjee, K., Doyen, L., Henzinger, T.A.: The cost of exactness in quantitative reachability. In: Aceto, L., Bacci, G., Bacci, G., Ingólfsdóttir, A., Legay, A., Mardare, R. (eds.) Models, Algorithms, Logics and Tools. LNCS, vol. 10460, pp. 367–381. Springer, Cham (2017). https://doi.org/10.1007/978-3-319-63121-9_18
10. Chockler, H., Halpern, J.Y.: Responsibility and blame: a structural-model approach. J. Artif. Int. Res. 22(1), 93–115 (2004)
11. Chockler, H., Halpern, J.Y., Kupferman, O.: What causes a system to satisfy a specification? ACM Trans. Comput. Logic 9(3), 20:1–20:26 (2008)
12. Cini, C., Francalanza, A.: An LTL proof system for runtime verification. In: Baier, C., Tinelli, C. (eds.) TACAS 2015. LNCS, vol. 9035, pp. 581–595. Springer, Heidelberg (2015). https://doi.org/10.1007/978-3-662-46681-0_54
13. Daca, P., Henzinger, T.A., Křetínský, J., Petrov, T.: Faster statistical model checking for unbounded temporal properties. In: Chechik, M., Raskin, J.-F. (eds.) TACAS 2016. LNCS, vol. 9636, pp. 112–129. Springer, Heidelberg (2016). https://doi.org/10.1007/978-3-662-49674-9_7

14. Dash, D., Voortman, M., De Jongh, M.: Sequences of mechanisms for causal reasoning in artificial intelligence. In: Proceedings of the 23rd International Joint Conference on Artificial Intelligence, IJCAI '13, pp. 839–845. AAAI Press (2013)
15. Eells, E.: Probabilistic Causality. Cambridge Studies in Probability, Induction and Decision Theory. Cambridge University Press, Cambridge (1991)
16. Eiter, T., Lukasiewicz, T.: Complexity results for explanations in the structural-model approach. Artif. Intell. **154**(1–2), 145–198 (2004)
17. Eiter, T., Lukasiewicz, T.: Causes and explanations in the structural-model approach: tractable cases. Artif. Intell. **170**(6–7), 542–580 (2006)
18. Esparza, J., Kiefer, S., Kretinsky, J., Weininger, M.: Online monitoring ω-regular properties in unknown Markov chains. Arxiv preprint, arXiv:2010.08347 (2020)
19. Faran, R., Kupferman, O.: Spanning the spectrum from safety to liveness. Acta Informatica **55**(8), 703–732 (2018). https://doi.org/10.1007/s00236-017-0307-4
20. Feigenbaum, J., Hendler, J.A., Jaggard, A.D., Weitzner, D.J., Wright, R.N.: Accountability and deterrence in online life. ACM, New York (2011)
21. Fenton-Glynn, L.: A proposed probabilistic extension of the halpern and pearl definition of 'actual cause'. Br. J. Philos. Sci. **68**(4), 1061–1124 (2016)
22. Gill, J.: Computational complexity of probabilistic turing machines. SIAM J. Comput. **6**(4), 675–695 (1977)
23. Gondi, K., Patel, Y., Sistla, A.P.: Monitoring the full range of ω-regular properties of stochastic systems. In: Jones, N.D., Müller-Olm, M. (eds.) VMCAI 2009. LNCS, vol. 5403, pp. 105–119. Springer, Heidelberg (2008). https://doi.org/10.1007/978-3-540-93900-9_12
24. Haase, C., Kiefer, S.: The odds of staying on budget. In: Halldórsson, M.M., Iwama, K., Kobayashi, N., Speckmann, B. (eds.) ICALP 2015. LNCS, vol. 9135, pp. 234–246. Springer, Heidelberg (2015). https://doi.org/10.1007/978-3-662-47666-6_19
25. Haase, C., Kiefer, S.: The complexity of the kth largest subset problem and related problems, **116**(2) (2016)
26. Halpern, J.Y.: A modification of the Halpern-Pearl definition of causality. In: Proceedings of IJCAI'15, pp. 3022–3033. AAAI Press (2015)
27. Halpern, J.Y., Pearl, J.: Causes and explanations: a structural-model approach: part 1: causes. In: Proceedings of the 17th Conference in Uncertainty in Artificial Intelligence (UAI), pp. 194–202 (2001)
28. Huang, Y., Kleinberg, S.: Fast and accurate causal inference from time series data. In: Proceedings of FLAIRS 2015, pp. 49–54. AAAI Press (2015)
29. Ibrahim, A., Pretschner, A.: From checking to inference: actual causality computations as optimization problems. In: Hung, D.V., Sokolsky, O. (eds.) ATVA 2020. LNCS, vol. 12302, pp. 343–359. Springer, Cham (2020). https://doi.org/10.1007/978-3-030-59152-6_19
30. Ibrahim, A., Pretschner, A., Klesel, T., Zibaei, E., Kacianka, S., Pretschner, A.: Actual causality canvas: a general framework for explanation-based socio-technical constructs. In: Proceedings of ECAI'20, pp. 2978–2985. IOS Press Ebooks (2020)
31. Kalajdzic, K., Bartocci, E., Smolka, S.A., Stoller, S.D., Grosu, R.: Runtime verification with particle filtering. In: Legay, A., Bensalem, S. (eds.) RV 2013. LNCS, vol. 8174, pp. 149–166. Springer, Heidelberg (2013). https://doi.org/10.1007/978-3-642-40787-1_9
32. Kleinberg, S.: A logic for causal inference in time series with discrete and continuous variables. In: Proceedings of IJCAI'11, pp. 943–950 (2011)
33. Kleinberg, S., Hripcsak, G.: A review of causal inference for biomedical informatics. J. Biomed. Inform. **44**(6), 1102–12 (2011)

34. Kleinberg, S., Mishra, B.: The temporal logic of causal structures. In: Proceedings of the Twenty-Fifth Conference on Uncertainty in Artificial Intelligence (UAI), pp. 303–312 (2009)
35. Kleinberg, S., Mishra, B.: The temporal logic of token causes. In: Proceedings of KR'10, pp. 575–577. AAAI Press (2010)
36. Miller, T.: Explanation in artificial intelligence: insights from the social sciences. Artif. Intell. **267**, 1–38 (2017)
37. Pearl, J.: Causality, 2nd edn. Cambridge University Press, Cambridge (2009)
38. Piribauer, J., Baier, C.: Partial and conditional expectations in Markov decision processes with integer weights. In: Bojańczyk, M., Simpson, A. (eds.) FoSSaCS 2019. LNCS, vol. 11425, pp. 436–452. Springer, Cham (2019). https://doi.org/10.1007/978-3-030-17127-8_25
39. Reichenbach, H.: The Direction of Time. Dover Publications, Mineola (1956)
40. Sistla, A.P., Srinivas, A.R.: Monitoring temporal properties of stochastic systems. In: Logozzo, F., Peled, D.A., Zuck, L.D. (eds.) VMCAI 2008. LNCS, vol. 4905, pp. 294–308. Springer, Heidelberg (2008). https://doi.org/10.1007/978-3-540-78163-9_25
41. Stoller, S.D.: Runtime verification with state estimation. In: Khurshid, S., Sen, K. (eds.) RV 2011. LNCS, vol. 7186, pp. 193–207. Springer, Heidelberg (2012). https://doi.org/10.1007/978-3-642-29860-8_15
42. Toda, S.: PP is as hard as the polynomial-time hierarchy, **20**, 865–877 (1991)
43. Vennekens, J., Bruynooghe, M., Denecker, M.: Embracing events in causal modelling: interventions and counterfactuals in CP-logic. In: Janhunen, T., Niemelä, I. (eds.) JELIA 2010. LNCS (LNAI), vol. 6341, pp. 313–325. Springer, Heidelberg (2010). https://doi.org/10.1007/978-3-642-15675-5_27
44. Zheng, M., Kleinberg, S.: A method for automating token causal explanation and discovery. In: Proceedings of FLAIRS'17 (2017)

TEMPEST - Synthesis Tool for Reactive Systems and Shields in Probabilistic Environments

Stefan Pranger[1]([☒]), Bettina Könighofer[1,2], Lukas Posch[1], and Roderick Bloem[1,2]

[1] Institute IAIK, Graz University of Technology, Graz, Austria
stefan.pranger@student.tugraz.at, bettina.koenighofer@iaik.tugraz.at
[2] Silicon Austria Labs, TU Graz SAL-DES Lab, Graz, Austria

Abstract. We present `Tempest`, a synthesis tool to automatically create correct-by-construction reactive systems and shields from qualitative or quantitative specifications in probabilistic environments. A shield is a special type of reactive system used for run-time enforcement; i.e., a shield enforces a given qualitative or quantitative specification of a running system while interfering with its operation as little as possible. Shields that enforce a qualitative or quantitative specification are called safety-shields or optimal-shields, respectively. Safety-shields can be implemented as pre-shields or as post-shields, optimal-shields are implemented as post-shields. Pre-shields are placed before the system and restrict the choices of the system. Post-shields are implemented after the system and are able to overwrite the system's output. `Tempest` is based on the probabilistic model checker `Storm`, adding model checking algorithms for stochastic games with safety and mean-payoff objectives. To the best of our knowledge, `Tempest` is the only synthesis tool able to solve 2$\frac{1}{2}$-player games with mean-payoff objectives without restrictions on the state space. Furthermore, `Tempest` adds the functionality to synthesize safe and optimal strategies that implement reactive systems and shields.

1 Introduction

Reactive synthesis aims to automatically construct correct and efficient systems w.r.t. a formal specification and has been increasingly used in a wide range of safety-critical applications. A natural model for reactive synthesis is to model some inputs from the environment probabilistically and some adversarially. For adversarial inputs, the synthesized system assumes the worst case, for probabilistic inputs the average case. The corresponding synthesis problem is mapped to solving a *competitive stochastic turn-based game*, i.e., a 2$\frac{1}{2}$-player game. *Qualitative specifications* specify the functional requirements of reactive systems. With

This project has received funding from the European Union's Horizon 2020 research and innovation programme under grant agreement N° 956123 - FOCETA.

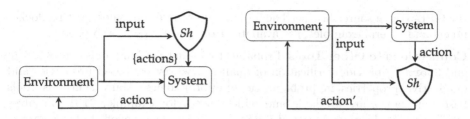

Fig. 1. *Left:* Pre-shielding. *Right:* Post-shielding.

a *quantitative specification* such as *mean-payoff objectives*, we can measure how well a system satisfies the specification.

Shield synthesis defines a synthesis framework to construct run-time enforcement modules called *shields* to guarantee the correctness of running systems. The concept of shielding is very general. Shields that enforce qualitative objectives are so-called *safety-shields* [1], which we distinguish between pre- and post-shielding as depicted in Fig. 1. In *pre-shielding*, the shield is implemented before the system and restricts the choices for the system to a set of correct actions. Pre-shielding is becoming increasingly important in the setting of safe reinforcement learning [8]. In *post-shielding*, the shield monitors the actions selected by the system and corrects them if the chosen action could lead to a specification violation. Shields that enforce quantitative measures are called *optimal-shields* [2] and are implemented as post-shields. `Tempest` is able to synthesize optimal-shields that enforce a mean-payoff objective. Optimal-shields that enforce multiple quantitative objectives can be obtained via a linear combination to give an approximate solution of a single mean-payoff objective. For instance, the decision whether an optimal-shield should interfere could be based on first, a *performance objective* to be minimized by the shield, and second, an *interference cost* for changing the output of the system. An optimal-shield can then be computed *by minimizing a single mean-payoff objective* obtained by combining both measures, thus guaranteeing maximal performance with minimal interference.

Tempest Capabilities. The core functionality of `Tempest` is the synthesis of reactive systems and shields in environments that incorporate uncertainty. To the best of our knowledge, `Tempest` is the only tool able to solve $2\frac{1}{2}$-player games with mean-payoff objectives and qualitative objectives given in probabilistic temporal logics, without any restrictions on the state space. Furthermore, `Tempest` is designed as a synthesis tool. Therefore, the computed strategies can intuitively be used as the synthesized system, which is not the case for many game-solving tools. `Tempest` is the first tool available for the synthesis of shields and is able to synthesize pre-safety and post-safety-shields, and optimal-shields.

Implementation and Availability. The tool is written in C++ and is built on top of the code-base of the model checker `Storm` [7], extending existing features to provide the capability of solving stochastic games. `Tempest` is available under the GPL-3 open source license. The tool and its source code, along with a docker image and several examples, are available from the Tempest web page[1].

Connections to Other Tools. Probabilistic model checking tools like PRISM [9] and Storm [7] provide verification of quantitative reward-based properties and qualitative properties in probabilistic temporal logics. Many synthesis tools based on games are available and widely used, for example, GIST [3] solves qualitative stochastic games and QUASY [4] solves mean-payoff 2-player games. PRISM-games 3.0 [6] is able to solve turn-based stochastic multi-player games under a variety of properties including long-run average [5]. However, for solving long-run average objectives, PRISM-games needs the game to be a *controllable multi-chain*, i.e., one of the players needs to be able to reach every end-component from any state with probability one. *This is a strong assumption on the structure of the game graph, which many models used in synthesis do not fulfill.* In contrast, Tempest does not rely on any assumptions on the structure of the game graph.

2   Model and Property Specification

Tempest Model Specification. Tempest supports turn-based *stochastic multi-player games* (SMGs) and uses PRISM-games' modelling language to describe the game [6]. The players are divided in two competing coalitions, where the first team is working together to satisfy or optimize a property given in rPATL [5]. In each state, one player chooses an available distribution to determine the next state. A *strategy* for a player determines the choices made by the player.

Tempest Property Specification. For the *synthesis of reactive systems*, Tempest uses the property specification language of PRISM-games to express properties in rPATL [5]. We give a few examples that can be used in Tempest:

- $\langle\langle 1, 2 \rangle\rangle P_{max=?}[F\ target]$: Using the operator $P_{max=?}$, Tempest computes a strategy for the player coalition of player 1 and 2 that guarantees to reach *target* with the largest probability.
- $\langle\langle 1, 2 \rangle\rangle R^r_{max=?}[S]$: Using the operators R and S, Tempest synthesizes a strategy that maximizes the expected averaged reward r in the *long-run*.

Synthesis of Safety-Shields. Let the *safety-value* of an action in a certain state be the maximal probability to stay safe within the next k steps when executing this action. A safety-shield decides whether an action is blocked in a certain state based on either an *absolute* threshold γ, or a *relative* threshold λ. A shield using an absolute threshold blocks all actions with a safety-value smaller than γ. Using a relative threshold λ, actions are blocked with a safety-value smaller than the best safety-value achievable in the current state times λ. The syntax for safety-shielding requires to specify the type of shielding using the keywords PreSafety and PostSafety, and to define the used threshold. Following, we demonstrate how Tempest extends the PRISM's property specification language.

---

[1] https://tempest-synthesis.org.

- $\langle PreSafety, \gamma = 0.9 \rangle \langle\langle shield \rangle\rangle P_{max=?}[G^{<=14} \, !crash]$: By using this property, Tempest synthesizes a pre-safety-shield that allows all actions that do not cause a crash with a maximal probability of 0.9 within the next 14 time steps.
- $\langle PostSafety, \lambda = 0.95 \rangle \langle\langle shield \rangle\rangle P_{max=?}[G^{<=14} \, !crash]$: Tempest synthesizes a post-safety-shield that blocks all actions using the relative threshold λ.

Synthesis of Optimal-Shields. The property starts with the keyword Optimal followed by the expression used to compute the long run average. For example:

- $\langle Optimal \rangle \langle\langle shield \rangle\rangle R^r_{min=?}[S]$: Tempest computes an optimal shield that guarantees the long-run average reward of r.

3   Tempest Synthesis of Strategies

Tempest computes a memoryless deterministic strategy, implementing a reactive system or a shield, under which the specified property can be guaranteed. The strategy is computed using *value iteration* to solve the coalition game. Figure 2 shows sample outputs of the strategies of the first experiment given in Sect. 4, implementing pre-safety and post-safety-shields. In the pre-shielding case, the strategy provides for any state a list of allowed actions with its corresponding safety-value. The strategy for post-shielding defines for every state and available action, the action to be forwarded by the shield.

```
Pre-Safety-Shield with absolute comparison (gamma = 0.8):
  state_id [label]: 'allowed actions' [<value>: (<action_id label)>]:

0 [move=0 & x1=0 & y1=0 & x2=4 & y2=4]:   1.0:(0 {e}); 1:(1 {s})
3 [move=0 & x1=1 & y1=0 & x2=3 & y2=4]:   0.9:(0 {e}); 1:(2 {w})
4 [move=0 & x1=1 & y1=0 & x2=4 & y2=4]:   0.9:(1 {s}); 1:(3 {n})
     .....


Post-Safety-Shield with relative comparison (lambda = 0.95):
  state_id [label]: 'forwarded actions' [<action_id> label: <forwarded_action_id> label]:

0 [move=0 & x1=0 & y1=0 & x2=4  & y2=4]:   0{e}:0{e}; 1{s}:1{s}
3 [move=0 & x1=1 & y1=0 & x2=3  & y2=4]:   0{e}:2{w}; 2{w}:2{w}
4 [move=0 & x1=1 & y1=0 & x2=4  & y2=4]:   1{s}:3{n}; 3{n}:3{n}
     .....
```

Fig. 2. Synthesized strategies implementing a pre-safety-shield (*top*) and a post-safety-shield (*bottom*).

4   Tempest in Action

High-Level Planning in Robotics. A classical application of reactive synthesis is the domain of automated high-level planning in robotics. We consider

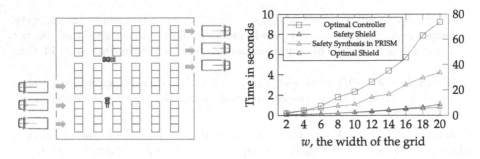

Fig. 3. *Left:* Warehouse floor plan with 6 × 3 shelves. *Right:* Synthesis-times for controller synthesis, safety-shield synthesis and optimal-shield synthesis.

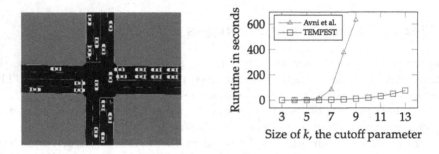

Fig. 4. *Left:* Synthesis times for safety-shield synthesis. *Right:* Comparison of synthesis times for optimal-shields: Tempest vs Avni et al.'s implementation [2].

a warehouse floor plan with several shelves, see Fig. 3 (left). To parametrise the experiment, we consider floor plans with n × 3 shelves with $2 \leq n \leq 20$. A robot operates together among other robots within the warehouse. Tempest can be used in this setting to synthesize controllers for the robot that perform certain tasks, as well as shields used to ensure safe operation of the robot, or to guarantee performance. **Controller synthesis:** Using Tempest, we synthesize a controller for the robot that repeatedly picks up packages from one of the entrances and delivers them to the exits. We use the mean-payoff criterion to specify that the stochastic shortest paths should be taken. **Safety-shield synthesis:** A safety-shield can be synthesized to enforce collision avoidance with other robots. In the experiments, we used a finite horizon of 14 steps and a relative threshold of $\lambda = 0.9$. **Optimal-shield synthesis:** During operation, a corridor may be blocked. A robot should not unnecessarily wait for the corridor to be traversable when alternative paths exist. We synthesize an optimal-shield that penalizes 'waiting' and is able to enforce a detour when waiting gets too expensive. **Results.** The models, parameters, and properties used for all experiments can be found on the Tempest website(see footnote 3). The results for the synthesis-times are depicted in Fig. 3 (right). The sizes of state space of the game graphs range from 5184 states for $n = 2$ to 186.624 states for $n = 20$. The results for optimal-shields use the axis on the right hand-side. The times for creating pre-safety and post-safety-shields are identical. To compare our results, we tried to compute a strategy for the optimal controller in PRISM-games 3.0 which resulted in an error. By proper modelling, we were able to synthesize safe controllers comparable to the safety-shield using PRISM-games, resulting in better synthesis-times for Tempest.

Optimal-Shielding in Urban Traffic Control. Avni et al. [2] synthesize optimal-shields that overwrite the commands of a traffic-light controller modeled in the traffic simulator SUMO. The optimal-shield needs to balance the number of waiting cars per incoming road with the cost for interfering with the traffic light controller. The example is parametrised with the cut-off parameter k that defines the maximal modelled number of waiting cars per road. The comparison of the synthesis-times from Avni et.al.'s implementation and Tempest are shown in Fig. 4 (right), showing a difference by orders of magnitudes in favor of Tempest.

5   Conclusion and Future Work

We have introduced Tempest, a tool for the synthesis of reactive systems and shields with properties given in rPATL capturing qualitative and quantitative objectives with probabilities. Currently, Tempest supports perfect-information SMGs. In future work, we will investigate in efficient techniques to deal with partial information. Furthermore, we will extend Tempest to support strategies with finite memory with deterministic and stochastic-updates.

Acknowledgements. We thank both Tim Quatmann and Joost-Pieter Katoen for their continuous help on getting acquainted with the source code of Storm.

References

1. Alshiekh, M., Bloem, R., Ehlers, R., Könighofer, B., Niekum, S., Topcu, U.: Safe reinforcement learning via shielding. In: Proceedings of the Thirty-Second AAAI Conference on Artificial Intelligence, (AAAI-18), New Orleans, Louisiana, USA, 2–7 February 2018, pp. 2669–2678. AAAI Press (2018)
2. Avni, G., Bloem, R., Chatterjee, K., Henzinger, T.A., Könighofer, B., Pranger, S.: Run-time optimization for learned controllers through quantitative games. In: Dillig, I., Tasiran, S. (eds.) CAV 2019. LNCS, vol. 11561, pp. 630–649. Springer, Cham (2019). https://doi.org/10.1007/978-3-030-25540-4_36
3. Chatterjee, K., Henzinger, T.A., Jobstmann, B., Radhakrishna, A.: Gist: a solver for probabilistic games. In: Touili, T., Cook, B., Jackson, P. (eds.) CAV 2010. LNCS, vol. 6174, pp. 665–669. Springer, Heidelberg (2010). https://doi.org/10.1007/978-3-642-14295-6_57
4. Chatterjee, K., Henzinger, T.A., Jobstmann, B., Singh, R.: QUASY: quantitative synthesis tool. In: Abdulla, P.A., Leino, K.R.M. (eds.) TACAS 2011. LNCS, vol. 6605, pp. 267–271. Springer, Heidelberg (2011). https://doi.org/10.1007/978-3-642-19835-9_24

5. Chen, T., Forejt, V., Kwiatkowska, M.Z., Parker, D., Simaitis, A.: Automatic verification of competitive stochastic systems. Formal Methods Syst. Des. **1**, 61–92 (2013)
6. Chen, T., Forejt, V., Kwiatkowska, M., Parker, D., Simaitis, A.: PRISM-games: a model checker for stochastic multi-player games. In: Piterman, N., Smolka, S.A. (eds.) TACAS 2013. LNCS, vol. 7795, pp. 185–191. Springer, Heidelberg (2013). https://doi.org/10.1007/978-3-642-36742-7_13
7. Dehnert, C., Junges, S., Katoen, J.-P., Volk, M.: A storm is coming: a modern probabilistic model checker. In: Majumdar, R., Kunčak, V. (eds.) CAV 2017. LNCS, vol. 10427, pp. 592–600. Springer, Cham (2017). https://doi.org/10.1007/978-3-319-63390-9_31
8. Jansen, N., Könighofer, B., Junges, S., Serban, A., Bloem, R.: Safe reinforcement learning using probabilistic shields (invited paper). In: 31st International Conference on Concurrency Theory, CONCUR 2020, 1–4 September 2020, Vienna, Austria (Virtual Conference), LIPIcs, pp. 3:1–3:16. Schloss Dagstuhl - Leibniz-Zentrum für Informatik (2020)
9. Kwiatkowska, M., Norman, G., Parker, D.: PRISM 4.0: verification of probabilistic real-time systems. In: Gopalakrishnan, G., Qadeer, S. (eds.) CAV 2011. LNCS, vol. 6806, pp. 585–591. Springer, Heidelberg (2011). https://doi.org/10.1007/978-3-642-22110-1_47

AQUA: Automated Quantized Inference for Probabilistic Programs

Zixin Huang$^{(\boxtimes)}$, Saikat Dutta, and Sasa Misailovic

University of Illinois at Urbana-Champaign, Urbana, IL 61801, USA
{zixinh2,saikatd2,misailo}@illinois.edu

Abstract. We present AQUA, a new probabilistic inference algorithm that operates on probabilistic programs with continuous posterior distributions. AQUA approximates programs via an efficient quantization of the continuous distributions. It represents the distributions of random variables using quantized value intervals (Interval Cube) and corresponding probability densities (Density Cube). AQUA's analysis transforms Interval and Density Cubes to compute the posterior distribution with bounded error. We also present an adaptive algorithm for selecting the size and the granularity of the Interval and Density Cubes.

We evaluate AQUA on 24 programs from the literature. AQUA solved all of 24 benchmarks in less than 43 s (median 1.35 s) with a high-level of accuracy. We show that AQUA is more accurate than state-of-the-art approximate algorithms (Stan's NUTS and ADVI) and supports programs that are out of reach of exact inference tools, such as PSI and SPPL.

1 Introduction

Many modern applications (e.g., in machine learning, robotics, autonomous driving, medical diagnostics, and financial forecasting) need to make decisions under uncertainty. Probabilistic programming languages (PPLs) offer an intuitive way to model uncertainty by representing complex probabilistic models as simple programs [5]. They expose randomness and Bayesian inference as first-class abstractions by extending standard languages with statements for sampling from probability distributions and probabilistic conditioning. The underlying programming system then automates the intricate details of the probabilistic inference.

Probabilistic inference is a computationally hard problem. Most current approaches that emerged from the statistics and machine learning communities applied aggressive numeric approximations, such as Markov Chain Monte Carlo sampling (MCMC) or Variational Inference (VI). However, these approaches often cannot obtain the level of accuracy that is required in applications such as algorithmic fairness [2], security/privacy [22], sensitivity analysis [1,13], or software testing [8].

Symbolic techniques for inference have been resurging as a more accurate alternative. They use a symbolic representation of the model's state (e.g., elementary functions, piecewise-linear functions, or hypercubes), and compute the

Z. Hou and V. Ganesh (Eds.): ATVA 2021, LNCS 12971, pp. 229–246, 2021.
https://doi.org/10.1007/978-3-030-88885-5_16

posterior distribution algebraically [8,16,19] or closely approximate programs using volume computation [2,20,22]. However, these approaches are often limited by the classes of programs they can solve. For instance, continuous programs pose a major challenge for these approaches due to integrals in posterior calculation. State-of-the-art symbolic solvers cannot solve many integrals exactly (often, the integrals do not have a closed form). Similarly, volume computation approaches have a limited support for continuous distributions (e.g., do not allow for conditioning on continuous random variables) and/or compute the probability of a single event, not the entire posterior distribution. *An intriguing research question is how to approximate multi-dimensional continuous distributions in a principled manner that allows for more expressive programs and can solve programs that are out of reach of existing tools for exact inference.*

AQUA. We present AQUA, a novel system for symbolic inference that uses quantization of probability density function for delivering scalable and precise solutions for a broad range of probabilistic programs. AQUA's inference algorithm approximates the original continuous program via an efficient quantization of the continuous distributions by using multi-dimensional tensor representations that we call *Interval Cube and Density Cube*. The Interval Cube stores the quantized value ranges of variables in the probabilistic program. The Density Cube approximates the joint posterior distribution by recording the probability of each hypercube contained in the interval cube.

AQUA's analysis transforms the symbolic state to compute quantized approximate posterior distribution. We derive the bounds for the approximation error (due to the quantization and integration) and show that our inference converges in distribution to the true posterior. We also present an adaptive algorithm for automatically selecting the granularity of the Interval and Density Cubes.

Example. Figure 1 presents a probabilistic program that represents the distribution of two random variables. In the program, we have two random variables a and b, each having **uniform** *prior* distribution (Lines 3–4). We then condition the model on 40 data points Y, assuming that each point is normally distributed with the mean a+b (Lines 5–6). We finally query for the joint *posterior* distribution (i.e., the distribution of latent variables a and b after observing the data on Line 6).

```
1  D=40
2  Y=[3.4,0.3,...]
3  a~uniform(-10,10)
4  b~uniform(-10,10)
5  for (i in 1:D)
6    Y[i]~normal(a+b,1)
7  return a,b
```

Fig. 1. Example

Figure 2 presents AQUA's results: (a) shows the prior of the two variables, (b) shows the likelihood (observation) on a single data point, and (c) shows the posterior distribution. On each plot, the X-axis and Y-axis represent a and b values, and the Z-axis values are the probability densities computed by AQUA. AQUA computes the result in 0.76 s, whereas an MCMC based inference algorithm (NUTS) produces a less accurate posterior within the same amount of time (Fig. 2(d)).

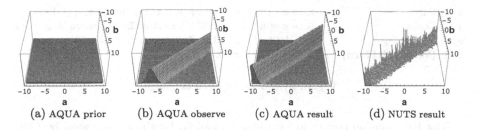

(a) AQUA prior   (b) AQUA observe   (c) AQUA result   (d) NUTS result

Fig. 2. AQUA estimated probabilistic density and NUTS histogram

Evaluation. We evaluate our implementation of AQUA on a set of 24 probabilistic programs from the literature. We compare AQUA with exact inference – PSI [8] and SPPL [19] – and approximate inference – MCMC and VI implemetations in Stan [5]. We show that AQUA can solve programs that are out of reach for PSI and SPPL. Our results show AQUA solved all benchmarks in less than 43 s (median 1.35 s). It is significantly more accurate than VI for all programs (for the Kolmogorov-Smirnov metric). AQUA is substantially more accurate than MCMC for 10 programs, even when MCMC is given substantially more time to complete. We also present a case study that shows AQUA can precisely capture the tails of the distribution of robust models.

Contributions. This paper makes the following contributions:

- **Inference Algorithm:** We present AQUA, a novel inference algorithm that works on general, real-world probabilistic programs with continuous distributions based on quantization and symbolic computation.
- **Quantization with Interval and Density Cubes:** Our analysis defines symbolic transformers on the abstract state consisting of the Interval and Density Cubes. We also present theoretical bounds on the quality of approximation.
- **Inference Algorithm Optimizations:** We present algorithm extensions that automatically refine the size/granularity of the analysis to satisfy a given precision threshold and aggressively reduce the analysis overhead of local variables.
- **Evaluation:** Our experiments show that AQUA is more accurate than approximate inference algorithms (Stan's MCMC/VI) and supports programs with conditioning on continuous distributions that are out of reach of exact inference tools (PSI and SPPL).

2   Preliminaries

Language Syntax and Semantics. Figure 3 describes the syntax of a probabilistic program using an imperative, first-order intermediate representation, drawing from Storm-IR [6,7]. It has statements for sampling from distributions[1] and conditioning on data with `factor` and `observe`.

---

[1] We support common continuous distributions including Normal, Uniform, Exponential, Beta, Gamma, Student-T, Laplace, Triangular, and any mixture of the above distributions.

```
x  ∈ Vars              E := c | x | E[E*] | E op E | d(E*).pdf(E*) | f(E*)
c  ∈ Consts            S := x = E | x ~ d(E*) | factor(E) | observe(d(E*),x)
op ∈ {+,−,*,>,...}          | if (E) S* else S* | for x ∈ 1..N; {S*}
d  ∈ {Normal,Uniform,...}  P := S+; return x+
```

Fig. 3. Syntax of AQUA's language

The language semantics are standard, inspired by those presented by Gorinova et al. [11] (We present the detailed semantics rules in the Appendix, available in the full version of the paper). In summary, a probabilistic program evaluates the *posterior probability density function*. Our operational semantics for a program defines its effect on the program state, σ, which maps variables to values. A value V can either be a constant c or an array of values $[c_1, c_2, ...]$. The notations $\sigma(x)$ and $\sigma(x \mapsto V)$ denote accessing and updating a variable x respectively. We refer to the return variables of the program as the *global variables*, and the others as *local variables*. We allow local variables to have discrete distributions (e.g. Bernoulli), as long as the density of the global variables are Lipschitz continuous. We define a special variable $\mathcal{L} \in \mathbb{R}^+$ which tracks the *unnormalized posterior density* of the probabilistic program. We initialize $\sigma(\mathcal{L})$ to 1.0 at the start of the program.

Probability Density. We review several basic terms from the probability theory. Let $\boldsymbol{x}$ be the set of variables with values in V, and $\mathcal{D}$ be the set of observed data points. Then, the posterior probability density function is $p(\boldsymbol{x}|\mathcal{D}) : V \rightarrow \mathbb{R}$, such that $\int_{\boldsymbol{x} \in V} p(\boldsymbol{x}|\mathcal{D}) d\boldsymbol{x} = 1$. The distribution $p(\boldsymbol{x}|\mathcal{D})$ can be calculated from the *unnormalized probability density function* $f(\boldsymbol{x}, \mathcal{D}) : V \rightarrow \mathbb{R}$, by $p(\boldsymbol{x}|\mathcal{D}) = \frac{1}{z} f(\boldsymbol{x}, \mathcal{D})$, where z is the normalizing constant: $z = \int f(\boldsymbol{x}, \mathcal{D}) d\boldsymbol{x}$. If $\boldsymbol{x}_{-i}$ contains all the variables in $\boldsymbol{x}$ excluding x_i, we define the *marginal probability density function* of x_i as $p(x_i|\mathcal{D}) = \int p(\boldsymbol{x}|\mathcal{D}) d\boldsymbol{x}_{-i}$. Hereon, we omit data symbol $\mathcal{D}$ to write $p(\boldsymbol{x})$ and $f(\boldsymbol{x})$ when clear from the context. In the semantics, $f(\boldsymbol{x})$ is represented by $\sigma(\mathcal{L})$.

3   AQUA's Probabilistic Inference Using Density Cubes

3.1   Notations and Basic Definitions

We represent the closed, bounded set $\{x \in \mathbb{R} | a \leq x \leq b\}$ with its lower-bound $a \in \mathbb{R}$ and upper-bound $b \in \mathbb{R}$. We denote this abstraction as an **interval** $I = [a, b] \in \mathbb{R}^2$. We refer to the lower and upper bound of I as $\underline{I}$ and $\overline{I}$, respectively $(\underline{I}, \overline{I} \in \mathbb{R})$.

A probabilistic program lifts a normal program operating on single values to a *distribution* over values. Hence, a probabilistic program represents a joint distribution over its variables. For our symbolic analysis, to represent the quantized values of variables, we define tensors of intervals which we will refer to as *Interval Cube*. We also assign a probability density to each interval in the Interval Cube. We will refer to this assignment of densities as *Density Cube*. If there are N variables in the program, the Density Cube will be an N-dimensional tensor.

Table 1. Correspondence of symbolic analysis and concrete analysis

Concrete	Symbolic
Value $\sigma(x)$	Interval Cube $\sigma^{\#}(x)$
Density $\sigma(\mathcal{L})$	Density Cube $\sigma^{\#}(P)$
State : $(\mathcal{P}(\textbf{Vars} \mapsto \textbf{Value}) \mapsto [0,1])$	**Astate** : $(\mathcal{P}(\textbf{Vars} \mapsto \text{Interval Cube}) \mapsto \text{Density Cube})$
$[\![E]\!]$: **State**$\mapsto$**Value**	$[\![E]\!]^{\#}$: **Astate**$\mapsto$Interval Cube
$[\![S]\!]$: **State**$\mapsto$**State**	$[\![S]\!]^{\#}$: **Astate**$\mapsto$**Astate**

Definition 1 (Interval Cube). We represent the value of a variable x with Interval Cube, $\boldsymbol{I}^{x}_{M_1,M_2,\ldots,M_N}$ where $[M_1, M_2, \ldots, M_N]$ represents the shape of the Interval Cube and each $M_i \in \mathbb{N}$ is the *number of intervals (splits)* along the i-th dimension. Each element of $\boldsymbol{I}^{x}_{M_1,M_2,\ldots,M_N}$ is a single interval. We let $\mathbb{I}$ be the set of all Interval Cubes. For a constant c, we denote its Interval Cube as $[c]$, meaning a singleton interval with both lower and upper bounds being c.

To simplify the notation, we hereon denote the shape of the hypercube as $\boldsymbol{M} = [M_1, M_2, \ldots, M_N]$ and each index in the hypercube is $\boldsymbol{m} \in \mathbb{M}$, $\mathbb{M} = \{[m_1, \ldots, m_N] \mid m_i \in [1, \ldots, M_i], i \in \{1, \ldots, N\}\}$. We write $\boldsymbol{K} = \boldsymbol{M}_1 \odot \boldsymbol{M}_2$ as the element-wise product (Hadamard product) of two shape vectors, namely $K_i = M_{1i} \times M_{2i}, i \in \{1, \ldots, N\}$. We use $\boldsymbol{m}_1$ to denote the index of a Interval Cube with shape $\boldsymbol{M}_1$, $\boldsymbol{m}_1 = [m_1, \ldots, m_N]$, $m_i \in \{1, \ldots, M_{1i}\}$, and similarly we use $\boldsymbol{m}_2$ for index in $\boldsymbol{M}_2$, and $\boldsymbol{k}$ for index in $\boldsymbol{K}$.

Definition 2 (Density Cube). For a given probabilistic program *Prog* with N variables, we define the Density Cube with shape $\boldsymbol{M}$ as $\boldsymbol{P}^{Prog}_{\boldsymbol{M}}$, where

$$\boldsymbol{P}^{Prog}_{\boldsymbol{M}}(\boldsymbol{m}) = p_{\boldsymbol{m}}, \text{ for each index } \boldsymbol{m} \in \mathbb{M},$$

and $p_{\boldsymbol{m}}$ denotes the value of the unnormalized probability density function at the lower bound of the corresponding interval in the Interval Cube. The densities at the lower bound of intervals will help us do numerical integration for posterior calculation. Further, $\boldsymbol{P}^{Prog}_{\boldsymbol{M}} \in \mathbb{R}^{M}$, and $p_{\boldsymbol{m}} \in \mathbb{R}$.

Definition 3 (Symbolic Domain). Our *symbolic state* has two components, a map from variables to Interval Cubes, and a Density Cube representing the joint density approximation. Let **Var** denote the set of variables, and $\mathcal{P}$ be the power set, the domain of the symbolic state is $\Sigma = \mathcal{P}(\text{Var} \mapsto \mathbb{I}) \times \mathbb{R}^{M}$ a symbolic state $\sigma^{\#} \in \Sigma$ will have the form

$$\sigma^{\#} = \left\langle \{x_1 \mapsto \boldsymbol{I}^{x_1}_{\boldsymbol{M}_1}, x_2 \mapsto \boldsymbol{I}^{x_2}_{\boldsymbol{M}_2}, \ldots, x_i \mapsto \boldsymbol{I}^{x_i}_{\boldsymbol{M}_i}, \ldots\}, P \mapsto \boldsymbol{P}^{Prog}_{\boldsymbol{M}} \right\rangle.$$

The symbolic domain expresses a piecewise constant interpolation of the joint probability density at a program point. Hereon, we refer to the set of all the variables in the state $\sigma^{\#}$ as $\boldsymbol{x} = \{x_1, x_2, \ldots, x_N\}$.

$$[\![E]\!]^{\#} \mapsto (\textbf{Astate} \mapsto \text{Interval Cube})$$

$$[\![x]\!]^{\#} := \lambda\sigma^{\#}.\sigma^{\#}(x)$$

$$[\![c]\!]^{\#} := \lambda\sigma^{\#}.[c]$$

$$[\![E_1[E_2]]\!]^{\#} := \lambda\sigma^{\#}.\text{let } [c,c] = [\![E_2]\!]^{\#}\sigma^{\#} \text{ in } [\![E_1[c]]\!]^{\#}\sigma^{\#}$$

$$[\![E_1 \text{ op } E_2]\!]^{\#} := \lambda\sigma^{\#}.\text{let } \boldsymbol{I}_{M_1}^{E_1} = [\![E_1]\!]^{\#}\sigma^{\#}, \boldsymbol{I}_{M_2}^{E_2} = [\![E_2]\!]^{\#}\sigma^{\#}, \boldsymbol{K} = \boldsymbol{M}_1 \odot \boldsymbol{M}_2$$

$$\text{in } \boldsymbol{I}_K^{E_1 \text{ op } E_2}, \text{ where } \boldsymbol{I}_K^{E_1 \text{ op } E_2}(\boldsymbol{k}) = \boldsymbol{I}_{M_1}^{E_1}(\boldsymbol{m}_1) \text{ op } \boldsymbol{I}_{M_1}^{E_2}(\boldsymbol{m}_2)$$

$$[\![d(E_1,...,E_{n-1}).\text{pdf}(E_n)]\!]^{\#} := \lambda\sigma^{\#}.\text{let } \boldsymbol{I}_{M_1}^{E_1} = [\![E_1]\!]^{\#}\sigma^{\#},...,\boldsymbol{I}_{M_n}^{E_n} = [\![E_n]\!]^{\#}\sigma^{\#}, \boldsymbol{K} = \bigodot_{i=1}^{n} \boldsymbol{M}_i,$$

$$\text{in } \boldsymbol{I}_K^{\text{dpdf}}, \text{ where } \boldsymbol{I}_K^{\text{dpdf}}(\boldsymbol{k}) = d\_\text{pdf}(\boldsymbol{I}_{M_n}^{E_n}(\boldsymbol{m}_n), \boldsymbol{I}_{M_1}^{E_1}(\boldsymbol{m}_1),...,\boldsymbol{I}_{M_{n-1}}^{E_{n-1}}(\boldsymbol{m}_{n-1}))$$

Fig. 4. Analysis of Expressions

3.2 Analysis

We approximate the posterior density function of variables in our symbolic states. Table 1 presents the correspondence of the objects in concrete semantics to symbolic states. While a concrete state has a single valuation of variables and evaluates to a single density value, our symbolic state stores all possible variable values in Interval Cube and corresponding probability densities in Density Cube. As the concrete semantics for a expression maps state to values, the symbolic semantics map symbolic state to Interval Cube; and as the concrete semantics for a statement map state to state, our symbolic semantics map symbolic state to symbolic state.

Analysis of Expressions. The symbolic transformer $[\![E]\!]^{\#}$ on an expression E takes a symbolic state $\sigma^{\#}$: **Astate** as input, and outputs an Interval Cube. Figure 4 presents the rules. We explain two important cases in detail:

- $[\![E_1 \text{ op } E_2]\!]^{\#}$: For the arithmetic/boolean operation on two Interval Cubes, which may not always have the same shape, the resulting Interval Cube needs to contain all possible value combinations. Specifically, for $\boldsymbol{I}_{M_1}^{E_1}$ with shape $\boldsymbol{M}_1 = [M_{11},...,M_{1N}]$ and $\boldsymbol{I}_{M_2}^{E_2}$ with shape $\boldsymbol{M}_2 = [M_{21},...,M_{2N}]$, the result $\boldsymbol{I}_K^{E_1 \text{ op } E_2}$ has shape $\boldsymbol{K} = [K_1,...,K_N]$ with $K_i = M_{1i} \times M_{2i}$ to capture all the combinations of elements from $\boldsymbol{I}_{M_1}^{E_1}$ and $\boldsymbol{I}_{M_2}^{E_2}$. If $\boldsymbol{M}_1$ and $\boldsymbol{M}_2$ are not of the same length, we reshape both $\boldsymbol{I}_{M_1}^{E_1}$ and $\boldsymbol{I}_{M_2}^{E_2}$ to have the same dimension, by letting some M_{1i} or M_{2i} to have value 1. We let the arithmetic or boolean operation on the interval pairs be $\boldsymbol{I}_{M_1}^{E_1}(\boldsymbol{m}_1) \text{ op } \boldsymbol{I}_{M_2}^{E_2}(\boldsymbol{m}_2) := [\underline{\boldsymbol{I}_{M_1}^{E_1}(\boldsymbol{m}_1) \text{ op } \boldsymbol{I}_{M_2}^{E_2}(\boldsymbol{m}_2)}, \overline{\boldsymbol{I}_{M_1}^{E_1}(\boldsymbol{m}_1)} \text{ op } \overline{\boldsymbol{I}_{M_2}^{E_2}(\boldsymbol{m}_2)}]$. We handle the case with multiple intervals analogously. This operation on multiple Interval Cubes can be implemented efficiently with the *broadcast* function in tensor libraries.
- $[\![d(E_1,...,E_{n-1}).\text{pdf}(E_n)]\!]$: Similar to arithmetic operator, we apply the mathematical density $d\_\text{pdf}(\_)$ of the distribution d whose parameters (e.g.,

$$[\![S]\!]^{\#} \mapsto (\textbf{Astate} \mapsto \textbf{Astate})$$

$$[\![\text{skip}]\!]^{\#} := \lambda\sigma^{\#}.\sigma^{\#}$$

$$[\![S_1;S_2]\!]^{\#} := \lambda\sigma^{\#}.[\![S_2]\!]^{\#}([\![S_1]\!]^{\#}\sigma^{\#})$$

$$[\![x=E]\!]^{\#} := \lambda\sigma^{\#}.\text{let } I = [\![E]\!]^{\#}\sigma^{\#} \text{ in } \sigma^{\#}(x \mapsto I)$$

$$[\![x \sim d(E_1,...,E_n)]\!]^{\#} := \lambda\sigma^{\#}.\text{let } \boldsymbol{P}_{\boldsymbol{M}_0} = \sigma^{\#}(P),\, \boldsymbol{I}_{\boldsymbol{K}}^{\text{dpdf}} = [\![d(E_1,...,E_n).\text{pdf}(x)]\!]^{\#}\sigma^{\#},\text{ in}$$

$$\text{let } \boldsymbol{M} = \boldsymbol{M}_0 \odot \boldsymbol{K}, \text{ in } \sigma^{\#}(P \mapsto \boldsymbol{P}'_{\boldsymbol{M}}),$$

$$\text{where } \boldsymbol{P}'_{\boldsymbol{M}}(\boldsymbol{m}) = \boldsymbol{P}_{\boldsymbol{M}_0}(\boldsymbol{m}_0) \cdot \boldsymbol{I}_{\boldsymbol{K}}^{\text{dpdf}}(\boldsymbol{k}), \text{ for all } \boldsymbol{m} = \boldsymbol{m}_0 \odot \boldsymbol{k},$$

$$\boldsymbol{m}_0 \in \{[m_{01},...,m_{0N}] | m_{0i} \in \{1,...,M_{0N}\}\}, [M_{01},...,M_{0N}] = \boldsymbol{M}_0,$$

$$\boldsymbol{k} \in \{[k_1,...,k_N] | k_i \in \{1,...,K_N\}\}, [K_1,...,K_N] = \boldsymbol{K}$$

$$[\![\text{factor}(E)]\!]^{\#} := \lambda\sigma^{\#}.\text{let} \boldsymbol{P}_{\boldsymbol{M}_0} = \sigma^{\#}(P),\, \boldsymbol{I}_{\boldsymbol{K}} = [\![E]\!]^{\#}\sigma^{\#},\, \boldsymbol{M} = \boldsymbol{M}_0 \odot \boldsymbol{K}$$

$$\text{in } \sigma^{\#}(P \mapsto \boldsymbol{P}'_{\boldsymbol{M}}), \text{ where } \boldsymbol{P}'_{\boldsymbol{M}}(\boldsymbol{m}) = \boldsymbol{P}_{\boldsymbol{M}_0}(\boldsymbol{m}_0) \cdot \boldsymbol{I}_{\boldsymbol{K}}(\boldsymbol{k})$$

$$\text{where } \boldsymbol{P}'_{\boldsymbol{M}}, \boldsymbol{P}_{\boldsymbol{M}_0} \text{ and } \boldsymbol{P}_{\boldsymbol{K}} \text{ are as above}$$

$$[\![\text{observe}(d(E_1,...,E_n),x)]\!]^{\#} := \lambda\sigma^{\#}.[\![\text{factor}(d(E_1,...,E_n).\text{pdf}(x))]\!]^{\#}\sigma^{\#}$$

$$[\![\text{if }(E) \text{ then } \{S_1\} \text{ else } \{S_2\}]\!]^{\#} := \lambda\sigma^{\#}.\left([\![\text{factor}(E);S_1]\!]^{\#}\sigma^{\#}\right) \sqcup \left([\![\text{factor}(1\text{-}E);S_2]\!]^{\#}\sigma^{\#}\right)$$

$$[\![\text{for }(i \text{ in } E_1..E_2)\, S]\!]^{\#} := \lambda\sigma^{\#}.[\![i=E_1;\text{if }(i \leq E_2)\text{then}\{S;\text{for }(i \text{ in } E_1+1..E_2)S\}\text{else}\{\text{skip}\}]\!]^{\#}\sigma^{\#}$$

Fig. 5. Analysis of Statements

mean, location, shape or variance) are intervals obtained by evaluating $E_1, \ldots, E_{n-1}$, and it takes the intervals of E_n for which we seek the density. We denote the shape of the result Interval Cube as $\boldsymbol{K}$, which is computed from the shape of the input Interval Cubes.

Analysis of Statements. Figure 5 presents the transformers $[\![S]\!]^{\#}$ on statements S, which takes an abstract state $\sigma^{\#}$: **Astate** as input, and outputs an abstract state. We explain two important rules where we modify Density Cube (the remaining statements are standard or rely on these two rules):

- $[\![x \sim d(E_1, \ldots, E_n)]\!]^{\#}$, $[\![\text{factor}(E)]\!]^{\#}$: We first evaluate $d.\text{pdf}(\_)$ of E into Interval Cube, and multiply the current Density Cube with the lower bound of intervals from the Interval Cube. Then at the lower bound of each interval, the density is the same as the one from concrete semantics (Lemma 7). Intuitively, we discretize the density function and use the density at the lower bound to represent each interval. For convenience, our discretization uses the density at the lower bound. Using the density at the upper bound or the midpoint is also possible, and our accuracy guarantee (Theorem 10) still holds.
- $[\![\text{if}(E) \text{ then } \{S_1\} \text{ else } \{S_2\}]\!]^{\#}$: We first solve the result from two branches one conditioning on E and the other on $1 - E$. The true boolean expressions evaluate to 1 and false to 0 in our analysis, and we get the interval cubes for E and $1 - E$ from expression rules (Fig. 4). We then *Join* the result states by adding up the Density Cubes from both branches.

Definition 4 (Joins). *Join* ($\sqcup$) adds the Density Cubes from two states. Formally, $\sigma_1^{\#} \sqcup \sigma_2^{\#} = \sigma_1^{\#}(P \mapsto \boldsymbol{P}_{M_1,M_2,\ldots,M_N}^{Prog})$, where each element in $\boldsymbol{P}_{M_1,M_2,\ldots,M_N}^{Prog}$ at location $\boldsymbol{m}$ is $\sigma_1^{\#}(P)(\boldsymbol{m}) + \sigma_1^{\#}(P)(\boldsymbol{m})$, with $\boldsymbol{m} = [m_1, m_2, \ldots, m_N]$, $m_i \in \{1, \ldots, M_i\}$. Since we already initialized the global variables with their Interval Cube, $\sigma_1^{\#}$ and $\sigma_2^{\#}$ should have the same variables and Interval Cubes. Then the joint probability density P is changed to the sum of the densities from both states. Similarly, we can define *Meet* ($\sqcap$) by product of $\sigma_1^{\#}(P)(\boldsymbol{m})$ and $\sigma_1^{\#}(P)(\boldsymbol{m})$.

Algorithm. Algorithm 1 takes as input a probabilistic program *Prog*, the shape vector $\boldsymbol{M}$ where each element M_i is the number of intervals for variable x_i, and the interval bounds $\boldsymbol{C}$ (optional). In Sect. 4, we describe an adaptive scheme to automatically search for a proper $\boldsymbol{C}$ for the analysis.

First, it initializes the probability density variable P with the single interval [1.0] (Line 2). Then, it splits the value domain for each x_i in *SampledVars*, which are variables sampled from a prior distribution $x_i \sim d(E_1, \ldots, E_n)$ and not from deterministic assignments, into M_i equi-length intervals in C_i (in the function *GetInitIntervals*, Line 3–5). M_i is the i-th element in $\boldsymbol{M}$, and C_i is the i-th element in $\boldsymbol{C}$.

The algorithm follows the analysis rules to get the state at the end of the program (Line 6). Then it computes the joint probability density estimation $\hat{f}$, as a piecewise function of $\sigma^{\#}(P)$ (Line 7).

The result $\hat{f}(\boldsymbol{x})$ is an approximation of the true unnormalized probability density function $f(\boldsymbol{x})$. In the concrete domain, the posterior probabilistic density function is calculated as $p(\boldsymbol{x}) = \frac{1}{z}f(\boldsymbol{x})$, but the integration $z = \int f(\boldsymbol{x})d\boldsymbol{x}$ is often intractable. We compute our approximation $\hat{z}$ using integration on the piecewise function:

Definition 5 (Integration for Normalizing Constant). Suppose there are N sampled variables $\boldsymbol{x}$ in the program, and let $\boldsymbol{C} = \bigotimes_{i=1}^{N}[a_i, b_i] \subset \mathbb{R}^N$ for each $x_i \in [a_i, b_i] \subset \mathbb{R}$ be the bounded domain used in the analysis ($\bigotimes$ represents the Cartesian Product on intervals on $\mathbb{R}$). We initialize $\sigma^{\#}[\boldsymbol{x}] = \boldsymbol{C}$ in the analysis. Then $z = \int_{\boldsymbol{C}} f(\boldsymbol{x})\, d\boldsymbol{x}$ is approximated with $\hat{z} = \int_{\sigma^{\#}[\boldsymbol{x}]} \hat{f}(\boldsymbol{x})\, d\boldsymbol{x}$
$$= \sum_{\boldsymbol{m} \in \mathbb{M}}(\prod_{i=1}^{N}(\overline{\boldsymbol{I}_{M_i}^{x_i}(\boldsymbol{m})} - \boldsymbol{I}_{M_i}^{x_i}(\boldsymbol{m})) \cdot \boldsymbol{P}_{M}^{P}(\boldsymbol{m})).$$

The algorithm finally computes the posterior and the marginals for every variable (Lines 8–11). When the program has N variables, and each variable has the same number of intervals M, Algorithm 1 has the time complexity $\mathcal{O}(N \cdot M^N)$ and space complexity $\mathcal{O}(M^N)$.

Algorithm 1. Posterior Interval Analysis Algorithm

1: **procedure** POSTERIORANALYSIS(*Prog*, M, C)
2:   $\sigma^{\#}_{init} \leftarrow \{P \mapsto [1]\}$ ▷ Initialize with probability 1
3:   **for** $x_i \in SampledVars(Prog)$ **do**
4:     $\sigma^{\#}_{init}[x_i] \leftarrow GetInitIntervals(x_i, M_i, C_i)$
5:   **end for**
6:   $\sigma^{\#} \leftarrow [\![Prog]\!]\sigma^{\#}_{init}$ ▷ Apply analysis rules
7:   $\hat{f}(\boldsymbol{x}) \leftarrow PiecewiseFunc(\sigma^{\#}(P))$
8:   $\hat{z} \leftarrow \int_{\sigma^{\#}[\boldsymbol{x}]} \hat{f}(\boldsymbol{x}) \, d\boldsymbol{x}; \quad \hat{p}(\boldsymbol{x}) \leftarrow \frac{1}{\hat{z}}\hat{f}(\boldsymbol{x})$ ▷ Normalize the Posterior
9:   **for** $x_i \in SampledVars(Prog)$ **do**
10:     $Marginal[x_i] \leftarrow \frac{1}{z}\int_{\sigma^{\#}[\boldsymbol{x}_{-i}]} \hat{p}(\boldsymbol{x}) \, d\boldsymbol{x}_{-i}$ ▷ Marginalize
11:   **end for**
12: **return** $(\hat{p}, Marginal)$
13: **end procedure**

3.3 Formal Guarantee of Accuracy

In this section we formally derive how well the symbolic state $\sigma^{\#}$ approximates the joint unnormalized density function f and the posterior density function p.

Definition 6 (Concretization of Symbolic States). Define γ as the concretization function, s.t. $\gamma(\sigma^{\#}) = \hat{f}$, where $\hat{f}(\boldsymbol{x}) = \sigma^{\#}(P)(\boldsymbol{m})$ if $\boldsymbol{x} \in \bigotimes_{i=1}^{N}[\underline{I^{x_i}_{M_i}}(\boldsymbol{m}), \overline{I^{x_i}_{M_i}}(\boldsymbol{m})) \subset \mathbb{R}^N$ for any $\boldsymbol{m}$, and 0 otherwise.

Lemma 7 shows that at any program point, the error is bounded if we use the analysis result $\gamma(\sigma^{\#}) = \hat{f}$ as an approximation of joint density function f, and the error will reduce by the more number of intervals. To simplify the presentation, we use $\underline{\boldsymbol{x}}^{(m)} = [\underline{I^{x_1}_{M_1}}(\boldsymbol{m}), \ldots, \underline{I^{x_N}_{M_N}}(\boldsymbol{m})]$ for all variables, and analogously for $\overline{\boldsymbol{x}}^{(m)}$.

Lemma 7 (Discretization Error). *The error of discretization is* $|\hat{f}(\boldsymbol{x}) - f(\boldsymbol{x})| \leq \mu \cdot \max_m \|\overline{\boldsymbol{x}}^{(m)} - \underline{\boldsymbol{x}}^{(m)}\|$ *if* $\boldsymbol{x} \neq \underline{\boldsymbol{x}}^{(m)}$, *and if* $\boldsymbol{x} = \underline{\boldsymbol{x}}^{(m)}$ *the error is 0.*

Proof Sketch. We show that at any program point, (1) $\sigma^{\#}(P)(\boldsymbol{m}) = f(\boldsymbol{x})$ when $\boldsymbol{x} = \underline{\boldsymbol{x}}^{(m)}$, meaning the abstract transformers are exact at the lower bounds, and (2) f is μ-Lipschitz continuous. By definition of μ-Lipschitz continuous, $|f(\boldsymbol{x}_1) - f(\boldsymbol{x}_2)| \leq \mu \cdot \|\boldsymbol{x}_1 - \boldsymbol{x}_2\|$, we can prove the Lemma. The proof is by structural induction: we first show at initialization of the program, $\sigma^{\#}$ satisfies (1) and (2) because $f(\boldsymbol{x}) = 1.0$ and $\sigma^{\#}(P)(\boldsymbol{m}) = [1.0]$. Then for each statement, we show if the pre-state satisfies (1), the post-state has $\sigma^{\#}(P)(\boldsymbol{m}) = f(\underline{\boldsymbol{x}}^{(m)})$; and if the pre-state satisfies (2), f is Lipschitz continuous. We present the full proof in the Appendix.   □

The error of AQUA's approximation to the normalizing constant z is also bounded:

Lemma 8 (Integration Error). *Let $U = \prod_{i=1}^{N}(b_i - a_i)$ be the volume of C. For all the probability distributions supported in our language, the error is $|z - \hat{z}| \leq U\mu \max_m \|\overline{\boldsymbol{x}}^{(m)} - \boldsymbol{x}^{(m)}\|$. If we use M equal-length intervals for each variable, $|z - \hat{z}| \leq U\mu\frac{1}{M}(\sum_{i=1}^{N}(b_i - a_i)^2)^{\frac{1}{2}}$. Then $|z - \hat{z}| \to 0$ as $M \to \infty$.*

Proof Sketch. Recall, all posteriors f in our language (Sect. 2) are Lipschitz continuous. We derive the error bound by applying the Lipschitz continuous property of f and the triangle inequality. We present the full proof in the Appendix. □

Moreover, the integration error bound above will decrease when we decrease the interval length, or increase the number of intervals. Then at the end of the analysis, we approximate the *posterior probability density function $p(\boldsymbol{x})$* on C as:

Definition 9 (Posterior Probability Density Approximation). Define $\hat{p}(\boldsymbol{x}) = \frac{1}{\hat{z}}\hat{f}(\boldsymbol{x})$ as the approximation of $p(\boldsymbol{x})$.

Now we show the end-to-end error of the analysis. As Theorem 10 states, by applying sufficiently many intervals, the random variables following AQUA's posterior estimation in C will *converge in distribution* to the true posterior in C. Without loss of generality, suppose we apply at least M equal-length intervals for each variable in its domain $[a_i, b_i]$, i.e. $M = \min\{M_1, M_2, \ldots, M_N\}$. And we refer $\hat{p}_M(\boldsymbol{x})$ as AQUA's approximation of $p(\boldsymbol{x})$ by applying at least M equal-length intervals for each variable.

Theorem 10 (Convergence of Posterior Density Approximation). *Define $F_C(\boldsymbol{x}) = \frac{1}{z}\int_{-\infty}^{\boldsymbol{x}} 1_{[\boldsymbol{u} \in C]} \cdot p(\boldsymbol{u})d\boldsymbol{u}$ as the true cumulative distribution function (CDF) on C, where $z = \int_C p(\boldsymbol{x})d\boldsymbol{x}$, and $\hat{F}_{C,M}(\boldsymbol{x}) = \int_{-\infty}^{\boldsymbol{x}} \hat{p}_M(\boldsymbol{u})d\boldsymbol{u}$ as the approximate CDF. Then*

$$\lim_{M \to \infty} \hat{F}_{C,M}(\boldsymbol{x}) = F_C(\boldsymbol{x}).$$

Proof Sketch. By combining the error bounds in Lemma 7 and Lemma 8 and applying triangle inequality, we can show the end-to-end error is bounded by $|\hat{F}_{C,t}(\boldsymbol{x}) - F_C(\boldsymbol{x})| \leq \frac{1}{M \cdot \hat{z}z}(\theta\mu z + U\mu F_C(\boldsymbol{x}))$, where $\theta = \|\boldsymbol{x} - \boldsymbol{a}\|$ is the distance from $\boldsymbol{x}$ to $\boldsymbol{a} = [a_1, a_2, \ldots, a_N]$. Recall $C = \bigotimes_{i=1}^{N}[a_i, b_i]$, so $\boldsymbol{a}$ is the lower bound of C. Then θ, μ (Lipschitz constant of f), z (normalizing constant), U (volume of C), and $F_C(\boldsymbol{x})$ are all constants regarding M, and $\hat{z} \to z > 0$ as $M \to \infty$. Hence $|\hat{F}_{C,t}(\boldsymbol{x}) - F_C(\boldsymbol{x})| \to 0$ as $M \to \infty$. □

We allow a user to provide a bounded domain C, or infer it with automatically with a heuristic (Sect. 4). Although AQUA's formal guarantee is in a bounded domain, it can give runtime warnings when any prior or likelihood has probability greater than a given threshold on the rest of the domain $\mathbb{R}^N - C$. If AQUA does not give any warning, the final error caused by truncating infinite domain into C will be smaller than the threshold.

Algorithm 2. Posterior Interval Analysis with Adaptive Interval

1: **procedure** POSTERIORADAPTIVEANALYSIS($Prog,M,t_0,t_{dist}$)
2:    $C \leftarrow GetInitBounds(Prog,t_0)$ ▷ $C = [C_1, C_2, \ldots, C_N]$
3:    $changed \leftarrow$ True
4:    **while** $changed$ **do**   ▷ Stop if C no longer changes
5:       $(\hat{p}, Marginal) \leftarrow$ POSTERIORANALYSIS($Prog, M, C$)   ▷ Apply analysis on C
6:       $changed \leftarrow$ False
7:       **for** $x_i \in SampledVars(Prog)$ **do**   ▷ Adapt C_i for each variable
8:          $\hat{p}_i(x_i) \leftarrow Marginal[x_i]$
9:          **if** $\exists x_i \in C_i$, $\hat{p}_i(x_i) < t_{dist}$ **then**
10:             $C_i \leftarrow [\inf\{x_i|\hat{p}_i(x_i) > t_{dist}\}, \sup\{x_i|\hat{p}_i(x_i) > t_{dist}\}]$
11:             $changed \leftarrow$ True
12:          **end if**
13:       **end for**
14:    **end while**
15: **return** $(\hat{p}, Marginal)$
16: **end procedure**

---

4   AQUA Analysis Optimizations

Adaptive Intervals. To find the suitable bounded intervals $C = [C_1, C_2, \ldots, C_N]$ that cover most probability, we design a adaptive algorithm (Algorithm 2) to adjust C the based on the result from last run. Algorithm 2 takes as inputs the program, the vector of number of intervals, and two thresholds t_0 and t_{dist} for deciding the interval bounds C. Increasing C_i or increasing the number of intervals in C_i will help reduce the approximation error.

The function $GetInitBounds$ (Line 2) takes the prior distribution of each x_i as a rough estimate of the distribution to determine an initial interval split. If the domain of the prior distribution is bounded in $[a_i, b_i]$ where $-\infty < a_i < b_i < \infty$, e.g. $\mathtt{x_i} \sim \mathtt{uniform(a,b)}$, AQUA divides $[a_i, b_i]$ into M_i equi-length intervals, each with length $(b_i - a_i)/M_i$, where M_i is given in M by the user. If the distribution is not bounded, e.g. $\mathtt{x_i} \sim \mathtt{normal(0,1)}$, the user can specify a threshold t_0 for AQUA to infer C_is such that values from the prior being out of C_is has probability smaller than t_0. Otherwise by default we set $t_0 = 4 \cdot 10^{-32}$.

In each iteration, the algorithm applies the analysis on the current C (line 5) and check if we need to adapt C. We adapt C when any variable x_i has density value $\hat{p}_i(x_i)$ being almost about 0 - smaller than the user provided threshold t_{dist} (e.g. 10^{-8}) (line 8–10). We shrink C_i to focus on the smallest area with density greater than a given threshold t_{dist}. With the same number of intervals M_i, the smaller C_i will produce thiner intervals and result in more accurate results. Practically, this adaptive algorithm is as accurate but is much more efficient than naively increasing the number of intervals M_i on the whole initial domain C_i. Suppose the program takes A adaptive iterations, and it has N variables and each variable has the same number of intervals M, Algorithm 2 has the time complexity $\mathcal{O}(A \cdot N \cdot M^N)$ and the space complexity $\mathcal{O}(M^N)$. In our experiments, A is usually less than 5.

Improving Inference for Many Local Variables. In this optimization we change the analysis of statements in Sect. 3 to marginalize the local variables as soon as possible. Local variables are those defined and only used in local blocks (e.g. in for-loop and if-then-else from Fig. 5).

By marginalizing out the local variables, we avoid repeatedly computing the joint density on the unused variables. For example, in a robust model one may naively calculate the joint density via $\hat{f}(x) = \prod_{i=1}^{D} \mathrm{d\_pdf}(x, w_i)$, where w_is are local variables defined in each loop body. This requires keeping a $(D+1)$-dimensional density cube to capture all the variables x and w_is. Instead, our optimization divides the above product into calculating the individual $\mathrm{d\_pdf}(x, w_i)$, when w_i leaves its scope, so we do not carry the current w_i to the next iteration. In each iteration we only operate on a 2-dimensional Density Cube for variables x and a single w_i. If out of N variables in the program D are local variables we will have a time complexity $\mathcal{O}(N \cdot M^{N-D})$ for Algorithm 1 (while the original is $\mathcal{O}(N \cdot M^N)$).

5   Methodology

We evaluate AQUA on 24 probabilistic programs collected from existing literature. We compare the execution time of AQUA on these programs with other probabilistic programming languages: Stan [5], PSI [8], and SPPL [19]. We implement AQUA in Java using ND4J library for tensor computation, and run all experiments on Intel Xeon 3.6 GHz machine with 6 cores and 32 GB RAM. For numerical stability, we use log probability/density (instead of original probability/density) for Density Cube.

Benchmarks. Table 2 presents the benchmarks obtained from the literature. Column **Description** summarizes the task of each program. Column **Distributions** shows the distributions of observable and latent variables. For example, the distributions in program "prior_mix" are one Bernoulli (B), one Mixture of two Normals ($N+N$), and 10 Student-T distributions (T^{10}). All posterior distributions are continuous. Column **#D** shows the number of data observations, **#N** shows the number of random variables in the program.

Comparing Posterior Distributions. The Kolmogorov-Smirnov (KS) statistic measures the distance between two probability distributions. We use the KS statistic for the accuracy evaluation in the analysis. Let F_{truth} and $\hat{F}$ denote the posterior distributions of the variable x from the original input data and the noisy data respectively, the *KS statistic* is defined as $KS = \sup_x \left| F_{truth}(x) - \hat{F}(x) \right|$, namely, the maximum difference in the cumulative distribution functions. The KS statistic takes a value between 0 (most close distributions) and 1 (most different distributions). Therefore, smaller KS statistic implies better accuracy.

Table 2. Program description and characteristics

	Description	Distributions	#D	#N
prior_mix	Mixture model [9]	$B \times (N + N) \times T^{10}$	10	1
zeroone	Bayesian neural network [3]	$U^2 \times M^{20}$	20	2
tug	Causal cognition model [10]	$U^2 \times (N + N)^2 \times B^{40}$	40	2
altermu	Model with param symmetry [18]	$N^3 \times N^{40}$	40	3
altermu2	Model with param symmetry [18]	$U^2 \times N^{40}$	40	2
neural	Bayesian neural network [17]	$U^2 \times (B \times M)^{39}$	39	2
normal_mixture	Mixture model with mixing rate [21]	$N^2 \times Be \times (B \times (N + N))^{63}$	63	3
mix_asym_prior	Mixture model with scale params [21]	$N^2 \times G^2 \times (B \times (N + N))^{40}$	40	4
logistic	Logistic regression [21]	$U^2 \times (B \times M)^{100}$	100	2
logistic_RW	Reweighted logistic regression [21,24]	$U^2 \times Be^{100} \times (B \times M)^{100}$	100	102
anova	Linear regression [21]	$U^2 \times N^{40}$	40	2
anova_RP	Localized linear regression [21,23]	$U^2 \times G^{40} \times N^{40}$	40	42
anova_RW	Reweighted linear regression [21,24]	$U^2 \times Be^{40} \times N^{40}$	40	42
lightspeed	Linear regression [21]	$N \times U \times N^{66}$	66	2
lightspeed_RP	Localized linear regression [21,23]	$N \times U \times G^{66} \times N^{66}$	66	68
lightspeed_RW	Reweighted linear regression [21,24]	$N \times U \times Be^{66} \times N^{66}$	66	68
unemployment	Linear regression [21]	$N^2 \times U \times N^{40}$	40	3
unemployment_RP	Localized linear regression [21,23]	$N^2 \times U \times G^{40} \times N^{40}$	40	43
unemployment_RW	Reweighted linear regression [21,24]	$N^2 \times U \times Be^{40} \times N^{40}$	40	43
timeseries	Timeseries analysis [21]	$U^3 \times N^{39}$	39	3
gammaTransform	Transformed param [19]	G	0	3
GPA	Hybrid continuous & discrete distr. [14]	$B \times (B \times (A + U) + B \times (A + U))$	1	3
radar_query1	Bayesian network in robotics [8]	$B \times (A + B) \times U \times N \times (Tr + Tr)$	2	6
radar_query2	Bayesian network in robotics [8]	$B \times (A + B) \times U^2 \times N \times Tr$	1	6

Distributions: A: Atomic, B: Bernoulli, Be: Beta, G: Gamma, M: Softmax, N: Normal, T: Student-T, Tr: Triangular, U: Uniform. '+' represents the mixture of two distributions, and '×' represents the product of the individual density functions in the joint probability density function.

Experimental Setup. We manually derived the *ground truth* posterior distributions for all the programs. We run AQUA with the adaptive algorithm described in Sect. 4. We use the equal number of $M = \max\{60, \lceil 40000^{(1/N)} \rceil\}$ intervals for each variable, where N is the number of sampled variables, so that the total number intervals $M^N \geq 40000$. Rounding up the total number of intervals to 40000 does not significantly affect time but will guarantee more accurate results. We test Stan on its two major inference algorithms, NUTS (a variant of MCMC) and ADVI (a variant of variational inference). For fair comparison, we allow running VI/NUTS until it reaches the same accuracy level (in KS distance) as AQUA and report the average time, or until it reaches the maximum iterations (fixed at 400000 for both VI and NUTS). We set the timeout to be 20 min for all the inference tools.

6 Evaluation

6.1 Runtime and Accuracy Comparison

Table 3 presents the runtime and accuracy comparison of AQUA with Stan, PSI, and SPPL. Column **Program** shows the name of the probabilistic program.

Table 3. Runtime Comparison for AQUA, Stan, PSI, and SPPL. Stan column shows time needed reach AQUA's accuracy.

Program	AQUA		Stan VI		Stan NUTS		PSI	SPPL
	Time(s)	Error	Time(s)	Error	Time(s)	Error	Time (s)	Time (s)
prior_mix	4.77	0.02	0.53	0.31	5.67	0.19	inte	⊘
zeroone	0.98	0.00	0.44	0.21	630.73	0.21	91.16	⊘
tug	0.83	0.01	1.20	0.25	519.94	0.06	inte	⊘
altermu	1.35	0.00	0.96	0.31	29.46	0.03	inte	⊘
altermu2	0.76	0.00	0.75	0.34	25.98	0.07	inte	⊘
neural	0.85	0.01	0.82	0.03	5.10	0.01	t.o.	⊘
normal_mixture	1.19	0.02	1.02	0.12	25.67	0.04	t.o.	⊘
mix_asym_prior	24.63	0.02	1.04	0.09	16.41	0.03	t.o.	⊘
logistic	0.99	0.02	0.74	0.07	17.31	0.02	t.o.	⊘
logistic_RW	1.87	0.01	15.37	0.09	72.45	0.02	t.o.	⊘
anova	0.90	0.01	0.75	0.07	6.72	0.02	inte	⊘
anova_RP	1.55	0.01	6.89	0.07	77.48	0.02	t.o.	⊘
anova_RW	1.40	0.01	6.93	0.06	24.67	0.02	t.o.	⊘
lightspeed	0.74	0.00	0.71	0.04	3.56	0.00	inte	⊘
lightspeed_RP	1.37	0.01	6.18	0.06	61.37	0.02	t.o.	⊘
lightspeed_RW	1.09	0.02	6.19	0.05	61.37	0.05	t.o.	⊘
unemployment	1.44	0.02	0.64	0.21	5.07	0.01	inte	⊘
unemployment_RP	42.34	0.01	6.78	0.25	12.46	0.01	t.o.	⊘
unemployment_RW	27.41	0.02	7.07	0.23	2.53	0.01	t.o.	⊘
timeseries	1.55	0.01	0.87	0.23	12.66	0.01	inte	⊘
gammaTransform	0.72	0.00	0.62	0.05	3.01	0.01	inte	1.30
GPA	0.46	0.02	⊘	⊘	⊘	⊘	0.12	0.05
radar_query1	0.87	0.01	⊘	⊘	⊘	⊘	inte	⊘
radar_query2	1.82	0.02	⊘	⊘	⊘	⊘	inte	⊘
Avg	5.08	0.01	3.17	0.15	77.12	0.04	⊘	⊘
Median	1.35	0.01	0.99	0.10	20.99	0.02	⊘	⊘

[*time*] : VI or NUTS takes more time than AQUA, or AQUA take more time than VI and NUTS.
[*error*] Has the error (in terms of a KS distance) larger than 0.01 from the best solution.
"⊘": the PPL cannot work on the program. "t.o.": timeout, "inte": evaluates to unsolved integrals.

Columns **Time (s)** show the execution time (in seconds) of each tool, averaged across 5 runs. We report the total time for computing joint density and marginals for all sampled variables. Columns **Error** show the error (KS distance, Sect. 5) of each tool vs. the ground truth when run for the same time, averaged across 5 runs.

Overall, **AQUA** (Column 2–3) solves the probabilistic programs with average time 5.08 s, median time 1.35 s. For 20 out of 24 programs, it takes less than two seconds to compute the results. AQUA results in average error 0.01, median error 0.01, and maximum error 0.02. With our optimization on local variables (Sect. 4), we are able to handle the 7 robust programs which have 42–102 variables, which might timeout with a naive approach.

Stan VI (Column 4–5) finishes fast but results in significantly larger error than AQUA or Stan NUTS. The average error from VI is 0.15, minimum error is 0.03 and maximum error is 0.34. For all cases, VI cannot reach the same accuracy level as AQUA. While VI often fits the posterior means correctly but

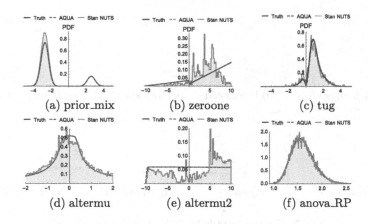

Fig. 6. Programs handled by AQUA for which Stan NUTS is imprecise.

it is not able to capture the joint distribution shape especially when it is non-Gaussian (it is a well known characteristic of VI). **Stan NUTS** (Column 6–7) takes more time than AQUA to reach the same level of accuracy of AQUA, although in theory NUTS will converge to the true distribution with enough iterations. AQUA provides the similar (with difference <0.01) or even better accuracy (with smaller KS distance) in all cases for NUTS and NUTS fails to reach the same accuracy level by the maximum number of iterations in 12 cases.

PSI (Column 8) and **SPPL** (Column 9) are not able to give result in many cases. PSI does not finish running within 20 min in 11 cases, or evaluates to unsolved integrals in 11 cases, since the exact integration in posterior calculation is often intractable. SPPL does not allow transformed variables in `factor` statements, which is essential to specify the likelihood of the variables given observed data, and thus is inapplicable to most of the programs.

Figure 6 presents the posterior densities from six programs where Stan NUTS was not able to reach the same accuracy level of AQUA, within maximum iterations. X-axis shows the value of a variable in the program, Y-axis shows the posterior probability density of the variable. A solid blue line shows the ground truth, a dashed red line shows the density function computed from AQUA, the gray histogram shows the density estimated with samples from Stan NUTS after running for the same time as AQUA. For each program we present the posterior from one variable (the first one in alphabetical order); the posteriors from other variables show a similar pattern. These examples show that AQUA is able to closely track the density of mixture models with large difference in densities (**prior_mix**), non-differentiable distributions (**zeroone** and **tug**), models with variable symmetries (in **altermu** and **altermu2** such symmetries can cause non-identifiability of variables from data), and some robust models with strong correlation between variables that can form complicated posterior geometries (**anova_RP**).

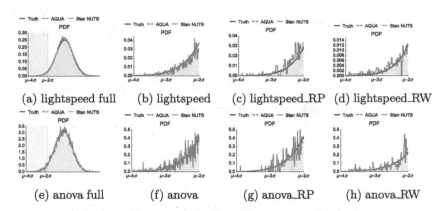

Fig. 7. Capturing tails by AQUA and Stan NUTS

6.2   Estimating the Tails of Posterior Distribution

We illustrate AQUA's ability to capture tails on several robust models. The distribution for robust models are often more spread-out than the original model, as they are designed to capture outliers in the data. We consider two different robust models: (1) Reparameterized-Localization (RP) [23], which assumes that each data point is from its distribution with a local variance variable; (2) Reweighting (RW) [24], which down-weights potential outliers in the data. We show the results from AQUA and NUTS running for the same amount of time, together with the ground truth. We omit VI since its accuracy is significantly worse.

Figure 7 presents the comparison of AQUA and NUTS. Plots (a),(e) are the full posterior distributions of original distribution. We highlight the left tail $[\mu - 4\sigma, \mu - 2\sigma]$, where μ is the posterior mean of and σ its standard deviation. Plots (b),(f) show the magnified tails from original distribution, plots (c),(g) show the tails from the RP transformation, and (d),(h) show the tails from RW transformation. AQUA is able to capture the tails precisely for both original and robust models, while Stan NUTS is less precise on the robust models (e.g., its KS metric is 0.05 compared to AQUA's 0.02).

7   Related Work

Symbolic Inference. Researchers have proposed several symbolic inference techniques in recent years [8,12,16,19]. Each of these techniques have limitations which AQUA improves upon. DICE [12] only supports discrete distributions. Hakaru [16] and PSI [8], which do exact inference using computer algebra, often cannot solve integrals for complicated probabilistic programs with continuous distributions (as our evaluation also shows for PSI). SPPL [19] does not allow users to specify the likelihood on transformed variables with continuous distributions. QCoral [4] and SYMPAIS [15] combine symbolic execution with sampling to solve the satisfaction probability of constraints, but they do not output the whole posterior. In contrast, AQUA supports a wide range of probabilistic models with continuous distribution, involving transformed or correlated random variables, and provides scalable, exact (or near exact), and interpretable solutions.

Volume Computation. Several works use volume computation methods to make a precise approximation of probabilistic inference [2,20,22]. These approaches have constraints on the form of programs they support, regarding conditioning and continuous distributions. For instance, Sweet et al. [22] support only discrete and FairSquare [2] approximates Gaussians with only five intervals; FairSquare [2] and Sankaranarayanan et al. [20] compute only the probability of an event, not the entire posterior. None of these systems can support conditioning on continuous variables, and thus we have not used them in our evaluation.

8 Conclusion

AQUA is a new inference algorithm which works on general, real-world probabilistic programs with continuous distributions. By using quantization with symbolic inference, AQUA solved all benchmarks in less than 43 s (median 1.35 s). Our evaluation shows that AQUA is more accurate than approximate algorithms and supports programs that are out of reach of state-of-the-art exact inference tools.

Acknowledgements. This research was supported in part by NSF Grants No. CCF-1846354, CCF-1956374, CCF-2008883, and Facebook PhD Fellowship.

References

1. Aguirre, A., Barthe, G., Hsu, J., Kaminski, B.L., Katoen, J.P., Matheja, C.: A pre-expectation calculus for probabilistic sensitivity. POPL (2021)
2. Albarghouthi, A., D'Antoni, L., Drews, S., Nori, A.: Fairsquare: probabilistic verification of program fairness. OOPSLA (2017)
3. Bissiri, P., Holmes, C., Walker, S.: A general framework for updating belief distributions. J. R. Stat. Soc. Ser. B Stat. Methodol. **78**(5), 1103 (2016)
4. Borges, M., Filieri, A., d'Amorim, M., Păsăreanu, C.S., Visser, W.: Compositional solution space quantification for probabilistic software analysis. PLDI (2014)
5. Carpenter, B., Gelman, A., Hoffman, M., Lee, D., et al.: Stan: a probabilistic programming language. JSTATSOFT **20**(2) (2016)
6. Dutta, S., Legunsen, O., Huang, Z., Misailovic, S.: Testing probabilistic programming systems. In: FSE (2018)
7. Dutta, S., Zhang, W., Huang, Z., Misailovic, S.: Storm: program reduction for testing and debugging probabilistic programming systems. In: FSE (2019)
8. Gehr, T., Misailovic, S., Vechev, M.: PSI: exact symbolic inference for probabilistic programs. In: Chaudhuri, S., Farzan, A. (eds.) CAV 2016. LNCS, vol. 9779, pp. 62–83. Springer, Cham (2016). https://doi.org/10.1007/978-3-319-41528-4_4
9. Gelman, A., Stern, H.S., Carlin, J.B., Dunson, D.B., Vehtari, A., Rubin, D.B.: Bayesian Data Analysis. Chapman and Hall/CRC (2013)

10. Goodman, N., Tenenbaum, J.: Probabilistic Models of Cognition. http:// probmods.org/
11. Gorinova, M.I., Gordon, A.D., Sutton, C.: Probabilistic programming with densities in SlicStan: efficient, flexible, and deterministic. POPL (2019)
12. Holtzen, S., Van den Broeck, G., Millstein, T.: Scaling exact inference for discrete probabilistic programs. OOPSLA (2020)
13. Huang, Z., Wang, Z., Misailovic, S.: PSense: automatic sensitivity analysis for probabilistic programs. In: Lahiri, S.K., Wang, C. (eds.) ATVA 2018. LNCS, vol. 11138, pp. 387–403. Springer, Cham (2018). https://doi.org/10.1007/978-3-030-01090-4_23
14. Laurel, J., Misailovic, S.: Continualization of probabilistic programs with correction. ESOP (2020)
15. Luo, Y., Filieri, A., Zhou, Y.: SYMPAIS: symbolic parallel adaptive importance sampling for probabilistic program analysis. arXiv preprint arXiv:2010.05050 (2020)
16. Narayanan, P., Carette, J., Romano, W., Shan, C., Zinkov, R.: Probabilistic inference by program transformation in Hakaru (system description). In: Kiselyov, O., King, A. (eds.) FLOPS 2016. LNCS, vol. 9613, pp. 62–79. Springer, Cham (2016). https://doi.org/10.1007/978-3-319-29604-3_5
17. Neal, R.M.: Bayesian Learning for Neural Networks. Springer, Heidelberg (2012)
18. Nishihara, R., Minka, T., Tarlow, D.: Detecting parameter symmetries in probabilistic models. arXiv preprint arXiv:1312.5386 (2013)
19. Saad, F.A., Rinard, M.C., Mansinghka, V.K.: SPPL: a probabilistic programming system with exact and scalable symbolic inference. PLDI (2021)
20. Sankaranarayanan, S., Chakarov, A., Gulwani, S.: Static analysis for probabilistic programs: Inferring whole program properties from finitely many paths. PLDI (2013)
21. (2018). https://github.com/stan-dev/example-models
22. Sweet, I., Trilla, J.M.C., Scherrer, C., Hicks, M., Magill, S.: What's the over/under? probabilistic bounds on information leakage. POST (2018)
23. Wang, C., Blei, D.M.: A general method for robust Bayesian modeling. Bayesian Anal. **13**(4), 1159–1187 (2018)
24. Wang, Y., Kucukelbir, A., Blei, D.M.: Robust probabilistic modeling with Bayesian data reweighting. ICML (2017)

Software and Hardware Verification

Proving SIFA Protection of Masked Redundant Circuits

Vedad Hadžić[✉], Robert Primas, and Roderick Bloem

Graz University of Technology, Graz, Austria
{vedad.hadzic,robert.primas,roderick.bloem}@iaik.tugraz.at
https://www.iaik.tugraz.at/

Abstract. Implementation attacks like side-channel and fault attacks pose a considerable threat to cryptographic devices that are physically accessible by an attacker. As a consequence, devices like smart cards implement corresponding countermeasures like redundant computation and masking. Recently, statistically ineffective fault attacks (SIFA) were shown to be able to circumvent these classical countermeasure techniques. We present a new approach for verifying the SIFA protection of arbitrary masked implementations in both hardware and software. The proposed method uses Boolean dependency analysis, factorization, and known properties of masked computations to show whether the fault detection mechanism of redundant masked circuits can leak information about the processed secret values. We implemented this new method in a tool called *Danira*, which can show the SIFA resistance of cryptographic implementations like AES S-Boxes within minutes.

1 Introduction

Cryptographic primitives are primarily designed to withstand mathematical attacks in a black-box setting. However, when these primitives are deployed in the real world, they find themselves in a grey-box setting in which an attacker may try to force faulty computations or observe additional physical side-channel information, such as instantaneous power consumption. This improved attacker capability simplifies the extraction of secrets like cryptographic keys.

Active implementation attacks, such as fault analysis [7,9], and passive side-channel attacks, like power or electromagnetic (EM) analysis [26,27], are among the most serious threats for implementations of cryptographic algorithms. A common algorithmic countermeasure strategy against these attacks is the combination of masking against power analysis with redundant computation against fault attacks. *Masking* is a secret-sharing technique where one splits a cryptographic computation into $d + 1$ random shares. This technique ensures that the

---

This work was supported by the *Austrian Research Promotion Agency (FFG)* via the **FERMION** project (grant number 867542, ICT of the Future), and the K-project **DeSSnet** (funded in the context of COMET). We refer to the online appendix [22] for the formal proofs of the presented lemmas and theorems.

© Springer Nature Switzerland AG 2021
Z. Hou and V. Ganesh (Eds.): ATVA 2021, LNCS 12971, pp. 249–265, 2021.
https://doi.org/10.1007/978-3-030-88885-5_17

observation of up to d intermediate values of that masked computation does not reveal any information about native (unmasked) values [6,15,20,21,24]. *Redundant computation* tries to prevent the release of faulty cryptographic computations caused by environmental influences or malicious tampering such as voltage glitches, lasers, or rapid temperature variations. Without this countermeasure, an attacker with access to faulty computations can learn information about the used cryptographic key in many different ways [3,16,23].

Researchers long believed that the combination of redundancy and masking could adequately deal with active and passive implementation attacks. However, it was recently shown that when using *statistical ineffective fault attacks* (SIFA), even such protected cryptographic implementations are vulnerable to rather straightforward implementation attacks [12–14]. The key observation behind SIFA attacks is that a cryptographic key may correlate with the suppression of a faulted cryptographic computation. Thus, the attacker can obtain information about this key by observing whether the output of a faulted cryptographic computation is suppressed by a redundancy countermeasure or not.

For example, if a 1-bit signal carries a secret value, and the attacker can force this signal to zero, they can learn the secret value by observing whether or not this fault is detected. While this simplified example is obvious, SIFA is interesting because it works even if the fault injection targets just one share of a masked secret. In fact, SIFA is exploitable even if the attacker does not know the exact effect of a fault injection on the faulted value [12].

Most proposed mitigation techniques against SIFA so far use error correction, which is however costly when combined with masking [11,29]. Another recently proposed SIFA mitigation tries to solve this issue with a careful combination of redundancy, masking, and reversible computing [10], achieving protection against SIFA without significant overheads. The authors give detailed *circuit* descriptions of protected cipher components that can be mapped into concrete software or hardware implementations. However, even minor modifications of the circuit description due to human error, compilers, or synthesis tools, although preserving functional equivalence, may make the circuit vulnerable to SIFA. Consequently, there is a high demand for tooling that can support designers in building efficient cryptographic implementations resistant against power analysis and fault attacks, including SIFA.

1.1   Related Work

The empirical and formal verification of power analysis and fault attack countermeasures is an already well established topic in the cryptographic research community [1,4,8,17–19,25]. On a conceptual level, the verification of masking countermeasures—ensuring that individual computations are unrelated to any cryptographic secret—does perform statistical independence checks that could also be adapted for verifying SIFA protection, i.e., that cryptographic secrets do not correlate with the suppression of a faulted cryptographic computation. However, in the following we argue that such existing tools either cannot be easily adapted for SIFA verification, or would come with performance overheads that make them unattractive for practical use.

Tools like REBECCA [8] and its successor COCO [19] use correlation tracking to show statistical independence in (sequential) masked hardware circuits. Although their method ignores the *strength* and *sign* of correlations for performance reasons, the remaining information is still sufficient to show standard probing resistance of masked circuits. However, these approximations are not applicable for SIFA verification. Since REBECCA and COCO do not track the *sign* of correlations, there is no way to distinguish the correlation sets of a negated value from a non-negated value. Due to the nature of bit-flip faults, this method leads to falsely reported leaks due to the structure of the fault-detection mechanism. Similarly, tools like `maskVerif` [4] rely on security proofs for a gate's input signals to prove the gate's security. According to our investigation, since the fault-detection mechanism combines the shares in its sub-formulas, a leakage report is triggered even though the value cannot be observed.

Exact methods like SILVER [25] use some form of model counting to track exact probability distributions of values within masked circuits and check whether the correlation strength is zero for all secret values. These methods could be adopted for SIFA verification, e.g., by using a strategy as outlined in Fig. 1 but will lead to verification runtimes significantly higher compared to the approach that we will present in this paper.

Besides masking verification tools, there also exists VerFI [2], a verification tool dedicated to fault attacks that, amongst others, does have the capability to verify SIFA protection of a given circuit in certain scenarios. More precisely, VerFI can detect SIFA vulnerability of a given circuits using an empirical and simulation-based approach that essentially checks if either (1) all fault injections are being corrected through error correction methods, or (2) all fault injections are being detected via redundancy methods. This empirical approach can be used for error-correction-based SIFA countermeasures, however, VerFI is not suited for the verification of, e.g., the more efficient SIFA countermeasure design by Daemen et al. [10] that does not need be able to correct any possible fault injection.

1.2 Contribution

The contribution of this paper is threefold and consists of a method and its implementation, its evaluation, and resulting SIFA-resistant circuit artifacts.

Method. We present a formal verification approach to determine whether a masked redundant cipher implementation is SIFA resistant within a well-defined attacker model. Our verification approach checks whether the output of the fault-detection mechanism correlates with secrets used in the computation. We present three properties and their respective checking methods that serve as sufficient conditions for SIFA protection. *(Incompleteness):* If a function δ does not functionally depend on all shares of a secret s, it cannot leak the secret. *(Hiding):* If a function δ can be written as $m \oplus \delta'$, where m is a uniformly distributed random variable and δ' is functionally independent of m, δ does not leak information about any secrets. *(Inferred independence):* For a function $\delta = \bigvee_i \delta_i$, if all linear combinations of its partial functions δ_i are statistically independent of a secret s, δ cannot leak the secret s. We present an algorithm that uses these sufficient but not necessary conditions to prove the security of circuits. Our tool *Danira* implements this algorithm and is, to our knowledge, the first tool for formal verification of SIFA resistance of masked redundant circuits.

Evaluation. We provide an experimental evaluation of our method. Because the sufficient conditions may not be able to prove SIFA resistance, we show in our experimental section that the approach gives precise results for a representative range of secure circuits. If *Danira* cannot prove resistance, it provides fault locations that might leak information about the secrets. We show that *Danira* can accurately prove security or find bugs in S-Boxes, the non-linear parts of cryptographic implementations, in minutes or even seconds. With respect to SIFA verification, masked linear layers do not need any further analysis as fault injections in these components are not exploitable with SIFA. Ultimately, we give practical examples illustrating that, even when a design is secure against SIFA on paper, vulnerabilities may arise as a result of simple compiler/synthesis optimizations, which can then however be identified with *Danira*.

Artifacts. As a direct result of this work, we present the first SIFA-resistant Verilog implementations of Daemen et al. [10] designs for a masked AES S-Box, the KECCAK χ_3 S-Box, and all classes of quadratic 4-bit S-Boxes.

2   Preliminaries

Masking is an algorithmic countermeasure that, while primarily intended to prevent power analysis attacks, also plays an essential role in SIFA attacks. In a masked cipher implementation, each input, output, and intermediate variable is split into $d + 1$ *shares* so that their XOR is equal to the original *native variable* [24]. In Boolean masking, a native variable s is split random shares $s_0 \ldots s_d$ that satisfy $s = s_0 \oplus \ldots \oplus s_d$. As long as an attacker cannot observe a set of values statistically dependent on all $d + 1$ shares of a native value, the computation is secure against classical power analysis techniques. Dealing with linear functions is trivial as they can be computed on each share individually. However, implementing masking for non-linear functions (S-Boxes) requires computations on all shares, which is more challenging to implement securely and correctly, and thus the main interest in the literature.

Redundant computation is an implementation-level fault attack countermeasure for cryptographic computations. The main idea is to perform the same computation several times and release a result only if the redundant computations match. This check prevents cases where an attacker forces faults in the computation, leading to incorrect results that correlate with native secrets [3]. Figure 1 shows the structure of a fault detection mechanism for redundant computations. If an attacker introduces a fault and the outputs do not match, output δ signals the faults and prevents the release of the result.

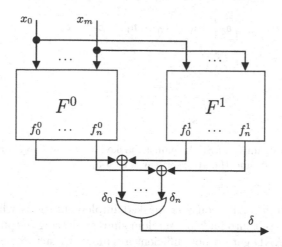

Fig. 1. A redundant computation with inputs $x_0, \ldots, x_m$, which are passed to both computation instances F^0 and F^1. The disjunction of differences $\delta_0, \ldots, \delta_n$ is used to determine whether there was a fault in one of the computation instances.

Statistical ineffective fault attacks (SIFA), first presented at CHES 2018 by Dobraunig et al., is a relatively new type of fault attack technique capable of circumventing common fault/power analysis countermeasures, while being applicable to a wide variety of block ciphers or AEAD schemes [12–14, 28]. When performing SIFA, an attacker calls a cryptographic operation (e.g. block cipher) with varying inputs, injects a fault during each of the computations, and only collects outputs in cases where the fault injection did not cause a faulty computation result (i.e. the output is not suppressed). This *filtered* set of outputs can then be used to perform a key recovery attack on a block cipher as follows.

A typical block cipher design of an iterated round function, consisting of a linear and non-linear layer, that mixes the current state with the cryptographic key such that in the end, each bit of the block cipher output is uniformly distributed. If we now consider, e.g., an AND computation that occurs in the non-linear layer of a (later) round function, one can observe that a fault-induced difference in one operand only propagates to the AND output if the other operand is '1'. Hence, if an attacker repeatedly calls a block cipher with varying inputs, while injecting the same difference in each computation, and only collecting outputs that are correct (not suppressed), a certain intermediate value should show a bias towards '0'. Given such a set of faulted but correct block cipher outputs, an attacker can now make a partial key guess of the last round key and calculate back to the faulted operation for each collected output (ciphertext). If the partial key guess was correct, the observed distribution of an intermediate value at that location should be biased. Otherwise, if the observed distribution is uniform, the key guess was wrong. For a more complete attack description targeting the AES-128 block cipher we refer to the description in [12].

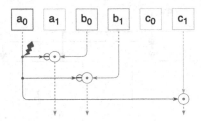

Fig. 2. Simplified example of SIFA against masked χ_3 using two shares. The induced difference cancels out, and the attacker learns $b_0 \lor b_1 \lor c_1$.

If we now additionally consider masked implementations where each intermediate value is split into multiple random shares, filtering outputs based on the operand of one AND gate is not sufficient anymore. In fact, for SIFA to work in masked scenarios, the attacker needs to work with fault inductions that cause a difference that propagates into multiple AND gates that use the shares of one native value as other operands. We show this with a small example inspired by Daemen et al. [10].

Example 1. Consider a masked S-Box implementation that operates on shared inputs and outputs. For simplicity, assume that we repeatedly call this S-Box with uniformly distributed inputs and observe the corresponding outputs. Since an S-Box is a bijective function, uniformly distributed inputs should give uniformly distributed outputs. Figure 2 shows a reduced depiction of a masked χ_3 S-Box, the smaller version of χ_5, which is used in KECCAK (SHA-3). The S-Box takes a 3-bit input, represented by bits a, b and c. Therefore a first-order masked version of χ_3 takes the bits $a_0, a_1, b_0, b_1, c_0, c_1$ as input, with $a = a_0 \oplus a_1$, etc. If we assume a fault targeting a_0 at the specified location, the induced bit-difference propagates into three AND-gates that take the bits b_0, b_1, and c_1 as the other inputs. In this case, the bit-difference cancels out and produces a value $\delta = b_0 \lor b_1 \lor c_1$. When a fault is not detected, an attacker knows that b_0, b_1, and c_1 are all zero, and therefore, b is zero as well. In this concrete case, the attacker uses a fault injection to filter out computations where the distribution of b is biased, and uses them to recover the key

Efficient SIFA countermeasures were presented at CHES 2020 [10]. Their SIFA mitigation strategy has almost no overhead and builds upon a careful combination of masking, redundant computation, and reversible computing. They show that, by building non-linear operations from incomplete and invertible building blocks, they achieve implementations where a single fault in the computation is either (1) not exploitable by SIFA, or (2) detectable via redundant computations. This approach is comparably easy to implement for small S-Boxes and can also be extended to larger S-Boxes such as the AES S-Box.

Boolean formulas are a symbolic composition of Boolean variables using logic operators. For a propositional boolean formula f, we write $\mathrm{Var}(f)$ to refer to the variables that occur in f. When clear from context, we write V to denote a superset of all used variables, $i.e.$, $\mathrm{Var}(f) \subseteq V$. The *partial evaluation* of f, where a variable q is assigned a value $p \in \mathbb{B}$ is written as $f[q \leftarrow p]$. Given a set of variables Q and an assignment $\alpha : Q \to \mathbb{B}$, we write $f[\alpha]$ to denote the partial evaluation of f where each variable in Q is assigned according to α.

We say that a formula f is *functionally dependent* on a variable x if and only if the concrete value of $x \in \mathbb{B}$ has an influence on the value of $f \in \mathbb{B}$. Henceforth, for a given formula f, we write $\mathcal{D}(f) \subseteq \mathrm{Var}(f)$ to denote the set of variables that f functionally depends on. That is, $x \in \mathcal{D}(f)$ if and only if there exists $\alpha : \mathrm{Var}(f) \setminus \{x\} \to \mathbb{B}$, such that $f[\alpha][x \leftarrow \bot] \oplus f[\alpha][x \leftarrow \top] = \top$. The above property can be checked by a SAT solver.

To discuss information leakage caused by a fault, we first define what it means for a formula f to contain information about another formula g. We define the weight of a Boolean function as $\#_V(f) = |\{\alpha : V \to \mathbb{B} \mid f[\alpha] = \top\}|$. Formulas f and g are *statistically dependent* if and only if $\#_V(f \wedge g) \cdot \#_V(\neg f) \neq \#_V(\neg f \wedge g) \cdot \#_V(f)$. That is, regardless of the observed value of f, the proportion of assignments α for which $g[\alpha] = \top$ is constant.

Example 2. Let $V = \{a, b, c\}$ be a set of variables. Let $f = a \wedge b$, $g = \neg a \vee c$, and $h = b \oplus c$ be Boolean formulas. Formulas f and g are statistically dependent because $\#_V(f \wedge g) \cdot \#_V(\neg f) = 6$ and $\#_V(\neg f \wedge g) \cdot \#_V(f) = 10$. Indeed, if $f[\alpha] = \top$, then probably $g[\alpha] = \bot$, whereas if $f[\alpha] = \bot$, then $g[\alpha] = \top$ is just as likely as $g[\alpha] = \bot$. The formulas f and h are statistically independent because $\#_V(f \wedge h) \cdot \#_V(\neg f) = 6$ and $\#_V(\neg f \wedge h) \cdot \#_V(f) = 6$.

We say that a Boolean formula f is *balanced* if and only if $\#_V(f) = \#_V(\neg f) = 2^{|V|-1}$. A Boolean variable x, interpreted as a formula, is inherently balanced for any variable set $x \in V$ as there are $2^{|V|-1}$ assignments $\alpha : V \to \mathbb{B}$ with $\alpha(x) = \top$. Lemma 1 states that this can be extended to functions of the form $f = x \oplus g$.

Lemma 1. *Let* $f = x \oplus g$ *be a Boolean formula with* $x \notin \mathrm{Var}(g)$. *We have that* f *is balanced.*

We measure the *Boolean distance* of two formulas f and g as the number of assignments where their values are different. This is equivalent to the weight of their difference $\#_V(f \oplus g)$. Lemma 2 states the connection between statistical independence and Boolean distance.

Lemma 2. *Let* f *and* g *be Boolean formulas and let* f *be balanced. Formulas* f *and* g *are statistically independent if and only if their difference is balanced.*

3 Verification Method

In this section, we introduce a method for verifying resistance against SIFA. That is, we show how to verify whether the fault-detection mechanism could give away information about native secrets processed by a software computation or hardware circuit. Our method focuses on proving the statistical independence of the fault-detection value δ and any of the secrets $s \in S$. We do not show this directly and instead try to prove the statistical independence using the *incompleteness, hiding*, and *inferred statistical independence* properties we introduce in this section. However, we first define the exact attack model considered in this verification approach.

3.1   Attack Model

Formally proving resistance against SIFA requires a definition of the attacker's capabilities and the exact information they observe. We use an attack model that is very similar to the one introduced by Daemen et al. [10]. We consider redundant masked implementations of S-Boxes that the attacker can query. Figure 1 shows a diagram of such an implementation, where the outputs of the two computation units are used to compute the fault-detection value δ. With SIFA, the value of δ is the only information the attacker receives from the computation. The goal of an attacker is to learn information about the native secret values processed by the computation. The inputs of the computation are categorized as masks and secret shares. In the rest of the section, we say that M is the set of mask variables, and S is the set of formulas representing the secrets. We, therefore, have the set of input variables $V = M \cup \bigcup_{s \in S} \mathrm{Var}(s)$.

As SIFA is a fault attack, the attacker has the technical capabilities to introduce the fault that changes the value of an intermediate computation. If we represent δ as a computational circuit, a fault modifies the output of precisely one logic gate used during the computation. In our attack model, we consider faults that can negate the value of the gate by causing a bit-flip, which also captures many other fault models such as stuck-at faults for masked circuits [10]. The attacker's goal is to find a fault location that would cause a statistical dependency between δ and one of the formulas $s \in S$. Our verification does not currently take into account the possible effects of "glitchy" fault injections, i.e., faults with specific timing behavior that causes the output of gates to change (glitch) several times before reaching a stable logic state While it has been shown that such effects need to be taken into account for implementing masking correctly in hardware, it is currently not clear if, or to what extend, they are relevant for SIFA attacks in realistic attacker settings.

Proposition 1. *A computation with a fault-detection value δ is SIFA resistant against a fault-inducing attacker if δ is statistically independent of all native secrets $s \in S$.*

3.2   Incompleteness

First, we prove that a fault-detection formula δ that does not functionally depend on all shares of a secret s, cannot be statistically dependent on s. A syntactic version of this property is known as *non-interference* in the literature [4,5]. Intuitively, if one of the shares is absent from the formula δ, then an attacker cannot infer anything about s without this missing piece of information. Definition 1 formally states this intuition of *incomplete* secrets. Lemma 3 states that *incompleteness* is sufficient for statistical independence.

Definition 1. *Let f be a formula, and s be a secret represented by the formula $s_0 \oplus \dots \oplus s_d$, where the shares s_i are variables. We say that a secret s is incomplete in formula f whenever $\mathcal{D}(s) \not\subseteq \mathcal{D}(f)$.*

Lemma 3. *Let secret $s = s_0 \oplus \dots \oplus s_d$ be incomplete in the fault-detection formula δ. Then δ and s are statistically independent.*

3.3 Hiding

Assume that the formula δ is functionally dependent on all shares of a secret $s = s_0 \oplus \dots \oplus s_d$, i.e., $\mathcal{D}(s) \subseteq \mathcal{D}(\delta)$. Incompleteness, as defined in Definition 1, is thus not fulfilled. However, δ and s could still be statistically independent. Intuitively, if δ is balanced and masked by some uniformly random value, it cannot statistically correlate with any secret $s \in S$.

Definition 2. *A uniformly random variable x hides a secret $s \in S$ in the error-detection formula δ whenever $\delta = x \oplus f$, with $x \notin \mathcal{D}(s) \cup \mathcal{D}(f)$.*

Not all variables can hide secrets. Masks hide secrets because they are uniformly random by definition. Although individual shares s_i of a secret $s \in S$ are guaranteed to be uniformly random, their corresponding native secrets are not. Consequently, when investigating the hiding property from Definition 2, we only consider masks and shares of incomplete secrets in δ, as stated in Lemma 4.

Lemma 4. *Let δ be a formula, S' be the set of secrets that are incomplete in δ, i.e., $S' = \{s \in S \mid \mathcal{D}(s) \cap \mathcal{D}(\delta) \neq \emptyset\}$, M be the uniformly random mask variables, and X be the union $X = M \cup \bigcup_{s \in S'} \mathcal{D}(s)$. If there exists an $x \in X$ that hides a secret $s \in S$, then δ and s are statistically independent.*

Lemma 5 presents a method that tests whether the factorization needed for the *hiding* property is possible. The method uses a SAT solver and is similar to the method that checks functional dependencies.

Lemma 5. *Let f be a Boolean formula and $x \in \mathrm{Var}(f)$ be a variable. Then $f = x \oplus f\,[x \leftarrow \bot]$ if and only if $f\,[x \leftarrow \bot] \oplus f\,[x \leftarrow \top] = \top$.*

It is enough to find one uniformly random variable x to show that δ is statistically independent of all secrets $s \in S$. As discussed earlier, not all variables in $\mathrm{Var}(\delta)$ are eligible for the hiding property. Thus, our verification method only checks the hiding property after determining incomplete secrets first.

3.4   Inferred Statistical Independence

Although incompleteness and hiding are enough in most cases, the structure of δ can make them inapplicable. Therefore, it is possible that δ functionally depends on some secret s, and no uniformly random value hides s in δ. Example 3 illustrates this situation.

Example 3. Let δ be the fault-detection formula with $\delta = \delta_0 \vee \delta_1$, $\delta_0 = x \oplus s_0$ and $\delta_1 = y \oplus s_1$ be its sub-formulas, $M = \{x, y\}$ be the masks, and $s = s_0 \oplus s_1$ be a secret. Formula δ is functionally dependent on both s_0 and s_1, since there are no assignments $\alpha : \mathrm{Var}(\delta) \setminus \{s_i\} \to \mathbb{B}$ such that $\delta[\alpha][s_i \leftarrow \bot] \oplus \delta[\alpha][s_i \leftarrow \top] = \top$. Similarly, δ cannot be factorized into either $\delta = x \oplus \delta[x \leftarrow \bot]$ or $\delta = y \oplus \delta[y \leftarrow \bot]$, so neither x nor y hide s. However δ is indeed statistically independent of s because $\#_{\mathrm{Var}(\delta)}(\delta \wedge s) \cdot \#_{\mathrm{Var}(\delta)}(\neg \delta) = \#_{\mathrm{Var}(\delta)}(\neg \delta \wedge s) \cdot \#_{\mathrm{Var}(\delta)}(\delta) = 24$.

Therefore, because of the structure of the fault-detection formula δ, there is a real possibility that the incompleteness and hiding checks are not sufficient to show that δ does not statistically depend on any secrets. However, this can be mitigated by inferring whether δ is statistically independent of s by looking at its sub-formulas δ_i instead. Lemma 6 introduces a method for inferring the statistical independence of two Boolean formulas f and g, where one has the topmost operation OR, just like δ, and the other is a balanced function, just like a secret. This property is inspired by correlation propagation used in REBECCA [8].

Lemma 6. *Let $f = a \vee b$ and g be Boolean formulas with the variable sets $\mathrm{Var}(f) \subseteq V$ and $\mathrm{Var}(g) \subseteq V$. If $\bot$, a, b, and $a \oplus b$ are statistically independent of g, then f is also statistically independent of g.*

Therefore, at least in the case where $\delta = \delta_0 \vee \delta_1$, we can infer that δ is statistically independent of a secret s, as long as δ_0, δ_1, and s fulfill the conditions of Lemma 6. Example 4 illustrates this.

Example 4. Let δ, δ_0, δ_1 and s be as in Example 3. By Lemma 1, s is balanced. The hiding property applies for δ_0, δ_1 and $\delta_0 \oplus \delta_1$, where x, y, and $x \oplus y$ can be factorized out respectively. According to Lemma 2, all of the prerequisites for Lemma 6 are met, so we are able to show that δ is indeed statistically independent of s, without testing the statistical independence definition explicitly.

However, in general, δ will be a formula of the form $\delta = \bigvee_{i=1}^{n} \delta_i$. Although it is possible to apply Lemma 6 recursively, it is not ideal because we run into the same problem we demonstrated in Example 3, just one recursive application later. Luckily, Lemma 6 can be generalized to OR operations with multiple arguments, as shown in Theorem 1.

Theorem 1. *Let $\Phi = \{\phi_1, \ldots, \phi_n\}$ be a set of Boolean formulas, $f = \bigvee_{i=1}^{n} \phi_i$ be their disjunction, g be another Boolean formula, and $\mathrm{Var}(f) \subseteq V$ and $\mathrm{Var}(g) \subseteq V$ be their variables. If for all $\Psi \in \mathcal{P}(\Phi)$, where $\mathcal{P}(\cdot)$ is the power-set operation, $f' = \bigoplus_{\psi \in \Psi} \psi$ is statistically independent of g, then so is f.*

Theorem 1 suggests that if we prove that all linear combinations of the error lines δ_i are statistically independent of a secret s, then we have indirectly shown that their disjunction δ is also statistically independent of s. Additionally, the condition of Theorem 1 can be further simplified because some of the linear combinations produced by $X \in \mathcal{P}(\Phi)$ could be equivalent. Instead of considering Φ, we could instead consider the maximal linearly independent subset of Φ.

Lemma 7. *Let Φ and g be as in Theorem 1. Let $\Phi' \subseteq \Phi$ be a linearly independent subset of Φ, i.e., $\forall \phi \in \Phi'. \forall \Psi \subseteq \Phi' \setminus \{\phi\}. \phi \neq \bigoplus_{\psi \in \Psi} \psi$, and let Φ' be maximal, i.e., $\forall \phi \in \Phi \backslash \Phi'. \exists \Psi \subseteq \Phi'. \phi = \bigoplus_{\psi \in \Psi} \psi$. If for all $\Psi \subseteq \Phi'$, $\bigoplus_{\psi \in \Psi} \psi$ is statistically independent of g, then the same holds for all $\Psi \subseteq \Phi$.*

As stated in Lemma 7, instead of considering all linear combinations in Φ, it is sufficient to consider only linear combinations of its maximally linearly independent subset Φ' when applying Theorem 1. In many cases, this substantially reduces the number of checks our verification method performed.

3.5   Approximating Statistical Independence

Theorem 1, together with the optimized condition from Lemma 7, is powerful enough to show that, given the mentioned conditions for δ_i, δ is statistically independent of a secret s. The statistical independence of the linear combinations of δ_i can be shown using the *incompleteness* and *hiding* properties discussed in Sects. 3.2 and 3.3. However, issuing exponentially many satisfiability queries required by Theorem 1 is still undesirable. Therefore, we introduce an over-approximation which only calls the SAT solver to perform factorization and functional dependency tests for each relevant δ_i with all variables in $\mathrm{Var}(\delta_i)$. We then use the gathered data to over-approximate the incompleteness and hiding properties for all linear combinations of δ_i.

In general a Boolean formula f can be rewritten as an equivalent formula $f = g \oplus h$. Here $g = \bigoplus_{x \in X} x$ is the linear sub-formula where $X \subseteq \mathrm{Var}(f)$ is a set of variable symbols for which Lemma 5 applies, i.e., $f[x \leftarrow \perp] \oplus f[x \leftarrow \top] = \top$. Consequently, h is the remaining sub-formula of f, i.e., $h = f[\alpha]$ where $\alpha : X \mapsto \perp$ assigns $\perp$ to all variables in X. Henceforth, we write $\mathcal{C}(f)$ to denote the maximal set of variables that can be factorized out of f via Lemma 5, i.e., $\mathcal{C}(f) = \{x \mid x \in \mathrm{Var}(f), f[x \leftarrow \perp] \oplus f[x \leftarrow \top] = \top\}$. Furthermore, call $f = f^{\mathrm{lin}} \oplus f^{\mathrm{nl}}$ the maximal factorization, where $f^{\mathrm{lin}} = \bigoplus_{x \in \mathcal{C}(f)} x$, $f^{\mathrm{nl}} = f[\alpha]$ and $\alpha : \mathcal{C}(f) \mapsto \perp$. Knowing both $\mathcal{C}(f)$ and $\mathcal{D}(f)$ allows us to perform easy hiding and incompleteness checks for f against some linear formula f'. Additionally, $\mathcal{C}(\cdot)$ and $\mathcal{D}(\cdot)$ allow us to approximate the maximal factorization for linear combinations $f = \bigoplus_{i=1}^{n} \phi_i$, where ϕ_i themselves are also formulas.

Lemma 8. *Let $f = \bigoplus_{i=1}^{n} \phi_i$ be a formula with sub-formulas ϕ_i. The variable set $\widehat{\mathcal{C}}(f) = \triangle_{i=1}^{n} \mathcal{C}(\phi_i) \setminus \bigcup_{i=1}^{n} \mathcal{D}(\phi_i^{\mathrm{nl}})$ is an under-approximation of $\mathcal{C}(f)$. Similarly, the set $\widehat{\mathcal{D}}(f) = \triangle_{i=1}^{n} \mathcal{C}(\phi_i) \cup \bigcup_{i=1}^{n} \mathcal{D}(\phi_i^{\mathrm{nl}})$ is an over-approximation of $\mathcal{D}(f)$.*[1]

---

[1] Operator $\triangle$ signifies symmetric difference: $A \triangle B = (A \cup B) \setminus (A \cap B)$.

Algorithm 1: *Danira* algorithm for verifying SIFA resistance

---

$\quad$ **Input** $\quad$: fault detection formulas $\{\delta_1, \ldots, \delta_n\}$, $\delta := \bigvee_{i=1}^{n} \delta_i$
$\qquad\qquad$ masks M, secrets $S = \{s^1, \ldots, s^d\}$
$\quad$ **Output**: **secure** or **unknown**

1 $\;R := M$; $\qquad\qquad\qquad\qquad\qquad\qquad$ // variables that hide
2 $\;K := \emptyset$; $\qquad\qquad\qquad\qquad\qquad\qquad$ // complete secrets
3 $\;$**for** $s \in S$ **do**
4 $\quad\;$ **if** $\mathcal{D}(s) \subseteq \mathcal{D}(\delta)$ **then** $\;K := K \cup \{s\}$; $\qquad$ // mark as complete
5 $\quad\;$ **if** $\mathcal{D}(s) \nsubseteq \mathcal{D}(\delta)$ **then** $\;R := R \cup (\mathcal{D}(s) \cap \mathcal{D}(\delta))$; $\;$ // shares can hide
6 $\;$**if** $K = \emptyset$ **or** $R \cap \mathcal{C}(\delta) \neq \emptyset$ **then return secure**; $\quad$ // incomplete or hidden
7 $\;G := \emptyset$; $\qquad\qquad\qquad\qquad\qquad\qquad$ // basis of δ_i formulas
8 $\;$**for** $i \in \{1, \ldots, n\}$ **do**
9 $\quad\;$ **if** $\forall G' \subseteq G.\, \delta_i \neq \bigoplus_{g \in G'} g$ **then** $G := G \cup \{\delta_i\}$; $\;$ // include δ_i in basis G
10 $\;$**for** $G' \subseteq G$ **do**
11 $\quad\;$ $\phi = \bigoplus_{g \in G'} g$; $\qquad\qquad\qquad\qquad\;$ // comb. of sub-formulas
12 $\quad\;$ **if** $\forall s \in K.\mathcal{D}(s) \nsubseteq \widehat{\mathcal{D}}(\phi)$ **then continue**; $\quad$ // no secrets complete
13 $\quad\;$ **if** $R \cap \widehat{\mathcal{C}}(\phi) \neq \emptyset$ **then continue**; $\qquad\;$ // secrets are hidden
14 $\quad\;$ **return unknown** ; $\qquad\qquad\qquad\;$ // ϕ maybe dependent
15 **return secure** ; $\qquad\qquad\qquad\qquad\;$ // all ϕ independent

---

These two approximations are much easier to compute than the real variable sets $\mathcal{C}(\delta)$ and $\mathcal{D}(\delta)$. Ideally, we first compute $\mathcal{D}(\delta_i)$ and $\mathcal{C}(\delta_i)$ for each of the fault-detection values δ_i using a SAT solver. Afterward, when checking all their linear combinations, we only use fast set computation operations from Lemma 8. Since $\widehat{\mathcal{D}}(\cdot)$ is an over-approximation, it must contain all functional dependencies and possibly some spurious ones. If we show the incompleteness of a secret s with $\widehat{\mathcal{D}}(\cdot)$, we would have gotten the same result with $\mathcal{D}(\cdot)$. Similarly, $\widehat{\mathcal{C}}(\cdot)$ contains a subset of the variables that can be factorized out of the formula. It is still a factorization, although it is not guaranteed to be maximal like $\mathcal{C}(\cdot)$. Therefore, if we show that a secret is hidden by some uniformly random variable using $\widehat{\mathcal{C}}(\cdot)$, it is guaranteed to be hidden.

3.6 Verification Algorithm

In this section, we summarize how the verification algorithm works. In particular, we focus on the order of checks performed by the algorithm and show how they correspond to the previous exposition. As described in Sect. 3.1, the attacker can introduce a fault in any sub-formula ϕ of δ. The verification method summarized in Algorithm 1 is given the faulted δ and its sub-formulas δ_i, the set of masks M, and the set of formulas S representing each secret as a linear combination of its shares. The show algorithm considers only one fault at a time, and our tool *Danira* runs it separately for each possible fault location.

First, the algorithm computes the set K of complete secrets, *i.e.*, secrets for which δ functionally depends on all its shares. Simultaneously, the algorithm

Procedure Chi3: Implementation of a masked KECCAK χ_3 S-Box [10]

Input : $\{a_0, a_1\}, \{b_0, b_1\}, \{c_0, c_1\}, M = \{m_r, m_t\}$
Output: $\{r_0, r_1\}, \{s_0, s_1\}, \{t_0, t_1\}$

1 $m_s := m_r \oplus m_t$;	9 $t_1 := t_1 \oplus x_3$;	17 $r_1 := r_1 \oplus x_3$;	25 $s_1 := s_1 \oplus x_3$;
2 $x_0 := \neg b_0 \wedge c_1$;	10 $x_0 := \neg c_0 \wedge a_1$;	18 $x_0 := \neg a_0 \wedge b_1$;	26 $r_0 := r_0 \oplus a_0$;
3 $x_2 := a_1 \wedge b_1$;	11 $x_2 := b_1 \wedge c_1$;	19 $x_2 := c_1 \wedge a_1$;	27 $t_1 := t_1 \oplus c_1$;
4 $x_1 := \neg b_0 \wedge c_0$;	12 $x_1 := \neg c_0 \wedge a_0$;	20 $x_1 := \neg a_0 \wedge b_0$;	28 $s_0 := s_0 \oplus b_0$;
5 $x_3 := a_1 \wedge b_0$;	13 $x_3 := b_1 \wedge c_0$;	21 $x_3 := c_1 \wedge a_0$;	29 $r_1 := r_1 \oplus a_1$;
6 $r_0 := x_0 \oplus m_r$;	14 $s_0 := x_0 \oplus m_s$;	22 $t_0 := x_0 \oplus m_t$;	30 $t_0 := t_0 \oplus c_0$;
7 $t_1 := x_2 \oplus m_t$;	15 $r_1 := x_2 \oplus m_r$;	23 $s_1 := x_2 \oplus m_s$;	31 $s_1 := s_1 \oplus b_1$;
8 $r_0 := r_0 \oplus x_1$;	16 $s_0 := s_0 \oplus x_1$;	24 $t_0 := t_0 \oplus x_1$;	

computes the set R of uniformly random values that contains all masks M and shares of incomplete secrets $s \notin K$. In the rest of the algorithm, only values in R can hide secrets. If there are no complete secrets in K or a uniformly random variable from R can be factorized out of δ and hides all secrets in K, we know that δ is statistically independent of the secrets S.

Next, the algorithm computes a maximal linearly independent subset G of fault-detection values δ_i. As discussed previously in Lemma 6, it is sufficient to apply Theorem 1 to this subset when proving statistical independence. The algorithm computes the approximations $\widehat{\mathcal{D}}(\phi)$ and $\widehat{\mathcal{C}}(\phi)$ for all possible linear combinations ϕ from G. It uses the approximations to check whether any of the secrets in K are complete in $\widehat{\mathcal{D}}(\phi)$, and if they are, whether any of the random values from R appear in $\widehat{\mathcal{C}}(\phi)$ and hide them. If we were able to show statistical independence of secrets for all ϕ, Algorithm 1 declares the computation secure for the given fault.

Theorem 2. *Algorithm 1 is sound: if it returns **secure**, the analyzed fault in the attack model from Sect. 3.1 is not exploitable via SIFA.*   □

4   Case Studies

This section evaluates our new verification approach against the secured implementations presented by Daemen et al. [10]. *Danira*[2] uses the netlist of a combinatorial circuit as the input. It interprets the inputs as variables and the intermediate computations as Boolean formulas. From a theoretical standpoint, it does not matter whether the analyzed circuit has a state or not because we only consider the outputs after the computation finishes.

In the rest of this section, we consider the SIFA-resistant masked implementations of KECCAK χ_3, all classes of quadratic 4-bit S-Boxes, and an AES S-Box [10]. We argue that without a sophisticated verification method, it is extremely easy to introduce bugs that produce correct computations but break the theoretical SIFA-resistance guarantees.

---

[2] *Danira*'s code is available at https://extgit.iaik.tugraz.at/scos/danira.

Finally, we summarize the performance of *Danira* on several versions of the same designs.

4.1   Masked Keccak χ_3

The KECCAK permutation χ_3 is a simple circuit with three inputs and three outputs used in many lightweight ciphers. Implementing a masked version is straightforward because of its low polynomial degree. Chi3 shows the masked computation of χ_3 proposed by Daemen et al. [10]. The secrets processed by the circuit are $a = a_0 \oplus a_1$, $b = b_0 \oplus b_1$ and $c = c_0 \oplus c_1$, whereas m_r and m_t are used as uniformly random masks. The results of the computation r, s, and t are also split into two shares, respectively. The circuit was designed in such a way that the outputs are used for fault detection. Given two redundant computations of Chi3 with outputs $\{r_0, r_1, s_0, s_1, t_0, t_1\}$ and $\{r'_0, r'_1, s'_0, s'_1, t'_0, t'_1\}$, the fault-detection values are defined as $\delta_1 = r_0 \oplus r'_0, \ldots, \delta_6 = t_1 \oplus t'_1$.

Each line of Chi3 is a possible fault location according to our attack model in Sect. 3.1. Introducing a bit-flip fault means negating the result of one such line in one of the redundant computations. Our verification method goes through each of the fault locations, negates the result at that point in the computation, and generates the fault-detection formulas $\delta_1, \ldots, \delta_6$. We specify $S = \{a, b, c\}$ and $M = \{m_r, m_t\}$, and run Algorithm 1 to see if the considered fault could leak information about the secrets.

We implemented the netlist for Chi3 manually, and *Danira* was able to verify that the design proposed in [10] was indeed SIFA resistant. However, when we synthesized an equivalent RTL design with Yosys, *Danira* reported that it could not prove SIFA resistance. In the synthesized netlist, Yosys introduced a temporary gate $v_0 = \neg b_0$ which it used to simplify Line 2 to $x_0 := v_0 \wedge c_1$ and Line 4 to $x_1 := v_0 \wedge c_0$. Although this makes sense from an optimization perspective because it effectively reduces the size of the circuit by one gate, it breaks the SIFA resistance. A fault at this new gate v_0 in the synthesized design is the same as two faults at Lines 2 and 4. As a result, δ becomes statistically dependent on c, which the attacker can exploit. Unfortunately, this demonstrates that *(1)* an analysis on the gate level is unavoidable and *(2)* they must be implemented manually, as synthesis tools or compilers break SIFA resistance while maintaining functional correctness.

4.2   Masked AES S-Box

Compared to χ_3, the AES S-Box is a significantly more complex circuit of high polynomial degree. The authors of the CHES paper [10] propose a high-level sketch of a SIFA-resistant masked AES S-Box. There are many ways to implement this high-level description and achieving SIFA resistance is not trivial. After several failed attempts, we managed to implement a protected version of the proposed AES S-Box with the help of our new verification tool. We are convinced that correctly protecting a circuit as large as an AES S-Box is infeasible without the help of an automated verification method such as *Danira*.

Table 1. Performance of *Danira* (D) and a modified version of SILVER [25] (S) for different masked designs. Correct (incorrect) designs are denoted by ✔ (✘). In all cases, the reused gate was the exploitable fault location.

Design	Gates	$(\wedge)$	$(\oplus)$	Result	D (s)	S (s)
KECCAK χ_3, full Chi3	37	12	25	✔	0.06	0.24
KECCAK χ_3, reuse $\neg b_0$	36	12	24	✘	0.05	0.07
KECCAK χ_3, reuse $\neg c_0$	36	12	24	✘	0.06	0.12
KECCAK χ_3, reuse $\neg a_0$	36	12	24	✘	0.06	0.18
4-bit perm. $\mathcal{Q}_4^4$ [10]	10	4	6	✔	0.03	0.10
4-bit perm. $\mathcal{Q}_{12}^4$ [10]	20	8	12	✔	0.05	0.16
4-bit perm. $\mathcal{Q}_{293}^4$ [10]	30	12	18	✔	0.05	0.23
4-bit perm. $\mathcal{Q}_{294}^4$ [10]	30	12	18	✔	0.04	0.21
4-bit perm. $\mathcal{Q}_{299}^4$ [10]	50	20	30	✔	0.07	0.41
4-bit perm. $\mathcal{Q}_{300}^4$ [10]	36	12	24	✔	0.06	0.26
AES S-Box, reuse g_{104}	631	144	487	✘	14.67	551.1
AES S-Box, reuse g_{240}	631	144	487	✘	83.28	1336.7
AES S-Box, reuse g_{360}	631	144	487	✘	135.04	1941.7
AES S-Box, full [10]	634	144	490	✔	184.39	3297.4

4.3 Performance Evaluation

This section gives a breakdown of *Danira*'s performance on correctly (and incorrectly) protected implementations. We performed all experiments on a notebook with an eight-core *Intel i7-8550U 1.8GHz* CPU and *16* GiB of memory.

As shown in Table 1, *Danira* instantly verified (or falsified) all tested KECCAK χ_3 and quadratic 4-bit S-Box designs. We also demonstrate that for KECCAK χ_3 and the AES S-Box, even one re-used gate leads to vulnerabilities. *Danira* verifies the SIFA resistance of our implementation in about three minutes. For the AES S-Boxes, *Danira* performs significantly better than a version SILVER [25] which we extended to verify SIFA resistance. However, although this shows *Danira*'s potential, our extension of SILVER with construct as shown in Fig. 1 is not perfect and could be further improved by its authors.

In summary, the results of our experiments in Table 1 indicate that: (1) the over-approximation we introduce in this paper is strong enough to prove SIFA resistance for secure designs, and (2) our verification method applied by *Danira* is fast enough for complex masked implementations.

5 Conclusion

Protecting masked implementations against SIFA is not straightforward. Designers can make mistakes when implementing a specification that is supposed to be secure. Additionally, compilers and synthesis tools can introduce simplifications that break the SIFA-resistance guarantees. *Danira* solves these problems using simple yet effective properties of redundant masked implementations to show whether they are SIFA resistant. As demonstrated by our case studies, *Danira* is able to verify designs that may be used in actual embedded systems. In cases where *Danira* cannot prove the security of a design, it gives a developer detailed debugging information about a problematic fault location.

References

1. Arribas, V., Nikova, S., Rijmen, V.: VerMI: verification tool for masked implementations. In: ICECS (2018)
2. Arribas, V., Wegener, F., Moradi, A., Nikova, S.: Cryptographic fault diagnosis using VerFI. IACR Cryptology ePrint Archive (2019)
3. Bar-El, H., Choukri, H., Naccache, D., Tunstall, M., Whelan, C.: The sorcerer's apprentice guide to fault attacks. Proc. IEEE **94**(2) (2006)
4. Barthe, G., Belaïd, S., Cassiers, G., Fouque, P.-A., Grégoire, B., Standaert, F.-X.: maskVerif: automated verification of higher-order masking in presence of physical defaults. In: Sako, K., Schneider, S., Ryan, P.Y.A. (eds.) ESORICS 2019. LNCS, vol. 11735, pp. 300–318. Springer, Cham (2019). https://doi.org/10.1007/978-3-030-29959-0_15
5. Barthe, G., Belaïd, S., Dupressoir, F., Fouque, P.-A., Grégoire, B., Strub, P.-Y.: Verified proofs of higher-order masking. In: Oswald, E., Fischlin, M. (eds.) EUROCRYPT 2015. LNCS, vol. 9056, pp. 457–485. Springer, Heidelberg (2015). https://doi.org/10.1007/978-3-662-46800-5_18
6. Barthe, G., Dupressoir, F., Faust, S., Grégoire, B., Standaert, F.-X., Strub, P.-Y.: Parallel implementations of masking schemes and the bounded moment leakage model. In: Coron, J.-S., Nielsen, J.B. (eds.) EUROCRYPT 2017. LNCS, vol. 10210, pp. 535–566. Springer, Cham (2017). https://doi.org/10.1007/978-3-319-56620-7_19
7. Biham, E., Shamir, A.: Differential fault analysis of secret key cryptosystems. In: Kaliski, B.S. (ed.) CRYPTO 1997. LNCS, vol. 1294, pp. 513–525. Springer, Heidelberg (1997). https://doi.org/10.1007/BFb0052259
8. Bloem, R., Gross, H., Iusupov, R., Könighofer, B., Mangard, S., Winter, J.: Formal verification of masked hardware implementations in the presence of glitches. In: Nielsen, J.B., Rijmen, V. (eds.) EUROCRYPT 2018. LNCS, vol. 10821, pp. 321–353. Springer, Cham (2018). https://doi.org/10.1007/978-3-319-78375-8_11
9. Boneh, D., DeMillo, R.A., Lipton, R.J.: On the importance of checking cryptographic protocols for faults. In: Fumy, W. (ed.) EUROCRYPT 1997. LNCS, vol. 1233, pp. 37–51. Springer, Heidelberg (1997). https://doi.org/10.1007/3-540-69053-0_4
10. Daemen, J., Dobraunig, C., Eichlseder, M., Groß, H., Mendel, F., Primas, R.: Protecting against statistical ineffective fault attacks. TCHES (2020)
11. Dhooghe, S., Nikova, S.: My gadget just cares for me - how NINA can prove security against combined attacks. In: Jarecki, S. (ed.) CT-RSA 2020. LNCS, vol. 12006, pp. 35–55. Springer, Cham (2020). https://doi.org/10.1007/978-3-030-40186-3_3
12. Dobraunig, C., Eichlseder, M., Gross, H., Mangard, S., Mendel, F., Primas, R.: Statistical ineffective fault attacks on masked AES with fault countermeasures. In: Peyrin, T., Galbraith, S. (eds.) ASIACRYPT 2018. LNCS, vol. 11273, pp. 315–342. Springer, Cham (2018). https://doi.org/10.1007/978-3-030-03329-3_11

13. Dobraunig, C., Eichlseder, M., Korak, T., Mangard, S., Mendel, F., Primas, R.: SIFA: exploiting ineffective fault inductions on symmetric cryptography. TCHES (2018)
14. Dobraunig, C., Mangard, S., Mendel, F., Primas, R.: Fault attacks on nonce-based authenticated encryption: application to Keyak and Ketje. In: Cid, C., Jacobson, M., Jr. (eds.) SAC 2018. LNCS, vol. 11349, pp. 257–277. Springer, Cham (2019). https://doi.org/10.1007/978-3-030-10970-7_12
15. Faust, S., Grosso, V., Merino Del Pozo, S., Paglialonga, C., Standaert, F.-X.: Composable masking schemes in the presence of physical defaults & the robust probing model. TCHES (2018)
16. Fuhr, T., Jaulmes, É., Lomné, V., Thillard, A.: Fault attacks on AES with faulty ciphertexts only. In: FDTC (2013)
17. Gao, P., Xie, H., Zhang, J., Song, F., Chen, T.: Quantitative verification of masked arithmetic programs against side-channel attacks. In: TACAS (2019)
18. Gao, P., Zhang, J., Song, F., Wang, C.: Verifying and quantifying side-channel resistance of masked software implementations. TOSEM 28(3) (2019)
19. Gigerl, B., Hadzic, V., Primas, R., Mangard, S., Bloem, R.: COCO: co-design and co-verification of masked software implementations on CPUs. In: USENIX (2021)
20. Groß, H., Iusupov, R., Bloem, R.: Generic low-latency masking in hardware. IACR Transactions on Cryptographic Hardware and Embedded Systems (2018)
21. Gross, H., Mangard, S.: Reconciling $d + 1$ masking in hardware and software. In: Fischer, W., Homma, N. (eds.) CHES 2017. LNCS, vol. 10529, pp. 115–136. Springer, Cham (2017). https://doi.org/10.1007/978-3-319-66787-4_6
22. Hadzic, V., Primas, R., Bloem, R.: Proving SIFA protection of masked redundant circuits. CoRR, abs/2107 (2021)
23. Hutter, M., Schmidt, J.-M.: The temperature side channel and heating fault attacks. In: Francillon, A., Rohatgi, P. (eds.) CARDIS 2013. LNCS, vol. 8419, pp. 219–235. Springer, Cham (2014). https://doi.org/10.1007/978-3-319-08302-5_15
24. Ishai, Y., Sahai, A., Wagner, D.: Private circuits: securing hardware against probing attacks. In: Boneh, D. (ed.) CRYPTO 2003. LNCS, vol. 2729, pp. 463–481. Springer, Heidelberg (2003). https://doi.org/10.1007/978-3-540-45146-4_27
25. Knichel, D., Sasdrich, P., Moradi, A.: SILVER – statistical independence and leakage verification. In: Moriai, S., Wang, H. (eds.) ASIACRYPT 2020. LNCS, vol. 12491, pp. 787–816. Springer, Cham (2020). https://doi.org/10.1007/978-3-030-64837-4_26
26. Kocher, P., Jaffe, J., Jun, B.: Differential power analysis. In: Wiener, M. (ed.) CRYPTO 1999. LNCS, vol. 1666, pp. 388–397. Springer, Heidelberg (1999). https://doi.org/10.1007/3-540-48405-1_25
27. Quisquater, J.-J., Samyde, D.: ElectroMagnetic Analysis (EMA): measures and counter-measures for smart cards. In: Attali, I., Jensen, T. (eds.) E-smart 2001. LNCS, vol. 2140, pp. 200–210. Springer, Heidelberg (2001). https://doi.org/10.1007/3-540-45418-7_17
28. Ramezanpour, K., Ampadu, P., Diehl, W.: A statistical fault analysis methodology for the ascon authenticated cipher. In: HOST (2019)
29. Saha, S., Jap, D., Roy, D.B., Chakraborty, A., Bhasin, S., Mukhopadhyay, D.: A framework to counter statistical ineffective fault analysis of block ciphers using domain transformation and error correction. TIFS (2020)

Verification by Gambling on Program Slices

Murad Akhundov[1]([✉]), Federico Mora[2], Nick Feng[1], Vincent Hui[1],
and Marsha Chechik[1]

[1] University of Toronto, Toronto, Canada
{murad,fengnick,vhui,chechik}@cs.toronto.edu
[2] University of California, Berkeley, Berkeley, USA
fmora@cs.berkeley.edu

Abstract. Automated software verification is a computationally hard
problem that is often exasperated by irrelevant context. Existing verification engines address this problem with slicing techniques that are
either too cautious, producing large verification condition queries, or too
aggressive, sacrificing soundness. In this paper, we present a novel technique, called Qicc, that is aggressive, sound, and "a little risky." Specifically, we use procedure extraction to generate a small set of verification
queries that we check with existing verification engines. If any query in
the set passes verification, then the original program will pass verification. However, there is no guarantee that such a query will exist, so Qicc
may waste time searching. We study the effectiveness of Qicc when it is
combined with two different verification engines, finding that Qicc's extra
cost is small while the rewards it brings to the analysis are significant.
We evaluated Qicc on a case study—the verification of a cryptographic
function in BusyBox—and found that Qicc succeeds when paired with
two different verifiers, while both verifiers are unsuccessful on their own.

1 Introduction

Automated software verification tools take as input an implementation annotated with specifications and aim to return a correctness proof, or a counterexample. Over the years, a wide range of automated verification techniques have
been proposed, including those based on bounded model checking, k-induction,
and predicate abstraction [3,6,9,11]. These techniques differ substantially and
succeed on different kinds of verification tasks; however, they all have one thing
in common: a better encoded problem leads to better engine performance [21].

One technique for improving problem encodings is *program slicing* [4,23].
Program slicing techniques take a program and a slicing criterion, and return a
subset of the input program based on that criterion. In the realm of verification,
these techniques have been used as sound pre-processing steps that eliminate
irrelevant context and focus the underlying verification engine on the properties
in question. For example, verification engines usually eliminate lines of code that
cannot affect assertions. When verification problems are too large, recent work
has suggested using slicing as an unsound pre-processing step, the idea being

© Springer Nature Switzerland AG 2021
Z. Hou and V. Ganesh (Eds.): ATVA 2021, LNCS 12971, pp. 266–282, 2021.
https://doi.org/10.1007/978-3-030-88885-5_18

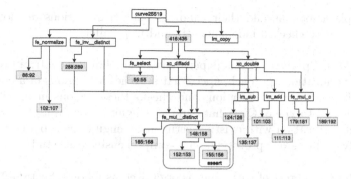

Fig. 1. Interprocedural region hierarchies of `curve25519`. Every node is a region. White nodes are functions, and blue nodes are parts of functions labeled by corresponding start and end lines of code. Arrows denote region containment. For example, the function `curve25519` calls the function `fe_select` inside a region at lines 416–436.

that an approximate answer is better than no answer at all [7]. In this paper, we seek to retain the soundness of the former use, while achieving the reductions of the latter use. We do this with a novel application of a classic program slicing technique called *procedure extraction* [16]. Procedure extraction takes a program and a set of program locations, and returns a minimal procedure that captures the behaviour of these locations. Traditionally, procedure extraction has been applied to program refactoring by automatically grouping features into functions [16]. The main challenge in applying it to verification is in deciding which program locations to extract. If we extract too many locations, the slice will remain large; if we extract too few, the slice may miss some important context.

In this paper, we propose an approach that "gambles" on a few well-thought-out slices. The cost of each gamble is small, but the reward is potentially big, often allowing us to solve previously non-terminating cases. To get an intuition for our approach, consider the example in Fig. 1 which shows the *interprocedural region hierarchies* of the `curve25519` function inside BusyBox's TLS library. We formally define regions in Sect. 2. For now, consider regions to be contiguous portions of the control-flow graph of a program with a single entry location and a single exit location. Regions can be nested, and Fig. 1 shows this nesting for `curve25519`. `curve25519` is a Diffie-Hellman function that takes a private key and returns a corresponding public key using elliptic curve cryptography, and our goal is to check whether its assertions hold. We highlight one of these assertions with a red "assert" in Fig. 1. When given the entire program as input, existing verification engines, e.g., CBMC [5] and UltimateAutomizer [14], struggle to prove this assertion (and the other assertions in the program) because they are overwhelmed by the size of the problem. However, as we discuss in more detail in Sect. 4.5, the part of the program inside the red rectangle is sufficient to prove that this assertion always holds, and focusing verifiers on this part of the program is sufficient to have them succeed. Our approach searches the regions of a program until it finds such a sufficient part of the program. When there are multiple assertions and their candidate sufficient regions do not overlap, assertions can be checked independently and in parallel.

Contributions. Specifically, this paper makes the following contributions. 1. We develop a verification approach, Qicc, that searches for regions of a control-flow graph sufficient to prove assertions and checks these regions in parallel. 2. We implement a prototype of Qicc that handles a significant subset of C, and allows concurrent verification with existing verification engines as a parameter. 3. We empirically evaluate our prototype on a comprehensive case study.

Organization. The rest of this paper is organized as follows. Section 2 gives the necessary formal background. Section 3 describes our approach and proves its correctness. Section 4.1 reports on the implementation. Section 4 evaluates the performance of Qicc when paired with different verification engines. Section 5 surveys related approaches. We conclude in Sect. 6.

2   Background

This section provides a brief overview of *control-flow automata* (CFA) which we use to model programs and specifications; *regions* which are the isolated components of CFAs that can be verified in isolation; and *cyclic region bodies* which are a special case of regions that Qicc identifies and attempts to verify.

Control Flow Automata. We represent programs using *control flow automata (CFA)* borrowed from Beyer et al. [2]. Formally, a CFA (L, l_i, L_f, V, G) has a finite set of program locations L, an initial location l_i, a set of final locations L_f, a finite set of program variables V, and a finite set of control-flow edges $G \in L \times O \times L$. The set O of program operations contains assignment and assumption operations. *Assignments* are denoted by $v \leftarrow t$, where v is a program variable in V and t is a term of the same type as v. *Assumptions* are denoted by $[b]$, where b is a boolean term. *Terms* are defined inductively: constants and variables are terms, and a function application $f(t_1, t_2...t_n)$ of function $f : D_1, D_2...D_n \rightarrow D_r$ over input terms $t_1, t_2...t_n$ of type $D_1, D_2...D_n$ yields a term of type D_r. A state of a CFA is a valuation for all variables in V together with a location.

A control-flow edge $l \xrightarrow{o} l'$ represents the transfer of control from location l to l' after successfully executing an operation o. An assignment $v \leftarrow t$ is successfully executed on edge $l \xrightarrow{v \leftarrow t} l'$ if the value of v at state $s' = \{\sigma', l'\}$ is the same as the value of t at state $s = \{\sigma, l\}$. An assumption is successfully executed on edge $l \xrightarrow{[b]} l'$ if b evaluates to $\top$ at state $s = \{\sigma, l\}$. A *program path* $l_1 \xrightarrow{o_1} l_2 \xrightarrow{o_2} ... \xrightarrow{o_n} l_n$ is a sequence of edges representing a transition from the source location l_1 to the target location l_n. The path is *feasible* if every operation on the path can be successfully executed in sequence. The path is *complete* if the source location is l_i and the target location is some $l_f \in L_f$.

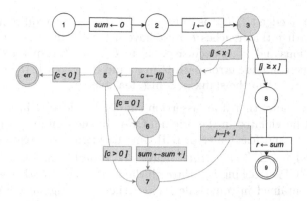

Fig. 2. An illustration of a region r (highlighted in red) in a CFA (based on the motivating example of Feng et al. [10]). The region has 3 as the initial location, and 3 and l_{err} as its final locations. A path from 1 to any location in the region must have a local suffix in r, e.g., the path 12345 has a local suffix 345. (Color figure online)

Program Safety and Assertions. We express safety properties with assertions in the program. Intuitively, an assertion takes a predicate p as input, and checks whether p evaluates to $\top$ while executing the program. We capture this intuition formally in CFAs, by representing assertions as control-flow edges $l \xrightarrow{[\neg p]} l_{err}$, where the target location l_{err} is a special final location representing assertion violation, and p is the asserted predicate. We require l_{err} to be reachable only through assertion edges. We say a path is *an error path* if it ends in l_{err}. An error path is *complete* if it starts from l_i, and *feasible* if every operation on the path is successfully executed.

Definition 1 (Program Safety). *A program is safe with respect to program assertions if and only if its CFA has no complete and feasible error path. In this case, we say that the program satisfies the assertion or property. If a program is not safe, then we say that the program violates the assertion or property.*

Sub-CFA and Region. $f' = (L', l'_i, L'_f, V, G')$ is a sub-CFA of $f = (L, l_i, L_f, V, G)$, where $L' \subseteq L$, $l_{err} \in L'_f$ and $G' \subseteq G$. A region r is a special sub-CFA that further requires that every path that starts at l_i and ends at some location $l' \in L' \setminus l_{err}$ must contain a local suffix which starts at l'_i and contains locations and edges exclusively from L' and G', respectively. This requirement allows r to be treated as a standalone CFA. Figure 2 illustrates an example of r (highlighted in red) in a CFA. Since l_{err} appears in both f and r, we have the following property:

Theorem 1 (Error Suffix). *Suppose $r = (L', l'_i, L'_f, V, G')$ is a region of CFA $f = (L, l_i, L_f, V, G)$, and r contains an edge $l \xrightarrow{o} l_{err}$. If f has a complete error path p that ends with $l \xrightarrow{o} l_{err}$, then there exists a complete error path p' in r, and $|p| \geq |p'|$. Moreover, if path p is feasible, then p' is also feasible.*

Proof. Since the edge $l \xrightarrow{o} l_{err}$ is in G', and $l \in L'$, by the requirement of region, every error path p that reaches l must have a local suffix that starts at l'_i and contains locations and edges exclusively from L' and G', respectively. Therefore, the suffix is the complete error path p' in r, and $|p| \geq |p'|$. If the complete error path p is feasible, then the suffix p' is also feasible. $\qquad\square$

Theorem 1 shows that if an assertion cannot be violated in a region r, then it also cannot be violated in the original CFA. In the example in Fig. 2, if there are no complete and feasible error paths in the highlighted region that reaches l_{err} through edge 5 $\xrightarrow{[c<0]} l_{err}$, then there is no complete and feasible error path in the original CFA reaching l_{err} through the same edge. In other words, if every assertion is contained in some safe region, then the original CFA is also safe. Therefore, a region is a sound program slice for assertion verification.

Domination, Backedge, Reducibility, and Strongly Connected Components. Let f be a CFA (L, l_i, L_f, V, G). A location $i \in L$ *dominates* a location $j \in L$ if every path from l_i to j passes through i. An edge $j \xrightarrow{op} i$ is *a backedge* if i dominates j. Graph G is *reducible* if it becomes acyclic after removing all of its backedges. A *strongly connected component* (SCC) S of f is the maximal sub-graph of G with the property that there is a path from every location in S to every other location in S. A node i is an *entry point* of S if $i \in S$ and there exists a location $n \notin S$ and an edge $n \to i$. Our definition of *reducible* is equivalent to the following: a CFA is reducible if every strongly connected sub-CFA has a single entry [13].

Cyclic Regions and Cyclic Region Bodies. Let f be a CFA (L, l_i, L_f, V, G), and e be a backedge $j \xrightarrow{op} i \in G$. The *cyclic region* of e is defined to be the smallest set of locations L' and edges G' such that: (1) $i, j \in L'$, $e \in G'$, (2) if some location $a \neq i$ is in L' then its predecessors location b ($\exists$ edge $b \xrightarrow{op} a \in G$) is also in L', and (3) G' is a strongly connected component. We call i the *head* of the cyclic region. A cyclic region can be also seen as a region $r = (L', i, L'_f, V, G')$, where L'_f is the set of final locations in L_f or locations with external edges $e'_{ext} \in G \setminus G'$. The inclusion of predecessors up to i in condition (2) ensures that every complete path to some location $l \in L'$ must have a local suffix that starts with i. In the example in Fig. 2, the highlighted region is a cyclic region of backedge 7 $\xrightarrow{j \leftarrow j+1}$ 3 with region head 3.

The *body* of a cyclic region r is $b = (L', i, L'_f, V, G'')$, where the graph G'' is constructed from G' by removing all the backedges to the region head i. The body of a cyclic region r is also a region: for every local suffix p in r there exists a local suffix of p which does not contain the removed backedges of G'', by taking the suffix from the last appearance of the region head in p. For the example in Fig. 2, we obtain the highlighted region r by excluding the backedge 7 $\xrightarrow{j \leftarrow j+1}$ 3 from r's graph. The path 34567345 in r has a local suffix 345 in the cyclic region.

3   Qicc

The goal of Qicc is to expedite verification of assertions by trying to remove irrelevant context. Qicc is aggressive, in that it attempts to solve the problem

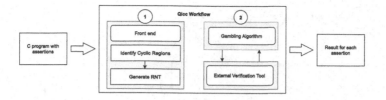

Fig. 3. Qicc architecture

with the least amount of context possible and then gradually adds context until it is sufficient. It would be too expensive to attempt every possible region, so Qicc prioritizes those that are easy to identify, quick to check, and likely to work. Specifically, Qicc prioritizes cyclic region bodies, as defined in Sect. 2. This heuristic is good because cycles can be very expensive to handle—especially with techniques like Bounded Model Checking [3]. For the example in Fig. 4a, Qicc starts by trying to verify the green region in isolation, and if that context is insufficient, it attempts a larger region (green and red). If that context is still insufficient, Qicc will attempt the entire CFA for the complete context.

In this section, we describe how Qicc works. We begin with cyclic region identification (front-end step in Fig. 3) and show why checking region bodies is sound. We then describe the verification step that gambles on program slices and calls an external verifier X. We refer to the combination as Qicc+X.

3.1 Cyclic Region Identification

Algorithm 1: RNT Gen	**Algorithm 2:** InnerFinder
Data: Reducible CFA, f	**Data:** Region γ
Result: Region Nesting Tree T	**Mutate:** Region Nesting Tree T
1 $\sigma \leftarrow$ new Stack()	**Result:** Set of regions inside γ
/* T is an association map */	1 components $\leftarrow$ Tarjan(γ)
2 T.addChild(ROOT, f)	2 InnerRegions $\leftarrow$ set()
3 $\sigma \leftarrow$ push(σ, f)	3 **for** $S \leftarrow$ components **do**
4 **while** $\neg$isEmpty(σ) **do**	4 $\quad$ **if** size(S) > 1 **then**
5 $\quad \gamma \leftarrow$ pop(σ)	5 $\quad\quad S_{body} \leftarrow$ RegionBody(S)
6 $\quad$ IRs$\leftarrow$ InnerFinder(γ, T)	6 $\quad\quad T$.addChild(γ, S_{body})
7 $\quad \sigma \leftarrow$ pushAll(σ, IRs)	7 $\quad\quad$ InnerRegions.add(S_{body})
8 **return** T	8 **return** InnerRegions

The first step of our approach is to identify all cyclic regions in the input program's CFA. Suppose $r_1 = (L_1, i_1, L_{f1}, V, G_1)$ and $r_2 = (L_2, i_2, L_{f2}, V, G_2)$ are two cyclic regions in a CFA f. We say that r_1 is an inner region of r_2 if $L_1 \subseteq L_2$, $G_1 \subseteq G_2$, and r_2's head i_2 dominates r_1's head i_1. A *Region Nesting Tree* (RNT) T for the CFA f is a tree of *cyclic region bodies* based on the nesting relationship. The root of T is f and its children are the bodies of cyclic regions that are not nested in other cyclic regions. If r_1 is nested in r_2, then r_1's body b_1 is *a descendent* of r_2's body b_2. b_1 is *a direct child* of b_2 if b_2 is the unique immediate

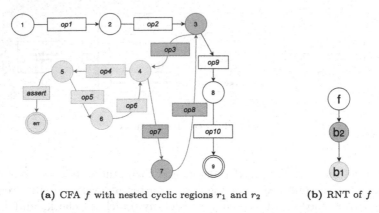

(a) CFA f with nested cyclic regions r_1 and r_2 **(b)** RNT of f

Fig. 4. (a) An illustration of a CFA f with nested cyclic regions. Region r_1 (green) of backedge 6 $\xrightarrow{op6}$ 4 has locations 4,5,6 and l_{err}. Region r_2 (green and red) of backedge 7 $\xrightarrow{op8}$ 3 has locations 3,4,5,6,7 and l_{err}. r_1 is an inner region of r_2 since r_2's head 3 dominates r_1's head 4, and r_1 is a sub-CFA of r_2. (b) The *region nesting tree* (RNT) of f where b_1 and b_2 are the body of regions of r_1 and r_2, respectively.

ancestor of b_1. Figure 4b shows the RNT T of the CFA f in Fig. 4a. The root of T is f. r_2's body b_2 is a direct child f. r_1's body b_1 is a direct child of b_2, which is also the leaf of T.

The identification algorithm is described in Algorithm 1. It takes as input a *reducible* CFA f and returns all cyclic regions, organized in an RNT T. Algorithm 1 first makes f to be the root of T (line 2), and pushes f into a stack σ (line 3), which is the set of sub-CFAs that may have inner cyclic regions. Algorithm 1 pops a sub-CFA γ from σ, and identifies the inner regions in γ by calling InnerFinder (Algorithm 2). Algorithm 2 first identifies all *Strongly Connected Components (SCCs)* in γ using Tarjan's Algorithm [22] (line 1). Since f is assumed to be reducible, every SCC S in γ is a cyclic region. Therefore, S's body S_{body} is added as a child of γ in T (line 6). Notice that S_{body} is not an SCC because the backedge to the *entry* is removed. Therefore, we push every identified S_{body} onto σ (line 7 in Algorithm 1) to find inner cyclic regions. The algorithm continues popping sub-CFAs from σ until it becomes empty, and finally returns T.

In the example in Fig. 4a, Algorithm 1 first identified r_2 as the SCC of f, and added r_2's body b_2 (backedge 7 $\xrightarrow{op8}$ 3 is removed) as a child of f in T. Then the algorithm searched on b_2 for SCC, and identified r_1. r_1's body b_1 (backedge 6 $\xrightarrow{op6}$ 4 is removed) is added as b_2's child. Finally, the algorithm failed to find SCC in b_2, and returned T.

Theorem 2 (RNT Gen Correctness). *Every node in the RNT T returned by Algorithm 1 is either f or the body of some cyclic region in f.*

Proof. Every node is added to T by finding an SCC of a sub-CFA of f, treating S as a cyclic region, and adding the body of S to T (line 6 of InnerFinder).

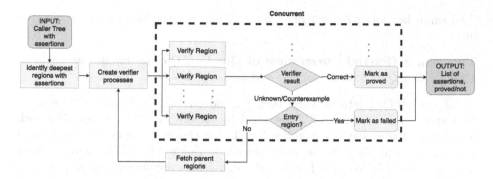

Fig. 5. The concurrent Gambling algorithm.

Therefore, it is sufficient to show that for every SCC S explored by `InnerFinder`, S is indeed a cyclic region of f.

In the first iteration, `InnerFinder` explores f. By the definition of SCCs, the `components` at line 6 of `InnerFinder` are all sub-CFAs of f, and are all cyclic (every node can reach every other node). Since f is reducible, every SCC including the members of `components` will have a single entry point and will be reducible (since sub-CFAs cannot introduce new edges into existing cycles). Let S_i be the ith SCC of `components` and let i be its single entry point. There must be a backedge e to i or else i would not be in the SCC. Therefore, by the definition of cyclic regions, the cyclic region of e is exactly S_i, as desired. In subsequent iterations the same argument is repeated, but with a new reducible CFA given to `InnerFinder`.   □

Theorem 2 together with Theorem 1 ensure that every node in the RNT is a sound program slice to be verified against assertions. This is important for establishing the correctness of Qicc's verification process.

3.2 Gambling

The RNT T returned by Algorithm 1 is a tree of possible regions that Qicc can verify to establish safety for the input CFA f. For every assertion edge $e = l \xrightarrow{assert} l_{err}$ in f, Qicc identifies the initial region $b \in T$ where no descendent of b contains the edge e. Qicc then verifies the assertion e in b by calling a verifier. If verification succeeds, then e is marked safe, and Qicc moves to the next assertion. If verification fails, then Qicc verifies the parent of b, and repeats the verification process by climbing up T until the root f is verified. Qicc returns "safe" if and only if every assertion is marked safe. Qicc returns an assertion violation if and only if some assertion is violated in T's root, f. For an input f in Fig. 4a and the RNT in Fig. 4b, Qicc identifies b_1 as the initial region that contains the assertion edge $e = 5 \xrightarrow{assert} l_{err}$, and verifies it against e. If the verification fails, then b_1's parent b_2 is checked. If the verification on b_2 still fails, then the entire CFA f is verified with the complete context. Qicc returns "safe" if e cannot be violated in one of b_1, b_2 or f, and returns "unsafe" if e is violated in f.

Theorem 3 (Partial Correctness of Qicc). *If Qicc terminates on an input CFA f, then Qicc returns "safe" if and only if f is safe.*

Proof. $\Longrightarrow$: If Qicc returns "safe", then f is indeed safe: By Theorem 2, we know that every node in the RNT T returned by Algorithm 1 is a region. For each assertion, if there exists a region $r \in T$ such that the assertion cannot be violated in r (safe region), then the assertion cannot be violated in f (Theorem 1). Since Qicc returns "safe" when it finds a safe region for every assertion, no assertion can be violated in f, and f is safe.

$\Longleftarrow$: If f is safe, then Qicc returns "safe": Suppose f is "safe", then f is a safe region where no assertion is violated. Since f is a node in the RNT T, Qicc eventually verifies f against all assertions inside, and returns "safe".

Optimizations: Batch Verification and Concurrent Verification. We highlight two key optimizations of Qicc, *batch verification* and *concurrent verification*. Instead of checking every assertion separately in a region b, *batch verification* allows all assertions to be verified in b at the same time. If verification is successful, then all assertions in b are marked safe. If verification is unsuccessful, the violated assertion is disabled in b, and b is verified again with the rest of assertions until every assertion is either safe or disabled in b. When batch verification is enabled, *concurrent verification* allows two regions r_1 and r_2 in the RNT T to be verified concurrently if they contain different assertions, Fig. 5 displays the logic that can be done concurrently. If two regions have some shared assertions, then the verification result is shared and propagated from one to the other. We evaluate the impact of these optimizations in the next section.

4   Evaluation

In this section, we describe a prototype implementation of Qicc, report on the results of a systematic evaluation, and present a case-study.

4.1   Implementation

We implemented the Qicc front-end region identification and the RNT generation algorithms in OCaml as CIL plugins [20]. We used TypeScript to implement the gambling algorithm to interface with the underlying solvers. Our implementation is limited to a subset of C without recursion, and focuses on a restricted version of cyclic regions which corresponds to the intuitive notion of loops. In addition, our implementation only supports regions with a single entry and where the backedge is not a goto statement. Our gambling algorithm does not support mutual recursion, as it would form a cycle in the verification task tree, but lack of support for regular recursion and regions described are implementation-based. Qicc can be parametrized by different verifiers – the current implementation interfaces with CBMC and Ultimate Automizer [5,14]. We refer to these instances as Qicc+CBMC and Qicc+UA, respectively. Qicc interacts with the verifiers by extracting each selected region as a function, and the verifier is provided with an entry function for each step in the gambling algorithm. Please refer to supplementary material for the tool source and usage instructions[1].

4.2 Experimental Design

In this section, we evaluate Qicc's performance as a slicer for program verification techniques and report the performance advantage Qicc provides when coupled with different verifiers; we first study its effect on bounded-model-checking [3] (i.e., Qicc+CBMC) before extending the study to other techniques. Since Qicc was designed to take advantage of cases where region bodies are sufficient to prove the assertion, we say that Qicc *hits* when that is the case and *misses* otherwise. We aim, in particular, to answer the following research questions:

RQ1: What is the benefit of Qicc+CBMC when it hits? What is the cost of Qicc+CBMC when it misses?
RQ2: Does the performance benefit of Qicc extend to other verifiers?
RQ3: Can Qicc scale to large, real-world, programs?

To answer these questions, we first present a thorough systematic comparison of Qicc+CBMC with CBMC, to assess benefits of a hit and costs of a miss in different scenarios. Second, we present a smaller systematic study using Ultimate Automizer (UA) [14] (i.e., Qicc+UA vs. UA) that shows how our technique has potential beyond BMCs. Third, we show how Qicc+CBMC and Qicc+UA were able to quickly prove that array bounds are respected in a real-world program while neither CBMC nor UA were able to terminate on this example. All experiments were conducted on Ubuntu 18.04 with 8 GB of memory, and a quad-core Intel Core i7 processor at 1.8 Ghz.

4.3 RQ1: Bounded Model Checking Systematic Analysis

Since Qicc's main goal is to reduce the performance penalty caused by cycles, we compared Qicc+CBMC and CBMC on 33 different configurations of synthetic loops and the benchmark as-is (baseline case).

Loop Bounds. We first categorize loops by their bound type: *small static bounds vs. large static bounds*, and *arbitrary/unbounded*. The bound type estimates the difficulty of verification for a bounded model checker (BMC): loops with small static bounds are cheap for a BMC to unroll, and only a small number of unrollings is necessary to convert these into equivalent loop-free programs. Loops with large static bounds are usually expensive to unroll

```
1 int main(){
2   int n, x = 1;
3   while (n < 1000){
4     assert(x == 1);
5     n += x;}}
```

Fig. 6. An program with an assertion inside a loop

[1] https://github.com/MuradAkh/Qicc.

(a) Baseline/Linear

(b) Single 1

(c) Single 2

```
1 [fact]
2 [assert]
```

```
1 loop:
2     [fact]
3     [assert]
```

```
1 [fact]
2 loop:
3     [assert]
```

(d) Double 1

(e) Double 2

(f) Double 3

```
1 loop:
2     loop:
3         [fact]
4         [assert]
```

```
1 loop:
2     [fact]
3     loop:
4         [assert]
```

```
1 [fact]
2 loop:
3     loop:
4         [assert]
```

Fig. 7. Loop structures used to generate synthetic cases for the systematic study

and solve: the complexity of the loop body and degree of internal nesting both increase its difficulty. Lastly, loops with arbitrary or nondeterministic bounds cannot be verified successfully with a BMC because BMC cannot statically determine the number of necessary loop unrollings. For the purpose of our evaluation, we used 10 and 200 as small and large loop bounds, respectively.

Loop Structure Scenarios. We create six general categories of relationships between loops and assertions to perform our analysis. We illustrate these relationships in Fig. 7, where *assert* denotes the location of the assertion, and *fact* denotes the location of *the furthest fact* required to guarantee the assertion always holds. For example, in Fig. 6, to prove that x == 1 on line 5, we need to know that x was initialised to 1 on line 2. In scenarios Single 2 and Double 3, Qicc is guaranteed to miss, as a required fact is outside of the loop. In the baseline scenario, Qicc is expected to perform as well as the underlying tool (plus a small baseline overhead). In Double 1 and Single 1, Qicc is guaranteed to hit, as all the necessary information lies within the inner loop. Finally, in Double 2, Qicc is guaranteed to miss once and then hit, as the furthest fact is between two loops. Figure 6 falls into Single 2 scenario. In each of these scenarios, we will vary the loop bounds to create cases.

Experiments. Every valid combination of loop structure and bound type yields 34 scenarios - one baseline scenario, 3 loop bounds for both of the single loop scenarios, and 9 permutations of loop bounds for all three of the double loop scenarios. We used 14 existing benchmarks adapted from SV-COMP [1] to generate 476 (14 * 34) synthetic scenarios. This process involved adding synthetic loops; loops that were already present in the SV-COMP benchmark were left as-is. For all runs, we enabled the unwinding-assertions command-line option and set the unrolling limit to 200. When the unwinding assertions option is disabled, unbounded loops are considered to have the unrolling limit n as the bound. We ran all experiments with a 600 s timeout.

Table 1. Instances solved by CBMC and Qicc+CBMC.

Bounds/Structures	Solved instances, CBMC/Qicc+CBMC				
	Single 1	Single 2	Double 1	Double 2	Double 3
Small	13/13	13/13	8/13	13/13	13/13
Large	7/13	13/13	4/13	7/13	13/13
Arbitrary	0/13	0/0	0/13	0/0	0/0
Small/large			6/13	13/13	13/13
Small/arbitrary			0/13	0/0	0/0
Large/small			6/13	7/13	13/13
Large/arbitrary			0/13	0/0	0/0
Arbitrary/small			0/13	0/13	0/0
Arbitrary/large			0/13	0/13	0/0

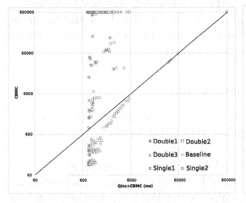 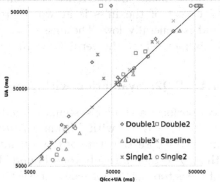

Fig. 8. Systematic study runtimes, CBMC vs Qicc+CBMC

Fig. 9. Systematic study runtimes, UA vs Qicc+UA

Results and Analysis. Table 1 displays the number of solved instances. The columns represent different loop structures introduced earlier, and the rows represent possible bounds for loops in those structures. Qicc+CBMC is always able to solve instances that CBMC solves; in addition, Qicc is able to handle other instances where it hits, specifically in Double 1, Double 2, and Single 1 categories.

Figure 8 plots the runtime of CBMC vs. Qicc+CBMC on all generated cases. The figure shows that in scenarios where Qicc was guaranteed to hit (Single 1 and Double 1), the performance benefit of Qicc+CBMC was very substantial, and Qicc+CBMC was able to solve 19 (out of 39 in this category) and 93 (out of 126) more cases than CBMC, respectively. For cases where Qicc was guaranteed to miss (Double 3 and Single 2), the overhead was very manageable, and Qicc+CBMC was able to solve the same number of instances as CBMC within the time bound. In the case of Double 2, where Qicc missed once and hit once,

Table 2. The number of solved instances in the systematic study, by loop structure

Bounds/Structures	Number of solved instances					
	Baseline	Single 1	Single 2	Double 1	Double 2	Double 3
UA	9	8	8	6	6	8
Qicc+UA	9	9	9	9	9	8

the timing benefit was still significant, and Qicc+CBMC was able to solve 89 (out of 126) more cases than CBMC. We can also see that our technique is most helpful with large loops, although in Double 1 scenario Qicc is able to solve more cases even with only small loops. In the baseline case (with no synthetic loops and no opportunity for Qicc to hit), both configurations solve 13/14 instances.

Answer to RQ1: When Qicc hits, its potential performance benefit is significant, and can make the difference between CBMC terminating and not terminating. The cost of the miss is at worst proportional to the depth of the program, and is generally low. The misses are proportionally more impactful on simpler examples, where the verification cost is small anyway.

4.4   RQ2: Evaluation with Automata Verifier

We perform a similar systematic analysis to the one described in Sect. 4.3 but replacing CBMC with Ultimate Automizer (UA) [14] as the underlying verifier. We chose the state-of-the-art automata-based model checker UA to show that Qicc generalizes beyond bounded-model-checking techniques, and because of UA's top-tier performance at SV-COMP [1]. We used the same loop structure scenarios as in the BMC evaluation. Unlike in the BMC evaluation, the loop bound was not varied as we found that it had no direct impact on UA's performance. Table 2 shows the number of instances solved by UA and Qicc+UA. Qicc+UA was able to solve 8 more cases than UA, particularly when loops were doubly nested (Double 1), and even in scenarios where Qicc missed once and hit once (Double 2). Figure 9 shows runtime for all the runs. As in case of CBMC, the overhead of a miss is minor, as no points are significantly below the diagonal apart from cheap cases. We can see hits can yield substantial performance benefit as a number of cases are significantly above the diagonal. Because of UA's inherent randomness, Qicc+UA sometimes outperformed UA in cases where this was not expected, and vice-versa; the linear cases above the diagonal in Fig. 9 are clear examples of the former. In order to show that the number of successful solves was not affected by randomness, we reran cases where Qicc+UA or UA did not terminate, but no further cases terminated after the re-run.

Answer to RQ2: Qicc shows potential when combined with an automata-based model checking technique. Just like with CBMC, the cost of a miss is low. The benefit of a hit is not as consistent as with CBMC, but Qicc+UA outperforms UA in some cases.

4.5   RQ3: Case Study

We now aim to show that Qicc can be effectively applied to real programs. To do this, we verify static array bounds in a larger (400-line) file from busybox (see networking/tls_fe.c in the busybox repository). The only modification made to the file was the encoding of arrays with pointers, as our implementation does not fully support C array syntax. As part of the study, we added assertions to check bounds of all instances of references to array elements.

Results and Analysis. Neither CBMC nor UA were able to prove the assertions without Qicc. CBMC was unable to complete the unrolling process without running out of memory. The unrolling limit was set to 253, same as the largest loop bound in the program. UA did not run out of memory but did not terminate within 2 h. Qicc+UA terminated in 55s in sequential mode and 35s in concurrent, meanwhile Qicc+CBMC terminated in 13s and 11s for sequential and concurrent modes respectively.

Qicc+UA saw a 20-second performance boost when proving the assertions concurrently (one thread per assertion). The performance benefit was more significant for Qicc+UA as UA has a larger baseline runtime overhead. Our case study contained 13 assertions and our machine had 4 cores, so not all threads were able to run in parallel. Because of this, we expect a significant performance boost on machines with more cores.

Answer to RQ3: Qicc improves the performance of both UA and CBMC on a real example. Furthermore, verifying assertions concurrently yields a substantial performance boost.

4.6   Threats to Validity

We have identified two threats to validity of our evaluation. Our case study was limited to verifying array bounds on a single program, and it may not scale well on other verification tasks, where the fact is further away from an assertion. However, our systematic analysis used a variety of verification tasks with different types of loops, showing that the cost of a miss is often negligible.

Second, we have not investigated the frequency of hits or misses in real-world programs. However, our results show that the cost of a miss is likely far smaller than the benefit of a hit. The cost of a miss can be further reduced using multiple processor cores, allowing a child and a parent region to be executed concurrently.

5   Related Work

In this section, we describe tools and techniques most relevant to our approach. We include problem reduction techniques that either have similar goals, or make similar simplifications to Qicc's region identification and isolation.

Program Slicing. Program slicing, proposed by Weiser et al. [23], is a family of strategies that look for the minimal section of a program relevant to preserving a specific behavior. Slicing complements safety verification techniques in that it scopes down the potential region [8] impacting an assertion; a more specifically scoped region makes verification more tractable. For example, Cook et al. prototyped a CBMC slicer based on approximating the *cone-of-influence* of program variables [7]. Qicc is a program slicer based on assuming *locality* of assertions—that proving assertions is made easier by using and isolating nearby context. Qicc uses *regions* as the program slice for speeding up verification.

Program Transformations for Verification. The problem of exploiting relevant context for program verification was previously explored by Lai et al. [19] and Wei et al. [12] in the context of *mixed semantics*. They outlined a program transformation that lifts out assertions from procedure calls using the fact that execution returns to the caller only when contained assertions are safe. As a side-effect, their transformation also ensures that neighboring context is prioritized to prove an assertion. Their alternative approach starts with information from the outermost context (i.e., the region where an assertion is moved out to) first in contrast to Qicc, which starts from the innermost inlined context.

Differential Program Verifiers. SymDiff [17] and 2Clever [10] are *differential program verifiers* that reason about a program's semantic differences after a change. Both techniques exploit a similar loop transformation to Qicc. SymDiff encodes each loop iteration as an inlined tail-recursive procedure [18]. 2Clever, which specifically targets changes made relative to an unchanging context, applies a variation of our *procedure extraction*-based transformation. SymDiff and 2Clever differ from Qicc as they target differential verification (and, in particular, do not target program safety (error reachability)), and they do not reason about segments in isolation.

Checking Array Properties. To check properties in large arrays, Jana et al. [15] removed loop head and in-lined the body, assigning non-deterministic values to loop variables. Unlike Qicc, their approach still performs verification on the entire program rather than on an isolated segment. However, this approach may be effective in cases where Qicc fails to achieve convergence.

6   Conclusion

Large, complicated programs challenge verification engines which need to discover relevant context in a large space. We implemented a prototype of Qicc, instantiated it with two existing verifiers, CBMC and UA, and evaluated both instantiations, Qicc+CBMC and Qicc+UA, on 476 and 84 systematically generated test cases, respectively. We found that Qicc+CBMC solved 312 cases compared to 162 cases solved by CBMC alone; and Qicc+UA solved 53 cases compared to 45 cases solved by UA alone. We then evaluated both pairs on a case study, verification of a cryptographic function in BusyBox. Qicc+CBMC and Qicc+UA both succeeded in the verification task whereby both CBMC and UA failed. Qicc's overhead is reasonable, while its benefits are large.

To further improve performance, in the future we plan to add a mechanism to reuse information from previously attempted proofs and insert additional facts into loop bodies as assumptions. We also intend to insert additional facts such as constant variables that can be identified using static analysis. We expect that these improvements will greatly expand the number of cases where Qicc is able to improve performance of the underlying verification tool.

Acknowledgments. This work was supported in part by NSF grants CNS-1739816 and CCF-1837132, by the DARPA LOGiCS project under contract FA8750-20-C-0156, by the iCyPhy center, by gifts from Intel, Amazon, and Microsoft, and by NSERC and General Motors.

References

1. Beyer, D.: Advances in automatic software verification: SV-COMP 2020. In: Biere, A., Parker, D. (eds.) TACAS 2020. LNCS, vol. 12079, pp. 347–367. Springer, Cham (2020). https://doi.org/10.1007/978-3-030-45237-7_21
2. Beyer, D., Gulwani, S., Schmidt, D.A.: Combining model checking and data-flow analysis. In: Clarke, E., Henzinger, T., Veith, H., Bloem, R. (eds.) Handbook of Model Checking, pp. 493–540. Springer, Cham (2018). https://doi.org/10.1007/978-3-319-10575-8_16
3. Biere, A., Cimatti, A., Clarke, E.M., Strichman, O., Zhu, Y., et al.: Bounded Model Checking. Adv. Comput. **58**(11), 117–148 (2003)
4. Chalupa, M., Strejček, J.: Evaluation of program slicing in software verification. In: Ahrendt, W., Tapia Tarifa, S.L. (eds.) IFM 2019. LNCS, vol. 11918, pp. 101–119. Springer, Cham (2019). https://doi.org/10.1007/978-3-030-34968-4_6
5. Clarke, E., Kroening, D., Lerda, F.: A tool for checking ANSI-C programs. In: Jensen, K., Podelski, A. (eds.) TACAS 2004. LNCS, vol. 2988, pp. 168–176. Springer, Heidelberg (2004). https://doi.org/10.1007/978-3-540-24730-2_15
6. Clarke, E., Kroening, D., Sharygina, N., Yorav, K.: Predicate abstraction of ANSI-C programs using SAT. Formal Methods Syst. Des. **25**(2–3), 105–127 (2004)
7. Cook, B., et al.: Using model checking tools to triage the severity of security bugs in the Xen hypervisor. In: Proceedings of FMCAD 2020 (2020)
8. DeMillo, R.A., Pan, H., Spafford, E.H.: Critical slicing for software fault localization. ACM SIGSOFT Softw. Eng. Notes **21**(3), 121–134 (1996)
9. Donaldson, A.F., Haller, L., Kroening, D., Rümmer, P.: Software verification using k-induction. In: Yahav, E. (ed.) SAS 2011. LNCS, vol. 6887, pp. 351–368. Springer, Heidelberg (2011). https://doi.org/10.1007/978-3-642-23702-7_26
10. Feng, N., Hui, V., Mora, F., Chechik, M.: Scaling client-specific equivalence checking via impact boundary search. In: Proceedings of ASE 2020. ACM (2020)
11. Gadelha, M.Y., Ismail, H.I., Cordeiro, L.C.: Handling loops in bounded model checking of C programs via k-induction. STTT **19**(1), 97–114 (2017)
12. Gurfinkel, A., Wei, O., Chechik, M.: Model checking recursive programs with exact predicate abstraction. In: Cha, S.S., Choi, J.-Y., Kim, M., Lee, I., Viswanathan, M. (eds.) ATVA 2008. LNCS, vol. 5311, pp. 95–110. Springer, Heidelberg (2008). https://doi.org/10.1007/978-3-540-88387-6_9
13. Hecht, M.S., Ullman, J.D.: Characterizations of reducible flow graphs. J. ACM **21**(3), 367–375 (1974)

14. Heizmann, M., et al.: Ultimate automizer with SMTInterpol. In: Piterman, N., Smolka, S.A. (eds.) TACAS 2013. LNCS, vol. 7795, pp. 641–643. Springer, Heidelberg (2013). https://doi.org/10.1007/978-3-642-36742-7_53
15. Jana, A., Khedker, U.P., Datar, A., Venkatesh, R., Niyas, C.: Scaling bounded model checking by transforming programs with arrays. In: Hermenegildo, M.V., Lopez-Garcia, P. (eds.) LOPSTR 2016. LNCS, vol. 10184, pp. 275–292. Springer, Cham (2017). https://doi.org/10.1007/978-3-319-63139-4_16
16. Komondoor, R., Horwitz, S.: Semantics-preserving procedure extraction. In: Proceedings of POPL 2000, pp. 155–169 (2000)
17. Lahiri, S.K., Hawblitzel, C., Kawaguchi, M., Rebêlo, H.: SYMDIFF: a language-agnostic semantic diff tool for imperative programs. In: Madhusudan, P., Seshia, S.A. (eds.) CAV 2012. LNCS, vol. 7358, pp. 712–717. Springer, Heidelberg (2012). https://doi.org/10.1007/978-3-642-31424-7_54
18. Lahiri, S.K., McMillan, K.L., Sharma, R., Hawblitzel, C.: Differential assertion checking. In: Proceedings of ESEC/FSE 2013, pp. 345–355. ACM (2013)
19. Lai, A., Qadeer, S.: A program transformation for faster goal-directed search. In: Proceedings of FMCAD 2014, pp. 147–154. IEEE (2014)
20. Necula, G.C., McPeak, S., Rahul, S.P., Weimer, W.: CIL: intermediate language and tools for analysis and transformation of C programs. In: Horspool, R.N. (ed.) CC 2002. LNCS, vol. 2304, pp. 213–228. Springer, Heidelberg (2002). https://doi.org/10.1007/3-540-45937-5_16
21. Prasad, M.R., Biere, A., Gupta, A.: A survey of recent advances in SAT-based formal verification. Int. J. Softw. Tools Technol. Transfer **7**(2), 156–173 (2005)
22. Tarjan, R.: Depth-first search and linear graph algorithms. SIAM J. Comput. **1**(2), 146–160 (1972)
23. Weiser, M.: Program slicing. In: Proceedings of ICSE 1981, pp. 439–449. IEEE Press (1981)

Runtime Enforcement of Hyperproperties

Norine Coenen[1], Bernd Finkbeiner[1], Christopher Hahn[1(✉)], Jana Hofmann[1],
and Yannick Schillo[2]

[1] CISPA Helmholtz Center for Information Security, Saarbrücken, Germany
{norine.coenen,finkbeiner,christopher.hahn,jana.hofmann}@cispa.de
[2] Saarland University, Saarbrücken, Germany
s8yaschi@stud.uni-saarland.de

Abstract. An enforcement mechanism monitors a reactive system for
undesired behavior at runtime and corrects the system's output in case
it violates the given specification. In this paper, we study the enforcement problem for *hyperproperties*, i.e., properties that relate multiple
computation traces to each other. We elaborate the notion of *sound* and
transparent enforcement mechanisms for hyperproperties in two trace
input models: 1) the parallel trace input model, where the number of
traces is known a-priori and all traces are produced and processed in
parallel and 2) the sequential trace input model, where traces are processed sequentially and no a-priori bound on the number of traces is
known. For both models, we study enforcement algorithms for specifications given as formulas in universally quantified HyperLTL, a temporal
logic for hyperproperties. For the parallel model, we describe an enforcement mechanism based on parity games. For the sequential model, we
show that enforcement is in general undecidable and present algorithms
for reasonable simplifications of the problem (partial guarantees or the
restriction to safety properties). Furthermore, we report on experimental
results of our prototype implementation for the parallel model.

1 Introduction

Runtime enforcement combines the strengths of dynamic and static verification
by monitoring the output of a running system and also *correcting* it in case it
violates a given specification. Enforcement mechanisms thus provide formal guarantees for settings in which a system needs to be kept alive while also fulfilling
critical properties. Privacy policies, for example, cannot be ensured by shutting
down the system to prevent a leakage: an attacker could gain information just
from the fact that the execution stopped.

Runtime enforcement has been successfully applied in settings where specifications are given as *trace properties* [14,16]. Not every system behavior, however, can be specified as a trace property. Many security and privacy policies are

This work was partially supported by the German Research Foundation (DFG) as part
of the Collaborative Research Center "Foundations of Perspicuous Software Systems"
(TRR 248, 389792660) and by the European Research Council (ERC) Grant OSARES
(No. 683300).

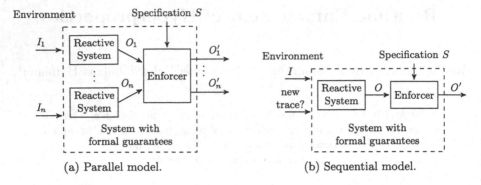

(a) Parallel model.   (b) Sequential model.

Fig. 1. Runtime enforcement for a reactive system. In case the input-output-relation would violate the specification S, the enforcer corrects the output.

hyperproperties [6], which generalize trace properties by relating multiple execution traces to each other. Examples are noninterference [30,37], observational determinism [41], and the detection of out-of-the-ordinary values in multiple data streams [27]. Previous work on runtime enforcement of hyperproperties either abstractly studied the class of enforceable hyperproperties [32] or security policies [38], or provided solutions for specific security policies like noninterference [12,28,38]. Our contribution is two-fold.

First, conceptually, we show that hyperproperty enforcement of reactive systems needs to solve challenging variants of the synthesis problem and that the concrete formulation depends on the given trace input model. We distinguish two input models 1) the parallel trace input model, where the number of traces is known a-priori and all traces are produced and processed in parallel and 2) the sequential trace input model, where traces are processed sequentially and no a-priori bound on the number of traces is known. Figure 1 depicts the general setting in these input models. In the parallel trace input model, the enforcement mechanism observes n traces at the same time. This is, for example, the natural model if a system runs in secure multi-execution [10]. In the sequential trace input model, system runs are observed in sessions, i.e., one at a time. An additional input indicates that a new session (i.e., trace) starts. Instances of this model naturally appear, for example, in web-based applications.

Second, algorithmically, we describe enforcement mechanisms for a concrete specification language. The best-studied temporal logic for hyperproperties is HyperLTL [7]. It extends LTL with trace variables and explicit trace quantification to relate multiple computation traces to each other. HyperLTL can express many standard information flow policies [7]. In particular, it is flexible enough to state different application-tailored specifications. We focus on universally quantified formulas, a fragment in which most of the enforceable hyperproperties naturally reside. For both trace input models, we develop enforcement mechanisms based on parity game solving. For the sequential model, we show that the problem is undecidable in general but provide algorithms for the simpler case that the enforcer only guarantees a correct continuation for the rest of the current session. Furthermore, we describe an algorithm for the case that the specification describes a safety property. Our algorithms monitor for *losing* prefixes, i.e., so-far observed traces for which the system has no winning strategy against an adversarial environment. We ensure that our enforcement mechansims are *sound* by detecting losing prefixes at the earliest possible point in time. Furthermore, they are *transparent*, i.e., non-losing prefixes are not altered.

We accompany our findings with a prototype implementation for the parallel model and conduct two experiments: 1) we enforce symmetry in mutual exclusion algorithms and 2) we enforce the information flow policy observational determinism. We will see that enforcing such complex HyperLTL specifications can scale to large traces once the initial parity game solving succeeds.

Related Work. HyperLTL has been studied extensively, for example, its expressiveness [5,8] as well as its verification [7,9,21,22], synthesis [18], and monitoring problem [4,19,20,24,39]. Especially relevant is the work on realizability monitoring for LTL [11] using parity games. Existing work on runtime enforcement includes algorithms for safety properties [3,40], real-time properties [17,36], concurrent software specifications [29], and concrete security policies [12,28,38]. For a tutorial on variants of runtime enforcement see [14]. Close related work is [32], which also studies the enforcement of general hyperproperties but independently of a concrete specification language (in contrast to our work). Systems are also assumed to be reactive and black-box, but there is no distinction between different trace input models. While we employ parity game solving, their enforcement mechanism executes several copies of the system to obtain executions that are related by the specification.

2   Preliminaries

Let Σ be an alphabet of atomic propositions. We assume that Σ can be partitioned into inputs and outputs, i.e., $\Sigma = I \mathbin{\dot\cup} O$. A finite sequence $t \in (2^{\Sigma})^*$ is a *finite trace*, an infinite sequence $t \in (2^{\Sigma})^{\omega}$ is an *infinite trace*. We write $t[i]$ for the $(i+1)$-th position of a trace, $t[0..i]$ for its prefix of length $i+1$, and $t[i,\infty]$ for the suffix from position i. A hyperproperty H is a set of sets of infinite traces.

HyperLTL. HyperLTL [7] is a linear temporal hyperlogic that extends LTL [35] with prenex trace quantification. The syntax of HyperLTL is given with respect to an alphabet Σ and a set $\mathcal{V}$ of trace variables.

$$\varphi ::= \forall \pi. \varphi \mid \exists \pi. \varphi \mid \psi$$
$$\psi ::= a_{\pi} \mid \neg \psi \mid \psi \vee \psi \mid \bigcirc \psi \mid \psi \mathcal{U} \psi$$

where $a \in \Sigma$ and $\pi \in \mathcal{V}$. The atomic proposition a is indexed with the trace variable π it refers to. We assume that formulas contain no free trace variables.

HyperLTL formulas are evaluated on a set $T \subseteq (2^\Sigma)^\omega$ of infinite traces and a trace assignment function $\Pi : \mathcal{V} \to T$. We use $\Pi[\pi \mapsto t]$ for the assignment that returns $\Pi(\pi')$ for $\pi' \neq \pi$ and t otherwise. Furthermore, let $\Pi[i, \infty]$ be defined as $\Pi[i, \infty](\pi) = \Pi(\pi)[i, \infty]$. The semantics of HyperLTL is defined as follows:

$$
\begin{aligned}
T, \Pi &\models a_\pi & &\text{iff} & &a \in \Pi(\pi)[0] \\
T, \Pi &\models \neg\psi & &\text{iff} & &T, \Pi \not\models \psi \\
T, \Pi &\models \psi_1 \vee \psi_2 & &\text{iff} & &T, \Pi \models \psi_1 \text{ or } T, \Pi \models \psi_2 \\
T, \Pi &\models \bigcirc\psi & &\text{iff} & &T, \Pi[1, \infty] \models \psi \\
T, \Pi &\models \psi_1 \mathcal{U} \psi_2 & &\text{iff} & &\exists i \geq 0 . T, \Pi[i, \infty] \models \psi_2 \text{ and } \forall 0 \leq j < i . T, \Pi[j, \infty] \models \psi_1 \\
T, \Pi &\models \exists\pi.\varphi & &\text{iff} & &\exists t \in T . T, \Pi[\pi \mapsto t] \models \varphi \\
T, \Pi &\models \forall\pi.\varphi & &\text{iff} & &\forall t \in T . T, \Pi[\pi \mapsto t] \models \varphi
\end{aligned}
$$

We also use the derived boolean connectives $\wedge, \to, \leftrightarrow$ as well as the derived temporal operators $\Diamond\varphi \equiv true\,\mathcal{U}\,\varphi$, $\Box\varphi \equiv \neg(\Diamond\neg\varphi)$, and $\varphi\,\mathcal{W}\,\psi \equiv (\varphi\,\mathcal{U}\,\psi) \vee \Box\varphi$. A trace set T satisfies a HyperLTL formula φ if $T, \emptyset \models \varphi$, where $\emptyset$ denotes the empty trace assignment.

Parity Games. A parity game $\mathcal{G}$ is a two-player game on a directed graph arena, where the states $V = V_0 \,\dot\cup\, V_1$ are partitioned among the two players P_0 and P_1. States belonging to P_0 and P_1 are required to alternate along every path. States are labeled with a coloring function $c : V \to \mathbb{N}$. Player P_0 wins the game if they have a strategy to enforce that the highest color occurring infinitely often in a run starting in the initial state is even. The winning region of a parity game is the set of states from which player P_0 has a winning strategy. A given LTL formula φ can be translated to a parity game $\mathcal{G}_\varphi$ in doubly-exponential time [13]. Formula φ is realizable iff player P_0 wins the game $\mathcal{G}_\varphi$. Its winning strategy σ_0 induces the reactive strategy σ representing a system implementation that satisfies φ.

3   Hyperproperty Enforcement

In this section, we develop a formal definition of hyperproperty enforcement mechanisms for reactive systems modeled with the parallel and the sequential trace input model. To this end, we first formally describe reactive systems under the two trace input models by the *prefixes* they can produce. Next, we develop the two basic requirements on enforcement mechanisms, *soundness* and *transparency* [14,15], for our settings. Soundness is traditionally formulated as the enforced system should be correct w.r.t. the specification.
Transparency (also known as precision [32]) states that

the behavior of the system is modified in a minimal way, i.e., the longest correct prefix should be preserved by the enforcement mechanism.

(a) Prefix in the parallel model.   (b) Prefix in the sequential model.

Fig. 2. Visualization of prefixes in trace input models.

In the context of reactive systems, formal definitions for soundness and transparency need to be formulated in terms of strategies that describe how the enforcement mechanism reacts to the inputs from the environment and outputs produced by the system. We therefore define soundness and transparency based on the notion of *losing prefixes* (i.e. prefixes for that no winning strategy exists) inspired by work on monitoring reactive systems [11]. We will see that the definition of losing prefixes depends heavily on the chosen trace input model. Especially the sequential model defines an interesting new kind of synthesis problem, which varies significantly from the known HyperLTL synthesis problem.

As is common in the study of runtime techniques for reactive systems, we make the following reasonable assumptions. First, reactive systems are treated as *black boxes*, i.e., two reactive systems with the same observable input-output behavior are considered to be equal. Thus, enforcement mechanisms cannot base their decisions on implementation details. Second, w.l.o.g. and to simplify presentation, we assume execution traces to have *infinite length*. Finite traces can always be interpreted as infinite traces, e.g., by adding end^ω. To reason about finite traces, on the other hand, definitions like the semantics of HyperLTL would need to accommodate many special cases like traces of different lengths. Lastly, we assume that control stays with the enforcer after a violation occurred instead of only correcting the error and handing control back to the system afterwards. Since we aim to provide formal guarantees, these two problems are equivalent: if only the error was corrected, the enforcement mechanism would still need to ensure that the correction does not make the specification unrealizable in the future, i.e., it would need to provide a strategy how to react to all future inputs.

3.1 Trace Input Models

We distinguish two *trace input models* [19], the parallel and the sequential model. The trace input models describe how a reactive system is employed and how its traces are obtained (see Fig. 1). We formally define the input models by the prefixes they can produce. The definitions are visualized in Fig. 2. In the parallel model, a fixed number of n systems are executed in parallel, producing n events at a time.

Definition 1 (Prefix in the Parallel Model). *An n-tuple of finite traces $U = (u_1, \dots u_n) \in ((2^\Sigma)^*)^n$ is a prefix of $V = (v_1, \dots v_n) \in ((2^\Sigma)^{*/\omega})^n$ (written $U \preceq V$) in the parallel model with n traces iff each u_i is a prefix of v_i (also denoted by $u_i \preceq v_i$).*

The prefix definition models the allowed executions of a system under the parallel trace input model: If the system produces U and after a few more steps produces V, then $U \preceq V$. Note that the prefix definition is transitive: U can be a prefix of another prefix (then the traces in V are of finite length) or a prefix of infinite-length traces.

In the sequential model, the traces are produced one by one and there is no a-priori known bound on the number of traces.

Definition 2 (Prefix in the Sequential Model). *Let* $U = (u_1, \ldots, u_n) \in ((2^\Sigma)^\omega)^*$ *be a sequence of traces and* $u \in (2^\Sigma)^*$ *be a finite trace. Let furthermore* $V = (v_1, \ldots, v_n, \ldots)$ *be a (possibly infinite) sequence of traces with* $v_i \in (2^\Sigma)^\omega$, *and* $v \in (2^\Sigma)^*$ *be a finite trace. We call* (U, u) *a prefix of* (V, v) *(written* $(U, u) \preceq (V, v)$) *iff either 1)* $U = V$ *and* $u \preceq v$ *or 2)* $V = u_1, \ldots, u_n, v_{n+1}, \ldots$ *and* $u \preceq v_{n+1}$.

We additionally say that $(U, u) \preceq V$ if $(U, u) \preceq (V, \epsilon)$, where ϵ is the empty trace. To continue an existing prefix (U, u), the system either extends the started trace u or finishes u and continues with additional traces. Traces in U are of infinite length and describe finished sessions. This means that they cannot be modified after the start of a new session. Again, prefixes in this model are transitive and are also defined for infinite sets.

Remark 1. We defined prefixes tailored to the trace input models to precisely capture the influence of the models on the enforcement problem. Usually, a set of traces T is defined as prefix of a set of traces T' if and only if $\forall t \in T. \exists t' \in T'. t \preceq t'$ [6]. A prefix in the sequential model, however, *cannot* be captured by the traditional prefix definition, as it does not admit infinite traces in a prefix.

3.2 Losing Prefixes for Hyperproperties

Losing prefixes describe *when* an enforcer has to intervene based on possible strategies for future inputs. As we will see, the definition of losing prefixes, and thus the definition of the enforcement problem, differs significantly for both input models. For the rest of this section, let H denote an arbitrary hyperproperty.

We first define strategies for the parallel model with n parallel sessions. In the enforcement setting, a strategy receives a previously recorded prefix. Depending on that prefix, the enforcer's strategy might react differently to future inputs. We therefore define a *prefixed strategy* as a higher-order function $\sigma : ((2^\Sigma)^*)^n \to ((2^I)^*)^n \to (2^O)^n$ over $\Sigma = I \dot\cup O$. The strategy first receives a prefix (produced by the system), then a sequence of inputs on all n traces, and reacts with an output for all traces. We define a losing prefix as follows.

Definition 3 (Losing Prefix in the Parallel Model). *A strategy* $\sigma(U)$ *is losing for* H *with* $U = (u_1, \ldots, u_n) \in ((2^\Sigma)^*)^n$ *if there are input sequences* $(v_1, \ldots, v_n) \in ((2^I)^\omega)^n$ *such that the following set is not in* H:

$$\bigcup_{1 \leq i \leq n} \{u_i \cdot (v_i[0] \cup \sigma_U(\epsilon)(i)) \cdot (v_i[1] \cup \sigma_U(v_i[0])(i)) \cdot (v_i[2] \cup \sigma_U(v_i[0]v_i[1])(i)) \ldots\},$$

where $\sigma_U = \sigma(U)$ *and* $\sigma_U(\cdot)(i)$ *denotes the* i-*th output that* σ *produces.*

We say that $\sigma(U)$ is winning if it is not losing. A prefix U is winning if there is a strategy σ such that $\sigma(U)$ is winning. Lastly, σ is winning if $\sigma(\epsilon)$ is winning and for all non-empty winning prefixes U, $\sigma(U)$ is winning.

Similar to the parallel model, a prefixed strategy in the sequential model is a function $\sigma : ((2^\Sigma)^\omega)^* \times (2^\Sigma)^* \to (2^I)^* \to 2^O$ over $\Sigma = I \cupdot O$. The definition of a losing prefix is the following.

Definition 4 (Losing Prefix in the Sequential Model). *In the sequential model, a strategy σ is losing with a prefix (U, u) for H, if there are input sequences $V = (v_0, v_1, \ldots)$ with $v_i \in (2^I)^\omega$, such that the set $U \cup \{t_0, t_1, \ldots\}$ is not in H, where $t_0, t_1, \ldots$ are defined as follows.*

$$
\begin{aligned}
t_0 &:= \quad u \cdot (v_0[0] \cup \sigma(U, u)(\epsilon)) \cdot (v_0[1] \cup \sigma(U, u)(v_0[0])) \cdot \ldots \\
t_1 &:= \quad (v_1[0] \cup \sigma(U \cup \{t_0\}, \epsilon)(\epsilon)) \cdot (v_1[1] \cup \sigma(U \cup \{t_0\}, \epsilon)(v_1[0])) \cdot \ldots \\
t_2 &:= \quad (v_2[0] \cup \sigma(U \cup \{t_0, t_1\}, \epsilon)(\epsilon)) \cdot (v_2[1] \cup \sigma(U \cup \{t_0, t_1\}, \epsilon)(v_2[0])) \cdot \ldots
\end{aligned}
$$

Winning prefixes and strategies are defined analogously to the parallel model.

Remark 2. The above definitions illustrate that enforcing hyperproperties in the sequential model defines an intriguing but complex problem. Strategies react to inputs based on the observed prefix. The *same* input sequence can therefore be answered differently in the first session and, say, in the third session. The enforcement problem thus not simply combines monitoring and synthesis but formulates a different kind of problem.

3.3   Enforcement Mechanisms

With the definitions of the previous sections, we adapt the notions of sound and transparent enforcement mechanisms to hyperproperties under the two trace input models. We define an enforcement mechanism *enf* for a hyperproperty H to be a computable function which transforms a black-box reactive system S with trace input model $\mathcal{M}$ into a reactive system $enf(S)$ with the same input model.

Definition 5 (Soundness). *enf is sound if for all reactive systems S and all input sequences in model $\mathcal{M}$, the set of traces produced by $enf(S)$ is in H.*

Definition 6 (Transparency). *enf is transparent if the following holds: Let U be a prefix producible by S with input sequence s_I. If U is winning, then for any prefix V producible by $enf(S)$ with input sequence s_I' where $s_I \preceq s_I'$, it holds that $U \preceq V$.*

We now have everything in place to define when a hyperproperty is enforceable for a given input model.

Definition 7 (Enforceable Hyperproperties). *A hyperproperty H is enforceable if there is a sound and transparent enforcement mechanism.*

It is now straightforward to see that in order to obtain a sound and transparent enforcement mechanism, we need to construct a winning strategy for H.

Proposition 1. *Let H be a hyperproperty and $\mathcal{M}$ be an input model. Assume that it is decidable whether a prefix U is losing in model $\mathcal{M}$ for H. Then there exists a sound and transparent enforcement mechanism enf for H iff there exists a winning strategy in $\mathcal{M}$ for H.*

The above proposition describes how to construct enforcement algorithms: We need to solve the synthesis problem posed by the respective trace input model. However, we have to restrict ourselves to properties that can be monitored for losing prefixes. This is only natural: for example, the property expressed by the HyperLTL formula $\exists \pi. \square a_\pi$ can in general not be enforced since it contains a hyperliveness [6] aspect: There is always the possibility for the required trace π to occur in a future session (c.f. monitorable hyperproperties in [1,19]). We therefore describe algorithms for HyperLTL specifications from the universal fragment $\forall \pi_1 \ldots \forall \pi_k. \varphi$ of HyperLTL. Additionally, we assume that the specification describes a property whose counterexamples have losing prefixes.

Before jumping to concrete algorithms, we describe two example scenarios of hyperproperty enforcement with different trace input models.

Example 1 (Fairness in Contract Signing). Contract signing protocols let multiple parties negotiate a contract. In this setting, fairness requires that in every situation where Bob can obtain Alice's signature, Alice must also be able to obtain Bob's signature. Due to the asymmetric nature of contract signing protocols (one party has to commit first), fairness is difficult to achieve (see, e.g., [33]). Many protocols rely on a trusted third party (TTP) to guarantee fairness. The TTP may negotiate multiple contracts in parallel sessions. The natural trace input model is therefore the parallel model. Fairness forbids the existence of two traces π and π' that have the same prefix of inputs, followed in π by Bob requesting (R^B) and receiving the signed contract (S^B), and in π' by Alice requesting (R^A), but *not* receiving the signed contract $(\neg S^A)$:

$$\forall \pi. \forall \pi'. \neg((\bigwedge_{i \in I}(i_\pi \leftrightarrow i_{\pi'}))\; \mathcal{U}\; (R_\pi^B \wedge R_{\pi'}^A \wedge \bigcirc(S_\pi^B \wedge \neg S_{\pi'}^A)))$$

Example 2 (Privacy in Fitness Trackers). Wearables track a wide range of extremely private health data which can leak an astonishing amount of insight into your health. For instance, it has been found that observing out-of-the-ordinary heart rate values correlates with diseases like the common cold or even Lyme disease [27]. Consider the following setting. A fitness tracker continuously collects data that is stored locally on the user's device. Additionally, the data is synced with an external cloud. While locally stored data should be left untouched, uploaded data has to be enforced to comply with information flow policies. Each day, a new stream of data is uploaded, hence the sequential trace input model would be appropriate. Comparing newer streams with older streams allows for the detection of anomalies. We formalize an exemplary property of this scenario in HyperLTL. Let *HR* be the set of possible heart rates. Let furthermore *active* denote whether the user is currently exercising. Then the following property ensures that unusually high heart rate values are not reported to the cloud:

$$\forall \pi. \forall \pi'. \Box((active_\pi \leftrightarrow active_{\pi'}) \rightarrow \bigwedge_{r \in HR} (r_\pi \leftrightarrow r_{\pi'}))$$

4   Enforcement Algorithms for HyperLTL Specifications

For both trace input models, we present sound and transparent enforcement algorithms for universal HyperLTL formulas defining hyperproperties with losing prefixes. First, we construct an algorithm for the parallel input model based on parity game solving. For the sequential trace input model, we first show that the problem is undecidable in the general case. Next, we provide an algorithm that only finishes the remainder of the current session. This simplifies the problem because the existence of a correct future session is not guaranteed. For this setting, we then present a simpler algorithm that is restricted to safety specifications.

4.1   Parallel Trace Input Model

In short, we proceed as follows: First, since we know the number of traces, we can translate the HyperLTL formula to an equivalent LTL formula. For that formula, we construct a realizability monitor based on the LTL monitor described in [11]. The monitor is a parity game, which we use to detect minimal losing prefixes and to provide a valid continuation for the original HyperLTL formula.

Assume that the input model contains n traces. Let a HyperLTL formula $\forall \pi_1 \ldots \forall \pi_k. \varphi$ over $\Sigma = I \dot\cup O$ be given, where φ is quantifier free. We construct an LTL formula φ_{LTL}^n over $\Sigma' = \{a_i \mid a \in \Sigma, 1 \leq i \leq n\}$ as follows:

$$\varphi_{\mathrm{LTL}}^n := \bigwedge_{i_1,\ldots,i_k \in [1,n]} \varphi[\forall a \in AP : a_{\pi_1} \mapsto a_{i_1}, \ldots, a_{\pi_k} \mapsto a_{i_k}]$$

The formula φ_{LTL}^n enumerates all possible combinations to choose k traces – one for each quantifier – from the set of n traces in the model. We use the notation $\varphi[\forall a \in AP : a_{\pi_1} \mapsto a_{i_1}, \ldots, a_{\pi_k} \mapsto a_{i_k}]$ to indicate that in φ, atomic propositions with trace variables are replaced by atomic propositions indexed with one of the n traces. We define $I' = \{a_i \mid a \in I, 1 \leq i \leq n\}$ and O' analogously. Since n is known upfront, we only write φ_{LTL}.

Our algorithm exploits that for every LTL formula φ, there exists an equivalent parity game $\mathcal{G}_\varphi$ such that φ is realizable iff player P_0 is winning in the initial state with strategy σ_0 [13]. For a finite trace u, φ is realizable with prefix u iff the play induced by u ends in a state q that is in the winning region of

---

Algorithm 1. HyperLTL enforcement algorithm for the parallel input model.

1: **procedure** INITIALIZE(ψ, n)
2:     $\varphi_{LTL} :=$ TOLTL(ψ, n);
3:     (game, q_0) := TOPARITY(φ_{LTL});
4:     winR := SOLVEPARITY(game);
5:     **if** $q_0 \notin$ winR **then**
6:         **raise** error;
7:     **return**(game, winR, q_0);

8: **procedure** ENFORCE(game, lastq)
9:     sig := GETSTRAT(game, lastq);
10:     **while** true **do**
11:         o := sig(lastq);
12:         lastq := MOVE(game, lastq, o);
13:         **output**(o);
14:         i := GETNEXTINPUT( );
15:         $i_{LTL} :=$ TOLTL(i);
16:         lastq := MOVE(game, lastq, i_{LTL});

17: **procedure** MONITOR(game, winR, q)
18:     lastq := q;
19:     **while** true **do**
20:         o := GETNEXTOUTPUT( );
21:         $o_{LTL} :=$ TOLTL(o);
22:         q := MOVE(game, lastq, o_{LTL});
23:         **if** q $\notin$ winR **then**
24:             **return**(game, lastq);
25:         i := GETNEXTINPUT( );
26:         $i_{LTL} :=$ TOLTL(i);
27:         q := MOVE(game, q, i_{LTL});
28:         lastq := q;

---

player P_0. The algorithm to enforce the HyperLTL formula calls the following three procedures – depicted in Algorithm 1 – in the appropriate order.

Initialize: Construct φ_{LTL} and the induced parity game $\mathcal{G}_\varphi$. Solve the game $\mathcal{G}_\varphi$, i.e. compute the winning region for player P_0. If the initial state $q_0 \in V_0$ is losing, raise an error. Otherwise start monitoring in the initial state.

Monitor: Assume the game is currently in state $q \in V_0$. Get the next outputs $(o_1, \ldots, o_n) \in O^n$ produced by the n traces of the system and translate them to $o_{LTL} \subseteq O'$ by subscripting them as described for formula φ_{LTL}. Move with o_{LTL} to the next state. This state is in V_1. Check if the reached state is still in the winning region. If not, it is a losing state, so we do not approve the system's output but let the enforcer take over and call ENFORCE on the last state. If the state is still in the winning region, we process the next inputs $(i_1, \ldots, i_n)$, translate them to i_{LTL}, and move with i_{LTL} to the next state in the game, again in V_0. While the game does not leave the winning region, the property is still realizable and the enforcer does not need to intervene.

Enforce: By construction, we start with a state $q \in V_0$ that is in the winning region, i.e., there is a positional winning strategy $\sigma : V_0 \to 2^{O'}$ for player P_0. Using this strategy, we output $\sigma(q)$ and continue with the next incoming input i_{LTL} to the next state in V_0. Continue with this strategy for any incoming input.

Correctness and Complexity. By construction, since we never leave the winning region, the enforced system fulfills the specification and the enforcer is sound. It is also transparent: As long as the prefix produced by the system is not losing, the enforcer does not intervene. The algorithm has triple exponential complexity in the number of traces n: The size of φ_{LTL} is exponential in n

and constructing the parity game is doubly exponential in the size of φ_{LTL} [13]. Solving the parity game only requires quasi-polynomial time [34]. Note, however, that all of the above steps are part of the initialization. At runtime, the algorithm only follows the game arena. If the enforcer is only supposed to correct a single output and afterwards hand back control to the system, the algorithm could be easily adapted accordingly.

4.2 Sequential Trace Input Model

Deciding whether a prefix is losing in the sequential model is harder than in the parallel model. In the sequential model, strategies are defined w.r.t. the traces seen so far – they incrementally upgrade their knowledge with every new trace. In general, the question whether there exists a sound and transparent enforcement mechanism for universal HyperLTL specifications is undecidable.

Theorem 1. *In the sequential model, it is undecidable whether a HyperLTL formula φ from the universal fragment is enforceable.*

Proof. We encode the classic realizability problem of universal HyperLTL, which is undecidable [18], into the sequential model enforcement problem for universal HyperLTL. HyperLTL realizability asks if there exists a strategy $\sigma\colon (2^I)^* \to 2^O$ such that the set of traces constructed from every possible input sequence satisfies the formula φ, i.e. whether $\{(w[0]\cup\sigma(\epsilon))\cdot(w[1]\cup\sigma(w[0]))\cdot(w[2]\cup\sigma(w[0..1]))\cdot \ldots \mid w \in (2^I)^\omega\}, \emptyset \models \varphi$. Let a universal HyperLTL formula φ over $\Sigma = I \,\dot\cup\, O$ be given. We construct $\psi := \varphi \wedge \forall\pi.\forall\pi'.(\bigwedge_{o\in O} o_\pi \leftrightarrow o_{\pi'})\ \mathcal{W}\ (\bigvee_{i\in I} i_\pi \nleftrightarrow i_{\pi'})$. The universal HyperLTL formula ψ requires the strategy to choose the same outputs as long as the inputs are the same. The choice of the strategy must therefore be independent of earlier sessions, i.e., $\sigma(U,\epsilon)(s_I) = \sigma(U',\epsilon)(s_I)$ for all sets of traces U, U' and input sequences s_I. Any trace set that fulfills ψ can therefore be arranged in a traditional HyperLTL strategy tree branching on the inputs and labeling the nodes with the outputs. Assume the enforcer has to take over control after the first event when enforcing ψ. Thus, there is a sound and transparent enforcement mechanism for ψ iff φ is realizable.   □

Finishing the Current Session. As the general problem is undecidable, we study the problem where the enforcer takes over control only for the rest of the current session. For the next session, the existence of a solution is not guaranteed. This approach is especially reasonable if we are confident that errors occur only sporadically. We adapt the algorithm presented for the parallel model. Let a HyperLTL formula $\forall\pi_1.\ldots.\forall\pi_k.\ \varphi$ over $\Sigma = I \,\dot\cup\, O$ be given, where φ is quantifier free. As for the parallel model, we translate the formula into an LTL formula φ_{LTL}^n. We first do so for the first session with $n = 1$. We construct and solve the parity game for that formula, and use it to monitor the incoming events and to enforce the rest of the session if necessary. For the next session, we construct φ_{LTL}^n for $n = 2$ and add an additional conjunct encoding the observed trace t_1. The resulting formula induces a parity game that monitors and enforces the second trace. Like this, we can always enforce the current trace in relation to all

Algorithm 2. HyperLTL enforcement algorithm for the sequential trace input model.

1: **procedure** ENFORCESEQUENTIAL(ψ)
2:     n := 1;
3:     φ_{traces} := true;
4:     **while** true **do**
5:         ψ_{curr} := TOLTL(ψ, n) $\wedge$ φ_{traces};
6:         (game, winR, q_0) := INITIALIZE'(ψ_{curr});
7:         res := MONITOR'(game, winR, q_0);
8:         **if** res == ('ok', t) **then**
9:             φ_{traces} := φ_{traces} $\wedge$ TOLTL(t);
10:        **else if** res = ('losing', t, (game, lastq)) **then**
11:            t' := ENFORCE'(game, lastq);
12:            φ_{traces} := φ_{traces} $\wedge$ TOLTL(t $\cdot$ t');
13:        n++;

---

traces seen so far. Algorithm 2 depicts the algorithm calling similar procedures as in Algorithm 1 (for which we therefore do not give any pseudo code). INITIALIZE' is already given an LTL formula and, therefore, does not translate its input to LTL. MONITOR' returns a tuple including the reason for its termination ('ok' when the trace finished and 'losing' when a losing prefix was detected). Additionally, the monitor returns the trace seen so far (not including the event that led to a losing prefix), which will be added to φ_{traces}. ENFORCE' enforces the rest of the session and afterwards returns the produced trace, which is then encoded in the LTL formula (TOLTL(t)).

Correctness and Complexity. Soundness and transparency follow from the fact that for the n-th session, the algorithm reduces the problem to the parallel setting with n traces, with the first $n - 1$ traces being fixed and encoded into the LTL formula φ_{LTL}^n. We construct a new parity game from φ_{LTL}^n after each finished session. The algorithm is thus of non-elementary complexity.

Safety Specifications. If we restrict ourselves to formulas $\psi = \forall \pi_1 \ldots \forall \pi_k. \varphi$, where φ is a *safety* formula, we can improve the complexity of the algorithm. Note, however, that not every property with losing prefixes is a safety property: for the formula $\forall \pi. \square(o_\pi \rightarrow \Diamond i_\pi)$ with $o \in O$ and $i \in I$, any prefix with o set at some point is losing. However, the formula does not belong to the safety fragment. Given a safety formula φ, we can translate it to a safety game [25] instead of a parity game. The LTL formula we create with every new trace is built incrementally, i.e., with every finished trace we only ever add new conjuncts. With safety games, we can thus recycle the winning region from the game of the previous trace. The algorithm proceeds as follows. 1) Translate φ into an LTL formula φ_{LTL}^1 for $n = 1$. 2) Build the safety game $\mathcal{G}_{\varphi_{\text{LTL}}}^1$ for φ_{LTL}^1 and solve it. Monitor the incoming events of trace t_1 as before. Enforce the rest of the trace if necessary. 3) Once the session is terminated, generate the LTL formula $\varphi_{\text{LTL}}^2 = \varphi_{\text{LTL}}^1 \wedge \varphi_{\text{diff}}^2$. As φ_{LTL}^2 is a conjunction of the old formula and a new conjunct φ_{diff}^2, we only need to generate the safety game $\mathcal{G}^2_{\text{diff}}$ and then build the product of $\mathcal{G}^2_{\text{diff}}$ with the winning region of $\mathcal{G}^1_{\varphi_{\text{LTL}}}$. We solve the resulting game and monitor (and potentially enforce) as before. The algorithm incrementally refines the safety game and enforces the rest of a session if needed. The construction recycles parts of the game computed for the previous session. We thus avoid the costly translation to a parity game for every new session. While constructing the safety game from the LTL specification has still doubly exponential complexity [25], solving safety games can be done in linear time [2].

5   Experimental Evaluation

We implemented the algorithm for the parallel trace input model in our proto-type tool REHyper[1], which is written in Rust. We use Strix [31] for the generation of the parity game. We determine the winning region and the positional strategies of the game with PGSolver [23]. All experiments ran on an Intel Xeon CPU E3-1240 v5 3.50 GHz, with 8 GB memory running Debian 10.6. We evaluate our prototype with two experiments. In the first, we enforce a non-trivial formulation of fairness in a mutual exclusion protocol. In the second, we enforce the information flow policy *observational determinism* on randomly generated traces.

5.1   Enforcing Symmetry in Mutual Exclusion Algorithms

Mutual exclusion algorithms like Lamport's bakery protocol ensure that multiple threads can safely access a shared resource. To ensure fair access to the resource, we want the protocol to be symmetric, i.e., for any two traces where the roles of the two processes are swapped, the grants are swapped accordingly. Since symmetry requires the comparison of two traces, it is a hyperproperty.

For our experiment, we used a Verilog implementation of the Bakery protocol [26], which has been proven to violate the following symmetry formulation [22]:

$$\forall \pi. \forall \pi'. (pc(0)_\pi = pc(1)_{\pi'} \wedge pc(1)_\pi = pc(0)_{\pi'}) \mathcal{W} \neg (pause_\pi = pause_{\pi'} \wedge$$
$$\text{sym}(sel_\pi, sel_{\pi'}) \wedge \text{sym}(break_\pi, break_{\pi'}) \wedge sel_\pi < 3 \wedge sel_{\pi'} < 3) \ .$$

The specification states that for any two traces, the program counters need to be symmetrical in the two processes as long as the processes are scheduled (*select*) and ties are broken (*break*) symmetrically. Both *pause* and *sel* < 3 handle further implementation details. The AIGER translation [22] of the protocol has 5 inputs and 46 outputs. To enforce the above formula, only 10 of the outputs are relevant. We enforced symmetry of the bakery protocol on simulated pairs of traces produced by the protocol. Table 1 shows our results for different trace lengths and trace generation techniques. We report the average runtime over 10 runs as well as minimal and maximal times along with the number of times

---

[1] REHyper is available at https://github.com/reactive-systems/REHyper.

Table 1. Enforcing symmetry in the Bakery protocol on pairs of traces. Times are given in seconds.

|t|	Random traces				Symmetric traces			
	avg	min	max	#enforced	avg	min	max	#enforced
500	0.003	0.003	0.003	0	0.013	0.008	0.020	10
1000	0.005	0.005	0.005	0	0.024	0.015	0.039	10
5.000	0.026	0.024	0.045	0	0.078	0.065	0.097	10
10.000	0.049	0.047	0.064	0	0.153	0.129	0.178	10

the enforcer needed to intervene. The symmetry assumptions are fairly specific and are unlikely to be reproduced by random input simulation. In a second experiment, we therefore generated pairs of symmetric traces. Here, the enforcer had to intervene every time, which produced only a small overhead.

The required game was constructed and solved in 313 seconds. For sets of more than two traces, the construction of the parity game did not return within two hours. The case study shows that the tool performs without significant overhead at runtime and can easily handle very long traces. The bottleneck is the initial parity game construction and solving.

5.2 Enforcing Observational Determinism

In our second experiment, we enforced observational determinism, given as the HyperLTL formula $\forall\pi.\forall\pi'.(o_\pi \leftrightarrow o_{\pi'})\mathcal{W}(i_\pi \leftrightarrow i_{\pi'})$. The formula states that for any two execution traces, the observable outputs have to agree as long as the observable inputs agree. Observational determinism is a prototypical information-flow policy used in many experiments and case studies for Hyper-LTL (e.g. [4,18,22]). We generated traces using the following scalable generation scheme: At each position, each input and output bit is flipped with a certain probability (0.5% or 1%). This results in instances where observational determinism randomly breaks. Table 2 shows our results. Each line corresponds to 100 randomly generated instances of the given size (number of inputs/outputs and traces, and length of the sessions). We report the initialization time that is needed to generate and solve the parity game. Furthermore, we report average, minimal, and maximal enforcement time as well as the number of instances where the enforcer intervened. All times are reported in seconds. The bottleneck is again the time needed to construct and solve the parity game. At runtime, which is the crucial aspect, the enforcer performs efficiently. The higher bit flip probability did not lead to more enforcements: For traces of length 10000, the probability that the enforcer intervenes is relatively high already at a bit flip probability of 0.5%.

Table 2. Enforcing observational determinism. Times are given in seconds.

Benchmark size				Init time	0.5% bit flip probability				1% bit flip probability			
# i	# o	# t	|t|		avg	min	max	#enf'ed	avg	min	max	#enf'ed
1	1	3	10000	0.517	0.014	0.013	0.017	60	0.013	0.013	0.015	60
		8	10000	65.67	0.524	0.517	0.625	99	0.524	0.517	0.588	97
2	2	4	10000	0.869	0.025	0.024	0.030	73	0.032	0.031	0.043	77
		5	10000	21.189	0.038	0.037	0.041	90	0.038	0.037	0.042	86
3	3	2	10000	0.633	0.019	0.018	0.022	47	0.023	0.023	0.025	54
		4	5000	132.849	0.022	0.021	0.026	77	0.021	0.021	0.021	71
		4	10000		0.038	0.036	0.056	77	0.037	0.037	0.042	77
4	4	3	1000		0.010	0.008	0.015	71	0.009	0.008	0.018	68
		3	5000	43.885	0.023	0.021	0.033	72	0.022	0.021	0.025	78
		3	10000		0.038	0.037	0.050	76	0.038	0.037	0.041	75

6 Conclusion

We studied the runtime enforcement problem for hyperproperties. Depending on the trace input model, we showed that the enforcement problem boils down to detecting losing prefixes and solving a custom synthesis problem. For both input models, we provided enforcement algorithms for specifications given in the universally quantified fragment of the temporal hyperlogic HyperLTL. While the problem for the sequential trace input model is in general undecidable, we showed that enforcing HyperLTL specifications becomes decidable under the reasonable restriction to only finish the current session. For the parallel model, we provided an enforcement mechanism based on parity game solving. Our prototype tool implements this algorithm for the parallel model. We conducted experiments on two case studies enforcing complex HyperLTL specifications for reactive systems with the parallel model. Our results show that once the initial parity game solving succeeds, our approach has only little overhead at runtime and scales to long traces.

References

1. Agrawal, S., Bonakdarpour, B.: Runtime verification of k-safety hyperproperties in HyperLTL. In: CSF 2016 (2016)
2. Beeri, C.: On the membership problem for functional and multivalued dependencies in relational databases. ACM Trans. Database Syst. 5(3), 241–259 (1980)
3. Bloem, R., Könighofer, B., Könighofer, R., Wang, C.: Shield synthesis: runtime enforcement for reactive systems. CoRR abs/1501.02573 (2015)
4. Bonakdarpour, B., Finkbeiner, B.: The complexity of monitoring hyperproperties. In: CSF 2018 (2018)
5. Bozzelli, L., Maubert, B., Pinchinat, S.: Unifying hyper and epistemic temporal logics. In: Pitts, A. (ed.) FoSSaCS 2015. LNCS, vol. 9034, pp. 167–182. Springer, Heidelberg (2015). https://doi.org/10.1007/978-3-662-46678-0_11

6. Clarkson, M.R., Schneider, F.B.: Hyperproperties. In: CSF 2008 (2008)

7. Clarkson, M.R., Finkbeiner, B., Koleini, M., Micinski, K.K., Rabe, M.N., Sánchez, C.: Temporal logics for hyperproperties. In: Abadi, M., Kremer, S. (eds.) POST 2014. LNCS, vol. 8414, pp. 265–284. Springer, Heidelberg (2014). https://doi.org/10.1007/978-3-642-54792-8_15

8. Coenen, N., Finkbeiner, B., Hahn, C., Hofmann, J.: The hierarchy of hyperlogics. In: LICS 2019 (2019)

9. Coenen, N., Finkbeiner, B., Sánchez, C., Tentrup, L.: Verifying hyperliveness. In: Dillig, I., Tasiran, S. (eds.) CAV 2019. LNCS, vol. 11561, pp. 121–139. Springer, Cham (2019). https://doi.org/10.1007/978-3-030-25540-4_7

10. Devriese, D., Piessens, F.: Noninterference through secure multi-execution. In: S&P 2010 (2010)

11. Ehlers, R., Finkbeiner, B.: Monitoring realizability. In: Khurshid, S., Sen, K. (eds.) RV 2011. LNCS, vol. 7186, pp. 427–441. Springer, Heidelberg (2012). https://doi.org/10.1007/978-3-642-29860-8_34

12. Erlingsson, U., Schneider, F.B.: SASI enforcement of security policies: a retrospective. In: NSPW 1999 (1999)

13. Esparza, Javier, Křetínský, Jan, Raskin, Jean-François., Sickert, Salomon: From LTL and limit-deterministic Büchi automata to deterministic parity automata. In: Legay, Axel, Margaria, Tiziana (eds.) TACAS 2017. LNCS, vol. 10205, pp. 426–442. Springer, Heidelberg (2017). https://doi.org/10.1007/978-3-662-54577-5_25

14. Falcone, Y.: You should better enforce than verify. In: Barringer, H., et al. (eds.) RV 2010. LNCS, vol. 6418, pp. 89–105. Springer, Heidelberg (2010). https://doi.org/10.1007/978-3-642-16612-9_9

15. Falcone, Y., Fernandez, J., Mounier, L.: What can you verify and enforce at runtime? Int. J. Softw. Tools Technol. Transf. **14**(3), 349–382 (2012). https://doi.org/10.1007/s10009-011-0196-8

16. Falcone, Y., Mounier, L., Fernandez, J.C., Richier, J.L.: Runtime enforcement monitors: composition, synthesis, and enforcement abilities. Form. Methods Syst. Des. **38**, 223–262 (2011). https://doi.org/10.1007/s10703-011-0114-4

17. Falcone, Y., Pinisetty, S.: On the runtime enforcement of timed properties. In: Finkbeiner, B., Mariani, L. (eds.) RV 2019. LNCS, vol. 11757, pp. 48–69. Springer, Cham (2019). https://doi.org/10.1007/978-3-030-32079-9_4

18. Finkbeiner, B., Hahn, C., Lukert, P., Stenger, M., Tentrup, L.: Synthesizing reactive systems from hyperproperties. In: Chockler, H., Weissenbacher, G. (eds.) CAV 2018. LNCS, vol. 10981, pp. 289–306. Springer, Cham (2018). https://doi.org/10.1007/978-3-319-96145-3_16

19. Finkbeiner, B., Hahn, C., Stenger, M., Tentrup, L.: Monitoring hyperproperties. Form. Methods Syst. Des. **54**(3), 336–363 (2019). https://doi.org/10.1007/s10703-019-00334-z

20. Finkbeiner, B., Hahn, C., Stenger, M., Tentrup, L.: RVHyper: a runtime verification tool for temporal hyperproperties. In: Beyer, D., Huisman, M. (eds.) TACAS 2018. LNCS, vol. 10806, pp. 194–200. Springer, Cham (2018). https://doi.org/10.1007/978-3-319-89963-3_11

21. Finkbeiner, B., Hahn, C., Torfah, H.: Model checking quantitative hyperproperties. In: Chockler, H., Weissenbacher, G. (eds.) CAV 2018. LNCS, vol. 10981, pp. 144–163. Springer, Cham (2018). https://doi.org/10.1007/978-3-319-96145-3_8

22. Finkbeiner, B., Rabe, M.N., Sánchez, C.: Algorithms for model checking HyperLTL and HyperCTL*. In: Kroening, D., Păsăreanu, C.S. (eds.) CAV 2015. LNCS, vol. 9206, pp. 30–48. Springer, Cham (2015). https://doi.org/10.1007/978-3-319-21690-4_3

23. Friedmann, O., Lange, M.: The PGSolver Collection of Parity Game Solvers Version 3 (2010)
24. Hahn, C., Stenger, M., Tentrup, L.: Constraint-based monitoring of hyperproperties. In: Vojnar, T., Zhang, L. (eds.) TACAS 2019. LNCS, vol. 11428, pp. 115–131. Springer, Cham (2019). https://doi.org/10.1007/978-3-030-17465-1_7
25. Kupferman, O., Vardi, M.Y.: Model checking of safety properties. In: Halbwachs, N., Peled, D. (eds.) CAV 1999. LNCS, vol. 1633, pp. 172–183. Springer, Heidelberg (1999). https://doi.org/10.1007/3-540-48683-6_17
26. Lamport, L.: A new solution of Dijkstra's concurrent programming problem. Commun. ACM **17**(8), 453–455 (1974)
27. Li, X., et al.: Digital health: tracking physiomes and activity using wearable biosensors reveals useful health-related information. PLoS Biol. **15**, e2001402 (2017)
28. Ligatti, J., Bauer, L., Walker, D.: Run-time enforcement of nonsafety policies. ACM Trans. Inf. Syst. Secur. **12**(3), 1–41 (2009)
29. Luo, Q., Roundefinedu, G.: EnforceMOP: a runtime property enforcement system for multithreaded programs. In: ISSTA 2013 (2013)
30. McLean, J.: Proving noninterference and functional correctness using traces. J. Comput. Secur. **1**(1), 37–58 (1992)
31. Meyer, P.J., Sickert, S., Luttenberger, M.: Strix: explicit reactive synthesis strikes back! In: Chockler, H., Weissenbacher, G. (eds.) CAV 2018. LNCS, vol. 10981, pp. 578–586. Springer, Cham (2018). https://doi.org/10.1007/978-3-319-96145-3_31
32. Ngo, M., Massacci, F., Milushev, D., Piessens, F.: Runtime enforcement of security policies on black box reactive programs. In: POPL 2015 (2015)
33. Norman, G., Shmatikov, V.: Analysis of probabilistic contract signing. J. Comput. Secur. **14**(6), 561–589 (2006)
34. Parys, P.: Parity games: Zielonka's algorithm in quasi-polynomial time. In: MFCS 2019 (2019)
35. Pnueli, A.: The temporal logic of programs. In: SFCS 1977 (1977)
36. Renard, M., Falcone, Y., Rollet, A., Jéron, T., Marchand, H.: Optimal enforcement of (timed) properties with uncontrollable events. In: MSCS 2019 (2019)
37. Roscoe, A.W.: CSP and determinism in security modelling. In: S&P 1995 (1995)
38. Schneider, F.B.: Enforceable security policies. ACM Trans. Inf. Syst. Secur. **3**, 30–50 (2000)
39. Stucki, S., Sánchez, C., Schneider, G., Bonakdarpour, B.: Gray-box monitoring of hyperproperties. In: ter Beek, M.H., McIver, A., Oliveira, J.N. (eds.) FM 2019. LNCS, vol. 11800, pp. 406–424. Springer, Cham (2019). https://doi.org/10.1007/978-3-030-30942-8_25
40. Wu, M., Zeng, H., Wang, C.: Synthesizing runtime enforcer of safety properties under burst error. In: Rayadurgam, S., Tkachuk, O. (eds.) NFM 2016. LNCS, vol. 9690, pp. 65–81. Springer, Cham (2016). https://doi.org/10.1007/978-3-319-40648-0_6
41. Zdancewic, S., Myers, A.C.: Observational determinism for concurrent program security. In: CSFW-16 (2003)

System Synthesis and Approximation

Compositional Synthesis of Modular Systems

Bernd Finkbeiner[ID] and Noemi Passing[✉][ID]

CISPA Helmholtz Center for Information Security, Saarbrücken, Germany
{finkbeiner,noemi.passing}@cispa.de

Abstract. Given the advances in reactive synthesis, it is a natural next step to consider more complex multi-process systems. Distributed synthesis, however, is not yet scalable. Compositional approaches can be a game changer. Here, the challenge is to decompose a given specification of the global system behavior into requirements on the individual processes. In this paper, we introduce a compositional synthesis algorithm that, for each process, constructs, in addition to the implementation, a certificate that captures the necessary interface between the processes. The certificates then allow for constructing separate requirements for the individual processes. By bounding the size of the certificates, we can bias the synthesis procedure towards solutions that are desirable in the sense that the assumptions between the processes are small. Our experimental results show that our approach is much faster than standard methods for distributed synthesis as long as reasonably small certificates exist.

1 Introduction

In the last decade, there have been breakthroughs in terms of realistic applications and practical tools for reactive synthesis, demonstrating that concentrating on *what* a system should do instead of *how* it should be done is feasible. A natural next step is to consider complex multi-process systems. For distributed systems, though, there are no scalable tools that are capable of automatically synthesizing strategies from formal specifications for arbitrary system architectures.

For the scalability of verification algorithms, compositionality, i.e., breaking down the verification of a complex system into several smaller tasks over individual components, has proven to be a key technique [21]. For synthesis, however, developing compositional approaches is much more challenging: In practice, an individual process can rarely guarantee the satisfaction of the specification alone. Typically, there exist input sequences that prevent a process from satisfying the specification. The other processes in the system then ensure that these sequences are not produced. Thus, a process needs information about the strategies of the

This work was partially supported by the German Research Foundation (DFG) as part of the Collaborative Research Center "Foundations of Perspicuous Software Systems" (TRR 248, 389792660), and by the European Research Council (ERC) Grant OSARES (No. 683300).

© Springer Nature Switzerland AG 2021
Z. Hou and V. Ganesh (Eds.): ATVA 2021, LNCS 12971, pp. 303–319, 2021.
https://doi.org/10.1007/978-3-030-88885-5_20

other processes to be able to satisfy the specification. Hence, distributed synthesis cannot easily be broken down into tasks over the individual processes.

In this paper, we introduce a compositional synthesis algorithm addressing this problem by synthesizing additional *guarantees on the behavior* of every process. These guarantees, the so-called *certificates*, then provide essential information for the individual synthesis tasks: A strategy is only required to satisfy the specification if the other processes do not deviate from their guaranteed behavior. This allows for considering a process independent of the other processes' strategies. Our algorithm is an extension of bounded synthesis [14] that incorporates the search for certificates into the synthesis task for the strategies.

The benefits of synthesizing additional certificates are threefold. First, it *guides the synthesis procedure*: Bounded synthesis searches for strategies up to a given size. Beyond that, our algorithm introduces a bound on the size of the certificates. Hence, it bounds the size of the interface between the processes and thus the size of the assumptions made by them. By starting with small bounds and by only increasing them if the specification is unrealizable for the given bounds, the algorithm restricts synthesis to search for solutions with small interfaces.

Second, the certificates *increase the understandability* of the synthesized solution: It is challenging to recognize the interconnections in a distributed system. The certificates capture which information a process needs about the behavior of the other processes to be able to satisfy the specification, immediately encapsulating the system's interconnections. Furthermore, the certificates abstract from behavior that is irrelevant for the satisfaction of the specification. This allows for analyzing the strategies locally without considering the whole system's behavior.

Third, synthesizing certificates *enables modularity* of the system: The strategies only depend on the certificates of the other processes, not on their particular strategies. As long as the processes do not deviate from their certificates, the parallel composition of the strategies satisfies the specification. Hence, the certificates form a contract between the processes. After defining the contract, the strategies can be exchanged safely with other ones that respect the contract. Thus, strategies can be adapted flexibly without synthesizing a solution for the whole system again if requirements that do not affect the contract change.

We introduce two representations of certificates, as LTL formulas and as labeled transition systems. We show soundness and completeness of our certifying synthesis algorithm for both of them. Furthermore, we present a technique for determining *relevant processes* for each process. This allows us to reduce the number of certificates that a process has to consider to satisfy the specification while maintaining soundness and completeness. Focusing on the representation of certificates as transition systems, we present an algorithm for synthesizing certificates that is based on a reduction to a SAT constraint system.

We implemented the algorithm and compared it to an extension [2] of the synthesis tool BoSy [9] to distributed systems and to a compositional synthesis algorithm based on dominant strategies [7]. The results clearly demonstrate the advantage of synthesizing certificates: If solutions with a small interface between the processes exist, our algorithm outperforms the other synthesis tools significantly. Otherwise, the overhead of synthesizing additional guarantees is small.

Further details and all proofs are available in the full version of this paper [13].

Related Work: There are several approaches to compositional synthesis for monolithic systems [10–12,16,17]. As we are considering distributed systems, we focus on distributed synthesis algorithms. Assume-guarantee synthesis [5] is closest to our approach. There, each process provides a guarantee on its own behavior and makes an assumption on the behavior of the other processes. If there is a strategy for each process that satisfies the specification under the hypothesis that the other processes respect the assumption, and if its guarantee implies the assumptions of the other processes, a solution for the whole system is found. In contrast to our approach, most assume-guarantee synthesis algorithms [1,3–5] either rely on the user to provide the assumptions or require that a strategy profile on which the strategies can synchronize is constructed prior to synthesis.

A recent extension of assume-guarantee synthesis [19] algorithmically synthesizes assume-guarantee contracts for each process. In contrast to our approach, the guarantees do not necessarily imply the assumptions of the other processes. Thus, the algorithm needs to iteratively refine assumptions and guarantees until a valid contract is found. This iteration is circumvented in our algorithm since only assumptions that are guaranteed by the other processes are used.

Using a weaker winning condition for synthesis, remorse-free dominance [6], avoids the explicit construction of assumptions and guarantees [7]. The assumptions are implicit, but they do not always suffice. Thus, although a dependency analysis of the specification allows for solutions for further, more interconnected systems and specifications [12], compositional solutions do not always exist.

2   Running Example

In many modern factories, autonomous robots are a crucial component in the production line. The correctness of their implementation is essential and therefore they are a natural target for synthesis. Consider a factory with two robots that carry production parts from one machine to another. In the factory, there is a crossing that is used by both robots. The robots are required to prevent a crash: $\varphi_{safe} := \Box \neg((at\_crossing_1 \wedge go_1) \wedge (at\_crossing_2 \wedge go_2))$, where $at\_crossing_i$ is an input variable denoting that robot r_i arrived at the crossing, and go_i is an output variable of robot r_i denoting that r_i moves ahead. Moreover, both robots need to cross the intersection at some point in time after arriving there: $\varphi_{cross_i} := \Box(at\_crossing_i \rightarrow \bigcirc \Diamond go_i)$. In addition to these requirements, both robots have further objectives φ_{add_i} that are specific to their area of application. For instance, they may capture which machines have to be approached.

None of the robots can satisfy $\varphi_{safe} \wedge \varphi_{cross_i}$ alone: The crossing needs to be entered eventually by r_i but no matter when it is entered, r_j might enter it at the same time. Thus, strategies cannot be synthesized individually without information on the other robot's behavior. Due to φ_{add_i}, the parallel composition of the strategies can be large and complex. Hence, understanding why the overall specification is met and recognizing the individual strategies is challenging.

If both robots commit to their behavior at crossings, a robot r_i can satisfy $\varphi_{safe} \wedge \varphi_{cross_i}$ individually since it is allowed to assume that the other robot does not deviate from its guaranteed behavior, the so-called certificate. For instance, if r_2 commits to always giving priority to r_1, entering the crossing regardless of r_2 satisfies $\varphi_{safe} \wedge \varphi_{cross_1}$ for r_1. If r_1 guarantees to not block crossings, r_2 can satisfy $\varphi_{safe} \wedge \varphi_{cross_2}$ as well. Hence, if both robots can satisfy the whole part of the specification that affects them, i.e., $\varphi_i = \varphi_{safe} \wedge \varphi_{cross_i} \wedge \varphi_{add_i}$, under the assumption that the other robot sticks to its certificate, then the parallel composition of their strategies satisfies the whole specification. Furthermore, we then know that the robots do not interfere in any other situation. Thus, the certificates provide insight in the required communication of the robots.

Moreover, when analyzing the strategy s_i of r_i, only taking r_j's certificate into account abstracts away r_j's behavior aside from crossings. This allows us to focus on the relevant aspects of r_j's behavior for r_i, making it significantly easier to understand why r_i's strategy satisfies φ_i. Lastly, the certificates form a contract of safe behavior at crossings: If r_i's additional objectives change, it suffices to synthesize a new strategy for r_i. Provided r_i does not change its behavior at crossings, r_j's strategy can be left unchanged.

3   Preliminaries

Notation. In the following, we denote the prefix of length t of an infinite word $\sigma = \sigma_1 \sigma_2 \cdots \in (2^V)^\omega$ by $\sigma_{..t} := \sigma_1 \ldots \sigma_t$. Moreover, for a set X and an infinite word $\sigma = \sigma_1 \sigma_2 \cdots \in (2^V)^\omega$, we define $\sigma \cap X = (\sigma_1 \cap X)(\sigma_2 \cap X) \cdots \in (2^X)^\omega$.

LTL. Linear-time temporal logic (LTL) [20] is a specification language for linear-time properties. Let Σ be a finite set of atomic propositions and let $a \in \Sigma$. The syntax of LTL is given by $\varphi, \psi :: = a \mid \neg\varphi \mid \varphi \vee \psi \mid \varphi \wedge \psi \mid \bigcirc \varphi \mid \varphi \mathcal{U} \psi$. We define $\Diamond \varphi = true \mathcal{U} \varphi$, and $\Box \varphi = \neg \Diamond \neg \varphi$ and use the standard semantics. The language $\mathcal{L}(\varphi)$ of a formula φ is the set of infinite words that satisfy φ. The atomic propositions in φ are denoted by $\mathrm{prop}(\varphi)$. We represent a formula $\varphi = \xi_1 \wedge \cdots \wedge \xi_k$ also by the set of its conjuncts, i.e., $\varphi = \{\xi_1, \ldots, \xi_k\}$.

Automata. A universal co-Büchi automaton $\mathcal{A} = (Q, q_0, \delta, F)$ over a finite alphabet Σ consists of a finite set of states Q, an initial state $q_0 \in Q$, a transition relation $\delta : Q \times 2^\Sigma \times Q$, and a set $F \subseteq Q$ of rejecting states. For an infinite word $\sigma = \sigma_0 \sigma_1 \cdots \in (2^\Sigma)^\omega$, a run of σ on $\mathcal{A}$ is an infinite sequence $q_0 q_1 \cdots \in Q^\omega$ of states with $(q_i, \sigma_i, q_{i+1}) \in \delta$ for all $i \geq 0$. A run is accepting if it contains only finitely many visits to rejecting states. $\mathcal{A}$ accepts a word σ if all runs of σ on $\mathcal{A}$ are accepting. The language $\mathcal{L}(\mathcal{A})$ of $\mathcal{A}$ is the set of all accepted words. An LTL specification φ can be translated into an equivalent universal co-Büchi automaton $\mathcal{A}_\varphi$, i.e., with $\mathcal{L}(\varphi) = \mathcal{L}(\mathcal{A}_\varphi)$, with a single exponential blow up [18].

Architectures. An architecture is a tuple $A = (P, V, I, O)$, where P is a set of processes consisting of the environment process env and a set of n system processes $P^- = P \setminus \{env\}$, V is a set of variables, $I = \langle I_1, \ldots, I_n \rangle$ assigns a set

$I_j \subseteq V$ of input variables to each system process p_j, and $O = \langle O_{env}, O_1, \ldots O_n \rangle$ assigns a set $O_j \subseteq V$ of output variables to each process p_j. For all $p_j, p_k \in P^-$ with $j \neq k$, we have $I_j \cap O_j = \emptyset$ and $O_j \cap O_k = \emptyset$. The variables V_j of $p_j \in P^-$ are its inputs and outputs, i.e., $V_j = I_j \cup O_j$. The variables V of the whole system are defined by $V = \bigcup_{p_j \in P^-} V_j$. We define $inp = \bigcup_{p_j \in P^-} I_j$ and $out = \bigcup_{p_j \in P^-} O_j$. An architecture is called distributed if $|P^-| \geq 2$ and monolithic otherwise. In the remainder of this paper, we assume that a distributed architecture is given.

Transition Systems. Given sets I and O of input and output variables, a Moore transition system (TS) $\mathcal{T} = (T, t_0, \tau, o)$ consists of a finite set of states T, an initial state t_0, a transition function $\tau : T \times 2^I \to T$, and a labeling function $o : T \to 2^O$. For an input sequence $\gamma = \gamma_0 \gamma_1 \ldots \in (2^I)^\omega$, $\mathcal{T}$ produces a path $\pi = (t_0, \gamma_0 \cup o(t_0))(t_1, \gamma_1 \cup o(t_1)) \ldots \in (T \times 2^{I \cup O})^\omega$, where $(t_j, \gamma_j, t_{j+1}) \in \tau$. The projection of a path to the variables is called trace. The parallel composition of two TS $\mathcal{T}_1 = (T_1, t_0^1, \tau_1, o_1)$, $\mathcal{T}_2 = (T_2, t_0^2, \tau_2, o_2)$, is given by $\mathcal{T}_1 \| \mathcal{T}_2 = (T, t_0, \tau, o)$, with $T = T_1 \times T_2$, $t_0 = (t_0^1, t_0^2)$, $\tau((t, t'), i) = (\tau_1(t, i_1 \cap I_1), \tau_2(t', i_2 \cap I_2))$, and $o((t, t')) = o_1(t) \cup o_2(t')$. A TS $\mathcal{T}_1 = (T_1, t_0^1, \tau_1, o_1)$ over I and O_1 *simulates* $\mathcal{T}_2 = (T_2, t_0^2, \tau_2, o_2)$ over I and O_2 with $O_1 \subseteq O_2$, denoted $\mathcal{T}_2 \preceq \mathcal{T}_1$, if there is a simulation relation $R : T_2 \times T_1$ with $(t_0^2, t_0^1) \in R$, $\forall (t_2, t_1) \in R$. $o(t_2) \cap O_1 = o(t_1)$, and $\forall t_2' \in T_2. \forall i \in 2^I. (\tau_2(t_2, i) = t_2') \to (\exists t_1' \in T_1. \tau_1(t_1, i) = t_1' \wedge (t_2', t_1') \in R)$.

Strategies. We model a strategy s_i of $p_i \in P^-$ as a Moore transition system $\mathcal{T}_i$ over I_i and O_i. The trace produced by $\mathcal{T}_i$ on $\gamma \in (2^{I_i})^\omega$ is called the *computation* of s_i on γ, denoted $comp(s_i, \gamma)$. For an LTL formula φ over V, s_i satisfies φ, denoted $s_i \models \varphi$, if $comp(s, \gamma) \cup \gamma' \models \varphi$ holds for all $\gamma \in (2^{I_i})^\omega$, $\gamma' \in (2^{V \setminus V_i})^\omega$.

Synthesis. For a specification φ, synthesis derives strategies $s_1, \ldots, s_n$ for the system processes such that $s_1 \| \ldots \| s_n \models \varphi$ holds. If such strategies exist, φ is realizable in the architecture. Bounded synthesis [14] additionally bounds the size of the strategies. The search for strategies is encoded into a constraint system that is satisfiable if, and only if, φ is realizable for the bound. There are SMT, SAT, QBF, and DQBF encodings for monolithic [8] and distributed [2] architectures.

4   Compositional Synthesis with Certificates

In this section, we describe a sound and complete compositional synthesis algorithm for distributed systems. The main idea is to synthesize strategies for the system processes individually. Hence, in contrast to classical distributed synthesis, where strategies $s_1, \ldots, s_n$ are synthesized such that $s_1 \| \ldots \| s_n \models \varphi$ holds, we require that $s_i \models \varphi_i$ holds for all system processes $p_i \in P^-$. Here, φ_i is a subformula of φ that, intuitively, captures the part of φ that affects p_i. As long as φ_i contains all parts of φ that restrict the behavior of s_i, the satisfaction of φ by the parallel composition of all strategies is guaranteed. Computing specification decompositions is not the main focus of this paper; in fact, our algorithm can be used with any decomposition that fulfills the above requirement. There is work on obtaining small subspecifications, e.g., [11], we, however, use an easy decomposition algorithm in the remainder of this paper for simplicity:

Definition 1 (Specification Decomposition). *Let* $\varphi = \xi_1 \wedge \cdots \wedge \xi_k$ *be an LTL formula. The decomposition of* φ *is a vector* $\langle \varphi_1, \ldots, \varphi_n \rangle$ *of LTL formulas with* $\varphi_i = \{\xi_j \mid \xi_j \in \varphi \wedge (\text{prop}(\xi_j) \cap O_i \neq \emptyset \vee \text{prop}(\xi_j) \cap out = \emptyset)\}$.

Intuitively, the subspecification φ_i contains all conjuncts of φ that contain outputs of p_i as well as all input-only conjuncts. In the remainder of this paper, we assume that both $\text{prop}(\varphi) \subseteq V$ and $\mathcal{L}(\varphi) \in (2^V)^\omega$ hold for all specifications φ. Then, every atomic proposition occurring in a formula φ is an input or output of at least one system process and thus $\bigwedge_{p_i \in P^-} \varphi_i = \varphi$ holds.

Although we decompose the specification, a process p_i usually cannot guarantee the satisfaction of φ_i alone; rather, it depends on the cooperation of the other processes. For instance, robot r_1 from Sect. 2 cannot guarantee that no crash will occur when entering the crossing since r_2 can enter it at the same point in time. Thus, we additionally synthesize a *guarantee on the behavior* of each process, the so-called *certificate*. The certificates then provide essential information to the processes: If p_i commits to a certificate, the other processes can rely on p_i's strategy to not deviate from this behavior. In particular, the strategies only need to satisfy the specification as long as the other processes stick to their certificates. Thus, a process is not required to react to *all* behaviors of the other processes but only to those that truly occur when the processes interact.

In this section, we represent the certificate of $p_i \in P^-$ by an LTL formula ψ_i. For instance, robot r_2 may guarantee to always give priority to r_1 at crossings, yielding the certificate $\psi_2 = \square((at\_crossing_1 \wedge at\_crossing_2) \rightarrow \bigcirc \neg go_2)$. Since r_1 can assume that r_2 does not deviate from its certificate ψ_2, a strategy for r_1 that enters crossings regardless of r_2 satisfies $\varphi_{safe} \wedge \varphi_{cross_1}$.

To ensure that p_i does not deviate from its own certificate, we require its strategy s_i to satisfy the LTL formula ψ_i describing it. To model that s_i only has to satisfy its specification if the other processes stick to their certificates, it has to satisfy $\Psi_i \rightarrow \varphi_i$, where $\Psi_i = \{\psi_j \mid p_j \in P^- \setminus \{p_i\}\}$, i.e., Ψ_i is the conjunction of the certificates of the other processes. Using this, we define certifying synthesis:

Definition 2 (Certifying Synthesis). *Let* φ *be an LTL formula with decomposition* $\langle \varphi_1, \ldots, \varphi_n \rangle$. *Certifying synthesis derives strategies* $s_1, \ldots, s_n$ *and LTL certificates* $\psi_1, \ldots, \psi_n$ *for the system processes such that* $s_i \models \psi_i \wedge (\Psi_i \rightarrow \varphi_i)$ *holds for all* $p_i \in P^-$, *where* $\Psi_i = \{\psi_j \mid p_j \in P^- \setminus \{p_i\}\}$.

Classical distributed synthesis algorithms reason *globally* about the satisfaction of the full specification by the parallel composition of the synthesized strategies. Certifying synthesis, in contrast, reasons *locally* about the satisfaction of the subspecifications for the individual processes, i.e., without considering the parallel composition of the strategies. This greatly improves the understandability of the correctness of synthesized solutions since we are able to consider the strategies separately. Furthermore, local reasoning is still sound and complete:

Theorem 1 (Soundness and Completeness). *Let* φ *be an LTL formula and let* $\mathcal{S} = \langle s_1, \ldots, s_n \rangle$ *be a vector of strategies for the system processes. There exists a vector* $\Psi = \langle \psi_1, \ldots, \psi_n \rangle$ *of LTL certificates such that* $(\mathcal{S}, \Psi)$ *is a solution of certifying synthesis for* φ *if, and only if* $s_1 \| \ldots \| s_n \models \varphi$ *holds.*

Soundness of certifying synthesis follows from the fact that every system process is required to satisfy its own certificate. Completeness is obtained since every strategy can serve as its own certificate: Intuitively, if $s_1 \| \ldots \| s_n \models \varphi$, then LTL certificates that capture the exact behavior of the corresponding strategy satisfy the requirements of certifying synthesis. The proof is given in [13].

Thus, certifying synthesis enables local reasoning and therefore better understandability of the solution as well as modularity of the system, while ensuring to find correct solutions for all specifications that are realizable in the architecture. Furthermore, the parallel composition of the strategies obtained with certifying synthesis for a specification φ is a solution for the whole system.

5 Certifying Synthesis with Deterministic Certificates

There are several quality measures for certificates, for instance their size. We, however, focus on certificates that are *easy to synthesize*: To determine whether a strategy sticks to its own certificate, a check for language containment has to be performed. Yet, efficient algorithms only exist for deterministic properties [23]. While certificates represented by LTL formulas are easily human-readable, they can be nondeterministic. Thus, the ω-automaton representing the LTL certificate needs to be determinized, yielding an exponential blowup in its size [22].

In this section, we introduce a representation of certificates that ensures determinism to avoid the blowup. Note that while enforcing determinism might yield larger certificates, it does not rule out any strategy that can be found with nondeterministic certificates: Since strategies are per se deterministic, there exists at least one deterministic certificate for them: The strategy itself.

We model the guaranteed behavior g_i of a system process p_i as a labeled transition system $\mathcal{T}_i^G$, called *guarantee transition system* (GTS), over inputs I_i and *guarantee output variables* $O_i^G \subseteq O_i$. Only considering a subset of O_i as output variables allows the certificate to abstract from outputs of p_i whose valuation is irrelevant for all other system processes. In the following, we assume the guarantee output variables of p_i to be both an output of p_i and an input of some other system process, i.e., $O_i^G := O_i \cap inp$. Intuitively, a variable $v \in O_i \setminus O_i^G$ cannot be observed by any other process. Thus, a guarantee on its behavior does not influence any other system process and hence it can be omitted. The variables V_i^G of the GTS of $p_i \in P^-$ are then given by $V_i^G := I_i \cup O_i^G$.

In certifying synthesis, it is essential that a strategy only needs to satisfy the specification if the other processes do not deviate from their certificates. In the previous section, we used an implication in the local objective to model this. When representing certificates as transition systems, we use *valid histories* to determine whether a sequence matches the certificates of the other processes.

Definition 3 (Valid History). *Let $\mathcal{G}_i$ be a set of guarantee transition systems. A valid history of length t with respect to $\mathcal{G}_i$ is a finite sequence $\sigma \in (2^V)^*$ of length t, where for all $g_j \in \mathcal{G}_i$, $\sigma_k \cap O_j^G = comp(g_j, \hat{\sigma} \cap I_j)_k \cap O_j^G$ holds for all points in time k with $1 \le k \le t$ and all infinite extensions $\hat{\sigma}$ of σ. The set of all valid histories of length t with respect to $\mathcal{G}_i$ is denoted by $\mathcal{H}_{\mathcal{G}_i}^t$.*

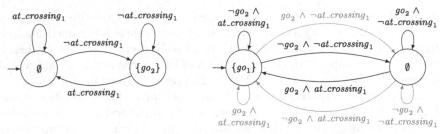

(a) Guarantee transition system for r_2 (b) Strategy transition system for r_1

Fig. 1. Strategy and GTS for robots r_1 and r_2 from Sect. 2, respectively. The labels of the states denote the output of the TS in the respective state.

Intuitively, a valid history respecting a set $\mathcal{G}_i$ of guarantee transition systems is a finite sequence that is a prefix of a computation of all GTS in $\mathcal{G}_i$. Thus, a valid history can be produced by the parallel composition of the GTS. Note that since strategies cannot look into the future, a finite word satisfies the requirements of a valid history either for all of its infinite extensions or for none of them.

As an example for valid histories, consider the manufacturing robots again. Assume that r_2 guarantees to always give priority to r_1 at crossings and to move forward if r_1 is not at the crossing. A GTS g_2 for r_2 is depicted in Fig. 1a. Since r_2 never outputs go_2 if r_1 is at the crossing (left state), the finite sequence $\{at\_crossing_1\}\{go_2\}$ is no valid history respecting g_2. Since r_2 outputs go_2 otherwise (right state), e.g., $\{at\_crossing_2\}\{go_2\}$ is a valid history respecting g_2.

We use valid histories to determine whether the other processes stick to their certificates. Thus, intuitively, a strategy is required to satisfy the specification if its computation is a valid history respecting the GTS of the other processes:

Definition 4 (Local Satisfaction). *Let $\mathcal{G}_i$ be a set of guarantee transition systems. A strategy s_i for $p_i \in P^-$ locally satisfies an LTL formula φ_i with respect to $\mathcal{G}_i$, denoted $s_i \models_{\mathcal{G}_i} \varphi_i$, if $comp(s_i, \gamma) \cup \gamma' \models \varphi_i$ holds for all $\gamma \in (2^{I_i})^\omega$, $\gamma' \in (2^{V \setminus V_i})^\omega$ with $comp(s_i, \gamma)_{..t} \cup \gamma'_{..t} \in \mathcal{H}^t_{\mathcal{G}_i}$ for all points in time t.*

If r_2, for instance, sticks to its guaranteed behavior g_2 depicted in Fig. 1a, then r_1 can enter crossings regardless of r_2. Such a strategy s_1 for r_1 is shown in Fig. 1b. Since neither $\sigma := \{at\_crossing_1\}\{go_2\}$ nor any finite sequence containing σ is a valid history respecting g_2, no transition for input go_2 has to be considered for local satisfaction when r_1 is at the crossing (left state of s_1). Therefore, these transitions are depicted in gray. Analogously, no transition for $\neg go_2$ has to be considered when r_1 is not at the crossing (right state). The other transitions match valid histories and thus they are taken into account. Since no crash occurs when considering the black transitions only, $s_1 \models_{\{g_2\}} \varphi_{safe}$ holds.

Using local satisfaction, we now define certifying synthesis in the setting where certificates are represented by labeled transition systems: Given an architecture A and a specification φ, certifying synthesis for φ derives strategies $s_1, \ldots, s_n$ and *guarantee transition systems* $g_1, \ldots, g_n$ for the system processes.

For all $p_i \in P^-$, we require s_i to locally satisfy its specification with respect to the guarantee transition systems of the other processes, i.e., $s_i \models_{\mathcal{G}_i} \varphi_i$, where $\mathcal{G}_i = \{g_j \mid p_j \in P^- \setminus \{p_i\}\}$. To ensure that a strategy does not deviate from its own certificate, g_i is required to simulate s_i, i.e., $s_i \preceq g_i$ needs to hold.

In the following, we show that solutions of certifying synthesis with LTL certificates can be translated into solutions with GTS and vice versa. Given a solution of certifying synthesis with GTS, the main idea is to construct LTL certificates that capture the exact behavior of the GTS. For the formal certificate translation and its proof of correctness, we refer to [13].

Lemma 1. *Let φ be an LTL formula. Let $\mathcal{S}$ and $\mathcal{G}$ be vectors of strategies and guarantee transition systems, respectively, for the system processes. If $(\mathcal{S}, \mathcal{G})$ is a solution of certifying synthesis for φ, then there exists a vector Ψ of LTL certificates such that $(\mathcal{S}, \Psi)$ is a solution for certifying synthesis for φ as well.*

Given a solution of certifying synthesis with LTL certificates, we can construct GTS that match the strategies of the given solution. Then, these strategies as well as the GTS form a solution of certifying synthesis with GTS. The full construction and its proof of correctness is given in [13].

Lemma 2. *Let φ be an LTL formula. Let $\mathcal{S}$ and Ψ be vectors of strategies and LTL certificates, respectively, for the system processes. If $(\mathcal{S}, \Psi)$ is a solution of certifying synthesis for φ, then there exists a vector $\mathcal{G}$ of guarantee transition system such that $(\mathcal{S}, \mathcal{G})$ is a solution for certifying synthesis for φ as well.*

Hence, we can translate solutions of certifying synthesis with LTL formulas and with GTS into each other. Thus, we can reuse the results from Sect. 4, in particular Theorem 1, and then soundness and completeness of certifying synthesis with guarantee transition systems follows with Lemmas 1 and 2:

Theorem 2 (Soundness and Completeness with GTS). *Let φ be an LTL formula. Let $\mathcal{S} = \langle s_1, \ldots, s_n \rangle$ be a vector of strategies for the system processes. Then, there exists a vector $\mathcal{G}$ of guarantee transition systems such that $(\mathcal{S}, \mathcal{G})$ is a solution of certifying synthesis for φ if, and only if, $s_1 \| \ldots \| s_n \models \varphi$ holds.*

Thus, similar to LTL certificates, certifying synthesis with GTS allows for local reasoning and thus enables modularity of the system while it still ensures that correct solutions for all realizable specifications are found. In particular, enforcing deterministic certificates does not rule out strategies that can be obtained with either nondeterministic certificates or with classical distributed synthesis.

As an example of the whole synthesis procedure of a distributed system with certifying synthesis and GTS, consider the manufacturing robots from Sect. 2. For simplicity, suppose that the robots do not have individual additional requirements φ_{add_i}. Hence, the full specification is given by $\varphi_{safe} \wedge \varphi_{cross_1} \wedge \varphi_{cross_2}$. Since go_i is an output variable of robot r_i, we obtain the subspecifications $\varphi_i = \varphi_{safe} \wedge \varphi_{cross_i}$. A solution of certifying synthesis is then given by the strategies and GTS depicted in Figs. 1 and 2. Note that s_2 only locally satisfies φ_{cross_2} with respect to g_1 when assuming that r_1 is not immediately again at

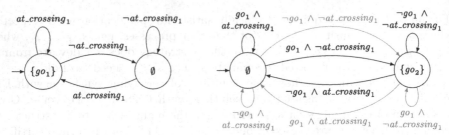

(a) Guarantee transition system for r_1 (b) Strategy transition system for r_2

Fig. 2. GTS and strategy for robots r_1 and r_2 from Sect. 2, respectively. The labels of the states denote the output of the TS in the respective state.

the intersection after crossing it. However, there are solutions with slightly more complicated certificates that do not need this assumption. The parallel composition of s_1 and s_2 yields a strategy that allows r_1 to move forwards if it is at the crossing and that allows r_2 to move forwards otherwise.

6   Computing Relevant Processes

Both representations of certificates introduced in the last two sections consider the certificates of *all* other system processes in the local objective of every system process p_i. This is not always necessary since in some cases φ_i is satisfiable by a strategy for p_i even if another process deviates from its guaranteed behavior.

In this section, we present an optimization of certifying synthesis that reduces the number of considered certificates. We compute a set of *relevant processes* $\mathcal{R}_i \subseteq P^- \setminus \{p_i\}$ for every $p_i \in P^-$. Certifying synthesis then only considers the certificates of the relevant processes: For LTL certificates, it requires that $s_i \models \psi_i \wedge (\Psi_i^{\mathcal{R}} \rightarrow \varphi_i)$ holds, where $\Psi_i^{\mathcal{R}} = \{\psi_j \in \Psi \mid p_j \in \mathcal{R}_i\}$. For GTS, both $s_i \preceq g_i$ and $s_i \models_{\mathcal{G}_i^{\mathcal{R}}} \varphi_i$ need to hold, where $\mathcal{G}_i^{\mathcal{R}} = \{g_j \in \mathcal{G} \mid p_j \in \mathcal{R}_i\}$. Such solutions of certifying synthesis are denoted by $(\mathcal{S}, \Psi)_{\mathcal{R}}$ and $(\mathcal{S}, \mathcal{G})_{\mathcal{R}}$, respectively.

The construction of the relevant processes $\mathcal{R}_i$ has to ensure that certifying synthesis is still sound and complete. In the following, we introduce a definition of relevant processes that does so. It excludes processes from p_i's set of relevant processes $\mathcal{R}_i$ whose output variables do not occur in the subspecification φ_i:

Definition 5 (Relevant Processes). *Let φ be an LTL formula with decomposition $\langle \varphi_1, \ldots, \varphi_n \rangle$. The relevant processes $\mathcal{R}_i \subseteq P^- \setminus \{p_i\}$ of system process $p_i \in P^-$ are given by $\mathcal{R}_i = \{p_j \in P^- \setminus \{p_i\} \mid O_j \cap \mathrm{prop}(\varphi_i) \neq \emptyset\}$.*

Intuitively, since $O_j \cap \mathrm{prop}(\varphi_i) = \emptyset$ holds for a process $p_j \in P^- \setminus \mathcal{R}_i$ with $i \neq j$, the subspecification φ_i does not restrict the satisfying valuations of the output variables of p_j. Thus, in particular, if a sequence satisfies φ_i, then it does so for any valuations of the variables in O_j. Hence, the guaranteed behavior of p_j does not influence the satisfiability of φ_i and thus p_i does not need to consider it. The proof of the following theorem stating this property is given in [13].

Theorem 3 (Correctness of Relevant Processes). *Let φ be an LTL formula. Let $\mathcal{S} = \langle s_1, \ldots, s_n \rangle$ be a vector of strategies for the system processes.*

1. *Let Ψ be a vector of LTL certificates. If $(\mathcal{S}, \Psi)_\mathcal{R}$ is a solution of certifying synthesis for φ, then $s_1 \| \ldots \| s_n \models \varphi$ holds. If $s_1 \| \ldots \| s_n \models \varphi$ holds, then there exists a vector Ψ' of LTL certificates and a vector $\mathcal{S}'$ of strategies such that $(\mathcal{S}', \Psi')_\mathcal{R}$ is a solution of certifying synthesis for φ.*
2. *Let $\mathcal{G}$ be a vector of guarantee transition systems. If $(\mathcal{S}, \mathcal{G})_\mathcal{R}$ is a solution of certifying synthesis for φ, then $s_1 \| \ldots \| s_n \models \varphi$. If $s_1 \| \ldots \| s_n \models \varphi$ holds, then there exists a vector $\mathcal{G}'$ of guarantee transition systems and a vector $\mathcal{S}'$ of strategies such that $(\mathcal{S}', \mathcal{G}')_\mathcal{R}$ is a solution of certifying synthesis for φ.*

Note that for certifying synthesis with relevant processes, we can only guarantee that for every vector of strategies $\langle s_1, \ldots, s_n \rangle$ whose parallel composition satisfies the specification, there exist *some* strategies that are a solution of certifying synthesis. These strategies are not necessarily $s_1, \ldots, s_n$: A strategy s_i may make use of the certificate of a process p_j outside of $\mathcal{R}_i$. That is, it may violate its specification φ_i on an input sequence that does not stick to g_j although φ_i is satisfiable for this input. Strategy s_i is not required to satisfy φ_i on this input, a strategy that may only consider the certificates of the relevant processes, however, is. As long as the definition of relevant processes allows for finding *some* solution of certifying synthesis, like the one introduced in this section does as a result of Theorem 3, certifying synthesis is nevertheless sound and complete.

7 Synthesizing Certificates

In this section, we describe an algorithm for practically synthesizing strategies and deterministic certificates represented by GTS. Our approach is based on *bounded synthesis* [14] and bounds the size of the strategies and of the certificates. This allows for producing size-optimal solutions in either terms of strategies or certificates. Like for monolithic bounded synthesis [8,14], we encode the search for a solution of certifying synthesis of a certain size into a SAT constraint system. We reuse parts of the constraint system for monolithic systems.

An essential part of bounded synthesis is to determine whether a strategy satisfies an LTL formula φ_i. To do so, we first construct the equivalent universal co-Büchi automaton $\mathcal{A}_i$ with $\mathcal{L}(\mathcal{A}_i) = \mathcal{L}(\varphi_i)$. Then, we check whether $\mathcal{A}_i$ accepts $comp(s_i, \gamma) \cup \gamma'$ for all $\gamma \in (2^{I_i})^\omega$, $\gamma' \in (2^{V \setminus V_i})^\omega$, i.e., whether all runs of $\mathcal{A}_i$ induced by $comp(s_i, \gamma) \cup \gamma'$ contain only finitely many visits to rejecting states. So far, we used *local satisfaction* to formalize that in compositional synthesis with GTS a strategy only needs to satisfy its specification as long as the other processes stick to their guarantees. That is, we changed the satisfaction condition. To reuse existing algorithms for bounded synthesis and, in particular, for checking whether a strategy is winning, however, we incorporate this property of certifying synthesis into the labeled transition system representing the strategy instead. In fact, we utilize the following observation: A finite run of a universal co-Büchi automaton can never visit a rejecting state infinitely often.

Hence, by ensuring that the automaton produces finite runs on all sequences that deviate from a guarantee, checking whether a strategy satisfies a specification can still be done by checking whether the runs of the corresponding automaton induced by the computations of the strategy visit a rejecting state only finitely often.

Therefore, we represent strategies by *incomplete* transition systems in the following. The domain of definition of their transition function is defined such that the computation of a strategy is infinite if, and only if, the other processes stick to their guarantees. To formalize this, we utilize valid histories:

Definition 6 (Local Strategy). *A local strategy s_i for process $p_i \in P^-$ with respect to a set $\mathcal{G}_i$ of GTS is represented by a TS $\mathcal{T}_i = (T, t_0, \tau, o)$ with a partial transition function $\tau : T \times 2^{I_i} \rightharpoonup T$. The domain of definition of τ is defined such that $comp(s_i, \gamma)$ is infinite for $\gamma \in (2^{I_i})^\omega$ if, and only if, there exists $\gamma' \in (2^{V \setminus V_i})^\omega$ such that $comp(s_i, \gamma)_{..t} \cup \gamma'_{..t} \in \mathcal{H}^t_{\mathcal{G}_i}$ holds for all points in time t.*

As an example, consider strategy s_1 for robot r_1 and guarantee transition system g_2 for robot r_2, both depicted in Fig. 1, again. From s_1, we can construct a local strategy s'_1 for r_1 with respect to g_2 by eliminating the gray transitions.

We now define certifying synthesis with local strategies: Given a specification φ, certifying synthesis derives GTS $g_1, \ldots, g_n$ and *local strategies* $s_1, \ldots, s_n$ respecting these guarantees, such that for all $p_i \in P^-$, $s_i \preceq g_i$ holds and all runs of $\mathcal{A}_i$ induced by $comp(s_i, \gamma) \cup \gamma'$ contain finitely many visits to rejecting states for all $\gamma \in (2^{I_i})^\omega$, $\gamma' \in (2^{V \setminus V_i})^\omega$, where $\mathcal{A}_i$ is a universal co-Büchi automaton with $\mathcal{L}(\mathcal{A}_i) = \mathcal{L}(\varphi_i)$. Thus, we can reuse existing algorithms for checking satisfaction of a formula in our certifying synthesis algorithm when synthesizing local strategies instead of complete ones. Similar to monolithic bounded synthesis, we construct a constraint system encoding the search for local strategies and GTS:

Theorem 4. *Let A be an architecture, let φ be an LTL formula, and let $\mathcal{B}$ be the size bounds. There is a SAT constraint system $\mathcal{C}_{A,\varphi,\mathcal{B}}$ such that (1) if $\mathcal{C}_{A,\varphi,\mathcal{B}}$ is satisfiable, then φ is realizable in A, (2) if φ is realizable in A for the bounds $\mathcal{B}$ and additionally $\mathrm{prop}(\varphi_i) \subseteq V_i$ holds for all $p_i \in P^-$, then $\mathcal{C}_{A,\varphi,\mathcal{B}}$ is satisfiable.*

Intuitively, the constraint system $\mathcal{C}_{A,\varphi,\mathcal{B}}$ consists of n slightly adapted copies of the SAT constraint system for monolithic systems [8,14] as well as additional constraints that ensure that the synthesized local strategies correspond to the synthesized guarantees and that they indeed fulfill the conditions of certifying synthesis. The constraint system $\mathcal{C}_{A,\varphi,\mathcal{B}}$ is presented in [13].

Note that we build a *single* constraint system for the whole certifying synthesis task. That is, the strategies and certificates of the individual processes are not synthesized completely independently. This is one of the main differences of our approach to the negotiation-based assume-guarantee synthesis algorithm [19]. While this prevents separate synthesis tasks and thus parallelizability, it eliminates the need for a negotiation between the processes. Moreover, it allows for completeness of the synthesis algorithm. Although the synthesis tasks are not fully separated, the constraint system $\mathcal{C}_{A,\varphi,\mathcal{B}}$ is in most cases still significantly smaller and easier to solve than the one of classical distributed synthesis.

As indicated in Theorem 4, certifying synthesis with local strategies is not complete in general: We can only ensure completeness if the satisfaction of each subspecification solely depends on the variables that the corresponding process can observe. This incompleteness is due to a slight difference in the satisfaction of a specification with local strategies and local satisfaction with complete strategies: The latter requires a strategy s_i to satisfy φ_i if *all processes* stick to their guarantees. The former, in contrast, requires s_i to satisfy φ_i if *all processes producing observable outputs* stick to their guarantees. Hence, if p_i cannot observe whether p_j sticks to its guarantee, satisfaction with local strategies requires s_i to satisfy φ_i even if p_j deviates, while local satisfaction does not.

This slight change in definition is needed in order to incorporate the requirements of certifying synthesis into the transition system representing the strategy and thus to be able to reuse existing bounded synthesis frameworks. Although this advantage is at general completenesses expanse, we experienced that in practice many distributed systems, at least after rewriting the specification, indeed satisfy the condition that is needed for completeness in our approximation of certifying synthesis. In fact, all benchmarks described in Sect. 8 satisfy it.

8   Experimental Results

We have implemented certifying synthesis with local strategies and guarantee transition systems. It expects an LTL formula and its decomposition as well as the system architecture, and bounds on the sizes of the strategies and certificates as input. Specification decomposition can easily be automated by, e.g., implementing Definition 1. The implementation extends the synthesis tool BoSy [9] for monolithic systems to certifying synthesis for distributed systems. In particular, we extend and adapt BoSy's SAT encoding [8] as described in [13].

We compare our implementation to two extensions of BoSy: One for distributed systems [2] and one for synthesizing individual dominant strategies, implementing the compositional synthesis algorithm presented in [7]. The results are shown in Table 1. We used the SMT encoding of distributed BoSy since the other ones either cause memory errors on almost all benchmarks (SAT), or do not support most of our architectures (QBF). Since the running times of the underlying SMT solver vary immensely, we report on the average running time of 10 runs. Synthesizing individual dominant strategies is incomplete and hence we can only report on results for half of our benchmarks. We could not compare our implementation to the iterative assume-guarantee synthesis tool Agnes [19], since it currently does not support most of our architectures or specifications.

The first four benchmarks stem from the synthesis competition [15]. The latch is parameterized in the number of bits, the generalized buffer in the number of senders, the load balancer in the number of servers, and the shift benchmark in the number of inputs. The fourth benchmark is a ripple-carry adder that is parameterized in the number of bits and the last benchmark describes the manufacturing robots from Sect. 2 and is parameterized in the size of the objectives φ_{add_i} of the robots. The system architectures are given in [13].

Table 1. Experimental results on scalable benchmarks. Reported is the parameter and the running time in seconds. We used a machine with a 3.1 GHz Dual-Core Intel Core i5 processor and 16 GB of RAM, and a timeout of 60 min. For dist. BoSy, we use the SMT encoding and give the average runtime of 10 runs.

Benchmark	Param.	Cert. Synth.	Dist. BoSy	Dom. Strat.
n-ary Latch	2	**0.89**	41.26	4.75
	3	**0.91**	TO	6.40
	...	...	...	...
	6	**12.26**	TO	13.89
	7	105.69	TO	**15.06**
Generalized Buffer	1	**1.20**	6.59	5.23
	2	**2.72**	3012.51	10.53
	3	**122.09**	TO	961.60
Load Balancer	1	**0.98**	1.89	2.18
	2	**1.64**	2.39	–
Shift	2	**1.10**	1.99	4.76
	3	**1.13**	4.16	7.04
	4	**1.14**	TO	11.13
	...	...	...	...
	7	**9.01**	TO	16.08
	8	71.89	TO	**19.38**
Ripple-Carry Adder	1	**0.878**	1.83	–
	2	**2.09**	36.84	–
	3	**106.45**	TO	–
Manufacturing Robots	2	**1.10**	2.45	–
	4	**1.18**	2.43	–
	6	**1.67**	3.20	–
	8	**2.88**	5.67	–
	10	**48.83**	221.16	–
	12	**1.44**	TO	–
	...	...	...	...
	42	**373.90**	TO	–

For the latch, the generalized buffer, the ripple-carry adder, and the shift, certifying synthesis clearly outperforms distributed BoSy. For many parameters, BoSy does not terminate within 60min, while certifying synthesis solves the tasks in less than 13 s. For these benchmarks, a process does not need to know the full behavior of the other processes. Hence, the certificates are notably smaller than the strategies. A process of the ripple-carry adder, for instance, only needs information about the carry bit of the previous process, the sum bit is irrelevant.

For the load balancer, in contrast, the certificates need to contain the full behavior of the processes. Hence, the benefit of the compositional approach lies solely in the specification decomposition. This advantage suffices to produce a solution faster than distributed BoSy. Yet, for other benchmarks with full certificates, the overhead of synthesizing certificates dominates the benefit of specification decomposition for larger parameters, showcasing that certifying synthesis is particularly beneficial if a small interface between the processes exists.

The manufacturing robot benchmark is designed such that the interface between the processes stays small for all parameters. Hence, it demonstrates the advantage of abstracting from irrelevant behavior. Certifying synthesis clearly outperforms distributed BoSy on all instances. The parameter corresponds to the minimal solution size with distributed BoSy which does not directly correspond to the solution size with certifying synthesis. Thus, the running times do not grow in parallel. For more details on this benchmark we refer to [13].

Thus, certifying synthesis is extremely beneficial for specifications where small certificates exist. This directly corresponds to the existence of a small interface between the processes of the system. Hence, bounding the size of the certificates indeed guides the synthesis procedure in finding solutions fast.

When synthesizing dominant strategies, the weaker winning condition poses implicit assumptions on the behavior of the other processes. These assumptions do not always suffice: There are no independent dominant strategies for the load balancer, the ripple-carry adder, and the robots. While certifying synthesis performs better for the generalized buffer, the slight overhead of synthesizing explicit certificates becomes clear for the latch and the shift: For larger parameters, synthesizing dominant strategies outperforms certifying synthesis. Yet, the implicit assumptions do not encapsulate the required interface between the processes and thus they do not increase the understandability of the system's interconnections.

9   Conclusions

We have presented a synthesis algorithm that reduces the complexity of distributed synthesis by decomposing the synthesis task into smaller ones for the individual processes. To ensure completeness, the algorithm synthesizes additional certificates that capture a certain behavior a process commits to. A process then makes use of the certificates of the other processes by only requiring its strategy to satisfy the specification if the other processes do not deviate from their certificates. Synthesizing additional certificates increases the understandability of the system and the solution since the certificates capture the interconnections of the processes and which agreements they have to establish. Moreover, the certificates form a contract between the processes: The synthesized strategies can be substituted as long as the new strategy still complies with the contract, i.e., as long as it does not deviate from the guaranteed behavior, enabling modularity.

We have introduced two representations of the certificates, as LTL formulas and as labeled transition systems. Both ensure soundness and completeness of the compositional certifying synthesis algorithm. For the latter representation, we presented an encoding of the search for strategies and certificates into a SAT constraint solving problem. Moreover, we have introduced a technique for reducing the number of certificates that a process needs to consider by determining relevant processes. We have implemented the certifying synthesis algorithm and compared it to two extensions of the synthesis tool BoSy to distributed systems. The results clearly show the advantage of compositional approaches as well as of guiding the synthesis procedure by bounding the size of the certificates: For benchmarks where small interfaces between the processes exist, certifying synthesis outperforms the other distributed synthesis tools significantly. If no solution with small interfaces exist, the overhead of certifying synthesis is small.

References

1. Alur, R., Moarref, S., Topcu, U.: Pattern-based refinement of assume-guarantee specifications in reactive synthesis. In: Baier, C., Tinelli, C. (eds.) TACAS 2015. LNCS, vol. 9035, pp. 501–516. Springer, Heidelberg (2015). https://doi.org/10.1007/978-3-662-46681-0_49
2. Baumeister, J.E.: Encodings of bounded synthesis for distributed systems. Bachelor's thesis, Saarland University (2017)
3. Bloem, R., Chatterjee, K., Jacobs, S., Könighofer, R.: Assume-guarantee synthesis for concurrent reactive programs with partial information. In: Baier, C., Tinelli, C. (eds.) TACAS 2015. LNCS, vol. 9035, pp. 517–532. Springer, Heidelberg (2015). https://doi.org/10.1007/978-3-662-46681-0_50
4. Brenguier, R., Raskin, J.-F., Sankur, O.: Assume-admissible synthesis. Acta Informatica 54(1), 41–83 (2016). https://doi.org/10.1007/s00236-016-0273-2
5. Chatterjee, K., Henzinger, T.A.: Assume-guarantee synthesis. In: Grumberg, O., Huth, M. (eds.) TACAS 2007. LNCS, vol. 4424, pp. 261–275. Springer, Heidelberg (2007). https://doi.org/10.1007/978-3-540-71209-1_21
6. Damm, W., Finkbeiner, B.: Does it pay to extend the perimeter of a world model? In: Butler, M., Schulte, W. (eds.) FM 2011. LNCS, vol. 6664, pp. 12–26. Springer, Heidelberg (2011). https://doi.org/10.1007/978-3-642-21437-0_4
7. Damm, W., Finkbeiner, B.: Automatic compositional synthesis of distributed systems. In: Jones, C., Pihlajasaari, P., Sun, J. (eds.) FM 2014. LNCS, vol. 8442, pp. 179–193. Springer, Cham (2014). https://doi.org/10.1007/978-3-319-06410-9_13
8. Faymonville, P., Finkbeiner, B., Rabe, M.N., Tentrup, L.: Encodings of bounded synthesis. In: Legay, A., Margaria, T. (eds.) TACAS 2017. LNCS, vol. 10205, pp. 354–370. Springer, Heidelberg (2017). https://doi.org/10.1007/978-3-662-54577-5_20
9. Faymonville, P., Finkbeiner, B., Tentrup, L.: BoSy: an experimentation framework for bounded synthesis. In: Majumdar, R., Kunčak, V. (eds.) CAV 2017. LNCS, vol. 10427, pp. 325–332. Springer, Cham (2017). https://doi.org/10.1007/978-3-319-63390-9_17
10. Filiot, E., Jin, N., Raskin, J.-F.: Compositional algorithms for LTL synthesis. In: Bouajjani, A., Chin, W.-N. (eds.) ATVA 2010. LNCS, vol. 6252, pp. 112–127. Springer, Heidelberg (2010). https://doi.org/10.1007/978-3-642-15643-4_10

11. Finkbeiner, B., Geier, G., Passing, N.: Specification decomposition for reactive synthesis. In: Dutle, A., Moscato, M.M., Titolo, L., Muñoz, C.A., Perez, I. (eds.) NFM 2021. LNCS, vol. 12673, pp. 113–130. Springer, Cham (2021). https://doi.org/10.1007/978-3-030-76384-8_8
12. Finkbeiner, B., Passing, N.: Dependency-based compositional synthesis. In: Hung, D.V., Sokolsky, O. (eds.) ATVA 2020. LNCS, vol. 12302, pp. 447–463. Springer, Cham (2020). https://doi.org/10.1007/978-3-030-59152-6_25
13. Finkbeiner, B., Passing, N.: Compositional synthesis of modular systems (Full Version). CoRR abs/2106.14783 (2021)
14. Finkbeiner, B., Schewe, S.: Bounded synthesis. Int. J. Softw. Tools Technol. Transfer 15(5), 519–539 (2012). https://doi.org/10.1007/s10009-012-0228-z
15. Jacobs, S., et al.: The 5th reactive synthesis competition (SYNTCOMP 2018): benchmarks, participants & results. CoRR abs/1904.07736 (2019)
16. Kugler, H., Segall, I.: Compositional synthesis of reactive systems from live sequence chart specifications. In: Kowalewski, S., Philippou, A. (eds.) TACAS 2009. LNCS, vol. 5505, pp. 77–91. Springer, Heidelberg (2009). https://doi.org/10.1007/978-3-642-00768-2_9
17. Kupferman, O., Piterman, N., Vardi, M.Y.: Safraless compositional synthesis. In: Ball, T., Jones, R.B. (eds.) CAV 2006. LNCS, vol. 4144, pp. 31–44. Springer, Heidelberg (2006). https://doi.org/10.1007/11817963_6
18. Kupferman, O., Vardi, M.Y.: Safraless decision procedures. In: FOCS (2005)
19. Majumdar, R., Mallik, K., Schmuck, A., Zufferey, D.: Assume-guarantee distributed synthesis. IEEE Trans. Comput. Aided Des. Integr. Circuits Syst. 39, 3215–3226 (2020)
20. Pnueli, A.: The temporal logic of programs. In: FOCS (1977)
21. de Roever, W.P., Langmaack, H., Pnueli, A. (eds.): Compositionality: The Significant Difference, COMPOS (1998)
22. Safra, S.: On the complexity of omega-automata. In: FOCS (1988)
23. Touati, H.J., Brayton, R.K., Kurshan, R.P.: Testing language containment for omega-automata using BDD's. Inf. Comput. 118, 101–109 (1995)

Event-B Refinement for Continuous Behaviours Approximation

Guillaume Dupont[✉], Yamine Aït-Ameur, Marc Pantel, and Neeraj K. Singh

INPT-ENSEEIHT/IRIT, University of Toulouse, Toulouse, France
{guillaume.dupont,yamine,marc.pantel,nsingh}@enseeiht.fr

Abstract. Hybrid systems are systems that integrate both discrete and continuous behaviours. The hybrid nature of such systems renders them difficult to model and verify in a single formal method. One of the key point when modelling these continuous features is the richness of the behaviours they may exhibit. In practice, continuous dynamics are expressed using complex differential equations, and are often difficult to handle during the implementation and validation process. To overcome this issue, controller designers use approximation allowing to substitute dynamics that have a close behaviour. Despite that it is based on sound, exact mathematics, this operation is rarely rigorous, and is performed prior to controller design, making it implicit in the resulting system.

In this paper, we propose a general formalised approach to approximation. It relies on the definition of a Galois connection, and refinement is used to embed it, explicitly, into a high-level development operation, associated to particular correctness constraints and useful properties. Two types of usage for approximation are presented and discussed in the light of existing cases studies, as to showcase their particularities on the modelling and proving sides.

Keywords: Hybrid systems · Approximation · Event-B · Refinement · Proof

1 Introduction

Computers have quickly found a place in modern applications, where they interact with "real-world", physical elements, such as motors, pistons or other *actuators*, thanks to advances in the domains of miniaturisation, real-time and embedded systems in general. Such systems, that integrate discrete behaviours (computers, controllers) together with continuous behaviours (actuators, plants) are called *hybrid systems* [14].

This hybrid nature poses an important challenge when it comes to modelling and verifying this kind of systems: formal methods in general are adapted to discrete behaviours (e.g. with state-based semantics and discrete steps), while continuous features are better handled using *control theory*, including continuous mathematics and differential equations. The difficulty is thus to integrate both these aspects at the same level during the modelling and verification process

© Springer Nature Switzerland AG 2021
Z. Hou and V. Ganesh (Eds.): ATVA 2021, LNCS 12971, pp. 320–336, 2021.
https://doi.org/10.1007/978-3-030-88885-5_21

for such systems, and to enable *close collaboration* between them, so that the constraints of one influence the design of the other, and *vice versa*.

A good example of such a high level of integration is *approximation*.

Approximation. Approximation is overall a common operation in control theory. The idea is that the equations describing a system are generally complex, due to an important number of variables (dimensions) and parameters to take into account, together with a large variety of phenomena that interact in numerous ways with each other. However, this level of detail is hardly relevant when designing the actual controller: factorisation, omission and other kinds of simplification may be used in order to derive simpler dynamics, with a somewhat similar behaviour as the complex one. Although it is based on sound mathematics, this operation is rarely *explicitly formalised*; it relies mainly on "known recipes", numerical simulations and a substantial amount of tweaking. Besides, approximation is usually performed upstream of program design, meaning it does not appear in the verification process, although system's dynamics fundamentally dictates the behaviour of its controller.

This traditional approach to approximation is a concern of system design: it renders maintenance and adaptation of the system to new constraints difficult without system re-designing, and enables the appearance of *magic numbers* and other *ad hoc* rules, hard to track down and to handle in a proper way.

Previous Work. We have proposed a generic approach for handling hybrid systems using the Event-B formal method [1], under the form of a *formal framework* [7,9]. This framework proposes 1) a number of extensions to Event-B's language, allowing to define and handle continuous dynamics within a model and 2) a set of *formal design patterns* to guide hybrid system design, using high-level development operations. In particular, in [8], we sketched a possible formalisation of approximation in Event-B, as a *refinement-based* development operation, and its use on a case study borrowed from the literature. Additionally, we explored another possible use of approximation in [7], where it is used to support the linearisation of a complex differential equation.

Objective of the Paper. The first goal of this paper is to *formalise* the approaches previously proposed in order to present a general formal setting for approximation. In particular, we define approximation as a high-level development operation that is bounded by specific constraints to ensure correctness, as well as powerful properties that can be used during the verification process.

To this extent, we define approximation as a *Galois connection*, and support it with *refinement*. This enables the use of such an operation as a powerful proving and modelling technique: a (concrete) model approximating another (abstract) model inherits its properties "for free", provided these properties hold on the abstract model and the approximation has been proven correct.

Expressing approximation this way allows to expose two distinct uses for it:

– *Downward* approximation, where a complex, accurate system is refined into a simpler one, usually for implementation purposes;

– *Upward* approximation, where a simpler system, with easier verification, is refined into a more complex and accurate one.

In this paper, we investigate both of these scenarios and provide concrete examples of their application in real-world cases studies.

Organisation of the Paper. Next section gives an overview of the Event-B method used for our formal developments. Section 3 presents the framework we have proposed to handle the modelling of hybrid systems. In Sect. 4, the mathematical theory of approximation together with relevant definitions are introduced. The core contribution is presented in Sect. 5 with the formalisation of *downward* and *upward* approximation in Event-B. Related work is discussed in Sect. 6. Last, Sect. 7 concludes and identifies some future research perspectives.

2   Event-B

As mentioned previously, the central idea of this paper is to use *refinement* as a means of providing support for approximation. This feature encourages the use of Event-B, as refinement is a built-in operation. In this Section, we review the fundamental concepts of Event-B, particularly its refinement relation. We also present the *theories* extension mechanism which is extensively used throughout our work.

Table 1. Event-B Model structure: contexts and machines

Context	Machine	Refinement
CONTEXT Ctx	**MACHINE** M^A	**MACHINE** M^C
SETS s	**SEES** Ctx	**REFINES** M^A
CONSTANTS c	**VARIABLES** x^A	**VARIABLES** x^C
AXIOMS A	**INVARIANTS** $I^A(x^A)$	**INVARIANTS** $J(x^A, x^C) \wedge I^C(x^C)$
THEOREMS T_{ctx}	**THEOREMS** $T_{mch}(x^A)$	...
END	**VARIANT** $V(x^A)$	**EVENTS**
	EVENTS	**EVENT** evt^C
	EVENT evt^A	**REFINES** evt^A
	ANY α^A	**ANY** α^C
	WHERE $G^A(x^A, \alpha^A)$	**WHERE** $G^C(x^C, \alpha^C)$
	THEN	**WITH**
	$x^A :\mid BAP^A(\alpha^A, x^A, x^{A'})$	$x^{A'}, \alpha^A \colon W(\alpha^A, \alpha^C, x^A, x^{A'}, x^C, x^{C'})$
	END	**THEN**
	...	$x^C :\mid BAP^C(\alpha^C, x^C, x^{C'})$
		END
		...
(a)	(b)	(c)

Event-B is a correct-by-construction, formal method for system design [1]. An Event-B model consists of a set of components linked together. *Contexts* (Table 1.a) collect the static parts of the model: constants, sets/types and general properties (axioms and theorems). *Machines* (Table 1.b) hold the dynamic parts of the model, expressed in the form of an abstract *state* (a set of variables) together with *guarded events*, which encode transformations of this state (defining a guarded state-transitions system). A machine is associated with various *invariants* and *theorems*, which are properties on the state that must always hold. A *variant* may also be defined, and used to prove convergence properties on the set of events. Generated proof obligations, when discharged, ensure that these properties hold.

Each event is defined by its *guard* (WHERE clause) that states when the event may be *triggered*, and its *action* (THEN clause), in the form of a *Before-After Predicate* (BAP), denoted by the "becomes-such-that" operator (:|), and that links the current value of the variable (x) with its "new" value, after the event is effectively executed (x'). An EVENT may also define different *parameters* using the ANY clause. These parameters serve as quantification of the event.

Refinement. Refinement is a relation between machines that can be used as a development operation. It defines a simulation relationship between the state transitions of a machine an its refinement. The core idea of refinement is to constraint or specify a model as to enrich it step by step while preserving its properties: if the abstract machine verifies a certain property, and if refinement is *correct*, then the resulting concrete machine also verifies this property, without the need to prove it again.

On the modelling side, refinement is indicated by the REFINES clause in the machine header and for each event (Table 1.c). Refinement allows, concretely, to add or substitute variables and event parameters, add invariants, add or modify events, and strengthen guards, all while ensuring that it is *proven correct*.

Verification. Any Event-B model is associated with *proof obligations* (POs) that are generated mechanically using substitution calculus. These obligations must be discharged (proved) in order to establish correctness of the model.

Regarding refinement, correctness is established if 1) concrete events may not be triggered when abstract events cannot (guard strengthening) and 2) concrete action is allowed by abstract action (simulation). In order to prove this correctness, especially in the case of substituting variables and parameters, it is generally necessary to express the relationship between the abstract and the concrete variables and/or parameters, in the form of a *gluing invariant* and *witnesses* (WITH clause).

Extension Mechanism. Event-B's expression language is based on set theory and first-order logic, making it mathematically low-level, and thus highly expressive. However, this language can be cumbersome when dealing with higher-level or complex constructs. For this reason, an extension to this language has been proposed, using *theories* [5]. Formally, a theory is a set of type-generic *data-types* together with constructive and/or axiomatic *operators* and *properties*, encapsulated in a special component that can then be referenced in Event-B models.

Tooling Support. Event-B is associated to the Rodin IDE[1], equipped with various modelling and proof tools for designing and validating Event-B models. Rodin also supports the design of theories, thanks to the *theory plug-in*.

---

[1] http://www.event-b.org/index.html.

3 Hybrid Systems in Event-B

Event-B is tailored to discrete systems by virtue of its semantics. However, because its expression language is based on pure set theory and first-order logic, it is possible to embed the basic building blocks required to handle continuous behaviours in this method.

In our previous work [9], we proposed a method for expressing continuous dynamics in Event-B models using *continuous variables* (functions of time), and *continuous before-after predicates*.

3.1 Continuous Variables

As previously stated, a continuous variable x_p is defined as a (partial) function of time, valued in some set S, usually a real vector space (i.e., $S = \mathbb{R}^n, n \in \mathbb{N}$). The function is *partial* (and we write $x_p \in \mathbb{R}^+ \nrightarrow S$) because it is not defined for every instant: if we take 0 as the origin of time and denote with t the current time (or "present"), then x_p is *at least defined* on time interval $[0, t]$: $[0, t] \subseteq \operatorname{dom}(x_p)$.

Because continuous variables are *functions*, it is difficult to describe their behaviour using discrete assignment (e.g. one cannot write $x_p := 5$). As a result, we adapted the concept of discrete assignment and proposed a way to describe *continuous* assignments, using *continuous before-after predicates* (CBAP).

Definition 1 (Continuous Before-After Predicate). *Let $t, t' \in \mathbb{R}^+$ two time points with $t' > t$. Let $x_p \in \mathbb{R}^+ \nrightarrow S$ a continuous state variable. Finally, let $\mathcal{P} \subseteq (\mathbb{R}^+ \nrightarrow S) \times (\mathbb{R}^+ \nrightarrow S)$ a predicate on the before and after values of the state variable and $H \subseteq S$ an evolution domain constraining the evolution of x_p. The* **continuous before-after predicate** *modelling the change of x_p on time interval $[t, t']$ following predicate $\mathcal{P}$ and constrained by evolution domain H, denoted $x_p :|_{t \to t'} \mathcal{P} \& H$, is defined as so:*

$$x_p :|_{t \to t'} \mathcal{P}(x_p, x'_p) \& H \equiv [0, t[\lhd x'_p = [0, t[\lhd x_p \qquad (PP)$$

$$\wedge \mathcal{P}([0, t] \lhd x_p, [t, t'] \lhd x'_p) \qquad (PR)$$

$$\wedge \forall t^* \in [t, t'], x_p(t^*) \in H \qquad (LI)$$

Informally, the expression $x_p :|_{t \to t'} \mathcal{P}(x_p, x'_p) \& H$ denotes that *variable x_p becomes such that*: 1) it remains unchanged on the interval $[0, t[$ (past preservation *PP*), 2) its "new" value on interval $[t, t']$ ($[t, t'] \lhd x'_p$) is linked to its value on $[0, t]$ ($[0, t] \lhd x'_p$) through predicate $\mathcal{P}$ (predicate *PR*), and 3) its value on the interval $[t, t']$ remains in the evolution domain H (local invariant *LI*).

3.2 Continuous Refinement

Event-B allows to refine a system by introducing new behaviours and constraints, while ensuring that the new features do not violate the system's properties (see Sect. 2). Formally, there are two types of refinement: *behavioural* refinement, in which the system's behaviour is extended or constrained (e.g. adding events, refining events guards and actions while preserving simulation relationship), and *data* refinement, in which we replace the expression of the state of the system by another (substituting variables and parameters).

In the context of continuous dynamics, we cannot really "add behaviour": while it is true that a new (discrete instantaneous) event may occur between two events, it is not possible to imagine a new continuous section woven inside an existing one, i.e. "add" of a new part of function on $[t_1, t_2]$.

If we reintroduce the notion of refinement as similarity of observational behaviour, we can formulate a general form of refinement for continuous variables.

Definition 2 (Continuous Refinement). *Let $x_p^A \in \mathbb{R}^+ \nrightarrow S^A$ (resp. $x_p^C \in \mathbb{R}^+ \nrightarrow S^C$) be an abstract (resp. concrete) continuous state variable, and $\mathcal{O} \in S^C \leftrightarrow S^A$ an **observation relation** between the state spaces of these variables. x_p^A is **continuously refined** by x_p^C on time interval $[0, t]$ if: $x_p^A \in_{[0,t]} \mathcal{O} \circ x_p^C$, or, in expanded form: $\forall t^* \in [0, t], x_p^A(t^*) \in \mathcal{O}[\{x_p^C(t^*)\}]$.*

This predicate, which *glues* continuous states x_p^A and x_p^C, is known as a **gluing invariant**. When writing models, it is given as a system invariant, and must therefore be proven to hold for every event.

3.3   Embedding Continuous Features Using Theories

We use Event-B's theory extension (see Sect. 2) to encode the definitions previously given as well as various useful continuous features for using them in Event-B models and proofs. Figure 1 gives an excerpt of the resulting theories.

```
THEORY DiffEq
TYPE PARAMETERS E , F , ...
DATATYPE
    DE(F) constructors ode(f : R × F ↠ F, η₀ : F, t₀ : R) , ...
OPERATORS
    solutionOf predicate (D : ℙ(R), η : R ↠ F, ℰ : DE(F))
        well−definedness condition D ⊆ dom(η)
    Solvable predicate (D : ℙ(R), ℰ : DE(F))
        direct definition ∃η · η ∈ R ↠ F ∧ D ⊆ dom(η) ∧ solutionOf(D, η, ℰ)
    :|ₜ→ₜ′ predicate (t, t′ : R,  xₚ, x′ₚ : R ↠ F, 𝒫 : ℙ((R ↠ F) × (R ↠ F)), H : ℙ(F))
        ...
```

Fig. 1. Continuous feature theory extract

One of the interest of the theory is to define the **DE**(F) data-type to represent differential equations. This type is associated with several *constructors* (e.g. **ode**) that allows to define various nature of differential equations (e.g. *ordinary differential equations*).

Additionally, this type is associated to operators for handling it in models and proofs. The **solutionOf** predicate characterise that a given function (η) is solution of the given equation ($\mathcal{E}$) on the given domain (D). Similarly, **Solvable** allows characterising an equation that admits a solution on interval D.

Note that we also formalise the continuous evolution operators of Sect. 3.1.

4   A Theory of Approximation

In a process similar to our achievements for continuous features, we envision to incorporate, in Event-B, the general and useful concept of approximation, together with related properties and constraints.

In this Section, we present a formalisation of approximation that ends up being a Galois connection. Such a formalisation enables the use of the constructs and properties related to approximation with refinement, and thus to define the notion of *approximate refinement.*

4.1   Foundational Constructs

In the following, we consider a *metric space* (E, d) where d is a distance. It is a reasonable assumption since continuous state variables usually evolve in normed vector spaces $S = \mathbb{R}^n, n \in \mathbb{N}^*$, which are *complete metric spaces.*

Approximation Operator. The idea of approximation is to *relax equality.* Instead of stating that two points are identical, we characterise the fact that they are "close enough" from each other, by a constant δ as formalised by Definition 3.

Definition 3 (Approximation). *Let $\delta \in \mathbb{R}, \delta \geq 0$ and $x, y \in E$. x is **approximately equal** to y by δ (x is a δ-approximation of y), noted $x \approx^\delta y$ if: $x \approx^\delta y \equiv d(x, y) \leq \delta$.*

For convenience, we provide a "lifted" version of this operator for functions on a given domain.

Definition 4 (Function Approximation). *Let $\delta \in \mathbb{R}, \delta \geq 0$, D be a set and $X \subseteq D$. Let $f, g \in D \nrightarrow E$ with $X \subseteq \mathrm{dom}(f)$ and $X \subseteq \mathrm{dom}(g)$. f is a δ-approximation of g if: $f \approx^\delta_X g \equiv \forall x \in X, f(x) \approx^\delta g(x)$.*

Expansion and Shrinking. This form of "relaxed equality", by itself, is not sufficient to be used in a refinement. Its purpose is to define two important operations, which are essentially *relaxed* and *strengthened* versions of inclusion.

Definition 5 (δ-Expansion). *Let $\delta \in \mathbb{R}, \delta \geq 0$ and $S \subseteq E$. The δ-expansion of S, denoted $\mathcal{E}_\delta(S)$, is defined by: $\mathcal{E}_\delta(S) = \{y \in E \mid \exists x \in S, x \approx^\delta y\} = \{y \in E \mid \exists x \in S, d(x, y) \leq \delta\}$.*

Intuitively, given a set S, the δ-expansion of S, $\mathcal{E}_\delta(S)$ includes S, such that any of its points is at most δ away from a point of S. It consists of S with some "headroom" (see Fig. 2a).

Definition 6 (δ-Shrinking). *Let $\delta \in \mathbb{R}, \delta \geq 0$ and $S \subseteq E$. The δ-shrinking of S, denoted $\mathcal{S}_\delta(S)$, is defined by: $\mathcal{S}_\delta(S) = \{x \in S \mid \inf_{y \in E \setminus S} d(x, y) > \delta\} = \{x \in S \mid \forall y \in E \setminus S, d(x, y) > \delta\}$.*

Intuitively, given a set S, the δ-shrinking of S, $\mathcal{S}_\delta(S)$ is included in S, such that any of its points 1) is included in S and 2) at least δ away from the *border* of S (See Fig. 2b).

(a) δ-Expansion   (b) δ-Shrinking

Fig. 2. Graphical representation of the expansion and shrinking operators

Approximated Predicates. Shrinking and expansion sets, used for approximation, are formalised as predicates (useful for automatic provers) by introducing a relaxed version of set membership.

Definition 7 (δ-Membership). *Let $\delta \in \mathbb{R}, \delta \geq 0$, $x \in E$ and $S \subseteq E$. x is a δ-member of S, noted $x \in^{\delta} S$, if: $x \in^{\delta} S \equiv x \in \mathcal{E}_{\delta}(S) \equiv \exists y \in S, d(x,y) \leq \delta$.*

Similarly to the lifted version of approximation, we define a convenient extension to δ-membership, for functions that yield a *set* (also called *multi-valued* functions). This extension is particularly useful to define gluing invariant involving approximation (see Sect. 5.1).

Definition 8 (Multi-Valued Functions Extension). *Let $\delta \in \mathbb{R}, \delta \geq 0$, $f \in D \nrightarrow E$ and $\Sigma \in D \nrightarrow \mathbb{P}(E)$. Let $X \subseteq D$ with $X \subseteq \mathrm{dom}(f)$ and $X \subseteq \mathrm{dom}(\Sigma)$. We define $f \in^{\delta}_{X} \Sigma$ by: $f \in^{\delta}_{X} \Sigma \equiv \forall x \in X, f(x) \in^{\delta} \Sigma(x)$.*

4.2 Properties of Approximation

Approximation constructs are accompanied by a number of useful properties exploited during the modelling and proving process in approximate refinement.

Shrinking and Closed Balls. For a set S, shrinking has the interesting property that any point that is at most δ away from a point of $\mathcal{S}(S)$ belongs to S. More formally, this property is captured by Theorem 1.

Theorem 1 (δ-Shrinking and Closed Ball Inclusion). *Let $\delta \in \mathbb{R}, \delta \geq 0$, $S \subseteq E$. For any $x \in \mathcal{S}_{\delta}(S)$, $\bar{\mathcal{B}}(x,\delta) \subseteq S$.*

We recall that a *closed ball* $\bar{\mathcal{B}}(x,\delta)$ of centre x and radius δ (for the given distance d) is the set of points that are not farther than δ from x. Formally: $\bar{\mathcal{B}}(x,\delta) = \{y \in E \mid d(x,y) \leq \delta\}$

Predicate Strengthening. The use of predicates with approximation disallows using interesting substitution properties (e.g. when $x = y$, substitution of an occurrence of x by y is allowed). Fortunately, approximation is accompanied with a weaker form of substitution, useful for refinement-related proof obligations, often based on predicate strengthening, i.e. of the form $\dots \wedge P^C \Rightarrow P^A$.

Theorem 2 (Sufficient Conditions for Predicate Strengthening). *Let* $\mathcal{O} \in S^C \leftrightarrow S^A$ *a relation on* S^C *and* S^A *and* $x^A \in S^A$ *and* $x^C \in S^C$ *two variables such that* $x^A \in^\delta \mathcal{O}[\{x^C\}]$. *Let* $P^C \subseteq S^C$ *and* $P^A \subseteq S^A$ *two subsets (representing predicates), with* $x^C \in P^C$.
*Then, a **sufficient condition for proving** $x^A \in P^A$ is:* $\mathcal{O}[P^C] \subseteq \mathcal{S}_\delta(P^A)$; *or, dually:* $\mathcal{E}_\delta(\mathcal{O}[P^C]) \subseteq P^A$.

Note that we superpose the notions of predicates and sets. This is possible in set theory thanks to the *axiom of comprehension*: if $P(x)$ is a predicate on x, then it can be represented by the set $\{\hat{x} \mid P(\hat{x})\}$ of elements that satisfy this predicate. Again, such predicates are useful for the proof tools that rewrites sets as first order logic predicate (e.g. to use SMT solvers).

Galois Connection. Expansion and shrinking are related by a particular link, informally stated as "nearly the opposite operation" of the other. In fact, expansion and shrinking are *adjoints*, they form a *Galois connection.*

Let us consider expansion and shrinking as functions on the partially ordered set $(\mathbb{P}(E), \subseteq)$. Then, Theorem 3 states important properties.

Theorem 3 (Expansion–Shrinking Galois Connection). *Let* $\delta \in \mathbb{R}, \delta \geq 0$. $(\mathcal{E}_\delta, \mathcal{S}_\delta)$ *is a Galois connection on the partially ordered set* $(\mathbb{P}(E), \subseteq)$ *(to itself).*

This theorem entails the following properties.

1. $\forall\, T, S \subseteq E$ with $T \subseteq S$ then $\mathcal{E}_\delta(T) \subseteq \mathcal{E}_\delta(S)$ and $\mathcal{S}_\delta(T) \subseteq \mathcal{S}_\delta(S)$ ($\mathcal{E}_\delta$ and $\mathcal{S}_\delta$ are monotone)
2. $\forall S \subseteq E$, then $\mathcal{E}_\delta(\mathcal{S}_\delta(S)) \subseteq S$ and $S \subseteq \mathcal{S}_\delta(\mathcal{E}_\delta(S))$

Note that these properties are central for data refinement in the approximate refinement we introduce. They are helpful to define the gluing invariants guaranteeing refinement correctness.

0-Approximation. We note that, when $\delta = 0$, approximated operators become exact operators: 0-approximation is equality, 0-membership is exact set membership, and 0-shrinking and 0-expansion are exact set inclusion.

4.3   Encoding Approximation in Event-B Using Theories

In the same way as for continuous features, approximation is not available as a built-in operator in the Event-B method. Therefore, we have encoded it with an algebraic theory as a set of explicit operators of an Event-B theory, so that it can be used in models (see Fig. 3).

The proposed approximation Event-B theory defines explicitly the various approximation operators, which are the core building blocks of approximation as a development operation. It also defines expansion and shrinking, and their various properties, in particular a formalisation of Theorem 2 (SPS and EPS).

The complete theory is accessible at https://www.irit.fr/~Guillaume. Dupont/models.php.

```
THEORY Approximation
IMPORT DiffEq
TYPE PARAMETERS E, F
OPERATORS
  ≈δ  predicate  (x, y : E,  δ : ℝ)
  ∈δ  predicate  (x : E,  S : ℙ(E),  δ : ℝ)
  ℰδ  expression  (S : ℙ(E),  δ : ℝ+)
     direct definition  {y ∈ E | ∃x · x ∈ S ∧ x ≈δ y}
  Sδ  expression  (S : ℙ(E),  δ : ℝ+)
     direct definition  {x ∈ S | ∀y · y ∈ E \ S ⇒ ¬(x ≈δ y)}
  ...
THEOREMS
  SPS:  —  Shrinking Predicate Strengthening
     ∀𝒪, Pᴬ, Pᶜ, xᴬ, xᶜ · 𝒪 ∈ Sᶜ ↔ Sᴬ ∧ ...
  EPS:  —  Expansion Predicate Strengthening
     ∀𝒪, Pᴬ, Pᶜ, xᴬ, xᶜ · 𝒪 ∈ Sᶜ ↔ Sᴬ ∧ ...
```

Fig. 3. Approximation theory extract

5   Approximation and Refinement: Two Scenarios of Use

The approximation link between variables x^A and x^C, sets S^A and S^C or functions f^A and f^C presented in the previous section allows to *glue* these concepts in two models relying on the defined Galois connection. This relationship, formalised in Event-B, enables the definition of gluing invariants in so-called *approximate refinement*. This operation may be carried out in two directions:

- **Downward approximation** in a refinement of an abstract *exact system* with a concrete *approximate system*. For instance, starting with complex exact dynamics and linearising it for implementation.
- **Upward approximation** where an abstract *approximated system* is refined with a concrete *exact system*. For instance starting with simple dynamics on which proof is easier and introducing the actual, richer behaviour while preserving its properties.

5.1   Approximate Gluing Invariant

Definition 2 presented a general form for continuous refinement, based on (exact) set membership. The concepts presented in Sect. 4 allow to relax this set membership predicate by introducing $\in^\delta$, and thus to define *approximate (continuous) refinement* of data as follows.

Definition 9 (Approximate Continuous Refinement). *With the same notations as for Definition 2 and given* $\delta \in \mathbb{R}, \delta \geq 0$, x_p^A *is* δ-*approximately (continuously) refined by* x_p^C *on time interval* $[0, t]$ *if:* $x_p^A \in_{[0,t]}^{\delta} \mathcal{O} \circ x_p^C$.

This predicate uses approximated set-membership; it is a relaxed version of the continuous gluing invariant presented in Sect. 3.2, and is referred to as **approximate gluing invariant** in the rest of this paper.

Informally, the idea of this approximate gluing invariant is to map the abstract value not only to some concrete values, but also to an area of radius δ around these concrete values, to give some headroom.

5.2 Downward Approximation Scenario

In the case of *downward approximation*, an abstract machine models the exact dynamics of the studied hybrid system, which is usually physically accurate but not adapted to implementation due to its complexity. The designer manages to prove properties on the "real-world" system, and then must perform an approximation operation, based on **shrinking**, to derive a system closer to implementation, while maintaining its properties using refinement.

A typical downward approximation scenario is the case of linearisation. For instance, consider a hybrid system with dynamics characterised by a complex, non-linear differential equation, not easy to handle at implementation. The development strategy is to establish safety on the complex, abstract system, and then linearise it with a correct approximate refinement to obtain a concrete system. The challenge in this case is to find sufficient constraints on the concrete system so that the approximation holds, and thus that safety is ensured while deviations allowed by the approximation are taken into account.

The general form of this scenario is given in listing of Fig. 4, where machine M_exact with continuous state $x_p^A \in \mathbb{R} \rightarrow S^A$ and featuring event **Event**^{A}, is refined by machine M_approx with continuous state $x_p^C \in \mathbb{R} \rightarrow S^C$ and featuring event **Event**^{C}, refining event **Event**^{A}.

Machine M_exact is associated to a safety invariant on x_p^A, synthesised as a set $\mathcal{I}^A \subseteq S^A$ (safA). This invariant is updated in M_approx, yielding safC.

MACHINE M_exact	MACHINE M_approx REFINES M_exact
VARIABLES t, x_p^A	VARIABLES t, x_p^C
INVARIANTS	INVARIANTS
inv0: $t \in \mathbb{R}$	inv1: $x_p^A \in \mathbb{R} \rightarrow S^A$
inv1: $x_p^A \in \mathbb{R} \rightarrow S^A$	inv2: $[0,t] \subseteq \mathrm{dom}(x_p^A)$
inv2: $[0,t] \subseteq \mathrm{dom}(x_p^A)$	inv3: $x_p^A \in_{[0,t]}^{\delta} \mathcal{O} \circ x_p^C$
safA:	safC: $\forall \tau \cdot \tau \in [0,t] \Rightarrow \mathcal{O}[\{x_p^C(\tau)\}] \subseteq \mathcal{S}_\delta(\mathcal{I}^A)$
$\quad \forall \tau \cdot \tau \in [0,t] \Rightarrow x_p^A(\tau) \in \mathcal{I}^A$	EVENTS
EVENTS	Event^C REFINES Event^A
Event^A	ANY t'
ANY t'	WHERE $\mathcal{O}[\{x_p^C(t)\}] \subseteq \mathcal{S}_\delta(\mathcal{G}^A)$
WHERE $x_p^A(t) \in \mathcal{G}^A$	WITH $x_p^{A'} \in_{[0,t']}^{\delta} \mathcal{O} \circ x_p^{C'}$
THEN $x_p^A :|_{t \rightarrow t'} \mathcal{P}^A(x_p^A, x_p^{A'})$ & H^A	THEN $x_p^C :|_{t \rightarrow t'} \mathcal{P}^C(x_p^C, x_p^{C'})$ & $\mathcal{O}[\{x_p^C(t)\}] \subseteq \mathcal{S}_\delta(H^A)$

Fig. 4. Downward approximation general scenario

Related Proof Obligations. This application of approximation revolves around the use of the *approximate gluing invariant* (inv3), which is also used as witness (WITH clause) for the refining event ensuring its preservation.

The other key point in this scenario is the proposed predicate strengthening: **shrinking** $\mathcal{S}_\delta$ is used to strengthen the abstract guard (WHERE clause) and evolution domain (& operator), so that the system remains *within bounds*, even with the slight headroom given by δ.

Note that the guard strengthening proof obligation in this case is as follows:
$$\mathcal{O}[\{x_p^C(t)\}] \subseteq \mathcal{S}_\delta(\mathcal{G}^A) \wedge x_p^A \in_{[0,t]}^{\delta} \mathcal{O} \circ x_p^C \Rightarrow x_p^A(t) \in \mathcal{G}^A.$$

It is trivially proven using Theorem 2, with $P^C = \{x_p^C(t)\}$ and $P^A = \mathcal{G}^A$, and by remarking that $x_p^C(t) \in \{x_p^C(t)\}$.

A similar reasoning is applied to invariant preservation as it is an another case of predicate strengthening. It follows that, in this general form, approximate refinement is correct by construction; i.e. given any guard $\mathcal{G}^A$, invariant $\mathcal{I}^A$ and evolution domain H^A of the abstract machine, it is possible to derive the updated guard, invariant and evolution domain of the concrete machine, so that approximation is correct.

In practice when giving the concrete machine, it is possible to obtain a correct approximation with any predicate that is *stricter* than the one given in Fig. 4. In particular, if the guard of the concrete event is of the form $x_p^C(t) \in \mathcal{G}^C$ then it is sufficient to have $\mathcal{O}[\mathcal{G}^C] \subseteq \mathcal{S}_\delta(\mathcal{G}^A)$ (again using Theorem 2), and similarly for invariant and evolution domain.

A Case Study. Downward approximation has been used to address the well-known *inverted pendulum* case study [7]. In this setup, physics and trigonometry are used to derive a first differential equation that is non-linear (because of the term $\sin(\theta)$ and $\cos(\theta)$). When θ is below a given bound, it is possible to *linearise* this equation, replacing $\sin(\theta)$ by θ_L and $\cos(\theta)$ by 1, thanks to approximation.

$$\begin{cases} \ddot{\theta} + \omega_0^2 \sin(\theta) = u\cos(\theta) \\ |\theta| < \theta_{max} \end{cases} \implies \begin{cases} \ddot{\theta}_L + \omega_0^2\theta_L = u_L \\ |\theta_L| < \theta_{max} - \delta \end{cases} \text{ with } \theta \approx^\delta \theta_L \quad (1)$$

As shown in Eq. 1, the resulting differential equation is linear, and its solutions approximate the original, non-linear one. More details can be found in [7] and the complete Event-B models can be accessed from https://www.irit.fr/~Guillaume.Dupont/models.php.

5.3   Upward Approximation Scenario

In the case of *upward approximation*, the abstract machine presents simpler dynamics than the hybrid system to design, for which formal verification is easier, but not accurate with regard to the actual behaviour of the system. In this first model, the designer sets a *target safe evolution domain* and then performs formal verification on an **expansion** of this evolution domain. Then, a safe approximation (in a refinement) is explicitly provided, that removes the expansion while ensuring that the properties are maintained.

This type of situation can be encountered when the verification and proving of the properties of the actual system is hard. In this case, approximation is actually performed *a priori*: the entry point of the refinement chain is the **approximated system**, in contrast with downward approximation where the entry point is the "raw", non-approximated system. In this case, approximation is merely a *proving technique*; approximate refinement allows to eliminate approximation, and to obtain an exact system fulfilling the required properties, in particular the properties preserved by refinement.

The general form for this scenario is given in Fig. 5. The abstract model corresponding to machine M_approx is the approximate one. It consists of a continuous variable $x_p^A \in \mathbb{R} \twoheadrightarrow S^A$ and an event $\mathbf{Event}^A$. This model is refined by the exact machine M_approx consisting of continuous variable $x_p^C \in \mathbb{R} \twoheadrightarrow S^C$ and event $\mathbf{Event}^C$, refining $\mathbf{Event}^A$.

```
MACHINE M_approx
VARIABLES t, x_p^A
INVARIANTS
  inv0:  t ∈ ℝ
  inv1:  x_p^A ∈ ℝ ⇸ S^A
  inv2:  [0, t] ⊆ dom(x_p^A)
  safA:  ∀τ · τ ∈ [0, t] ⇒ x_p^A(τ) ∈ 𝓔_δ(𝓞[𝓘^C])
EVENTS
  Event^A
  ANY t'
  WHERE x_p^A(t) ∈ 𝓔_δ(𝓞[𝓖^C])
  THEN x_p^A :|_{t→t'} 𝓟^A(x_p^A, x_p^{A'}) & 𝓔_δ(𝓞[H^A])
```

```
MACHINE M_exact
VARIABLES t, x_p^C
INVARIANTS
  inv1:  x_p^A ∈ ℝ ⇸ S^A
  inv2:  [0, t] ⊆ dom(x_p^A)
  inv3:  x_p^A ∈_{[0,t]}^δ 𝓞 ∘ x_p^C
  safC:  ∀τ · τ ∈ [0, t] ⇒ x_p^C(τ) ∈ 𝓘^C
EVENTS
  Event^C REFINES Event^A
  ANY t'
  WHERE x_p^C(t)𝓖^C
  WITH x_p^{A'} ∈_β^δ [0, t']𝓞 ∘ x_p^{C'}
  THEN x_p^C :|_{t→t'} 𝓟^C(x_p^C, x_p^{C'}) & H^C
```

Fig. 5. Upward approximation general scenario

Compared to the other scenario, the approximation is carried out using the *same* approximate gluing invariant (inv3), also used as a witness (WITH) for the refining event, as to ensure its preservation.

However the major key point for this usage of approximation is that the provided safety invariant for the abstract machine (safA) is *obtained from the concrete safety invariant* (safC). In other words, safC is the "target" (required) safety evolution domain, and safA is an *expansion* of this domain. Observe that, as expected, this usage of approximate refinement *eliminates approximation* (i.e. removes the expansion $\mathcal{E}_\delta$ introduced in the abstract model) while preserving the useful properties established on the abstract, approximated system.

Related Proof Obligations. In this particular case, the guard strengthening proof obligation is of the form: $x_p^C(t) \in \mathcal{G}^C \wedge x_p^A \in_{[0,t]}^\delta \mathcal{O} \circ x_p^C \Rightarrow x_p^A(t) \in \mathcal{E}_\delta(\mathcal{O}[\mathcal{G}^C])$.

This is again trivially proven using Theorem 2, with $P^C = \mathcal{G}^C$ and $P^A = \mathcal{E}_\delta(\mathcal{O}[\mathcal{G}^C])$, and by observing that $\mathcal{E}_\delta(\mathcal{O}[\mathcal{G}^C]) \subseteq \mathcal{E}_\delta(\mathcal{O}[\mathcal{G}^C])$.

This reasoning can be used for invariant preservation, so the proposed approximate refinement for this general form is correct by construction. Given the *target* guard $\mathcal{G}^C$, invariant $\mathcal{I}^C$ and evolution domain H^C, it is possible to derive the updated guard, invariant and evolution domain of the abstract machine, so that approximation is correct.

Similarly to the downward scenario, it is possible, in practice, to establish a correct approximation for any predicate that is *stricter* than the one given in Fig. 5. Formally, if the guard of the abstract event is of the form $x_p^A(t) \in \mathcal{G}^A$, then it is sufficient to prove that $\mathcal{E}_\delta(\mathcal{O}[\mathcal{G}^C]) \subseteq \mathcal{S}_\delta(\mathcal{G}^A)$ to establish guard strengthening (using Theorem 2), and similarly for invariant and evolution domain.

A Case Study. Upward approximation is demonstrated on the case study of a robot visiting targets [8], borrowed from the work of [11]. The robot is described by complex dynamics (p^C, v^C position and speed) and control command (u^C, w^C), that model the physical properties of its actuators. These complex dynamics can be approximated with simpler ones (p^A and control u^A), on which formal verification is easier, with $p^A \approx^\delta p^C$ approximation (see Eq. 2).

The strategy is, first, to model the simpler (approximated) system, perform formal verification on it, and then use approximate refinement to correctly approximate it to obtain the concrete (exact) system.

$$\begin{cases} p^A = u^A \\ d(p^A, \mathbf{0}) \leq A + \delta \end{cases} \implies \begin{cases} \dot{v}^C = \frac{1}{2}u^C - K(p^C - w^C) - v^C \\ \dot{p}^C = v^C, \dot{w}^C = u^C \\ d(p^C, \mathbf{0}) \leq A \end{cases} \quad \text{with } p^A \approx^\delta p^C$$

$$(2)$$

More details can be found in [8] and the complete Event-B models can be accessed from https://www.irit.fr/~Guillaume.Dupont/models.php.

6   Related Work and Assessment

A number of solutions have been proposed to handle formal modelling of hybrid systems using various formal methods. In many cases, the main idea consists in incorporating continuous features in existing (discrete) formalisms, and to design means to reason on these features, through the use of theorems, proof rules or even entire proof systems. Below, we focus on the use of approximation.

Controller Annotation. In this kind of bottom-up approach, a controller program usually written in C language is annotated with control information (e.g. differential equations), for example using Frama-C [4] or ACSL [13]. Proof obligations are generated and discharged using Coq or Isabelle/HOL (respectively), together with advanced libraries dealing with continuous features. In this context, approximations are carried out implicitly: floating point numbers are projected to reals, and the behaviour found in the controller is generally an integrated, discretised version of the differential equation given in the annotation.

Built-in Approximation. Hybrid model-checkers are widely used to analyse hybrid system behaviours, and in particular reachability. In practice, the hybrid system is modelled as a hybrid automaton [2], and the verification procedure is generally undecidable for non-linear systems [12]. As this latter point is extremely constraining, hybrid model-checkers for non-linear dynamics use approximation and bounded exploration. For instance, tools such as d/dt [3], SpaceEx [10] and Flow* [6] use *flowpipe* over-approximation within the decision procedure.

Preliminary Approximation. The problem of having approximation as part of the algorithm is that it is generally difficult to control. To overcome this issue, one may perform approximation *before* applying model-checking techniques on the model. In the work of Girard et al. [11], the authors propose the concept of *approximate bi-simulation* to characterise the notion of *close observational behaviour* between two systems. In the case studies they address, the authors manage to establish such a relationship between a complex system and a linear one, and perform model-checking on this latter. Then, by virtue of the properties of approximate bi-simulation, they deduce the required properties for the original complex system.

It is to be noted that approximate bi-simulation is rigorously proven *on paper*, and is presented as a verification technique (rather than an explicit, formalised development operation).

Assessment. Compared to our approach, the formal approaches for dealing with hybrid systems reviewed above generally lack *high-level development operations*, often because they are thought to be used *after* the design process. The direct consequence is that, in many cases, approximation is *implicit* (part of the model), or even carried out *outside* of the verification process (rigorous paper proof).

Our main contribution in this regard is the integration of approximation in the underlying formal method as a formalised, tool-supported, refinement-based development operation, so that it is made *explicit* and overall part of the model. It is seen as complementary to the previously reviewed approaches.

7 Conclusion

The work presented in this paper is twofold. On the one hand, it presents an algebraic theory of approximation of reals, which allows to extend Event-B with an approximation relation and the associated operators. This approximation relation defines a Galois connection connecting dynamics and their approximation. On the other hand, it demonstrates how classical refinement can be used rigorously to link a model and its approximate model of a hybrid system.

This refinement operation may be used in two ways. The first (downward approximation) enables the refinement of a hybrid system characterised by a non-linear differential equation into a linear system by approximating it. The second method is dual (upward approximation), it allows to refine a linear system approximating a non-linear system. It is worth noting that the introduced approximation relation is 1) explicit since it is formalised in an algebraic theory, allowing for the characterisation of its properties and the proof of theorems, and 2) used in both directions of the adjunct functions of the Galois connection it defines, i.e. from exact to approximate and *vice versa*. This capability is of primary importance as traditional approaches either do not formalise the approximation (although rigorously defined) or embed it implicitly in the verification tools.

Last, the Event-B method, particularly refinement, and the Rodin IDE proved capable of expressing the evolution of hybrid systems in the presence of approximation. The defined approximation has been used in two case studies presented in this paper. This operation is part of the framework we established in our previous work [7].

The work presented in this paper lays important theoretical foundations for new directions of research. First, approximation, as defined in this paper, is general; it may be refined into specific types of approximation (e.g., polynomial approximation, linearisation, interpolation...). Moreover, it may be used as a base for other operations of a similar nature, and in particular *discretisation*.

From a more theoretic point of view, this formalisation of approximation exhibits a type of *continuous refinement* that differs significantly from discrete refinement. Another direction is to investigate other types of continuous refinement and their properties, and how they can be integrated into a formal method like Event-B as high-level development operation.

References

1. Abrial, J.R.: Modeling in Event-B: System and Software Engineering, 1st edn. Cambridge University Press, New York (2010)
2. Alur, R., et al.: The algorithmic analysis of hybrid systems. Theor. Comput. Sci. **138**(1), 3–34 (1995). Hybrid Systems
3. Asarin, E., Dang, T., Maler, O.: The d/dt tool for verification of hybrid systems. In: Brinksma, E., Larsen, K.G. (eds.) CAV 2002. LNCS, vol. 2404, pp. 365–370. Springer, Heidelberg (2002). https://doi.org/10.1007/3-540-45657-0_30
4. Boldo, S., Clément, F., Filliâtre, J.C., Mayero, M., Melquiond, G., Weis, P.: Trusting computations: a mechanized proof from partial differential equations to actual program. Comput. Math. Appl. **68**(3), 325–352 (2014)
5. Butler, M., Maamria, I.: Practical theory extension in Event-B. In: Liu, Z., Woodcock, J., Zhu, H. (eds.) Theories of Programming and Formal Methods. LNCS, vol. 8051, pp. 67–81. Springer, Heidelberg (2013). https://doi.org/10.1007/978-3-642-39698-4_5
6. Chen, X., Ábrahám, E., Sankaranarayanan, S.: Flow*: an analyzer for non-linear hybrid systems. In: Sharygina, N., Veith, H. (eds.) CAV 2013. LNCS, vol. 8044, pp. 258–263. Springer, Heidelberg (2013). https://doi.org/10.1007/978-3-642-39799-8_18
7. Dupont, G., Aït-Ameur, Y., Pantel, M., Singh, N.K.: An Event-B based generic framework for hybrid systems formal modelling. In: Dongol, B., Troubitsyna, E. (eds.) IFM 2020. LNCS, vol. 12546, pp. 82–102. Springer, Cham (2020). https://doi.org/10.1007/978-3-030-63461-2_5
8. Dupont, G., Aït-Ameur, Y., Singh, N.K., Ishikawa, F., Kobayashi, T., Pantel, M.: Embedding approximation in Event-B: safe hybrid system design using proof and refinement. In: Lin, S.-W., Hou, Z., Mahony, B. (eds.) ICFEM 2020. LNCS, vol. 12531, pp. 251–267. Springer, Cham (2020). https://doi.org/10.1007/978-3-030-63406-3_15
9. Dupont, G., Aït-Ameur, Y., Singh, N.K., Pantel, M.: Event-B hybridation: a proof and refinement-based framework for modelling hybrid systems. ACM Trans. Embed. Comput. Syst. **20**(4) (2021, to appear)
10. Frehse, G., et al.: SpaceEx: scalable verification of hybrid systems. In: Gopalakrishnan, G., Qadeer, S. (eds.) CAV 2011. LNCS, vol. 6806, pp. 379–395. Springer, Heidelberg (2011). https://doi.org/10.1007/978-3-642-22110-1_30

11. Girard, A., Julius, A.A., Pappas, G.J.: Approximate simulation relations for hybrid systems. Discret. Event Dyn. Syst. **18**(2), 163–179 (2008)
12. Henzinger, T.A., Kopke, P.W., Puri, A., Varaiya, P.: What's decidable about hybrid automata? J. Comput. Syst. Sci. **57**(1), 94–124 (1998)
13. Herencia-Zapana, H., et al.: PVS linear algebra libraries for verification of control software algorithms in C/ACSL. In: Goodloe, A.E., Person, S. (eds.) NFM 2012. LNCS, vol. 7226, pp. 147–161. Springer, Heidelberg (2012). https://doi.org/10.1007/978-3-642-28891-3_15
14. Lee, E.A.: Cyber physical systems: design challenges. In: 11th IEEE International Symposium ISORC, pp. 363–369. IEEE Computer Society (2008)

Incorporating Monitors in Reactive Synthesis Without Paying the Price

Shaun Azzopardi(✉)⬛, Nir Piterman⬛, and Gerardo Schneider⬛

University of Gothenburg, Gothenburg, Sweden
{shaun.azzopardi,nir.piterman,gerardo.schneider}@gu.se

Abstract. Temporal synthesis attempts to construct reactive programs that satisfy a given declarative (LTL) formula. Practitioners have found it challenging to work exclusively with declarative specifications, and have found languages that combine modelling with declarative specifications more useful. Synthesised controllers may also need to work with pre-existing or manually constructed programs. In this paper we explore an approach that combines synthesis of declarative specifications in the presence of an existing behaviour model as a monitor, with the benefit of not having to reason about the state space of the monitor. We suggest a formal language with automata monitors as non-repeating and repeating triggers for LTL formulas. We use symbolic automata with memory as triggers, resulting in a strictly more expressive and succinct language than existing regular expression triggers. We give a compositional synthesis procedure for this language, where reasoning about the monitor state space is minimal. To show the advantages of our approach we apply it to specifications requiring counting and constraints over arbitrarily long sequence of events, where we can also see the power of parametrisation, easily handled in our approach. We provide a tool to construct controllers (in the form of symbolic automata) for our language.

Keywords: Synthesis · Temporal logic · Symbolic automata · Monitoring

1 Introduction

Synthesis of programs from declarative specifications is an attractive prospect. Although thought prohibitive due to the theoretical hardness of LTL synthesis, recent improvements have made it a more reasonable endeavour, e.g. the identification of GR(1) [24], for which synthesis is easier, and development of tools such as Strix [20,22] whose decomposition method allows for practical synthesis of full LTL. Limitations remain in the context of LTL, due to the inherent hardness of the problem. Beyond LTL there are also directions where the practicality of synthesis is not clear.

This research is funded by the ERC consolidator grant D-SynMA under the European Union's Horizon 2020 research and innovation programme (grant agreement No. 772459).

© Springer Nature Switzerland AG 2021
Z. Hou and V. Ganesh (Eds.): ATVA 2021, LNCS 12971, pp. 337–353, 2021.
https://doi.org/10.1007/978-3-030-88885-5_22

In addition to these algorithmic challenges, there are additional methodological challenges. Practitioners have identified that it is sometimes very challenging to write declarative specifications, and suggested to use additional modelling [15,21]. Furthermore, synthesised parts need to work alongside pre-existing or manually constructed parts (cf. [19]). This, however, further exacerbates the algorithmic challenge as the state-space of the additional parts needs to be reasoned about by the synthesis algorithm.

We argue that modelling could also be a practical way of dealing with some of the algorithmic challenges and advocate a partial use of synthesis, leaving parts that are impractical for synthesis to be manually modelled. This leaves the question of how to combine the two parts.

We suggest to compose automata with synthesised controllers by transfer of control rather than co-operation. We define a specification language with repeating and non-repeating *trigger* properties (cf. [2,17]). Triggers are defined as environment observing automata/monitors, which transfer control to LTL formulas. Both aspects – control transfer and triggers – are familiar to practitioners and would be easy to use: control transfer is natural for software; and triggers are heavily used in industrial verification languages (cf. [2]).

We aim at triggers that are rich, succinct and easy to write. Thus, we use monitors extracted from symbolic executable automata inspired by DATEs [9]. Expressiveness of automata is increased by having variables that are updated by guarded transitions, which means that automata can be infinite-state (but the benefits remain if they are restricted to finite-state). This choice of monitors allows to push multiple other interesting concerns that are difficult for LTL synthesis to the monitor side. Experience of using such monitors in the runtime verification community suggests that they are indeed easy to write [13].

Our contributions are as follows. We formally define our specification language "monitor-triggered temporal logic". We show that the way we combine monitors with LTL indeed bypasses the need to reason about the state-space of monitors. Thus, avoiding some of the algorithmic challenges of synthesis. We briefly present our synthesis tool. We give examples highlighting the benefits of using monitors, focusing on counting (with appropriate counter variables updated by monitor transitions) and parametrisation (with unspecified parameter variables that can be instantiated to any required value). Full proofs of the propositions and theorems claimed can be found in [4].

Related Work. In the literature we find several approaches that use monitors in the context of synthesis. Ulus and Belta use monitors with reactive control for robotic system navigation, with monitors used for lower-level control (e.g. to identify the next goal locations), and controllers used for high-level control to avoid conflicts between different robots [28]. Wenchao et al. consider human-in-the-loop systems, where occasionally the input of a human is required. The controller monitors the environment for any possible violations, and invokes the human operator when necessary [18].[1] The use of monitors in these approaches is *ad hoc*, a more general approach is that of the Spectra language [21]. Essentially, Spectra monitors have an initial state, and several safety transition rules of the form $p \rightarrow q$, where p is a proposition on some low-level variables, and q defines the **next** value of the monitor variable. This monitor variable can be used in the higher-level controller specification. The approach here is more general than ours in a sense, since we limit ourselves to using monitors as triggers, however our monitors are more succinct and expressive.

The notion of triggers in temporal logic is not new, with regular expressions being used as triggers for LTL formulas in different languages [2,11,14,27]. Complexity wise, Kupferman et al. show how the synthesis of these trigger properties is 2EXPTIME-complete [17]. However, in order to support such logics algorithms would have to incorporate the entire state-space of the automata induced by the regular expression triggers. We are not aware of implementations supporting synthesis from such extensions of LTL. Using automata directly within the language, as we do, may be more succinct and convenient. We also include a *repetition* of trigger formulas in a way that is different from these extensions. However, the main difference is in avoiding the need to reason about the triggering parts.

Our combination of monitors and LTL formulas can be seen as a control-flow composition [19]. Lustig and Vardi discuss how to synthesise a control-flow composition that satisfies an LTL formula given an existing library of components. They consider all components to be given and synthesise the composition itself. Differently, we assume the composition to be given and synthesise a controller for the LTL part. Other work given a global specification reduces it according to that of the existing components, resulting in a specification for the required missing component [26]. This is at a higher level than our work, since we start with specifications for each component.

2   Preliminaries

We write σ for infinite traces over an event alphabet Σ. We use the notation $\sigma_{i,j}$, where $i, j \in \mathbb{N}$ and $i \leq j$, to refer to the sub-trace of σ starting from position i, ending at (including) position j. We write σ_i for $\sigma_{i,i}$, and $\sigma_{i,\infty}$ for the suffix of σ starting at i.

Linear Temporal Logic (LTL). General LTL (ϕ) and co-safety LTL (φ) are defined over a set of propositions $\mathcal{P}$ respectively as follows, where $e \in \mathcal{P}$:

$$\phi \stackrel{\text{def}}{=} \mathbf{tt} \mid \mathbf{ff} \mid e \mid \neg e \mid \phi \wedge \phi \mid \phi \vee \phi \mid X\phi \mid \phi U\phi \mid G\phi$$

$$\varphi \stackrel{\text{def}}{=} \mathbf{tt} \mid \mathbf{ff} \mid e \mid \neg e \mid \varphi \wedge \varphi \mid \varphi \vee \varphi \mid X\varphi \mid \varphi U\varphi$$

We also define and use $F\phi \stackrel{\text{def}}{=} \mathbf{tt}U\phi$ and $\phi W\phi' \stackrel{\text{def}}{=} (\phi U\phi') \vee G\phi$. We write $\sigma \vdash \phi$ for $\sigma_{0,\infty} \vdash \phi$. We omit the standard semantics of LTL [23].

---

[1] We can think of our approach as dual, where the monitor invokes the synthesised controller when necessary.

Mealy Machines. A *Mealy machine* is a tuple $C = \langle S, s_0, \Sigma_{in}, \Sigma_{out}, \rightarrow, F \rangle$, where S is the set of states, s_0 the initial state, Σ_{in} the set of input events, Σ_{out} the set of output events, $\rightarrow: S \times \Sigma_{in} \mapsto \Sigma_{out} \times S$ the complete deterministic transition function, and $F \subseteq S$ a set of accepting states. For $(s, I, O, s') \in \rightarrow$ we write $s \xrightarrow{I/O} s'$.

Notice that by definition for every state $s \in S$ and every $I \in \Sigma_{in}$ there is $O \in \Sigma_{out}$ and s' such that $s \xrightarrow{I/O} s'$. A *run* of the Mealy machine C is $r = s_0, s_1, \ldots$ such that for every $i \geq 0$ we have $s_i \xrightarrow{I_i/O_i} s_{i+1}$ for some I_i and O_i. A run r *produces* the word $w = \sigma_0, \sigma_1, \ldots$, where $\sigma_i = I_i \cup O_i$. We say that C produces the word w if there exists a run r producing w. We say that C *accepts* a prefix u of w if $s_{|u|} \in F$.

Realisability. An LTL formula φ over set of events $\mathcal{P} = \mathcal{P}_{in} \cup \mathcal{P}_{out}$ is *realisable* if there exists a Mealy machine C over input events $2^{\mathcal{P}_{in}}$ and output events $2^{\mathcal{P}_{out}}$ such that for all words w produced by C we have $w \vdash \varphi$. We say C realises φ.

Theorem 1 ([25]). *Given an LTL formula φ it is decidable in 2EXPTIME whether φ is realisable. If φ is realisable the same algorithm can be used to construct a Mealy machine C_φ realising φ.*

2.1 Flagging Monitors

We introduce our own simplified version of DATEs [3,9], *flagging monitors*, as a formalism for defining runtime monitors. Flagging monitors (monitors, for short) are different from DATEs in that they work in discrete time, and events are in the form of sets. Monitors are designed such that once they *flag* (accept) they never flag again. This is modeled by having *flagging* states, which are used to signal that monitoring has ended successfully. We also use *sink* states, from which it is assured the monitor cannot flag in the future. We ensure that the monitor flags only upon determining a matching sub-trace, and thus a monitor upon reaching a flagging state can never flag again.

Monitor. A *monitor* is a tuple $D = \langle \Sigma, \mathbb{V}, \Theta, Q, \theta_0, q_0, F, \bot, \rightarrow \rangle$, where Σ is the event alphabet, $\mathbb{V}$ is a set of typed variables, Θ is the set of possible valuations of $\mathbb{V}$, Q is a finite set of states, $\theta_0 \in \Theta$ is the initial variable valuation, $q_0 \in Q$ is the initial state, $F \subseteq (Q \setminus \{q_0\})$ is the set of *flagging states* (we often use $q_F \in F$), $\bot \in Q$ is a *sink* state, and $\rightarrow \in Q_\top \times (\Sigma \times \Theta \mapsto \{true, false\}) \times (\Sigma \times \Theta \mapsto \Theta) \mapsto Q$ is the *deterministic transition function*, from $Q_\top \overset{\text{def}}{=} Q \setminus \{\bot\}$, activated if a guard holds on the input event and the current variable valuation, while it may perform some action to transform the valuation.

For $(q, g, a, q') \in \rightarrow$ we write $q \xrightarrow{g \mapsto a} q'$, and we will be using E as the input event parameter for both g and a. We omit g when it is the *true* guard, and a when it is the *null* action. We use $D_{\langle * \rangle}$ for the monitor that accepts on every event, i.e. $\langle \Sigma, V, \Theta, \{q_0, q_F, \bot\}, \theta_0, q_0, \{q_F\}, \bot, \{q_0 \xrightarrow{true \mapsto null} q_F\} \rangle$.

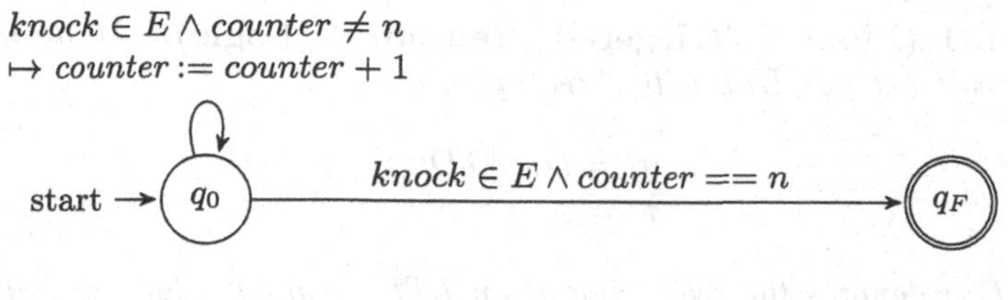

$knock \in E \wedge counter \neq n$
$\mapsto counter := counter + 1$

Fig. 1. Monitor that counts the number of knocks, and flags after n knocks.

For example, the monitor in Fig. 1 keeps a counter that counts the number of *knock* events, and flags when the number of knocks is exactly n.

We give an operational semantics to *monitors*, with configurations as pairs of states and valuations, with transitions between configurations tagged by events.

Monitor Semantics. The semantics of flagging monitors [3] is given over configurations of type $Q \times \Theta$, with transitions labeled by Σ, and the transition $\rightarrow$ defined by the following rules: (1) A transition from a non-flagging and non-sink configuration is taken when the guard holds on the event and valuation, and then the latter is updated according to the transition's action; (2) If there is no available transition whose guard holds true on the current valuation then transition to the same configuration (stutter); (3) A sink configuration cannot be left; and (4) A flag configuration always transitions to the sink configuration. We use $\Rightarrow$ for the transitive closure of $\rightarrow$.[2]

Flagging Trace. A finite trace is said to be flagging if it reaches a flagging state. $\sigma_{i,j} \Vdash D \stackrel{\text{def}}{=} \exists q_F, \theta' \cdot (q_0, \theta_0) \stackrel{\sigma_{i,j}}{\Rightarrow} (q_F, \theta')$.

The semantics ensures that every extension of a flagging trace is non-flagging.

Proposition 1. $\forall \sigma \in \Sigma^\omega \cdot \forall n \in \mathbb{N} \cdot \sigma_{i,j} \Vdash D \wedge n > 0 \implies \sigma_{i,j+n} \not\Vdash D$.

We can also easily show that $D_{\langle * \rangle}$ accepts all traces of length one.

Proposition 2. $\forall \sigma \in \Sigma^\omega$ *and* $\forall i \in \mathbb{N} \cdot \sigma_{i,i} \Vdash D_{\langle * \rangle}$.

3   Monitors as Triggers for LTL Formulas

We suggest a simple kind of interaction between monitors and LTL, where monitors are used as *triggers* for LTL. Previous work has considered the use of a trigger operator that activates the checking of an LTL expression when a certain regular expression matches [2]. Our approach here is similar, except that we maintain a stricter separation between the monitored and temporal logic parts.

Our language combining monitors with LTL has three operators: (i) monitors as a trigger for an LTL formula; (ii) repetition of the trigger formula (when the LTL formula is co-safety); and (iii) assumptions in the form of LTL formulas.

---

[2] See [4] for full formal semantics.

Definition 1 (Monitor-Triggered Temporal Logic). *Monitor-triggered temporal logic extends LTL with three operators:*

$$\pi' = D\!:\!\phi \mid (D; \varphi)^*$$
$$\pi = \phi \to \pi'$$

Formula $D\!:\!\phi$ denotes the triggering of an LTL formula ϕ by a monitor D. We call formulas of this form simple-trigger LTL. Formula $(D; \varphi)^*$ repeats infinitely the triggering of a co-safety LTL formula φ by a monitor D. We call formulas of this form repeating-trigger LTL. Finally, $\phi \to \pi'$ models a specification with an LTL assumption ϕ. LTL formulas are defined over a set of propositions $\mathcal{P} = \mathcal{P}_{in} \cup \mathcal{P}_{out}$ and monitors over the alphabet $\Sigma = 2^{\mathcal{P}_{in}}$.

In formulas of the form $D\!:\!\phi$ if D flags then the suffix must satisfy ϕ. In formulas of the form $(D; \varphi)^*$, the monitor restarts after satisfaction of the co-safety formula φ. For example, if D is the monitor in Fig. 1 and $\varphi = (open \wedge X(greet \wedge X\,close)))$, then $D\!:\!\varphi$ would accept every trace that waits for knocks, and at the nth knock opens the door, then greets, and then closes the door. On the other hand, $(D; \varphi)^*$ requires the trace to arbitrarily repeat this behaviour.

To support repeating triggers, we define the notion of tight satisfaction.

Definition 2 (Tight Co-safety LTL Satisfaction). *A finite trace is said to tightly satisfy a co-safety LTL formula if it satisfies the formula and no strict prefix satisfies the formula: $\sigma_{i,j} \Vdash \varphi \overset{\text{def}}{=} \sigma_{i,j} \vdash \varphi \wedge (\forall k \cdot i \leq k < j \implies \sigma_{i,k} \not\vdash \varphi)$. We also call such a trace a tight witness for the LTL formula.*

Note that here a tight witness is not necessarily a minimal witness (in the sense that all of its extensions satisfy the LTL formula). For example, for every set of propositions P, a trace $\langle P \rangle$ is a minimal witness for $X\mathsf{tt}$ [6]. However it is not a tight witness in our sense, since $\langle P \rangle \not\vdash X\mathsf{tt}$. On the other hand $\langle P, P \rangle$ is a tight witness since $\langle P, P \rangle \vdash X\mathsf{tt}$ and every prefix of it does not satisfy $X\mathsf{tt}$.

Notice that it would not be simple to just use finite trace semantics for full LTL [5,6,11,12,16]. Consider for example, the trace $\langle\{a\}\rangle$, which satisfies Ga. It is not clear how to define tight satisfaction in order to start the monitor again. For example, $\langle\{a\}\rangle$ can be extended to $\langle\{a\}, \{a\}\rangle$ and still satisfy Ga. Hence formulas of the form $(D; \varphi)^*$ are restricted to co-safety LTL, where satisfaction over finite traces is well-defined and accepted.

We now define the trace semantics of the trigger and repetition operators.

Definition 3 (Monitor-Trigger Temporal Logic Semantics).

1. *An infinite trace satisfies a simple-trigger LTL formula if when a prefix of it causes the monitor to flag then the corresponding suffix (including the last element of the prefix) satisfies the LTL formula:*

$$\sigma_{i,\infty} \vdash D\!:\!\phi \overset{\text{def}}{=} \exists j \cdot i \leq j \wedge (\sigma_{i,j} \Vdash D \implies \sigma_{j,\infty} \vdash \phi) \qquad \text{where } i \in \mathbb{N}.$$

2. *A finite trace satisfies one step of a repeating-trigger LTL formula if a prefix of it causes the monitor to flag and the corresponding suffix (including the last element of the prefix) tightly satisfies the co-safety LTL formula:*

$$\sigma_{i,k} \vdash D; \varphi \overset{\text{def}}{=} \exists j \cdot i \leq j \leq k \wedge (\sigma_{i,j} \Vdash D \wedge \sigma_{j,k} \Vdash \varphi) \qquad \text{where } i, k \in \mathbb{N}.$$

3. *An infinite trace satisfies a repeating-trigger LTL formula if when a prefix of it matches the monitor then the corresponding infinite suffix matches the LTL formula:*

$$\sigma \vdash (D; \varphi)^* \overset{\text{def}}{=} \forall i \cdot \sigma_{0,i} \Vdash D \implies \exists j \cdot j \geq i \wedge \sigma_{0,j} \vdash D; \varphi \wedge \sigma_{j+1,\infty} \vdash (D; \varphi)^*.$$

4. *An infinite trace satisfies a specification π' with an assumption ϕ when if it satisfies ϕ it also satisfies π':*

$$\sigma \vdash \phi \to \pi' \overset{\text{def}}{=} \sigma \vdash \phi \implies \sigma \vdash \pi'.$$

An interesting aspect of this semantics is that in a formula $D; \varphi$, D and φ share an event, and the same for $D{:}\phi$. This is a choice we make to allow for message-passing between the two later on. Here it does not limit us, since not sharing a time step can be simulated by adding a further transition with a *true* guard before flagging, or by simply transforming ϕ into $X\phi$.

This semantics ensures that given an infinite trace, when a finite sub-trace satisfies $D; \varphi$, extensions of the sub-trace do not also satisfy it.

Proposition 3. $\sigma_{i,j} \vdash D; \varphi \implies \forall k > j \cdot \sigma_{i,k} \not\vdash D; \varphi.$

We can prove that a trace σ satisfies an LTL formula ϕ iff it also satisfies the formula where ϕ is triggered by the empty *monitor*.

Proposition 4. $\sigma \vdash \phi \iff \sigma \vdash D_{\langle * \rangle}{:}\phi.$

Moreover, we can show that adding these monitors as triggers for LTL formulas results in a language that is more powerful than LTL.

Theorem 2. *Our language is strictly more expressive than LTL.*

Proof. Proposition 4 shows that every LTL formula ϕ can be written in our language as $D_{\langle * \rangle}; \phi$. LTL cannot express the property that each even time step must have p be true [29] (regardless of what is true at odd steps). In our language $(D_{\langle * \rangle}; p \wedge X\mathbf{tt})^*$ specifies that p is true in every even time step, and $(D_{\langle * \rangle}; Xp)^*$ specifies that p is true in every odd time step. $\square$

Our logic is even more expressive, for example Fig. 2 shows a monitor that flags upon the average occurrence of an event falling below a certain level. We note that, in general, we have not restricted the types of variables of a monitor to range over finite domains. Thus, a monitor could also identify context-free or context-sensitive languages or, indeed, be Turing powerful. However, Theorem 2 holds even if we consider only monitors whose variables have finite domains, or even monitors without variables.

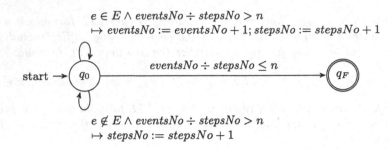

Fig. 2. Monitor that keeps track of the number of time steps, and the number of occurrences of e, while flagging is the average occurrence of e goes below n.

4   Synthesising Monitor-Triggered Controllers

We have so far discussed our language from a satisfaction viewpoint. However we are interested in synthesising systems that enforce the specifications in our language. In this section we present our synthesis approach, which relies on the synthesis of controllers for LTL formulas.

Consider a specification $\pi = \gamma \rightarrow \pi'$, where π' is either of the form $D{:}\phi$ or $(D; \varphi)^*$. We focus on specifications where the assumption γ is restricted to conjunctions of simple invariants, transition invariants, and recurrence properties. Formally, we have the following:

$$\alpha \stackrel{\text{def}}{=} \mathbf{tt} \mid \mathbf{ff} \mid a \mid \neg\alpha \mid \alpha \wedge \alpha \mid \alpha \vee \alpha$$
$$\beta \stackrel{\text{def}}{=} \alpha \mid X\alpha \mid \beta \wedge \beta \mid \beta \vee \beta$$
$$\gamma \stackrel{\text{def}}{=} G\beta \mid GF\alpha \mid \gamma \wedge \gamma$$

That is, α are Boolean combinations of propositions, β allows next operators without nesting them, and γ is a conjunction of invariants of Boolean formulas, Boolean formulas that include next, or recurrence of Boolean formulas. We discuss below the case of general assumptions.

Let $\pi = \gamma \rightarrow (D{:}\phi)$. Then $t(\pi)$ is the formula $\gamma \rightarrow \phi$. Let $\pi = \gamma \rightarrow (D; \varphi)^*$. Then $t(\pi)$ is the formula $\gamma \rightarrow \varphi$. That is, $t(\pi)$ is the specification obtained by considering the implication of the assumption γ and the LTL formula.

4.1   Tight Synthesis for Co-safety Implication Formulas

Let π contain a repeating trigger and let $t(\pi) = \gamma \rightarrow \varphi$, where φ is a co-safety formula. Suppose that $t(\pi)$ is realisable and let $C_{t(\pi)}$ be a Mealy machine realising $t(\pi)$.

Definition 4. *A Mealy machine C tightly realises a formula of the form $\gamma \rightarrow \varphi$, where φ is a co-safety formula, if it realises $\gamma \rightarrow \varphi$ and in addition for every word w produced by C such that $w \vdash \gamma$ there exists a prefix u of w such that C accepts u, $u_{0,|u|} \Vdash \varphi$, and for every $u' < u$ we have C does not accept u.*

That is, when the antecedent γ holds, the Mealy machine accepts the *tight witness* for satisfaction of φ.

Theorem 3. *The formula* $t(\pi) = \gamma \to \varphi$ *is tightly realisable iff it is realisable. A Mealy machine tightly realising* $t(\pi)$ *can be constructed from* $C_{t(\pi)}$ *with the same complexity.*

Proof (sketch). We can construct a deterministic finite automaton that is at most doubly exponential in ϕ, that accepts all finite prefixes that satisfy ϕ. Its product with $C_{t(\pi)}$ results in a Mealy machine that accepts all prefixes that satisfy $t(\pi)$, in particular the shortest prefix, as required for realisability.

Note that in the case of tight realisability we can give a controller with a set of accepting states that enable us to accept upon observing tight witnesses. In the case where we are only concerned about non-tight realisability we assume the controller does not have any accepting states.

4.2   Monitor-Triggered Synthesis

We are now ready to handle synthesis for monitor-triggered LTL.

Definition 5. *A monitor-triggered LTL formula* π *over set of events* $\mathcal{P}_{in}$ *and* $\mathcal{P}_{out}$ *is realisable if there exists a Mealy machine* C *over input events* $2^{\mathcal{P}_{in}}$ *and output events* $2^{\mathcal{P}_{out}}$ *such that for all words* w *produced by* C *we have* $w \vdash \pi$. *We say that* C *realises* π.

In the case of simple triggers, we combine the monitor with a Mealy machine realising $t(\pi)$. In the case of repeating triggers, we combine the monitor with a Mealy machine tightly realising $t(\pi)$. In what follows we define the behaviour of the combination of a monitor and a Mealy machine.

Consider a specification $\pi = \gamma \to \pi'$, where π' is either $M{:}\phi$ or $(M;\varphi)^*$.

Theorem 4. *Let* $C_{t(\pi)}$ *be a Mealy machine realising* $t(\pi)$ *when* π' *is a simple-trigger LTL, and tightly realising* $t(\pi)$ *when* π' *is a repeating-trigger LTL. Then there is a Mealy machine* $M \blacktriangleright C_{t(\pi)}$ *that realises* π.

Proof (sketch). $M \blacktriangleright C_{t(\pi)}$ can be constructed over states that correspond to a tuple of M states, valuations, and $C_{t(\pi)}$ states. Monitor transitions can be unfolded into Mealy machine transitions with no outputs, according to their semantics. Transitions to a flagging state can be composed with transitions from the initial state of $C_{t(\pi)}$. For the repeating case, transitions to final states of $C_{t(\pi)}$ are made instead to point back to the initial configuration (initial state and valuation of M, and initial state of $C_{t(\pi)}$). Execution happens only in one machine at a time, except for the shared transition in the repeating case. We can show by induction the correctness of this construction.

The opposite of Theorem 4 is, however, not true. If π is realisable then it does not necessarily mean that $t(\pi)$ is also realisable. Consider a specification with a monitor that never flags, and which thus any Mealy machine realises. Another example is with a monitor that only flags upon seeing the event set $\{a\}$, and an LTL formula of the form $(b \implies \textbf{ff}) \wedge (a \implies c)$ (where a and b are input events, and c an output event). The LTL formula is clearly unrealisable given the first conjunct, however the combination of the monitor with a controller for LTL's second conjunct would realise the corresponding specification. Thus the construction in Theorem 4 is only sound but not complete, i.e., we have a procedure to produce controllers for our language only when the underlying LTL formula (modulo the assumption) is realisable, or when the monitor cannot flag.

Corollary 1. *If M cannot flag, or $t(\pi)$ is realisable, then π is realisable.*

We recall that we have restricted the assumptions to a combination of invariants, transition invariants, and recurrence properties. Such assumptions are "state-less". That is, identifying whether a word satisfies an assumption does not require to follow the state of the assumption. Thus, in our synthesis procedure it is enough for the controller to check whether the assumption holds without worrying about what happened during the run of the monitor that triggered it. In particular, if (safety) assumptions are violated only during the run of monitors, our Mealy machine will still enforce satisfaction of the implied formula. In order to treat more general assumptions, we would have to either analyse the structure of the monitor in order to identify in which "assumption states" the controller could be started or give a precondition for synthesis by requiring that the controller could start from an arbitrary "assumption state", which we leave for future work. Similarly, understanding the conditions the monitor enforces and using them as assumptions would allow us to get closer to completeness of Theorem 4. One coarse abstraction is simply the disjunction of the monitor's flagging transitions' guards as initial assumptions for the LTL formula.

5 Tool Support

We created a proof-of-concept automated tool[3] to support the theory presented in this paper. Implemented in Python, this tool currently accepts as input a monitor written in a syntax inspired by that of LARVA [3,10], and an LTL specification, while it outputs a symbolic representation of the Mealy machine constructed in the proof of Theorem 4, in the form of a monitor with outputs.

The proof of Theorem 3 is constructive and provides an optimal algorithm to synthesise tight controllers using standard automata techniques. For this tool we have instead opted to re-use an existing synthesis tool, Strix [20,22] due to its efficiency. To force Strix to synthesise a tight controller (for repeating triggers), the tool performs a transformation to the co-safety guarantees to output a new event that is only output once a tight witness is detected. This transformation

---

[3] https://github.com/dSynMa/syMTri

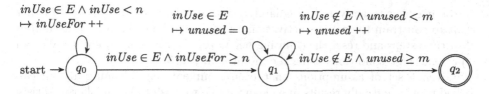

$inUse \in E \wedge inUse < n$
$\mapsto inUseFor{++}$

$inUse \in E$
$\mapsto unused = 0$

$inUse \notin E \wedge unused < m$
$\mapsto unused{++}$

start $\rightarrow$ q_0 $inUse \in E \wedge inUseFor \geq n$ q_1 $inUse \notin E \wedge unused \geq m$ q_2

Fig. 3. Flagging monitor that checks that the room has been in use for n time steps, after which when there is a period of m time steps where the room is empty it flags.

works well on our case studies, but is exponential in the worst-case. This is due to the need for disambiguating disjunctions. For example, given $\psi_1 \vee \psi_2$ we cannot in general easily be sure which disjunct the controller will decide to enforce; instead we disambiguate it to $(\psi_1 \wedge \neg\psi_2) \vee (\neg\psi_1 \wedge \psi_2) \vee (\psi_1 \wedge \psi_2)$ (cf. [8]).

6 Case Studies

We have applied our monitor approach mainly in the setting of conditions on the sequence of environment events, for which synthesis techniques can be particularly inefficient. We will consider a case study involving such conditions, where several events need to be observed before a robot can start cleaning a room. Furthermore we consider a problem from SYNTCOMP 2020 on which all tools timed out due to exponential blowup as the parameter values increase, relating to observing two event buses. We show how our approach using monitors avoids the pitfalls of existing approaches with regards to these kinds of specifications.

6.1 Event Counting

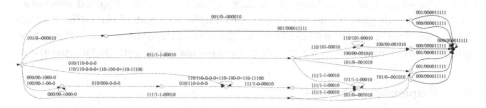

Fig. 4. Tight controller for cleaning robot, with rightmost state as accepting state. (1 (0) in position i means event i (not) occurs, and - when we do not care).

Consider a break room that is used by people intermittently during the day, and that needs to be cleaned periodically by a cleaning robot. We do not want to activate the robot every time the room is unclean to not disturb people on their break. Instead our procedure involves checking that the room is in use for a certain amount n of time steps. We also do not want the cleaning robot to be too eager or to activate immediately upon an empty room. Thus we further want to constrain the robot's activation on the room being empty for a number of m time steps and reset the counting whenever the room is not empty. We can represent these conditions using the monitor in Fig. 3.

Given a set of assumptions on the environment (e.g. cleaning an unclean locked room eventually results in a clean room), we wish the controller to satisfy that eventually the room will be clean, after which the robot leaves the room and opens the door to the public: $F(isClean \ \& \ (XF \ !inRoom) \ \& \ (XF \ !doorLocked))$.[4] Our tool synthesises Fig. 4 as a tight controller for this.

Representing the first monitor condition in LTL is not difficult ($\neg pW(p \wedge X(\neg pWp \wedge ...)))$, where proposition p corresponds to $inRoom$ and W is the weak until operator. The second condition is different, given the possible resetting of the count, but still easily representable in LTL $((\bigvee_{i=0}^{m-1} X^i p)W(\bigwedge_{i=0}^{m-1} X^i \neg p))$. Setting $n, m = 2$, and φ to be what we require out of the cleaning robot in one step, then a step of our specification (*without repetition*) in LTL is:

$$\psi = \neg pW(p \wedge X(\neg pW(p \wedge X((p \vee Xp)W(\neg p \wedge X(\neg p \wedge \varphi)))))).$$

In fact Strix confirms this to be realisable, and produces an appropriate Mealy Machine with eighty transitions, the size of which increases with each increase in any of the parameters.

However, using our approach all we require is Fig. 3 and Fig. 4. By representing the counting part of the specification using a monitor we can create a specification much more succinct than the LTL one, while its representation is of the same size for each value of the parameter. Moreover in LTL it is not clear how to reproduce our repeating triggers.

The difference is that the traditional approaches explicitly enumerate every possible behaviour and state of the controller at runtime, which can get very large. In our approach we are instead doing this symbolically, and allowing the particular behaviour of the environment at runtime to drive our symbolic monitor. The extra cost associated with this is the semantics of guard evaluation and maintaining variable states. For this example, the cost of the variable states (only two variables) is much smaller than the cost of the Strix generated machine, while guards simply check for membership and use basic arithmetic operations.

6.2   Sequences of Events

We consider a benchmark from SYNTCOMP 2020 [1][5], that generates formulas of the form, e.g. for $n = 2$, $F(p_0 \wedge F(p_1)) \wedge F(q_0 \wedge F(q_1)) \iff GFacc$. Strix [20], the best-performing tool in the LTL tracks of the competition, was successful when the bus size was small, however timed out for $n = m = 12$ (and above). The issue here is that the generated strategy must take into account every possible interleaving of the two sequences, which quickly causes a state space explosion.

---

[4] The full specification is available with our tool.
[5] The considered benchmark corresponds to files of the form `ltl2dba_beta_<n>.tlsf`.

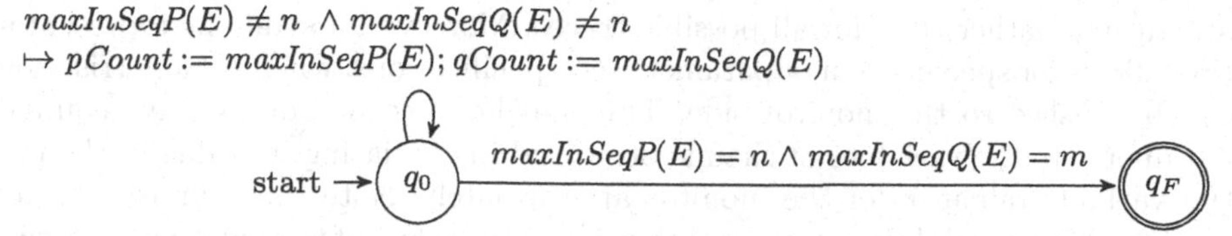

$maxInSeqP(E) \neq n \;\wedge\; maxInSeqQ(E) \neq n$
$\mapsto pCount := maxInSeqP(E); qCount := maxInSeqQ(E)$

Fig. 5. Event ordering in two buses.

With our approach we can represent the left-hand side in constant-size for any n and m, as illustrated in Fig. 5, where $maxInSeqX$ is a function that returns the maximal j such that $\forall k \in [xCount, j] \cdot x_k \in E$. The benefits apply however complex the right-hand side.

To replicate the whole LTL formula we can use $M{:}GFacc$, where M is the monitor in Fig. 5. This is somewhat different from the original specification, where a necessary and sufficient relation was specified. One would be tempted to specify this as (for $n = 1$) $(M; (Facc))^*$, however the monitor is not active while the controller is activated, thus p_1 and q_1 may occur in tandem with acc but be missed by the monitor. Although this is not of consequence towards the satisfaction of the formula here (p_1 should occur infinitely often), this is not generally the case. On the other hand $M{:}GFacc$ captures that upon the first activation of M there is no need to monitor the environment's behaviour anymore, and thus is equivalent to the original specification for control.

7 Discussion

The case studies we considered in the previous section focused on counting and waiting for sequence of events. We expect other useful applications of monitors as triggers, given they can be used to specify more sophisticated quantitative properties out of reach for LTL, e.g. see Fig. 2 [10].

We have highlighted how our approach extends the scope of use of reactive synthesis. It is clear that we can gain in scalability and expressiveness, but there is a price to pay: the "trigger" part. In general, to avoid lack of guarantees one can avoid working directly with automata, and instead use regular expressions or co-safety LTL formulas (under our notion of tight satisfaction) as triggers. Standard inexpensive monitor synthesis [7] could then be used to generate a monitor. In the case of more expressive manually-written monitors, which is standard for runtime verification (e.g. [9]), in practice one can easily apply model checking to the monitor to ensure it satisfies specific properties (e.g. no infinite loops).

There are certain benefits to using a symbolic representation, including succinct representation, and easy parametrisation. The Mealy machine construction we give in the proof of Theorem 4 is in fact not carried out by our tool, but instead it produces a symbolic monitor with outputs that essentially performs the construction on-the-fly. The cost of unfolding is then only paid for the trace at runtime, rather than for all possible traces. Moreover, a symbolic representation allows for specification of parametrised specifications, when parametrisation can be pushed to the monitor side. This can be done by adding any required parameter to the variables of the monitor, and instantiating its value in the initial variable valuation of the monitor appropriately. Note that our results are agnostic of the initial valuation, and thus hold regardless of the parameter values.

We have not yet discussed conjunction of trigger formulas, e.g. $(M_1; \psi_1)^* \wedge (M_2; \psi_2)^*$. Conjunction is easy when the output events of ψ_1 and ψ_2 respectively talk about are independent from each other. Our controller construction can be used independently for each. Similarly, when the properties are safety properties there is no difficulty. However, when, e.g., ψ_1 is a liveness property with at least one output event correlated with an output event of ψ_2, then conjunction is more difficult, due to possible interaction between the two possibly concurrent controllers. We are investigating a solution for this issue of concurrency of controllers by identifying appropriate assumptions about the monitor.

Theorem 2 compares our expressive power to that of LTL. We also mention that we do not restrict the variables used by monitors. Thus, even when comparing with languages that include regular expressions or automata [2,11,17] our language would be more expressive. If we were to restrict monitors to be finite state, then, as these languages can express all ω-regular languages, it is clear that they would be able to express our specifications. We note, however, that the repeating trigger operator is not directly expressible in these languages. Thus, the translation involves a conversion of our specification to an automaton and embedding this automaton in "their" specification. The conversion of our specification to an automaton includes both the enumeration of the states of the monitor and the exponential translation of LTL to (tight) automata.

8   Conclusions

We have explored synthesis for specifications that combine modelling and declarative aspects, in the form of symbolic monitors triggers for LTL formulas. We have shown how this extends the scope of synthesis by allowing parts of a specification that are hard for synthesis to be instead handled in the monitor part. The synthesis algorithm we give synthesises the LTL part without requiring the need to reason about the monitor. Moreover, we have implemented this approach and applied it to several case studies involving counting and monitoring multiple sequences of events that can be impossible or hard for LTL synthesis. We showed how by exploiting the symbolic nature of the monitors we can create fixed-size parameterised controllers for some parameterised specifications.

Future Work. Our work opens the door to a number of interesting research avenues, both by using richer monitor triggers and by exploring different interactions between triggers and controllers. We discuss below just a few such possibilities. In all the cases below the challenges lie not only in providing a new language to capture the extension but rather in the theoretical framework with a proof that the integration is sound.

A first intuitive extension is to add real-time to the monitors, to express properties like *"compute the average use of a certain resource every week and activate the controller to act differently depending on whether the average is bigger (or smaller) than a certain amount"*. While extending the monitor with real-time is quite straightforward (our monitors are restricted versions of DATEs [9] which already contain timers and stopwatches), the challenge will be to combine it with the controller in a suitable manner. Having real-time monitors running in parallel with controllers would enable for instance the possibility to add timeouts to activities performed by the controllers.

Currently we have a strict alternation between the execution of the monitor and the controller: we would like to explore under which conditions the two can instead run in parallel. This would allow the controller to react to the monitor only when certain complex condition hold while the controller is active doing other things (e.g., the monitor might send an interruption request to the controller when a certain sequence of events happens within a certain amount of time, while the controller is busy ensuring a fairness property).

We could also have many triggers that run in parallel activating different controllers, or even some meta-monitor that acts as an orchestrator to enable and disable controllers depending on certain conditions. This might require to extend/modify the semantics since the interaction might be done asynchronously.

We would like to address the limitation of controller synthesis concerning what to do when the assumptions are not satisfied. It is well-known that in order to be able to automatically synthesise a controller very often one must have strong assumptions, and nothing is said in case the assumptions are not satisfied. We would like to explore the use of monitors to monitor the violation of assumptions and interact with the controller in order to coordinate how to handle those situations (we can for instance envisage a procedure that automatically extends the controller with transitions that takes the controller to a recovery state if the assumptions are violated).

References

1. Syntcomp 2020. http://www.syntcomp.org/syntcomp-2020-results/
2. Armoni, R., et al.: The ForSpec temporal logic: a new temporal property-specification language. In: Katoen, J.-P., Stevens, P. (eds.) TACAS 2002. LNCS, vol. 2280, pp. 296–311. Springer, Heidelberg (2002). https://doi.org/10.1007/3-540-46002-0_21
3. Azzopardi, S., Ellul, J., Pace, G.J.: Monitoring smart contracts: ContractLarva and open challenges beyond. In: Colombo, C., Leucker, M. (eds.) RV 2018. LNCS, vol. 11237, pp. 113–137. Springer, Cham (2018). https://doi.org/10.1007/978-3-030-03769-7_8
4. Azzopardi, S., Piterman, N., Schneider, G.: Incorporating monitors in reactive synthesis without paying the price. arXiv e-prints arXiv:2107.00929, July 2021
5. Bartocci, E., Bloem, R., Nickovic, D., Roeck, F.: A counting semantics for monitoring LTL specifications over finite traces. In: Chockler, H., Weissenbacher, G. (eds.) CAV 2018. LNCS, vol. 10981, pp. 547–564. Springer, Cham (2018). https://doi.org/10.1007/978-3-319-96145-3_29

6. Bauer, A., Leucker, M., Schallhart, C.: The good, the bad, and the ugly, but how ugly is ugly? In: Sokolsky, O., Taşıran, S. (eds.) RV 2007. LNCS, vol. 4839, pp. 126–138. Springer, Heidelberg (2007). https://doi.org/10.1007/978-3-540-77395-5_11

7. Bauer, A., Leucker, M., Schallhart, C.: Runtime verification for LTL and TLTL. ACM Trans. Softw. Eng. Methodol. **20**(4), 1–64 (2011)

8. Benedikt, M., Lenhardt, R., Worrell, J.: LTL model checking of interval Markov chains. In: Piterman, N., Smolka, S.A. (eds.) TACAS 2013. LNCS, vol. 7795, pp. 32–46. Springer, Heidelberg (2013). https://doi.org/10.1007/978-3-642-36742-7_3

9. Colombo, C., Pace, G.J., Schneider, G.: Dynamic event-based runtime monitoring of real-time and contextual properties. In: Cofer, D., Fantechi, A. (eds.) FMICS 2008. LNCS, vol. 5596, pp. 135–149. Springer, Heidelberg (2009). https://doi.org/10.1007/978-3-642-03240-0_13

10. Colombo, C., Pace, G.J., Schneider, G.: LARVA – safer monitoring of real-time Java programs. In: SEFM 2009, pp. 33–37. IEEE Computer Society (2009)

11. De Giacomo, G., Vardi, M.Y.: Linear temporal logic and linear dynamic logic on finite traces. In: IJCAI 2013, pp. 854–860. AAAI Press (2013)

12. Eisner, C., Fisman, D., Havlicek, J., Lustig, Y., McIsaac, A., Van Campenhout, D.: Reasoning with temporal logic on truncated paths. In: Hunt, W.A., Somenzi, F. (eds.) CAV 2003. LNCS, vol. 2725, pp. 27–39. Springer, Heidelberg (2003). https://doi.org/10.1007/978-3-540-45069-6_3

13. Falcone, Y., Krstić, S., Reger, G., Traytel, D.: A taxonomy for classifying runtime verification tools. Int. J. Softw. Tools Technol. Transfer **23**(2), 255–284 (2021). https://doi.org/10.1007/s10009-021-00609-z

14. Faymonville, P., Zimmermann, M.: Parametric linear dynamic logic. Inf. Comput. **253**, 237–256 (2017). https://doi.org/10.1016/j.ic.2016.07.009

15. Filippidis, I., Murray, R.M., Holzmann, G.J.: A multi-paradigm language for reactive synthesis. In: SYNT 2015, pp. 73–97 (2015)

16. Fisman, D., Kugler, H.: Temporal reasoning on incomplete paths. In: Margaria, T., Steffen, B. (eds.) ISoLA 2018. LNCS, vol. 11245, pp. 28–52. Springer, Cham (2018). https://doi.org/10.1007/978-3-030-03421-4_3

17. Kupferman, O., Vardi, M.Y.: Synthesis of trigger properties. In: Clarke, E.M., Voronkov, A. (eds.) LPAR 2010. LNCS (LNAI), vol. 6355, pp. 312–331. Springer, Heidelberg (2010). https://doi.org/10.1007/978-3-642-17511-4_18

18. Li, W., Sadigh, D., Sastry, S.S., Seshia, S.A.: Synthesis for human-in-the-loop control systems. In: Ábrahám, E., Havelund, K. (eds.) TACAS 2014. LNCS, vol. 8413, pp. 470–484. Springer, Heidelberg (2014). https://doi.org/10.1007/978-3-642-54862-8_40

19. Lustig, Y., Vardi, M.Y.: Synthesis from component libraries. In: de Alfaro, L. (ed.) FoSSaCS 2009. LNCS, vol. 5504, pp. 395–409. Springer, Heidelberg (2009). https://doi.org/10.1007/978-3-642-00596-1_28

20. Luttenberger, M., Meyer, P.J., Sickert, S.: Practical synthesis of reactive systems from LTL specifications via parity games. Acta Inform. **2**, 3–36 (2019). https://doi.org/10.1007/s00236-019-00349-3

21. Maoz, S., Ringert, J.O.: Spectra: a specification language for reactive systems (2019)

22. Meyer, P.J., Sickert, S., Luttenberger, M.: Strix: explicit reactive synthesis strikes back! In: Chockler, H., Weissenbacher, G. (eds.) CAV 2018. LNCS, vol. 10981, pp. 578–586. Springer, Cham (2018). https://doi.org/10.1007/978-3-319-96145-3_31

23. Piterman, N., Pnueli, A.: Temporal logic and fair discrete systems. In: Clarke, E., Henzinger, T., Veith, H., Bloem, R. (eds.) Handbook of Model Checking, pp. 27–73. Springer, Cham (2018). https://doi.org/10.1007/978-3-319-10575-8_2

24. Piterman, N., Pnueli, A., Sa'ar, Y.: Synthesis of reactive(1) designs. In: Emerson, E.A., Namjoshi, K.S. (eds.) VMCAI 2006. LNCS, vol. 3855, pp. 364–380. Springer, Heidelberg (2005). https://doi.org/10.1007/11609773_24

25. Pnueli, A., Rosner, R.: On the synthesis of a reactive module. In: POPL, pp. 179–190. ACM Press (1989)

26. Raclet, J.: Residual for component specifications. Electron. Notes Theor. Comput. Sci. **215**, 93–110 (2008). https://doi.org/10.1016/j.entcs.2008.06.023

27. Sistla, A.P., Wolfson, O.: Temporal triggers in active databases. IEEE Trans. Knowl. Data Eng. **7**(3), 471–486 (1995)

28. Ulus, D., Belta, C.: Reactive control meets runtime verification: a case study of navigation. In: Finkbeiner, B., Mariani, L. (eds.) RV 2019. LNCS, vol. 11757, pp. 368–374. Springer, Cham (2019). https://doi.org/10.1007/978-3-030-32079-9_21

29. Wolper, P.: Temporal logic can be more expressive. Inf. Control **56**(1/2), 72–99 (1983)

Verification of Machine Learning

pyNeVer: A Framework for Learning and Verification of Neural Networks

Dario Guidotti[1], Luca Pulina[2], and Armando Tacchella[1($\boxtimes$)]

[1] University of Genoa, Genoa, Italy
dario.guidotti@edu.unige.it, armando.tacchella@unige.it
[2] University of Sassari, Sassari, Italy
lpulina@uniss.it

1 Summary

Automated verification of neural networks (NNs) was first proposed in [1] and it is an established research topic with several contributions to date—see, e.g., [2]. The taxonomy proposed in [2] suggests a division among verification tools providing deterministic guarantees, e.g., Marabou [3], and those providing sound approximations, e.g., ERAN [4] and NNV [5]. PYNEVER borrows basic techniques from [5] and casts them into an abstraction approach inspired by [4]; like ERAN and NNV, it features complete verification methods, but it features a distinctive abstraction mechanism. Networks comprising layers of affine transformations and layers of activation functions such as Rectified Linear Units (ReLUs) and sigmoids are abstracted to mappings between polytopes represented as generalized star sets [6]; the main novelty is that the abstraction level of each layer can be controlled down to a single neuron to support various refinement policies. Additionally, PYNEVER can also load popular datasets and NN models in ONNX [7] and PYTORCH [8] formats, and supports training of NNs carried out transparently through PYTORCH. Additionally, NNs can be manipulated through network slimming and weight pruning to ease verification—see [9]. Here we focus on verification with PYNEVER and provide a brief experimental account. PYNEVER sources, documentation and examples are accessible at

https://github.com/NeVerTools/pyNeVer

In the remainder of this section, we briefly introduce some basic definitions and notation used in the paper.

Star Sets. To represent polytopes and define abstract computations we consider a subclass of *generalized star sets*, introduced in [6] and defined as follows— the notation is adapted from [10]. Given a *basis matrix* $V \in \mathbb{R}^{n \times m}$ obtained arranging a set of m *basis vectors* $\{v_1, \ldots, v_m\}$ in columns, a point $c \in \mathbb{R}^n$ called *center* and a *predicate* $R : \mathbb{R}^m \to \{\top, \bot\}$, a generalized star set is a tuple $\Theta = (c, V, R)$ yielding the set of points:

$$\llbracket \Theta \rrbracket \equiv \{z \in \mathbb{R}^n \mid z = Vx + c \text{ such that } R(x_1, \ldots, x_m) = \top\}. \quad (1)$$

© Springer Nature Switzerland AG 2021
Z. Hou and V. Ganesh (Eds.): ATVA 2021, LNCS 12971, pp. 357–363, 2021.
https://doi.org/10.1007/978-3-030-88885-5_23

In the following we denote $[\![\Theta]\!]$ also as Θ. We consider only star sets such that $R(x) := Cx \le d$, where $C \in \mathbb{R}^{p \times m}$ and $d \in \mathbb{R}^p$ for $p \ge 1$, i.e., R is a conjunction of p linear constraints; we further require that the set $Y = \{y \in \mathbb{R}^m \mid Cy \le d\}$ is bounded. We refer to generalized star sets obeying our restrictions simply as *stars*, and it is easy to show that such sets are polytopes in $\mathbb{R}^n$ whose set we represent as $\langle \mathbb{R}^n \rangle$. Given a star $\Theta = (c, V, R)$ and an affine mapping $f : R^n \to R^m$ with $f = Ax + b$, the affine mapping of the star is defined as $f(\Theta) = (\hat{c}, \hat{V}, R)$ where $\hat{c} = Ac + b$ and $\hat{V} = AV$. Notice that, if $\Theta \in \langle \mathbb{R}^n \rangle$ then also $f(\Theta) \in \langle \mathbb{R}^m \rangle$, i.e., the affine transformation of a polytope is still a polytope.

Neural networks. Given a finite number p of functions $f_1 : \mathbb{R}^n \to \mathbb{R}^{n_1}, \dots, f_p :$ $\mathbb{R}^{n_{p-1}} \to \mathbb{R}^m$—also called *layers*—we define a *feed forward neural network* as a function $\nu : \mathbb{R}^n \to \mathbb{R}^m$ obtained through the compositions of the layers, i.e., $\nu(x) = f_p(f_{p-1}(\dots f_1(x) \dots))$. The layer f_1 is called *input layer*, the layer f_p is called *output layer*, and the remaining layers are called *hidden*. Given $x \in \mathbb{R}^n$, we consider two types of layers: the mapping $f(x) = Ax + b$ with $A \in \mathbb{R}^{m \times n}$ and $b \in \mathbb{R}^m$ is an *affine layer* implementing the linear mapping $f : \mathbb{R}^n \to \mathbb{R}^m$; the mapping $f(x) = (\sigma_1(x_1), \dots, \sigma_n(x_n))$ is a *functional layer* $f : \mathbb{R}^n \to \mathbb{R}^n$ consisting of n *activation functions*—also called *neurons*; usually $\sigma_i = \sigma$ for all $i \in [1, n]$, i.e., the function σ is applied to each component of the vector x. We consider two kinds of activation functions $\sigma : \mathbb{R} \to \mathbb{R}$ that find widespread adoption: the *ReLU* function defined as $\sigma(r) = max(0, r)$, and the *logistic* function—of the family of *sigmoids*—defined as $\sigma(r) = \frac{1}{1+e^{-r}}$. For a neural network $f : \mathbb{R}^n \to \mathbb{R}^n$, the task of *classification* is about assigning to every input vector $x \in \mathbb{R}^n$ one out of m labels: an input x is assigned to a class k when $\nu(x)_k > \nu(x)_j$ for all $j \in [1, m]$ and $j \ne k$; the task of *regression* is about approximating a functional mapping from $\mathbb{R}^n$ to $\mathbb{R}^m$.

2   Abstraction Algorithms

In Algorithm 1 we detail the abstract mapping of a ReLU node—abstraction of sigmoid nodes and affine transformations are also implemented. Let us assume that the concrete functional layer contains n activation functions. The function COMPUTE_LAYER takes as input an indexed list of N stars $\Theta_1, \dots, \Theta_N$ representing an abstraction of the input and an indexed list of n positive integers called *refinement levels*. For each neuron, the refinement level tunes the grain of the abstraction: level 0 corresponds to the coarsest abstraction that we consider and the greater the level, the finer the abstraction grain becomes. In the case of ReLUs, all non-zero levels map to the same (precise) refinement, i.e., a piece-wise affine mapping. Notice that, since each neuron features its own refinement level, Algorithm 1 controls abstraction down to the single neuron as expected, enabling the computation of layers with mixed degrees of abstraction. The output of function COMPUTE_LAYER is still an indexed list of stars, that can be obtained by independently processing the stars in the input list. For this reason, the **for** loop starting at line 3 is parallelized in the actual implementation. Given a single input star $\Theta_i \in \langle \mathbb{R}^n \rangle$, each of the n dimensions is

Algorithm 1. Abstraction of the ReLU activation function.

```
1: function COMPUTE_LAYER(input = [Θ_1, ..., Θ_N], refine = [r_1, ..., r_n])
2:     output = []
3:     for i = 1 : N do
4:         stars = [Θ_i]
5:         for j = 1 : n do stars = COMPUTE_RELU(stars, j, refine[j], n)
6:         APPEND(output, stars)
7:     return output

8: function COMPUTE_RELU(input = [Γ_1, ..., Γ_K], j, level, n)
9:     output = []
10:    for k = 1 : K do
11:        (lb, ub) = GET_BOUNDS(input[k], j)
12:        M = [e_1 ... e_{j-1} 0^n e_{j+1} ... e_n]
13:        if lb ≥ 0 then S = input[k]
14:        else if ub ≤ 0 then S = M * input[k]
15:        else
16:            if level > 0 then
17:                Θ_low = input[k] ∧ z_j < 0;  Θ_upp = input[k] ∧ z_j ≥ 0
18:                S = [M * Θ_low, Θ_upp]
19:            else
20:                (c, V, Cx ≤ d) = input[k]
21:                C_1 = [0 0 ... - 1] ∈ R^{1×m+1}, d_1 = 0
22:                C_2 = [V_j - 1] ∈ R^{1×m+1}, d_2 = -c_j
23:                C_3 = [(-ub)/(ub-lb) V_j - 1] ∈ R^{1×m+1}, d_3 = (ub)/(ub-lb)(c_j - lb)
24:                C_0 = [C 0^{m×1}], d_0 = d
25:                Ĉ = [C_0; C_1; C_2; C_3], d̂ = [d_0; d_1; d_2; d_3]
26:                V̂ = MV, V̂ = [V̂ e_j]
27:                S = (Mc, V̂, Ĉx̂ ≤ d̂)
28:            APPEND(output, S)
29:    return output
```

processed in turn by the **for** loop starting at line 5 and involving the function COMPUTE_RELU. Notice that the stars obtained processing the j-th dimension are fed again to COMPUTE_RELU in order to process the $j + 1$-th dimension. The function APPEND(p_1, p_2) (line 6) takes an indexed list p_1 and either an element or another indexed list p_2 and appends it to p_1. For each star given as input, the function COMPUTE_RELU first computes the lower and upper bounds of the star along the j-th dimension by solving a linear-programming problem—function GET_BOUNDS at line 11. Independently from the abstraction level, if $lb \geq 0$ then the ReLU acts as an identity function (line 13), whereas if $ub \leq 0$ then the j-th dimension is zeroed (line 14). The "asterisk" operator (*) takes a matrix M, a star $\Gamma = (c, V, R)$ and returns the star (Mc, MV, R). In this case, M is composed of the standard orthonormal basis in $\mathbb{R}^n$ arranged in columns, with the exception of the j-th dimension which is zeroed. When $lb < 0$ and $ub > 0$ we must consider the refinement level. For any non-zero level, the input star is "split" into two stars, one considering all the points $z < 0$ (Θ_{low}) and the other considering points $z \geq 0$ (Θ_{upp}) along dimension j. Both Θ_{low} and Θ_{upp} are obtained by adding to the input star $input[k]$ the appropriate constraints. Notice that, if the analysis at lines 17–18 is applied throughout the network, and the input abstraction is precise, then the abstract output range will also be precise, i.e., it will coincide with the concrete one: we call *complete* the analysis of PYNEVER

Table 1. Performances of PYNEVER on a subset of ACAS XU networks. Columns PROPERTY and NET report the property and the network considered, respectively. The other columns report the verification time (TIME) and the result of verification (VERIFIED) for complete, mixed and over-approximate analyses, respectively.

PROPERTY	NET	COMPLETE		MIXED		OVERAPPROX	
		TIME	VERIFIED	TIME	VERIFIED	TIME	VERIFIED
# 3	1_1	460	T	25	T	2	F
	1_3	83	T	11	T	3	F
	2_3	33	T	9	T	2	F
	4_3	319	T	31	T	3	F
	5_1	44	T	10	T	2	F
# 4	1_1	143	T	11	F	3	F
	1_3	96	T	16	F	3	F
	3_2	67	T	20	T	3	F
	4_2	177	T	15	T	3	F

in this case. Currently, PYNEVER does not attempt to merge stars. Therefore, in the complete analysis, the number of stars is worst-case exponential—see [5]. If the refinement level is 0, then the ReLU is abstracPted using the tightest polyhedral abstraction available, i.e. a triangle with vertices in $(lb, 0)$, $(0, 0)$ and (ub, ub). The computation of the resulting star is carried out from line 21 to line 25. Intuitively, given the predicates of the input star $Cx \leq d$, the matrix C and the vector d are modified to constrain the output star within the points inside the triangle defining the abstraction, given the points of the input star. If the analysis at lines 21–25 is carried out throughout the network, assuming that the input star contains all potential input points, then the output star will be a (sound) over-approximation of the concrete output range: we call *over-approximate* the analysis of PYNEVER in this case. As we mentioned before, we can mix different levels of abstraction, down to the single neuron: we call *mixed* an analysis that adopts different levels of abstraction.

3   Experimental Evaluation

In this section, we provide some empirical results about PYNEVER[1]. Our experiments are focused on the verification task, i.e., given a neural network $\nu : \mathbb{R}^n \to \mathbb{R}^m$ we wish to verify algorithmically that it complies to stated *post-conditions* on the output as long as it satisfies *pre-conditions* on the input. In the first experiment, we compare the three different verification methodologies available in PYNEVER, namely complete, mixed and over-approximate analysis. In this experiment, the mixed strategy is implemented by refining a fixed

---

[1] All experiments ran on a laptop equipped with an Intel i7-8565 CPU (8 core at 1.8 GHz) and 16 GB of memory with Ubuntu 20 operating system.

Table 2. Performances of a pool of state-of-the-art tools on a subset of ACAS XU networks. The table is organized similarly to Table 1. In the results, "<1" indicates that the CPU time spent was less than 1 s, while a dash ("−") denotes that the tool exhausted the available memory.

P	NET	ERAN$_{cp}$		ERAN$_{cz}$		ERAN$_{op}$		ERAN$_{oz}$		MARABOU		NNV$_c$		NNV$_o$	
		TIME	VER	TIME	VER	TIME	VER	TIME	VER	TIME	VER	TIME	VER	TIME	VER
# 3	1_1	139	T	73	T	105	F	65	F	7073	T	329	T	1	F
	1_3	9	T	−	−	9	T	36	F	3451	T	37	T	<1	F
	2_3	4	T	3	T	4	T	2	T	966	T	17	T	<1	F
	4_3	4	T	4	T	4	T	5	T	1452	T	112	T	<1	F
	5_1	7	T	3	T	8	T	4	T	763	T	17	T	<1	F
# 4	1_1	11	T	6	T	11	T	7	T	2401	T	141	T	1	F
	1_3	8	T	3	T	8	T	3	T	756	T	41	T	<1	F
	3_2	4	T	3	T	5	T	2	T	63	T	21	T	<1	F
	4_2	4	T	2	T	4	T	2	T	44	T	59	T	<1	F

amount of neurons in each layer. The results that we present are obtained refining at most a single neuron for each layer. Clearly, different refinement heuristics may yield different results, but a thorough experimentation of such heuristics is beyond the scope of this paper. Here, we just wish to show how combining concrete and over-approximate analysis, even with a very straightforward approach, may yield improvements in the overall verification time. For the comparison, we consider networks and properties from the ACAS Xu evaluation [11]. ACAS Xu is an airborne collision avoidance system based on NNs whose purpose is to issue advisory commands to an autonomous vehicle (ownship) about evasive maneuvers to be performed in case another vehicle (intruder) comes too close. In particular, we selected Property 3 and 4 since they can be easily expressed as a single verification query in our tool. In the words of [11], these safety properties *"deal with situations where the intruder is directly ahead of the ownship, and state that the NN will never issue a COC (clear of conflict) advisory"*. Considering the analysis in [11], each property can be assessed on 42 different networks depending on the choice of two parameters. Among the 84 networks available, we selected those for which our over-approximate analysis was not able to find a definitive answer, ending with a total of 9 networks. Notice that Property 3 and Property 4 are always satisfied in these networks. Table 1 shows the results of this experiment. Looking at the table, we can see that the complete analysis of PYNEVER is able to answer all the queries, whereas the over-approximate analysis does not succeed on any of them. Considering the results of the mixed analysis, we see that PYNEVER is able to answer all but two queries and the total amount of CPU time spent is noticeably less than the complete analysis and uniformly closer to the one reported for the over-approximate one. Arguably, the mixed methodology provides a good trade-off between precision and speed.

Our second experiment aims to compare PYNEVER to a pool of state-of-the-art tools. In particular, we consider four versions of ERAN [12,13], i.e.

the ones resulting from the combination of complete (c) and over-approximate (o) methodologies, using either polytopes (p) or zonotopes (z); we consider also Marabou [3], and two versions of NNV [10] featuring both complete and over-approximate methodologies (NNV_c and NNV_o, respectively). We report the results in Table 2, where we denote ERAN versions with $ERAN_{xy}$, where $x \in \{c, o\}$ indicates the analysis, while $y \in \{p, z\}$ denotes the polyhedron type. Focusing on complete analyses, i.e., the results of $ERAN_{cp}$, $ERAN_{cz}$, Marabou and NNV_c, and comparing them with the related results of PYNEVER reported in Table 1, we can see that the complete analysis of PYNEVER is in the same ballpark as all but one of the other tools—$ERAN_{cz}$ exhausts available memory in one query. The same comparison, but focusing on over-approximation techniques, yields a different result: ERAN seems to strike a better balance between speed and precision since it is able to verify the properties even when using over-approximation. On the other hand, the performances of PYNEVER are on the same page with the ones reported for NNV_o. Finally, looking at Table 1 and focusing on the results related to the mixed analysis, we can see that it outperforms NNV_o and it is close to $ERAN_{op}$ and $ERAN_{oz}$ in terms of verified properties.

References

1. Pulina, L., Tacchella, A.: An abstraction-refinement approach to verification of artificial neural networks. In: Touili, T., Cook, B., Jackson, P. (eds.) CAV 2010. LNCS, vol. 6174, pp. 243–257. Springer, Heidelberg (2010). https://doi.org/10.1007/978-3-642-14295-6_24
2. Huang, X., et al.: Safety and trustworthiness of deep neural networks: A survey. arXiv preprint arXiv:1812.08342 (2018)
3. Katz, G., et al.: The marabou framework for verification and analysis of deep neural networks. In: Dillig, I., Tasiran, S. (eds.) CAV 2019. LNCS, vol. 11561, pp. 443–452. Springer, Cham (2019). https://doi.org/10.1007/978-3-030-25540-4_26
4. Singh, G., Gehr, T., Püschel, M., Vechev, M.T.: Boosting robustness certification of neural networks. In: Proceedings of the ICLR 2019 (2019)
5. Tran, H., et al.: NNV: the neural network verification tool for deep neural networks and learning-enabled cyber-physical systems. CoRR, abs/2004.05519 (2020)
6. Bak, S., Duggirala, P.S.: Simulation-equivalent reachability of large linear systems with inputs. In: Majumdar, R., Kunčak, V. (eds.) CAV 2017. LNCS, vol. 10426, pp. 401–420. Springer, Cham (2017). https://doi.org/10.1007/978-3-319-63387-9_20
7. Open Neural Network Exchange the open standard for machine learning interoperability. https://onnx.ai/
8. Paszke, A., et al.: Pytorch: an imperative style, high-performance deep learning library. In: Proceedings of the NIPS 2019, pp. 8024–8035 (2019)
9. Guidotti, D., Leofante, F., Pulina, L., Tacchella, A.: Verification of neural networks: enhancing scalability through pruning. In: Proceedings of the ECAI 2020, volume 325 of Frontiers in Artificial Intelligence and Applications, pp. 2505–2512. IOS Press (2020)
10. Tran, H.D., et al.: Star-based reachability analysis of deep neural networks. In: ter Beek, M.H., McIver, A., Oliveira, J.N. (eds.) FM 2019. LNCS, vol. 11800, pp. 670–686. Springer, Cham (2019). https://doi.org/10.1007/978-3-030-30942-8_39

11. Katz, G., Barrett, C., Dill, D.L., Julian, K., Kochenderfer, M.J.: Reluplex: an efficient SMT solver for verifying deep neural networks. In: Majumdar, R., Kunčak, V. (eds.) CAV 2017. LNCS, vol. 10426, pp. 97–117. Springer, Cham (2017). https://doi.org/10.1007/978-3-319-63387-9_5
12. Singh, G., Gehr, T., Mirman, M., Püschel, M., Vechev, M.T.: Fast and effective robustness certification. In: Proceedings of the NIPS 2018, pp. 10825–10836 (2018)
13. Singh, G., Gehr, T., Püschel, M., Vechev, M.T.: An abstract domain for certifying neural networks. Proc. ACM Program. Lang. 3(POPL):41:1–41:30 (2019)

Property-Directed Verification
and Robustness Certification
of Recurrent Neural Networks

Igor Khmelnitsky[1,2], Daniel Neider[3], Rajarshi Roy[3(✉)], Xuan Xie[3],
Benoît Barbot[4], Benedikt Bollig[1], Alain Finkel[1,7], Serge Haddad[1,2],
Martin Leucker[5], and Lina Ye[1,2,6]

[1] Université Paris-Saclay, CNRS, ENS Paris-Saclay, LMF, Gif-sur-Yvette, France
[2] Inria, Paris, France
[3] Max Planck Institute for Software Systems, Kaiserslautern, Germany
`rajarshi@mpi-sws.org`
[4] Université Paris-Est Créteil, Créteil, France
[5] Institute for Software Engineering and Programming Languages,
Universität zu Lübeck, Lübeck, Germany
[6] CentraleSupélec, Université Paris-Saclay, Gif-sur-Yvette, France
[7] Institut Universitaire de France, Paris, France

Abstract. This paper presents a property-directed approach to verifying recurrent neural networks (RNNs). To this end, we learn a deterministic finite automaton as a *surrogate model* from a given RNN using active automata learning. This model may then be analyzed using *model checking* as a verification technique. The term *property-directed* reflects the idea that our procedure is guided and controlled by the given property rather than performing the two steps separately. We show that this not only allows us to discover *small* counterexamples fast, but also to generalize them by pumping towards faulty flows hinting at the underlying error in the RNN. We also show that our method can be efficiently used for *adversarial robustness certification* of RNNs.

1 Introduction

Recurrent neural networks (RNNs) are a state-of-the-art tool to represent and learn sequence-based models. They have applications in time-series prediction, sentiment analysis, and many more. In particular, they are increasingly used in safety-critical applications and act, for example, as controllers in cyber-physical systems [1]. Thus, there is a growing need for formal verification. However, research in this domain is only at the beginning. While formal-methods based

The first four authors contributed equally, the remaining authors are ordered alphabetically. This work was partly supported by the PHC PROCOPE 2020 project LeaRNNify (number 44707TK), funded by DAAD and Campus France and the Deutsche Forschungsgemeinschaft (DFG, German Research Foundation) grant number 434592664.

© Springer Nature Switzerland AG 2021
Z. Hou and V. Ganesh (Eds.): ATVA 2021, LNCS 12971, pp. 364–380, 2021.
https://doi.org/10.1007/978-3-030-88885-5_24

techniques such as *model checking* [4] have been successfully used in practice and reached a certain level of industrial acceptance, a transfer to machine-learning algorithms has yet to take place. We apply it on machine-learning artifacts rather than on the algorithm.

An emerging research stream aims at extracting, from RNNs, state-based formalisms such as finite automata [3,16,17,20,21,25]. Finite automata turned out to be useful for understanding and analyzing all kinds of systems using testing or model checking. In the field of formal verification, it has proven to be beneficial to run the extraction and verification process simultaneously. Moreover, the state space of RNNs tends to be prohibitively large, or even infinite, and so do incremental abstractions thereof. Motivated by these facts, we propose an intertwined approach to verifying RNNs, where, in an incremental fashion, grammatical inference and model checking go hand-in-hand. Our approach is inspired by black-box checking [22], which *exploits* the property to be verified *during* the verification process. Our procedure can be used to find misclassified examples or to verify a system that the given RNN controls.

Property-Directed Verification. Let us give a glimpse of our method. We consider an RNN R as a binary classifier of finite sequences over a finite alphabet Σ. In other words, R represents the set of strings that are classified as positive. We denote this set by $L(R)$ and call it the *language* of R. Note that $L(R) \subseteq \Sigma^*$. We would like to know whether R is compatible with a given specification A, written $R \models A$. Here, we assume that A is given as a (deterministic) finite automaton. Finite automata are algorithmically feasible, albeit having a reasonable expressive power: many abstract specification languages such as temporal logics or regular expressions can be compiled into finite automata [10].

But what does $R \models A$ actually mean? In fact, there are various options. If A provides a complete characterization of the sequences that are to be classified as positive, then $\models$ refers to language equivalence, i.e., $L(R) = L(A)$. Note that this would imply that $L(R)$ is supposed to be a regular language, which may rarely be the case in practice. Therefore, we will focus on checking inclusion $L(R) \subseteq L(A)$, which is more versatile as we explain next.

Suppose N is a finite automaton representing a negative specification, i.e., R must classify words in $L(N)$ as negative at any cost. In other words, R does not produce false positives. This amounts to checking that $L(R) \subseteq L(\overline{N})$ where $\overline{N}$ is the "complement automaton" of N. For instance, assume that R is supposed to recognize valid XML documents over a finite predefined set of tags. Seen as a set of strings, this is not a regular language. However, we can still check whether $L(R)$ only contains words where every opening tag <*tag-name*> is eventually followed by a closing tag </*tag-name*> (while the number of opening and the number of closing tags may differ). As negative specification, we can then take an automaton N accepting the corresponding *regular* set of strings. For example, <book><author></author><author></book> $\in L(N)$, since the second occurrence of <author> is not followed by some </author> anymore. On the other hand, we have <book><author><author></author></book> $\in L(\overline{N})$, as <book> and <author> are always eventually followed by their closing counterpart.

Symmetrically, suppose P is a finite automaton representing a *positive* specification so that we can find false negative classifications: If P represents the words that R *must classify as positive*, we would like to know whether $L(P) \subseteq L(R)$. Our procedure can be run using the complement of P as specification and inverting the outputs of R, i.e., we check, equivalently, $L(\overline{R}) \subseteq L(\overline{P})$.

An important instance of this setting is *adversarial robustness certification*, which measures a neural network's resilience against adversarial examples. Given a (regular) set of words L classified as positive by the given RNN, the RNN is *robust* wrt. L if slight modifications in a word from L do not alter the RNN's judgement. This notion actually relies on a distance function. Then, P is the set of words whose distance to a word in L is bounded by a predefined threshold, which is regular for several popular distances such as the *Hamming* or *Levenshtein distance*. Similarly, we can also check whether the neighborhood of a regular set of words preserves a negative classification.

So, in all these cases, we are faced with the question of whether the language of an RNN R is contained in the (regular) language of a finite automaton A. Our approach to this problem relies on black-box checking [22], which has been designed as a combination of model checking and testing in order to verify finite-state systems and is based on Angluin's L* learning algorithm [2]. L* produces a sequel of *hypothesis* automata based on queries to R. Every such hypothesis $\mathcal{H}$ may already share some structural properties with R. So, instead of checking conformance of $\mathcal{H}$ with R, it is worthwhile to first check $L(\mathcal{H}) \subseteq L(A)$ using classical model-checking algorithms. If the answer is affirmative, we apply statistical model checking to check $L(R) \subseteq L(\mathcal{H})$ to confirm the result. Otherwise, a counterexample is exploited to refine $\mathcal{H}$, starting a new cycle in L*. Just like in black-box checking, our experimental results suggest that the process of interweaving automata learning and model checking is beneficial in the verification of RNNs and offers advantages over more obvious approaches such as (pure) statistical model checking or running automata extraction and model checking in sequence. A further key advantage of our approach is that, unlike in statistical model checking, we often find a *family* of counterexamples, in terms of loops in the hypothesis automaton, which testify conceptual problems of the given RNN.

Note that, though we only cover the case of binary classifiers, our framework is in principle applicable to multiple labels using one-vs-all classification.

Related Work. Mayr and Yovine describe an adaptation of the PAC variant of Angluin's L* algorithm that can be applied to neural networks [17]. As L* is not guaranteed to terminate when facing non-regular languages, the authors impose a bound on the number of states of the hypotheses and on the length of the words for membership queries. In [16,18], Mayr et al. propose *on-the-fly property checking* where one learns an automaton approximating the intersection of the RNN language and the complement of the property to be verified. Like the RNN, the property is considered as a black box, only decidability of the word problem is required. Therefore, the approach is suitable for non-regular specifications.

Weiss et al. introduce a different technique to extract finite automata from RNNs [25]. It also relies on Angluin's L* but, moreover, uses an orthogonal abstraction of the given RNN to perform equivalence checks between them.

The paper [1] studies formal verification of systems where an RNN-based agent interacts with a linearly definable environment. The verification procedure proceeds by a reduction to feed-forward neural networks (FFNNs). It is complete and fully automatic. This is at the expense of the expressive power of the specification language, which is restricted to properties that only depend on bounded prefixes of the system's executions. In our approach, we do not restrict the kind of regular property to verify. The work [13] also reduces the verification of RNNs to FFNN verification. To do so, the authors calculate inductive invariants, thereby avoiding a blowup in the network size. The effectiveness of their approach is demonstrated on audio signal systems. Like in [1], a time interval is imposed in which a given property is verified.

For adversarial robustness certification, Ryou et al. [23] compute a convex relaxation of the non-linear operations found in the recurrent cells for certifying the robustness of RNNs. The authors show the effectiveness of their approach in speech recognition. Besides, MARBLE [8] builds a probabilistic model to quantize the robustness of RNNs. However, these approaches are white-box based and demand the full structure and information of neural networks. Instead, our approach is based on learning with black-box checking.

Elboher et al. present a counter-example guided verification framework whose workflow shares similarities with our property-guided verification [9]. However, their approach addresses FFNNs rather than RNNs. For recent progress in the area of safety and robustness verification of deep neural networks, see [15].

Outline. In Sect. 2, we recall basic notions such as RNNs and finite automata. Section 3 describes two basic algorithms for the verification of RNNs, before we present property-directed verification in Sect. 4. How to handle adversarial robustness certification is discussed in Sect. 5. The experimental evaluation and a thorough discussion can be found in Sect. 6.

2   Preliminaries

In this section, we provide definitions of basic concepts such as languages, recurrent neural networks, finite automata, and Angluin's L* algorithm.

Words and Languages. Let Σ be an alphabet, i.e., a nonempty finite set, whose elements are called *letters*. A (finite) word w over Σ is a sequence $a_1 \ldots a_n$ of letters $a_i \in \Sigma$. The length of w is defined as $|w| = n$. The unique word of length 0 is called the *empty word* and denoted by λ. We let Σ^* refer to the set of all words over Σ. Any set $L \subseteq \Sigma^*$ is called a *language* (over Σ). Its complement is $\overline{L} = \{w \in \Sigma^* \mid w \notin L\}$. For two languages $L_1, L_2 \subseteq \Sigma^*$, we let $L_1 \setminus L_2 = L_1 \cap \overline{L_2}$. The symmetric difference of L_1 and L_2 is defined as $L_1 \oplus L_2 = (L_1 \setminus L_2) \cup (L_2 \setminus L_1)$.

Probability Distributions. In order to sample words over Σ, we assume a probability distribution $(p_a)_{a \in \Sigma}$ on Σ (by default, we pick the uniform distribution) and a "termination" probability $p \in (0, 1]$. Together, they determine a natural probability distribution on Σ^* given, for $w = a_1 \ldots a_n \in \Sigma^*$, by $\Pr(w) = p_{a_1} \cdot \ldots \cdot p_{a_n} \cdot (1 - p)^n \cdot p$. According to the geometric distribution, the expected length of a word is $(1/p) - 1$, with a variance of $(1 - p)/p^2$. Let $0 < \varepsilon < 1$ be an error parameter and $L_1, L_2 \subseteq \Sigma^*$ be languages. We call L_1 ε-*approximately correct* wrt. L_2 if $\Pr(L_1 \setminus L_2) = \sum_{w \in L_1 \setminus L_2} \Pr(w) < \varepsilon$.

Finite Automata and Recurrent Neural Networks. We employ two kinds of language acceptors: finite automata and recurrent neural networks.

Recurrent neural networks (RNNs) are a generic term for artificial neural networks that process sequential data. They are particularly suitable for classifying sequences of varying length, which is essential in domains such as natural language processing (NLP) or time-series prediction. For the purposes of this paper, it is sufficient to think of an RNN R as an effective function $R : \Sigma^* \to \{0, 1\}$, which determines its language as $L(R) = \{w \in \Sigma^* \mid R(w) = 1\}$. Its complement $\overline{R}$ is defined by $\overline{R}(w) = 1 - R(w)$ for all $w \in \Sigma^*$. There are several ways to effectively represent R. Among the most popular architectures are (simple) Elman RNNs, long short-term memory (LSTM) [11], and GRUs [6]. Their expressive power depends on the exact architecture, but generally goes beyond the power of finite automata, i.e., the class of regular languages.

A *deterministic finite automaton (DFA)* over Σ is a tuple $A = (Q, \delta, q_0, F)$ where Q is a finite set of states, $q_0 \in Q$ is the initial state, $F \subseteq Q$ is the set of final states, and $\delta : Q \times \Sigma \to Q$ is the transition function. We assume familiarity with basic automata theory and leave it at mentioning that the language $L(A)$ of A is defined as the set of words from Σ^* that δ guides into a final state when starting in q_0. That is, for the complement DFA $\overline{A} = (Q, \delta, q_0, Q \setminus F)$, we get $L(\overline{A}) = \overline{L(A)} = \Sigma^* \setminus L(A)$. It is well-known that high-level specifications such as LTL formulas over finite words [10] or regular expressions can be compiled into corresponding DFAs.

We sometimes use RNNs and DFAs synonymous for their respective languages. For example, we say that R is ε-approximately correct wrt. A if $L(R)$ is ε-approximately correct wrt. $L(A)$.

Angluin's Algorithm. Angluin introduced L*, a classical instance of a learning algorithm in the presence of a minimally adequate teacher (MAT) [2]. We do not detail the algorithm here but only define the interfaces that we need to embed L* into our framework. Given any regular language $L \subseteq \Sigma^*$, the algorithm L* eventually outputs the unique minimal DFA $\mathcal{H}$ such that $L(\mathcal{H}) = L$. The crux is that, while Σ is given, L is a priori unknown and can only be accessed through *membership queries (MQ)* and *equivalence queries (EQ)*:

(MQ) $w \overset{?}{\in} L$ for a given word $w \in \Sigma^*$. Thus, the answer is either yes or no.
(EQ) $L(\mathcal{H}) \overset{?}{=} L$ for a given DFA $\mathcal{H}$. Again, the answer is either yes or no. If the answer is no, one also gets a counterexample word from the symmetric difference $L(\mathcal{H}) \oplus L$.

Algorithm 1: SMC
Input: RNN R, DFA A, $\varepsilon, \gamma \in (0,1)$
1 **for** $i = 1, \ldots, \log(2/\gamma)/(2\varepsilon^2)$ **do**
2 $\quad$ $w \leftarrow$ sampleWord()
3 $\quad$ **if** $w \in L(R) \setminus L(A)$ **then**
4 $\quad\quad$ | **return** "Counterexample w"
5
6 **end**
7 **return** "Property satisfied"

Algorithm 2: AAMC
Input: RNN R and DFA A
1 $A_R \leftarrow$ Approximation(R)
2 **if** $\exists w \in L(A_R) \setminus L(A)$ **then**
3 $\quad$ | **return** "Counterexample w"
4 **else return** "Property satisfied"

Algorithm 3: PDV
Input: RNN R, DFA A, $\varepsilon, \gamma \in (0,1)$
1 Initialize L*
2 **while** *true* **do**
3 $\quad$ $\mathcal{H} \leftarrow$ hypothesis provided by L*
4 $\quad$ Check $L(\mathcal{H}) \subseteq L(A)$
5 $\quad$ **if** $L(\mathcal{H}) \subseteq L(A)$ **then**
6 $\quad\quad$ Check $L(R) \subseteq L(\mathcal{H})$ using Alg. 1
7 $\quad\quad$ **if** $L(R) \subseteq L(\mathcal{H})$ **then**
8 $\quad\quad\quad$ | **return** "Property satisfied"
9 $\quad\quad$ **else** Feed counterexample to L*
10 $\quad$ **else**
11 $\quad\quad$ Let $w \in L(\mathcal{H}) \setminus L(A)$
12 $\quad\quad$ **if** $w \in L(R)$ **then**
13 $\quad\quad\quad$ | **return** "Counterexample w"
14 $\quad\quad$ **else** Feed counterexample w to L*
15 $\quad$ **end**
16 **end**

Essentially, L* asks MQs until it considers that it has a consistent data set to come up with a hypothesis DFA $\mathcal{H}$, which then undergoes an EQ. If the latter succeeds, then the algorithm stops. Otherwise, the counterexample and possibly more membership queries are used to refine the hypothesis. The algorithm provides the following guarantee: If MQs and EQs are answered according to a given regular language $L \subseteq \Sigma^*$, then the algorithm eventually outputs, after polynomially[1] many steps, the unique minimal DFA $\mathcal{H}$ such that $L(\mathcal{H}) = L$.

3 Verification Approaches

Before we present (in Sect. 4) our method of verifying RNNs, we here describe two simple approaches. The experiments will later compare all three algorithms wrt. their performance.

Statistical Model Checking (SMC). One obvious approach for checking whether the RNN under test R satisfies a given specification A, i.e., to check whether $L(R) \subseteq L(A)$, is by a form of random testing. The idea is to generate a finite test suite $T \subset \Sigma^*$ and to check, for each $w \in T$, whether for $w \in L(R)$ also $w \in L(A)$ holds. If not, each such w is a *counterexample*. On the other hand, if none of the words turns out to be a counterexample, the property holds on R with a certain error probability. The algorithm is sketched as Algorithm 1

Note that the test suite is sampled according to a probability distribution on Σ^*. Recall that our choice depends on two parameters: a probability distribution on Σ and a "termination" probability, both are described in Sect. 2.

---

[1] In the index of the right congruence associated with L and in the size of the longest counterexample obtained as a reply to an EQ.

Theorem 1. (Correctness of SMC). *If Algorithm 1, with $\varepsilon, \gamma \in (0,1)$, terminates with "Counterexample w", then w is mistakenly classified by R as positive. If it terminates with "Property satisfied", then R is ε-approximately correct wrt. A with probability at least $1 - \gamma$.*

While the approach works in principle, it has several drawbacks for its practical application. The size of the test suite may be quite huge and it may take a while both finding a counterexample or proving correctness.

Moreover, the correctness result and the algorithm assume that the words to be tested are chosen according to a random distribution that somehow also has to take into account the RNN as well as the property automaton.

It has been reported that this method does not work well in practice [25] and our experiments support these findings.

Automaton Abstraction and Model Checking (AAMC). As model checking is mainly working for finite-state systems, a straightforward idea would be to (a) *approximate* the RNN R by a finite automaton A_R such that $L(R) \approx L(A_R)$ and (b) to check whether $L(A_R) \subseteq L(A)$ using model checking. The algorithmic schema is depicted in Algorithm 2.

Here, we can instantiate Approximation() by the DFA-extraction algorithms from [17] or [25]. In fact, for approximating an RNN by a finite-state system, several approaches have been studied in the literature, which can be, roughly, divided into two approaches: (a) *abstraction* and (b) *automata learning*. In the first approach, the state space of the RNN is mapped to equivalence classes according to certain predicates. The second approach uses automata-learning techniques such as Angluin's L*. The approach [25] is an intertwined version combining both ideas.

Therefore, there are different instances of AAMC, varying in the approximation approach. Note that, for verification as language inclusion, as considered here, it actually suffices to learn an over-approximation A_R such that $L(R) \subsetneq L(A_R)$.

While the approach seems promising at first hand, its correctness has two glitches. First, the result "Property satisfied" depends on the quality of the approximation. Second, any returned counterexample w may be *spurious*: w is a counterexample with respect to A_R satisfying A but may not be a counterexample for R satisfying A. If $w \in L(R)$, then it is indeed a counterexample, but if not, it is spurious—an indication that the approximation needs to be refined. If the automaton is obtained using abstraction techniques (such as predicate abstraction) that guarantee over-approximations, well-known principles like CEGAR [7] may be used to refine it. In the automata-learning setting, w may be used as a counterexample for the learning algorithm to improve the approximation. Repeating the latter idea suggests an interplay between automata learning and verification—and this is the idea that we follow in this paper. However, rather than starting from some approximation with a certain quality that is later refined according to the RNN and the property, we perform a direct, *property-directed* approach.

4   Property-Directed Verification of RNNs

We are now ready to present our algorithm for property-directed verification (PDV). The underlying idea is to replace the EQ in Angluin's L* algorithm with a combination of classical model checking and statistical model checking, which are used as an alternative to EQs. This approach, which we call *property-directed verification of RNNs*, is outlined as Algorithm 3 and works as follows.

After initialization of L* and the corresponding data structure, L* automatically generates and asks MQs to the given RNN R until it comes up with a first hypothesis DFA $\mathcal{H}$ (Line 3). In particular, the language $L(\mathcal{H})$ is consistent with the MQs asked so far.

At an early stage of the algorithm, $\mathcal{H}$ is generally small. However, it already shares some characteristics with R. So it is worth checking, using standard automata algorithms, whether there is no mismatch yet between $\mathcal{H}$ and A, i.e., whether $L(\mathcal{H}) \subseteq L(A)$ holds (Line 4). Because otherwise (Line 10), a counterexample word $w \in L(\mathcal{H}) \setminus L(A)$ is already a candidate for being a misclassified input for R. If indeed $w \in L(R)$, w is mistakenly considered positive by R so that R violates the specification A. The algorithm then outputs "Counterexample w" (Line 13). If, on the other hand, R happens to agree with A on a negative classification of w, then there is a mismatch between R and the hypothesis $\mathcal{H}$ (Line 14). In that case, w is fed back to L* to refine $\mathcal{H}$.

Now, let us consider the case that $L(\mathcal{H}) \subseteq L(A)$ holds (Line 5). If, in addition, we can establish $L(R) \subseteq L(\mathcal{H})$, we conclude that $L(R) \subseteq L(A)$ and output "Property satisfied" (Line 8). This inclusion test (Line 6) relies on statistical model checking using given parameters $\varepsilon, \gamma > 0$ (cf. Algorithm 1). If the test passes, we have some statistical guarantee of correctness of R (cf. Theorem 1). Otherwise, we obtain a word $w \in L(R) \setminus L(\mathcal{H})$ witnessing a discrepancy between R and $\mathcal{H}$ that will be exploited to refine $\mathcal{H}$ (Line 9).

Overall, in the event that the algorithm terminates, we have the following theorem (with proof in the appendix) that assures the soundness of a returned counterexample and provides the statistical guarantees on the property satisfaction, depending on the result of the algorithm:

Theorem 2. (Correctness of PDV). *Suppose Algorithm 3 terminates, using SMC for inclusion checking with parameters ε and γ. If it outputs "Counterexample w", then w is mistakenly classified by R as positive. If it outputs "Property satisfied", then R is ε-approximately correct wrt. A with probability at least $1 - \gamma$.*

Although we cannot hope that Algorithm 3 will always terminate, we demonstrate empirically that it is an effective way for the verification of RNNs.

5   Adversarial Robustness Certification

Our method can especially be used for *adversarial robustness certification*, which is parameterized by a distance function $dist : \Sigma^* \times \Sigma^* \to [0, \infty]$ satisfying, for all words $w_1, w_2, w_3 \in \Sigma^*$: (i) $dist(w_1, w_2) = 0$ iff $w_1 = w_2$, (ii) $dist(w_1, w_2) = dist(w_2, w_1)$, and (iii) $dist(w_1, w_3) \leq dist(w_1, w_2) + dist(w_2, w_3)$. Popular distance functions are *Hamming distance* and *Levenshtein distance*. The Hamming distance between $w_1, w_2 \in \Sigma^*$ is the number of positions in which w_1 differs from w_2, provided $|w_1| = |w_2|$ (otherwise, the distance is ∞). The Levenshtein distance (edit distance) between w_1 and w_2 is the minimal number of operations among substitution, insertion, and deletion that are required to transform w_1 into w_2. For $L \subseteq \Sigma^*$ and $r \in \mathbb{N}$, we let $\mathcal{N}_r(L) = \{w' \in \Sigma^* \mid dist(w, w') \leq r$ for some $w \in L\}$ be the *r-neighborhood* of L. If L is regular and *dist* is the Hamming or Levenshtein distance, then $\mathcal{N}_r(L)$ is regular (for efficient constructions of *Levenshtein automata* when L is a singleton, see [24]).

Let R be an RNN, $L \subseteq \Sigma^*$ be a regular language such that $L \subseteq L(R)$, $r \in \mathbb{N}$, and $0 < \varepsilon < 1$. We call R *ε-adversarially robust* (wrt. L and r) if $\Pr(\mathcal{N}_r(L) \setminus L(R)) < \varepsilon$. Accordingly, every word from $\mathcal{N}_r(L) \setminus L(R)$ is an *adversarial example*. Thus, checking adversarial robustness amounts to checking the inclusion $L(\overline{R}) \subseteq \mathcal{N}_r(L)$ through one of the above-mentioned algorithms.

Note that, even when L is a finite set, $\mathcal{N}_r(L)$ can be too large for exhaustive exploration so that PDV, in combination with SMC, is particularly promising, as we demonstrate in our experimental evaluation.

From the definitions and Theorem 2, we get:

Lemma 1. *Suppose Algorithm 3, for input $\overline{R}$ and a DFA A recognizing $\overline{\mathcal{N}_r(L)}$, terminates, using SMC for inclusion checking with parameters ε and γ. If it outputs "Counterexample w", then w is an adversarial example. Otherwise, R is ε-adversarially robust (wrt. L and r) with probability at least $1 - \gamma$.*

Similarly, we can handle the case where $L \cap L(R) = \emptyset$. Then, R is ε-*adversarially robust* if $\Pr(L(R) \cap \mathcal{N}_r(L)) < \varepsilon$, and every word in $L(R) \cap \mathcal{N}_r(L)$ is an *adversarial example*. Overall, this case amounts to checking $L(R) \subseteq \overline{\mathcal{N}_r(L)}$.

6   Experimental Evaluation

We now present an experimental evaluation of the three algorithms SMC, AAMC, and PDV, and provide a comparison of their performance on LSTM networks [11] (a variant of RNNs using LSTM units). The algorithms have been implemented[2] in Python 3.6 using PyTorch 19.09 and Numpy library. The experiments of adversarial robustness certification were run on Macbook Pro 13 with the macOS. The other experiments were run on NVIDIA DGX-2 with an Ubuntu OS.

Optimization For Equivalence Queries. In [17], the authors implement AAMC but with an optimization that was originally shown in [2]. This optimization concerns the number of samples required for checking the equivalence between the hypothesis and the taught language. This number depends on ε, γ and the number of previous equivalence queries n and is calculated by $\frac{1}{\varepsilon}\left(\log\frac{1}{\gamma} + \log(2)(n+1)\right)$. We adopt this optimization in AAMC and PDV as well (Algorithm 2 in Line 1 and Algorithm 3 in Line 6).

---

[2] Available at https://github.com/LeaRNNify/Property-directed-verification.

Table 1. Experimental results

Type	Avg time (s)	Avg len	#Mistakes	Avg MQs
SMC	92	111	**122**	286063
AAMC	444	**7**	30	3701916
PDV	**21**	11	109	**28318**

6.1 Evaluation on Randomly Generated DFAs

Synthetic Benchmarks. To compare the algorithms, we implemented the following procedure, which generates a random DFA A_{rand}, an RNN R that learned $L(A_{\mathsf{rand}})$, and a finite set of specification DFAs: (1) choose a random DFA $A_{\mathsf{rand}} = (Q, \delta, q_0, F)$, with $|Q| \leq 30$, over an alphabet Σ with $|\Sigma| = 5$; (2) randomly sample words from Σ^* as described in Sect. 2 in order to create a training set and a test set; (3) train an RNN R with hidden dimension $20|Q|$ and $1 + |Q|/10$ layers—if the accuracy of R on the training set is larger than 95%, continue, otherwise restart the procedure; (4) choose randomly up to five sets $F_i \subseteq Q \setminus F$ to define specification DFAs $A_i = (Q, \delta, q_0, F \cup F_i)$. Using this procedure, we created 30 DFAs/RNNs and 138 specifications.

Experimental Results. Given an RNN R and a specification DFA A, we checked whether R satisfies A using Algorithms 1–3, i.e., SMC, AAMC, and PDV, with $\varepsilon, \gamma = 5 \cdot 10^{-4}$.

Table 1 summarizes the executions of the three algorithms on our 138 random instances. The columns of the table are as follows: (i) *Avg time* was counted in seconds and all the algorithms were timed out after 10 min; (ii) *Avg len* is the average length of the found counterexamples (if one was found); (iii) *#Mistakes* is the number of random instances for which a mistake was found; (iv) *Avg MQs* is the average number of membership queries asked to the RNN.

Note that not only is PDV faster and finds more errors than AAMC, the average number of states of the final DFA is also much smaller: **26** states with PDV and **319** with AAMC. Furthermore, it asked more than 10 times less MQs to the RNN. Comparing PDV to SMC, it is 4.5 times faster and the average length of counterexamples it found is 10 times smaller, even though with a little fewer mistakes discovered.

Faulty Flows. One of the advantages of extracting DFAs in order to detect mistakes in a given RNN is the possibility to find not only one mistake but a "faulty flow". For example, Fig. 1 shows one hypothesis DFA extracted with PDV, based on which we found a mistake in the corresponding RNN. The counterexample we found was *abcee*. One can see that the word *abce* is a loop in the DFA. Hence, we can suspect that this could be a "faulty flow". Checking the words $w_n = (abce)^n e$ for $n \in \{1, \ldots, 100\}$, we observed that, for any $n \in \{1, \ldots, 100\}$, the word w_n was in the RNN language but not in the specification.

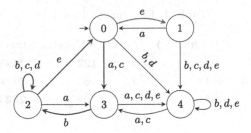

Fig. 1. Faulty Flow in DFA extracted through PDV

To automate the reasoning above, we did the following: Given an RNN R, a specification A, the extracted DFA $\mathcal{H}$, and the counterexample w: (1) build the cross product DFA $\mathcal{H} \times \overline{A}$; (2) for every prefix w_1 of the counterexample $w = w_1 w_2$, denote by s_{w_1} the state to which the prefix w_1 leads in $\mathcal{H} \times \overline{A}$—for any loop ℓ starting from s_{w_1}, check if $w_n = w_1 \ell^n w_2$ is a counterexample for $n \in \{1, \ldots, 100\}$; (3) if w_n is a counterexample for more than 20 times, declare a "faulty flow". Using this procedure, we managed to find faulty flows in 81/109 of the counterexamples that were found by PDV.

6.2 Adversarial Robustness Certification

We also examined PDV for adversarial robustness certification, following the ideas explained in Sect. 5, both on synthetic as well as real-world examples.

Synthetic Benchmarks. For a given DFA (representing one of the languages described below), we randomly sampled words from Σ^* by using the DFA and created a training set and a test set. For RNN training, we proceeded like in step (3) for the benchmarks in Sect. 6.1. Moreover, for certification, we randomly sampled 100 positive words and 100 negative words from the test set. For a given word w, we then let $L = \{w\}$ and considered $\mathcal{N}_r(L)$ where $r = 1, \ldots, 5$.

Given an RNN R, we checked whether R satisfies adversarial robustness using the certification methods PDV, SMC, and *neighborhood-automata generation SMC (NAG-SMC)*, with $\varepsilon, \gamma = 0.01$. In SMC, we randomly modified the input word within a certain distance to generate words in the neighborhood. In NAG-SMC, on the other hand, we first generated a neighborhood automaton of the input word, and sampled words that are accepted by the automaton. Here, we followed the algorithm by Bernardi and Giménez [5], who introduce a method for generating a uniformly random word of length n in a given regular language with mean time bit-complexity $O(n)$.

Figure 2, which is a set of scatter plots, shows the results of the average time of executing the algorithms on the languages that we describe below. The x-axis and y-axis are both time in seconds, and each data point represents one adversarial robustness certification procedure. The length of words are from 50 to 500 and follow the normal distribution.

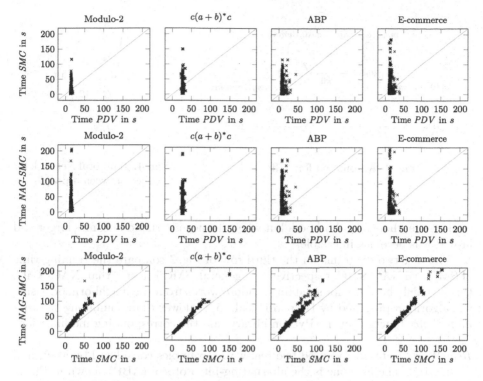

Fig. 2. Comparison of three algorithms on the regular languages

Simple Regular Ranguages. As a sanity check of our approach, we considered the following two regular languages and distance functions: $L_1 = ((a + b)(a + b))^*$ (also called *modulo-2 language*) with Hamming distance; $L_2 = c(a + b)^* c$ with distance function *dist* such that $dist(w_1, w_2)$ is the Hamming distance if $w_1, w_2 \in L_2$ and $|w_1| = |w_2|$, and $dist(w_1, w_2) = \infty$ otherwise. The size of the Hamming neighbourhood will exponentially grow with the distance.

The accuracies of the trained RNNs reached 100%. All three approaches successfully reported "adversarially robust" for the certified RNNs.

The first two diagrams on the first row of Fig. 2 compare the runtimes of PDV and SMC on the two regular-language datasets, resp., whereas the first two diagrams on the second row compare the runtimes of PDV and NAG-SMC. We make two main observations. First, on average, the running time of PDV (avg. 15.70 s) is faster than SMC (avg. 24.04 s) and NAG-SMC (avg. 32.5 s), which shows clearly that combining symbolically checking robustness on the extracted model and statistical approximation checking is more efficient than pure statistical approaches. Second, although SMC and NAG-SMC are able to certify short words (whose length is smaller than 30) faster, when the length of words is greater, they have to spend more time (which is more than 60 s) for certification. This is because, for short words, statistical approaches can easily

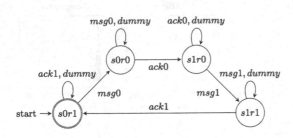

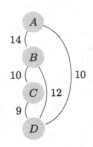

Fig. 3. Automaton for ABP

Fig. 4. Temporal Network for contact between 4 people

explore the whole neighborhood, but when the neighborhood becomes larger and larger, this becomes infeasible.

The first two diagrams on the third row of Fig. 2 compare the running time of SMC and NAG-SMC, respectively. In general, SMC is faster than NAG-SMC, this is mainly because, for sampling random words from the neighborhood, using the algorithm proposed by Bernardi et al. [5] is slower than combining the *random.choice* function in the Python library and the corresponding modification.

Real-World Dataset. We used two real-world examples considered by Mayr and Yovine [17]. The first one is the alternating-bit protocol (ABP) shown in Fig. 3. However, we add a special letter *dummy* in the alphabet and a self-loop transition labeled with *dummy* on every state. We use the number of insertions of the letter *dummy* as the distance function. The second example is a variant of an example from the E-commerce website [19]. There are seven letters in the original automaton. Similarly, we also add *dummy* and self-loop transition in every state (omitted in the figure for simplicity). Again, we use the number of insertions of *dummy* as the distance function.

The accuracies of the trained RNNs also reach 100%. For certification, the three approaches can certify the adversarial robustness for the RNNs as well.

The last two diagrams on the first (resp. second) row of Fig. 2 compare the runtime of PDV and SMC (resp. PDV and NAG-SMC) on the ABP and the E-commerce dataset. The data points in the first and second row have a vertical shape. The reason is that the running time of PDV is usually relatively stable (10–20 s), while the running time of SMC and NAG-SMC increases linearly with the word length.

The last two diagrams on the third row of Fig. 2 compare the runtimes of SMC and NAG-SMC on the two datasets. Here, the data points have a diagonal shape, but for NAG-SMC, when the word length is long (more than 300), it usually spends more time than SMC. This is mainly because it is inefficient to construct the neighborhood automaton and sample random words from the neighborhood.

6.3   RNNs Identifying Contact Sequences

Contact tracing [14] has proven to be increasingly effective in curbing the spread of infectious diseases. In particular, analyzing contact sequences—sequences of individuals who have been in close contact in a certain order—can be crucial in identifying individuals who might be at risk during an epidemic. We, thus, look at RNNs which can potentially aid contact tracing by identifying possible contact sequences. However, in order to deploy such RNNs in practice, one would require them to be verified adequately. One does not want to alert individuals unnecessarily even if they are safe or overlook individuals who could be at risk.

In a real-world setting, one would obtain contact sequences from contact-tracing information available from, for instance, contact-tracing apps. However, such data is often difficult to procure due to privacy issues. Thus, in order to mimic a real life scenario, we use data available from www.sociopatterns. org, which contains information about interaction of humans in public places (hospitals, schools, etc.) presented as temporal networks.

Formally, a *temporal network* $G = (V, E)$ [12] is a graph structure consisting of a set of vertices V and a set of labeled edges E, where the labels represent the timestamp during which the edge was active. Figure 4 is a simple temporal network, which can be perceived as contact graph of four workers in an office where edge labels represent the time of meeting between them. A *time-respecting path* $\pi \in V^*$—a sequence of vertices such that there exists a sequence of edges with increasing time labels—depicts a contact sequence in such a network. In the above example, $CDAB$ is a time-respecting path while $ABCD$ is not.

Benchmarks. For our experiment, given a temporal network G, we generated an RNN R recognizing contact sequences as follows:

1. We created training and test data for the RNN by generating (i) valid time-respecting paths (of lengths between 5 and 15) using labeled edges from G, and (ii) invalid time-respecting paths, by considering a valid path and randomly introducing breaks in the path. The number of time-respecting paths in the training set is twice the size of the number of labeled edges in G, while the test set is one-fifth the size of the training set.
2. We trained RNN R with hidden dimension $|V|$ (minimum 100) as well as $\lfloor 2 + |V|/100 \rfloor$ layers on the training data. We considered only those RNNs that could be trained within 5 h with high accuracy (avg. 99%) on the test data.
3. We used a DFA that accepts all possible paths (disregarding the time labels) in the network as the specification, which would allow us to check whether the RNN learned unwanted edges between vertices.

Using this process, from the seven temporal networks, we generated seven RNNs and seven specification DFAs. We ran SMC, PDV, and AAMC on the generated RNNs, using the same parameters as used for the random instances.

Table 2. Results of model-checking algorithm on RNN identifying contact sequences

Case	Alg.	Counter-example len.	Extracted DFA size	Time (s)	Case	Alg.	Counter-example len.	Extracted DFA size	Time (s)
Across	SMC	3		0.3	Within	SMC	2		0.28
Kenyan	AAMC	2	328	624.76	Kenyan	AAMC	2	178	620.30
Household	PDV	2	2	0.22	Household	PDV	2	2	0.27
	SMC	2		0.23		SMC	71		1.51
Workplace	AAMC	2	111	604.99	Conference	AAMC	2	38	876.19
	PDV	2	2	0.77		PDV	2	2	0.33
	SMC	5		0.33		SMC	3		0.48
Highschool	AAMC	2	91	627.30	Workplace	AAMC	2	87	621.44
2011	PDV	2	2	0.19	2015	PDV	2	2	1.11
	SMC	7		0.24					
Hospital	AAMC	2	36	614.76					
	PDV	2	2	0.006					

Results. Table 2 notes the length of counterexample, the extracted DFA size (only for PDV and AAMC), and the running time of the algorithms. We make three main observations. First, the counterexamples obtained by PDV and AAMC (avg. length 2), are much more succinct than those by SMC (avg. length 13.1). Small counterexamples help in identifying the underlying error in the RNN, while long and random counterexamples provide much less insight. For example, from the counterexamples obtained from PDV and AAMC, we learned that the RNN overlooked certain edges or identified wrong edges. This result highlights the demerit of SMC, which has also been observed by [25]. Second, the running time of SMC and PDV (avg. 0.48 s and 0.41 s) is comparable, while that of AAMC is prohibitively large (avg. 655.68 s), indicating that model checking on small and rough abstractions of the RNN produces superior results. Third, the extracted DFA size, in case of AAMC (avg. size 124.14), is always larger compared to PDV (avg. size 2), indicating that RNNs are quite difficult to be approximated by small DFAs and this slows down the model-checking process as well. Again, our experiments confirm that PDV produces succinct counterexamples reasonably fast.

7   Conclusion

We proposed property-directed verification (PDV) as a new verification method for formally verifying RNNs with respect to regular specifications, with adversarial robustness certification as one important application. It is straightforward to extend our ideas to the setting of Moore/Mealy machines supporting the setting of richer classes of RNN classifiers, but this is left as part of future work. Another future work is to investigate the applicability of our approach for RNNs representing more expressive languages, such as context-free ones. Finally, we plan to extend the PDV algorithm for the formal verification of RNN-based agent environment systems, and to compare it with the existing results.

References

1. Akintunde, M.E., Kevorchian, A., Lomuscio, A., Pirovano, E.: Verification of RNN-based neural agent-environment systems. In: Proceedings of AAAI 2019, pp. 6006–6013. AAAI Press (2019). https://doi.org/10.1609/aaai.v33i01.33016006
2. Angluin, D.: Learning regular sets from queries and counterexamples. Inf. Comput. **75**(2), 87–106 (1987)
3. Ayache, S., Eyraud, R., Goudian, N.: Explaining black boxes on sequential data using weighted automata. In: Proceedings of ICGI 2018, Proceedings of Machine Learning Research, vol. 93, pp. 81–103. PMLR (2018)
4. Baier, C., Katoen, J.: Principles of Model Checking. MIT Press, Cambridge (2008)
5. Bernardi, O., Giménez, O.: A linear algorithm for the random sampling from regular languages. Algorithmica **62**(1–2), 130–145 (2012)
6. Cho, K., et al.: Learning phrase representations using RNN encoder-decoder for statistical machine translation. In: Proceedings of the EMNLP, pp. 1724–1734. ACL (2014)
7. Clarke, E., Grumberg, O., Jha, S., Lu, Y., Veith, H.: Counterexample-guided abstraction refinement. In: Emerson, E.A., Sistla, A.P. (eds.) CAV 2000. LNCS, vol. 1855, pp. 154–169. Springer, Heidelberg (2000). https://doi.org/10.1007/10722167_15
8. Du, X., Li, Y., Xie, X., Ma, L., Liu, Y., Zhao, J.: Marble: model-based robustness analysis of stateful deep learning systems. In: ASE 2020, pp. 423–435. IEEE (2020)
9. Elboher, Y.Y., Gottschlich, J., Katz, G.: An abstraction-based framework for neural network verification. In: Lahiri, S.K., Wang, C. (eds.) CAV 2020. LNCS, vol. 12224, pp. 43–65. Springer, Cham (2020). https://doi.org/10.1007/978-3-030-53288-8_3
10. Giacomo, G.D., Vardi, M.Y.: Synthesis for LTL and LDL on finite traces. In: Proceedings of IJCAI 2015, pp. 1558–1564. AAAI Press (2015)
11. Hochreiter, S., Schmidhuber, J.: Long short-term memory. Neural Comput. **9**(8), 1735–1780 (1997)
12. Holme, P.: Temporal networks. In: Encyclopedia of Social Network Analysis and Mining, pp. 2119–2129. Springer, Heidelberg (2014)
13. Jacoby, Y., Barrett, C.W., Katz, G.: Verifying recurrent neural networks using invariant inference. CoRR abs/2004.02462 (2020)
14. Keck, C.: Principles of Public Health Practice. Cengage Learning (2002)
15. Kwiatkowska, M.Z.: Safety verification for deep neural networks with provable guarantees (Invited Paper). In: Proceedings of CONCUR 2019. Leibniz International Proceedings in Informatics (LIPIcs), vol. 140, pp. 1:1–1:5. Schloss Dagstuhl-Leibniz-Zentrum fuer Informatik (2019)
16. Mayr, F., Visca, R., Yovine, S.: On-the-fly black-box probably approximately correct checking of recurrent neural networks. In: Holzinger, A., Kieseberg, P., Tjoa, A.M., Weippl, E. (eds.) CD-MAKE 2020. LNCS, vol. 12279, pp. 343–363. Springer, Cham (2020). https://doi.org/10.1007/978-3-030-57321-8_19
17. Mayr, F., Yovine, S.: Regular inference on artificial neural networks. In: Holzinger, A., Kieseberg, P., Tjoa, A.M., Weippl, E. (eds.) CD-MAKE 2018. LNCS, vol. 11015, pp. 350–369. Springer, Cham (2018). https://doi.org/10.1007/978-3-319-99740-7_25
18. Mayr, F., Yovine, S., Visca, R.: Property checking with interpretable error characterization for recurrent neural networks. Mach. Learn. Knowl. Extr. **3**(1), 205–227 (2021)

19. Merten, M.: Active automata learning for real life applications. Ph.D. thesis, Dortmund University of Technology (2013)
20. Okudono, T., Waga, M., Sekiyama, T., Hasuo, I.: Weighted automata extraction from recurrent neural networks via regression on state spaces. In: Proceedings of AAAI 2020, pp. 5306–5314. AAAI Press (2020)
21. Omlin, C.W., Giles, C.L.: Extraction of rules from discrete-time recurrent neural networks. Neural Netw. **9**(1), 41–52 (1996)
22. Peled, D.A., Vardi, M.Y., Yannakakis, M.: Black box checking. J. Autom. Lang. Comb. **7**(2), 225–246 (2002)
23. Ryou, W., Chen, J., Balunovic, M., Singh, G., Dan, A.M., Vechev, M.T.: Fast and effective robustness certification for recurrent neural networks. CoRR abs/2005.13300 (2020)
24. Schulz, K.U., Mihov, S.: Fast string correction with Levenshtein automata. Int. J. Document Anal. Recogn. **5**(1), 67–85 (2002)
25. Weiss, G., Goldberg, Y., Yahav, E.: Extracting automata from recurrent neural networks using queries and counterexamples. In: Proceedings of ICML 2018. Proceedings of Machine Learning Research, vol. 80, pp. 5244–5253. PMLR (2018)

Author Index

Printed in the United States
by Baker & Taylor Publisher Services